MEMOIRS
OF A
BUCCANEER

DAMPIER'S NEW VOYAGE
ROUND THE WORLD, 1697

WILLIAM DAMPIER

DOVER PUBLICATIONS, INC.
MINEOLA, NEW YORK

Bibliographical Note

This Dover edition, first published in 2007, is an unabridged republication of the 1968 Dover reprint of the work originally published in 1927 by Argonaut Press, London, under the title *A New Voyage Round the World.* The current reprint includes the Introduction by Percy G. Adams written especially for the first Dover edition.

International Standard Book Number: 0-486-45726-5

Manufactured in the United States of America
Dover Publications, Inc., 31 East 2nd Street, Mineola, N.Y. 11501

CONTENTS

ILLUSTRATIONS AND MAPS

*Retitled *Memoirs of a Buccaneer* for the 2007 Dover reprint.

INTRODUCTION TO THE DOVER EDITION

IN a modern classic called *The Road to Xanadu*, John Livingston Lowes demonstrated beyond question that the "twilight realms" of Coleridge's consciousness were stocked with facts and images out of the great writers of travel literature. But travel writers have always been a storehouse of facts as well as an inspiration to the imagination. From the Middle Ages to Eugene O'Neill, Marco Polo has remained a favorite. Caliban is only one evidence that Shakespeare knew the voyagers. Milton's commonplace book shows how carefully he read the many volumes of *Purchas his Pilgrimage*, and Wordsworth not only owned collections of older voyages like that of the Churchills but enjoyed the travelers of his own day like Crèvecoeur and Bartram. Perhaps the dean of these influential and fascinating writers was William Dampier.

From the appearance of *A New Voyage round the World* in 1697, Dampier was admired and imitated by scientists, mariners, and writers. The Royal Society immediately placed a digest of his book in its *Philosophical Transactions*. Defoe borrowed his facts, parodied his title, and studied his style. Swift, in order to build on the famous writer's prestige, let Lemuel Gulliver follow in his footsteps and call him Cousin Dampier. Sir Hans Sloane, a foremost scientist, became the traveler's personal friend, had his picture painted, and borrowed from him when he wrote his own book about the Indies. Debrosses, compiler of one of the foremost collections of voyages in the eighteenth century, marveled, "Where is it possible to find navigators like William Dampier?" "The Cook of a former age," he was recommended to apprentice seamen by admirals like Howe and Nelson, and Coleridge's admiration was so great that in *Table Talk* he offered Dampier as a model for all military and naval writers.

Such a variety of admirers suggests a variety of attractions in Dampier's books. His plain style and adventurous life appealed to the creators of the modern novel. His careful and thorough data on places, winds, and currents made him an indispensable part of any circumnavigator's library for a hundred years. His graphic descriptions of plants and animals not only elicited the praise of scientists and geographers but forced subsequent travelers to adopt his methods and be less superficial. His wealth of exotic knowledge of all kinds provided a kaleidoscope of images for poets and novelists. All of this thoroughness and variety were the reasons John Masefield could say that Dampier's were "the best books of voyages in the language."

A great travel writer is hardly the product of a miracle, however. It is true that William Dampier was endowed with certain characteristics more or less superior in quality—a keen eye, a curious mind that led him in new directions, ambition, courage, patience in recording and revising notes—but he was also fortunate in his environment. Born in 1652 he lived during an exciting time of discovery and exploration, of political intrigues, of treaties made and broken, of wars declared and undeclared. It was the romantic age of buccaneers and privateers and pirates, but it was also an age of reason in which the Royal Society and the Académie des Sciences had begun to inculcate the modern scientific attitude. It is not surprising then that in such a world William Dampier, like many other ambitious and orphaned boys of his day, would become an apprentice sailor and seek his fortune in faraway lands and uncharted seas.

By the time he was twenty he had sailed to Newfoundland and to the East Indies, and by the age of twenty-six he had served in the British navy, briefly managed a plantation in Jamaica, engaged in trading all over the West Indies, and spent three years as a logwood cutter around the Bay of Campeche in Mexico. In 1678 he returned to England long enough to take a wife he was destined to see only occasionally in the remainder of his wandering life.

Back in Jamaica he left the ship on which he was serving to go for over eight years with Coxon, Sawkins, Sharp, and other notorious buccaneers on daring expeditions against Spanish towns and shipping. One of his first experiences with them was to assist in the razing of Porto Bello in an attack almost as famous as the one made on that Central American town by Henry Morgan earlier. All of these stories are recounted best by Dampier's contemporaries, Basil Ringrose and John Esquemeling, in *The Buccaneers of America.** Then after two scorching marches across the Isthmus of Panama, after helping to capture Spanish ships in the Pacific and raid Spanish towns on the west coast of the New World, after a voyage around the Horn and a stay of some months in Virginia, after a return to the Pacific—after all this Dampier sailed west with his buccaneers, left them in protest in the East Indies, lived an adventurous life as trader and gunner for some three years, and finally returned to England around the Cape of Good Hope taking with him a painted East Indian called Prince Jeoly, who created a stir in London and whom he sold because there was no money left from his years of buccaneering.

And yet there was one very tangible residue—the journal he had begun to keep at Porto Bello and which he guarded so zealously while crossing swollen rivers in Central America, while attacking Spanish ships and

---

* Reprinted by Dover Publications, Inc., in 1967.

towns, while jumping from one berth to another in the East Indies, and while slipping through a porthole to escape his more or less enforced life as chief gunner at Fort St. George in Sumatra. It was a part of this journal, altered and revised by its author, which was published in 1697 by James Knapton as *A New Voyage round the World* and which brought its author both fame and popularity. His book was dedicated to one President of the Royal Society, and another, Sir Hans Sloane, sponsored him in society and among government circles. He dined with Samuel Pepys and John Evelyn, and he appeared before the Council of Trade and Plantations as an authority on Spanish America.

A second volume of his journal was published two years later, shortly after he was taken into the British navy and made captain of the *Roebuck* for a voyage to New Holland and New Guinea. With fifty men and boys he managed to reach the East Indies, but on the way back his rotten old ship gave out and he and his crew were picked up and brought home. Again there was a journal, published in two parts, in 1703 and 1709, as *A Voyage to New Holland*, and this time he returned with a collection of plants which, at the request of the Royal Society, he turned over to Dr. John Woodward. Much less happy for his reputation, he thought, was the court martial that convicted him of cruelty for putting his recalcitrant lieutenant in chains. But while the voyage demonstrated that Dampier was too impatient with subordinates to be an ideal commander, he remained a favorite among men of affairs and learning. He met the Queen and kissed her hand, and he was given a new command.

Just after seeing the first part of *A Voyage to New Holland* through the press, Dampier sailed away on the *Saint George*, accompanied by the *Cinque Ports*, with private sponsors and a commission from the Queen to harass the Spanish. But the greatest of travel writers was destined never to be a firm and daring and lucky leader in the tradition of Francis Drake and Woodes Rogers and George Anson. After the Captain of the *Cinque Ports* died, Lieutenant Stradling, who succeeded to his command, left the expedition at Panama; and in the Pacific, Dampiers' mate went off with a Spanish prize ship and twenty-one of his crew. Now there were sixty-four ill-equipped, sickly, and mutinous men to handle a leaky, worn-out boat. When some of the crew blamed Dampier for indecisive leadership in the loss of the Manila Galleon, a famed Spanish treasure ship that sailed annually between Manila and Acapulco, the mate William Funnell and thirty-four more men deserted on another prize and sailed east and home. Eventually Dampier's most ill-fated voyage ended, but only after the crew abandoned the rotten-bottomed *Saint George* for a captured Spanish brigantine and underwent hardships in the eastern Pacific, including the confiscation by the Dutch of their ship and goods. This second of William Dampier's circumnavigations lasted four years and had even less to show in the way of tangible rewards, for this time he failed to bring home either exotic plants or a painted prince. Nor did he publish a journal.

But there was a kind of journal. The mate who left him in the Pacific, William Funnell, arrived in London before his Captain and persuaded Dampier's publisher James Knapton to print an account of the voyage that presented the deserters' side of the story and was damaging to Dampier. Furthermore, Funnell and the publisher very obviously tried to capitalize on the substantial reputation of the absent travel writer, for the book appeared without an author's name and was entitled *Account of William Dampier's Expedition into the South Seas in the Ship St. George*. It was a trick to be pulled often thereafter when anonymous accounts, sometimes four or five in number, were to come out quickly after almost every one of the well known eighteenth-century circumnavigations of the globe. When Dampier did return he answered Funnell's distorted and often untruthful charges with only a few pages of hurried notes.

But again the reputation of William Dampier suffered little, for in 1708 during the War of the Spanish Succession, he sailed once more, on his third and final and only really successful voyage round the world. This time, however, he was not the captain. Woodes Rogers, one of the world's great leaders, was the diplomatic, courageous, firm commander of the two ships that harassed the Spanish all up and down the west coast of America and climaxed its voyage by capturing the Manila Galleon, the first taken by British privateers since Drake and Cavendish. Even more memorable from that trip was the rescue of Alexander Selkirk from the island of Juan Fernández in the Pacific. Although on this voyage Dampier kept no journal, two excellent accounts of it did appear, one by Woodes Rogers, who sailed on the *Duke*, called *A Cruising Voyage Round the World* (1712),* and the other by Captain Edward Cooke of the *Dutchess*. Both journals show over and over that Dampier's position as pilot was an honored one and that his advice was constantly sought and respected. This was his last voyage and his last public performance, for he died in 1715.

Although a busy and exciting life is a great asset to a travel writer, he also needs good models to guide and inspire him, and Dampier was born

* Reprinted by Dover Publications, Inc., in 1970.

into a period that provided such models. Sir John Mandeville's adventures, written in the Middle Ages, were still attractive to readers of Dampier's day and have remained popular ever since. Late in the sixteenth century Richard Hakluyt edited what was to be the most honored of all collections of voyages, an edition which Samuel Purchas would supplement in 1625. If Pliny's *Natural History* is added to all these volumes of older voyages, the result would be for Dampier's day a literary tradition that might lead to greatness.

But there were other, more recent, factors in Dampier's environment that made him the most important writer in an increasingly important tradition. The Jesuits of France had been going out with other early travelers to all parts of the uncivilized world and in letters and books were beginning to be known not only for their bravery in Canada, or Abyssinia, or China, but for their erudition in describing customs, geography, and natural history. Chardin, Tavernier, and other Frenchmen who went to the East had published accounts of their travels which were eventually to become popular and authoritative. Spanish inhabitants of and visitors in the New World—Herrera, d'Acosta, Oviedo, and especially Garcilaso de Vega—were being culled for information that would supplement that taken from British, French, and Italian travel writers to make huge volumes of geographical facts amassed best by the Dutch but also by such British editors as John Ogilby. These began to appear in English only when Dampier was a young man. Although he claimed correctly not to have borrowed any of their information, quotations and references in *A New Voyage* prove that he profited from the best of these travelers who wrote before him—Tavernier in Asia and Africa, Thomas Gage in Mexico, Captain Robert Knox on Ceylon, Sir John Narborough around the world, and Duquesne to the East Indies.

One of the most important influences on him was the Royal Society. When he was in his teens, that newly formed body of philosophers, scientists, and men of letters, realizing the possibilities inherent in travel writing, published a set of "directions" for those who intended to go to distant continents urging them to record exactly and minutely what they saw, even to bring back samples or drawings, in short, to be "auxiliaries" of science. These "directions" were again published, with additions by Robert Boyle, noted scientist and President of the Royal Society, and then included in the prefaces of such eighteenth-century collections of travels as those by the Churchills and J. F. Bernard. The drawings, the maps, and the natural history details of Dampier's books demonstrate clearly that he attempted to follow these directions.

Most immediately an influence on the form and style of Dampier's book, as well as an inspiration for his keeping a journal, was *The Buccaneers of America*. The first three parts of this volume, written by the buccaneer-surgeon John Esquemeling, were published in Dutch in Amsterdam in 1678 and then quickly translated into other European languages, appearing in English in 1684. The next year a fourth part was added in English, the work of Basil Ringrose, another buccaneer. Although Dampier began keeping his own journal before he could have seen either of these English accounts, his notes subsequent to 1685 make frequent references to *The Buccaneers of America*, especially to that part written by his "ingenious friend Mr. Ringrose," whose death in a Spanish ambush in Mexico is recorded in *A New Voyage*. Both Esquemeling and Ringrose often paused while narrating an adventure to describe a town, an island, or occasionally a plant or animal, a practice followed by Dampier and perfected by him. Furthermore, after 1685, when Ringrose's part of *The Buccaneers* was published, Dampier became much more detailed and much more faithful in keeping his own journal, most certainly to avoid repeating what Ringrose had said but perhaps also because he hoped to outdo his successful "worthy consort."

William Dampier then, like writers in all literary genres, shows the influence of a tradition and of his predecessors, but he himself passed on that tradition so well that more than anyone else he ushered in what has been truly called the silver age of travel literature. Near the end of the seventeenth century a Frenchman claimed that in his country "voyagers have come into credit and now hold first place" with the reading public, having supplanted the popular romances. By the third quarter of the eighteenth century dozens of great collections of voyages had been published in all the countries of western Europe, among them the editions of Churchill, Harris, Debrosses, Prévost, and Smollett. For editing one such collection, John Hawkesworth received six times the sum paid Henry Fielding for what is perhaps the best novel of the century. By the end of that century a French bibliographer named Boucher was to be convinced that "never have there appeared so many voyages" to be read not only by the "ordinary" person but to be studied by "naturalists and geographers, artists and archeologists, even by political scientists, economists, and moral philosophers." After analyzing the publishing trends of the period, Edward Arber has concluded that for at least the early eighteenth century the most widely read books were travels, collections of voyages, and geographical compilations and that "James Knapton set the fashion in this, with Dampier's *Voyages*."

But few of his successors and imitators in the silver age could match the master. Although *A New Voyage* begins rather slowly—the account of Dampier's first circumnavigation starting only in the fourth chapter—its author recorded many intriguing, even exciting, adventures in the journal form which he normally followed. There are sea fights against apparently superior odds, dangerous reconnoitering forays on the coast of Spanish America, bloody ambushes, captives taken, traded, or shot, and narrow escapes from enemy fireships, crippling illness, and frightful storms. But while we read on because of the excitement, we learn much that supplements the facts given in *The Buccaneers of America* and other books about the Spanish Main. We learn how and where the buccaneers were forced to careen and clean their ships in order to protect the hulls and sail faster than the prospective prize. We learn how buccaneer crews deposed a captain or elected a new one or deserted at will. We learn how they captured natives to gain information about towns to be raided, how they treated captives, how they drank to excess, how they were sometimes gentle, often quarrelsome, occasionally murderous. With Esquemeling, Ringrose, and Raveneau de Lussan, Dampier is one of the chief eyewitness historians of buccaneering.

A New Voyage is great travel literature, however, because it provides more than a gripping narrative and more than information about the last of the notorious buccaneering expeditions. In one typical chapter its keen-eyed author was able to maintain interest while describing the curious manatee, the cacao and mangrove trees, the booby, Man-of-War, and noddy birds, and the Mosquito Indians of Central America. And in such descriptions he was able to be attractive without exaggeration, the favorite vice of travelers of all ages. He refused, for example, to believe in cannibals because in all his travels he had never seen or heard of one; and his ten or twelve feet for the maximum length of the clever manatee, or sea cow, is startling in its accuracy when we consider the exorbitant claims of other seventeenth- and eighteenth-century travelers. Such accuracy and thoroughness, supported by colorful anecdotes, would cause the renowned scientist-traveler Baron Humboldt to say one hundred years later that illustrious savants such as Condamine had added little to the observations of William Dampier.

Perhaps as attractive as any other feature in *A New Voyage* is the slow unfolding of the personality of its author. By 1697, the year of his book and of the Treaty of Ryswick, buccaneering had become a thing of the past, and so Dampier was forced to defend his actions. As a result, he carefully explained how in Jamaica he was the last man aboard his trading ship to desert and join the buccaneers, how he failed to condone the murder of rebellious or useless hostages, and how he expostulated with the buccaneers when they took Captain Swan's ship and left him to be murdered in Mindanao. Or he was forced to avoid certain embarrassing subjects. Never referring to his buccaneer associates by any name other than the respected one of "privateers," he failed to mention the arrant act of piracy performed when his fellows stole a handsome new ship from friendly Dutch owners, rechristened it the *Batchelor's Delight*, and sailed off on a plundering voyage. Such acts as this brought on "troubles" which he and Lionel Wafer and others of his friends faced in Virginia, where, we know, some of them at least were imprisoned and had their buccaneering gains confiscated.

Nevertheless, while he showed that in 1697 he was on the defensive because of the life he described in his book, he also displayed many admirable characteristics. Curious, ambitious, and encyclopedic in his quest for facts, he told how he forsook Captain Davis for Captain Swan simply "to get some knowledge of the northern parts" of North America. Level headed and compassionate, he managed to pacify his piratical fellows in the East Indies and persuade them to put him ashore when they refused to follow his advice and return for their abandoned captain. Once ashore he was joined by friends who preferred to follow him in an uncertain life among savages than to follow others in a certain life as pirates. Fair minded always, he once thought his own crew "unreasonable" for not dividing Spanish spoils with another crew engaged in related adventures. Not lacking in generosity, he was willing to puff his buccaneer-surgeon friend Lionel Wafter's account of the Isthmus because, he said "Mr. Wafer is better able to do it than any Man I know." Although Dampier's journals and other journals show that he avoided the drunkenness so prevalent aboard ships in his day, he was obviously liked and respected. He told with some pride, for example, how a sophisticated French captain and his lieutenant invited him more than once to visit them aboard their ship for dinner and urged him to leave the English buccaneers and come with them to France. After meeting Dampier in his book, one is not surprised to discover how socially acceptable he became in London.

Nor is it surprising that *A New Voyage* was so influential, that it "set the fashion" for travelers of succeeding generations. Dampier's "Golden Dreams" of taking America from Spain, of civilizing the Indians, of developing a great British trade in the west would inspire Daniel Defoe to draw up plans for such a project, tear them up before King William could see them, and then redo them for Lord Harley and forever after be accused of being responsible for the South Sea Bubble. The French Defoe who wrote *The Voyages of Francois Coreal* would advocate those same Golden Dreams for any country which might be missionary and humanitarian enough to dry the tears of the Indians and treat them like humans. Almost as influential would be Dampier's conviction that there was a Northwest Passage practical enough to be used by ships sailing across northern Canada; for a hundred years at least, the search for that elusive passage would go on taking up the time of ships, academies of science, and business men and projectors like Benjamin Franklin. Even more influential would be *A New Voyage's* account of the rescue from Juan Fernández of the Mosquito Indian Will, who lived there for three years and became one of the two chief models for literally thousands of Robinsonades, the other being Alexander Selkirk, who a dozen years later was to be rescued from the same island by the privateers commanded by Woodes Rogers but piloted by the same William Dampier who had so carefully described Will's ingenious and patient planning of his lonely life. *A New Voyage*, in fact, set many fashions—for scientists, explorers, circumnavigators, projectors, historians, poets, and authors of novels, voyages, and pseudo-voyages. The social and literary chronicler can hardly fail to look back with respect on its author, whom Coleridge out of his vast knowledge of travel literature called so fondly, "Old Dampier, a rough sailor, but a man of exquisite mind."

PERCY G. ADAMS

Baton Rouge, Louisiana
February, 1967

AFTER reading Sir Albert Gray's excellent Introduction to this edition of Dampier's *New Voyage round the World*, I was at once convinced that nothing remained to be said except from the bibliographical side.

At the very outset of my researches I was faced with a mass of contradictory and incorrect references—the work of past cataloguers for whom the intricacies of the numerous issues and editions had proved too complicated. Even now I cannot state with absolute certainty that the results of my work have produced a bibliography of Dampier's works complete in every detail. At the same time, it is gratifying to know that the Library of the British Museum has accepted it, and has found it necessary to revise *in toto* the pages of the General Catalogue containing the Dampier entries. Although the Bodleian does not possess copies of all the various editions, the Librarian tells me that those they have confirm my statements.

After his return to England in 1691 Dampier must have prepared his MS. for the press during the intervals between the numerous short voyages he made in the next half dozen years.

The *New Voyage* appeared in 1697 and was an immediate success, a second edition following the same year. A third edition was published in 1698. Both these later editions had *partially* embodied an "errata" sheet which was affixed to the end of the first edition. Dampier's publisher, James Knapton, encouraged by the success of the work, demanded more material for a further volume. This consisted of *A Supplement to the Voyage round the World*, together with the *Voyages to Campeachy* and the *Discourse on the Trade Winds*. It was issued in 1699 under the general title of *Voyages and Discoveries*, and bore the imprint "Vol. II." With it a fourth edition of the *New Voyage* appeared, also dated 1699. It had been more carefully revised, and the *complete* "errata" sheet from the first edition had been embodied[1].

It now bore the imprint "Vol. I" on the title-page. An Index (unpaginated) to both volumes appeared in Vol. II.

This year (1699) was a great publishing year for Knapton, for beside the Dampier volumes he had also issued Lionel Wafer's *New Voyage and Description of the Isthmus of America* and William Hacke's *Collection of Original Voyages*, which consisted of Cowley's *Voyage round the Globe*, Sharp's *Journey*

---

[1] *E.g.* the "errata" sheet tells us that on p. 501 "Malucca" should read "Malacca." In spite of the 2nd and 3rd editions being "corrected," we find this unchanged till the 4th edition of 1699.

over the Isthmus of Darien[1], Wood's *Magellan* and Roberts' *Levant*. As we shall see shortly, all these were to be incorporated in a later edition of "Dampier's Voyages."

Now, although the 1699 edition of Dampier can be correctly described as a two volume work, each volume was reprinted as occasion demanded[2].

The *New Voyage*, in reality, still remained an individual work. Thus the 5th edition appeared in 1703, and the 6th in 1717.

Meanwhile the *Voyages and Discoveries* had reached its 2nd edition in 1700 and 3rd in 1705. But with the 5th edition of the *New Voyage* in 1703 appeared the 1st edition of Dampier's third volume, the *Voyage to New Holland*. It proved a success, although it took six years to be exhausted. The 2nd edition appeared in 1709, and with it was also issued the 1st edition of the *Continuation of the New Voyage*.

Thus, it was not until 1709 that all Dampier's volumes had appeared, and although Librarians often speak of the "three volume Dampier," they must remember that each volume bore a different date and each date represented a different edition of that volume. Thus, there was no "three volume Dampier" in the generally-accepted meaning of the term, and nothing could prevent such a set being made up of any odd editions. In fact, this is, to a large extent, exactly what happened, and one will find a 1st edition of the *New Voyage* bound up conformably with, say, a 2nd edition of *Voyages and Discoveries* and a mixed edition of the two parts of *New Holland*.

We now come to the four volume edition of 1729, of which the present work forms a reprint of Vol. I.

Knapton conceived the idea of issuing all his "explorer" volumes in one collection. Accordingly, he first reprinted the three volumes of Dampier's *Voyages* (omitting the dedication in Vol. I). The *New Voyage* was called "Seventh edition corrected," and *Voyages and Discoveries* was the fourth edition (though unnamed as such). Vol. III consisted of the *New Holland* voyage followed by a reprint of Wafer's *Voyages*. Both parts of the *New Holland* voyage now appeared for the first time in continuous pagination[3]. Wafer's *Voyages* formed the 3rd edition, as the first had appeared in 1699 and the 2nd in 1704. Vol. IV contained the voyages of Funnell, Cowley, Sharp, Wood, and Roberts.

We have already noted the previous issue of the four latter voyages, and

[1] Sharp's *Voyages and Adventures in the South Sea* had already appeared in 1684.

[2] This is proved by the "advertisements" at the end of the other volumes published by Knapton in 1699.

[3] They were reprinted as one narrative in Harris' *Collection of Voyages* (*Navigantium atque Itinerantium Bibliotheca*), 1744.

A

New Voyage

ROUND THE

WORLD.

Deſcribing particularly,

The *Iſthmus* of *America*, ſeveral Coaſts
and Iſlands in the *Weſt Indies* , the
Iſles of *Cape Verd*, the Paſſage by *Terra
del Fuego*, the *South Sea* Coaſts of *Chili*,
Peru, and *Mexico*; the Iſle of *Guam* one
of the *Ladrones*, *Mindanao*, and other
Philippine and *Eaſt-India* Iſlands near
Cambodia, *China*, *Formoſa*, *Luconia*, *Ce-
lebes*, &c. *New Holland*, *Sumatra*, *Nicobar*
Iſles; the *Cape* of *Good Hope*, and *Santa
Hellena*.

THEIR
Soil, Rivers, Harbours, Plants, Fruits, Animals, and Inhabitants.

THEIR
Cuſtoms, Religion, Government, Trade, *&c.*

By *William Dampier*.

Illuſtrated with Particular Maps and Draughts.

LONDON,
Printed for *James Knapton*, at the *Crown* in St *Paul*'s
Church-yard. M DC XCVII.

Title-page of the first edition of "A New Voyage Round the World"

Funnell's *Voyage round the World*, which was an account of Dampier's *St George* voyage, had been published by Knapton in 1707.

With regard to the MS. copy of Dampier's *New Voyage* (Sloane MSS. 3236) little need be said here, as Sir Albert Gray has treated it in the conclusion of his Introduction. I would merely note that the brief passage referring to New Holland was printed in *Early Voyages to Terra Australis*, Hakluyt Society, 1859, pp. 108–111. The volume also reprinted those portions of the printed edition of the *New Voyage to New Holland* which contained direct reference to Australia.

It would be superfluous to mention all the reprints of Dampier's *Voyages* after 1729. I would, therefore, merely draw attention to the "Collections of Voyages," in which Dampier's *Voyages*, and those of Funnell, Cowley, etc., appeared.

HARRIS. 1744–48. Vol. I. Dampier, Funnell, Cowley.

Allgemeine Historie. 1747–77. Vol. XII. Dampier, Wood. (Cowley's *Voyage* appeared in Vol. XVIII.)

CALLANDER. 1766–68. Vol. II. Dampier, Sharp, Cowley, Wafer. (Funnell's *Voyage* appeared in Vol. III.)

New Collection. . 1767. Vol. III, p. 608. Dampier.

World Displayed. 1767–68. Vol. VI, p. 609. Dampier.

[DAVID HENRY.] *English Navigators.* 1774. Vol. I. Dampier, Cowley.

PINKERTON. 1808–14. Vol. XI. Dampier.

KERR. 1811–24. Vol. X. Dampier, Funnell, Cowley.

LAHARPE. 1816. Vol. XV. Dampier.

The following table shows, at a glance, the correlation of the different editions of the works which constitute "Dampier's Voyages."

New Voyage		Voyages and Discoveries		Voyage to New Holland			
				Part I		Part II	
Edition	Date	Edition	Date	Edition	Date	Edition	Date
[1st]	1697	—	—	—	—	—	—
2nd	1697	—	—	—	—	—	—
3rd	1698	—	—	—	—	—	—
4th	1699	[1st]	1699	—	—	—	—
5th	1703	2nd	1700	[1st]	1703	—	—
6th	1717	3rd	1705	2nd	1709	[1st]	1709
7th	1729	[4th?]	1729	3rd	1729	[2nd?]	1729

DAMPIER's *New Voyage* on its publication won immediate success, and has ever since maintained its place in the front rank among the most notable records of maritime adventure. It stands midway between the epic tales of Hakluyt and the official narratives of the world voyages of Anson and Cook. As a record of buccaneering it comes between the applauded filibustering of Hawkins and Drake and the condemned piracy of the eighteenth century. The stories of the buccaneers are on the verge of romance. On an episode in the life of one of them Defoe founded one of the great romances of all time—"a most circumstantial and elaborate lie," as Leslie Stephen calls it, "for which we are all grateful." No buccaneer's story has had anything like the popularity of *Robinson Crusoe*: but it may be noted that when Defoe essayed to tell lying tales of pirates, such as Capt. Avery, founded on Dampier and other writers of fact, the subsequent popularity has been with the true story.

¶ In his Preface Dampier describes his book as "composed of a mixt relation of places and actions," a modest and inadequate indication which would hardly be approved by the advertising experts of the present day. The relation of places was, in fact, an extensive contribution to the geographical and ethnographical knowledge of his time. Nor does the description take count of the frequent excursions in the realm of natural history which diversify the main story with detailed accounts of tropical animals and plants, not highly scientific indeed, but accurate for the most part and novel to his readers.

¶ Another more general description is that of the title page, "A voyage round the world." A reader might presume from such a title some intention of circumnavigation at the start, and some continuous prosecution of the aim. Dampier, however, left England without any purpose of rounding the globe, and apparently had no mind to do so until, after many years of devotion to other pursuits, he found himself already halfway home. His was no single voyage, rather the haphazard resultant of episodical voyages, some only of which were in the line of circumnavigation; in the course of these voyages he must have sailed in a dozen ships, apart from canoes and other boats. He accomplished the grand tour, however, a feat which in his time could with luck have been achieved in two years;—it took him twelve and a half.

¶ Many men, who recount adventures in which they have borne a part, describe fully their own actions and conduct; some with a particularity trying to the reader's patience. Dampier is not one of these. In the *New Voyage*, which began when he was 27, he says nothing of his previous life and throughout shows a too strict reserve in regard to his share in the events related. To enable readers of the present volume to form some estimate of the man, a sketch of his life, however inadequate, has to be provided. The details of his subsequent career, which includes a second circumnavigation and two other notable voyages, would be hardly appropriate here. They will not be touched further than seems necessary for an appraisement of Dampier's conduct and character.

LIFE BEFORE THE *NEW VOYAGE*

¶ All that is known of Dampier's early life is told by himself in the first chapter of his *Voyages to the Bay of Campeachy*. He was born in the earlier half of 1652, the son of a farmer at East Coker, near Yeovil. His father died in 1662, and his mother in 1668. His parents had designed him for commercial life; he was sent to school, probably at Yeovil, and attended the Latin class. On the death of his mother his guardians "took other measures" and "removed me from the Latin school to learn writing and arithmetic," in other words, transferred him to the Modern Side. A year or so later, having had "very early inclinations to see the world," he was apprenticed to the master of a Weymouth ship and with him made a voyage to France and then to Newfoundland. He was "pinched with the rigour of that cold climate" and set his heart on a long voyage in summer seas. Soon after his return to London his chance came and, now 19 years of age, he embarked on a voyage to Bantam, serving before the mast. Returning home early in 1672, he spent the rest of the year with his brother in Somersetshire.

¶ He soon tired of home life and the Second Dutch War was now afoot. Dampier enlisted and fought under Sir Edward Spragge in his first two engagements. A day or two before the third, in which Sir Edward was killed, he fell sick and after a long illness went home to his brother. There, a neighbouring gentleman, Colonel Hillier, made him an offer of employment in the management of his plantation in Jamaica under a Mr Whalley, and he set forth in the *Content* of London, working his passage as a seaman, under agreement for his discharge on arrival. This he deemed necessary lest he should be "trepann'd and sold as a servant after my arrival in

Jamaica." For six months he worked with Mr Whalley on the plantation, "16 Mile Walk," *i.e.* from Spanish Town: then took service under Capt. Heming on his plantation at St Ann's, in the north of the island. He soon left an employment in which, as he says, he was clearly out of his element, and spent some months in trading cruises round the island, during which he "came acquainted with all the ports and bays about Jamaica and with their manufactures, as also with the benefit of the Land and Sea Winds." He thus early began his habits of close observation of men and nature. Now also began his practice of keeping a journal, which he had omitted in his voyage to Bantam.

¶ Between 1675 and 1678, Dampier spent about two years in cutting and loading logwood on the Bay of Campeachy, an occupation which he seemed to have enjoyed. The resistance of Spain to foreign intrusion was becoming feeble, and Dampier reckons there were 270 Englishmen engaged in the logwood trade. "It is not my business," he adds, "to determine how far we might have a right of cutting wood there." He did not, however, get rich on it, and at length in straitened circumstances was constrained to take a turn with some privateers along the gulf as far as Vera Cruz. For a short time he resumed work at Campeachy, thence returning to Jamaica and back to London (August, 1678). He gave himself only a six months' leave, during which he married Judith[1] ——, from the household of the Duke of Grafton (see page 285). It does not appear that they had any children, and nothing more is known of the wife till some 25 years later. He had to work for his living and now projected another expedition to Campeachy—"but it proved to be a voyage round the world."

HIS FIRST CIRCUMNAVIGATION[2]

¶ As has been noted, the circumnavigation was a haphazard tour interrupted by digressions as accidental and whimsical as some in the

---

[1] Her Christian name appears in a codicil to a revoked will of 1703.

[2] The following writers were comrades of Dampier in parts of the voyage. The extent to which they are more or less synoptical is shown by reference to the chapters of this book. (1) Basil Ringrose, Part IV of the *History of the Buccaneers*, Sloane MSS. 3820 (Dampier, Introduction and Chaps. I–III); (2) Lionel Wafer, *New Voyage and Description*, etc., 1699 (Dampier, Introduction and Chaps. I–III); (3) William Ambrosia Cowley, *Voyage round the World*, 1699 (Dampier, Chaps. IV–V); (4) Bartholomew Sharp, *Voyages and Adventures*, in the Dampier Voyages, 1727, Sloane MSS. 45, 46 B (Dampier, Introduction and Chaps. I–III); (5) John Cox, *An account of our Proceedings*, etc., Sloane MSS. 49 (Dampier, Chaps. I–III).

autobiography of Tristram Shandy. For the convenience of the reader I have divided the whole into eight stages, each of which is a more or less separate cruise, defined by change of direction, ship or captain.

FIRST STAGE

¶ Dampier set out on the memorable adventures recorded in the present volume in an early month of 1679, embarking as a passenger in the *Loyal Merchant* of London, Capt. Knapman. On arrival in Jamaica in April, he spent the remainder of the year there. Having bought a small estate in Dorsetshire, he was near returning home to complete the purchase when Mr Hobby invited him to join in a trading voyage to the Mosquito shore, and he "sent the writing of my new purchase" to England by the hands of friends. As fate would have it Mr Hobby put in to Negril Bay at the west end of Jamaica, where a squadron of buccaneers was assembled under Captains John Coxon, Sawkins, Bartholomew Sharp, and other worthies. The temptation which led many an honest man to the buccaneering life could not be resisted. "Mr Hobby's men all left him to go with them, upon an expedition they had contrived, leaving not one with him, beside myself." After three or four days Dampier went too, and no more is heard of Mr Hobby.

BUCCANEERING

¶ I allow myself at this point, following Shandean precedent, to interpose a digression on buccaneering. Under this polite West Indian synonym for piracy, the profession was at the zenith of its prosperity when Dampier joined in: it had acquired indeed some measure of respectability. Some knowledge of its history in the West Indies, and of the current state of public opinion in regard to it, is needed for understanding how a man of Dampier's character, and many like him, came to be associated with it, untroubled by more than occasional twinges of conscience.

¶ Earlier in the century the hunters of Hispaniola were waging a not unrighteous warfare against Spanish tyranny. From the *boucans*, frames or hurdles, on which their meat was roasted, they got the name of buccaneers. They obtained the assistance of French and English adventurers, and the war was extended to the sea. With the accession of more and more reckless spirits from Europe, whose only object was booty, the local justification was lost, and the buccaneers, whose exploits are told by Esquemeling, Dampier and Burney, and ever since followed with zest and sympathy by boys, young and old (including Charles Kingsley), were for the most part pirates[1]. The glamour which surrounds the buc-caneers can be partly accounted for. Their enterprises have seemed to be a continuation of those of Hawkins and Drake, the national heroes of the preceding century, and thus worthy of a measure of their praise[2]. True, the enemy in both cases was Spain, and in Dampier's time, despite the friendly policy of James I and Charles I, Spain was still regarded as the national foe. Spanish cruelties to the natives and to honest traders whom they imprisoned rankled in the hearts of Englishmen. There was, however, no national or religious enthusiasm behind the buccaneers, whose operations had a different origin and were instigated solely by motives of plunder. Mr Andrew Lang's description of the buccaneers[3] as "the most hideously ruthless miscreants that ever disgraced the earth and the sea" is true enough of the leaders of the preceding decades, such as l'Olonnois (French), Bartholomew Portuquez, Roche Braziliano (Dutch), and we may add Henry Morgan (Welsh). Even these villains had their several accounts for settlement with the Spaniards. L'Olonnois had been kidnapped and sold as a slave; Morgan, too, had been sold as a slave; Esquemeling, their historian, had been beaten, tortured and nearly starved to death. The captains whom Dampier served were of

[1] Some had commissions of various import from French or English authorities. Thus Captain Swan had one from the Duke of York, neither to give offence to the Spaniards nor to receive any affront from them. With this Swan, under plea of such an affront, "thought he had a lawful Commission of his own to right himself." Dampier had not seen the French commissions, but heard that they were "to fish, fowl and hunt," and were nominally confined to Hispaniola: the French, nevertheless, "make them a pretence for a general ravage in any part of America, by sea or land." (See page 137.) Captain Cook succeeded to one of these by right of seizing the French Captain Tristian's bark! Most of the buccaneers, however, did not trouble about commissions. In his threatening letter to the President of Panama, Captain Sawkins promised to visit that city when his force was ready, declaring, in language fine enough to glorify a better cause, that he would "bring our commissions on the muzzles of our guns, at which time he should read them as plain as the flame of gunpowder could make them" (Ringrose, *Hist. of the Buccaneers*, Part IV, Chap. VIII).

[2] "The exploits of Drake and Raleigh were imitated, upon a smaller scale indeed, but with equally desperate valour, by small bands of pirates, gathered from all nations, but chiefly French and English" (Sir W. Scott, *Rokeby*, Canto I, Note D). The scale was in fact much larger.

[3] "Essays in Little"; and Preface to Esquemeling's *History of the Buccaneers* (Broadway Translations), 1893.

a more humane stamp. The change may be seen by a comparison of the original Esquemeling with the supplement of Ringrose and with the stories of Dampier and the others of his time. Though engaged in a lawless war the later captains conducted it more according to the existing laws of war, and they treated their Spanish enemies with respect and occasional chivalry. As for the men comprising the crews, they were of no worse class than those who manned the ships of war or merchantmen of the time. They were simply children of fortune, some of good behaviour, some vicious and drunken, a few provided with education[1], many with none, like the mixed companies who some 60 or 70 years ago crowded to the goldfields of Australia and California.

¶ As the enterprises of the buccaneers were lawless, so were the relations of the captains and crews. Readers of this volume will note the fitful allegiance of the captains to the commander-in-chief, and of the crews to the captains. Dissensions led to frequent mutinies and desertions: these however seem to have been treated as no more abnormal than changes of weather. They were settled without violence, and in most cases amicably, the men following the captains they liked best.

¶ The troubles of Spanish America are rightly traced to the Bull of the Borgia Pope who divided the Spanish and Portuguese claims of conquest by lines of longitude, and to the exclusive commercial policy based on that award. The filibustering of the Elizabethan seamen was England's protest against the preposterous claim founded on a Papal decree, not sanctioned by more than sparse settlements on the vast coasts of two continents. As Sir Charles Lucas says, the Spaniards "claimed rather than possessed, and did little either in conquest or settlement."[2] England's protest brought forth the Spanish Armada; its destruction, however, did not produce a settlement of the international situation in America. More than 80 years later the operations of the buccaneers, insulting to Spain and cruelly destructive of Spanish life and property, impossible as they were for the English government to defend, led to the conclusion of the treaty of 1670. It was a one-sided agreement which protected for England little more than Jamaica, while for Spain the whole of her settlements on both sides of America were to be immune. Exemplifying the foolish ideas

[1] Ringrose, who was one of these, tells us of another, Richard Gopson, who died on the return journey across the Isthmus. He had been apprentice to a druggist in London but "was an ingenious man and a good scholar, and had with him a Greek Testament which he frequently read, and would translate *ex tempore* into English to such of the company as were disposed to hear him."

[2] *Hist. Geog. of the Brit. Colonies*, West Indies, p. 296.

of the time in regard to commercial policy it proposed to secure not mutual but exclusive trade. It provided that the subjects of the Confederates "shall abstain and forbear to sail and trade in the ports and havens which have fortifications, castles, magazines or warehouses, and in all places whatever possessed by the other party in the West Indies." The Governors of Jamaica did what they could, without sufficient power to their elbows, to carry the treaty into effect. Some buccaneers were punished, but when Dampier, nine years later, came on the scene, the game was more popular than ever and attracted many hundreds of adventurers from both England and France. At this time the French were more occupied with gaining a footing in Hispaniola, and thus most of the sea work "on the account," such was the euphemism, was done by the English[1].

¶ Trading between nations is a natural propensity, and an exclusive trade agreement was one certain to be resented and disregarded. The Spaniards on their side did little to ease the situation[2]. Englishmen and Frenchmen when they fell into their power were put to death or imprisoned with barbarous severities[3]. They did not on all occasions feel bound to keep their word with heretics. Their oppressive treatment of the natives led many tribes to give active or covert assistance to the intruders. Although at times, as we shall see, they fought with their old valour, in most cases they lived in a state of terror, vacated their towns at the first assault, and were held in contempt by the English freebooters.

¶ Public opinion at home was not seriously adverse to the buccaneers[4]. Morgan, the most notorious professor of the craft, after being alternately commissioned and prosecuted as a privateer, was knighted and appointed

---

[1] "Nulli melius piraticam exercent quam Angli," says Scaliger.

[2] Sir Henry Morgan does, however, in 1680 (*Cal. S.P. Amer. and W.I.*) mention the arrival at Port Royal of a "good English merchantman" which had been trading with the Spaniards on the Main. She reported a friendly reception of herself, but great desolation of the maritime towns through the frequent sacking of the privateers.

[3] See despatch of Sir Thomas Lynch, 26 July, 1683, in *Cal. S.P. Amer. and W.I.*

[4] The New Englanders heartily supported buccaneering and throve on it. On 25 Aug. 1684 Governor Cranfield records the arrival at Boston of a French privateer of 35 guns. When she was sighted the Bostonians sent a messenger and a pilot to convoy her into port in defiance of the King's Proclamation, which they tore down. He adds that the pirates were likely to leave the greatest part of their booty behind them (amounting to £700 a man), as they had bought up most of the choice goods in Boston. (*Cal. S.P. Amer. and W.I.*) Much further evidence is supplied by the official correspondence.

Lieutenant-Governor of Jamaica. Some of Dampier's associates, prosecuted on their return to England on charges of piracy, were acquitted or
liberated after short imprisonment. At this time, when larceny of a sheep
or ass was punishable with death, the penalty of piracy, under the statute
28 Hen. VIII, c. 15, unless accompanied by murder, was only fine and
imprisonment[1]. James II had proclaimed a pardon for buccaneers, and
the open confession of piracy, in Ringrose's and Dampier's narratives,
created little or no danger of prosecution: there was evidently no fear
even of adverse public criticism. In Dampier's case his book opened for
him the door of employment under Government.

SECOND STAGE

¶ The expedition contrived by the pirate leaders was an attack on
Portobello, the rich isthmus city near the site of the famous Nombre de
Dios[2]. The buccaneer force consisted of nine ships, two of them French,
and 477 men. The place was easily taken and, though it had been sacked
by Morgan only 11 years ago, the booty gave a dividend of £40 per man.
A proposal was now made, on the instigation of friendly Indians, to march
across the Isthmus to the city of Santa Maria. The French broke off:
they "were not willing to go to Panama, declaring themselves generally
against a long march by land." The force was thus reduced by two ships
and 111 men. Two of the captains with a party of seamen were left "to
guard our ships in our absence with which we intended to return home."
The expeditionary force of 331 men landed and marched forward
in seven companies carrying flags of various colours; "all or most of
them were armed with fuzee, pistol and hanger." The adventurous
march with this trivial armament was completed in ten days: Santa

---

[1] Under date 20 May, 1680, the Council of Jamaica wrote to the Commissioners of
Trade and Plantations of the "detestable depredations of some of our nation (who pass
for inhabitants of Jamaica) under colour of French commissions," referring to them as
"ravenous vermin." They suggested that piracy should be punished as felony without
benefit of clergy.

[2] The capture of Portobello is described in the *History of the Buccaneers*, Part III, Chap.
XII. The details of other events, shortly summarised by Dampier in his Chapter I, are
supplied by Basil Ringrose in Part IV of that *History*. For this first period my quotations
are from Ringrose. Another account of this stage of Dampier's voyage is given by Lionel
Wafer, the surgeon, in his *New Voyage and Description*, who was with him in one ship or
another till 25 August, 1685, when Davis and Swan parted company (see Chap. VIII).
Wafer's book was not published till after Dampier's, in 1699.

Maria was taken with no loss of men but produced little or no booty. The force, which had been provided by the Indians with 35 canoes, then got separated and one party appeared off Panama at the island of Perico, where were anchored "five great ships and three pretty big barks." The buccaneers numbered only 68 men in five canoes: they nevertheless attacked and took the barks after a desperate resistance. An Admiral was killed and in one of the barks the Spaniards lost 61 out of 86 men: all but eight of the rest were wounded. The buccaneers' casualties were 18 killed and 22 wounded. It was then found that the five ships were deserted, their crews having been transferred to man the barks; the biggest was *La Santissima Trinidad* of 400 tons. The freebooters found themselves in possession of more than sufficient shipping to carry them whither they would. The action, however, occasioned a second breach in the brotherhood. Captain Coxon, the Commander-in-Chief, was charged with backwardness in the engagement, and some "sticked not to defame or brand him with the note of cowardice." Coxon thereupon withdrew from the fleet taking 70 men with him, and recrossed the isthmus[1]. The next adventure, an attack on Puebla Nova, was a grievous failure, costing the death of Captain Sawkins, the new Commander-in-Chief, "a man as stout as could be, and beloved above any other that ever we had amongst us, as he well deserved."[2] A minority, 63 in number, who so lamented Sawkins that they could not serve his successor Sharp, mutinied and left for the isthmus in an old ship assigned to them. They had hardly gone when another mutiny broke out. The men on one of the prizes to which Captain Edmund Cook was appointed by Sharp refused to serve under him: Cook joined Sharp's ship and Captain Cox took over the command of the mutinous crew, with the status "as it were of Vice-Admiral."

¶ Off Guayaquil they captured a bark which they sank after replacing

[1] Coxon's subsequent career is told by Mr Masefield (vol. 1, p. 531). He spent the rest of his life in the Caribbean Sea, alternately in piracy and as a government agent in the suppression of piracy. Latterly he went trading with the Mosquito Indians and died among them in 1688.

[2] So wrote Ringrose (Sloane MSS. 3820). In his published story (*History of the Buccaneers*, Part IV), the passage appears thus: "A man who was as valiant and courageous as any could be, and likewise, next to Captain Sharp, the best beloved of our company or the most part thereof." The discrepancy is thus accounted for. Ringrose returned to England in 1682 and sailed again with Captain Swan in October, 1683. In his absence his MS. was doctored by Sharp, or his shipmate Hack, before its publication in 1685 in the supplement to the *History*. Sharp perhaps anticipated that Ringrose would never return to confute him; and he did not, being killed in Mexico, as we shall see, in February, 1686.

from her their rigging damaged in the encounter. A designed attack on Arica failed owing to heavy weather which prevented a landing from the boats. With little difficulty they next captured the city of La Serena, an exploit not even mentioned by Dampier, but described with much zest by Ringrose. The city had no less than seven great churches and each had its organ. The houses had charming gardens and orchards "as well and as neatly furnished as those in England, producing strawberries as big as walnuts and very delicious to the taste." Sad to relate, owing to the Spaniards' failure to pay the 95,000 pieces-of-eight demanded as ransom, this agreeable city was burned to the ground.

¶ At Juan Fernandez, the most southerly point of the cruise, another mutiny broke out. According to Ringrose there was a division of opinion, some for going home by way of the Straits of Magellan, others for a further cruise on the Pacific coast. Sharp was deposed from his command in favour of Watling. The ships left the island on 14 January, 1681, the crews in smouldering discontent. The leaders seem to have thought that the best chance of harmony lay in carrying out a successful *coup*: a second attack on Arica was accordingly resolved upon. At Iquique Island near that town information for the assault was demanded from four prisoners: that given by one old mestizo was hastily believed to be false, and he was summarily shot. This brutal act raised further dissension and Captain Sharp in one of his apocryphal additions to Ringrose's text states that after a vain protest, he, Pilate-fashion, "took water and washed his hands saying, 'Gentlemen, I am clear of the blood of this old man: and I will warrant you a hot day for this piece of cruelty whenever we come to fight at Arica!'" Ringrose says not a word of this, nor does Sharp himself in his own journal: he probably invented the lie because the attack on Arica in fact turned out a bloody and profitless affair. Captain Watling and both quartermasters—28 men in all—were killed; 18 others desperately wounded, and some, including three surgeons who were drinking instead of fighting or attending the wounded, were taken prisoners. The town was stormed with reckless courage and half taken against a stubborn defence. The Spaniards with superior numbers counter-attacked again and again and finally drove the marauders back to their ships[1]. Great expectations were thus disappointed, Arica being the port from which "is fetched all the plate that is carried to Lima, the head city of Peru."

---

[1] Cox attributes the failure at Arica to "having landed on Sunday, 30 January, it being the anniversary of King Charles the First, and a fatal day for the English to engage on."

On the death of Watling, Sharp resumed the command. Ringrose (as emended by Sharp himself) eulogises this captain as "a man of undaunted courage and of an excellent conduct," while according to Dampier the company were "not satisfied either with his courage or behaviour." The opinion of the crews was put to the test by voting at the island of Plata. The majority, including Ringrose, went for Sharp: the minority of 44, including Dampier and Wafer[1], seceded. At this point Dampier takes up the chronicle, but we part from Ringrose with regret[2].

¶ Now that Dampier tells his story in detail less commentary is needed. In Chapters I and III he has much to say about the friendly Mosquito Indians and their wonderful skill in striking fish, turtle and manatees. On this account they were "esteemed and coveted by all privateers," and some of them were always part of the ships' complements in the cruises on both sides of the Isthmus: they are the men to whom Dampier frequently refers as "strikers." In his account of the laborious journey of 23 days over the Isthmus (Chap. II)—the outward crossing had taken them only ten—the reader will specially note how he preserved his journal in a joint of bamboo, waxed at both ends. The exhausted party were taken on board Captain Tristian's ship on 24 May, 1681[3], and here is concluded the second stage of the voyage round the world. Since Portobello, the expedition had been a failure in capture of "plate." Other booty had to be discarded for want of neutral ports for its realisation, and Dampier's

[1] Wafer says: "I was of Mr Dampier's side in that matter and chose to go back to the Isthmus rather than stay under a Captain in whom we experienced neither courage nor conduct." It need not be inferred from this that Dampier took a lead in the mutiny. Wafer's book, published two years later, was addressed to readers presumably acquainted with Dampier's.

[2] His spirited and admirably written narrative shows him to have been a man of education, witness that on an emergency he was able to make shift with Latin for talk with a Spaniard. He went home with Captain Sharp and wrote his story which forms Part IV of the *History of the Buccaneers*. He came out again with Captain Cook to Virginia, where Dampier joined them. He was killed in an ambush near Santa Pecaque, in Mexico, February, 1686 (see page 189).

[3] Later they were there joined by Lionel Wafer, the chirurgeon, who had been severely injured by an explosion of powder during the transit, and was left with other stragglers in the charge of friendly Indians, with whom he remained some five months. Wafer, by reason of his medical skill, lived "in great splendour and repute," and was so "ador'd" by his hosts that they tattooed him "in yellow, red and blue, very bright and lovely." When he rejoined his friends at La Sound's Key, he was at first not recognised, and then with hilarity.

party brought back little or nothing. It was about 2½ years since he had left London.

¶ Dampier is so reticent about himself that it is difficult to hazard an opinion as to the part he took in this or any other buccaneering cruise. There is nothing to go upon: throughout the voyages of this volume he never commanded a ship nor an expedition: he does not tell us how he was rated, or what part he took in affairs—he gave his advice occasionally, and joined in the mutiny at Plata, intimating, however, that he took no active share in it. Nor does he appear to have been much in the forefront of battle, as Ringrose was. The only friendship he seems to have formed was with Ringrose, whom he called friend and "worthy consort." He is not even mentioned by Sharp, Cowley or Cox. His attitude towards the wild men with whom he associated was one of aloofness. His chief concern was the study of geography, the winds and tides, the plants and animals, and keeping his journal posted up.

THIRD STAGE

¶ From Captain Tristian, Dampier was transferred to another Frenchman, Captain Archemboe[1], but soon grew "weary of living with the French." Their sailors were "the saddest creatures that ever I was among." By insistence he compelled Captain Wright to add him with other English to his crew. The cruise in the Caribbean Sea described in Chapter III, though it brought the pirates little profit, gave Dampier plenty of time for his favourite studies and observations. He was at the island of Aves little more than a year after the disaster to Count d'Estrée's fleet (February, 1681) which he describes from hearsay. Off the Caracas coast he and 20 others took one of the ships and their share of the spoil and sailed off to Virginia. He does not specify the cause of the defection or the intention in choosing that destination. Of his 13 months' stay there he says no more than that he fell into troubles of some sort.

FOURTH STAGE

¶ In August, 1683, he again joins the buccaneers in the *Revenge*, Captain Cook. The cruise was a long one round the Horn and up the Pacific Coast as described in Chapters IV-IX. The course taken was to the Cape Verde islands and Sierra Leone. Here the buccaneers boarded and took a fine Danish vessel, the *Batchelor's Delight*, 36 guns, to which Cook transferred his crew. It was an act of piracy so flagrant, committed against a friendly nation, without such shadow of excuse as was deemed to justify harms to

---

[1] Probably Archambaut.

Spain, that Dampier is evidently ashamed to mention it. Cowley relates the incident without compunction. Dampier sailed with Cook till his death at Cape Blanco in June, 1684, thereafter with his successor, Captain Davis. On the *Batchelor's Delight* he found "the men more under command than I have ever seen privateers, yet I could not expect to find them at a minute's call." This is the only indication Dampier gives of his rating and Mr Masefield suggests with some probability that he was second master or master's mate under Ambrosia Cowley[1]. Cook was joined (March, 1684) by Captain Eaton in the *Nicholas*, and in October, at Plata, by Captain Swan in the *Cygnet*.

¶ Swan's case was a pitiful one: the *Cygnet*, fitted out by London merchants for lawful trade, had met Captain Peter Harris and a party of buccaneers at Nicoya with a considerable booty in hand. Swan's men, with whom he had already had difficulties at the Straits, were now seduced, and he was compelled to turn pirate. He was no backslider, however—it was by his order that Payta was burned to the ground in default of ransom (Chap. VI). Nevertheless his deflection from the path of virtue and duty weighed heavily on his mind. In a letter from Panama to a friend, quoted by Mr Masefield, he asks him to assure his employers that "I do all I can to preserve their interests and that what I do now I could in no wise prevent. So desire them to do what they can with the King for me, for as soon as I can I shall deliver myself to the King's justice." His view now was that if the buccaneers were backed by the Government "the King might make this whole kingdom of Peru tributary to him in two years' time." As he wrote, the attack on the Lima fleet was impending, and he adds in a message to his wife, "I shall, with God's help, do things which (were it with my Prince's leave) would make her a lady: but now I cannot tell but it may bring me to a halter." His end is told in Chapter XVI.

¶ The climax of this cruise was to have been the capture of the fleet carrying treasure from Lima to Panama. Davis and Swan had now (May, 1685) been joined by Captains Townley and Harris, and by a French contingent under Captain Gronet. The growth of the piratical

---

[1] William Ambrosia Cowley was master and pilot of the *Revenge* and sailed in her and the *Batchelor's Delight* until the parting of Captains Davis and Eaton (Sept. 1684). He joined Eaton and reached England by way of the East Indies in October, 1686, having deserted Eaton at the Philippines. He published his narrative, *Captain Cowley's Voyage round the World*, in 1699 (see further, Masefield, vol. I, p. 532). The book is interesting on some points of detail, but untrustworthy.

movement is seen in the numbers given by Dampier. The buccaneers had ten sail (six ships and four tenders, etc.) carrying no less than 960 men. They had, however, only 52 guns, these being in Davis' and Swan's ships. The Spaniards, on the other hand, had 14 sail, six of them "of good force," with 174 guns in all. Everything went against the pirates. While they had the weather-gage Gronet failed them: the Spaniards by a ruse obtained the weather-gage, and a running fight round the Bay ensued, from which the assailants were glad to escape. In the event of success there would have been no booty of plate, that having been already landed at Lavelia in view of a probable attack[1].

¶ The noteworthy events of this cruise, besides captures of casual prizes, are the taking and burning of Payta, and the abortive attempt on Guayaquil (Chap. VI); the taking and burning of Leon in Nicaragua, where was killed an old buccaneer who had fought with Cromwell in Ireland; and the parting of Davis and Swan[2] (Chap. VIII). Dampier, "not from any dislike to my old Captain but to get some knowledge of the Mexican Coast," joined up with Swan, who was minded to pass over to the East Indies, "which was a way very agreeable to my inclination." Thus is first inferentially expressed his intention of circumnavigation, more than 6½ years after he set out from England.

FIFTH STAGE

¶ On breaking with Davis, Swan's chief object in crossing the Pacific (Dampier probably sharing it) was to have done with buccaneering, and by honest trading to reinstate himself in the good graces of his employers. To induce his men to go with him, however, he was obliged

---

[1] The failure was attributed to Gronet, and he was cashiered, as Dampier relates at the close of Chap. VII. After a long cruise he fell in with Townley again and with him had better success. They sacked Grenada and Rio Lejo. Subsequently in April 1686 he sacked Guayaquil and took a large booty, but died of wounds received in the attack. Townley after parting with Gronet attacked and took Lavelia with much spoil, but in Aug. 1686 met his end in an action with Spanish ships in the Gulf of Panama (Masefield, vol. I, p. 538).

[2] Davis cruised for some time on the Pacific coast, returning with Lionel Wafer by way of the Horn to Virginia, where they settled for about three years. Arrested there for piracy they were sent to London for trial but were acquitted. After some years spent partly in London he returned to Jamaica, and on the outbreak of the War of the Spanish Succession joined a privateer in raids on the Spanish goldmines. His account of this adventure is appended to the 2nd edition of Wafer's book, 1704.

to hold out hopes of further piracy in the East Indies. At Guam in the Ladrones he made no attempt to pursue an Acapulco ship, being "now wholly averse to any hostile action." At Mindanao the party conducted themselves as traders and were hospitably entertained by the Sultan. Little trade was available and thoughts were entertained of settling there, the men being now weary lotus-eaters. The six months' residence at this place led to serious trouble: Swan became brutal and tyrannical towards his men, succumbed to the attractions of the town, and made long absences from his ship. Another mutiny was the result; the majority of the crew seized the ship, left Swan ashore, and sailed off under a new Captain—Read. Dampier's conduct on this occasion exhibits the same aloofness as on other occasions. He took no part in the men's conspiracy, nor, on the other hand, as it would seem, in the attempt to get Swan aboard. In spite of his better feelings, he became a pirate for another 18 months.

SIXTH STAGE

¶ The voyage under Captain Read, from the buccaneering point of view, was a complete failure. Though "our business was to pillage," only two prizes were taken and those of little account. Much sea and land, however, was explored, as is seen by the route—Manila, Pulo Condore, Formosa, Celebes, the north coast of Australia and the Nicobars. Here Dampier ended his buccaneering career of $8\frac{1}{2}$ years. The men had become more and more drunken, quarrelsome and unruly, and Dampier looked for an opportunity to escape from "this mad crew."[1] A canoe was obtained and Dampier, the surgeon and another Englishman, with a few natives, set out for Achin. In his terror during a storm which threatened to overwhelm their puny craft, Dampier "made sad reflections on my former life and look'd back with horror and detestation on actions which before I disliked but now I trembled at the remembrance of." In his escape from the dangers attendant on those actions, curiously enough he recognised the protection of Heaven. "I did also call to mind the many miraculous acts of God's Providence towards me in the whole course of my life."

¶ Whatever condemnation may be passed on Dampier's long association with pirates, it must be noted to his credit that during the whole period of this cruise in the Archipelago, while his companions were drinking and brawling, he was studiously recording his observations. His six months'

---

[1] See page 252: "I did ever abhor drunkenness, which now our men that were aboard abandon'd themselves wholly to."

residence at Mindanao provides us with a full description of plant and animal life as also of the inhabitants, their government, religion, manners and customs (Chaps. XI, XII). Here too comes on the scene that curious Prince Jeoly, the "painted Prince," whom Dampier brought to England for show and there sold as his only asset[1].

SEVENTH STAGE

¶ From Achin, and for the rest of the circumnavigation, Dampier was for the most part a mere passenger. First a voyage to Tonquin with Captain Welden (July, 1688–April, 1689): thence to Malacca and Fort George and back to Achin and Bencoulen, where he was employed as gunner in the English fort for five months. This section of his travels is omitted from the *New Voyage* and reserved for the *Voyage to Tonqueen*. At Achin, as will be seen in Chapter XVIII, he learns the further adventures of Captain Read and his crew whom he had deserted at the Nicobars.

EIGHTH STAGE

¶ His eventful voyage now draws to a close (Chaps. XIX and XX). Getting a passage from Bencoulen in the *Defence*, Captain Heath, Dampier arrived in the Downs on 16 September, 1691, 12½ years since he had left England. All buccaneer's visions of a home-coming with ample booty in bar gold or pieces-of-eight had vanished, and he landed with no more marketable commodities than a tattooed native.

DAMPIER'S SUBSEQUENT LIFE

¶ On his return to England Dampier was 39 years of age. Further great voyages were in store for him, each of which would require its own commentary. None, however, has been so attractive to the reading public as the *New Voyage*, it may be because the other expeditions, though comprising exploits and adventure, are hardly so attractive to law-abiding citizens as those to which additional zest is provided by contempt of law.
¶ For six years nothing is known of Dampier's life except that he was at Corunna in 1694, probably in a merchant ship. It is likely that he made other such voyages: in the intervals he was preparing his *New Voyage* for publication early in 1697. Its immediate success obtained for

---

[1] Mr Masefield quotes a broadsheet of the time (*Dampier Voy.* vol. I, p. 539) from which it appears that the Prince was on view at the Blue Boar's Head in Fleet Street.

him an appointment at the Customs House as land-carriage man, and in June of that year he was examined before the Council of Trade and Plantation with respect to possible settlements on the Isthmus of Darien. Early in 1698 he was again examined before the Council with regard to an expedition against the pirates to the east of the Cape of Good Hope. His advice may have been sought partly on account of his piratical experience and partly because his book had shown that he had little heart in the business.

The Roebuck *voyage*

¶ He now submitted to the Government proposals for a new voyage of exploration to New Holland, which were accepted. He was appointed captain of the *Roebuck*, 21 guns, his first command, at the age of 47. He tells the story of his cruise in his *Voyage to New Holland*, published in two parts, 1703 and 1709. The expedition went awry from the first and for divers causes. His ship was unseaworthy for a long voyage, and he quarrelled with his men, especially with his lieutenant, Fisher, whom he put in irons and handed over as a prisoner to the Portuguese governor at Bahia. At Shark's Bay, in Western Australia, scurvy and the lack of water and provisions broke his spirit and he turned homewards. After touching at Timor, Batavia and the Cape he got his crazy vessel as far as Ascension where she foundered. There he got a passage in a man-of-war to Barbados and so home in a merchantman. From the point of view of exploration the voyage was no great success: he might have anticipated Cook, Furneaux and Flinders, and he touched only the barren coast of Western Australia[1]. His failure was largely due to his employers who gave him an unseaworthy and badly provisioned ship, and to his mutinous crew. It would be unjust to attribute the failure to his incompetency as a leader of men: all that is to be said is that in the conditions he did not succeed as such.

¶ On his return he had to meet not only adverse criticism on his failure as an explorer, but also a court martial at the instance of Lieutenant Fisher. He was found guilty of "very hard and cruel usage towards Lieutenant Fisher," for which the court held there were no grounds. He was fined all his pay[2] and declared to be "not a fit person to be

[1] His name has, however, been rightly honoured in Australasia. There is the Dampier Strait at the west end of New Guinea and also a Dampier Island. Western Australia gives his name to a district and an archipelago: New South Wales to a county.

[2] That is his pay as captain: his pay as land-carriage man at the Customs was by special order paid to him during his absence and went to the support of his wife.

employed as Commander of any of His Majesty's Ships." We cannot
question the judgment of a court, the principal members of which were
Sir George Rooke and Sir Cloudesley Shovell. It was one which in our
time, when public opinion upholds legal decisions and requires govern-
ments to respect them, would be the end of an officer's career. It was
not so in Dampier's case. We need not here consider whether the Government disagreed with the judgment or merely disregarded it, because the
War of the Spanish Succession had now broken out and Dampier's
buccaneering experience was wanted on behalf of the country. Private
owners fitted out two privateers, the *St George* and the *Fame*, Dampier
being appointed to the former as Commander. Ten months after the
court martial he had an audience of the Queen to whom he was introduced
by the Lord High Admiral, and kissed hands on his mission.

The St George *voyage*

¶ The only account we possess of this privateering voyage is that of
William Funnell, who was rated mate of the *St George*, as he himself
claims, or as steward according to Dampier. Funnell is a dull and
malicious reporter and is not to be trusted when he deals with Dampier's
motives and conduct. Trouble began at the start, Captain Pulling in
the *Fame* deserting him in the Downs. His place was taken at Kinsale
(August, 1703) by Captain Pickering in the *Cinque Ports*. On the Brazilian
coast Pickering died and was succeeded by his lieutenant, Stradling.
More quarrelling ensued, enhanced by the hardships of the passage round
the Horn. Dissension between Stradling and his men led to the marooning
of Alexander Selkirk on Juan Fernandez. The failure to take two enemy
ships led to further recriminations and desertions. Dampier quarrelled
with Stradling and left him at Tobago: he quarrelled also with his own mate,
Clipperton, who went off with 21 men in a prize bark. After another
failure to capture a Manila bark, he was deserted by Funnell and 34 men.
His ship, being unseaworthy, was abandoned and with his now reduced
crew of about 30, in a prize brigantine, he crossed the Pacific to a Dutch
island where they were imprisoned. Dampier did not reach England till
the close of 1707. So began, continued and ended in disaster his second
voyage of circumnavigation. Meanwhile Funnell had already published
his damaging book[1]. Dampier would perhaps have written the story of

---

[1] Funnell by his references in his preface to the popularity of Dampier's previous work
evidently intended to forestall Dampier by passing off his book as another Dampier
voyage.

the voyage himself, but being already engaged to go to sea, he contented himself with publishing his *Vindication* in language strangely different from that of the *New Voyage*. Mr Masefield describes it as "angry and incoherent," but it may fairly be regarded as being no more than a collection of notes jotted down in indignation and hot haste, preparatory to a more reasoned vindication later[1].

The Duke *and* Dutchess *voyage*

¶ When Dampier returned from his second voyage as captain the merchants of Bristol were already organising a privateering expedition to the Pacific under Captain Woodes Rogers, and the honourable office of pilot was offered to Dampier. Of all his voyages this was probably the happiest to himself. The expedition was lawful and gave him no qualms of conscience; he was free from the cares and responsibilities of supreme command; he served under one of the most competent captains of the time, and his experience and ability as a navigator as well as his wise counsel enabled him to contribute largely to the success of the venture. The two vessels were the *Duke* and the *Dutchess*, Dampier sailing on the former with Rogers. In the list of officers he is described as "William Dampier, Pilot for the South Seas, who had been already three times there and twice round the World." Perhaps profiting by the experience of Dampier's previous ill-equipped expeditions, the merchants had provided the ships so liberally with provisions and gear that the 'tween decks were badly encumbered, and the ships "altogether in a very unfit state to engage an enemy." The crews indeed were of the same unpromising material with which Dampier was familiar. About one-third were foreigners, the rest landsmen, "tailors, tinkers, pedlars, fiddlers and haymakers." Between Cork, "where our crew were continually marrying," and the Canaries a dangerous mutiny broke out which Rogers promptly put down, imposing upon a ringleader the indignity of being whipped by a fellow-conspirator. Troubles with the crew were, however, to a large

---

[1] Funnell's *Voyage round the World* was published in 1707. Dampier got home later in that year and left again with Woodes Rogers 2 Aug. 1708. Some of Funnell's passages relating to Dampier and the *Vindicatio*, also the *Answers* to the *Vindication*, by John Welbe, a midshipman on board Captain Dampier's ship, are set out in Mr Masefield's admirable edition of the *Voyages*, vol. II, pp. 576–93. Welbe's answers are spiteful and probably in great part untrue. As Mr Masefield points out he contradicts them in a material particular in a subsequent letter of 1722 preserved in the Townshend MSS.

extent obviated by the payment of regular wages: the contract of employ-ment on the *St George* had been the vicious one of "no prey, no pay." Moreover, Rogers was wise enough to share his responsibility with his officers and all questions of importance were referred to Committees, Dampier's name being on nearly every list. Discipline was thus preserved and the cruise resulted in the capture of many prizes and a very large booty, which unhappily did not benefit Dampier, as the distribution was delayed till after his death[1].

¶ The most interesting feature of this voyage was the rescue of Alexander Selkirk from the island of Juan Fernandez, which the ships might not have hit without Dampier's knowledge of the winds. The meeting with his countrymen after his desolate life of four years is told by Woodes Rogers[2] with unconscious art, and one cannot help favourably comparing the inarticulate Selkirk with the expansive Ben Gunn of *Treasure Island*. Dampier took a leading part in the scene; he was able to tell Rogers that Selkirk was the best man in the *Cinque Ports* from which he had been marooned; so, says Rogers, "I immediately agreed with him to be a mate on board our ship."[3]

¶ After his return from his last voyage Dampier lived $3\frac{1}{2}$ years more, probably in London, where he died in the parish of St Stephen, Coleman Street, in March, 1715. His will dated 29 November, 1714, was proved on 23 March, 1715. He described himself as "diseased and weak of body, but of sound and perfect mind," and left nine-tenths of his property to his cousin, Grace Mercer, the remaining tenth to his brother, George Dampier, of Porton, in the County of Somerset. The large share of his property bequeathed to his cousin may indicate that she looked after him in his last years. His wife had probably predeceased him, as she is not mentioned in the will. By a previous will made before 1703 he had left a sum of £200 to his friend, Edward Southwell, to be disposed of as he should think best for his wife's use. On the starting of the *St George* cruise, however, he was constrained to put that sum into the venture.

[1] The booty amounted to about £170,000, a large share going to Woodes Rogers. He was able to rent the Bahama islands from the lords proprietors for 21 years and became their governor. (See Rogers, W., in the *Dict. Nat. Biog.*)

[2] Woodes Rogers published the account of the voyage, *A New Cruising Voyage round the World*, 1712.

[3] The various lives of Alexander Selkirk are well summarised in the *Dict. Nat. Biog.* It is probable that Selkirk did not alone provide the suggestion of Robinson Crusoe. Defoe had also before him Dampier's account of the rescue of the marooned Mosquito Indian in Chapter IV.

DAMPIER THE MAN

¶ Dampier is an attractive character, but do what one will, one cannot make a hero of him. Nor indeed does he seem to be quite in his right place on the roll of "Men of Action," with a biography by W. Clark Russell[1]. During the whole of the cruises comprised in the *New Voyage* he served either before the mast or as a subordinate officer and was never chosen for the command of a ship or an expedition; his advice does not appear to have been asked, and when proffered was seldom followed. He took no leading part in the various mutinies, keeping his mind to himself until he had to take one side or the other. He is once respectfully mentioned as "Mr William Dampier" by Cowley, but never once, so far as I have discovered, in the other narratives of Ringrose, Cox or Sharp. His whole time, so far as not interrupted by raids or the quarrels of his rowdy associates, was devoted to close observation of winds and tides, geography, plants and animal life. He was in fact a student carrying for the nonce the fuzee and hanger of a buccaneer. In happier days, and with a sounder scientific education, his status in a world cruise might have been that of Darwin on the *Beagle*.

¶ His first command of a ship at the age of 47 could not have been conferred owing to reputation as a leader of men. The *Roebuck* expedition was an official voyage of exploration initiated by his own suggestion, and the conduct of it was given to him, there can be little doubt, on the strength of his book, the *New Voyage*. The lack of success, however attributable to the unseaworthiness and ill-provisioning of the ship, and to the unmanageable crew, was not so damaging to his reputation as an explorer as was the judgment of the court martial to his capacity as a captain. His second chance, as privateersman in the *St George*, was equally unfortunate in the result. Here again he had to deal with an unseaworthy ship and dissolute crews. In both these cases he came home without his ship, and had to meet adverse criticism by recriminations. Whatever excuse may be found in the adverse conditions—and there is undoubtedly much—it can hardly be said that Dampier has established a claim to be regarded as a leader of men. His rough experience and scientific attainments no

---

[1] *Dampier*, by W. Clark Russell (Men of Action Series). The author is strangely inaccurate in some matters. He says it does not appear that Dampier was ever married, and he observes that after the *Roebuck* voyage Dampier had already twice circumnavigated the globe. The second round was that on which he started in the *St George*.

doubt made him a first-rate navigator, but a reputation as an explorer cannot be founded upon a single ineffectual visit to the coasts of Australia. ¶ Dampier's true distinction seems to me to lie in the scientific and literary merits of his writings. There is scientific research in all his books, notably in his *Discourse of Winds, Breezes, Storms, Tides and Currents,* a treatise which has preserved its usefulness to the present day. The exciting adventures of his buccaneering life are told in the modest and simple language of his time, which charms us equally in the autobiographical fiction of Swift and Defoe. As Leslie Stephen says of *Treasure Island,* we throw ourselves into the events, enjoy the thrilling excitement and do not bother ourselves with questions of psychology. His contributions to nautical science are extolled by those best qualified to judge. I will quote two naval authorities who testify also to the literary charm of the writing. First Captain Burney[1]: "It is not easy to name another voyager or traveller who has given more useful information to the world; to whom the merchant and mariner are so much indebted; or who has communicated his information in a more unembarrassed and intelligible a manner. And this he has done in a style perfectly unassuming, equally free from affectation and from the most distant appearance of invention." Admiral Smyth[2] is equally eulogistic: "The information he affords flows as from a mind which possesses the mastery of its subject, and is desirous to communicate it. He delights and instructs by the truth and discernment with which he narrates the incidents of a peculiar life; and describes the attractive and important realities of nature with a fidelity and sagacity that anticipate the deductions of philosophy. Hence he was the first who discovered and treated of the geological structure of sea coasts; and though the local magnetic attraction in ships had fallen under the notice of seamen, he was among the first to lead the way to its investigation since the facts that 'stumbled' him at the Cape of Good Hope, respecting the variations of the compass, excited the mind of Flinders, his ardent admirer, to study the anomaly. His sterling sense enabled him to give the character without the strict forms of science to his faithful delineations and physical suggestions: and inductive inquirers have rarely been so much indebted to any adventurer whose pursuits were so entirely remote from their subjects of speculation."

¶ Those who have excellently well adjudged Dampier's merits in science and literature have hardly done justice to his personal character. On the

---

[1] *A Chronological History of the Discoveries in the South Sea or Pacific Ocean,* 1803–17.

[2] *United Service Journal,* 1837, Parts II and III.

debit side some will reckon the unfortunate court martial, but any good man may, in the stress of difficulties attending a sea-command, exercise undue severity in the maintenance of his authority: and no doubt Lieutenant Fisher was a trying subordinate. The Admiralty do not seem to have taken quite the same view of the case as the court, as they shortly afterwards gave Dampier a privateer's commission. Then there is the fact that he was a buccaneer. On this point references have already been made to the laxity of public opinion on that subject in his day. It cannot be said that in joining the buccaneers Dampier mistook his vocation. That in modern parlance was research, and he could not in his day have obtained opportunities for research in the distant Caribbean and Pacific seas except with the buccaneers[1]. He was with them, but hardly one of them. As he was less of a buccaneer, so, as I believe, he was more of a gentleman. I have thus no need to claim or admit that "he was the mildest mannered man that ever scuttled ship or cut a throat." There is no evidence that he did either, and one likes to think he did not.

¶ Although he was not an active buccaneer he seems to have done his duty by his associates; at any rate no complaints against him in this respect are recorded. He took his share in their strenuous labour whether afloat or ashore, without mingling in their drinking bouts and quarrels; and all the while he was carefully writing up his journal day by day, and adding to his observations of Nature. He affords a bright example of strength of character in the pursuit of knowledge under the most adverse conditions.

¶ What is most conspicuous in Dampier's writings is his modesty and self-effacement; and I conclude that this, one of the hall-marks of a gentleman, was his demeanour in conversation and society. He unconsciously gives us a glimpse of his character when he tells us in Chapter III of the pressing invitation which he had from the captain and lieutenant of a French man-of-war to go back with them to France. Evidently charmed with his conversation, they saw how different a man he was from his ruffian associates. Though engaged in piracy he was always in favour of justice, and thus writes of Captain Davis' men (he being a Davis man himself) as being "so unreasonable, that they would not allow Captain Eaton's men an equal share with them in what they got" (page 97). It is a further tribute to his character that when he was at home he had

---

[1] Mr Masefield quotes one of Dampier's marginal notes on the Sloane MS. 3236: "I came into these seas this second time more to indulge my curiosity than to get wealth, though I must confess at that time I did think the trade lawful."

the patronage and help of Charles Montagu, Earl of Halifax, and the friendship of such men as Sir Robert Southwell, a president of the Royal Society, his son Edward Southwell, a Secretary of State for Ireland, and Sir Hans Sloane, who showed his respect for Dampier by having his portrait painted by Thomas Murray[1]—the face is that of a grave, thoughtful and resolute man. Much the most interesting sidelight on his social quality, however, is thrown by John Evelyn's record of his dinner with Mr Pepys on 6 August, 1698:

¶ "I dined with Mr Pepys, where was Captain Dampier, who had been a famous buccaneer, had brought hither the painted prince Job, and printed a relation of his very strange adventure, and his observations. He was now going abroad again by the King's encouragement, who furnished a ship of 290 tons. He seemed a more modest man than one would imagine by relation of the crew he had assorted with. He brought a map of his observations of the course of the winds in the South Seas, and assured us that the maps hitherto extant were all false as to the Pacific Sea, which he makes on the south of the line, that on the north end running by the coast of Peru being extremely tempestuous."

¶ It would seem that Evelyn expected to meet a swashbuckler and found a modest and courteous gentleman, with perhaps much to tell of his life's adventures, but for the moment chiefly concerned with his objection to calling an ocean pacific unless it is so. How pleasant it would have been for any person, however eminent, to have made a fourth at that dinner!

THE TEXT OF THE *NEW VOYAGE*

¶ When we come to investigate the text of this delightful book, we find some difficulties which have to be met and solved. The story and the scientific observations are undoubtedly Dampier's, for which he must have the entire credit. It was, however, charged against him in his own day that the literary style or polish was contributed by some unknown assistant or collaborator. This was believed by Swift, who evidently loved Dampier and was probably much influenced by him in his methods of narration as, indeed, is indicated by his reference to Dampier as Lemuel Gulliver's Cousin. That Dampier had some aid in preparing his work for the press is admitted by himself in the Preface to the *Voyage to New Holland*. He there refers to the charge that he has "published things digested and drawn up by others," and he retorts: "I think it so far a diminution to

---

[1] The picture, now in the National Portrait Gallery, is reproduced here.

WILLIAM DAMPIER (1652-1715).
*From the painting by T. Murray
in the National Portrait Gallery.*

one of my education and employment, to have what I write revised and corrected by friends; that on the contrary the best and most eminent authors are not ashamed to own the same thing, and look upon it as an advantage."

¶ It is difficult, if not impossible, now to discover the extent or nature of the assistance which Dampier obtained. The "copy" of the voyage as printed does not appear to exist, and the Sloane MS. account of it is in the clear script of a copyist, the marginal notes only being in Dampier's hand. The MS. is much shorter than the printed book. It comprises the story of the voyage, but lacks the observations in natural history: on the other hand, it includes (1) Wafer's account (taken "out of his own writing") of his life among the Indians of the Isthmus, (2) the account of the voyage of Captain Swan before he joined Dampier's party, and (3) the antecedent adventures of Captain Harris, all of which are omitted from the book. A perplexing factor is that the Sloane MS. contains in the copyist's writing the references (A), (B), etc., to the marginal notes afterwards supplied by Dampier. Other marginal notes are added, these indicated by a pointing hand. In some cases the marginal note is incorporated in the book, in others disregarded. Sometimes, too, a jotting from the journal as to an unimportant day's doing is omitted from the book. In some places the printed book alters the MS. in a material point[1]. Thus the MS. represents only one step in the preparation of the book text. Being in a copyist's hand, it may be only a fair copy of Dampier's not always quite legible writing: or it may be a version of his journal with some little polish administered by a literary friend. It is clear that his natural history notes were composed and kept separately from his journal. They comprise observations made at various places and at different and often subsequent periods of his travels: and they are sometimes pitch-forked into the book at odd junctures.

[1] For instance at page 13 (30 April 1681) we read "that we might the better work our escape from our enemies." In the MS. the words are "that we might the better work our designs on our enemies."

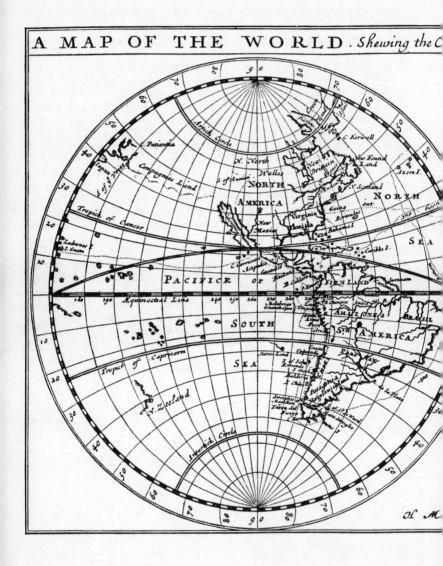

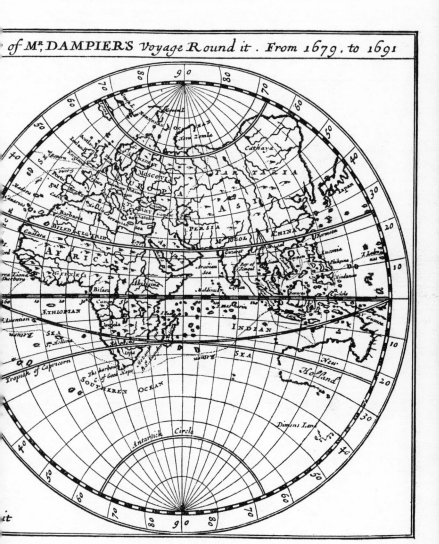

it

A NEW
VOYAGE
ROUND THE
WORLD.

Defcribing particularly

The *Ifthmus* of *America*, feveral Coafts and Iflands in the *Weft Indies*, the Ifles of *Cape Verde*, the Paffage by *Terra del Fuego*, the *South-Sea* Coafts of *Chili*, *Peru*, and *Mexico*; the Ifle of *Guam* one of the *Ladrones*, *Mindanao*, and other *Philippine* and *Eaft-India* Iflands near *Cambodia*, *China*, *Formofa*, *Luconia*, *Celebes*, &c. *New-Holland*, *Sumatra*, *Nicobar* Ifles; the Cape of *Good Hope*, and *Santa Hellena*.

Their Soil, Rivers, Harbours, Plants, Fruits, Animals, and Inhabitants.

Their Cuftoms, Religion, Government, Trade, &c.

VOL. I.

By Capt. *WILLIAM DAMPIER*.

Illuftrated with MAPS and DRAUGHTS.

The SEVENTH EDITION, Corrected.

LONDON:

Printed for JAMES and JOHN KNAPTON, at the Crown in St. *Paul*'s Church-Yard. MDCCXXIX.

To the Right Honourable

Charles Mountague, Esq;

President of the Royal Society,
One of the Lords Commissioners
of the Treasury, &c.

SIR,

May it please you to Pardon the Boldness of a Stranger to your Person, if upon the encouragement of Common Fame, he presumes so much upon your Candor, as to lay before you this Account of his Travels. As the Scene of them is not only Remote, but for the most part little frequented also, so there may be some things in them New even to you; and some, possibly, not altogether unuseful to the Publick: And that just Veneration which the World pays, as to your General Worth, so especially to that Zeal for the advancement of Knowledge, and the Interest of your Country, which you express upon all Occasions, gives you a particular Right to whatever may any way tend to the promoting these Interests, as an Offering due to your Merit. I have not so much of the vanity of a Traveller, as to be fond of telling stories, especially of this kind; nor can I think this plain piece of mine, deserves a place among your more Curious Collections: much less have I the Arrogance to use your Name by way of Patronage for the too obvious faults, both of the Author and the Work. Yet dare I avow, according to my narrow sphere and poor abilities, a hearty Zeal for the promoting of useful knowledge, and of any thing that may never so remotely tend to my Countries advantage: And I must own an Ambition of transmitting to the Publick through your hands, these Essays I have made toward those great ends, of which you are so deservedly esteemed the Patron. This hath been my design in this Publication, being desirous to bring in my Gleanings here and there in Remote Regions, to that general Magazine, of the knowledge of Foreign Parts, which the *Royal Society* thought you most worthy the Custody of, when they chose you for their *President*: and if in perusing these Papers, your Goodness shall so far distinguish the Experience of the Author from his Faults, as to judge him capable of serving his Country, either immediately, or by serving you, he will endeavour by some real proofs to show himself,

SIR,

Your Most Faithful,

Devoted, Humble Servant,

W. Dampier.

PREFACE

BEFORE the Reader proceed any further in the perusal of this Work, I must bespeak a little of his Patience here to take along with him this short account of it. It is composed of a mixt Relation of Places and Actions, in the same order of time in which they occurred: for which end I kept a Journal of every Day's Observations.

¶ In the Description of Places, their Product, &c. I have endeavoured to give what satisfaction I could to my Country-men; tho' possibly to the describing several things that may have been much better accounted for by others: Choosing to be more particular than might be needful, with respect to the intelligent Reader, rather than to omit what I thought might tend to the Information of Persons no less sensible and inquisitive, tho' not so Learned or Experienced. For which reason, my chief Care hath been to be as particular as was consistent with my intended brevity, in setting down such Observables as I met with. Nor have I given my self any great Trouble since my Return, to compare my Discoveries with those of others: The rather, because, should it so happen that I have described some places, or things which others have done before me, yet in different Accounts, even of the same things, it can hardly be but there will be some new Light afforded by each of them. But after all, considering that the main of this Voyage hath its Scene laid in long Tracts of the Remoter Parts, both of the *East* and *West-Indies*, some of which very seldom visited by *English*-men, and others as rarely by any *Europeans*, I may without vanity encourage the Reader to expect many things wholly new to him, and many others more fully described than he may have seen elsewhere; for which not only in this Voyage, tho' it self of many years continuance, but also several former long and distant Voyages have qualified me.

¶ As for the Actions of the Company among whom I made the greatest part of this Voyage, a Thread of which I have carried on thro' it, 'tis not to divert the Reader with them that I mention them, much less that I take any pleasure in relating them: but for method's sake, and for the Reader's satisfaction; who could not so well acquiesce in my Description of Places, &c. without knowing the particular Traverses I made among them; nor in these, without an Account of the Concomitant Circumstances: Besides, that I would not prejudice the Truth and Sincerity of my Relation, tho' by Omissions only. And as for the Traverses themselves, they make for

the Reader's advantage, how little soever for mine; since thereby I have
been the better inabled to gratify his Curiosity; as one who rambles about
a Country can give usually a better account of it, than a Carrier who jogs
on to his Inn, without ever going out of his Road.

¶ As to my Stile, it cannot be expected, that a Seaman should affect
Politeness; for were I able to do it, yet I think I should be little sollicitous
about it, in a work of this Nature. I have frequently indeed, divested my
self of Sea-Phrases, to gratify the Land Reader; for which the Seamen will
hardly forgive me: And yet, possibly, I shall not seem Complaisant enough
to the other; because I still retain the use of so many Sea-terms. I confess
I have not been at all scrupulous in this matter, either as to the one or the
other of these; for I am perswaded, that if what I say be intelligible, it
matters not greatly in what words it is express'd.

¶ For the same reason I have not been curious as to the spelling of the
Names of Places, Plants, Fruits, Animals, &c. which in any of these
remoter parts are given at the pleasure of Travellers, and vary according
to their different Humours: Neither have I confined my self to such
Names as are given by Learned Authors, or so much as enquired after
many of them. I write for my Countrymen; and have therefore, for the
most part, used such Names as are familiar to our *English* Seamen, and
those of our Colonies abroad, yet without neglecting others that occurr'd.
As it might suffice me to have given such Names and Descriptions as I
could; I shall leave to those of more leisure and opportunity the trouble of
comparing these with those which other Authors have assigned.

¶ The Reader will find as he goes along, some References to an Appendix,
which I once designed to this Book; as, to a Chapter about the Winds in
different parts of the World; to a Description of the Bay of *Campeachy* in
the *West-Indies*, where I lived long in a former Voyage; and to a particular
Chorographical Description of all the *South-Sea* Coast of *America*, partly
from a *Spanish MS*, and partly from my own and other Travellers Observations, besides those contained in this Book. But such an Appendix would
have swelled it too unreasonably: and therefore I chose rather to publish
it hereafter by its self, as opportunity shall serve. And the same must be
said also as to a particular Voyage from *Achin* in the Isle of *Sumatra*, to
Tonquin, *Malacca*, &c. which should have been inserted as part of this
General one; but it would have been too long, and therefore omitting it
for the present, I have carried on this, next way from *Sumatra* to *England*;
and so made the *Tour* of the *World* correspondent to the *Title*.

¶ For the better apprehending the Course of the Voyage, and the
Situation of the Places mentioned in it, I have caused several Maps to

be engraven, and some particular Draughts of my own Composure. Among them, there is in the Map of the *American Isthmus*, a new Scheme of the adjoining Bay of *Panama* and its Islands, which to some may seem superfluous after that which Mr. *Ringrose* hath published in the History of the *Buccaneers*; and which he offers as a very exact Draught. I must needs disagree with him in that, and doubt not but this which I here publish will be found more agreeable to that Bay, by one who shall have opportunity to examine it; for it is a contraction of a larger Map which I took from several Stations in the Bay it self. The Reader may judge how well I was able to do it, by my several Traverses about it, mentioned in this Book; those, particularly, which are described in the 7th Chapter, which I have caused to be marked out with a pricked Line; as the Course of my Voyage is generally in all the Maps, for the Reader's more easy tracing it.

¶ I have nothing more to add, but that there are here and there some mistakes made, as to expression, and the like, which will need a favourable Correction as they occur upon Reading. For instance, the Log of Wood lying out at some distance from Sides of the Boats described at *Guam*, and parallel to their Keel, which for distinction's sake I have called the little Boat, might more clearly and properly have been called the side Log, or by some such Name; for though fashioned at the Bottom and Ends Boat-wise, yet is not hollow at top, but solid throughout. In other places also I may not have express'd my self so fully as I ought: But any considerable Omission, that I shall recollect or be inform'd of, I shall indeavour to make up in those Accounts I have yet to publish; and for any Faults, I leave the Reader to the joint use of his Judgment and Candour.

THE INTRODUCTION

The Author's Departure from England, *and Arrival in* Jamaica. *His first going over the* Isthmus *of* America *into the* South-Seas: *His coasting along* Peru *and* Chili, *and back again, to his parting with Captain* Sharp *near the Isle of* Plata, *in order to return over Land.*

I FIRST set out of *England* on this Voyage at the beginning of the year 1679, in the *Loyal Merchant of London,* bound for *Jamaica,* Captain *Knapman* Commander. I went a Passenger, designing when I came thither, to go from thence to the Bay of *Campeachy,* in the Gulph of *Mexico,* to cut Log-wood: where in a former Voyage I had spent about three years in that employ; and so was well acquainted with the place and the work.
¶ We sailed with a prosperous Gale without any impediment or remarkable Passage in our Voyage: unless that when we came in Sight of the Island *Hispaniola,* and were coasting along on the South-side of it by the little Isles of *Vacca,* or *Ash,* I observed Captain *Knapman* was more vigilant than ordinary, keeping at a good distance off Shore, for fear of coming too near those small low Islands; as he did once, in a Voyage from *England,* about the Year 1673, losing his Ship there, by the Carelessness of his Mates. But we succeeded better; and arrived safe at *Port-Royal* in *Jamaica* some time in *April* 1679. and went immediately ashore.
¶ I had brought some Goods with me from *England,* which I intended to sell here, and stock my self with Rum and Sugar, Saws, Axes, Hats, Stockings, Shoes and such other Commodities, as I knew would sell among the *Campeachy* Log-wood-Cutters. Accordingly I sold my *English* Cargo at *Port-Royal*; but upon some maturer Considerations of my intended Voyage to *Campeachy,* I changed my Thoughts of that design, and continued at *Jamaica* all that Year, in Expectation of some other Business.
¶ I shall not trouble the Reader with my Observations at that Isle, so well known to *English*-men; nor with the Particulars of my own Affairs during my Stay there. But in short, having there made a Purchase of a small Estate in *Dorsetshire,* near my Native Country of *Somerset,* of one whose Title to it I was well assured of, I was just embarking my self for *England,* about *Christmas,* 1679. when one Mr. *Hobby* invited me to go first a short Trading Voyage to the Country of the *Moskito's,* of whom I shall speak in my first Chapter. I was willing to get up some Money

before my return, having laid out what I had at *Jamaica*; so I sent the Writing of my new Purchase along with the same Friends whom I should have accompanied to *England*, and went on board Mr. *Hobby*.

¶ Soon after our setting out we came to an anchor again in *Negril* Bay, at the West-end of *Jamaica*; but finding there Captain *Coxon*, *Sawkins*, *Sharp*, and other Privateers, Mr. *Hobby*'s Men all left him to go with them, upon an Expedition they had contrived, leaving not one with him, beside my self; and being thus left alone, after three or four days stay with Mr. *Hobby*, I was the more easily perswaded to go with them too.

¶ It was shortly after *Christmas* 1679 when we set out. The first Expedition was to *Portobel*; which being accomplished, it was resolved to march by Land over the Isthmus of *Darien*, upon some new Adventures in the *South-Seas*. Accordingly on the 5th of *April* 1680, we went ashore on the Isthmus, near *Golden-Island*, one of the *Sambaloes*, to the number of between three and four hundred Men, carrying with us such Provisions as were necessary, and Toys wherewith to gratify the *Wild Indians*, through whose Country we were to pass. In about nine days march we arrived at *Santa Maria*, and took it, and after a Stay there of about three days, we went on to the *South-Sea* Coast, and there embarked our selves in such Canoas and Periago's, as our *Indian* Friends furnished us withal. We were in Sight of *Panama* by the 23d of *April*, and having in vain attempted *Puebla Nova*, before which *Sawkins*, then Commander in chief, and others, were kill'd, we made some Stay at the neighbouring Isles of *Quibo*.

¶ Here we resolved to change our Course, and stand away to the southward for the Coast of *Peru*. Accordingly we left the Keys or Isles of *Quibo* the 6th of *June*, and spent the rest of the Year in that southern Course; for touching at the Isles of *Gorgonia* and *Plata*, we came to *Ylo*, a small Town on the Coast of *Peru*, and took it. This was in *October*, and in *November* we went thence to *Coquimbo* on the same Coast, and about *Christmas* were got as far as the Isle of *John Fernando*, which was the farthest of our Course to the Southward.

¶ After *Christmas* we went back again to the Northward, having a design upon *Arica*, a strong Town advantageously situated in the hollow of the Elbow, or bending of the *Peruvian* Coast. But being there repulsed with great Loss, we continued our Course northward, till by the middle of *April* we were come in sight of the Isle of *Plata*, a little to the southward of the Equinoctial Line.

¶ I have related this part of my Voyage thus summarily and concisely, as well because the World hath Accounts of it already, in the relations that Mr. *Ringrose* and others have given of Captain *Sharp*'s Expedition, who was made chief Commander, upon *Sawkin*'s being kill'd; as also, because in the prosecution of this Voyage I shall come to speak of these parts again, upon occasion of my going the second time into the *South-Seas*: and shall there describe at large the places both of the *North* and *South America*, as they occurred to me. And for this Reason, that I might avoid needless Repetitions, and hasten to such particulars, as the Publick hath hitherto had no account of, I have chosen to comprize the Relation of my Voyage hitherto in this short Compass, and place it as an Introduction before the rest, that the Reader may the better perceive where I mean to begin to be particular; for there I have plac'd the Title of my first Chapter.

¶ All therefore that I have to add to the Introduction, is this; That while we lay at the Isle of *John Fernando*, Captain *Sharp* was, by general Consent, displaced from being Commander; the Company being not satisfied either with his Courage or Behaviour. In his stead, Captain *Watling* was advanced: but he being killed shortly after before *Arica*, we were without a Commander during all the rest of our Return towards *Plata*. Now *Watling* being killed, a great number of the meaner sort began to be as earnest for choosing Captain *Sharp* again into the Vacancy, as before they had been as forward as any to turn him out: And on the other side, the abler and more experienced Men, being altogether dissatisfied with *Sharp*'s former Conduct, would by no means consent to have him chosen. In short, by that time we were come in Sight of the Island *Plata*, the difference between the contending Parties was grown so high, that they resolved to part Companies; having first made an Agreement, that which Party soever should upon Polling, appear to have the Majority, they should keep the Ship: And the other should content themselves with the Launch or Long-boat, and Canoas, and return back over the Isthmus, or go to seek their Fortune other-ways, as they would.

¶ Accordingly we put it to the Vote; and upon dividing, Captain *Sharp*'s Party carried it. I, who had never been pleased with his Management, though I had hitherto kept my Mind to my self, now declared my self on the side of those that were Out-voted; and according to our Agreement, we took our Shares of such Necessaries, as were fit to carry over Land with us, (for that was our Resolution:) and so prepared for our Departure.

MEMOIRS
OF A
BUCCANEER

WILLIAM DAMPIER'S
NEW VOYAGE ROUND
THE WORLD

CHAPTER I

An Account of the Author's Return out of the South-Seas, *to his Landing near* Cape St. Lawrence,
in the Isthmus of Darien: *With an Occasional Description of the* Moskito Indians.

APRIL the 17th 1681, about Ten a Clock in the Morning, being
12 Leagues N.W. from the Island *Plata*, we left Captain *Sharp*
and those who were willing to go with him in the Ship, and
imbarked into our Lanch and Canoas, designing for the River of *Santa
Maria*, in the Gulf of St. *Michael*, which is about 200 Leagues from the
Isle of *Plata*. We were in Number 44 white Men who bore Arms, a
Spanish Indian, who bore Arms also; and two *Moskito Indians*, who always
bear Arms amongst the Privateers, and are much valued by them for
striking Fish, and Turtle or Tortoise, and Manatee or Sea-Cow; and five
Slaves taken in the South-Seas, who fell to our share.

¶ The Craft which carried us was a Lanch, or Long-Boat, one Canoa,
and another Canoa which had been sawn asunder in the Middle, in order
to have made Bumkins, or Vessels for carrying Water, if we had not
separated from our Ship. This we join'd together again and made it
tight; providing Sails to help us along: And for 3 Days before we parted,
we sifted so much Flower as we could well carry, and rubb'd up 20 or
30 pound of Chocolate with Sugar to sweeten it; these Things and a
Kettle, the Slaves carried also on their Backs after we landed. And because there were some who designed to go with us that we knew were
not well able to march, we gave out, that if any Man faultred in the
Journey over Land he must expect to be shot to Death; for we knew that
the *Spaniards* would soon be after us, and one Man falling into their
Hands might be the ruin of us all, by giving an account of our Strength
and Condition; yet this would not deter 'em from going with us. We
had but little Wind when we parted from the Ship; but before 12 a Clock
the Seabreeze came in strong, which was like to founder us before we got

in with the shoar; for our security therefore, we cut up an old dry Hide that we brought with us, and barricadoed the Lanch all round with it to keep the Water out. About 10 a Clock at Night we got in about 7 Leagues to windward of Cape *Passao* under the *Line*, and then it proved calm; and we lay and drove all Night, being fatigu'd the preceeding Day. The 18th Day we had little Wind till the Afternoon; and then we made sail, standing along the shore to the Northward, having the Wind at S.S.W. and fair Weather.

¶ At 7 a Clock we came abrest of Cape *Passao*, and found a small Bark at an Anchor in a small Bay to Leeward of the Cape, which we took, our own Boats being too small to transport us. We took her just under the Equinoctial Line, she was not only a help to us, but in taking her we were safe from being described: we did not design to have meddled with any when we parted with our Consorts, nor to have seen any if we could have helped it. The Bark came from *Gallio* laden with Timber, and was bound for *Guiaquil*.

¶ The 19th Day in the Morning we came to an Anchor about 12 Leagues to the Southward of Cape *St. Francisco*, to put our new Bark into a better trim. In 3 or 4 Hours time we finished our Business, and came to sail again, and steered along the Coast with the Wind at S.S.W. intending to touch at *Gorgonia*.

¶ Being to the Northward of Cape St. *Francisco* we met with very wet Weather; but the Wind continuing we arrived at *Gorgonia* the 24th Day in the Morning, before it was light; we were afraid to approach it in the Day Time, for fear the *Spaniards* should lie there for us, it being the place where we careened lately, and there they might expect us.

¶ When we came ashore we found the *Spaniards* had been there to seek after us, by a House they had built, which would entertain 100 Men, and by a great Cross before the Doors. This was token enough that the *Spaniards* did expect us this Day again; therefore we examined our Prisoners if they knew any Thing of it, who confessed they had heard of a Pereago, (or large Canoa) that rowed with 14 Oars, which was kept in a River on the Main, and once in 2 or three Days came over to *Gorgonia* purposely to see for us; and that having discovered us, she was to make all speed to *Panama* with the News; where they had three Ships ready to send after us.

¶ We lay here all the Day, and scrubb'd our new Bark, that if ever we should be chased we might the better escape: we fill'd our Water, and in the Evening went from thence, having the Wind at S.W. a brisk gale.

¶ The 25th Day we had much Wind and Rain, and we lost the Canoa that had been cut and was joined together; we would have kept all our Canoas to carry us up the River, the Bark not being so convenient.

¶ The 27th Day we went from thence with a moderate gale of Wind at S.W. In the Afternoon we had excessive Showers of Rain.

¶ The 28th Day was very wet all the Morning; betwixt 10 and 11 it cleared up, and we saw two great Ships about a League and half to the Westward of us, we being then two Leagues from the shore, and about 10 Leagues to the Southward of point *Garrachina*. These Ships had been cruising between *Gorgonia* and the Gulf 6 Months; but whether our Prisoners did know it I cannot tell.

¶ We presently furled our Sails, and rowed in close under the shore, knowing that they were Cruisers; for if they had been bound to *Panama* this Wind would have carried them thither; and no Ships bound from *Panama* come on this side of the Bay, but keep the North-side of the Bay till as far as the Keys of *Quibo* to the Westward; and then if they are bound to the Southward they stand over and may fetch *Galleo*, or betwixt it and Cape *St. Francisco*.

¶ The Glare did not continue long before it rained again, and kept us from the fight of each other: but if they had seen and chased us, we were resolved to run our Bark and Canoas ashore, and take ourselves to the Mountains and travel over Land; for we knew that the *Indians* which lived in these parts never had any Commerce with the *Spaniards*; so we might have had a chance for our Lives.

¶ The 29th Day, at 9 a Clock in the Morning, we came to an Anchor at Point *Garrachina*, about 7 Leagues from the Gulf of St. *Michael*, which was the Place where we first came into the South-Seas, and the way by which we designed to return.

Here we lay all the Day, and went ashore and dried our Cloaths, clean'd our Guns, dried our Ammunition, and fixt our selves against our Enemies, if we should be attack'd; for we did expect to find some Opposition at Landing: we likewise kept a good Look-out all the Day, for fear of those two Ships that we saw the Day before.

¶ The 30th Day in the Morning at 8 a Clock we came into the Gulf of St. *Michael*'s Mouth; for we put from Point *Garrachina* in the Evening, designing to have reached the Islands in the Gulf before Day; that we might the better work our Escape from our Enemies, if we should find any of them waiting to stop our Passage.

¶ About 9 a Clock we came to an Anchor a Mile without a large Island, which lies 4 Miles from the Mouth of the River; we had other small Islands without us, and might have gone up into the River, having a

strong tide of flood, but would not adventure farther till we had lookt
well about us.

¶ We immediately sent a Canoa ashore on the Island, where we saw
(what we always feared) a Ship at the Mouth of the River, lying close by the
shore, and a large Tent by it, by which we found it would be a hard
Task for us to escape them.

¶ When the Canoa came aboard with this News, some of our Men were
a little disheartened; but it was no more than I ever expected.

¶ Our Care was now to get safe over Land, seeing we could not land
here according to our desire: Therefore before the Tide of Flood was
spent, we manned our Canoa and rowed again to the Island, to see if
the Enemy was yet in Motion. When we came ashore we dispersed our
selves all over the Island, to prevent our Enemies from coming any way
to view us; and presently after High-water we saw a small Canoa coming
over from the Ship to the Island that we were on; which made us all get
into our Canoa, and wait their coming; and we lay close till they came
within Pistol-shot of us, and then being ready, we started out and took
them. There were in her one white Man and two *Indians*; who being
examined, told us that the Ship which we saw at the River's Mouth,
had lain there six Months, guarding the River, waiting for our coming;
that she had 12 Guns, and 150 Seamen and Soldiers: that the Seamen
all lay aboard, but the Soldiers lay ashore in their Tents; that there were
300 Men at the Mines, who had all small Arms, and would be aboard in
two Tides Time. They likewise told us, that there were two Ships cruising
in the Bay, between this place and *Gorgonia*; the biggest had 20 Guns,
and 200 Men, the other 10 Guns, and 150 Men: Besides all this they told
us that the *Indians* on this side the Country were our Enemies; which was
the worse News of all. However we presently brought these Prisoners
aboard, and got under sail, turning out with the Tide of Ebb, for it was
not convenient to stay longer there.

¶ We did not long consider what to do; but intended to land that Night,
or the next Day betimes; for we did not question but we should either
get a good Commerce with the *Indians*, by such Toys as we had purposely
brought with us, or else force our way through their Country, in spight
of all their Opposition; and we did not fear what these *Spaniards* could do
against us, in case they should land and come after us. We had a strong
Southerly Wind, which blew right in; and the Tide of Ebb being far
spent, we could not turn out.

¶ I perswaded them to run into the River of *Congo*, which is a large
River, about three Leagues from the Island where we lay; which with

a Southerly Wind we could have done: and when we were got so high as the Tide flows, then we might have landed. But all the Arguments I could use were not of force sufficient to convince them that there was a large River so near us, but they would land somewhere, they neither did know how, where, nor when.

¶ When we had rowed and towed against the Wind all Night, we just got about Cape *St. Lorenzo* in the Morning; and sailed about 4 Miles farther to the Westward, and run into a small Creek within two Keys, or little Islands, and rowed up to the Head of the Creek, being about a Mile up, and there we landed *May* 1. 1681.

¶ We got out all our Provision and Cloaths, and then sunk our Vessel.

¶ While we were landing and fixing our Snap-sacks to march, our *Moskito Indians* struck a plentiful Dish of Fish, which we immediately drest, and therewith satisfied our Hunger.

¶ Having made mention of the *Moskito Indians*, it may not be amiss to conclude this Chapter with a short account of them. They are tall, well-made, raw-bon'd, lusty, strong, and nimble of Foot, long-visaged, lank black Hair, look stern, hard favour'd, and of a dark Copper-colour Complexion. They are but a small Nation or Family, and not 100 Men of them in Number, inhabiting on the Main on the North-side, near Cape *Gratia Dios*; between Cape *Honduras* and *Nicaragua*. They are very ingenious at throwing the Lance, Fisgig, Harpoon, or any manner of Dart, being bred to it from their Infancy; for the Children imitating their Parents, never go abroad without a Lance in their Hands, which they throw at any Object, till use hath made them Masters of the Art. Then they learn to put by a Lance, Arrow, or Dart: The manner is thus. Two Boys stand at a small distance, and dart a blunt stick at one another; each of them holding a small stick in his right Hand, with which he strikes away that which was darted at him. As they grow in Years they become more dexterous and courageous, and then they will stand a fair Mark, to any one that will shoot Arrows at them; which they will put by with a very small stick, no bigger than the Rod of a Fowling-piece; and when they are grown to be Men, they will guard themselves from Arrows, though they come very thick at them, provided two do not happen to come at once. They have extraordinary good Eyes, and will discry a Sail at Sea farther, and see any Thing better than we. Their chiefest Employment in their own Country is to strike Fish, Turtle, or Manatee, the manner of which I describe elsewhere, Chap. 3. For this they are esteemed and coveted by all Privateers; for one or two of them in a Ship, will maintain 100 Men: So that when we careen our Ships, we choose commonly such Places where there is plenty of Turtle or Manatee for these *Moskito* Men to strike: and it is very rare to find Privateers destitute of one or more of them, when the Commander, or most of the Men are *English*; but they do not love the *French*, and the *Spaniards* they hate mortally. When they come among Privateers, they get the use of Guns, and prove very good Marks-Men: they behave themselves very bold in fight, and never seem to flinch nor hang back; for they think that the white Men with whom they are, know better than they do when it is best to fight, and let the disadvantage of their Party be never so great, they will never yield nor give back while any of their Party stand. I could never perceive any Religion nor any Ceremonies, or superstitious Observations among them, being ready to imitate us in whatsoever they saw us do at any time. Only they seem to fear the Devil, whom they call *Wallesaw*; and they say he often appears to some among them, whom our Men commonly call their Priest, when they desire to speak with him on urgent Business; but the rest know not any thing of him, nor how he appears, otherwise than as these Priests tell them. Yet they all say they must not anger him, for then he will beat them, and that sometimes he carries away these their Priests. Thus much I have heard from some of them who speak good *English*.

¶ They marry but one Wife, with whom they live till Death separates them. At their first coming together, the Man makes a very small Plantation, for there is Land enough, and they may choose what spot they please. They delight to settle near the Sea, or by some River, for the sake of striking Fish, their beloved Employment.

¶ For within Land there are other *Indians*, with whom they are always at War. After the Man hath cleared a Spot of Land, and hath planted it, he seldom minds it afterwards, but leaves the managing of it to his Wife, and he goes out a striking. Sometimes he seeks only for Fish, at other times for Turtle, or Manatee, and whatever he gets he brings home to his Wife, and never stirs out to seek for more till it is all eaten. When hunger begins to bite, he either takes his Canoa and seeks for more Game at Sea, or walks out into the Woods and hunts about for Peccary, Warree, each a sort of wild Hogs or Deer; and seldom returns empty-handed, nor seeks for any more so long as any of it lasts. Their Plantations are so small, that they cannot subsist with what they produce: for their largest Plantations have not above 20 or 30 Plantain-Trees, a Bed of Yams and Potatoes, a Bush of *Indian* Pepper, and a small Spot of Pine-apples; which last Fruit is a main thing they delight in; for with these they make a sort of Drink which our Men call Pine-drink, much esteemed by these *Moskito*'s, and to which they invite each other to be merry, providing Fish and Flesh also. Whoever of them makes of this Liquor treats his Neighbours, making a little Canoa full at a time, and so enough to make them all drunk; and it is seldom that such Feasts are made, but the Party that makes them hath some design, either to be revenged for some Injury done him, or to debate of such Differences as have hapned between him and his Neighbours, and to examine into the Truth of such Matters. Yet before they are warmed with drink, they never speak one word of their Grievances: and the Women, who commonly know their Husband's Designs, prevent them from doing any Injury to each other, by hiding their Lances, Harpoons, Bows and Arrows, or any other Weapon that they have.

¶ The *Moskito*'s are in general very civil and kind to the *English*, of whom they receive a great deal of Respect, both when they are aboard their Ships, and also ashore, either in *Jamaica*, or elsewhere, whither they often come with the Seamen. We always humour them, letting them go any whither as they will, and return to their Country in any Vessel bound that way, if they please. They will have the Management of themselves in their striking, and will go in their own little Canoa, which our Men could not go in without danger of oversetting: nor will they then let any white Man come in their Canoa, but will go a striking in it just as they please: All which we allow them. For should we cross them, though they should see Shoals of Fish, or Turtle, or the like, they will purposely strike their Harpoons and Turtle-Irons aside, or so glance them as to kill nothing. They have no form of Government among them, but acknowledge the King of *England* for their Sovereign. They learn our Language, and take the Governour of *Jamaica* to be one of the greatest Princes in the World.

¶ While they are among the *English* they wear good Cloaths, and take delight to go neat and tight; but when they return again to their own Country they put by all their Cloaths, and go after their own Country fashion, wearing only a small Piece of Linen tied about their Wastes, hanging down to their Knees.

CHAPTER II

The Author's Land Journey *from the* South *to the* North Sea, *over the* Terra Firma, *or* Isthmus *of* Darien.

BEING landed *May* the 1st, we began our march about 3 a Clock in the Afternoon, directing our Course by our Pocket Compasses *N.E.* and having gone about 2 Miles, we came to the Foot of a Hill where we built small Hutts and lay all Night; having excessive Rains till 12 a Clock.

¶ The 2d Day in the Morning having fair Weather we ascended the Hill, and found a small *Indian* Path, which we followed till we found it run too much Easterly, and then doubting it would carry us out of the way, we climb'd some of the highest Trees on the Hill, which was not meanly furnished with as large and tall Trees as ever I saw: At length we discovered some Houses in a Valley on the North-side of the Hill, but it being steep could not descend on that Side, but followed the small Path which led us down the Hill on the East-side, where we presently found several other *Indian* Houses. The first that we came to at the Foot of the Hill had none but Women at home, who could not speak *Spanish*, but gave each of us a good Calabash or Shell-full of Corn-drink. The other Houses had some Men at home, but none that spoke *Spanish*; yet we made a shift to buy such Food as their Houses or Plantations afforded, which we drest and eat all together; having all sorts of our Provision in common, because none should live better than others, or pay dearer for any thing than it was worth. This Day we had marched 6 Mile.

¶ In the Evening the Husbands of those Women came home, and told us in broken *Spanish*, that they had been on board of the Guard-Ship, which we fled from two Days before, that we were now not above 3 Mile from the Mouth of the River *Congo*, and that they could go from thence aboard the Guard-Ship in half a Tide's time.

¶ This Evening we supped plentifully on Fowls, and Pecary; a sort of wild Hogs which we bought of the *Indians*; Yams, Potatoes and Plantains served us for Bread, whereof we had enough. After Supper we agreed with one of these *Indians* to guide us a Days march into the Country, towards the North-side; he was to have for his Pains a Hatchet, and his Bargain was to bring us to a certain *Indian's* Habitation, who could speak *Spanish*, from whom we were in hopes to be better satisfied of our Journey.

¶ The 3d Day having fair Weather, we began to stir betimes, and set out between 6 and 7 a Clock, marching through several old ruined Plantations. This Morning one of our Men being tired gave us the slip. By 12 a Clock we had gone 8 Mile, and arrived at the *Indian*'s House, who lived on the Bank of the River *Congo*, and spake very good *Spanish*; to whom we declared the Reason of this Visit.

¶ At first he seemed to be very dubious of entertaining any Discourse with us, and gave impertinent Answers to the Questions that we demanded of him; he told us he knew no way to the North-side of the Country, but could carry us to *Cheapo*, or *Santa Maria*, which we knew to be *Spanish* Garrisons; the one lying to the Eastward of us, the other to the Westward: either of them at least 20 Miles out of our way. We could get no other Answer from him, and all his Discourse was in such an angry Tone, as plainly declared he was not our Friend. However, we were forced to make a Virtue of Necessity, and humour him, for it was neither time nor place to be angry with the *Indians*; all our Lives lying in their Hand.

¶ We were now at a great Loss, not knowing what Course to take, for we tempted him with Beads, Money, Hatchets, Matcheats, or long Knives; but nothing would work on him, till one of our Men took a Sky-coloured Petticoat out of his Bag and put it on his Wife; who was so much pleased with the Present, that she immediately began to chatter to her Husband, and soon brought him into a better Humour. He could then tell us that he knew the Way to the North-side, and would have gone with us, but that he had cut his Foot two Days before, which made him uncapable of serving us himself: But he would take care that we should not want a Guide; and therefore he hired the same *Indian* who brought us hither, to conduct us two Days march further for another Hatchet. The old Man would have stayed us here all the Day, because it rained very hard; but our Business required more haste, our Enemies lying so near us, for he told us that he could go from his House aboard the Guard-Ship in a Tide's time; and this was the 4th Day since they saw us. So we marched 3 Miles farther, and then built Hutts, where we stayed all Night; it rained all the Afternoon, and the greatest Part of the Night.

¶ The 4th Day we began our March betimes, for the Forenoons were commonly fair, but much Rain Afternoon: tho' whether it rained or shined it was much at one with us, for I verily believe we crost the Rivers 30 times this Day: the *Indians* having no Paths to travel from one part of the Country to another; and therefore guided themselves by the Rivers. We marched this Day 12 Miles, and then built our Hutt, and lay down to sleep; but we always kept two Men on the Watch; otherwise our own Slaves might have knockt us on the Head while we slept. It rained violently all the Afternoon, and most part of the Night. We had much ado to kindle a Fire this Evening: our Hutts were but very mean or ordinary, and our Fire small, so that we could not dry our Cloaths, scarce warm our selves, and no sort of Food for the Belly; all which made it very hard with us. I confess these Hardships quite expell'd the Thoughts of an Enemy, for now having been 4 Days in the Country, we began to have but few other Cares than how to get Guides and Food, the *Spaniards* were seldom in our Thoughts.

❡ The 5th Day we set out in the morning betimes, and having travelled 7 Miles in those wild pathless Woods, by 10 a Clock in the Morning we arrived at a young *Spanish Indian*'s House, who had formerly lived with the Bishop of *Panama*. The young *Indian* was very brisk, spoke very good *Spanish*, and received us very kindly. This Plantation afforded us store of Provisions, Yams, and Potatoes, but nothing of any Flesh, besides 2 fat Monkeys we shot, part whereof we distributed to some of our Company, who were weak and sickly; for others we got Eggs, and such Refreshments as the *Indians* had, for we still provided for the Sick and Weak. We had a *Spanish Indian* in our Company, who first took up Arms with Captain *Sawkins*, and had been with us ever since his Death. He was persuaded to live here by the Master of the House, who promised him his Sister in Marriage, and to be assistant to him in clearing a Plantation: but we would not consent to part from him here, for fear of some Treachery, but promised to release him in two or three Days, when we were certainly out of danger of our Enemies. We stayed here all the Afternoon, and dried our Cloaths and Ammunition, cleared our Guns, and provided our selves for a March the next Morning.

❡ Our Chirurgeon, Mr. *Wafer*, came to a sad Disaster here: being drying his Powder, a careless Fellow passed by with his Pipe lighted, and set fire to his Powder, which blew up and scorched his Knee, and reduced him to that Condition, that he was not able to march; wherefore we allowed him a Slave to carry his things, being all of us the more concern'd at the Accident, because liable our selves every Moment to Misfortune, and none to look after us but him. This *Indian* Plantation was seated on the Bank of the River *Congo*, in a very fat Soil, and thus far we might have come in our Canoa, if I could have persuaded them to it.

❡ The 6th Day we set out again, having hired another Guide. Here we first crost the River *Congo* in a Canoa, having been from our first Landing on the West-side of the River, and being over, we marched to the Eastward two Miles, and came to another River, which we forded several Times, though it was very deep. Two of our Men were not able to keep Company with us, but came after us as they were able. The last time we forded the River, it was so deep, that our tallest Men stood in the deepest Place, and handed the sick, weak and short Men; by which means we all got over safe, except those two who were behind. Foreseeing a Necessity of wading through Rivers frequently in our Land-march, I took care before I left the Ship to provide my self a large Joint of Bambo, which I stopt at both Ends, closing it with Wax, so as to keep out any Water. In this I preserved my Journal and other Writings from being wet, tho' I was often forced to swim. When we were over this River, we sat down to wait the coming of our Consorts who were left behind, and in half an Hour they came. But the River by that time was so high, that they could not get over it, neither could we help them over, but bid them be of good comfort, and stay till the River did fall: But we marched two Miles farther by the Side of the River, and there built our Hutts, having gone this Day six Miles. We had scarce finished our Hutts, before the River rose much higher, and overflowing the Banks, obliged us to remove into higher ground: But the next Night came on before we could build more Hutts, so we lay straggling in the Woods, some under one Tree, some under another, as we could find conveniency, which might have been indifferent comfortable if the Weather had been fair; but the greatest Part of the Night we had extraordinary hard Rain, with much Lightning, and terrible Claps of Thunder. These Hardships and Inconveniencies made us all careless, and there was no Watch kept, (tho' I believe no body did sleep:) So our Slaves taking the opportunity, went away in the Night; all but one, who was hid in some hole and knew nothing of their design, or else fell asleep. Those that went away carried with them our Chirurgeon's Gun and all his Money.

¶ The next Morning being the 8th Day, we went to the River's side, and found it much fallen; and here our Guide would have us ford it again, which being deep, and the Current running swift, we could not. Then we contrived to swim over; those that could not swim, we were resolved to help over as well as we could: But this was not so feisable: for we should not be able to get all our Things over. At length we concluded to send one Man over with a Line, who should hale over all our Things first, and then get the Men over. This being agreed on, one *George Gayny* took the end of a Line and made it fast about his Neck, and left the other end ashore, and one Man stood by the Line, to clear it away to him. But when *Gayny* was in the midst of the Water, the Line in drawing after

him chanced to kink or grow entangled; and he that stood by to clear it
away, stopt the Line which turned *Gayny* on his back, and he that had
the Line in his Hand threw it all into the River after him, thinking he
might recover himself; but the Stream running very swift, and the Man
having three Hundred Dollars at his back, was carried down, and never
seen more by us. Those two Men whom we left behind the Day before,
told us afterwards that they found him lying dead in a Creek, where the
Eddy had driven him ashore, and the Money on his Back; but they
meddled not with any of it, being only in Care how to work their way
through a wild unknown Country. This put a Period to that Contrivance.
This was the fourth Man that we lost in this Land-Journey; for these two
Men that we left the Day before did not come to us till we were in the
North-Seas, so we yielded them also for lost. Being frustrated at getting
over the River this way, we looked about for a Tree to fell across the
River. At length we found one, which we cut down, and it reached clear
over: on this we passed to the other side, where we found a small Plantain
Walk, which we soon ransackt.

¶ While we were busy getting Plantains our Guide was gone, but in less
than two Hours came to us again, and brought with him an old *Indian*, to
whom he delivered up his Charge; and we gave him a Hatchet and
dismist him, and entered our selves under the Conduct of our new Guide:
who immediately led us away, and crost another River, and entered into
a large Valley of the fattest Land I did ever take notice of; the Trees were
not very thick, but the largest that I saw in all my Travels; We saw great
Tracks which were made by the Pecaries, but saw none of them. We
marched in this pleasant Country till 3 a Clock in the Afternoon, in all
about 4 Miles, and then arrived at the old Man's Country House, which
was only a Habitation for Hunting: there was a small Plantain Walk,
some Yams, and Potatoes. Here we took up our Quarters for this Day,
and refreshed ourselves with such Food as the Place afforded, and dryed
our Cloaths and Ammunition. At this Place our young *Spanish Indian*
provided to leave us, for now we thought our selves past Danger. This
was he that was perswaded to stay at the last House we came from, to
marry the young Man's Sister; and we dismissed him according to our
Promise.

¶ The 9th Day the old Man conducted us towards his own Habitation.
We marched about 5 Miles in this Valley; and then ascended a Hill, and
travelled about 5 Miles farther over two or three small Hills, before we
came to any Settlement. Half a Mile before we came to the Plantations
we light of a Path, which carried us to the *Indians* Habitations. We saw

many wooden Crosses erected in the way, which created some Jealousy in us that here were some *Spaniards*: Therefore we new primed all our Guns, and provided our selves for an Enemy; but coming into the Town found none but *Indians*, who were all got together in a large House to receive us: for the old Man had a little Boy with him, that he sent before.

¶ They made us welcome to such as they had, which was very mean; for these were new Plantations, the Corn being not eared. Potatoes, Yams, and Plantains they had none, but what they brought from their old Plantations. There was none of them spoke good *Spanish*: Two young Men could speak a little, it caused us to take more notice of them. To these we made a Present, and desired them to get us a Guide to conduct us to the North-side, or part of the way, which they promised to do themselves; if we would reward them for it, but told us we must lye still the next Day. But we thought our selves nearer the North-Sea than we were, and proposed to go without a Guide, rather than stay here a whole Day: However some of our Men who were tired resolved to stay behind; and Mr. *Wafer* our Chirurgeon, who marched in great Pain ever since his Knee was burned with Powder, was resolved to stay with them.

¶ The 10th Day we got up betimes, resolving to march, but the *Indians* opposed it as much as they could; but seeing they could not perswade us to stay, they came with us; and having taken leave of our Friends, we set out.

¶ Here therefore we left the Chirurgeon and two more, as we said, and marched away to the Eastward following our Guides. But we often looked on our Pocket Compasses, and shewed them to the Guides, pointing at the way that we would go, which made them shake their Heads, and say, they were pretty Things, but not convenient for us. After we had descended the Hills on which the Town stood, we came down into a Valley, and guided our selves by a River, which we crossed 22 Times; and having marched 9 Miles, we built Hutts and lay there all Night: This Evening I killed a Quaum, a large Bird as big as a Turkey, wherewith we treated our Guides, for we brought no Provision with us. This Night our last Slave run away.

¶ The eleventh Day we marched 10 Mile farther, and built Hutts at Night; but went supperless to Bed.

¶ The twelfth in the Morning we crossed a deep River, passing over it on a Tree, and marched 7 Mile in a low swampy Ground; and came to the side of a great deep River, but could not get over. We built Hutts upon its Banks and lay there all Night, upon our Barbecu's, or Frames of Sticks, raised about 3 Foot from the Ground.

¶ The thirteenth Day when we turned out, the River had overflowed its Banks, and was 2 foot deep in our Hutts, and our Guides went from us, not telling us their intent, which made us think they were returned home again. Now we began to repent our haste in coming from the Settlements, for we had no Food since we came from thence. Indeed we got Macaw-berries in this Place, wherewith we satisfied our selves this Day though coarsely.

¶ The fourteenth Day in the Morning betimes, our Guides came to us again; and the Waters being fallen within their bounds, they carried us to a Tree that stood on the Bank of the River, and told us if we could fell that Tree cross it, we might pass: if not, we could pass no farther. Therefore we set two of the best Ax-men that we had, who fell'd it exactly cross the River, and the Boughs just reached over; on this we passed very safe. We afterwards crossed another River three Times, with much Difficulty, and at 3 a Clock in the Afternoon we came to an *Indian* Settlement, where we met a drove of Monkeys, and killed 4 of them, and staied here all Night, having marched this Day 6 Miles. Here we got Plantains enough, and a kind Reception of the *Indian* that lived here all alone, except one Boy to wait on him.

¶ The fifteenth Day when we set out, the kind *Indian* and his Boy went with us in a Canoa, and set us over such Places as we could not ford: and being past those great Rivers, he returned back again, having helped us at least 2 Mile. We marched afterwards 5 Mile, and came to large Plantain Walks, where we took up our Quarters that Night; we there fed plentifully on Plantains, both ripe and green, and had fair Weather all the Day and Night. I think these were the largest Plantain-walks, and the biggest Plantains that ever I saw, but no House near them: We gathered what we pleased by our Guides Orders.

¶ The sixteenth Day we marched 3 Mile, and came to a large Settlement, where we abode all Day: Not a Man of us but wisht the Journey at an End; our Feet being blistered, and our Thighs stript with wading through so many Rivers; the way being almost continually through Rivers, or pathless Woods. In the afternoon five of us went to seek for Game, and kill'd 3 Monkeys, which we drest for Supper. Here we first began to have fair Weather, which continued with us till we came to the North-Seas.

¶ The eighteenth Day we set out at 10 a Clock, and the *Indians* with 5 Canoas carried us a League up a River; and when we landed, the kind *Indians* went with us and carried our Burdens. We marched 3 Mile farther, and then built our Hutts, having travelled from the last Settlements 6 Mile.

¶ The nineteenth Day our Guides lost their way, and we did not march above 2 Mile.

¶ The twentieth Day by 12 a Clock we came to *Cheapa* River. The Rivers we crost hitherto run all into the South-Seas; and this of *Cheapo* was the last we met with that run that way. Here an old Man who came from the last Settlements, distributed his burthen of Plantains amongst us, and taking his leave returned Home. Afterward we forded the River, and marched to the foot of a very high Mountain, where we lay all Night. This Day we marched about 9 Miles.

¶ The 21st Day some of the *Indians* returned back, and we marched up a very high Mountain; being on the Top, we went some Miles on a ridge, and steep on both sides; then descended a little, and came to a fine Spring, where we lay all Night, having gone this Day about 9 Miles, the Weather still very fair and clear.

¶ The 22d Day we marched over another very high Mountain, keeping on the ridge 5 Miles. When we came to the North-end, we to our great Comfort, saw the Sea; then we descended, and parted our selves into 3 Companies, and lay by the side of a River, which was the first we met that runs into the North-Sea.

¶ The 23d Day we came through several large Plantain Walks, and at 10 a Clock came to an *Indian* Habitation, not far from the *North-Seas*. Here we got Canoas to carry us down the River *Conception* to the Sea-side; having gone this Day 7 Miles. We found a great many *Indians* at the Mouth of the River. They had settled themselves here for the benefit of Trade with the Privateers; and their Commodities were Yams, Potatoes, Plantains, Sugar, Canes, Fowls, and Eggs.

¶ The *Indians* told us, that there had been a great many *English* and *French* Ships here, which were all gone but one *Barcolongo*, a *French* Privateer that lay at *La Sounds* Key or Island. This Island is about 3 Leagues from the Mouth of the River *Conception*, and is one of the *Samballoes*, a range of Islands reaching for about 20 Leagues, from Point *Samballas* to *Golden Island* Eastward. These Islands or Keys, as we call them, were first made the Rendezvous of Privateers in the Year 1679, being very convenient for careening, and had Names given to some of them by the Captains of the Privateers: as this *La Sounds* Key particularly.

¶ Thus we finished our Journey from the *South-Sea* to the *North* in 23 Days; in which time by my Account we travelled 110 Miles, crossing some very high Mountains; but our common March was in the Valleys among deep and dangerous Rivers. At our first landing in this Country, we were told that the *Indians* were our Enemies; we knew the Rivers to be deep,

the wet Season to be coming in; yet, excepting those we left behind, we
lost but one Man, who was drowned, as I said. Our first landing Place
on the *South* Coast was very disadvantageous, for we travelled at least
fifty Miles more than we need to have done, could we have gone up
Cheapo River, or *Santa Maria* River; for at either of these Places a Man
may pass from Sea to Sea in three Days time with ease. The *Indians* can
do it in a Day and a half, by which you may see how easy it is for a Party
of Men to travel over. I must confess the *Indians* did assist us very much,
and I question whether ever we had got over without their Assistance,
because they brought us from time to time to their Plantations, where we
always got Provision, which else we should have wanted. But if a Party
of 500 or 600 Men, or more, were minded to travel from the North to the
South-Seas, they may do it without asking leave of the *Indians*; though it
be much better to be Friends with them.

¶ On the 24th of *May*, (having lain one Night at the River's Mouth) we
all went on board the Privateer, who lay at *La Sound*'s Key. It was a
French Vessel, Captain *Tristian* Commander. The first thing we did was
to get such things as we could to gratify our *Indian* Guides, for we were
resolved to reward them to their Hearts content. This we did by giving
them Beads, Knives, Scissars, and Looking-glasses, which we bought of
the Privateers Crew: and half a Dollar a Man from each of us; which we
would have bestowed in Goods also, but could not get any, the Privateer
having no more Toys. They were so well satisfied with these, that they
returned with joy to their Friends; and were very kind to our Consorts
whom we left behind; as Mr. *Wafer* our Chirurgeon and the rest of them
told us, when they came to us some Months afterwards, as shall be said
hereafter.

¶ I might have given a further Account of several things relating to this
Country; the *Inland* Parts of which are so little known to the *Europeans*.
But I shall leave this Province to Mr. *Wafer*, who made a longer Abode
in it than I, and is better able to do it than any Man that I know, and is
now preparing a particular Description of this Country for the Press.

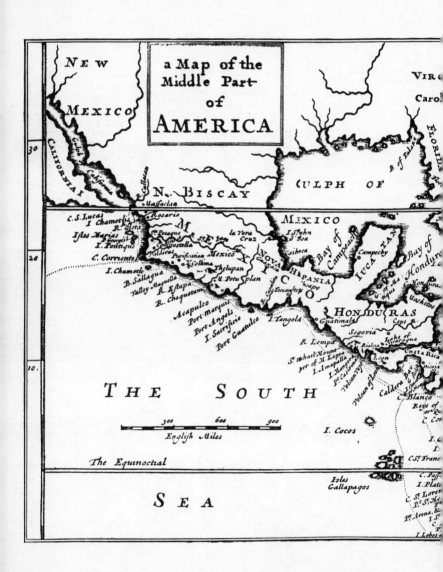

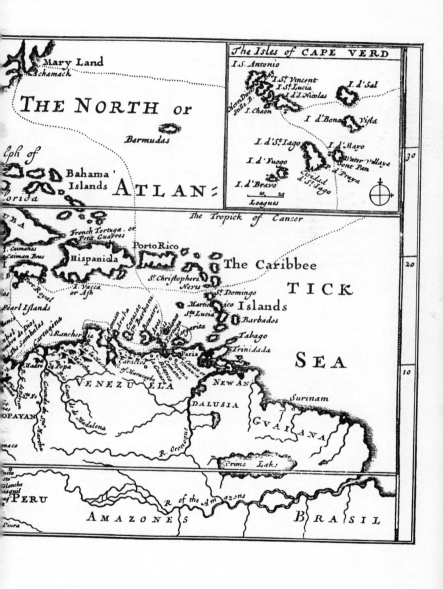

Mary Land
Achamack

THE NORTH or

Bermudas

lph of
Florida

Bahama
Islands   ATLAN:

The Isles of CAPE VERD

I.S. Antonio
I.S.t Vincent
I.S.t Lucia
I.d.S. Nicolas   I. d'Sal
Ieux Dieu
Salt. B.
I. Chaon   I. d'Bona   Vista

I. d'S.t Iago   I. d'Mayo
                  Water village
I. d'Fuogo   Port Pan
                  Ciudad   I. d'Praya
I. d'Bravo   d'S.t Iago

10   20
Leagues

30

The Tropick of Cancer

UBA   French Tortuga. or
           Petit Guavres
S. Caimanes   Porto Rico
Caiman Brac
        Hispaniola   The Caribbee
S.   I. Vacca
        or Ash   S.t Christophers   TICK
Peral Islands   Nevis
              Barbada   S.t Domingo   Islands
abel de Dios   Martinico
mbre Sombalos Rancheria   S.ta Lucia   Barbados
Madre de Popa   Curasao Bonaire
                     Aves   Tabago
res   Rio Grande de la   Margarita   Trinidada
OPAYAN   Madalena   VENEZUELA   SEA
                       Paris
maco   NEW AN
                        DALUSIA   Surinam
PERU   GUAIANA
                R. Oronoque
Piura   Prime Lake
                R. of the Amazons
        AMAZONES   BRASIL

30

20

10

CHAPTER III

The Author's cruising with the Privateers in the North-Seas *on the* West-India *Coast. They go to the Isle of St.* Andreas. *Of the* Cedars *there. The* Corn-Islands, *and their Inhabitants.* Bluefield's *River, and an account of the* Manatee *there, or* Sea-Cow; *with the Manner how the* Moskito Indians *kill them, and* Tortoise, &c. *The* Maho-*tree. The Savages of* Bocca-toro. *He touches again at Point* Samballas, *and its Islands. The Groves of* Sapadillaes *there, the* Soldier's *Insect, and* Manchaneel *Tree. The River of* Darien, *and the* Wild Indians *near it;* Monastery *of* Madre de Popa, Rio Grande, Santa Martha *Town, and the high Mountain there;* Rio la Hacha *Town,* Rancho Reys, *and* Pearl Fishery *there; the* Indian *Inhabitants and Country.* Dutch *Isle of* Querisao, &c. *Count* D'Estree's *unfortunate Expedition thither. Isle of* Bon Airy. *Isle of* Aves, *the* Booby *and* Man of War Bird: *The Wreck of* D'Estree's *Fleet, and Captain* Pain's *Adventure here. Little Isle of* Aves. *The Isles* Roca's, *the* Noddy *and* Tropick Bird, *Mineral Water,* Egg-Birds; *the* Mangrove Trees, black, red, *and white, Isle of* Tortuga, *its Salt Ponds. Isle of* Blanco; *the* Guano Animal, *their Variety; and the best* Sea Tortoise. *Modern Alterations in the* West-Indies. *The Coast of* Caraccus, *its remarkable Land, and Product of the best* Cacoa Nuts. *The* Cacoa *described at large, with the Husbandry of it. City of* Caraccos. La Guaire *Fort and Haven. Town of* Comana. Verina, *its famous best* Spanish *Tobacco. The rich Trade of the Coast of* Caraccos. *Of the* Sucking Fish, *or* Remora. *The Author's Arrival in* Virginia.

THE Privateer on board which we went being now cleaned, and our *Indian* Guides thus satisfied and set ashore, we set sail in two Days for *Springer's* Key, another of the *Samballoes* Isles, and about 7 or 8 Leagues from *La Sound's* Key. Here lay 8 Sail of Privateers more, *viz.*

Capt. *Coxen*, 10 Guns, 100 Men. ⎫
Capt. *Payne*, 10 Guns, 100 Men. ⎬ *English* Commanders
Capt. *Wright*, a Barcolongo. 4 Guns, 40 Men ⎨ and *Englishmen.*
Capt. *Williams*, a small Barcolongo. ⎭
Capt. *Yankes*, a Barcolongo, 4 Guns, about 60 Men, *English, Dutch* and *French*; himself a *Dutchman.*
Capt. *Archemboe*, 8 Guns, 40 Men. ⎫
Capt. *Tucker*, 6 Guns, 70 Men. ⎬ *French* Commanders
Capt. *Rose*, a Barcolongo. ⎭ and Men.

¶ An Hour before we came to the Fleet, Captain *Wright*, who had been sent to *Chagra* River, arrived at *Springer's* Key, with a large Canoa or Periago laden with Flower, which he took there. Some of the Prisoners belonging to the Periago, came from *Panama* not above six Days before he took her, and told the News of our coming over land, and likewise related the Condition and Strength of *Panama*, which was the main thing they enquired after; for Captain *Wright* was sent thither purposely to get a Prisoner that was able to inform them of the Strength of that City, because these Privateers designed to join all their Force, and by the Assistance of the *Indians*, (who had promised to be their Guides) to march over land to *Panama*; and there is no other way of getting Prisoners for that purpose, but by absconding between *Chagra* and *Portabell*, because there are much Goods brought that way from *Panama*; especially when the Armado lyeth at *Portabell*. All the Commanders were aboard of Captain *Wright* when we came into the Fleet; and were mighty inquisitive of the Prisoners to know the Truth of what they related concerning us. But as soon as they knew we were come, they immediately came aboard of Captain *Tristian*, being all overjoyed to see us; for Captain *Coxon*, and many others, had left us in the *South-Seas* about 12 Months since, and had never heard what became of us since that time. They enquired of us what we did there? how we lived? how far we had been? and what Discoveries we made in those Seas? After we had answered these general Questions, they began to be more particular in examining us concerning our Passage through the Country from the *South-Seas*. We related the whole matter; giving them an account of the Fatigues of our March, and the Inconveniencies we suffered by the Rains; and disheartned them quite from that design.

¶ Then they proposed several other Places where such a party of Men as were now got together might make a Voyage; but the Objections of some or other still hinder'd any proceeding: For the Privateers have an account of most Towns within 20 Leagues of the Sea, on all the Coast from *Trinidado* down to *La Vera Cruz*; and are able to give a near guess of the Strength and Riches of them: For they make it their Business to examine all Prisoners that fall into their Hands, concerning the Country, Town, or City that they belong to; whether born there, or how long they have known it? how many Families, whether most *Spaniards?* or whether the major part are not Copper-colour'd, as *Mulattoes*, *Mustesoes*, or *Indians?* whether rich, and what their Riches do consist in? and what their chiefest Manufactures? if fortified, how many great Guns, and what Number of small Arms? whether it is possible to come undescrib'd on them? How many Look-outs or Centinels; for such the *Spaniards* always keep? and how the Look-outs are placed? Whether possible to avoid the Look-outs, or take them? If any River or Creek comes near it, or where the best Landing; with innumerable other such Questions, which their Curiosities led them to demand. And if they have had any former

Discourse of such Places from other Prisoners, they compare one with the other; then examine again, and enquire if he or any of them are capable to be Guides to Conduct a Party of Men thither: if not, where and how any Prisoner may be taken that may do it; and from thence they afterwards lay their Schemes to prosecute whatever design they take in Hand.

¶ It was 7 or 8 Days after before any Resolution was taken, yet Consultations were held every Day. The *French* seemed very forward to go to any Town that the *English* could or would propose, because the Governour of *Pettit Guavos* (from whom the Privateers take Commissions) had recommended a Gentleman lately come from *France* to be General of the Expedition, and sent Word by Captain *Tucker*, with whom this Gentleman came, that they should, if possible, make an Attempt on some Town before he returned again. The *English* when they were in Company with the *French*, seem'd to approve of what the *French* said, but never looked on that General to be fit for the Service in Hand.

¶ At length it was concluded to go to a Town, the Name of which I have forgot; it lies a great way in the Country, but not such a tedious march as it would be from hence to *Panama*. Our way to it lay up *Carpenter*'s River, which is about 60 Leagues to the Westward of *Portabell*. Our greatest Obstruction in this Design was our want of Boats: therefore it was concluded to go with all our Fleet to St. *Andreas*, a small uninhabited Island lying near the Isle of *Providence*, to the Westward of it, in 13 deg. 15 Min. North Lat. and from *Portabell* N.N.W. about 70 Leagues; where we should be but a little way from *Carpenter*'s River. And besides, at this Island we might build Canoas, it being plentifully stored with large Cedars for such a purpose; and for this Reason the *Jamaica*-men come hither frequently to build Sloops; Cedar being very fit for Building, and it being to be had here at free-cost; beside other Wood. *Jamaica* is well stored with Cedars of its own, chiefly among the Rocky Mountains: these also of St. *Andreas* grow in stony Ground, and are the largest that ever I knew or heard of; the Bodies alone being ordinarily 40 or 50 Foot long, many 60 or 70 and upwards, and of a proportionable Bigness. The *Bermudas* Isles are well stored with them; so is *Virginia*, which is generally a sandy Soil. I saw none in the *East-Indies*, nor in the South-Sea Coast, except on the Isthmus as I came over it. We reckon the *Periagoes* and *Canoas* that are made of Cedar to be the best of any; they are nothing but the Tree it self made hollow Boatwise, with a flat bottom, and the Canoa generally sharp at both ends, the Periago at one only, with the other end flat. But what is commonly said of Cedar, that the Worm will not touch it, is a mistake, for I have seen of it very much Worm-eaten.

¶ All Things being thus concluded on, we sailed from thence, directing our course towards St. *Andreas*. We kept Company the first Day, but at Night it blew a hard gale at N.E. and some of our Ships bore away: the next Day others were forced to leave us, and the second Night we lost all our Company. I was now belonging to Captain *Archembo*, for all the rest of the Fleet were over-mann'd: Capt. *Archembo* wanting Men, we that came out of the South-Seas must either sail with him, or remain among the *Indians*. Indeed we found no Cause to dislike the Captain; but his *French* Seamen were the saddest Creatures that ever I was among; for tho' we had bad Weather that requir'd many Hands aloft, yet the biggest part of them never stirr'd out of their Hammocks, but to eat or ease themselves. We made a shift to find the Island the fourth Day, where we met Capt. *Wright*, who came thither the Day before, and had taken a *Spanish* Tartan, wherein were 30 Men, all well armed: She had 4 Patereroes and some long Guns plac'd in the Swivel on the Gunnel. They fought an Hour before they yielded. The News they related was, that they came from *Cartagena* in Company of 11 Armadilloes (which are small Vessels of War) to seek for the Fleet of Privateers lying in the *Samballoes*: That they parted from the Armadilloes 2 Days before: That they were ordered to search the *Samballoes* for us, and if they did not find us, then they were ordered to go to *Portabell*, and lay there till they had farther Intelligence of us, and he supposed these Armadilloes to be now there.

¶ We that came over Land out of the *South-Seas* being weary of living among the *French*, desired Captain *Wright* to fit up his Prize the Tartan, and make a Man of War of her for us, which he at first seemed to decline, because he was settled among the *French* in *Hispaniola*, and was very well beloved both by the Governour of *Pettit Guavos*, and all the Gentry; and they would resent it ill, that Captain *Wright*, who had no occasion of Men, should be so unkind to Captain *Archembo*, as to seduce his Men from him; he being so meanly mann'd that he could hardly sail his Ship with his *Frenchmen*. We told him we would no longer remain with Captain *Archembo*, but would go ashore there, and build Canoas to transport our selves down to the *Moskitoes*, if he would not entertain us; for Privateers are not obliged to any Ship, but free to go ashore where they please, or to go into any other Ship that will entertain them, only paying for their Provision.

¶ When Captain *Wright* saw our Resolutions, he agreed with us on Condition we should be under his Command, as one Ship's Company, to which we unanimously consented.

¶ We staid here about 10 Days, to see if any more of our Fleet would come to us; but there came no more of us to the Island but three, *viz.* Captain *Wright*, Captain *Archembo*, and Captain *Tucker*. Therefore we concluded the rest were bore away either for *Boccatora*, or *Bluefields* River on the Main; and we designed to seek them. We had fine Weather while we lay here, only some Tornadoes, or Thunder-shores: But in this Isle of St. *Andreas*, there being neither Fish, Fowl, nor Deer, and it being therefore but an ordinary Place for us, who had but little Provision, we sailed from hence again in quest of our scattered Fleet, directing our Course for some Islands lying near the Main, called by the Privateers the *Corn-Islands*; being in hopes to get Corn there. These Islands I take to be the same which are generally called in the Maps the *Pearl Islands*, lying about the Lat. of 12 D. 10 M. North. Here we arrived the next Day, and went ashore on one of them, but found none of the Inhabitants; for here are but a few poor naked *Indians* that live here; who have been so often plundered by the Privateers that they have but little Provision; and

when they see a Sail they hide themselves; otherwise Ships that come here would take them, and make Slaves of them; and I have seen some of them that have been Slaves. They are People of a mean Stature, yet strong Limbs; they are of a dark Copper-colour, black Hair, full round Faces, small black Eyes, their Eyebrows hanging over their Eyes, low Foreheads, short thick Noses, not high, but flattish; full Lips, and short Chins. They have a Fashion to cut Holes in the Lips of the Boys when they are young, close to their Chin; which they keep open with little Pegs till they are 14 or 15 Years old: then they wear Beards in them, made of Turtle or Tortoise-shell, in the form you see in the Margin. The little notch at the Upper-end they put in through the Lip, where it remains between the Teeth and the Lip; the Under-part hangs down over their Chin. This they commonly wear all Day, and when they sleep they take it out. They have likewise Holes bored in their Ears, both Men and Women when young; and by continual stretching them with great Pegs, they grow to be as big as a mill'd five Shilling-piece. Herein they wear pieces of Wood cut very round and smooth, so that their Ear seems to be all Wood, with a little Skin about it. Another Ornament the Women use is about their Legs, which they are very curious in; for from the Infancy of the Girls, their Mothers make fast a Piece of Cotton Cloath about the small of their Leg, from the Ankle to the Calf, very hard; which makes them have a very full Calf: This the Women wear to their dying Day. Both Men and Women go naked, only a Clout about their Wastes; yet they have but little Feet, though they go bare Foot. Finding no Provision here, we sailed towards *Bluefield* River, where we careened our Tartane; and there Captain *Archembo* and Captain *Tucker* left us, and went towards *Boccotoro*.

¶ This *Blewfield*'s River comes out between the Rivers of *Nicargua* and *Veragna*. At its Mouth is a fine sandy Bay, where Barks may clean: It is deep at its Mouth, but a Shole within; so that Ships may not enter, yet Barks of 60 or 70 Tuns may. It had this Name from Captain *Blewfield*, a famous Privateer living on *Providence* Island long before *Jamaica* was taken. Which Island of *Providence* was settled by the *English*, and belonged to the Earls of *Warwick*.

¶ In this River we found a Canoa coming down the Stream; and though we went with our Canoas to seek for Inhabitants, yet we found none, but saw in two or three Places signs that *Indians* had made on the Side of the River. The Canoa which we found was but meanly made for want of Tools, therefore we concluded these *Indians* have no Commerce with the *Spaniards*, nor with other *Indians* that have.

¶ While we lay here, our *Moskito* Men went in their Canoa, and struck us some Manatee, or Sea-Cow. Besides this *Blewfield*'s River, I have seen of the Manatee in the Bay of *Campeachy*, on the Coasts of *Bocca del Drago*, and *Bocco del Toro*, in the River of *Darien*, and among the South Keys or little Islands of *Cuba*. I have heard of their being found on the North of *Jamaica* a few, and in the Rivers of *Surinam* in great Multitudes, which is a very low Land. I have seen of them also at *Mindanea* one of the *Philippine* Islands, and on the Coast of *New Holland*. This Creature is about the Bigness of a Horse, and 10 or 12 Foot long. The Mouth of it is much like the Mouth of a Cow, having great thick Lips. The Eyes are no bigger than a small Pea; the Ears are only two small holes on each side of the Head. The Neck is short and thick, bigger than the Head. The biggest Part of this Creature is at the Shoulders, where it hath two large Fins, one on each side of its Belly. Under each of these Fins the Female hath a small Dug to suckle her young. From the Shoulders towards the Tail it retains its bigness for about a Foot, then groweth smaller and smaller to the very Tail, which is flat, and about 14 Inches broad, and 20 Inches long, and in the Middle 4 or 5 Inches thick, but about the Edges of it not above 2 Inches thick. From the Head to the Tail it is round and smooth without any Fin but those two before-mentioned. I have heard that some have weighed above 1200 *l.* but I never saw any so large. The Manatee delights to live in brackish Water; and they are commonly in Creeks and Rivers near the Sea. 'Tis for this Reason possibly they are not seen in the *South-Seas* (that ever I could observe) where the Coast is generally a bold Shore, that is, high Land and deep Water close home by it, with a high Sea or great Surges, except in the Bay of *Panama*; yet even there is no Manatee. Whereas the *West-Indies*, being as it were, one great Bay composed of many smaller, are mostly low Land and shoal Water, and afford proper Pasture (as I may say) for the Manatee. Sometimes we find them in salt Water, sometimes in fresh; but never far at Sea. And those that live in the Sea at such Places where there is no River nor Creek fit for them to enter, yet do commonly come once or twice in 24 Hours to the Mouth of any fresh Water River that is near their Place of Abode. They live on Grass 7 or 8 Inches long, and of a narrow Blade, which grows in the Sea in many places, especially among Islands near the Main. This Grass groweth likewise in Creeks, or in great Rivers near the Sides of them, in such places where there is but little Tide or Current. They never come ashore, nor into shallower Water than where they can swim. Their Flesh is white, both the Fat and the Lean, and extraordinary sweet, wholesome Meat. The Tail of a young Cow is most esteem'd; but if old both Head and Tail are very tough. A Calf that sucks is the most delicate Meat; Privateers commonly roast them; as they do also great pieces cut out of the Bellies of the old ones.

¶ The Skin of the Manatee is of great use to Privateers, for they cut them into Straps, which they make fast on the Sides of their Canoas thro' which they put their oars in rowing, instead of Tholes or Pegs. The Skin of the Bull, or of the Back of the Cow is too thick for this use; but of it they make Horse-whips, cutting them 2 or 3 Foot long: at the Handle they leave the full Substance of the Skin, and from thence cut it away tapering, but very even and square all the four Sides. While the Thongs are green they wist them, and hang them to dry; which in a Weeks time become as hard as Wood. The *Moskito* Men have always a small Canoa for their use to strike Fish, Tortoise, or Manatee, which they keep usually to themselves, and very neat and clean. They use no Oars but Paddles, the broad Part of which doth not go tapering towards the Staff, Pole or Shandle of it, as in the Oar; nor do they use it in the same manner, by laying it on the Side of the Vessel; but hold it perpendicular, griping the Staff hard with both Hands, and putting back the Water by main Strength, and very quick Strokes. One of the *Moskitoes* (for they go but two in a Canoa) sits in the Stern, the other kneels down in the Head, and both paddle till they come to the place where they expect their Game. Then they lye still or paddle very softly, looking well about them; and he that is in the Head of the Canoa lays down his Paddle, and stands up with his striking Staff in his Hand. This Staff is about 8 Foot long, almost as big as a Man's

Arm at the great End, in which there is a Hole to place his Harpoon in. At the other end of his Staff there is a piece of light Wood called Bobwood, with a Hole in it, through which the small End of the Staff comes; and on this piece of Bobwood there is a Line of 10 or 12 Fathom wound neatly about, and the End of the Line made fast to it. The other End of the Line is made fast to the Harpoon, which is at the great End of the Staff, and the *Moskito* Men keep about a Fathom of it loose in his Hand. When he strikes, the Harpoon presently comes out of the Staff, and as the Manatee swims away, the Line runs off from the Bob; and altho' at first both Staff and Bob may be carried under Water, yet as the Line runs off it will rise again. Then the *Moskito* Men paddle with all their might to get hold of the Bob again, and spend usually a quarter of an Hour before they get in. When the Manatee begins to be tired, it lieth still, and then the *Moskito* Men paddle to the Bob and take it up, and begin to hale in the Line. When the Manatee feels them he swims away again, with the Canoa after him; then he that steers must be nimble to turn the Head of the Canoa that way that his Consort points, who being in the Head of the Canoa, and holding the Line, both sees and feels which way the Manatee is swimming. Thus the Canoa is towed with a violent Motion, till the Manatee's Strength decays. Then they gather in the Line, which they are often forced to let all go to the very End. At length when the Creature's Strength is spent, they hale it up to the Canoa's side, and knock it on the Head, and tow it to the nearest Shore, where they make it fast and seek for another; which having taken, they get on shore with it to put it into their Canoa: For 'tis so heavy that they cannot lift it in, but they hale it up in shole Water, as near the Shore as they can, and then overset the Canoa, laying one side close to the Manatee. Then they roll in, which brings the Canoa upright again; and when they have heav'd out the Water, they fasten a line to the other Manatee that lieth afloat, and tow it after them. I have known two *Moskito* Men for a Week every Day bring aboard 2 Manatee in this manner; the least of which hath not weighed less than 600 Pound, and that in a very small Canoa, that three *Englishmen* would scarce adventure to go in. When they strike a Cow that hath a young one, they seldom miss the Calf, for she commonly takes her young under one of her Fins. But if the Calf is so big that she cannot carry it, or so frightned that she only minds to save her own Life, yet the young never leaves her till the *Moskito* Men have an opportunity to strike her.

¶ The manner of striking Manatee and Tortoise is much the same; only when they seek for Manatee they paddle so gently, that they make no noise, and never touch the side of their Canoa with their Paddle, because it is a Creature that hears very well. But they are not so nice when they seek for Tortoise, whose Eyes are better than his Ears. They strike the Tortoise with a square sharp Iron Peg, the other with a Harpoon. The *Moskito* Men make their own striking Instruments, as Harpoons,  Fish-hooks, and Tortoise-Irons or Pegs. These Pegs, or Tortoise-Irons are made 4 square, sharp at one End, and not much above an Inch in length, of such a Figure as you see in the Margin. The small Spike at the broad end hath a Line fasten'd to it, and goes also into a Hole at the end of the striking Staff, which when the Tortoise is struck flies off, the Iron and the end of the Line fastned to it going quite within the Shell, where 'tis so buried that the Tortoise cannot possibly escape.

¶ They make their Lines both for fishing and striking with the Bark of *Maho*; which is a sort of Tree or Shrub that grows plentifully all over the *West-Indies*, and whose Bark is made up of Strings, or Threads very strong. You may draw it off either in Flakes or small Threads, as you have Occasion. 'Tis fit for any manner of Cordage; and Privateers often make their Rigging of it. So much by way of Digression.

¶ When we had clean'd our Tartane we sailed from hence, bound for *Boca-toro*, which is an opening between 2 Islands about 10 Deg. 10 Min. North Lat. between the Rivers of *Veragne* and *Chagre*. Here we met with Captain *Yanky*, who told us that there had been a Fleet of *Spanish* Armadilloes to seek us: That Capt. *Tristian* having fallen to Leeward, was coming to *Boca-toro*, and fell in amongst them, supposing them to be our Fleet: That they fired and chased him, but he rowed and towed, and they supposed he got away: That Capt. *Pain* was likewise chaced by them and Capt. *Williams*; and that they had not seen them since they lay within the Islands: That the *Spaniards* never came in to him; and that Capt. *Coxon* was in at the careening Place.

¶ This *Boca-toro* is a place that the Privateers use to resort to, as much as any place on all the Coast, because here is plenty of green Tortoise, and a good careening Place. The *Indians* here have no Commerce with the *Spaniards*; but are very barbarous and will not be dealt with. They have destroyed many Privateers, as they did not long after this some of Capt. *Pain*'s Men; who having built a Tent ashore to put his Goods in while he careened his Ship, and some Men lying there with their Arms, in the Night the *Indians* crept softly into the Tent, and cut off the Heads of three or four Men, and made their escape; nor was this the first time they had served the Privateers so. There grow on this Coast *Vinelloes* in great quantity, with which Chocolate is perfumed. These I shall describe elsewhere.

¶ Our Fleet being thus scattered, there were now no hopes of getting together again; therefore every one did what they thought most conducing to obtain their Ends. Capt. *Wright*, with whom I now was, was resolved to cruise on the Coast of *Cartagene*; and it being now almost the Westerly Wind Season, we sailed from hence, and Capt. *Yanky* with us; and we consorted, because Capt. *Yanky* had no Commission, and was afraid the *French* would take away his Bark. We past by *Scuda*, a small Island (where 'tis said Sir *Francis Drake*'s Bowels were bury'd) and came to a small River to Westward of *Chagre*; where we took two new Canoas, and carry'd them with us into the *Samballoes*. We had the Wind at West, with much Rain; which brought us to *Point-Samballas*. Here Capt. *Wright* and Capt. *Yanky* left us in the Tartane to fix the Canoas, while they went on the Coast of *Cartagene* to seek for Provision. We cruised in among the Islands, and kept our *Moskito-men*, or Strikers out, who brought aboard some half-grown Tortoise; and some of us went ashore every Day to hunt for what we could find in the Woods: Sometimes we got *Pecary*, *Warree* or Deer; at other times we light on a drove of large fat Monkeys, or *Quames*, *Corrosoes*, (each a large sort of Fowl) Pigeons, Parrots, or Turtle-doves. We liv'd very well on what we got, not staying long in one place; but sometimes we would go on the Islands, where there grow great Groves of *Sapadilloes*, which is a sort of Fruit much like a Pear, but more juicy; and under those Trees we found plenty of *Soldiers*, a little kind of Animals that live in Shells, and have two great Claws like a Crab, and are good food. One time our Men found a great many large ones, and being sharp-set had them drest, but most of them were very sick afterwards, being poisoned by them: For on this Island were many *Manchaneel* Trees, whose Fruit is like a small Crab, and smells very well, but they are not wholesome; and we commonly take care of meddling with any Animals that eat them. And this we take for a general Rule; when we find any Fruits that we have not seen before, if we see them peck'd by Birds, we may freely eat, but if we see no such sign, we let them alone; for of this Fruit no Birds will taste. Many of these Islands have of these *Manchaneel* Trees growing on them.

¶ Thus cruising in among these Islands, at length we came again to *La Sound*'s Key; and the Day before having met with a *Jamaica* Sloop that was come over on the Coast to Trade, she went with us. It was in the Evening when we came to an Anchor, and the next Morning we fired two Guns for the *Indians* that lived on the Main to come aboard; for by this time we concluded we should hear from our five Men that we left in the

Heart of the Country among the *Indians*, this being about the latter End of *August*, and it was the Beginning of *May* when we parted from them. According to our Expectations the *Indians* came aboard, and brought our Friends with them: Mr. *Wafer* wore a Clout about him, and was painted like an *Indian*; and he was some time aboard before I knew him. One of them, named *Richard Cobson*, died within three or four Days after, and was buried on *La Sound*'s Key.

¶ After this we went to other Keys, to the Eastward of these, to meet Capt. *Wright* and Capt. *Yanky*, who met with a Fleet of Periagoes laden with *Indian* Corn, Hog and Fowls, going to *Cartagene*; being convoyed by a small Armadilly of two Guns and six Patereroes. Her they chaced ashore, and most of the Periagoes; but they got two of them off, and brought them away.

¶ Here Capt. *Wright*'s and Capt. *Yanky*'s Barks were clean'd; and we stock'd our selves with Corn, and then went towards the Coast of *Cartagene*. In our way thither we passed by the River of *Darien*; which is very broad at the Mouth, but not above 6 Foot Water on a Spring-tide; for the Tide riseth but little here. Capt. *Coxon*, about 6 Months before we came out of the *South-Seas*, went up this River with a party of Men: every Man carry'd a small strong Bag to put his Gold in; expecting great Riches there, tho' they got little or none. They rowed up about 100 Leagues before they came to any Settlement, and then found some *Spaniards*, who lived there to truck with the *Indians* for Gold; there being Gold Scales in every House. The *Spaniards* admired how they came so far from the Mouth of the River, because there are a sort of *Indians* living between that Place and the Sea, who are very dreadful to the *Spaniards*, and will not have any Commerce with them, nor with any white People. They use Trunks about 8 foot long, out of which they blow poisoned Darts; and are so silent in their Attacks on their Enemies, and retreat so nimbly again, that the *Spaniards* can never find them. Their Darts are made of Macaw-wood, being about the bigness and length of a Knitting-needle; one end is wound about with Cotton, the other end is extraordinary sharp and small; and is jagged with notches like a Harpoon: So that whatever it strikes into, it immediately breaks off, by the Weight of the biggest end; which it is not of strength to bear, (it being made so slender for that purpose) and is very difficult to be got out again, by reason of those notches. These *Indians* have always War with our *Darien* friendly *Indians*, and live on both sides this great River 50 or 60 Leagues from the Sea, but not near the Mouth of the River. There are abundance of *Manatee* in this River, and some Creeks belonging to it. This Relation I had from

several Men who accompanied Capt. *Coxon* in that discovery; and from
Mr. *Cook* in particular, who was with them, and is a very intelligent
Person: He is now chief Mate of a Ship bound to *Guinea*. To return
therefore to the Prosecution of our Voyage; meeting with nothing of note,
we passed by *Carthagene*; which is a City so well known, that I shall say
nothing of it. We sailed by in sight of it, for it lies open to the Sea: and
had a fair view of *Madre de Popa*, or *Nuestra Sennora de Popa*, a Monastery
of the Virgin *Mary*'s, standing on the top of a very steep Hill just behind
Cartagene. It is a Place of incredible Wealth, by reason of the Offerings
made here continually; and for this reason often in danger of being
visited by the Privateers, did not the neighbourhood of *Carthagene* keep
them in awe. 'Tis in short, the very *Loretto* of the *West-Indies*: It hath
innumerable Miracles related of it. Any Misfortune that befalls the
Privateers is attributed to this Lady's doing; and the *Spaniards* report that
she was aboard that Night the *Oxford* Man of War was blown up at the
Isle of *Vacca* near *Hispaniola*, and that she came home all wet; as belike
she often returns with her Cloaths dirty and torn with passing thro' Woods
and bad ways, when she has been out upon any Expedition; deserving
doubtless a new Suit for such eminent Pieces of Service.

¶ From hence we passed on to the *Rio Grande*, where we took up fresh
Water at Sea, a League off the Mouth of that River. From thence we
sailed Eastwards passing by St. *Martha* a large Town, and good harbour,
belonging to the *Spaniards*: yet hath it within these few Years been twice
taken by the Privateers. It stands close upon the Sea, and the Hill within
Land is a very large one, towering up a great heighth from a vast Body
of Land. I am of Opinion that it is higher than the Pike of *Tenariff*;
others also that have seen both think the same; tho' its bigness makes its
heighth less sensible. I have seen it in passing by, 30 Leagues off at Sea;
others, as they told me, above 60: and several have told me, that they
have seen at once, *Jamaica*, *Hispaniola*, and the high Land of *Santa Martha*;
and yet the nearest of these two Places is distant from it 120 Leagues;
and *Jamaica*, which is farthest off, is accounted near 150 Leagues; and I
question whether any Land on either of those two Islands may be seen
50 Leagues. It's Head is generally hid in the Clouds; but in clear Weather,
when the top appears, it looks white; supposed to be covered with Snow.
St. *Martha* lieth in the Lat. of 12 Deg. North.

¶ Being advanc'd 5 or 6 Leagues to the Eastward of *Santa Martha*, we
left our Ships at Anchor, and return'd back in our Canoa's to the River
Grande; entring it by a Mouth of it that disembogues it self near *Santa
Martha*: purposing to Attempt some Towns that lye a pretty way up that

River. But this Design meeting with Discouragements, we return'd to our Ships, and set sail to the *Rio la Hacha*. This hath been a strong *Spanish* Town, and is well built; but being often taken by the Privateers, the *Spaniards* deserted it some Time before our Arrival. It lieth to the West-ward of a River; and right against the Town is a good Road for Ships, the bottom clean and sandy. The *Jamaica* Sloops used often to come over to Trade here: and I am inform'd that the *Spaniards* have again settled themselves in it, and made it very strong. We enter'd the Fort, and brought two small Guns aboard. From thence we went to the *Rancho-Reys*, one or two small *Indian* Villages, where the *Spaniards* keep two Barks to fish for Pearl. The Pearl-banks lye about 4 or 5 Leagues off from the shore, as I have been told; thither the Fishing-Barks go and anchor; then the Divers go down to the Bottom, and fill a Basket (which is let down before) with Oysters; and when they come up, others go down, two at a Time; this they do till the Bark is full, and then go ashore, where the old Men, Women and Children of the *Indians* open the Oysters, there being a *Spanish* Overseer to look after the Pearl. Yet these *Indians* do very often secure the best Pearl for themselves, as many *Jamaica*-men can testifie who daily trade with them. The Meat they string up, and hang it a drying. At this place we went ashore, where we found one of the Barks, and saw great heaps of Oyster-shells, but the People all fled: Yet in another place, between this and *Rio La Receba* we took some of the *Indians*, who seem to be a stubborn sort of People: They are long visaged, black Hair, their Noses somewhat rising in the middle, and of a stern look. The *Spaniards* report them to be a very numerous Nation; and that they will not subject themselves to their Yoak. Yet they have *Spanish* Priests among them; and by trading have brought them to be somewhat sociable; ·but cannot keep a severe Hand over them. The Land is but barren, it being of a light Sand near the Sea, and most *Savannah*, or Champian; and the Grass but thin and coarse, yet they feed plenty of Cattle. Every Man knoweth his own, and looketh after them; but the Land is in common, except only their Houses or small Plantations where they live, which every Man maintains with some fence about it. They may remove from one place to another as they please, no Man having right to any Land but what he possesseth. This part of the Country is not so subject to Rain as to the Westward of *Santa Martha*; yet here are Tornadoes, or Thunder-showers; but neither so violent as on the Coast of *Portabell*, nor so frequent. The Westerly Winds in the Westerly Wind Season blow here, tho' not so strong nor lasting as on the Coasts of *Cartagene* and *Portabell*.

❡ When we had spent some Time here, we return'd again towards the

Coast of *Cartagene*; and being between *Rio Grande* and that place, we met
with Westerly Winds, which kept us still to the Eastward of *Cartagene* 3 or
4 Days; and then in the Morning we descryed a Sail off at Sea, and we
chased her at noon: Captain *Wright*, who sailed best, came up with her,
and engaged her; and in half an Hour after Captain *Yanky*, who sailed
better than the Tartan (the Vessel that I was in) came up with her likewise, and laid her aboard, then Captain *Wright* also; and they took her
before we came up. They lost 2 or 3 Men, and had 7 or 8 wounded. The
Prize was a Ship of 12 Guns and 40 Men, who had all good small Arms.
She was laden with Sugar and Tobacco, and 8 or 10 Tuns of Marmalett
on board: She came from *Saint Jago* on *Cuba*, and was bound to *Cartagene*.
¶ We went back with her to *Rio Grande*, to fix our Rigging which was
shattered in the Fight, and to consider what to do with her; for these
were Commodities of little use to us, and not worth going into a Port
with. At the *Rio Grande* Captain *Wright* demanded the Prize as his due
by virtue of his Commission: Captain *Yanky* said it was his due by the
Law of Privateers. Indeed Captain *Wright* had the most right to her,
having by his Commission protected Captain *Yanky* from the *French*, who
would have turned him out because he had no Commission; and he likewise began to engage her first. But the Company were all afraid that
Captain *Wright* would presently carry her into a Port; therefore most of
Capt. *Wright*'s Men stuck to Captain *Yanky*, and Captain *Wright* losing
his Prize burned his own Bark, and had Captain *Yanky*'s, it being bigger
than his own; the Tartan was sold to a *Jamaica* Trader, and Captain
Yanky commanded the Prize-Ship. We went again from hence to *Rio la
Hach*, and set the Prisoners ashore; and it being now the beginning of
November, we concluded to go to *Querisao* to sell our Sugar, if favoured
by Westerly Winds, which were now come in. We sailed from thence,
having fair Weather and Winds to our Mind, which brought us to *Querisao*,
a *Dutch* Island. Captain *Wright* went ashore to the Governour, and offered
him the Sail of the Sugar: But the Governour told him he had a great
Trade with the *Spaniards*, therefore he could not admit us in there; but
if we could go to St. *Thomas*, which is an Island, and free Port, belonging
to the *Danes*, and a Sanctuary for Privateers, he would send a Sloop with
such Goods as we wanted, and Money to buy the Sugar, which he would
take at a certain rate; but it was not agreed to.
¶ *Querisao* is the only Island of Importance that the *Dutch* have in the
West-Indies. It is about 5 Leagues in length, and may be 9 or 10 in
circumference: the Northermost point is laid down in North lat. 12 d.
40 m. and it is about 7 or 8 Leagues from the Main, near Cape *Roman*.

On the South side of the East-end is a good Harbour, call'd *Santa Barbara*; but the chiefest Harbour is about 3 Leagues from the S.E. end, on the South-side of it where the *Dutch* have a very good Town, and a very strong Fort. Ships bound in thither must be sure to keep close to the Harbour's Mouth, and have a Hasar or Rope ready to send one end ashore to the Fort: for there is no Anchoring at the entrance of the Harbour, and the Current always sets to the Westward. But being got in, it is a very secure Port for Ships, either to careen, or lye safe. At the East end are two Hills, one of them is much higher than the other, and steepest towards the North-side. The rest of the Island is indifferent level; where of late some rich Men have made Sugar-works; which formerly was all Pasture for Cattle: there are also some small Plantations of Potatoes and Yams, and they have still a great many Cattle on the Island; but it is not so much esteemed for its produce, as for its Situation for the Trade with the *Spaniard*. Formerly the Harbour was never without Ships from *Cartagene* and *Portabell*, that did use to buy of the *Dutch* 1000 or 1500 Negroes at once, besides great quantities of *European* Commodities; but of late that Trade is fallen into the Hands of the *English* at *Jamaica*: yet still the *Dutch* have a vast Trade over all the *West-Indies*, sending from *Holland* Ships of good force laden with *European* Goods, whereby they make very profitable returns. The *Dutch* have two other Islands here, but of little Moment in comparison of *Querisao*; the one lieth 7 or 8 Leagues to the Westward of *Querisao*, called *Aruba*; the other 9 or 10 Leagues to the Eastward of it, call'd *Bon-Airy*. From these Islands the *Dutch* fetch in Sloops Provision for *Querisao* to maintain their Garrison and Negroes. I was never at *Aruba*, therefore cannot say any Thing of it as to my own Knowledge; but by report it is much like *Bon-Airy*, which I shall describe, only not so big. Between *Querisao* and *Bon-Airy* is a small Island called *Little Querisao*, it is not above a League from *Great Querisao*. The King of *France* has long had an Eye on *Querisao*, and made some Attempts to take it, but never yet succeeded. I have heard that about 23 or 24 Years since the Governour had sold it to the *French*, but dy'd a small Time before the Fleet came to demand it, and by his Death that design failed. Afterwards, in the Year 1678, the Count *D'Estree*, who a Year before had taken the Isle of *Tobago* from the *Dutch*, was sent thither also with a Squadron of stout Ships, very well mann'd, and fitted with Bombs and Carcasses; intending to take it by storm. This Fleet first came to *Martinico*; where, while they staid, orders were sent to *Petit Guavers*, for all Privateers to repair thither, and assist the Count in his Design. There were but two Privateers Ships that went thither to him, which were mann'd partly with *French*, partly with

Englishmen. These set out with the Count; but in their way to *Querisao*,
the whole Fleet was lost on a Riff or Ridge of Rocks, that runs off from
the Isle of *Aves*; not above two Ships escaping, one of which was one of
the Privateers; and so that design perished.

¶ Wherefore not driving a Bargain for our Sugar with the Governour
of *Querisao*, we went from thence to *Bon-Airy*, another *Dutch* Island, where
we met a *Dutch* sloop come from *Europe*, laden with *Irish* Beef; which we
bought in exchange for some of our Sugar.

¶ *Bon-Airy* is the Eastermost of the *Dutch* Islands, and is the largest of the
three, though not the most considerable. The middle of the Island is laid
down in Lat. 12 d. 16 m. It is about 20 Leagues from the Main, and
9 or 10 from *Querisao*, and is accounted 16 or 17 Leagues round. The
Road is on the S.W. side, near the middle of the Island; where there is
a pretty deep Bay runs in. Ships that come from the Eastward luff up
close to the Eastern shore: and let go their Anchor in 60 fathom Water,
within half a Cabels length of the shore. But at the same Time they
must be ready with a Boat to carry a Hasar or Rope, and make it fast
ashore; otherwise when the Land-wind comes in the night, the Ship would
drive off to Sea again; for the Ground is so steep, that no Anchor can
hold if once it starts. About half a Mile to the Westward of this Anchoring-
place there is a small low Island, and a Channel between it and the main
Island.

¶ The Houses are about half a Mile within Land, right in the Road:
There is a Governour lives here, a Deputy to the Governour of *Querisao*,
and 7 or 8 Soldiers, with 5 or 6 Families of *Indians*. There is no Fort; and
the Soldiers in peaceable Times have little to do but to eat and sleep,
for they never watch but in Time of War. The *Indians* are Husbandmen,
and plant Maiz and *Guinea*-Corn, and some Yams, and Potatoes: but
their chiefest Business is about Cattle: for this Island is plentifully stocked
with Goats: and they send great Quantities every Year in Salt to *Querisao*.
There are some Horses, and Bulls and Cows; but I never saw any Sheep,
tho' I have been all over the Island. The South-side is plain low Land,
and there are several sorts of Trees, but none very large. There is a small
Spring of Water by the Houses, which serves the Inhabitants, tho' it is
blackish. At the West-end of the Island there is a good Spring of fresh
Water, and three or four *Indian* Families live there, but no Water nor
Houses at any other place. On the South-side near the East-end is a
good Salt-pond, where *Dutch* Sloops come for Salt.

¶ From *Bon-Airy* we went to the Isle of *Aves*, or Birds; so called from its
great plenty of Birds, as *Men-of-War* and *Boobies*; but especially *Boobies*.

The *Booby* is a Water-fowl, somewhat less than a Hen, of a light grayish Colour. I observed the *Boobies* of this Island to be whiter than others. This Bird hath a strong Bill, longer and bigger than a Crow's, and broader at the End: Her feet are flat like a Duck's Feet. It is a very simple Creature, and will hardly go out of a Man's way. In other places they build their Nests on the Ground, but here they build on Trees; which I never saw any where else; tho' I have seen of them in a great many Places. Their Flesh is black and eats fishy, but are often eaten by the Privateers. Their Numbers have been much lessened by the *French* Fleet which was lost here, as I shall give an account.

❡ The *Man-of-War* (as it is called by the *English*) is about the Bigness of a Kite, and in shape like it, but black; and the Neck is red. It lives on Fish, yet never lights on the Water, but soars aloft like a Kite, and when it sees its Prey, it flies down Head foremost to the Water's Edge very swiftly, takes its Prey out of the Sea with it Bill, and immediately mounts again as swiftly, and never touching the Water with his Bill. His Wings are very long; his Feet are like other Land-fowl, and he builds on Trees where he finds any; but where they are wanting, on the Ground.

❡ This Island *Aves* lies about 8 or 9 Leagues to the Eastward of the Island *Bon-Airy*, about 14 or 15 Leagues from the Main, and about the Lat. of 11 d. 45 m. North. It is but small, not above four Mile in length, and towards the East-end not half a Mile broad. On the North-side it is low Land, commonly overflown with the Tide; but on the South-side there is a great rocky Bank of Coral thrown up by the Sea. The West-end is, for near a Mile space, plain even Savannah Land, without any Trees. There are 2 or 3 Wells dug by Privateers, who often frequent this Island, because there is a good Harbour about the middle of it on the North-side where they may conveniently careen. The Riff or Bank of Rocks on which the *French* Fleet was lost, as I mentioned above, runs along from the East-end to the Northward about 3 Mile, then trends away to the Westward making, as it were a Half-Moon. This Riff breaks off all the Sea, and there is good Riding in even sandy Ground to the Westward of it. There are 2 or 3 small low sandy Keys or Islands within this Riff, about 3 Miles from the main Island. The Count *d'Estree* lost his Fleet here in this manner. Coming from the Eastward, he fell in on the Back of the Riff, and fired Guns to give warning to the rest of his Fleet: But they supposing their Admiral was engaged with Enemies, hoisted up their Topsails, and crouded all the Sails they could make, and ran full sail ashore after him; all within half a Mile of each other. For his Light being in the Main-Top was an unhappy Beacon for them to follow; and there escaped but one King's Ship and one Privateer. The Ships continued whole all Day, and the Men had time enough, most of them, to get ashore, yet many perished in the Wreck; and many of those that got safe on the Island, for want of being accustomed to such Hardships, died like rotten Sheep. But the Privateers who had been used to such Accidents lived merrily, from whom I had this relation: and they told me, that if they had gone to *Jamaica* with 30*l.* a Man in their Pockets, they could not have enjoyed themselves more: For they kept in a Gang by themselves, and watched when the Ships broke, to get the Goods that came from them, and though much was staved against the Rocks, yet abundance of Wine and Brandy floated over the Riff, where the Privateers waited to take it up. They lived here about three Weeks, waiting an opportunity to transport themselves back again to *Hispaniola*; in all which time they were never without two or three Hogsheads of Wine and Brandy in their Tents, and Barrels of Beef and Pork; which they could live on without Bread well enough, tho' the new Comers out of *France* could not. There were about Forty *Frenchmen* on board in one of the Ships where there was good store of Liquor, till the after-part of her broke away and floated over the Riff, and was carry'd away to Sea, with all the Men drinking and singing, who being in drink, did not mind the Danger, but were never heard of afterwards.

¶ In a short time after this great Shipwrack, Capt. *Pain*, Commander of a Privateer of six Guns, had a pleasant Accident befel him at this Island. He came hither to careen, intending to fit himself very well; for here lay driven on the Island, Masts, Yards, Timbers, and many things that he wanted, therefore he halled into the Harbour, close to the Island, and unrigg'd his Ship. Before he had done, a *Dutch* Ship of twenty Guns, was sent from *Querisao* to take up the Guns that were lost on the Riff: But seeing a Ship in the Harbour, and knowing her to be a *French* Privateer, they thought to take her first, and came within a Mile of her, and began to fire at her, intending to warp in the next Day, for it is very narrow going in. Capt. *Pain* got ashore some of his Guns, and did what he could to resist them; tho' he did in a manner conclude he must be taken. But while his Men were thus busied, he spy'd a *Dutch* Sloop turning to get into the Road, and saw her at the Evening anchor at the West-end of the Island. This gave him some hope of making his escape; which he did, by sending two Canoas in the Night aboard the Sloop, who took her, and got considerable Purchase in her; and he went away in her, making a good Reprizal, and leaving his own empty Ship to the *Dutch* Man of War.

¶ There is another Island to the Eastward of the Isle of *Aves*, about four League, called by Privateers the little Isle of *Aves*, which is over-grown with Mangrove Trees. I have seen it, but was never on it. There are no Inhabitants that I could learn on either of these Islands, but *Boobies* and a few other Birds.

¶ Whilst we were at the Isle of *Aves*, we careen'd Capt. *Wright*'s Bark, and scrubb'd the Sugar-prize, and got two Guns out of the Wrecks; continuing here till the Beginning of *Feb*. 168½.

¶ We went from hence to the Isles *Roca*'s, to careen the Sugar-prize, which the Isle of *Aves* was not a Place so convenient for. Accordingly we haled close to one of the small Islands, and got our Guns ashore the first thing we did, and built a Breast-work on the Point, and planted all our Guns there, to hinder an Enemy from coming to us while we lay on the Careen: Then we made a House, and cover'd it with our Sails, to put our Goods and Provisions in. While we lay here, a *French* Man of War of 36 Guns came thro' the Keys or little Islands; to whom we sold about 10 Tun of Sugar. I was aboard twice or thrice, and very kindly welcomed both by the Captain and his Lieutenant, who was a Cavalier of *Malta*; and they both offered me great Encouragement in *France*, if I would go with them; but I ever designed to continue with those of my own Nation.

¶ The Islands *Roca*'s are a Parcel of small uninhabited Islands, lying about the Lat. of 11 deg. 40 min. about 15 or 16 Leagues from the Main, and about 20 Leagues N.W. by W. from *Tortuga*, and 6 or 7 Leagues to the Westward of *Orchilla*, another Island lying about the same Distance from the Main; which Island I have seen, but was never at it. *Roca*'s stretch themselves East and West about 5 Leagues, and their breadth about 3 Leagues. The northernmost of these Islands is the most remarkable by reason of a high white rocky Hill at the West-end of it, which may be seen a great way; and on it there are abundance of Tropick-Birds, Men-of-War, Booby and Noddies, which breed there. The Booby and Man-of-War I have describ'd already. The Noddy is a small black Bird, about the Bigness of the *English* Blackbird, and indifferent good Meat. They build in Rocks. We never find them far off from Shore. I have seen of them in other places, but never saw any of their Nests, but in this Island, where there is great plenty of them. The Tropick-Bird is as big as a Pigeon, but round and plump like a Partridge. They are all white, except two or three Feathers in each Wing of a light Grey. Their Bills are of a yellowish Colour, thick and short. They have one long Feather, or rather a Quill about 7 Inches long, grows out at the Rump, which is all the Tail they have. They are never seen far without either Tropick, for which reason they are called Tropick-Birds. They are very good Food, and we meet with them a great way at Sea, and I never saw of them any where but at Sea and in this Island, where they build and are found in great plenty.

¶ By the Sea, on the South-side of that high Hill, there's fresh Water comes out of the Rocks, but so slowly, that it yield not above 40 Gallons in 24 Hours, and it tastes so copperish, or aluminous rather, and rough in the Mouth, that it seems very unpleasant at first drinking: But after two or three Days any Water will seem to have no taste.

¶ The middle of this Island is low plain Land, over-grown with long Grass, where there are Multitudes of small grey Fowls no bigger than a Blackbird, yet lay Eggs bigger than a Magpy's; and they are therefore by Privateers called Egg-birds. The East-end of the Island is over-grown with black Mangrove Trees.

¶ There are three sorts of Mangrove Trees, black, red and white. The black Mangrove is the largest Tree; the Body about as big as an Oak, and about 20 Feet high. It is very hard and serviceable Timber, but extra-ordinary heavy, therefore not much made use of for building. The red Mangrove groweth commonly by the Sea-side, or by Rivers or Creeks. The Body is not so big as that of the black Mangrove, but always grows out of many Roots about the Bigness of a Man's Leg, some bigger some less, which at about 6, 8, or 10 Foot above the Ground, join into one Trunk or Body, that seems to be supported by so many artificial Stakes. Where this sort of Tree grows, it is impossible to march, by reason of these Stakes, which grow so mixt one amongst another, that I have, when forced to go thro' them, gone half a Mile, and never set my Foot on the Ground, stepping from Root to Root. The Timber is hard and good for many uses. The Inside of the Bark is red, and it is used for tanning of Leather very much all over the *West-Indies*. The white Mangrove never groweth so big as the other two sorts, neither is it of any great use: Of the young Trees Privateers use to make Loom, or Handles for their Oars, for it is commonly straight, but not very strong, which is the Fault of them. Neither the black nor white Mangrove grow towering up from Stilts or rising Roots, as the red doth; but the Body immediately out of the Ground, like other Trees.

¶ The Land of this East-end is light Sand, which is sometimes overflown with the Sea at Spring-Tides. The Road for Ships is on the South-side, against the middle of the Island. The rest of the Islands of *Roca*'s are low. The next to this on the South-side is but small, flat, and even, without Trees, bearing only Grass. On the South-side of it is a Pond of brackish

Water, which sometimes Privateers use instead of better; there is likewise good Riding by it. About a League from this are two other Islands, not 200 Yards distant from each other; yet a deep Channel for Ships to pass thro'. They are both over-grown with red Mangrove Trees; which Trees, above any of the Mangroves, do flourish best in wet drowned Land, such as these two Islands are; only the East-Point of the westermost Island is dry Sand, without Tree or Bush. On this Point we careened, lying on the South-side of it.

¶ The other Islands are low, and have red Mangroves and other Trees on them. Here also Ships may ride, but no such place for careening as where we lay, because at that place Ships may hale close to the Shore; and if they had but four Guns on the Point, may secure the Channel, and hinder any Enemy from coming near them. I observ'd, that within among the Islands was good riding in many places, but not without the Islands, except to the Westward, or South West of them. For on the East or N.E. of these Islands, the common Trade-wind blows, and makes a great Sea: And to the Southward of them, there is no Ground under 70, or 80, or 100 Fathom, close by the Land.

¶ After we had filled what Water we could from hence, we set out again in *April* 1682, and came to *Salt-Tortuga*, so called to distinguish it from the Shoals of *Dry Tortugas*, near Cape *Florida*, and from the Isle of *Tortugas* by *Hispaniola*, which was called formerly *French Tortugas*; tho' not having heard any mention of that Name a great while, I am apt to think it is swallowed up in that of *Petit-Guavres*, the chief Garrison the *French* have in those Parts. This Island we arrived at is pretty large, uninhabited, and abounds with Salt. It is in Lat. 11 d. North, and lyeth West and a little northerly from *Margarita*, an Island inhabited by the *Spaniards*, strong and wealthy; it is distant from it about 14 Leagues, and 17 or 18 from Cape *Blanco* on the Main: A Ship being within these Islands, a little to the Southward may see at once the Main, *Magarita* and *Tortuga*, when it is clear Weather. The East-end of *Tortuga* is full of rugged, bare, broken Rocks, which stretch themselves a little way out to Sea. At the S.E. Part is an indifferent good Road for Ships, much frequented in peaceable times by Merchant-Ships, that come thither to lade Salt, in the Months of *May*, *June*, *July* and *August*. For at the East-end is a large Salt-pond, within 200 Paces of the Sea. The Salt begins to kern or grain in *April*, except it is a dry Season; for it is observed that Rain makes the Salt kern. I have seen above 20 Sail at a time in this Road come to lade Salt; and these Ships coming from some of the *Caribbe Islands*, are alway well stored with Rum, Sugar and Lime-juice to make Punch, to hearten their Men when

they are at work, getting and bringing aboard the Salt; and they commonly provide the more, in hopes to meet with Privateers, who resort hither in the aforesaid Months, purposely to keep a *Christmas*, as they call it; being sure to meet with Liquor enough to be merry with, and are very liberal to those that treat them. Near the West-end of the Island, on the South-side, there is a small Harbour and some fresh Water: That End of the Island is full of shrubby Trees, but the East-end is rocky and barren as to Trees, producing only coarse Grass. There are some Goats on it, but not many; and Turtle or Tortoise come upon the sandy Bays to lay their Eggs, and from thence the Island has its name. There is no riding any where but in the Roads where the Salt-ponds are, or in the Harbour.
¶ At this Isle we thought to have sold our Sugar among the *English* Ships that come hither for Salt; but failing there, we design'd for *Trinidada*, an Island near the Main, inhabited by the *Spaniards*, tolerably strong and wealthy; but the Current and Easterly Winds hindring us, we passed thro' between *Margarita* and the Main, and went to *Blanco*, a pretty large Island almost North of *Margarita*; about 30 Leagues from the Main, and in 11 d. 50 m. North Lat. It is a flat, even, low, uninhabited Island, dry and healthy: most Savannah of long Grass, and hath some Trees of *Lignum-Vitæ* growing in Spots, with shrubby Bushes of other Wood about them. It is plentifully stored with *Guano*'s, which are an Animal like a Lizard, but much bigger. The Body is as big as the small of a Man's Leg, and from the Hind-quarter the Tail grows tapering to the End, which is very small. If a Man takes hold of the Tail, except very near the Hind-quarter, it will part and break off in one of the Joints, and the *Guano* will get away. They lay Eggs, as most of those amphibious Creatures do, and are very good to eat. Their Flesh is much esteem'd by Privateers, who commonly dress them for their sick Men; for they make very good Broath. They are of divers Colours, as almost black, dark-brown, light-brown, dark-green, light-green, yellow and speckled. They all live as well in the Water as on Land, and some of them are constantly in the Water, and among Rocks: These are commonly black. Others that live in swampy wet Ground are commonly on Bushes and Trees, these are green. But such as live in dry Ground, as here at *Blanco*, are commonly yellow; yet these also will live in the Water, and are sometimes on Trees. The Road is on the N.W. End, against a small Cove, or little sandy Bay. There is no riding any where else, for it is deep Water, and steep close to the Land. There is one small Spring on the West-side, and there is sandy Bays round the Island, where Turtle or Tortoise come up in great abundance, going ashore in the Night. These that frequent this Island

are called green Turtle, and they are the best of that sort, both for Largeness and Sweetness of any in all the *West-Indies*. I would here give a particular Description of these, and other sorts of Turtle in these Seas; but because I shall have occasion to mention some other sort of Turtle when I come again into the *South-Seas*, that are very different from all these, I shall there give a general Account of all these several sorts at once, that the Difference between them may be the better discerned. Some of our modern Descriptions speak of Goats on this Island. I know not what there may have been formerly, but there are none now to my certain knowledge; for my self, and many more of our Crew, have been all over it. Indeed these parts have undergone great Changes in this last Age, as well in Places themselves, as in their Owners, and Commodities of them; particularly *Nombre de Dios*, a City once famous, and which still retains a considerable Name in some late Accounts, is now nothing but a Name. For I have lain ashoar in the Place where that City stood; but it is all over-grown with Wood, so as to leave no sign that any Town hath been there.

¶ We staid at the Isle of *Blanco* not above ten Days, and then went back to *Salt-Tortuga* again, where Capt. *Yanky* parted with us: And from thence, after about four Days, all which time our Men were drunk and quarrelling, we in Capt. *Wright*'s Ship went to the Coast of *Caraccos* on the main Land. This Coast is upon several Accounts very remarkable: 'Tis a continued Tract of high Ridges of Hills, and small Valleys intermixt, for about 20 Leagues, stretching East and West, but in such manner, that the Ridges of Hills and the Valleys alternately run pointing upon the Shore from South to North: The Valleys are some of them about 4 or 5, others not above 1 or 2 Furlongs wide, and in length from the Sea scarce any of them above 4 or 5 Mile at most; there being a long Ridge of Mountains at that distance from the Sea-Coast, and in a manner parallel to it, that joins those shorter Ridges, and closeth up the South-end of the Valleys, which at the North-ends of them lie open to the Sea, and make so many little sandy Bays, that are the only Landing-places on the Coast. Both the main Ridge and these shorter Ribs are very high Land, so that 3 or 4 Leagues off at Sea the Valleys scarce appear to the Eye, but all look like one great Mountain. From the Isles of *Roca*'s about 15, and from the Isle of *Aves* about 20 Leagues off, we see this Coast very plain from on board our Ships, yet when at Anchor on this Coast, we cannot see those Isles; tho' again from the Tops of these Hills, they appear as if at no great distance, like so many Hillocks in a Pond. These Hills are barren, except the lower Sides of them that are covered with some of the same rich black

Mould that fills the Valleys, and is as good as I have seen. In some of the
Valleys there's a strong red Clay, but in the general they are extreamly
fertile, well-water'd, and inhabited by *Spaniards* and their Negroes. They
have Maiz and Plantains for their Support, with *Indian* Fowls and some
Hogs. But the main Product of these Valleys, and indeed the only Com-.
modity it vends, are the Cacao-Nuts, of which the Chocolate is made.
The Cacao-Tree grows no where in the North-Seas but in the Bay of
Campeachy, on *Costa Rica*, between *Portabel* and *Nicaragua*, chiefly up
Carpenter's River; and on this Coast as high as the Isle of *Trinidada*. In
the South-Seas it grows in the River of *Guiaquil*, a little to the Southward
of the Line, and in the Valley of *Collima*, on the South-side of the Continent of *Mexico*; both which places I shall hereafter describe. Besides
these, I am confident there's no places in the World where the Cacao
grows, except those in *Jamaica*, of which there are now but few remaining,
of many and large Walks or Plantations of them found there by the
English at their first Arrival, and since planted by them; and even these,
tho' there is a great deal of Pains and Care bestowed on them, yet seldom
come to any thing, being generally blighted. The Nuts of this Coast of
Caraccos, tho' less than those of *Costa Rica*, which are large flat Nuts, yet
are better and fatter, in my Opinion, being so very oily, that we are
forced to use Water in rubbing them up; and the *Spaniards* that live here,
instead of parching them to get off the Shell before they pound or rub
them to make Chocolate, do in a manner burn them to dry up the Oil;
for else, they say, it would fill them too full of Blood, drinking Chocolate
as they do, five or six times a Day. My worthy Consort Mr. *Ringrose*
commends most the *Guiaquil* Nut; I presume, because he had little
Knowledge of the rest; for being intimately acquainted with him, I know
the Course of his Travels and Experience: But I am persuaded, had he
known the rest so well as I pretend to have done, who have at several
times been long used to, and in a manner lived upon all the several sorts
of them above-mentioned, he would prefer the *Caraccos* Nuts before any
other; yet possibly the drying up of these Nuts so much by the *Spaniards*
here, as I said, may lessen their Esteem with those *Europeans*, that use
their Chocolate ready rubb'd up: So that we always chose to make it up
our selves.

¶ The Cacao Tree hath a Body about a Foot and an half thick (the
largest sort) and 7 or 8 Foot high, to the Branches, which are large, and
spreading like an Oak, with a pretty thick, smooth, dark-green Leaf,
shaped like that of a Plumb-tree, but larger. The Nuts are inclosed in
Cods as big as both a Man's Fists put together: At the broad End of

which there is a small, tough, limber Stalk, by which they hang pendulous from the Body of the Tree, in all parts of it from top to bottom, scattered at irregular Distances, and from the greater Branches a little way up; especially at the Joints of them or Partings, where they hang thickest, but never on the smaller Boughs. There may be ordinarily about 20 or 30 of these Cods upon a well-bearing Tree; and they have two Crops of them in a Year, one in *December*, but the best in *June*. The Cod itself or Shell is almost half an Inch thick; neither spongy nor woody, but of a Substance between both, brittle, yet harder than the Rind of a Lemmon; like which its Surface is grained or knobbed, but more coarse and unequal. The Cods at first are of a dark green, but the Side of them next the Sun of a muddy red. As they grow ripe, the green turns to a fine bright yellow, and the muddy to a more lively, beautiful red, very pleasant to the Eye. They neither ripen, nor are gathered at once: But for three Weeks or a Month when the Season is, the Overseers of the Plantations go every Day about to see which are turned yellow; cutting at once, it may be, not above one from a Tree. The Cods thus gathered, they lay in several heaps to sweat, and then bursting the Shell with their Hands, they pull out the Nuts, which are the only Substance they contain, having no Stalk or Pith among them, and (excepting that these Nuts lie in regular Rows) are placed like the Grains of Maiz, but sticking together, and so closely stowed, that after they have been once separated, it would be hard to place them again in so narrow a compass. There are generally near 100 Nuts in a Cod; in proportion to the greatness of which, for it varies, the Nuts are bigger or less. When taken out they dry them in the Sun upon Matts spread on the Ground: After which they need no more Care, having a thin hard Skin of their own, and much Oil, which preserves them. Salt-Water will not hurt them; for we had our Bags rotten, lying in the bottom of our Ship, and yet the Nuts never the worse. They raise the young Trees of Nuts, set with the great End downward, in fine black Mould, and in the same Places where they are to bear; which they do in 4 or 5 Years Time, without the trouble of transplanting. There are ordinarily of these Trees, from 500 to 2000 and upward in a Plantation or Cacao-walk, as they call them; and they shelter the young Trees from the Weather with Plantains set about them for two or three Years; destroying all the Plantains by such Time the Cacao-Trees are of a pretty good Body, and able to endure the heat; which I take to be the most pernicious to them of any Thing; for tho' these Vallies lye open to the North Winds, unless a little shelter'd here and there, by some Groves of Plantain Trees which are purposely set near the Shores of the several

Bays, yet by all that I could either observe or learn, the Cacao's in this Country are never blighted, as I have often known them to be in other Places. Cacao-Nuts are used as Money in the Bay of *Campeachy*.

¶ The chief Town of this Country is called *Caraccos*; a good way within Land, 'tis a large wealthy Place, where live most of the Owners of these Cacao-walks that are in the Valleys by the Shore; the Plantations being managed by Overseers and Negroes. It is in a large Savannah Country, that abounds with Cattle; and a *Spaniard* of my Acquaintance, a very sensible Man who hath been there, tells me that 'tis very populous, and he judges it to be three Times as big as *Corunna* in *Gallicia*. The way to it is very steep and craggy, over that ridge of Hills, which I say closes up the Valleys and partition Hills of the Cacoa Coast. In this Coast it self the chief Place is *La Guaire*, a good Town close by the Sea; and though it has but a bad Harbour, yet it is much frequented by the *Spanish* Shipping; for the *Dutch* and *English* anchor in the sandy Bays that lie here and there, in the Mouths of several Valleys, and where there is very good riding. The Town is open, but hath a strong Fort; yet both were taken some Years since by Captain *Wright* and his Privateers. 'Tis seated about 4 or 5 Leagues to the Westward of Cape *Blanco*, which Cape is the Eastermost Boundary of this Coast of *Caraccos*. Further Eastward about 20 Leagues, is a great Lake or Branch of the Sea, called *Laguna de Venezuela*; about which are many rich Towns, but the Mouth of the Lake is shallow, that no Ship can enter. Near this Mouth is a Place called *Comana*, where the Privateers were once repulsed without daring to attempt it any more, being the only Place in the North-Seas they attempted in vain for many Years; and the *Spaniards* since throw it in their Teeth frequently, as a Word of reproach or defiance to them. Not far from that Place is *Verina*, a small Village and *Spanish* Plantation, famous for its Tobacco, reputed the best in the World.

¶ But to return to *Caraccos*, all this Coast is subject to dry Winds, generally North East, which caused us to have scabby Lips; and we always found it thus, and that in different Seasons of the Year, for I have been on this Coast several Times. In other respects it is very healthy, and a sweet clear Air. The *Spaniards* have Look-outs or Scouts on the Hills, and Breast-works in the Valleys, and most of their Negroes are furnished with Arms also for defence of the Bays. The *Dutch* have a very profitable Trade here, almost to themselves. I have known three or four great Ships at a Time on the Coast, each it may be of thirty or forty Guns. They carry hither all sorts of *European* Commodities, especially Linnen; making vast Returns, chiefly in Silver and Cacao. And I have often wondered and regretted it, that none of my own Countrymen find the way thither directly from *England*; for our *Jamaica-Men* trade thither indeed, and find the Sweet of it, tho' they carry *English* Commodities at second or third Hand.

¶ While we lay on this Coast, we went ashore in some of the Bays, and took 7 or 8 Tun of Cacao; and after that 3 Barks, one laden with Hides, the second with *European* Commodities, the third with Earthen-Ware and Brandy. With these 3 Barks we went again to the Island of *Roca*'s, where we shar'd our Commodities, and separated, having Vessels enough to transport us all whither we thought most convenient. Twenty of us (for we were about 60) took one of the Vessels and our share of the Goods, and went directly for *Virginia*. In our way thither we took several of the *Sucking-fishes*; for when we see them about the Ship, we cast out a Line and Hook, and they will take it with any manner of Bait, whether Fish or Flesh. The *Sucking-fish* is about the bigness of a large Whiting, and much of the same make towards the Tail, but the Head is flatter. From the Head to the middle of its Back, there groweth a sort of Flesh of a hard gristly Substance like that of the *Limpit* (a Shell-fish tapering up pira-midically) which sticks to the Rocks; or like the Head or Mouth of a Shell-Snail, but harder. This Excrescence is of a flat and oval form, about seven or eight Inches long, and five or six broad; and rising about half an Inch high. It is full of small ridges with which it will fasten itself to any thing that it meets with in the Sea, just as a Snail doth to a Wall. When any of them happen to come about a Ship, they seldom leave her, for they will feed on such filth as is daily thrown over-board, or on mere Excrements. When it is fair Weather, and but little Wind, they will play about the Ship; but in blustering Weather, or when the Ship sails quick, they commonly fasten themselves to the Ship's Bottom, from whence neither the Ship's Motion, tho' never so swift, nor the most tempestuous Sea can remove them. They will likewise fasten themselves to any other bigger Fish; for they never swim fast themselves, if they meet with any thing to carry them. I have found them sticking to a Shark, after it was hal'd in on the Deck, though a Shark is so strong and boisterous a Fish, and throws about him so vehemently for half an Hour together, it may be, when caught, that did not the Sucking-fish stick at no ordinary rate, it must needs be cast off by so much Violence. It is usual also to see them sticking to Turtle, to any old Trees, Planks, or the like, that lie driven at Sea. Any Knobs or Inequalities at a Ship's Bottom, are a great Hindrance to the Swiftness of its sailing; and 10 or 12 of these sticking to it, must needs retard it, as much, in a manner, as if its Bottom were foul. So that

I am inclined to think that this Fish is the *Remora*, of which the Antients tell such Stories; if it be not, I know no other that is, and I leave the Reader to judge. I have seen of these Sucking-fishes in great plenty in the Bay of *Campeachy*, and in all the Sea between that and the Coast of *Caraccos*, as about those Islands particularly I have lately described, *Rocas, Blanco, Tortugas*, &c. They have no Scales, and are very good Meat.

¶ We met nothing else worth Remark in our Voyage to *Virginia*; where we arrived in *July* 1682. That Country is so well known to our Nation, that I shall say nothing of it, nor shall I detain the Reader with the Story of my own Affairs, and the Trouble that befel me during about Thirteen Months of my Stay there; but in the next Chapter, enter immediately upon my Second Voyage into the *South-Seas*, and round the Globe.

CHAPTER IV

The Author's Voyage to the Isle of John Fernando *in the* South-Seas. *He arrives at the Isles of* Cape Verd. *Isle of* Sall; *its Salt-Ponds. The* Flamingo, *and its remarkable Nest. Ambergreece where found. The Isles of* St. Nicholas, Mayo, St. Jago, Fogo, *a burning Mountain; with the rest of the Isles of* Cape Verd. Sherborough *River on the Coast of* Guinea. *The Commodities and Negroes there: A Town of theirs describ'd. Tornadoes, Sharks, Flying-fish. A Sea deep and clear, yet pale. Isles of* Sibbel de Ward. *Small red Lobsters. Streight* Le Mair. *States Island.* Cape Horn *in* Terra del Fuego. *Their meeting with Capt.* Eaton *in the* South-Seas, *and their going together to the Isle of* John Fernando. *Of a* Moskito-Man *left there alone Three Years: His Art and Sagacity; with that of other* Indians. *The Island describ'd. The* Savannahs *of* America. *Goats at* John Fernando's. Seals. Sea-Lions. Snappers, *a sort of Fish. Rock-fish. The Bays, and natural Strength of this Island.*

BEING now entring upon the Relation of a new Voyage, which makes up the main Body of this Book, proceeding from *Virginia* by the way of *Terra del Fuego*, and the *South-Seas*, the *East-Indies*, and so on, till my return to *England* by the way of the *Cape of good Hope*, I shall give my Reader this short Account of my first Entrance upon it. Among those who accompanied Capt. *Sharp* into the *South-Seas* in our former Expedition, and leaving him there, return'd over Land, as is said in the Introduction, and in the 1st and 2d Chapters; there was one Mr. *Cook*, an *English* Native of St. *Christopher*'s, a *Cirole*, as we call all born of *European* Parents in the *West-Indies*. He was a sensible Man, and had been some Years a Privateer. At our joining our selves with those Privateers, we met at our coming again to the *North-Seas*; his Lot was to be with Captain

Yanky, who kept Company for some considerable time with Capt. *Wright*, in whose Ship I was, and parted with us at our 2d Anchoring at the Isle of *Tortugas*; as I have said in the last Chapter. After our parting, this Mr. *Cook* being Quarter-Master under Capt. *Yanky*, the second Place in the Ship, according to the Law of Privateers, laid Claim to a Ship they took from the *Spaniards*; and such of Capt. *Yanky*'s Men as were so disposed, particularly all those who came with us over Land went aboard this Prize-Ship under the new Capt. *Cook*. This Distribution was made at the Isle of *Vacca*, or the Isle of *Ash*, as we call it; and here they parted also such Goods as they had taken. But Capt. *Cook* having no Commission, as Capt. *Yanky*, Capt. *Tristian*, and some other *French* Commanders had, who lay then at that Island, and they grutching the *English* such a Vessel, they all joined together, plunder'd the *English* of their Ships, Goods and Arms, and turn'd them ashore. Yet Capt. *Tristian* took in about 8 or 10 of these *English*, and carried them with him to *Petit-Guavres*: of which Number Capt. *Cook* was one, and Capt. *Davis* another, who with the rest found means to seize the Ship as she lay at Anchor in the Road, Capt. *Tristian* and many of his Men being then ashore: and the *English* sending ashore such *Frenchmen* as remained in the Ship and were master'd by them, though superior in Number, stood away with her immediately for the Isle of *Vacca*, before any notice of this Surprize could reach the *French* Governour of that Isle; so deceiving him also by a Stratagem, they got on board the rest of their Countrymen, who had been left on that Island; and going thence they took a Ship newly come from *France* laden with Wines. They also took a Ship of good force, in which they resolved to embark themselves, and make a new Expedition into the *South-Seas*, to cruise on the Coast of *Chili* and *Peru*. But first they went for *Virginia* with their Prizes; where they arrived the *April* after my coming thither. The best of their Prizes carried 18 Guns; this they fitted up there with Sails, and every thing necessary for so long a Voyage; selling the Wines they had taken for such Provisions as they wanted. My self, and those of our Fellow-travellers over the *Isthmus* of *America*, who came with me to *Virginia* the Year before this (most of which had since made a short Voyage to *Carolina*, and were again return'd to *Virginia*) resolv'd to join our selves to these new Adventurers: and as many more engaged in the same Design as made our whole Crew consist of about 70 Men. So having furnish'd our selves with necessary Materials, and agreed upon some particular Rules, especially of Temperance and Sobriety, by reason of the length of our intended Voyage, we all went on board our Ship.

¶ *August* 23. 1683. we sailed from *Achamack* in *Virginia*, under the Com-

mand of Capt. *Cook* bound for the *South-Seas*. I shall not trouble the
Reader with an Account of every Day's Run, but hasten to the less
known Parts of the World, to give a Description of them; only relating
such memorable Accidents as hapned to us, and such Places as we
touched at by the way.

¶ We met nothing worth Observation till we came to the Islands of
Cape Verd, excepting a terrible Storm which we could not escape: This
hapned in a few Days after we left *Virginia*; with a S.S.E. Wind just in
our Teeth. The Storm lasted above a Week: It drencht us all like so
many drowned Rats, and was one of the worst Storms I ever was in.
One I met with in the *East-Indies* was more violent for the time; but of
not above 24 Hours continuance. After that Storm we had favourable
Winds and good Weather; and in a short time we arrived at the Island
Sall, which is one of the Eastermost of the *Cape Verd* Islands. Of these
there are in Number (so considerable as to bear distinct Names) and they
lie several Degrees off from *Cape Verd* in *Africk*, whence they receive that
Appellation; taking up about 5 Deg. of Longitude in breadth, and about
as many of Latitude in their length, *viz.* from near 14 to 19 North. They
are most inhabited by *Portuguese Banditti*. This of *Sall* is an Island lying
in the Lat. of 16. in Long. 19. deg. 33 m. West from the *Lizard* in *England*,
stretching from North to South about 8 or 9 Leagues, and not above a
League and an half or two Leagues wide. It hath its Name from the
abundance of Salt that is naturally congealed there, the whole Island
being full of large Salt-ponds. The Land is very barren, producing no
Tree that I could see, but some small shrubby Bushes by the Sea-side.
Neither could I discern any Grass; yet there are some poor Goats on it.

¶ I know not whether there are any other Beasts on the Island: There
are some wild Fowl, but I judge not many. I saw a few Flamingo's, which
is a sort of large Fowl, much like a Heron in shape, but bigger, and of a
reddish Colour. They delight to keep together in great Companies, and
feed in Mud or Ponds, or in such Places where there is not much Water:
They are very shy, therefore it is hard to shoot them. Yet I have lain
obscured in the Evening near a Place where they resort, and with two
more in my Company have killed 14 of them at once; the first Shot being
made while they were standing on the Ground, the other two as they rose.
They build their Nests in shallow Ponds, where there is much Mud, which
they scrape together, making little Hillocks, like small Islands, appearing
out of the Water a Foot and half high from the Bottom. They make the
Foundation of these Hillocks broad, bringing them up tapering to the
Top, where they leave a small hollow Pit to lay their Eggs in; and when

they either lay their Eggs or hatch them, they stand all the while, not on the Hillock, but close by it with their Legs on the Ground and in the Water, resting themselves against the Hillock, and covering the hollow Nest upon it with their Rumps: For their Legs are very long; and building thus, as they do, upon the Ground, they could neither draw their Legs conveniently into their Nests, nor sit down upon them otherwise than by resting their whole Bodies there, to the Prejudice of their Eggs or their Young, were it not for this admirable Contrivance, which they have by natural Instinct. They never lay more than two Eggs, and seldom fewer. The young ones cannot fly till they are almost full grown; but will run prodigiously fast; yet we have taken many of them. The Flesh of both young and old is lean and black, yet very good Meat, tasting neither fishy, nor any way unsavory. Their Tongues are large, having a large Knob of Fat at the Root, which is an excellent Bit: A Dish of *Flamingo*'s Tongues being fit for a Prince's Table.

¶ When many of them are standing together by a Pond's Side, being half a Mile distant from a Man, they appear to him like a Brick Wall; their Feathers being of the Colour of new red Brick: And they commonly stand upright and single, one by one, exactly in a row (except when feeding) and close by each other. The young ones at first are of a light grey; and as their Wing-feathers spring out, they grow darker; and never come to their right Colour, or any beautiful Shape, under ten or eleven Months old. I have seen *Flamingoes* at *Rio la Hacha*, and at an Island lying near the Main of *America*, right against *Querisao*, called by Privateers *Flamingo* Key, from the Multitude of these Fowls that breed there: And I never saw of their Nests and Young but here.

¶ There are not above 5 or 6 Men on this Island of *Sall*, and a poor Governor, as they called him, who came aboard in our Boat, and about 3 or 4 poor lean Goats for a Present to our Captain, telling him they were the best that the Island did afford. The Captain, minding more the Poverty of the Giver than the Value of the Present, gave him in requital a Coat to cloath him; for he had nothing but a few Rags on his Back, and an old Hat not worth three Farthings; which yet I believe he wore but seldom, for fear he should want before he might get another; for he told us there had not been a Ship in 3 Years before. We bought of him about 20 Bushels of Salt for a few old Cloaths: And he begged a little Powder and Shot. We stay'd here 3 Days; in which time one of these *Portuguese* offered to some of our Men a Lump of Ambergreece in exchange for some Cloaths, desiring them to keep it secret, for he said if the Governor should know it he should be hang'd. At length one

Mr. *Coppinger* bought for a small Matter; yet I believe he gave more than it was worth. We had not a Man in the Ship that knew Ambergreece; but I have since seen it in other places, and therefore am certain it was not right. It was of a dark colour, like Sheep Dung, and very soft, but of no smell, and possibly 'twas some of their Goat's Dung. I afterwards saw some sold at the *Nequebars* in the *East-Indies*, which was of a lighter Colour, but very hard, neither had it any smell; and this also, I suppose was a cheat. Yet it is certain that in both these Places there is *Ambergreece* found.

¶ I was told by one *John Read*, a *Bristol* Man, that he was Prentice to a Master who traded to these Islands of *Cape Verd*, and once as he was riding at an Anchor at *Fogo*, another of these Islands, there was a lump of it swam by the Ship, and the Boat being ashore he mist it; but knew it to be Ambergreece, having taken up a lump swimming in the like manner the Voyage before, and his Master having at several Times bought pieces of it of the Natives of the Isle of *Fogo*, so as to enrich himself thereby. And so at the *Nequebars*, *Englishmen* have bought, as I have been credible inform'd, great Quantities of very good Ambergreece. Yet the Inhabitants are so subtle that they will counterfeit it, both there and here: and I have heard that in the Gulf of *Florida*, whence much of it comes, the Native *Indians* there use the same Fraud.

¶ Upon this Occasion, I cannot omit to tell my Reader what I learnt from Mr. *Hill* the Chirurgeon, upon his shewing me once a piece of Ambergreece, which was thus. One Mr. *Benjamin Barker*, a Man that I have been long well acquainted with, and know him to be a very diligent and observing Person, and likewise very sober and credible, told this Mr. *Hill*, that being in the Bay of *Honduras* to procure Logwood, which grows there in great abundance, and passing in a Canoa over to one of the Islands in that Bay, he found upon the Shoar, on a sandy Bay there, a lump of Ambergreece, so large, that when carried to *Jamaica*, he found it to weigh a Hundred Pound and upwards. When he first found it, it lay dry, above the Mark which the Sea then came to at Highwater; and he observed in it a great Multitude of Beetles: It was of a dusky colour, towards black, and about the hardness of mellow Cheese, and of a very fragrant Smell: This that Mr. *Hill* shewed me, being some of it, which Mr. *Barker* gave him. Besides those already mentioned, all the Places where I have heard that Ambergreece hath been found, at *Bermudas*, and the *Bahama* Islands in the *West-Indies*, and that part of the Coast of *Africk* with its adjacent Islands, which reaches from *Mozambique* to the *Red-Sea*.

¶ We went from this Island of *Sall*, to St. *Nicholas*, another of the *Cape Verd* Islands, lying West South West from *Sall*, about 22 Leagues. We arrived there the next Day after we left the other, and anchored on the S.E. side of the Island. This is a pretty large Island; it is one of the biggest of all the *Cape-Verd*, and lieth in a triangular form. The longest side, which lieth to the East, is about 30 Leagues long, and the other two about 20 Leagues each. It is a mountainous barren Island, and rocky all round towards the Sea; yet in the Heart of it there are Valleys, where the *Portuguese*, which inhabit here, have Vineyards and Plantations, and Wood for fewel. Here are many Goats, which are but poor in Comparison with those in other Places, yet much better than those at *Sall*: There are likewise many Asses. The Governour of this Island came aboard us, with three or four Gentlemen more in his Company, who were all indifferently well cloathed, and accoutred with Swords and Pistols; but the rest that accompanied him to the Sea-side, which were about twenty or thirty Men more, were but in a ragged Garb. The Governour brought aboard some Wine made in the Island, which tasted much like *Madera* Wine: It was of a pale Colour, and lookt thick. He told us the chief Town was in the Valley fourteen Mile from the Bay where we rode; that he had there under him above one hundred Families, besides other Inhabitants that lived scattering in Valleys more remote. They were all very swarthy; the Governour was the clearest of them, yet of a dark tawny Complexion.

¶ At this Island we scrubb'd the bottom of our Ship, and here also we dug Wells ashore on the Bay, and filled all our Water, and after 5 or 6 Days stay, we went from hence to *Mayo*, another of the *Cape Verd* Islands, lying about forty Mile East and by South from the other; arriving there the next Day, and anchoring on the N.W. side of the Island. We sent our Boat on shore, intending to have purchased some Provision, as Beef or Goats, with which this Island is better stock'd than the rest of the Islands. But the Inhabitants would not suffer our Men to land; for about a Week before our Arrival there came an *English* Ship, the Men of which came ashore, pretending Friendship, and seiz'd on the Governour with some others, and carrying them aboard, made them send ashore for Cattle to ransom their Liberties: And yet after this set sail, and carried them away, and they had not heard of them since. The *English* Man that did this (as I was afterwards informed) was one Capt. *Bond* of *Bristol*. Whether ever he brought back those Men again I know not: He himself and most of his Men have since gone over to the *Spaniards*: and it was he who had like to have burnt our Ship after this in the Bay of *Panama*; as I shall have occasion to relate.

¶ This Isle of *Mayo* is but small, and invironed with sholes, yet a Place much frequented by Shipping for its great plenty of Salt: and though there is but bad landing, yet many Ships lade here every Year. Here are plenty of Bulls, Cows, and Goats; and at a certain Season of the Year, as *May*, *June*, *July*, and *August*, a sort of small Sea-Tortoise come hither to lay their Eggs; but these Turtle are not so sweet as those in the *West-Indies*. The Inhabitants plant Corn, Yams, Potatoes, and some Plantains, and breed a few Fowls; living very poor, yet much better than the Inhabitants of any other of these Islands, *St. Jago* excepted, which lieth four or five Leagues to the Westward of *Mayo*, and is the chief, the most fruitful, and best inhabited of all the Islands of *Cape Verd*; yet mountainous, and much barren Land in it.

¶ On the East-side of the Isle St. *Jago* is a good Port, which in peaceable Times especially is seldom without Ships; for this hath been long a Place which Ships have been wont to touch at for Water and Refreshments, as those outward-bound to the *East-Indies*, *English*, *French* and *Dutch*; many of the Ships bound to the Coast of *Guinea*, the *Dutch* to *Surinam*, and their own *Portuguese* Fleet going for *Brazil*, which is generally about the latter end of *September*: but few Ships call in here in their return to *Europe*. When any Ships are here the Country People bring down their Commodities to sell to the Seamen and Passengers, *viz.* Bullocks, Hogs, Goats, Fowls, Eggs, Plantains, and Coco-Nuts, which they will give in exchange for Shirts, Drawers, Handkerchiefs, Hats, Wastecoats, Breeches, or in a manner for any sort of Cloath, especially Linnen, for Woollen is not much esteemed there. They care not willingly to part with their Cattle of any sort but in exchange for Money, or Linnen, or some other valuable Commodity. Travellers must have a Care of these People, for they are very thievish; and if they see an Opportunity will snatch any Thing from you, and run away with it. We did not touch at this Island in this Voyage; but I was there before this in the Year 1670, when I saw a Fort here lying on the top of an Hill, and commanding the Harbour.

¶ The Governour of this Island is chief over all the rest of the Islands. I have been told that there are two large Towns on this Island, some small Villages, and a great many Inhabitants; and that they make a great deal of Wine, such as is that of St. *Nicholas*. I have not been on any other of the *Cape Verd* Islands, nor near them; but have seen most of them at a distance. They seem to be mountainous and barren; some of these before-mentioned being the most fruitful and most frequented by Strangers, especially St. *Jago* and *Mayo*. As to the rest of them, *Fogo* and *Brava* are two small Islands lying to the Westward of St. *Jago*, but of little note;

only *Fogo* is remarkable for its being a *Vulcano*: It is all of it one large Mountain of a good heighth, out of the top whereof issues Flames of Fire, yet only discerned in the Night: and then it may be seen a great way at Sea. Yet this Island is not without Inhabitants, who live at the foot of the Mountain near the Sea. Their Substance is much the same as in the other Islands; they have some Goats, Fowls, Plantains, Coco-Nuts, &c. as I am informed. Of the Plantains and Coco-Nuts I shall have occasion to speak when I come into the *East-Indies*; and shall defer the giving an Account of them till then.

¶ The remainder of these Islands of *Cape Verd*, are St. *Anthonia*, *St. Lucia*, *St. Vincente*, and *Bona Vista*: of which I know nothing considerable.

¶ Our entrance among these Islands was from the North East; for in our Passage from *Virginia* we ran pretty fair toward the Coast of *Gualata* in *Africk*, to preserve the Trade-wind, lest we should be born off too much to the Westward, and so lose the Islands. We anchored at the South of *Sall*, and passing by the South of St. *Nicholas* anchored again at *Mayo*, as hath been said; where we made the shorter stay, because we could get no Flesh among the Inhabitants, by reason of the regret they had at their Governour, and his Mens being carried away by Capt. *Bond*. So leaving the Isles of *Cape Verd* we stood away to the Southward with the Wind at E.N.E. intending to have touched no more till we came to the Streights of *Magellan*. But when we came into the Lat. of 10 deg. North, we met the Winds at S. by W. and S.S.W. therefore we altered our Resolutions, and steered away for the Coast of *Guinea*, and in few Days came to the Mouth of the River of *Sherboro*, which is an *English* Factory, lying South of *Sierra Liona*. We had one of our Men who was well acquainted there; and by his Direction we went in among the Shoals, and came to an Anchor.

¶ *Sherboro* was a good way from us, so I can give no account of the Place, or our Factory there; save that I have been informed, that there is a considerable Trade driven there for a sort of red Wood for dying, which grows in that Country very plentifully, 'tis called by our People *Cam-wood*. A little within the shoar where we anchored was a Town of Negroes, Natives of this Coast. It was skreened from our sight by a large Grove of Trees that grew between them and the shoar; but we went thither to them several Times, during the 3 or 4 Days of our stay here, to refresh our selves; and they as often came aboard us, bringing with them Plantains, Sugar-Canes, Palm-wines, Rice, Fowls, and Honey, which they sold us. They were no way shy of us, being well acquainted with the *English*, by reason of our *Guiena* Factories and Trade. This Town seem'd pretty large;

the Houses are but low and ordinary: but one great House in the midst of it, where their chief Men meet and receive Strangers: and here they treated us with Palm-wine. As to their Persons, they are like other Negroes. While we lay here we scrubb'd the bottom of our Ship, and then fill'd all our Water-casks; and buying up 2 Puncheons of Rice for our Voyage; we departed from hence about the middle of *November* 1683, prosecuting our intended Course towards the *Streights* of *Magellan*.

¶ We had but little Wind after we got out, and very hot Weather, with some fierce Tornadoes, commonly rising out of the N.E. which brought Thunder, Lightening, and Rain. These did not last long; sometimes not a quarter of an Hour, and then the Wind would shuffle about to the Southward again, and fall flat calm; for these Tornadoes commonly come against the Wind that is then blowing, as our Thunder-Clouds are often observed to do in *England*; but the Tornadoes I shall describe more largely in my Chapter of Winds, in the Appendix to this Book. At this Time many of our Men were taken with Fevers: yet we lost but one. While we lay in the Calms we caught several great Sharks; sometimes two or three in a Day, and eat them all, boiling and squeezing them dry, and then stewing them with Vinegar, Pepper, &c. for we had but little Flesh aboard. We took the Benefit of every Tornado, which came sometimes three or four in a Day, and carried what Sail we could to get to the Southward, for we had but little Wind when they were over; and those small Winds between the Tornadoes were much against us, at S. by E. and S.S.E. till we past the Equinoctial Line, which we crost about a degree to the Eastward of the Meridian of the Isle of St. *Jago*, one of the *Cape-Verd* Islands.

¶ At first we could scarcely lye S.W. but being got a degree to the Southward of the Line, the Wind veer'd most Easterly, and then we stemmed S.W. by S. and as we got farther to the Southward, so the Wind came about to the Eastward and freshened upon us. In the Lat. of 3 S. we had the Wind at S.E. In the Lat. of 5 we had it at E.S. where it stood a considerable Time, and blew a fresh Top-gallant gale. We then made the best use of it, steering on briskly with all the sail we could make; and this Wind, by the 18th of *January* carried us into the Lat. of 36 South. In all this Time we met with nothing worthy remark; not so much as a Fish, except flying Fish, which have been so often described, that I think it needless to do it.

¶ Here we found the Sea much changed from its natural greenness to a white, or palish Colour, which caused us to sound, supposing we might strike Ground: For whenever we find the Colour of the Sea to change, we know we are not far from Land, or shoals which stretch out into the Sea, running from some Land. But here we found no Ground with one hundred Fathom Line. I was this Day at noon by reckoning, 48 d. 50 m. West from the *Lizard*, the Variation by our Morning amplitude 15 d. 10 m. East, the Variation increasing. The 20th Day one of our Chirurgeons died much lamented, because we had but one more for such a dangerous Voyage.

¶ *January* 28. we made the *Sibbel de Wards*, which are 3 Islands lying in the lat. of 51 d. 25 m. South, and Longitude West from the *Lizard* in *England*, by my Account, 57 d. 28 m. the Variation here we found to be 23 d. 10 m. I had for a Month before we came hither, endeavoured to perswade Captain *Cook*, and his Company, to anchor at these Islands, where I told them we might probably get Water, as I then thought, and in case we should miss of it here, yet by being good Husbands of what we had, we might reach *John Fernando*'s in the *South-Seas*, before our Water was spent. This I urged to hinder their Designs of going through the Streights of *Magellan*, which I knew would prove very dangerous to us; the rather, because our Men being Privateers, and so more wilful, and less under Command, would not be so ready to give a watchful Attendance in a Passage so little known. For altho' these Men were more under Command than I had ever seen any Privateers, yet I could not expect to find them at a Minute's call in coming to an Anchor, or weighing Anchor: Beside, if ever we should have occasion to moor, or cast out two Anchors, we had not a Boat to carry out or weigh an Anchor. These Islands of *Sibbel de Wards* were so named by the *Dutch*. They are all three rocky barren Islands without any Tree, only some Dildoe-Bushes growing on them: And I do believe there is no Water on any one of them, for there was no Appearance of any Water. The two Northermost we could not come near; but the Southermost we came close by, but could not strike Ground till within two Cables length of the shore, and there found it to be foul rocky Ground.

¶ From the Time that we were in 10 d. South, till we came to these Islands, we had the Wind between E.N.E. and the N.N.E. fair Weather, and a brisk gale. The Day that we made these Islands, we saw great shoals of small Lobsters, which coloured the Sea in red spots, for a Mile in compass, and we drew some of them out of the Sea in our Water-buckets. They were no bigger than the top of a Man's little Finger, yet all their Claws, both great and small like a Lobster. I never saw any of this sort of Fish naturally red but here; for ours on the *English* Coast, which are black naturally, are not red till they are boiled: Neither did

I ever any where else meet with any Fish of the Lobster-shape so small
as these; unless, it may be, Shrimps or Prawns: Capt. *Swan* and Capt.
Eaton met also with shoals of this Fish in much the same Latitude and
Longitude.

¶ Leaving therefore the *Sibbel de Ward* Islands, as having neither good
Anchorage nor Water, we sailed on, directing our Course for the Streights
of *Magellan*. But the Winds hanging in the Wester-board, and blowing
hard, oft put us by our Topsails, so that we could not fetch it. The 6th
Day of *February* we fell in with the Streights *Le Mair*, which is very high
Land on both sides, and the Streights very narrow. We had the Wind at
N.N.W. a fresh gale; and seeing the Opening of the Streights, we ran in
with it, till within four Mile of the Mouth, and then it fell Calm, and we
found a strong Tide setting out of the Streights to the Northward, and
like to founder our Ship; but whether flood or ebb I know not; only it
made such a short cockling Sea, as if it had been in a Race, or place where
two Tides meet; for it ran every way, sometimes breaking in over our
Waste, sometimes over our Poop, sometimes over our Bow, and the Ship
tossed like an Egg shell, so that I never felt such uncertain Jerks in a Ship.
At 8 a Clock in the Evening we had a small Breeze at W.N.W. and steered
away to the Eastward, intending to go round the *States-Island*, the East-
end of which we reached the next Day by Noon, having a fresh Breeze
all Night.

¶ The 7th Day at Noon being off the East-end of *States-Island*, I had a
good Observation of the Sun, and found my self in Lat. 54 d. 52 m. South.

¶ At the East-end of *States-Island* are three small Islands, or rather Rocks,
pretty high, and white with the Dung of Fowls. Wherefore having
observed the Sun, we haled up South, designing to pass round to the
Southward of Cape *Horne*, which is the Southermost Land of *Terra del
Fuego*. The Winds hung in the Western quarter betwixt the N.W. and
the West, so that we could not get much to the Westward, and we never
saw *Terra del Fuego* after that Evening that we made the Streights *Le Mair*.
I have heard that there have been Smoaks and Fires on *Terra del Fuego*,
not on the tops of Hills, but in Plains and Valleys, seen by those who have
sailed thro' the Streights of *Magellan*; supposed to be made by the Natives.

¶ We did not see the Sun at rising or setting, in order to make an
amplitude after we left the *Sibbel de Wards*, till we got into the South-Sea:
Therefore I know not whether the Variation increased any more or no.
Indeed I had an Observation of the Sun at Noon, in lat. 59 d. 30 m. and
we were then standing to the Southward with the Wind at W. by N. and
that Night the Wind came about more to the Southward of the West, and

we tackt. I was then in lat. 60 by reckoning, which was the farthest South lat. that ever I was in.

¶ The 14th Day of *February* being in lat. 57, and to the West of Cape *Horne*, we had a violent Storm, which held us to the 3d Day of *March*, blowing commonly S.W. and S.W. by W. and W.S.W. thick Weather all the Time, with small drizling Rain, but not hard. We made a shift however to save 23 Barrels of Rain-water, besides what we drest our Victuals withal.

¶ *March* the 3d the Wind shifted at once, and came about at South, blowing a fierce gale of Wind; soon after it came about to the Eastward, and we stood into the South-Seas.

¶ The 9th Day having an Observation of the Sun, not having seen it of late, we found our selves in lat. 47 d. 10 m. and the Variation to be but 15 d. 30 m. East.

¶ The Wind stood at S.E. we had fair Weather, and a moderate Gale, and the 17th Day we were in lat. 36 by Observation, and then found the Variation to be but 8 d. East.

¶ The 19th Day when we looked out in the Morning we saw a Ship to the Southward of us, coming with all the Sail she could make after us: We lay muzled to let her come up with us, for we supposed her to be a *Spanish* Ship come from *Baldivia* bound to *Lima*: We being now to the Northward of *Baldivia* and this being the time of the Year when Ships that Trade thence to *Baldivia* return home. They had the same Opinion of us, and therefore made sure to take us, but coming nearer we both found our mistakes. This proved to be one Capt. *Eaton* in a Ship sent purposely from *London* to the *South-Seas*. We haled each other, and the Captain came on Board, and told us of his Actions on the Coast of *Brazil*, and in the River of *Plate*.

¶ He met Captain *Swan* (one that came from *England* to trade here) at the East Entrance into the Streights of *Magellan*, and they accompanied each other thro' the Streights, and were separated after they were thro' by the Storm before-mentioned. Both we and Capt. *Eaton* being bound for *John Fernando*'s Isle, we kept Company, and we spared him Bread and Beef, and he spared us Water, which he took in as he passed thro' the Streights.

¶ *March* the 22d 1684, we came in sight of the Island, and the next Day got in and anchored in a Bay at the South end of the Island, and 25 Fathom Water, not two Cables length from the Shore. We presently got out our Canoa, and went ashore to see for a *Moskito Indian*, whom we left here when we were chased hence by three *Spanish* Ships in the Year 1681, a little before we went to *Arica*; Capt. *Watlin* being then our Commander, after Capt. *Sharp* was turned out.

¶ This *Indian* lived here alone above three Years, and altho' he was several Times sought after by the *Spaniards*, who knew he was left on the Island, yet they could never find him. He was in the Woods, hunting for Goats, when Captain *Watlin* drew off his Men, and the Ship was under sail before he came back to shore. He had with him his Gun and a Knife, with a small Horn of Powder, and a few Shot; which being spent, he contrived a way by notching his Knife, to saw the Barrel of his Gun into small Pieces, wherewith he made Harpoons, Lances, Hooks and a long Knife, heating the pieces first in the Fire, which he struck with his Gun-flint, and a piece of the Barrel of his Gun, which he hardned; having learnt to do that among the *English*. The hot pieces of Iron he would Hammer out and bend as he pleased with Stones, and saw them with his jagged Knife; or grind them to an edge by long labour, and harden them to a good Temper as there was occasion. All this may seem strange to those that are not acquainted with the Sagacity of the *Indians*; but it is no more than these *Moskito* Men are accustomed to in their own Country, where they make their own Fishing and Striking Instruments, without either Forge or Anvil; tho' they spend a great deal of Time about them.

¶ Other wild *Indians* who have not the use of Iron, which the *Moskito* Men have from the *English*, make Hatches of a very hard Stone, with which they will cut down Trees, (the Cotton-Tree especially, which is a soft tender Wood) to build their Houses or make Canoas; and tho' in working their Canoas hollow, they cannot dig them so neat and thin, yet they will make them fit for their Service. This their Digging or Hatchet-work they help out by Fire; whether for the felling of Trees, or for the making the inside of their Canoa hollow. These Contrivances are used particularly by the Savage *Indians* of *Blewfield*'s River, described in the 3d Chapter, whose Canoas and Stone-Hatches I have seen. These Stone-hatches are about 10 Inches long, 4 broad, and three Inches thick in the middle. They are grownd away flat and sharp at both ends: Right in the midst, and clear round it they make a notch, so wide and deep that a Man might place his Finger along it, and taking a stick or withe about 4 foot long, they bind it round the Hatchet-head, in that notch, and so twisting it hard, use it as an handle or helve; the Head being held by it very fast. Nor are other wild *Indians* less ingenious. Those of *Patagonia*, particularly, head their Arrows with Flint, cut or ground; which I have seen and admired. But to return to our *Moskito* Man on the Isle of *J.*

Fernando. With such Instruments as he made in that manner, he got such Provision as the Island afforded; either Goats or Fish. He told us that at first he was forced to eat Seal, which is very ordinary Meat, before he had made Hooks: but afterwards he never killed any Seals but to make Lines, cutting their Skins into Thongs. He had a little House or Hut half a Mile from the Sea, which was lin'd with Goats Skin; his Couch or Barbecu of Sticks lying along about two foot distant from the Ground, was spread with the same, and was all his Bedding. He had no Cloaths left, having worn out those he brought from *Watlin*'s Ship, but only a Skin about his Waste. He saw our Ship the Day before we came to an Anchor, and did believe we were *English*, and therefore kill'd three Goats in the Morning, before we came to an Anchor, and drest them with Cabbage, to treat us when we came ashore. He came then to the Sea-side to congratulate our safe Arrival. And when we landed, a *Moskito Indian*, named *Robin*, first leap'd ashore, and running to his Brother *Moskito* Man, threw himself flat on his face at his feet, who helping him up, and embracing him, fell flat with his face on the Ground at *Robin*'s feet, and was by him taken up also. We stood with pleasure to behold the surprize, and tenderness, and solemnity of this Interview, which was exceedingly affectionate on both Sides; and when their Ceremonies of Civility were over, we also that stood gazing at them drew near, each of us embracing him we had found here, who was overjoyed to see so many of his old Friends come hither, as he thought purposely to fetch him. He was named *Will*, as the other was *Robin*. These were names given them by the *English*, for they had no Names among themselves; and they take it as a great favour to be named by any of us; and will complain for want of it, if we do not appoint them some name when they are with us: saying of themselves they are poor Men, and have no Name.

¶ This Island is in lat. 34 d. 45 m. and about 120 Leagues from the Main. It is about 12 Leagues round, full of high Hills, and small pleasant Valleys; which if manured, would probably produce any Thing proper for the Climate. The sides of the Mountains are part Savannahs, part Woodland. Savannahs are clear pieces of Land without Woods; not because more barren than the Wood-land, for they are frequently spots of as good Land as any, and often are intermixt with Wood-land. In the Bay of *Campeachy* are very large Savannahs, which I have seen full of Cattle: but about the River of *Plate* are the largest that ever I heard of, 50, 60, or 100 Miles in length; and *Jamaica*, *Cuba* and *Hispaniola*, have many Savannahs intermixt with Woods. Places cleared of Wood by Art and Labour do not go by this Name, but those only which are found so in the uninhabited parts of *America*, such as this Isle of *John Fernando*'s; or which were originally clear in other parts.

¶ The Grass in these Savannahs at *John Fernando*'s is not a long flaggy Grass, such as is usually in the Savannahs in the *West-Indies*, but a sort of kindly Grass, thick and flourishing the biggest part of the Year. The Woods afford divers sorts of Trees; some large and good Timber for Building, but none fit for Masts. The Cabbage Trees of this Isle are but small and low; yet afford a good Head, and the Cabbage very sweet. This Tree I shall describe in the Appendix, in the Bay of *Campeachy*.

¶ The Savannahs are stocked with Goats in great Herds: but those that live on the East-end of the Island are not so fat as those on the West-end; for though there is much more Grass, and plenty of Water in every Valley, nevertheless they thrive not so well here as on the West-end, where there is less Food; and yet there are found greater Flocks, and those too fatter and sweeter.

¶ The West-end of the Island is all high Champion Ground without any Valley, and but one place to land; there is neither Wood nor any fresh Water, and the Grass short and dry.

¶ Goats were first put on the Island by *John Fernando*, who first discovered it on his Voyage from *Lima* to *Baldivia*; (and discovered also another Island about the same bigness, 20 Leagues to the Westward of this.) From those Goats these were propagated, and the Island hath taken its Name from this its first Discoverer, who when he returned to *Lima*, desired a Patent for it, designing to settle here; and it was in his second Voyage hither that he set ashore three or four Goats, which have since by their increase, so well stock'd the whole Island. But he could never get a Patent for it, therefore it lies still destitute of Inhabitants, tho' doubtless capable of maintaining 4 or 500 Families, by what may be produced off the Land only. I speak much within compass; for the Savannahs would at present feed 1000 Head of Cattle, besides Goats, and the Land being cultivated would probably bear Corn, or Wheat, and good Pease, Yams, or Potatoes; for the Land in their Valleys and sides of the Mountains, is of a good black fruitful Mould. The Sea about it is likewise very productive of its Inhabitants. *Seals* swarm as thick about this Island, as if they had no other place in the World to live in; for there is not a Bay nor Rock that one can get ashore on, but is full of them. *Sea-Lions* are here in great Companies, and Fish, particularly Snappers and Rock-fish, are so plentiful, that two Men in an Hour's Time will take with Hook and Line as many as will serve 100 Men.

¶ The *Seals* are a sort of Creatures pretty well known, yet it may not be amiss to describe them. They are as big as Calves, the Head of them like a Dog, therefore called by the *Dutch* the *Sea-hounds*. Under each Shoulder grows a long thick Fin: These serve them to swim with when in the Sea, and are instead of Legs to them when on the Land for raising their Bodies up on end, by the Help of these Fins or Stumps, and so having their Tail-parts drawn close under them, they rebound as it were, and throw their Bodies forward, drawing their hinder Parts after them; and then again rising up, and springing forward with their fore Parts alternately, they lie tumbling thus up and down, all the while they are moving on Land. From their Shoulders to their Tails they grow tapering like Fish, and have two small Fins on each side the Rump; which is commonly covered with their Fins. These Fins serve instead of a Tail in the Sea; and on Land they sit on them, when they give suck to their young. Their Hair is of divers colours, as black, grey, dun, spotted, looking very sleek and pleasant when they come first out of the Sea: For these at *John Fernando*'s have fine thick short Furr; the like I have not taken notice of any where but in these Seas. Here are always Thousands, I might say possibly Millions of them, either sitting on the Bays, or going and coming in the Sea round the Island; which is covered with them (as they lie at the Top of the Water playing and sunning themselves) for a Mile or two from the Shore. When they come out of the Sea they bleat like Sheep for their Young; and tho' they pass through Hundreds of others young ones, before they come to their own, yet they will not suffer any of them to suck. The young ones are like Puppies, and lie much ashore; but when beaten by any of us, they, as well as the old ones, will make towards the Sea, and swim very swift and nimble; tho' on Shore they lie very sluggishly, and will not go out of our ways unless we beat them, but snap at us. A blow on the Nose soon kills them. Large Ships might here load themseves with Seals-skins, and Trane-oyl; for they are extraordinary fat. Seals are found as well in cold as hot Climates; and in the cold Places they love to get on Lumps of Ice, where they will lie and sun themselves, as here on the Land: They are frequent in the Northern Parts of *Europe* and *America*, and in the Southern Parts of *Africa*, as about the *Cape of Good Hope*, and at the *Streights of Magellan*: And tho' I never saw any in the *West-Indies*, but in the Bay of *Campeachy*, at certain Islands called the *Alceranes*, and at others called the *Desarts*; yet they are over all the *American* Coast of the *South-Seas*, from *Terra del Fuego*, up to the Equinoctial Line; but to the North of the Equinox again, in these Seas, I never saw any, till as far as 21 North Lat. Nor did I ever see any in the *East-Indies*. In general they seem to resort where there is plenty of Fish, for that is their Food;

and Fish, such as they feed on, as Cods, Groopers, &c. are most plentiful on rocky Coasts: and such is mostly this Western Coast of the South *America*; as I shall further relate.

❡ The *Sea-Lion* is a large Creature about 12 or 14 Foot long. The biggest Part of his Body is as big as a Bull: It is shaped like a *Seal*, but six times as big. The Head is like a Lion's Head; it hath a broad Face with many long Hairs growing about its Lips like a Cat. It has a great goggle Eye, the Teeth three Inches long, about the Bigness of a Man's Thumb: In Capt. *Sharp*'s time, some of our Men made Dice with them. They have no Hair on their Bodies like the *Seal*; they are of a dun Colour, and are all extraordinary fat; one of them being cut up and boiled, will yield a Hogshead of Oil, which is very sweet and wholsome to fry Meat withal. The lean Flesh is black, and of a coarse Grain; yet indifferent good Food. They will lie a Week at a time ashore if not disturbed. Where 3 or 4, or more of them come ashore together, they huddle one on another like Swine, and grunt like them, making a hideous Noise. They eat Fish, which I believe is their common Food.

❡ The *Snapper* is a Fish much like a *Roach*, but a great deal bigger. It hath a large Head and Mouth, and great Gills. The Back is of a bright Red, the Belly of a Silver Colour: The Scales are as broad as a Shilling. The *Snapper* is excellent Meat. They are in many Places in the *West-Indies*, and the *South-Seas*: I have not seen them any where beside.

❡ The *Rock-Fish* is called by Seamen a *Grooper*; the *Spaniards* call it a *Baccalao*, which is the Name for Cod, because it is much like it. It is rounder than the *Snapper*, of a dark brown Colour; and hath small Scales no bigger than a Silver-penny. This Fish is good sweet Meat, and is found in great plenty on all the Coast of *Peru* and *Chili*.

❡ There are only two Bays in the whole Island where Ships may anchor; these are both at the East-end, and in both of them is a Rivulet of good fresh Water. Either of these Bays may be fortified with little charge, to that degree that 50 Men in each may be able to keep off 1000; and there is no coming into these Bays from the West-end, but with great difficulty, over the Mountains, where if 3 Men are placed, they may keep down as many as come against them on any side. This was partly experienced by 5 *Englishmen* that Capt. *Davis* left here, who defended themselves against a great Body of *Spaniards* who landed in the Bays, and came here to destroy them; and tho' the second time one of their Consorts deserted and fled to the *Spaniards*, yet the other four kept their ground, and were afterwards taken in from hence by Capt. *Strong* of *London*.

❡ We remained at *John Fernando*'s sixteen Days; our sick Men were ashore all the time, and one of Captain *Eaton's* Doctors (for he had four in his Ship) tending and feeding them with Goat and several Herbs, whereof here is plenty growing in the Brooks; and their Diseases were chiefly Scorbutick.

CHAPTER V

The Author departs from John *Fernando's. Of the* Pacifick Sea. *Of the* Andes, *or high Mountains in* Peru *and* Chili. *A Prize taken. Isle of* Lobos: *Penguins and other Birds there. Three Prizes more. The Islands* Gallapago's: *The* Dildoe-*Tree,* Burton-*Wood,* Mammet-*Trees,* Guanoes, Land-Tortoise, *their several kind; Green Snakes, Turtle-Doves, Tortoise, or* Turtle-grass. *Sea-Turtle, their several Kinds. The Air and Weather at the* Gallapago's. *Some of the Islands described, their Soil, &c. The Island* Cocos *described, Cape* Blanco, *and the Bay of* Caldera; *the Savannahs there. Capt.* Cook *dies. Of* Nicoya, *and a red Wood for dying, and other Commodities. A narrow Escape of Twelve Men.* Lancewood. Volcan Vejo, *a burning Mountain on the Coast of* Ria Lexa. *A Tornado. The Island and Harbour of* Ria Lexa. *The Gulph of* Amapalla *and Point* Gasivina. *Isles of* Mangera *and* Amapalla. *The* Indian *Inhabitants.* Hog-Plumb-*Tree. Other Islands in the Gulph of* Amapalla. *Capt.* Eaton *and Capt.* Davis *careen their Ships here, and afterwards part.*

THE 8th of *April* 1684, we sailed from the Isle of *J. Fernando,* with the Wind at S.E. We were now two Ships in Company: Capt. *Cook's,* whose Ship I was in, and who here took the Sickness of which he died a while after, and Captain *Eaton's.* Our Passage lay now along the *Pacifick-Sea,* properly so called. For tho' it be usual with our Map-makers to give that Name to this whole Ocean, calling it *Mare Australe, Mal del Zur,* or *Mare Pacificum*; yet, in my Opinion, the Name of the *Pacifick-Sea* ought not to be extended from South to North farther than from 30 to about 4 Deg. South Latitude, and from the *American* Shore Westward indefinitely, with respect to my Observation; who have been in these parts 250 Leagues or more from Land, and still had the Sea very quiet from Winds. For in all this Tract of Water, of which I have spoken, there are no dark rainy Clouds, tho' often a thick Horizon, so as to hinder an Observation of the Sun with the Quadrant; and in the Morning hazy Weather frequently, and thick Mists, but scarce able to wet one. Nor are there in this Sea any Winds but the Trade-wind, no Tempests, no Tornadoes or Hurricanes (tho' North of the Equator, they are met with as well in this Ocean as in the Atlantick;) yet the Sea itself at the new and full of the Moon, runs with high, large, long Surges, but such as never break out at Sea, and so are safe enough; unless that where they fall in and break upon the Shore, they make it bad landing.

¶ In this Sea we made the best of our way toward the Line, till in the Lat. of 24 S. where we fell in with the main Land of the *South America*. All this course of the Land, both of *Chili* and *Peru* is vastly high; therefore we kept 12 or 14 Leagues off from shore, being unwilling to be seen by the *Spaniards* dwelling there. The Land (especially beyond this, from 24 deg. S. Lat. 17, and from 14 to 10) is of a most prodigious Heighth. It lies generally in Ridges parallel to the Shore, and 3 or 4 Ridges one with another, each surpassing other in heighth; and those that are farthest within Land, are much higher than others. They always appear blue when seen at Sea: sometimes they are obscured with Clouds, but not so often as the high Lands in other parts of the World, for here are seldom or never any Rains on these Hills, any more than in the Sea near it; neither are they subject to Fogs. These are the highest Mountains that ever I saw, far surpassing the *Pike* of *Tenariffe*; or *Santa Martha*, and I believe any Mountains in the World.

¶ I have seen very high Land in the Lat. of 30 South, but not so high as in the Latitudes before described. In Sir *John Narborough*'s Voyage also to *Baldivia* (a City on this Coast) mention is made of very high Land seen near *Baldivia*: and the *Spaniards*, with whom I have discoursed, have told me, that there is a very high Land all the way between *Coquimbo*, (which lies in about 30 d. South lat.) and *Baldivia*, which is in 40 South; so that by all likelihood these Ridges of Mountains do run in a continued Chain from one end of *Peru* and *Chili* to the other, all along this *South-Sea* Coast, called usually the *Andes*, or *Sierra Nuevada des Andes*. The excessive Height of these Mountains may possibly be the reason that there are no Rivers of note that fall into these Seas. Some small Rivers indeed there are, but very few of them, for in some places there is not one that comes out into the Sea in 150 or 200 Leagues, and where they are thickest they are 30 40 or 50 Leagues asunder, and too little and shallow to be navigable. Besides, some of these do not constantly run, but are dry at certain Seasons of the Year; as the River of *Ylo* runs flush with a quick Current at the latter End of *January*, and so continues till *June*, and then it decreaseth by degrees, growing less, and running slow till the latter End of *September*, when it fails wholly, and runs no more till *January* again: This I have seen at both Seasons in two former Voyages I made hither, and have been informed by the *Spaniards* that other Rivers on this Coast are of the like Nature, being rather Torrents or Land-floods caused by their Rains at certain Seasons far within Land, than perennial Streams.

¶ We kept still along in sight of this Coast, but at a good distance from it, encountring with nothing of note, till in the Lat. of 9 deg. 40 min. South, on the 3d of *May*, we descried a Sail to the Northward of us. She was plying to Windward, we chased her, and Capt. *Eaton* being a-Head soon took her: she came from *Guiaquil* about a Month before, laden with Timber, and was bound to *Lima*. Three Days before we took her, she came from *Santa*, whither she had gone for Water, and where they had news of our being in these Seas by an express from *Baldivia*, for, as we afterwards heard, Capt. *Swan* had been at *Baldivia* to seek a Trade there; and he having met Capt. *Eaton* in the Streights of *Magellan*, the *Spaniards* of *Baldivia* were doubtless informed of us by him, suspecting him also to be one of us, tho' he was not. Upon this News the Viceroy of *Lima* sent Expresses to all the Sea-Ports, that they might provide themselves against our Assaults.

¶ We immediately steered away for the Island *Lobos*, which lieth in Lat. 6. d. 24 m. South Lat. (I took the Elevation of it ashore with an Astrolabe) and it is 5 Leagues from the Main. It is called *Lobos de la Mar*, to distinguish it from another that is not far from it, and extreamly like it, called *Lobos de la Terra*, for it lies nearer the Main. *Lobos*, or *Lovos*, is the *Spanish* Name for a Seal, of which there are great plenty about these and several other Islands in these Seas that go by this Name.

¶ The 9th of *May* we arrived at this Isle of *Lobos de la Mar*, and came to an Anchor with our Prize. This *Lobos* consists indeed of two little Islands, each about a Mile round, of an indifferent height, a small Channel between, fit for Boats only; and several Rocks lying on the North-side of the Islands, a little way from shore. There is a small Cove or sandy Bay sheltered from the Winds, at the West-end of the Eastermost Island, where Ships may careen: The rest of the shore, as well round the two Islands as between them, is a rocky Coast, consisting of small Cliffs. Within Land they are both of them partly rocky, and partly sandy, barren, without any fresh Water, Tree, Shrub, Grass, or Herbs; or any Land Animals (for the Seals and Sea-Lions come ashore here) but Fowls, of which there are great Multitudes; as *Boobies*, but mostly *Penguins*, which I have seen plentifully all over the *South-Seas*, on the Coast of *Newfoundland*, and of the *Cape of good Hope*. They are a Sea-Fowl, about as big as a Duck, and such Feet; but a sharp Bill, feeding on Fish. They do not fly, but flutter, having rather Stumps like a young Goslin's, than Wings: And these are instead of Fins to them in the Water. Their Feathers are downy. Their Flesh is but ordinary Food; but their Eggs are good Meat. There is another sort of small black Fowl, that makes holes in the Sand for their Night

Habitations, whose Flesh is good sweet Meat. I never saw any of them but here, and at *John Fernando*'s.

¶ There is good Riding between the Eastermost Island and the Rocks, in ten, twelve, or fourteen Fathom, for the Wind is commonly at S. or S.S.E. and the Eastermost Island lying East and West, shelters that Road.

¶ Here we scrubb'd our Ships, and being in a readiness to sail, the Prisoners were examined, to know if any of them could conduct us to some Town where we might make some Attempt; for they had before informed us, that we were descried by the *Spaniards*, and by that we knew that they would send no Riches by Sea so long as we were here. Many Towns were considered on, as *Guiaquil*, *Zana*, *Truxillo*, and others: At last *Truxillo* was pitched on, as the most important; therefore the likeliest to make us a Voyage if we could conquer it: Which we did not much question, tho' we knew it to be a very populous City. But the greatest difficulty was in Landing; for *Guanchaquo*, which is the nearest Sea-Port to it, but six Miles off, is an ill place to Land, since sometimes the very Fishermen that live there, are not able to go in three or four Days. However the 17th of *May* in the Afternoon, our Men were mustered of both Ships Companies, and their Arms proved. We were in all 108 Men fit for Service, besides the sick: And the next Day we intended to sail and take the *Wood* Prize with us. But the next Day, one of our Men being ashore betimes on the Island, described three sail bound to the North-ward; two of them without the Island to the Westward, the other between it and the Continent.

¶ We soon got our Anchors up and chased: and Captain *Eaton*, who drew the least draught of Water, put through between the Westermost Island and the Rocks, and went after those two that were without the Islands. We in Captain *Cook*'s Ship went after the other, which stood in for the Main Land, but we soon fetched her up, and having taken her, stood in again with her to the Island; for we saw that Captain *Eaton* wanted no help, having taken both those that he went after. He came in with one of his Prizes; but the other was so far to Leeward, and so deep, that he could not then get her in, but he hoped to get her in the next Day: but being deep laden, as designed to go down before the Wind to *Panama*, she would not bear sail.

¶ The 19th Day she turned all Day, but got nothing nearer the Island. Our *Moskito*-strikers, according to their Custom, went and struck six Turtles; for here are indifferent plenty of them. These Ships that we took the Day before we came from *Guanchaquo*, all three laden with Flour, bound for *Panama*. Two of them were laden as deep as they could swim, the other was not above half laden, but was ordered by the Vice-Roy of *Lima* to sail with the other two, or else she should not sail till we were gone out of the Seas; for he hoped they might escape us by setting out early. In the biggest Ship was a Letter to the President of *Panama* from the Vice-Roy of *Lima*; assuring him, that there were Enemies come into that Sea; for which reason he had dispatched these three Ships with Flour, that they might not want; (for *Panama* is supplied from *Peru*;) and desired him to be frugal of it, for he knew not when he should send more. In this Ship were likewise 7 or 8 Tuns of Marmalade of Quinces, and a stately Mule sent to the President, and a very large Image of the Virgin *Mary* in Wood, carved and painted to adorn a new Church at *Panama*, and sent from *Lima* by the Vice-Roy; for this great Ship came from thence not long before. She brought also from *Lima* 800000 Pieces of Eight, to carry with her to *Panama*: but while she lay at *Guanchaco*, taking in her lading of Flour, the Merchants hearing of Capt. *Swan's* being in *Baldivia*, order'd the Money ashoar again. These Prisoners likewise informed us, that the Gentlemen (Inhabitants of *Truxillo*) were building a Fort at *Guanchaquo* (which is the Sea-Port for *Truxillo*) close by the Sea, purposely to hinder the designs of any that should attempt to land there. Upon this News we altered our former Resolutions, and resolved to go with our three Prizes to the *Gallapagos*; which are a great many large Islands, lying some under the Equator, others on each side of it. I shall here omit the description of *Truxillo*, because in my Appendix, at the latter end of the Book, I intend to give a general Relation of most of the Towns of note on this Coast, from *Baldivia* to *Panama*, and from thence towards *California*.

¶ The 19th Day in the Evening we sailed from the Island *Lobos*, with Captain *Eaton* in our Company. We carried the three Flour Prizes with us, but our first Prize laden with Timber, we left here at an Anchor; the Wind was at S. by E. which is the common Trade-wind here, and we steered away N.W. by N. intending to run into the Latitude of the Isles *Gallapagos*, and steer off West, because we did not know the certain distance, and therefore could not shape a direct course to them. When we came within 40 Minutes of the Equator, we steered West, having the Wind at South, a very moderate gentle Gale. It was the 31st Day of *May* when we first had sight of the Islands *Gallapagos*: Some of them appeared on our Weather-bow, some on our Lee-bow, others right a-Head. We at first sight trimm'd our Sails, and steered as nigh the Wind as we could, striving to get to the Southermost of them, but our Prizes being deep laden, their Sails but small and thin, and a very small Gale, they could not keep up with us; therefore we likewise edged away again, a point from the Wind, to keep near them; and in the Evening, the Ship that I was in, and Capt. *Eaton* anchored on the East-side of one of the Eastermost Islands, a Mile from the shoar, in sixteen Fathom Water, clean, white, hard Sand.

¶ The *Gallapagos* Islands are a great number of uninhabited Islands, lying under, and on both sides of the Equator. The Eastermost of them are about 110 Leagues from the Main. They are laid down in the Longitude of 181, reaching to the Westward as far as 176, therefore their Longitude from *England* Westward is about 68 degrees. But I believe our Hydrographers do not place them far enough to the Westward. The *Spaniards* who first discovered them, and in whose draughts alone they are laid down, report them to be a great number stretching North-West from the Line, as far as 5 degrees N. but we saw not above 14 or 15. They are some of them 7 or 8 Leagues long, and 3 or 4 broad. They are of a good heighth, most of them flat and even on the top; 4 or 5 of the Eastermost are rocky, barren and hilly, producing neither Tree, Herb, nor Grass, but a few Dildoe-trees, except by the Sea-side. The Dildoe-tree is a green prickly shrub, that grows about 10 or 12 foot high, without either Leaf or Fruit. It is as big as a Man's Leg, from the root to the top, and it is full of sharp prickles, growing in thick rows from top to bottom; this shrub is fit for no use, not so much as to burn. Close by the Sea there grows in some Places Bushes of Burton-wood, which is very good firing. This sort of Wood grows in many Places in the *West-Indies*, especially in the Bay of *Campeachy*, and the *Samballoes*. I did never see any in these Seas but here. There is Water on these barren Islands, in ponds and holes among the Rocks. Some other of these Islands are mostly plain and low, and the Land more fertile, producing Trees of divers sorts, unknown to us. Some of the Westermost of these Islands, are nine or ten Leagues long, and six or seven broad; the Mould deep and black. These produce Trees of great and tall Bodies, especially Mammee-trees, which grow here in great Groves. In these large Islands there are some pretty big Rivers; and in many of the other lesser Islands, there are Brooks of good Water. The *Spaniards* when they first discover'd these Islands, found Multitudes of Guanoes, and Land-turtle or Tortoise, and named them the *Gallapagos* Islands. I do believe there is no place in the World that is so plentifully stored with those Animals. The Guanoes here are fat and large as any that I ever saw; they are so tame, that a Man may knock down twenty in an Hour's Time with a Club. The Land-turtle are here so numerous, that 5 or 600 Men might subsist on them alone for several Months, without any other sort of Provision: They are extraordinary large and fat;

and so sweet, that no Pullet eats more pleasantly. One of the largest of these Creatures will weigh 150 or 200 weight, and some of them are 2 foot, or 2 foot 6 inches over the Challapee or Belly. I did never see any but at this place, that will weigh above 30 pound weight. I have heard that at the Isle of St. *Lawrence* or *Madagascar*, and at the *English* Forest, an Island near it, called also *Don Mascarin*, and now possessed by the *French*; there are very large ones, but whether so big, fat, and sweet as these, I know not. There are 3 or 4 sorts of these Creatures in the *West-Indies*. One is called by the *Spaniards, Hecatee*; these live most in fresh Water-ponds, and seldom come on Land. They weigh about 10 or 15 pound; they have small Legs and flat Feet, and small long Necks. Another sort is called *Tenapen*; these are a great deal less than the *Hecatee*; the Shell on their Backs is all carved naturally, finely wrought, and well clouded: the Backs of these are rounder than those before-mentioned; they are otherwise much of the same form: These delight to live in wet swampy places, or on the Land near such places. Both these sorts are very good Meat. They are in great plenty on the *Isles of Pines* near *Cuba*: there the *Spanish* Hunters when they meet them in the Woods bring them home to their Huts, and mark them by notching their Shells, then let them go; this they do to have them at Hand, for they never ramble far from thence. When these Hunters return to *Cuba*, after about a Month or six Weeks stay, they carry with them 3 or 400 or more, of these Creatures to sell; for they are very good Meat, and every Man knows his own by their Marks. These Tortoise in the *Gallapagoes* are more like the *Hecatee*, except that, as I said before, they are much bigger; and they have very long small Necks and little Heads. There are some green Snakes on these Islands, but no other Land Animal that I did ever see. There are great plenty of Turtle-Doves so tame, that a Man may kill 5 or 6 dozen in a Forenoon with a stick. They are somewhat less than a Pigeon, and are very good Meat, and commonly fat.

¶ There are good wide Channels between these Islands fit for Ships to pass, and in some places shole Water, where there grows plenty of Turtle-Grass; therefore these Islands are plentifully stored with Sea-Turtle, of that sort which is called the green Turtle. I have hitherto deferred the description of these Creatures, therefore I shall give it here. There are 4 sorts of Sea-turtle, *viz.* the Trunk-turtle, the Loggerhead, the Hawks-bill, and the Green-turtle. The Trunk-turtle is commonly bigger than the other, their Backs are higher and rounder, and their Flesh rank and not wholsome. The Loggerhead is so call'd, because it hath a great Head, much bigger than the other sorts; their flesh is likewise very rank, and seldom eaten but in case of Necessity: They feed on Moss that grows about Rocks. The Hawks-bill Turtle is the least kind, they are so call'd because their Mouths are long and small, somewhat resembling the Bill of a Hawk: on the Backs of these Hawks-bill Turtle grows that shell which is so much esteem'd for making Cabinets, Combs, and other things. The largest of them may have 3 pound and an half of shell; I have taken some that have had 3 pound 10 Ounces: But they commonly have a pound and half, or two pound; some not so much. These are but ordinary food, but generally sweeter than the Loggerhead: Yet these Hawks-bills, in some places are unwholsome, causing them that eat them to purge and vomit excessively, especially those between the *Samballoes* and *Portobel*. We meet with other Fish in the *West-Indies*, of the same malignant Nature: But I shall describe them in the Appendix. These Hawks-bill Turtles are better or worse, according to their feeding. In some places they feed on Grass, as the Green-Tortoise also doth; in other places they keep among Rocks, and feed on Moss, or Sea-Weeds; but these are not so sweet as those that eat Grass, neither is their Shell so clear; for they are commonly over-grown with Barnacles which spoil the shell; and their flesh is commonly yellow, especially the fat.

¶ Hawks-bill Turtle are in many places of the *West-Indies*: They have Islands and places peculiar to themselves, where they lay their Eggs, and seldom come among any other Turtle. These and all other Turtle lay Eggs in the Sand; their Time of laying is in *May*, *June*, *July*. Some begin sooner, some later. They lay 3 Times in a Season, and at each Time 80 or 90 Eggs. Their Eggs are as big as a Hen's Egg, and very round, covered only with a white tough Skin. There are some Bays on the North-side of *Jamaica*, where these Hawks-bills resort to lay. In the Bay of *Honduras* are Islands which they likewise make their breeding-places, and many places along all the Coast on the Main of the *West-Indies*, from *Trinidado* to *La Vera Cruz*, in the Bay of *Nova Hispania*. When a Sea-turtle turns out of the Sea to lay, she is at least an Hour before she returns again, for she is to go above High-water Mark, and if it be low-water when she comes ashore, she must rest once or twice, being heavy, before she comes to the place where she lays. When she hath found a place for her purpose, she makes a great hole with her Fins in the Sand, wherein she lays her Eggs, then covers them 2 foot deep with the same Sand which she threw out of the hole, and so returns. Sometimes they come up the Night before they intend to lay, and take a view of the place, and so having made a Tour, or Semi-circular March, they return to the Sea again, and they never fail to come ashore the next night to lay near that place. All sorts of Turtle use the same methods in laying. I knew a Man in *Jamaica*, that made 8 pound Sterling of the shell of these Hawks-bill Turtle, which he got in one Season, and in one small Bay, not half a Mile long. The manner of taking them is to watch the Bay, by walking from one part to the other all night, making no noise, nor keeping any sort of light. When the Turtle comes ashore, the Man that watches for them turns them on their Backs, then hales them above high-water mark, and leaves them till the Morning. A large green Turtle, with her weight and struggling, will puzzle 2 Men to turn her. The Hawks-bill Turtle are not only found in the *West-Indies*, but on the Coast of *Guinea*, and in the *East-Indies*. I never saw any in the *South-Seas*.

¶ The green Turtle are so called, because their shell is greener than any other. It is very thin and clear, and better clouded than the Hawks-bill; but 'tis used only for inlays, being extraordinary thin. These Turtles are generally larger than the Hawks-bill; one will weigh 2 or 3 hundred Pound. Their Backs are flatter than the Hawks-bill, their Heads round and small. Green Turtle are the sweetest of all the kinds: but there are degrees of them, both in respect to their flesh and their bigness. I have observed that at *Blanco* in the *West-Indies*, the green Turtle (which is the only kind there) are larger than any other in the North-Seas. There they will commonly weigh 280 or 300 pound: Their Fat is yellow, and the Lean white, and their Flesh extraordinary sweet. At *Boca Toro*, West of *Portobel*, they are not so large, their flesh not so white, nor the fat so yellow. Those in the Bay of *Honduras* and *Campeachy* are somewhat smaller still; their fat is green, and the lean of a darker colour than those at *Boca Toro*. I heard of a monstrous green Turtle once taken at *Port-Royal*, in the Bay of *Campeachy* that was four foot deep from the back to the belly, and the belly six foot broad; Capt. *Roch*'s Son, of about nine or ten Years of Age, went in it as in a Boat, on board his Father's Ship, about a quarter of a Mile from the shore. The leaves of Fat afforded eight Gallons of Oil. The Turtle that live among the Keys, or small Islands on the South-side of *Cuba*, are a mix'd sort, some bigger, some less; and so their flesh is of a mixt Colour, some green, some dark, some yellowish. With these *Port-Royal* in *Jamaica* is constantly supplied, by Sloops that come hither with Nets to take them. They carry them alive to *Jamaica*, where the Turtles have Wires made with Stakes in the Sea, to preserve them alive; and the Market is every Day plentifully stored with Turtle, it being the common Food there, chiefly for the ordinary sort of People.

¶ Green Turtle live on Grass, which grows in the Sea, in 3, 4, 5, or 6 Fathom Water, at most of the Places before-mentioned. This Grass is different from Manatee-grass, for that is a small blade; but this a quarter of an inch broad, and six Inches long. The Turtle of these Islands *Gallapagos*, are a sort of a bastard green Turtle; for their shell is thicker than other green Turtle in the *West* or *East-Indies*, and their flesh is not so sweet. They are larger than any other green Turtle; for it is common for these to be two or three foot deep, and their Callapees, or Bellies five foot wide: But there are other green Turtle in the *South-Seas* that are not so big as the smallest Hawks-bill. These are seen at the Island *Plata*, and other places thereabouts: They feed on Moss, and are very rank, but fat.

¶ Both these sorts are different from any others, for both He's and She's come ashore in the Day Time, and lie in the Sun; but in other places, none but the She's go ashore, and that in the Night only, to lay their Eggs. The best feeding for Turtle in the South Seas is among these *Gallapagos* Islands, for here is plenty of Grass.

¶ There is another sort of green Turtle in the *South-Seas* which are but small, yet pretty sweet: These lie Westward on the Coast of *Mexico*. One thing is very strange and remarkable in these Creatures; that at the breeding Time they leave for two or three Months their common haunts, where they feed most of the Year, and resort to other Places, only to lay their Eggs: And 'tis not thought that they eat any Thing during this Season: So that both He's and She's grow very lean; but the He's to that degree that none will eat them. The most remarkable Places that I did ever hear of for their breeding, is at an Island in the *West-Indies* called *Caimanes*, and the Isle *Ascention* in the *Western Ocean*: and when the breeding Time is past, there are none remaining. Doubtless they swim some hundreds of Leagues to come to those two Places: For it hath been often observed, that at *Caimanes*, at the breeding Time, there are found all those sort of Turtle before described. The *South-Keys* of *Cuba* are above 40 Leagues from thence, which is the nearest Place that these Creatures can come from; and it is most certain, that there could not live so many there as come here in one Season.

¶ Those that go to lay at *Ascention*, must needs travel much farther; for there is no Land nearer it than 300 Leagues: And it is certain, that these Creatures live always near the shore. In the *South-Sea* likewise, the *Gallapagos* is the place where they live the biggest part of the Year; yet they go from thence at their Season over to the Main, to lay their Eggs; which is 100 Leagues, the nearest Place. Altho' Multitudes of these Turtles go from their common Places of feeding and abode, to those laying Places, yet they do not all go: And at the Time when the Turtle resort to these Places to lay their Eggs, they are accompanied with abundance of Fish, especially Sharks; the Places which the Turtle then leave being at that Time destitute of Fish, which follow the Turtle.

¶ When the She's go thus to their Places to lay, the Male accompany them, and never leave them till they return: Both Male and Female are fat the beginning of the Season; but before they return, the Male, as I said, are so lean, that they are not fit to eat, but the Female are good to the very last; yet not so fat as at the beginning of the Season. It is reported of these Creatures, that they are nine Days engendering, and in the Water; the Male on the Female's Back. It is observable, that the Male, while engendering, do not easily forsake their Female: For I have gone and taken hold of the Male when engendring: and a very bad striker may strike them then, for the Male is not shy at all: But the Female seeing a Boat, when they rise to blow, would make her escape, but that the Male grasps her with his two fore Fins, and holds her fast. When they are thus coupled, it is best to strike the Female first, then you are sure of the Male also. These Creatures are thought to live to a great Age; and it is observed by the *Jamaica* Turtlers, that they are many Years before they come to their full growth.

¶ The Air of these Islands is temperate enough considering the Clime. Here is constantly a fresh Sea-breeze all Day, and cooling refreshing Winds in the Night: Therefore the Heat is not so violent here, as in most Places near the Equator. The time of the Year for the Rains is in *November*, *December* and *January*. Then there is oftentimes excessive hard tempestuous Weather, mixt with much Thunder and Lightning. Sometimes before and after these Months, there are moderate refreshing showers; but in *May*, *June*, *July* and *August*, the Weather is always very fair.

¶ We staid at one of these Islands, which lies under the Equator but one Night, because our Prizes could not get in to Anchor. We refresh'd our selves very well both with Land and Sea-Turtles; and the next Day we sailed from thence. The next Island of the *Gallapagos* that we came to, is but two Leagues from this: 'tis rocky and barren like this; it is about five or six Leagues long, and four broad. We anchored in the Afternoon, at the North-side of the Island, a Quarter of a Mile from the Shore, in 16 Fathom Water. It is steep all round this Island, and no anchoring only at this Place. Here it is but ordinary riding; for the Ground is so steep, that if an Anchor starts it never holds again; and the Wind is commonly off from the Land, except in the Night, when the Land-wind comes more from the West, for there it blows right along the Shoar, tho' but faintly. Here is no Water but in Ponds and Holes of the Rocks.

That which we first anchored at hath Water on the North-end, falling down in a Stream from high steep Rocks, upon the sandy Bay, where it may be taken up. As soon as we came to an Anchor, we made a Tent ashore for Capt. *Cook* who was sick. Here we found the Sea-Turtle lying ashore on the Sand; this is not customary in the *West-Indies*. We turned them on their Backs that they might not get away. The next Day more came up, when we found it to be their custom to lie in the Sun: So we never took care to turn them afterwards; but sent ashore the Cook every Morning, who killed as many as served for the Day. This Custom we observed all the time we lay here, feeding sometimes on Land-Turtle, sometimes on Sea-Turtle, there being plenty of either sort. Capt. *Davis* came hither again a second time; and then he went to other Islands on the West-side of these. There he found such plenty of Land-Turtle, that he and his Men eat nothing else for three Months that he staid there. They were so fat that he saved sixty Jars of Oil out of those that he spent: This Oil served instead of Butter, to eat with Doughboys or Dumplins, in his return out of these Seas. He found very convenient Places to careen, and good Channels between the Islands; and very good anchoring in many Places. There he found also plenty of Brooks of good Fresh-water, and Fire-wood enough, there being plenty of Trees fit for many uses. Capt. *Harris*, one that we shall speak of hereafter, came thither likewise, and found some Islands that had plenty of *Mammee-Trees*, and pretty large Rivers. The Sea about these Islands is plentifully stored with Fish, such as are at *John Fernando*'s. They are both large and fat, and as plentiful here as at *John Fernando*'s. Here are particularly abundance of Sharks. The North-part of this second Isle we anchored at, lies 28 min. North of the *Equator*. I took the Height of the Sun with an *Astrolabe*. These Isles of the *Gallapago*'s have plenty of Salt. We stay'd here but 12 Days; in which time we put ashore 5000 Packs of Flour for a Reserve, if we should have occasion of any before we left these Seas. Here one of our *Indian* Prisoners informed us that he was born at *Ria Lexa*, and that he would engage to carry us thither. He being examin'd of the Strength and Riches of it, satisfy'd the Company so well, that they were resolv'd to go thither.

❡ Having thus concluded; the 12th of *June* we sailed from hence, designing to touch at the Island *Cocos*, as well to put ashoar some Flour there, as to see the Island, because it was in our way to *Ria Lexa*. We steer'd North, till in Lat. 4 d. 40 min. intending then to steer W. by N. for we expected to have had the Wind at S. by E. or S.S.E. as we had on the South-side of the *Equator*. Thus I had formerly found the Winds near the Shoar in these Latitudes; but when we first parted from the

Gallapagos, we had the Wind at S. and as we sailed farther North, we had the Winds at S. by W. then at S.S.W. Winds which we did not expect. We thought at first that the Wind would come about again to the South; but when we came to sail off West to the Island *Cocos*, we had the Wind at S.W. by S. and could lie but W. by N. Yet we stood that course till we were in the Lat. 5 d. 40 m. N. and then despairing, as the Winds were, to find the Island *Cocos*, we steer'd over to the Main; for had we seen the Island then, we could not have fetcht it, being so far to the North of it.

¶ The Island *Cocos* is so named by the *Spaniards*, because there are abundance of Coco-Nut Trees growing on it. They are not only in one or two Places, but grow in great Groves, all round the Island, by the Sea. This is an uninhabited Island, it is 7 or 8 Leagues round, and pretty high in the middle, where it is destitute of Trees, but looks very green and pleasant, with an Herb called by the *Spaniards Gramadael*. It is low Land by the Sea-side.

¶ This Island is in 5 d. 15 m. North of the Equator; it is environed with Rocks, which makes it almost inaccessible: only at the N.E. End there is a small Harbour where Ships may safely enter and ride secure. In this Harbour there is a fine Brook of fresh Water running into the Sea. This is the Account that the *Spaniards* give of it, and I had the same also from Capt. *Eaton*, who was there afterward.

¶ Any who like us had not experienced the Nature of the Winds in these Parts, might reasonably expect that we could have sailed with a flown Sheet to *Ria Lexa*; but we found our selves mistaken, for as we came nearer the Shoar, we found the Winds right in our Teeth. But I shall refer my Reader to the Chapter of Winds in the Appendix, for a farther Account of this.

¶ We had very fair Weather, and small Winds in this Voyage from the *Gallapagos*, and at the Beginning of *July* we fell in with Cape *Blanco*, on the Main of *Mexico*. This is so called from two white Rocks lying off it. When we are off at Sea right against the Cape, they appear as part of the Cape; but being near the Shore, either to the Eastward or Westward of the Cape, they appear like two Ships under sail at first view, but coming nearer, they are like two high Towers; they being small, high and steep on all sides, and they are about half a Mile from the Cape. This Cape is in Lat. 9 d. 56 m. It is about the height of *Beachy-head* in *England*, on the Coast of *Sussex*. It is a full Point, with steep Rocks to the Sea. The Top of it is flat and even for about a Mile; then it gradually falls away on each side with a gentle Descent. It appears very pleasant, being cover'd with great lofty Trees. From the Cape on the N.W. side the Land runs

in N.E. for about 4 Leagues, making a small Bay, call'd by the *Spaniards*
Caldera. A League within Cape *Blanco*, on the N.W. side of it, and at the
Entrance of this Bay, there is a small Brook of very good Water running
into the Sea. Here the Land is low, making a saddling between 2 small
Hills. It is very rich Land, producing large tall Trees of many sorts; the
Mould is black and deep, which I have always taken notice of to be a fat
Soil. About a Mile from this Brook, towards the N.E. the Woodland
terminates. Here the Savannah Land begins, and runs some Leagues into
the Country, making many small Hills and Dales. These Savannahs are
not altogether clear of Trees, but are here and there sprinkled with small
Groves, which render them very delightful. The Grass which grows here
is very kindly, thick and long; I have seen none better in the *West-Indies*.
Toward the Bottom of the Bay, the Land by the Sea is low and full of
Mangroves, but farther in the Country the Land is high and mountainous.
The Mountains are part Woodland, part Savannah. The Trees in those
Woods are but small and short; and the Mountain Savannahs are cloathed
but with indifferent Grass. From the bottom of this Bay, it is but 14 or
15 Leagues, to the Lake of *Nicargua* on the North-Sea Coast: The way
between is somewhat mountainous, but most Savannah.

¶ Capt. *Cook*, who was then sick at *John Fernando*'s, continued so till we
came within 2 or 3 Leagues of Cape *Blanco*, and then died of a sudden;
tho' he seem'd that Morning to be as likely to live, as he had been some
Weeks before; but it is usual with sick Men coming from the Sea, where
they have nothing but the Sea-Air, to die off as soon as ever they come
within the view of the Land. About four Hours after we all came to an
Anchor, (namely the Ship that I was in, Captain *Eaton*, and the great
Meal Prize,) a League within the Cape, right against the Brook of fresh-
water, in 14 fathom clean hard Sand. Presently after we came to an
Anchor Capt. *Cook* was carried ashore to be buried, twelve Men carried
their Arms to guard those that were ordered to dig the Grave: for
although we saw no appearance of Inhabitants, yet we did not know but
the Country might be thick inhabited. And before Capt. *Cook* was
interred, three *Spanish Indians* came to the Place where our Men were
digging the Grave, and demanded what they were, and from whence they
came? To whom our Men answered, they came from *Lima*, and were
bound to *Ria Lexa*, but that the Captain of one of the Ships dying at Sea,
obliged them to come into this Place to give him Christian Burial. The
three *Spanish Indians* who were very shy at first, began to be very bold,
and drawing near, asked many silly Questions; and our Men did not stick
to sooth them up with as many Falsehoods, purposely to draw them into

their clutches. Our Men often laught at their temerity; and asked them if they never saw any *Spaniards* before? They told them, that they themselves were *Spaniards*, and that they lived among *Spaniards*, and that altho' they were born there, yet they had never seen 3 Ships there before: Our Men told them, that neither now might they have seen so many, if it had not been on an urgent occasion. At length they drill'd them by Discourse so near, that our Men laid hold on all three at once; but before Captain *Cook* was buried, one of them made his escape, the other two were brought off aboard our Ship. Captain *Eaton* immediately came aboard and examined them; they connfessed that they came purposely to view our Ship, and if possible, to inform themselves what we were; for the President of *Panama* not long before sent a Letter of advice to *Nicoya*, informing the Magistrates thereof, that some Enemies were come into these Seas, and that therefore it behoved them to be careful of themselves. *Nicoya* is a small Mulatto Town, about 12 or 14 Leagues East from hence, standing on the Banks of a River of that name. It is a Place very fit for building Ships, therefore most of the Inhabitants are Carpenters; who are commonly employed in building new, or repairing old Ships. It was here that Capt. *Sharp* (just after I left him, in the Year 1681.) got Carpenters to fix his Ship, before he returned to *England*: and for that reason it behoved the *Spaniards* to be careful, (according to the Governour of *Panama*'s Advice,) lest any Men at other times wanting such Necessaries as that Place afforded, might again be supplied there. These *Spanish Indians* told us likewise, that they were sent to the Place where they were taken in order to view our Ships, as fearing these were those mentioned by the President of *Panama*: It being demanded of them to give an account of the Estate and Riches of the Country; they said that the Inhabitants were most Husbandmen, who were imployed either in Planting and Manuring of Corn, or chiefly about Cattle; they having large Savannahs, which were well stored with Bulls, Cows and Horses; that by the Sea-side, in some Places, there grew some Red-wood, useful in Dying; of this they said there was little Profit made, because they were forced to send it to the Lake of *Nicargua*, which runs into the *North-Seas*: That they sent thither also great quantities of Bull and Cow-Hides, and brought from thence in Exchange *Europe* Commodities; as Hats, Linnen and Woollen, wherewith they cloathed themselves; that the Flesh of the Cattle turned to no other Profit than Sustenance for their Families; As for Butter and Cheese they make but little in those Parts. After they had given this Relation, they told us, that if we wanted Provision there was a Beef-Estantion, or Farm of Bulls and Cows about three Mile off, where we might kill what we pleased. This was welcome News, for we had no sort of Flesh since we left the *Gallapagos*; therefore Twenty-four of us immediately entered into two Boats, taking one of these *Spanish Indians* with us for a Pilot, and went ashore about a League from the Ship. There we haled up our Boats dry, and marched all away, following our Guide, who soon brought us to some Houses and a large Penn for Cattle. This Penn stood in a large Savannah, about two Mile from our Boats: There were a great many fat Bulls and Cows feeding in the Savannahs; some of us would have killed three or four to carry on board, but others opposed it, and said, it was better to stay all Night, and in the Morning drive the Cattle into the Pen, and then kill 20 or 30, or as many as we pleased. I was minded to return aboard, and endeavoured to perswade them all to go with me, but some would not, therefore I returned with 12, which was half, and left the other 12 behind. At this place I saw three or four Tun of the Red-wood; which I take to be that sort of Wood, called in *Jamaica* Blood-wood, or *Nicargua*-wood. We who returned aboard, met no one to oppose us, and the next Day we expected our Consorts that we left ashore, but none came; therefore at four a Clock in the Afternoon, ten Men went in our Canoa to see what was become of them: When they came to the Bay where we landed to go to the Estantion, they found our Men all on a small Rock, half a Mile from the shore, standing in the Water up to their Wastes. These Men had slept ashore in the House, and turned out betimes in the Morning to pen the Cattle; 2 or 3 went one way, and as many another way, to get the Cattle to the Pen, and others stood at the Pen to drive them in. When they were thus scattered, about 40 or 50 armed *Spaniards* came in among them. Our Men immediately called to each other, and drew together in a Body before the *Spaniards* could attack them; and marched to their Boat, which was hal'd up dry on the Sand. But when they came to the sandy Bay, they found their Boat all in Flames. This was a very unpleasing sight, for they knew not how to get aboard, unless they marched by Land to the Place where Capt. *Cook* was buried, which was near a League. The greatest part of the way was thick Woods, where the *Spaniards* might easily lay an Ambush for them, at which they are very expert. On the other side, the *Spaniards* now thought them secure; and therefore came to them, and asked them if they would be pleased to walk to their Plantations, with many other such flouts; but our Men answered never a Word. It was about half ebb, when one of our Men took notice of a Rock a good distance from the shore, just appearing above Water; he shewed it to his Consorts, and told them it would be a good Castle for them if they could get thither. They all wisht themselves there; for the *Spaniards*, who lay as yet at a good distance from them behind the Bushes, as secure of their Prey, began to whistle now and then a shot among them. Having therefore well considered the place together with the danger they were in, they proposed to send one of the tallest Men to try if the Sea between them and the Rock were fordable. This Counsel they presently put in Execution, and found it according to their desire. So they all marched over to the Rock, where they remained till the Canoa came to them; which was about seven Hours. It was the latter part of the Ebb when they first went over, and then the Rock was dry; but when the Tide of Flood returned again, the Rock was covered, and the Water still flowing; so that if our Canoa had staied but one Hour longer, they might have been in as great danger of their Lives from the Sea, as before from the *Spaniards*; for the Tide riseth here about eight foot. The *Spaniards* remained on the shore, expecting to see them destroyed, but never came from behind the Bushes, where they first planted themselves; they having not above 3 or 4 Hand-guns, the rest of them being armed with Lances. The *Spaniards* in these parts are very expert in heaving or darting the Lance; with which upon Occasion, they will do great Feats, especially in Ambuscades: And by their good Will, they care not for fighting otherwise, but content themselves with standing aloof, threatning and calling Names, at which they are as expert as the other; so that if their Tongues be quiet, we always take it for granted they have laid some Ambush. Before Night our Canoa came aboard, and brought our Men all safe. The next Day two Canoas were sent to the bottom of the Bay to seek for a large Canoa, which we were informed was there. The *Spaniards* have neither Ships nor Barks here, and but a few Canoas, which they seldom use: Neither are there any Fishermen here, as I judge, because Fish is very scarce; for I never saw any here, neither could any of our Men ever take any; and yet where-ever we come to an Anchor, we always send out our Strikers, and put our Hooks and Lines over-board, to try for Fish. The next Day our Men returned out of the Bay, and brought the Canoa with them, which they were sent for, and three or four Days afterwards the two Canoas were sent out again for another, which they likewise brought aboard. These Canoas were fitted with Thoats or Benches, Straps and Oars fit for Service; and one of these Captain *Eaton* had for his share, and we the other, which we fixt for landing Men when occasion required. While we lay here, we filled our Water, and cut a great many Looms, or Handles, or Staves for Oars; for here is plenty of Lance-wood, which is most proper for that use. I never saw any in the *South-Seas*, but in this Place: There is plenty of it in *Jamaica*, especially at a Place called *Blewfields* (not *Blewfields*

River which is on the Main) near the West-end of that Island. The Lance-wood grows strait like our young Ash; it is very hard, tough and heavy, therefore Privateers esteem it very much, not only to make Looms for Oars, but Scowring-Rods for their Guns; for they have seldom less than three or four spare Rods for fear one should break, and they are much better than Rods made of Ash.

¶ The Day before we went from hence, Mr. *Edward Davis*, the Company's Quarter-Master, was made Captain by consent of all the Company; for it was his Place by Succession. The 20th Day of *July* we sailed from this Bay of *Caldera*, with Capt. *Eaton*, and our Prize which we brought from *Gallapagos* in Company, directing our Course for *Ria Lexa*. The Wind was at North, which altho' but an ordinary Wind, yet carried us in three Days abrest of our intended Port.

¶ *Ria Lexa* is the most remarkable Land on all this Coast, for there is a high peeked burning Mountain, called by the *Spaniards Volcan-Vejo*, or the *Old Volcan*. This must be brought to bear N.E. then steer in directly with the Mountain, and that course will bring you to the Harbour. The Sea-winds are here at S.S.W. therefore Ships that come hither must take the Sea-winds, for there is no going in with the Land-wind. The *Volcan* may be easily known, because there is not any other so high a Mountain near it, neither is there any that appears in the like form all along the Coast; besides it smoaks all the Day, and in the Night it sometimes sends forth flames of Fire. This Mountain may be seen twenty Leagues; being within three Leagues of the Harbour, the entrance into it may be seen; there is a small flat low Island which makes the Harbour, it is about a Mile long, and a quarter of a Mile broad, and is from the Main about a Mile and half. There is a Channel at each end of the Island, the West Channel is the widest and safest, yet at the N.W. point of the Island there is a shole which Ships must take heed of going in. Being past that shole, you must keep close to the Island, for there is a whole sandy point strikes over from the Main almost half way. The East Channel is not so wide, besides there runs a stronger Tide; therefore Ships seldom or never go in that way. This Harbor is capable of receiving 200 Sail of Ships; the best riding is near the Main, where there is seven or eight fathom Water, clean hard Sand.

¶ *Ria Lexa* Town is two Leagues from hence, and there are 2 Creeks that run towards it; the Westermost comes near the back-side of the Town, the other runs up to the Town, but neither Ships nor Barks can go so far. These Creeks are very narrow, and the Land on each side drowned and full of red Mangrove-Trees. About a Mile and half below the Town, on the

Banks of the East-Creek, the *Spaniards* had cast up a strong Breast-work; it was likewise reported they had another on the West Creek, both so advantageously placed, that ten Men might with ease keep 200 Men from landing. I shall give a Description of the Town in my return hither, and therefore forbear to do it here. Wherefore to resume the Thread of our Course, we were now in sight of the *Volcan*, being by Estimation 7 or 8 Leagues from the shoar, and the Mountain bearing N.E. we took in our Topsails and hal'd up our Courses, intending to go with our Canoas into the Harbor in the Night. In the Evening we had a very hard Tornado, out of the N.E. with much Thunder, Lightning and Rain. The violence of the Wind did not last long, yet it was 11 a Clock at Night before we got out our Canoas, and then it was quite calm. We rowed in directly for the shoar, and thought to have reach'd it before Day, but it was 9 a Clock in the Morning before we got into the Harbor. When we came within a League of the Island of *Ria Lexa*, that makes the Harbour, we saw a House on it, and coming nearer we saw two or three Men, who stood and looked on us till we came within half a Mile of the Island, then they went into their Canoa, which lay on the inside of the Island, and rowed towards the Main; but we overtook them before they got over, and brought them back again to the Island. There was a Horseman right against us on the Main when we took the Canoa, who immediately rode away towards the Town as fast as he could. The rest of our Canoas rowed heavily, and did not come to the Island till 12 a Clock, therefore we were forced to stay for them. Before they came we examined the Prisoners, who told us, that they were set there to watch, for the Governour of *Ria Lexa* received a Letter about a Month before, wherein he was advised of some Enemies come into the Sea, and therefore admonished him to be careful; that immediately thereupon the Governour had caused a House to be built on this Island, and ordered four Men to be continually there to watch Night and Day; and if they saw any Ship coming thither they were to give notice of it. They said they did not expect to see Boats or Canoas, but lookt out for a Ship. At first they took us in our advanced Canoa to be some Men that had been cast away and lost our Ship; till seeing 3 or 4 Canoas more, they began to suspect what we were. They told us likewise, that the Horseman which we saw did come to them every Morning, and that in less than an Hour's time he could be at the Town. When Capt. *Eaton* and his Canoas came ashoar, we told them what had happened. It was now three Hours since the Horseman rode away, and we could not expect to get to the Town in less than two Hours; in which time the Governour having notice of our coming, might be provided to receive us at his Breast-works; therefore we thought it best to defer this Design till another time.

¶ There is a fine Spring of fresh Water on the Island; there are some Trees also, but the biggest Part is Savannah, whereon is good Grass, tho' there is no sort of Beast to eat it. This Island is in Lat. 12 d. 10 m. North. Here we stayed till 4 a Clock in the Afternoon; then our Ships being come within a League of the Shoar, we all went on board, and steered for the Gulf of *Amapalla*, intending there to careen our Ships.

¶ The 26th of *July* Capt. *Eaton* came aboard our Ship, to consult with Capt. *Davis*, how to get some *Indians* to assist us in careening: it was concluded, that when we came near the Gulf, Capt. *Davis* should take two Canoas well mann'd, and go before, and Capt. *Eaton* should stay aboard. According to this Agreement, Capt. *Davis* went away for the Gulf the next Day.

¶ The Gulf of *Amapalla* is a great Arm of the Sea running 8 or 10 Leagues into the Country. It is bounded on the South-side of its Entrance with Point *Casivina*, and on the N.W. side with St. *Michael*'s Mount. Both these places are very remarkable: Point *Casivina* is in Lat. 12 d. 40 m. North: It is a high round Point, which at Sea appears like an Island; because the Land within it is very low. St. *Michael*'s Mount is a very high peeked Hill, not very steep: the Land at the Foot of it on the S.E. side, is low and even, for at least a Mile. From this low Land the Gulf of *Amapalla* enters on that side. Between this low Land and Point *Casivina*, there are two considerable high Islands; the Southermost is called *Mangera*, the other is called *Amapalla*; and they are two Miles asunder.

¶ *Mangera* is a high round Island, about 2 Leagues in compass, appearing like a tall Grove. It is invironed with Rocks all round, only a small Cove, or sandy Bay on the N.E. side. The Mold and Soil of this Island is black, but not deep; it is mixt with Stones, yet very productive of large tall Timber Trees. In the middle of the Island there is an *Indian* Town, and a fair *Spanish* Church. The *Indians* have Plantations of Maiz round the Town, and some Plantains: They have a few Cocks and Hens, but no other sort of tame Fowl; neither have they any sort of Beast, but Cats and Dogs. There is a Path from the Town to the sandy Bay, but the way is steep and rocky. At this sandy Bay there are always 10 or 12 Canoas lie haled up dry, except when they are in use.

¶ *Amapalla* is a larger Island than *Mangera*; the Soil much the same. There are two Towns on it, about two Miles asunder; one on the North-side, the other on the East-side: That on the East-side is not above a Mile from the Sea; it stands on a Plain on the Top of an Hill, the Path to it is so steep and rocky, that a few Men might keep down a great Number only with Stones. There is a very fair Church standing in the midst of the Town. The other Town is not so big, yet it has a good handsome Church. One thing I have observed in all the *Indian* Towns under the *Spanish* Government, as well in these parts in the Bay of *Campeachy*, and elsewhere, that the Images of the Virgin *Mary* and other Saints, (with which all their Churches were filled) are still painted in an *Indian* Complexion, and partly in that Dress; but in those Towns which are inhabited chiefly by *Spaniards*, the Saints also conform themselves to the *Spanish* Garb and Complexion. The Houses here are but mean; the *Indians* of both Plains have good Field Maiz, remote from the Town: They have but few Plantains, but they have abundance of large Hog-plumb Trees, growing about their Houses. The Tree that bears this Fruit is as big as our largest Plumb-tree: The Leaf is of a dark green Colour, and as broad as the Leaf of a Plumb-tree; but they are shaped like the Haw-thorn Leaf. The Trees are very brittle Wood; the Fruit is oval, and as big as a small Horse-Plumb. It is at first very green, but when it is ripe, one side is yellow, the other red. It hath a great Stone, and but little Substance about it: The Fruit is pleasant enough; but I do not remember that ever I saw one thoroughly ripe, that had not a Maggot or two in it. I do not remember that I did ever see any of this Fruit in the *South-Seas*; but at this Place. In the Bay of *Campeachy* they are very plentiful, and in *Jamaica* they plant them to fence their Ground. These *Indians* have also some Fowls, as those at *Mangera*: No *Spaniards* dwell among them, but only one *Padre* or Priest, who serves for all three Towns; these two at *Amapalla*, and that at *Mangera*. They are under the Governour of the Town of St. *Michael*'s, at the Foot of St. *Michael*'s Mount, to whom they pay their Tribute in Maiz; being extreamly poor, yet very contented. They have nothing to make Money of, but their Plantations of Maiz and their Fowls; the *Padre* or Fryar hath his Tenths of it, and knows to a Peck how much every Man hath, and how many Fowls, of which they dare not kill one, tho' they are sick, without leave from him. There was (as I said) never another white Man on these Islands but the Fryar. He could speak the *Indian* Language, as all Fryars must that live among them. In this vast Country of *America* there are divers Nations of *Indians*, different in their Language, therefore those Fryars that are minded to live among any Nations of *Indians*, must learn the Language of those People they propose to teach. Although these here are but poor, yet the *Indians* in many other places have great Riches, which the *Spaniards* draw from them for Trifles: In such places the Fryars get plentiful Incomes; as particularly in the Bay

of *Campeachy*, where the *Indians* have large Cacao-walks; or in other places
where they plant Cochoneel-Trees, or Silvester-Trees; or where they
gather Vinelloes, and in such places where they gather Gold. In such
places as these, the Fryars do get a great deal of Wealth. There was but
one of all the *Indians* on both these Islands that could speak *Spanish*; he
could write *Spanish* also, being bred up purposely to keep the Registers
and Books of Account: He was Secretary to both Islands. They had a
Casica too, (a small sort of Magistrate the *Indians* have amongst themselves)
but he could neither write nor speak *Spanish*.

¶ There are a great many more Islands in this Bay, but none inhabited
as these. There is one pretty large Island belonging to a Nunnery, as the
Indians told us, this was stocked with Bulls and Cows; there were 3 or 4
Indians lived there to look after the Cattle, for the sake of which we often
frequented this Island, while we lay in the Bay: they are all low Islands,
except *Amapalla* and *Mangera*. There are two Channels to come into this
Gulph, one between Point *Casivina* and *Mangera*, the other between
Mangera and *Amapalla*: The latter is the best. The Riding-place is on the
East-side of *Amapalla*, right against a Spot of low Ground; for all the Island
except this one place is high Land. Running in farther, Ships may anchor
near the Main, on the N.E. side of the Island *Amapalla*. This is the place
most frequented by *Spaniards*: It is called the Port of *Martin Lopez*. This
Gulph or Lake runs in some Leagues beyond all the Islands; but it is
shole Water, and not capable of Ships.

¶ It was into this Gulph that Capt. *Davis* was gone with the two Canoas,
to endeavour for a Prisoner, to gain Intelligence, if possible, before our
Ships came in: He came the first Night to *Mangera*, but for want of a
Pilot, did not know where to look for the Town. In the Morning he found
a great many Canoas haled up on the Bay; and from that Bay found a
Path which led him and his Company to the Town. The *Indians* saw our
Ships in the Evening coming towards the Island, and being before informed of Enemies in the Sea, they kept Scouts out all Night for fear:
who seeing Capt. *Davis* coming, run into the Town, and alarmed all the
People. When Capt. *Davis* came thither, they all run into the Woods.
The Fryar happened to be there at this time; who being unable to ramble
into the Woods, fell into Capt. *Davis*'s, Hands: there were two *Indian* Boys
with him, who were likewise taken. Capt. *Davis* went only to get a Prisoner,
therefore was well satisfied with the Fryar, and immediately came down
to the Sea-side. He went from thence to the Island *Amapalla*, carrying
the Fryar and the two *Indian* Boys with him. These were his Pilots to
conduct him to the Landing-place, where they arrived about Noon. They

made no stay here, but left three or four Men to look after the Canoas, and Capt. *Davis* with the rest marched to the Town, taking the Fryar with them. The Town, as is before noted, is about a Mile from the Landing-place, standing in a Plain on the Top of a Hill, having a very steep Ascent to go to it. All the *Indians* stood on the Top of the Hill waiting Capt. *Davis*'s coming.

¶ The Secretary, mentioned before, had no great Kindness for the *Spaniards*. It was he that persuaded the *Indians* to wait Capt. *Davis* his coming; for they were all running into the Woods; but he told them, that if any of the *Spaniard*'s Enemies came thither, it was not to hurt them, but the *Spaniards* whose Slaves they were; and that their Poverty would protect them. This Man with the *Casica* stood more forward than the rest, at the Bank of the Hill, when Capt. *Davis* with his Company appeared beneath. They called out therefore in *Spanish*, demanding of our Men, What they were, and from whence they came? To whom Capt. *Davis* and his Men replied, They were *Biscayers*, and that they were sent thither by the King of *Spain* to clear those Seas from Enemies; that their Ships were coming into the Gulf to careen, and that they came thither before the Ships, to seek a convenient Place for it, as also to desire the *Indian*'s Assistance. The Secretary, who, as I said before, was the only Man that could speak *Spanish*, told them that they were welcome, for he had a great Respect for any *Old Spain* Men, especially for the *Biscayers*, of whom he had heard a very honourable Report; therefore he desired them to come up to their Town. Capt. *Davis* and his Men immediately ascending the Hill, the Fryar going before; and they were received with a great deal of Affection by the *Indians*. The *Casica* and Secretary embraced Capt. *Davis*, and the other *Indians* received his Men with the like Ceremony. These Salutations being ended, they all marched towards the Church, for that is the place of all publick Meetings, and all Plays and Pastimes are acted there also; therefore in the Churches belonging to *Indian* Towns they have all sorts of Vizards, and strange antick Dresses both for Men and Women, and abundance of Musical Hautboys and Strumstrums. The Strum-strum is made somewhat like a Cittern; most of those that the *Indians* use are made of a large Goad cut in the midst, and a thin Board laid over the Hollow, and which is fastned to the Sides; this serves for the Belly; over which the Strings are placed. The Nights before any Holidays, or the Nights ensuing, are the times when they all meet to make merry. Their Mirth consists in singing, dancing and sporting in those antick Habits, and using as many antick Gestures. If the Moon shine they use but few Torches, if not, the Church is full of light. There meet at these times all sorts of both Sexes. All the *Indians* that I have been acquainted with who are under the *Spaniards*, seem to be more melancholy than other *Indians* that are free; and at these publick Meetings, when they are in the greatest of their Jollity, their Mirth seems to be rather forced than real. Their Songs are very melancholy and doleful; so is their Musick: but whether it be natural to the *Indians* to be thus melancholy, or the Effect of their Slavery, I am not certain: But I have always been prone to believe, that they are then only condoling their Misfortunes, the Loss of their Country and Liberties: which altho' these that are now living do not know, nor remember what it was to be free, yet there seems to be a deep Impression of the Thoughts of the Slavery which the *Spaniards* have brought them under, increas'd probably by some Traditions of their antient Freedom.

¶ Capt. *Davis* intended when they were all in the Church to shut the Doors, and then make a Bargain with them, letting them know what he was, and so draw them afterwards by fair means to our assistance: the Fryar being with him, who had also promis'd to engage them to it: but before they were all in the Church, one of Capt. *Davis* his Men pusht one of the *Indians* to hasten him into the Church. The *Indian* immediately ran away, and all the rest taking the Alarm, sprang out of the Church like Deer; it was hard to say which was first: and Capt. *Davis*, who knew nothing of what hapned, was left in the Church only with the Fryar. When they were all fled, Capt. *Davis* his Men fired and killed the Secretary; and thus our Hopes perished by the Indiscretion of one foolish Fellow.

¶ In the Afternoon the Ships came into the Gulf between Point *Casivina* and *Mangera*, and anchored near the Island *Amapalla*, on the East-side, in 10 Fathom Water, clean hard Sand. In the Evening Capt. *Davis* and his Company came aboard, and brought the Fryar with them; who told Capt. *Davis*, that if the Secretary had not been kill'd, he could have sent him a Letter by one of the *Indians* that was taken at *Mangera*, and persuaded him to come to us; but now the only way was to send one of those *Indians* to seek the *Casica*, and that himself would instruct him what to say, and did not question but the *Casica* would come in on his word. The next Day we sent ashoar one of the *Indians*, who before Night returned with the *Casica* and six other *Indians*, who remained with us all the time that we staid here. These *Indians* did us good service; especially in piloting us to an Island where we kill'd Beef whenever we wanted; and for this their service we satisfied them to their Hearts content. It was at this Island *Amapalla* that a Party of *Englishmen* and *Frenchmen* came afterwards, and stay'd a great while, and at last landed on the Main, and marched over Land to the *Cape River*, which disembogues into the North Seas near *Cape*

Gratia Dios, and is therefore called the *Cape-River*: Near the Head of this River they made Bark-logs (which I shall describe in the next Chapter) and so went into the North-Seas. This was the way that Captain *Sharp* had proposed to go if he had been put to it; for this way was partly known by Privateers by the discovery that was made into the Country about 30 Years since, by a Party of *English* Men that went up that River in Canoas, about as far as the place where these *French* Men made their Bark-logs: there they landed and marched to a Town called *Segovia* in the Country. They were near a Month getting up the River, for there were many Cataracts, where they were often forced to leave the River, and hale their Canoas ashoar over the Land, till they were past the Cataracts, and then launch their Canoas again into the River. I have discoursed several Men that were in that Expedition, and if I mistake not, Captain *Sharp* was one of them. But to return to our Voyage in Hand; when both our Ships were clean, and our Water filled, Captain *Davis* and Captain *Eaton* broke off Consortships. Capt. *Eaton* took aboard of his Ship 400 Packs of Flour, and sailed out of the Gulf the second Day of *September*.

CHAPTER VI

THE third Day of *September*, 1684, we sent the Friar ashoar, and left the *Indians* in Possession of the Prize which we brought in hither, though she was still half laden with Flour, and we sailed out with the Land-Wind, passing between *Amapalla* and *Mangera*. When we were a League out, we saw a Canoa coming with Sail and Oars after us; therefore we shortned Sail and staid for her. She was a Canoa sent by the Governour of St. *Michael*'s Town to our Captain, desiring him not to carry away the Friar. The Messenger being told, that the Friar was set ashore again at *Amapalla*, he returned with joy, and we made Sail again, having the Wind at W.N.W. We steered towards the Coast of *Peru*; we had *Tornadoes* every Day till we made Cape St. *Francisco*, which from *June* to *November* are very common on these Coasts; and we had with the *Tornadoes* very much Thunder, Lightning and Rain. When the *Tornadoes* were over, the Winds, which while they lasted was most from the South-East, came about again to the West, and never failed us till we were in sight of Cape St. *Francisco*, where we found the Wind at South with fair Weather. This Cape is in lat. 01 d. 00 North. It is a high bluff, or full point of Land, cloathed with tall great Trees. Passing by this Point, coming from the North, you will see a small low Point, which you might suppose to be the Cape; but you are then past it, and presently afterwards it appears with three Points. The Land in the Country within this Cape is very high, and the Mountains commonly appear very black. When we came in with this Cape, we overtook Capt. *Eaton*, plying under the shoar: he in his Passage from *Amapalla*, while he was on that Coast, met with such terrible *Tornadoes* of Thunder and Lightning, that as he and all his Men related, they had never met with the like in any Place. They were very much affrighted by them, the Air smelling very much of Sulphur, and they apprehending themselves in great danger of being burnt by the Lightning. He touch'd at the Island *Cocos*, and put ashoar 200 Packs of Flour there, and loaded his Boat with Coco-Nuts, and took in fresh Water. In the Evening we separated again from Capt. *Eaton*; for he stood off to Sea, and we plied up under the shoar, making our best Advantage both of Sea and Land-Winds. The Sea-Winds are here at South, the Land-Winds at S.S.E. but sometimes when we came abrest of the River we should have the Wind at S.E.

¶ The 20th Day of *September* we came to the Island *Plata*, and anchored in 16 Fathom. We had very good Weather from the Time that we fell in with Cape St. *Francisco*; and were now fallen in again with the same Places from whence I begin the account of this Voyage in the first Chapter, having now compassed in the whole Continent of the South-*America*.

¶ The Island *Plata*, as some report, was so named by the *Spaniards*, after Sir *Francis Drake* took the *Cacafoga*, a Ship chiefly laden with Plate, which they say he brought hither, and divided it here with his Men. It is about four Mile long, and a Mile and half broad, and of a good heighth. It is bounded with high steep Cliffs clear round, only at one Place on the East-side. The top of it is flat and even, the Soil sandy and dry: the Trees it produceth are but small-bodied, low, and grow thin; and there are only three or four sorts of Trees, all unknown to us. I observed they were much over-grown with long Moss. There is good Grass, especially in the beginning of the Year. There is no Water on this Island but at one place on the East-side, close by the Sea; there it drills slowly down from the Rocks, where it may be received into Vessels. There was plenty of Goats, but they are now all destroyed. There is no other sort of Land-Animal that I did ever see: here are plenty of *Boobies* and *Men of War* Birds. The anchoring-Place is on the East-side, near the middle of the Island, close by the shoar, within 2 Cables length of the sandy Bay: there is about 18 or 20 Fathom good fast oazy Ground, and smooth Water; for the S.E. point of the Island shelters from the South-Winds which constantly blow here. From the S.E. point there strikes out a small shole a quarter of a Mile into the Sea, where there is commonly a great ripling or working of short Waves during all the Flood. The Tide runs pretty strong, the Flood to the South, and the Ebb to the North. There is good landing on the sandy Bay against the Anchoring-Place, from whence you may go up into the Island, and at no Place besides. There are 2 or 3 high, steep, small Rocks at the S.E. point, not a Cables length from the Island; and another much bigger at the N.E. end: it is deep Water all round, but at the anchoring-Place, and at the shole at the S.E. point. This Island lieth in lat. 01 d. 10 m. South. It is distant from Cape St. *Lorenzo* 4 or 5 Leagues, bearing from it W.S.W. and half a point westerly. At this Island are plenty of those small *Sea-Turtle* spoken of in my last Chapter.

¶ The 21st Day Captain *Eaton* came to an Anchor by us: he was very willing to have consorted with us again; but Captain *Davis*'s Men were so unreasonable, that they would not allow Captain *Eaton*'s Men an equal share with them in what they got: therefore Captain *Eaton* staid here but one Night, and the next Day sailed from hence, steering away to the Southward. We staid no longer than the Day ensuing, and then we sailed towards Point St. *Hellena*, intending there to land some Men purposely to get Prisoners for Intelligence.

¶ Point *Santa Hellena*, bears South from the Island *Plata*. It lies in lat. 2 d. 15 m. South. The Point is pretty high, flat, and even at top, overgrown with many great Thistles, but no sort of Tree; at a distance it appears like an Island, because the Land within it is very low.

¶ This Point strikes out West into the Sea, making a pretty large Bay on the North-side. A mile within the Point, on the sandy Bay, close by the Sea, there is a poor small *Indian* Village, called *Sancta Hellena*; the Land about it is low, sandy and barren, there are no Trees nor Grass growing near it; neither do the *Indians* produce any Fruit, Grain, or

Plant, but Water-Melons only, which are large and very sweet. There is no fresh Water at this Place, nor near it; therefore the Inhabitants are obliged to fetch all their Water from the River *Colanche*, which is in the bottom of the Bay, about 4 Leagues from it. Not far from this Town on the Bay, close by the Sea, about 5 paces from high-water Mark, there is a sort of *bituminous* Matter boils out of a little hole in the Earth; it is like thin *Tar*: the *Spaniards* call it *Algatrane*. By much boiling it becomes hard like Pitch. It is frequently used by the *Spaniards* instead of Pitch; and the *Indians* that inhabit here save it in Jars. It boils up most at high Water; and then the *Indians* are ready to receive it. These *Indians* are Fishermen, and go out to Sea on Bark-logs. Their chief Subsistence is Maiz, most of which they get from Ships that come hither from *Algatrane*. There is good anchoring to Leeward of the Point, right against the Village: but on the West-side of the Point it is deep Water, and no anchoring. The *Spaniards* do report, that there was once a very rich Ship driven ashoar here in Calm, for want of Wind to work her. As soon as ever she struck she heel'd off to Sea, 7 or 8 Fathom Water, where she lies to this Day; none having attempted to fish for her, because she lies deep, and there falls in here a great high Sea. When we were abrest of this Point, we sent away our Canoas in the Night to take the *Indian* Village. They landed in the Morning betimes close by the Town, and took some Prisoners. They took likewise a small Bark which the *Indians* had set on fire, but our Men quenched it, and took the *Indians* that did it; who being asked wherefore he set the Bark on fire, said, that there was an Order from the Vice-Roy lately set out, commanding all Seamen to burn their Vessels, if attacked by us, and betake themselves to their Boats. There was another Bark in a small Cove, a Mile from the Village, thither our Men went, thinking to take her, but the Seamen that were aboard set her in Flames and fled: In the Evening our Men came aboard, and brought the small Bark with them, the Fire of which they had quenched; and then we returned again towards *Plata*; where we arrived the 26th Day of *September*.

¶ In the Evening we sent out some Men in our Bark lately taken, and Canoas, to an *Indian* Village called *Manta*, two or three Leagues to the Westward of Cape St. *Lorenzo*; hoping there to get other Prisoners, for we could not learn from those we took at Point St. *Hellena*, the reason why the Vice-Roy should give such Orders to burn the Ships. They had a fresh Sea-breeze till about 12 a Clock at Night, and then it proved calm; wherefore they rowed away with their Canoas as near to the Town as they thought convenient, and lay still till Day.

¶ *Manta* is a small *Indian* Village on the Main, distant from the Island

Plata 7 or 8 Leagues. It stands so advantageously to be seen, being built on a small Ascent, that it makes a very fair prospect to the Sea; yet but a few poor scattering *Indian* Houses. There is a very fine Church, adorned with a great deal of carved Work. It was formerly a Habitation for *Spaniards*, but they are all removed from hence now. The Land about it is dry and sandy, bearing only a few shrubby Trees. These *Indians* plant no manner of Grain or Root, but are supplied from other places; and commonly keep a stock of Provision to relieve Ships that want; for this is the first Settlement that Ships can touch at, which come from *Panama*, bound to *Lima*, or any other Port in *Peru*. The Land being dry and sandy, is not fit to produce Crops of Maiz; which is the reason they plant none. There is a Spring of good Water between the Village and the Seas.

¶ On the back of the Town, a pretty way up in the Country, there is a very high Mountain, towring up like a Sugar-loaf, called *Monte Christo*. It is a very good Sea-mark, for there is none like it on all the Coast. The Body of this Mountain bears due South from *Manta*. About a Mile and half from the shore, right against the Village, there is a Rock, which is very dangerous, because it never appears above Water; neither doth the Sea break on it, because there is seldom any great Sea; yet it is now so well known, that all Ships bound to this place do easily avoid it. A Mile within this Rock there is good Anchoring in 6, 8, or 10 fathom Water, good hard Sand, and clear Ground: And a Mile from the Road on the West-side, there is a shoal running out a Mile into the Sea. From *Manta* to Cape St. *Lorenzo* the Land is plain and even, of an indifferent heighth. [See a farther Account of these Coasts in the Appendix.]

¶ As soon as ever the day appear'd our Men landed, and marched towards the Village, which was about a Mile and a half from their Landing-place: Some of the *Indians* who were stirring, saw them coming, and alarmed their Neighbours; so that all that were able got away. They took only two old Women, who both said, that it was reported that a great many Enemies were come over Land thro' the Country of *Darien* into the *South-Seas*, and that they were at present in Canoas and Periagoes: and that the Vice-Roy upon this News had set out the fore-mentioned order for burning their own Ships. Our Men found no sort of Provision here; the Vice-Roy having likewise sent orders to all Sea-ports to keep no Provision, but to just supply themselves. These Women also said, that the *Manta Indians* were sent over to the Island *Plata*, to destroy all the Goats there; which they performed about a Month agone. With this News our Men returned again, and arrived at *Plata* the next Day.

¶ We lay still at the Island *Plata*, being not resolved what to do; till the

2d Day of *Octob.* and then Capt. *Swan* in the *Cygnet of London* arrived there. He was fitted out by very eminent Merchants of that City, on a Design only to Trade with the *Spaniards* or *Indians*, having a very considerable Cargo well sorted for these parts of the World; but meeting with divers Disappointments, and being out of hopes to obtain a Trade in these Seas, his Men forced him to entertain a Company of Privateers which he met with near *Nicoya*, a Town whither he was going to seek a Trade, and these Privateers were bound thither in Boats to get a Ship. These were the Men that we had heard of at *Manta*; they came over Land under the Command of Capt. *Peter Harris*, Nephew to that Capt. *Harris* who was killed before *Panama*. Capt. *Swan* was still Commander of his own Ship, and Capt. *Harris* commanded a small Bark under Capt. *Swan*. There was much Joy on all sides when they arriv'd; and immediately hereupon Capt. *Davis* and Capt. *Swan* consorted, wishing for Capt. *Eaton* again. Our little Bark, which was taken at *Santa Hellena*, was immediately sent out to cruize, while the Ships were fitting; for Capt. *Swan*'s Ship being full of Goods, was not fit to entertain his new Guest, till the Goods were disposed of; therefore he by the Consent of the Super-cargo's, got up all his Goods on Deck, and sold to any one that would buy upon Trust: the rest was thrown over-board into the Sea, except fine Goods, as Silks, Muslins, Stockings, &c. and except the Iron, whereof he had a good Quantity, both wrought and in Bars: This was saved for Ballast.

¶ The third Day after our Bark was sent to cruize, she brought in a Prize of 400 Tuns, laden with Timber: They took her in the Bay of *Guiaquil*; she came from a Town of that Name, and was bound to *Lima*. The Commander of this Prize said that it was generally reported and believed at *Guiaquil*, that the Vice-Roy was fitting out 10 Sail of Frigots to drive us out of these Seas. This News made our unsettled Crew wish, that they had been persuaded to accept of Capt. *Eaton*'s Company on reasonable Terms. Capt. *Davis* and Capt. *Swan* had some discourse concerning Capt. *Eaton*; they at last concluded to send our small Bark towards the Coast of *Lima*, as far as the Island *Lobos*, to seek Capt. *Eaton*. This being approved by all Hands, she was clean'd the next Day, and sent away, mann'd with twenty Men, ten of Capt. *Davis*'s, and ten of *Swan*'s Men, and Capt. *Swan* writ a Letter directed to Capt. *Eaton*, desiring his Company, and the Isle of *Plata* was appointed for the general Rendezvous. When this Bark was gone, we turn'd another Bark, which we had, into a Fireship; having six or seven Carpenters, who soon fixt her; and while the Carpenters were at work about the Fireship, we scrubbed and clean'd our Men of War, as well as Time and Place would permit.

¶ The 19th Day of *October* we finished our Business, and the 20th Day we sailed towards the Island *Lobos*, where our Bark was ordered to stay for us, or meet us again at *Plata*. We had but little Wind, therefore it was the 23d Day before we passed by Point St. *Hellena*. The 25th Day we crossed over the Bay of *Guiaquil*. The 30th Day we doubled *Cape Blanco*. This Cape is in Lat. 3 d. 45 m. It is counted the worst Cape in all the *South-Seas* to double, passing to the Southward; for in all other places Ships may stand off to Sea 20 or 30 Leagues off, if they find they cannot get any thing under the Shoar; but here they dare not do it: for, by relation of the *Spaniards*, they find a Current setting N.W. which will carry a Ship off more in two Hours, than they can run in again in five. Besides, setting to the Northward they lose ground: therefore they always beat up in under the Shoar, which oft-times they find very difficult, because the Wind commonly blows very strong at S.S.W. or S. by W. without altering; for here are never any Land-winds. This Cape is of an indifferent Heighth: It is fenced with white Rocks to the Sea; for which reason, I believe, it hath this Name. The Land in the Country seems to be full of high, steep, rugged and barren Rocks.

¶ The 2d Day of *November* we got as high as *Payta*: we lay about six Leagues off Shoar all the Day, that the *Spaniards* might not see us; and in the Evening sent our Canoas ashoar to take it, mann'd with 110 Men.

¶ *Payta* is a small *Spanish* Sea-Port Town in the lat. of 5 d. 15 m. It is built on the Sand, close by the Sea, in a Nook, Elbow, or small Bay, under a pretty high Hill. There are not above 75 or 80 Houses, and two Churches. The Houses are but low and ill built. The Building in this Country of *Peru* is much alike on all the Sea-Coast. The Walls are built of Brick, made with Earth and Straw kneaded together: They are about three Foot long, two Foot broad, and a Foot and a half thick: They never burn them, but lay them a long time in the Sun to dry before they are used in building. In some places they have no Roofs, only Poles laid a-cross from the side Walls and covered with Matts; and then those Walls are carry'd up to a considerable Heighth. But where they build Roofs upon their Houses, the Walls are not made so high, as I said before. The Houses in general, all over this Kingdom, are but meanly built, one chief reason, with the common People especially, is the want of Materials to build withal; for however it be more within Land, yet here is neither Stone nor Timber to build with, nor any Materials but such Brick as I have described; and even the Stone which they have in some places is so brittle, that you may rub it into Sand with your Fingers. Another reason why they build so meanly is, because it never Rains; therefore they only

endeavour to fence themselves from the Sun. Yet their Walls, which are
built but with an ordinary sort of Brick, in comparison with what is made
in other parts of the World, continue a long time as firm as when first
made, having never any Winds nor Rains, to rot, moulder, or shake them.
However, the richer Sort have Timber, which they make use of in
building; but it is brought from other places.

¶ This dry Country commences to the Northward, from about Cape
Blanco to *Coquimbo*, in about 30 d. S. having no Rain that I could ever
observe or hear of; nor any green thing growing in the Mountains: neither
yet in the Valleys, except where here and there water'd with a few small
Rivers dispers'd up and down. So that the Northermost Parts of this
Tract of Land are supplied with Timber from *Guiaquil*, *Galleo*, *Tornato*,
and other places that are watered with Rains; where there are plenty of
all sorts of Timber. In the South Parts, as about *Guasco* and *Coquimbo*,
they fetch their Timber from the Island *Chiloe*, or other places thereabouts.
The Walls of Churches and rich Mens Houses are whitened with Lime,
both within and without; and the Doors and Posts are very large, and
adorned with carved Work, and the Beams also in the Churches: The
Inside of the Houses are hung round with rich embroidered, or painted
Cloths. They have likewise abundance of fine Pictures, which adds no
small Ornament to their Houses: these, I suppose, they have from *Old
Spain*. But the Houses of *Payta* are none of them so richly furnished. The
Churches were large and fairly carved: At one end of the Town there was
a small Fort close by the Sea, but no great Guns in it. This Fort, only
with Musquets, will command all the Bay, so as to hinder any Boats from
landing. There is another Fort on the Top of the Hill, just over the
Town, which commands both it and the lower Fort. There is neither
Wood nor Water to be had there: they fetch their Water from an *Indian*
Town called *Colan*, about two Leagues N.N.E. from *Payta*: for at *Colan*
there is a small River of fresh Water, which runs out into the Sea; from
whence Ships that touch at *Payta* are supplied with Water and other
Refreshments, as Fowls, Hogs, Plantains, Yams, and Maiz: *Payta* being
destitute of all these things, only as they fetch them from *Colan*, as they
have occasion.

¶ The *Indians* of *Colan* are all Fishermen: they go out to Sea and fish for
Bark-logs. Bark-logs are made of many round Logs of Wood, in manner
of a Raft, and very different according to the Use that they are designed
for, or the Humour of the People that make them, or the matter that they
are made of. If they are made for fishing, then they are only 3 or 4 Logs
of light Wood, of 7 or 8 Foot long, plac'd by the side of each other, pinn'd

fast together with wooden Pins, and bound hard with Withes. The Logs are so placed, that the middlemost are longer than those by the Sides, especially at the Head or Fore-part, which grows narrower gradually into an Angle or Point, the better to cut thro' the Water. Others are made to carry Goods: the Bottom of these is made of 20 or 30 great Trees of about 20, 30 or 40 Foot long, fasten'd like the other, side to side, and so shaped: on the Top of these they place another shorter Row of Trees across them, pinn'd fast to each other, and then pinn'd to the undermost Row: this double Row of Planks makes the bottom of the Float, and of a considerable breadth. From this bottom the Raft is raised to about 10 foot higher, with rows of Posts sometimes set upright, and supporting a floor or two: but those I observed were rais'd by thick Trees laid a-cross each other, as in Wood-Piles; only not close together, as in the bottom of the Float, but at the ends and sides only, so as to leave the middle all hollow like a Chamber; except that here and there a Beam goes across it, to keep the Float more compact. In this hollow, at about 4 foot heighth from the beams at the bottom, they lay small poles along, and close together, to make a floor for another Room, on the top of which also they lay another such floor made of Poles; and the entrances into both these Rooms is only by creeping between the great traverse Trees which make the Walls of this Sea-House. The lowest of these stories serves as a Cellar: there they lay great stones for Ballast, and their Jars of fresh Water closed up, and whatever may bear being wet; for by the weight of the Ballast and Cargo, the bottom of this Room, and of the whole Vessel, is sunk so deep, as to lie 2 or 3 feet within the Surface of the Water. The second story is for the Seamen, and their Necessaries. Above this second story the Goods are stowed, to what heighth they please, usually about 8 or 10 feet, and kept together by Poles set upright quite round: only there is a little space abaft for the Steers-men, (for they have a large Rudder) and afore for the Fire-hearth, to dress their Victuals, especially when they make long Voyages, as from *Lima* to *Truxillo*, or *Guiaquil*, or *Panama*, which last Voyage is 5 or 600 Leagues. In the midst of all, among the Goods rises a Mast, to which is fasten'd a large Sail, as in our West-Country Barges in the *Thames*. They always go before the Wind, being unable to Ply against it; and therefore are fit only for these Seas, where the Wind is always in a manner the same, not varying above a point or two all the way from *Lima*, till such time as they come into the Bay of *Panama*: and even there they meet with no great Sea; but sometimes Northerly Winds; and then they lower their Sails, and drive before it, waiting a change. All their Care then is only to keep off from Shoar; for they are so made that they cannot sink at Sea. These Rafts carry 60 or 70 Tuns of Goods and upwards; their Cargo is chiefly Wine, Oil, Flour, Sugar, *Quito*-Cloth, Soap, Goat-skins drest, &c. The Float is manag'd usually by 3 or 4 Men, who being unable to return with it against the Trade-wind, when they come to *Panama* dispose of the Goods and Bottom together; getting a Passage back again for themselves in some Ship or Boat bound to the Port they came from; and there they make a new Bark-log for their next Cargo.

¶ The smaller sort of Bark-logs, described before, which lie flat on the Water, and are used for Fishing, or carrying Water to Ships, or the like (half a Tun or a Tun at a time) are more governable than the other, tho' they have Masts and Sails too. With these they go out at Night by the help of the Land-wind (which is seldom wanting on this Coast) and return back in the Day Time with the Sea-wind.

¶ This sort of Floats are used in many Places both in the *East* and *West-Indies*. On the Coast *Coromandel* in the *East-Indies* they call them *Catamarians*. These are but one Log, or two sometimes of a sort of light Wood, and are made without Sail or Rudder, and so small, that they carry but one Man, whose Legs and Breech are always in the Water, and he manages his Log with a Paddle, appearing at a distance like a Man siting on a Fish's Back.

¶ The Country about *Payta* is mountainous and barren, like all the rest of the Kingdom of *Peru*. There is no Towns of Consequence nearer it than *Piura*, which is a large Town in the Country 40 Miles distant. It lieth, by report of our *Spanish* Prisoners, in a Valley, which is water'd with a small River, that disembogues it self into the Bay of *Chirapee*, in about 7 d. of North latitude. This Bay is nearer to *Piura* than *Payta*; yet all Goods imported by Sea for *Piura* are landed at *Payta*, for the Bay of *Chiropee* is full of dangerous sholes, and therefore not frequented by Shipping. The Road of *Payta* is one of the best on the Coast of *Peru*. It is sheltered from the South West by a point of Land, which makes a large Bay and smooth Water for Ships to ride in. There is room enough for a good Fleet of Ships, and good anchoring in any depth, from 6 Fathom Water to 20 Fathom. Right against the Town, the nearer the Town, the shallower the Water, and the smoother the riding, it is clean Sand all over the Bay. Most Ships passing either to the North or the South touch at this Place for Water, for tho' here is none at the Town, yet those *Indian* Fishermen of *Colan* will, and do supply all Ships very reasonably; and good Water is much prized on all this Coast through the Scarcity of it.

¶ *November* the 3d, at 6 a Clock in the Morning, our Men landed about 4 Miles to the South of the Town, and took some Prisoners that were sent thither to watch for fear of us; and these Prisoners said, that the Governour of *Piura* came with 100 armed Men to *Payta* the Night before, purposely to oppose our landing there, if we should attempt it.

¶ Our Men marched directly to the Fort on the Hill, and took it without the loss of one Man. Hereupon the Governour of *Piura* with all his Men, and the Inhabitants of the Town ran away as fast as they could. Then our Men entered the Town, and found it emptied both of Money and Goods; there was not so much as a Meal of Victuals left for them.

¶ The Prisoners told us a Ship had been here a little before and burnt a great Ship in the Road, but did not land their Men; and that here they put ashore all their Prisoners and Pilots. We knew this must be Captain *Eaton*'s Ship which had done this, and by these Circumstances we supposed he was gone to the *East-Indies*, it being always designed by him. The Prisoners told us also, That since Capt. *Eaton* was here, a small Bark had been off the Harbour, and taken a pair of Bark-logs a Fishing, and made the Fishermen bring aboard 20 or 30 Jars of fresh Water. This we supposed was our Bark that was sent to the *Lobos* to seek Capt. *Eaton*.

¶ In the Evening we came in with our Ships, and Anchored before the Town in 10 Fathom Water, near a Mile from the shore. Here we staid till the sixth Day, in hopes to get a Ransom from the Town. Our Captains demanded 300 Packs of Flour, 3000 Pound of Sugar, 25 Jars of Wine, and 1000 Jars of Water to be brought off to us; but we got nothing of it. Therefore Captain *Swan* ordered the Town to be fired, which was presently done. Then all our Men came aboard, and Captain *Swan* ordered the Bark which Capt. *Harris* commanded, to be burnt, because she did not sail well.

¶ At Night, when the Land-Wind came off, we sailed from hence towards *Lobos*. The 10th Day in the Evening we saw a Sail bearing N.W. by N. as far as we could well discern her on our Deck. We immediately chased, separating our selves, the better to meet her in the Night; but we mist her. Therefore the next Morning we again trimm'd sharp, and made the best of our way to *Lobos de la Mar*.

¶ The 14th Day we had sight of the Island *Lobos de Terra*: It bore East from us; we stood in towards it, and betwixt 7 and 8 a Clock in the Night came to an Anchor at the N.E. end of the Island, in 4 Fathom Water. This Island at Sea is of an indifferent height, and appears like *Lobos de la Mar*. About a quarter of a Mile from the North-end there is a great hollow Rock, and a good Channel between, where there is 7 Fathom Water. The 15th Day we went ashore, and found abundance of Penguins and Boobies, and Seal in great quantities. We sent aboard of all these to be drest, for we had not tasted any Flesh in a great while before; therefore some of us did eat very heartily. Captain *Swan*, to encourage his Men to eat this coarse Flesh, would commend it for extraordinary Food, comparing the Seal to a roasted Pig, the Boobies to Hens, and the Penguins to Ducks: this he did to train them to live contentedly on coarse Meat, not knowing but we might be forced to make use of such Food before we departed out of these Seas; for it is generally seen among Privateers, that nothing emboldens them sooner to Mutiny than want, which we could not well suffer in a Place where there are such quantities of these Animals to be had, if Men could be perswaded to be content with them.

¶ In the Afternoon we sailed from *Lobos de Terra*; with the Wind at S. by E. and arrived at *Lobos de la Mar* on the 19th Day. Here we found a Letter, left by our Bark that was sent to seek Capt. *Eaton*, by which we understood, that Capt. *Eaton* had been there, but was gone before they arrived, and had left no Letter to advise us which way he was gone; and that our Bark was again returned to *Plata*, in hopes to find us there, or meet us by the way, else resolving to stay for us there. We were sorry to hear that Capt. *Eaton* was gone, for now we did not expect to meet with him any more in these Seas.

¶ The 21st Day we sent out our *Moskito* Strikers for Turtle, who brought aboard enough to serve both Ships Companies; and this they did all the time that we abode here. While we lay at this Island, Captain *Swan* made new Yards, squarer than those he had before, and made his Sails larger, and our Ship's Company in the mean time split Plank for Fire-wood, and put aboard as many Planks as we could conveniently stow, for other uses: Here being Plank enough of all sorts, which we had brought hither in the first Prize that we took, and left here.

¶ The 26th Day in the Evening, we saw a small Bark about 3 Leagues N.N.W. from the Island, but we supposing her to be our own Bark, did not go after her. The next Morning she was two Leagues South of the Island, standing off to Sea; but we did not now chace her neither, altho' we knew she was not our Bark; for being to Windward of us, she could have made her escape, if we had chased her. This Bark, as we were afterwards informed, was sent out purposely to see if we were at this Island. Her Orders were, not to come too near, only to appear in sight; they supposing that if we were here we should soon be after her; as indeed it was a wonder we had not chased her: But our not doing so, and lying close under the Island undiscern'd by them, was a great Occasion of our coming upon *Puna* afterwards unexpectedly, they being now without fear of any Enemy so near them.

¶ The 28th Day we scrubbed our Ship's bottom, intending to sail the next Day towards *Guiaquil*; it being concluded upon to attempt that Town before we returned again to *Plata*. Accordingly, on the 29th Day in the Morning, we loosed from hence, steering directly for the Bay of *Guiaquil*. This Bay runs in between Cape *Blanco* on the South-side, and Point *Chandy* on the North. About 25 Leagues from C. *Blanco*, near the bottom of the Bay, there is a small Island called *Santa Clara*, which lies East and West: It is of an indifferent length, and it appears like a dead Man stretched out in a Shroud. The East-end represents the Head, and the West-end the Feet. Ships that are bound into the River of *Guiaquil* pass on the South-side, to avoid the sholes which lie on the North-side of it; whereon formerly Ships have been lost. It is reported by the *Spaniards*, that there is a very rich Wreck lies on the North-side of that Island, not far from it; and that some of the Plate hath been taken up by one who came from *Old-Spain*, with a Patent from the King to fish in those Seas for Wrecks; but he dying, the Project ceased, and the Wreck still remains as he left it; only the *Indians* by stealth do sometimes take up some of it; and they might have taken up much more, if it were not for the *Cat-fish* which swarms hereabouts.

¶ The *Cat-fish* is much like a *Whiting*, but the Head is flatter and bigger. It hath a great wide Mouth, and certain small Strings pointing out from each side of it, like Cat's Whiskers; and for that reason it is called a *Cat-fish*. It hath three Fins; one growing on the top of his back, and one on either side. Each of these Fins hath a stiff sharp Bone, which is very venomous if it strikes into a Man's Flesh; therefore it is dangerous diving where many of these Fish are. The *Indians* that adventured to search this Wreck, have to their Sorrow experienced it; some having lost their Lives, others the use of their Limbs by it: this we were informed of by an *Indian*, who himself had been fishing on it by stealth. I my self have known some white Men that have lost the use of their Hands, only by a small prick with the Fin of these Fish: Therefore when we catch them with a Hook, we tread on them to take the Hook out of their Mouths, or otherwise, in flurting about (as all Fish will when first taken) they might accidentally strike their sharp Fins into the Hands of those that caught them. Some of the Fish are seven or eight pound weight: some again, in some particular Places, are none of them bigger than a Man's Thumb, but their Fins are all alike venomous. They use to be at the Mouths of Rivers, or where there is much Mud and Oaze, and they are found all over the *American* Coast, both in the *North* and *South-Sea*, at least in the hot Countries, as also in the *East-Indies*: where sailing with Captain *Minchin* among certain Islands near the *Streights* of *Malacca*, he pointed to an Island, at which he told me he lost the use of his Hand by one of these, only in going to take the Hook out of its Mouth. The Wound was scarce visible, yet his Hand was much swoln, and the Pain lasted about 9 Weeks; during most part of which the raging Heat of it was almost ready to distract him. However, though the bony Fins of these Fish are so venomous, yet the Bones in their Bodies are not so; at least we never perceived any such effect in eating the Fish; and their Flesh is very sweet, delicious and wholesome Meat.

¶ From the Island *Santa Clara* to *Punta Arena* is 7 Leagues E.N.E. This *Punta Arena*, or *Sandy-Point*, is the Westermost Point of the Island *Puna*. Here all Ships bound into the River of *Guiaquil* anchor, and must wait for a Pilot, the entrance being very dangerous for Strangers.

¶ The Island *Puna* is a pretty large flat low Island, stretching East and West about 12 or 14 Leagues long, and about four or five Leagues wide. The Tide runs very strong all about this Island, but so many different ways, by reason of the Branches, Creeks, and Rivers that run into the Sea near it, that it casts up many dangerous sholes on all sides of it. There is in the Island only one *Indian* Town on the South-side of it, close by the Sea, and seven Leagues from *Point Arena*, which Town is also called *Puna*. The *Indians* of this Town are all Seamen, and are the only Pilots in these Seas, especially for this River. Their chiefest Employment, when they are not at Sea, is fishing. These Men are obliged by the *Spaniards* to keep good watch for Ships that anchor at Point *Arena*; which, as I said before, is 7 Leagues from the Town *Puna*. The place where they keep this watch is at a Point of Land on the Island *Puna*, that starts out into the Sea; from whence they can see all Ships that anchor at Point *Arena*. The *Indians* come thither in the Morning, and return at Night on Horseback. From this watching Point to Point *Arena* it is 4 Leagues, all drowned Mangrove-land: and in the midway between these two Points is another small Point, where these *Indians* are obliged to keep another Watch, when they fear an Enemy. The Centinel goes thither in a Canoa in the Morning, and returns at Night; for there is no coming thither by Land, through that Mangrove marshy Ground. The middle of the Island *Puna* is Savannah or Pasture. There are some ridges of good Wood-land, which is of a light yellow or sandy Mould, producing large tall Trees, most unknown even to Travellers: But there are plenty of *Palmeto*-Trees, which, because I am acquainted with, I shall describe. The *Palmeto*-Tree is about the bigness of an ordinary Ash: It is about 30 Foot high; the Body straight, without any limb, or branch, or leaf, except at the head only, where it spreads forth into many small Branches, not half so big as a Man's Arm, some no bigger than one's Finger: These Branches are about three or four Foot long, clear from any knot: At the end of the Branch there groweth one broad leaf, about the bigness of a large Fan. This, when it first shoots forth, grows in folds, like a Fan when it is closed; and still as it grows bigger so it opens, till it becomes like a Fan spread abroad. It is strengthened towards the stalk with many small ribs springing from thence, and growing into the leaf; which as they grow near the end of the leaf, grow thinner and smaller. The leaves that make the brush-part of the Flag-brooms which are brought into *England*, grow just in this manner; and are indeed a small kind of *Palmeto*; for there are of them of several Dimensions. In *Bermudas*, and elsewhere, they make Hats, Baskets, Brooms, Fans to blow the Fire instead of Bellows, with many other House-implements, of *Palmeto*-leaves. On the Ridges where these Trees grow, the *Indians* have here and there Plantations of Maiz, Yams, and Potatoes.

¶ There are in the Town of *Puna* about 20 Houses, and a small Church. The Houses stand all on Posts, 10 or 12 foot high, with Ladders on the outside to go up into them. I did never see the like Building any where but among the *Malayans* in the *East-Indies*. They are thatched with *Palmeto*-leaves, and their Chambers well boarded, in which last they exceed the *Malayans*. The best place for Ships to lie at an Anchor is against the middle of the Town. There is five Fathom Water within a Cables length of the shoar, and good soft deep Oaze where Ships may careen, or hale ashore; it stows 15 or 16 Foot Water up and down.

¶ From *Puna* to *Guiaquil* is reckoned 7 Leagues. It is 1 League before you come to the River of *Guiaquil's* Mouth, where it is about two Mile wide; from thence upwards the River lies pretty straight, without any considerable turnings. Both sides of the River are low swampy Land, overgrown with Red Mangroves, so that there is no landing. Four Mile before you come to the Town of *Guiaquil*, there's a low Island standing in the River. This Island divides the River into two Parts, making two very fair Channels for Ships to pass up and down. The S.W. Channel is the widest, the other is as deep, but narrower and narrower yet, by reason of many Trees and Bushes, which spread over the River, both from the Main and from the Island; and there are also several great stumps of Trees standing upright in the Water, on either side. The Island is above a Mile long. From the upper part of the Island to the Town of *Guiaquil*, is almost a League, and near as much from one side of the River to the other. In that spacious place Ships of the greatest Burthen may ride afloat; but the best place for Ships is nearest to that part of the Land where the Town stands; and this place is seldom without Ships. *Guiaquil* stands facing the Island, close by the River, partly on the side, and partly at the Foot of a gentle Hill declining towards the River, by which the lower-part of it is often overflown. There are two Forts, one standing on the low Ground, the other on the Hill. This Town makes a very fine Prospect, it being beautified with several Churches and other good Buildings. Here lives a Governour, who, as I have been informed, hath his Patent from the King of *Spain*. *Guiaquil* may be reckoned one of the chiefest Sea-Ports in the *South-Seas*: the Commodities which are exported from hence are Cacao, Hides, Tallow, Sarsaparilla, and other Drugs, and Woollen-Cloth, commonly called Cloth of *Quito*.

¶ The Cacao grows on both sides of the River above the Town. It is a small Nut, like the *Campeachy* Nut: I think, the smallest of the two; they produce as much Cacao here as serves all the Kingdom of *Peru*; and much of it is sent to *Acapulco*, and from thence to the *Philippine Islands*.

¶ Sarsaparilla grows in the Water by the sides of the River, as I have been informed.

¶ The *Quito*-Cloth comes from a rich Town in the Country within Land called *Quito*. There is a great deal made, both Serges and Broad-Cloth. This Cloth is not very fine, but it is worn by the common sort of People throughout the whole Kingdom of *Peru*. This, and all other Commodities, which come from *Quito*, are shipt off at *Guiaquil* for other Parts; and all imported Goods for the City of *Quito* pass by *Guiaquil*: By which it may appear that *Guiaquil* is a Place of no mean Trade.

¶ *Quito*, as I have been informed, is a very populous City, seated in the heart of the Country. It is inhabited partly by *Spaniards*; but the major part of its Inhabitants are *Indians*, under the *Spanish* Government.

¶ It is invironed with Mountains of a vast heighth, from whose Bowels many great Rivers have their rise. These Mountains abound in Gold, which by violent Rains is wash'd with the Sand into the adjacent Brooks, where the *Indians* resort in Troops, washing away the Sand, and putting up the Gold-dust in their Calabashes or Gourd-Shells: But for the manner of gathering the Gold I refer you to Mr. *Wafer*'s Book: Only I shall remark here, that *Quito* is the Place in all the Kingdom of *Peru* that abounds most with this rich Metal, as I have been often informed.

¶ The Country is subject to great Rains, and very thick Fogs, especially the Valleys. For that reason it is very unwholsome and sickly. The chiefest Distempers are Fevers, violent Head-ach, Pains in the Bowels, and Fluxes. I know no Place where Gold is found but what is very unhealthy;

as I shall more particularly relate when I come to speak of *Achin* in the Isle of *Sumatra* in the *East-Indies*. *Guiaquil* is not so sickly as *Quito* and other Towns farther within Land; yet in Comparison with the Towns that are on the Coast of *Mare Pacifico*, South of Cape *Blanco*, it is very sickly.

¶ It was to this Town of *Guiaquil* that we were bound; therefore we left our Ships off Cape *Blanco*, and ran into the Bay of *Guiaquil* with our Bark and Canoas, steering in for the Island *Santa Clara*, where we arrived the next Day after we left our Ships, and from thence we sent away two Canoas the next Evening to Point *Arena*. At this Point there are abundance of Oysters, and other Shell-fish, as Cockles and Muscles; therefore the *Indians* of *Puna* often come hither to get these Fish. Our Canoas got over before Day, and absconded in a Creek, to wait for the coming of the *Puna Indians*. The next Morning some of them, according to their Custom, came thither on Bark-logs, at the latter part of the Ebb, and were all taken by our Men. The next Day, by their advice, the two Watchmen of the *Indian* Town *Puna* were taken by our Men, and all its Inhabitants, not one escaping. The next Ebb they took a small Bark laden with *Quito*-Cloth. She came from *Guiaquil* that Tide, and was bound to *Lima*, they having advice that we were gone off the Coast, by the Bark which I said we saw while we lay at the Island *Lobos*. The Master of this Cloth-bark informed our Men, that there were three Barks coming from *Guiaquil*, laden with Negroes: he said they would come from thence the next Tide. The same Tide of Ebb that they took the Cloth-bark, they sent a Canoa to our Bark, where the biggest part of the Men were, to hasten them away with speed to the *Indian* Town. The Bark was now riding at Point *Arena*; and the next Flood she came with all the Men, and the rest of the Canoas to *Puna*. The Tide of Flood being now far spent, we lay at this Town till the last of the Ebb, and then rowed away, leaving five Men aboard our Bark, who were ordered to lie still till eight a Clock the next Morning, and not to fire at any Boat or Bark, but after that time they might fire at any Object: For it was supposed, that before that time we should be Masters of *Guiaquil*. We had not rowed above two Mile, before we met and took one of the three Barks laden with Negroes; the Master of her said, that the other two would come from *Guiaquil* the next Tide of Ebb. We cut her Main-mast down, and left her at an Anchor. It was now strong Flood, and therefore we rowed with all speed towards the Town, in hopes to get thither before the Flood was down, but we found it farther than we did expect it to be, or else our Canoas being very full of Men, did not row so fast as we would have them. The Day broke when we were two Leagues from the Town, and then we had not above an

Hours Flood more; therefore our Captains desired the *Indian* Pilot to direct us to some Creek where we might abscond all Day, which was immediately done, and one Canoa was sent toward *Puna* to our Bark, to order them not to move nor fire till the next Day. But she came too late to countermand the first Orders; for the two Barks before-mentioned laden with Negroes, come from the Town the last quarter of the Evening Tide, and lay in the River, close by the shoar on one side, and we rowed upon the other side and mist them; neither did they see nor hear us. As soon as the Flood was spent, the two Barks weighed and went down with the Ebb, towards *Puna*. Our Bark seeing them coming directly towards them, and both full of Men, supposed that we by some Accident had been destroyed, and that the two Barks were mann'd with *Spanish* Soldiers, and sent to take our Ships, and therefore they fired three Guns at them a League before they came near. The two *Spanish* Barks immediately came to an Anchor, and the Masters got into their Boats, and rowed for the shoar; but our Canoa that was sent from us took them both. The firing of these three Guns made a great disorder among our advanced Men, for most of them did believe they were heard at *Guiaquil*, and that therefore it could be no Profit to lie still in the Creek; but either row away to the Town, or back again to our Ships. It was now quarter Ebb, therefore we could not move upwards, if we had been disposed so to do. At length Capt. *Davis* said, he would immediately land in the Creek where they lay, and march directly to the Town, if but forty Men would accompany him: And without saying more Words, he landed among the Mangroves in the Marshes. Those that were so minded followed him, to the Number of forty or fifty. Capt. *Swan* lay still with the rest of the Party in the Creek, for they thought it impossible to do any good that way. Capt. *Davis* and his Men were absent about four Hours, and then returned all wet, and quite tired, and could not find any Passage out into the firm Land. He had been so far, that he almost despaired of getting back again: For a Man cannot pass thro' those red Mangroves but with very much labour. When Capt. *Davis* was returned, we concluded to be going towards the Town the beginning of the next Flood; and if we found that the Town was alarmed, we purposed to return again without attempting any thing there. As soon as it was flood we rowed away, and passed by the Island thro' the N.E. Channel, which is the narrowest. There are so many Stumps in the River, that it is very dangerous passing in the Night (and that is the time we always take for such Attempts) for the River runs very swift, and one of our Canoas stuck on a Stump, and had certainly overset, if she had not been immediately rescued by others. When we were come almost to the end of the Island, there was a Musquet fired at us out of the Bushes on the Main. We then had the Town open before us, and presently saw lighted Torches, or Candles, all the Town over; whereas before the Gun was fired there was but one Light: therefore we now concluded we were discovered: Yet many of our Men said, that it was a Holy-day the next Day, as it was indeed, and that therefore the *Spaniards* were making Fire-works, which they often do in the Night against such times. We rowed therefore a little farther, and found firm Land, and Capt. *Davis* pitched his Canoa ashore and landed with his Men. Capt. *Swan,* and most of his Men did not think it convenient to attempt any thing, seeing the Town was alarmed; but at last, being upbraided with Cowardize, Captain *Swan* and his Men landed also. The place where we landed was about two Mile from the Town: It was all overgrown with Woods so thick, that we could not march thro' in the Night; and therefore we sat down, waiting for the light of the Day. We had two *Indian* Pilots with us; one that had been with us a Month, who having received some Abuses from a Gentleman of *Guiaquil,* to be revenged offered his Service to us, and we found him very faithful: The other was taken by us not above two or three Days before, and he seemed to be as willing as the other to assist us. This latter was led by one of Capt. *Davis*'s Men, who shewed himself very forward to go to the Town, and upbraided others with faint-heartedness: Yet this Man (as he afterwards confessed) notwithstanding his Courage, privately cut the String that the Guide was made fast with, and let him go to the Town by himself, not caring to follow him; but when he thought the Guide was got far enough from us, he cried out that the Pilot was gone, and that some Body had cut the Cord that tied him. This put every Man in a moving Posture to seek the *Indian,* but all in vain; and our Consternation was great, being in the dark and among Woods; so the design was wholly dashed, for not a Man after that had the Heart to speak of going farther. Here we staid till Day, and then rowed out into the middle of the River, where we had a fair view of the Town; which, as I said before, makes a very pleasant Prospect. We lay still about half an Hour, being a Mile, or something better from the Town. They did not fire one Gun at us, nor we at them. Thus our design on *Guiaquil* failed: Yet Capt. *Townley,* and Capt. *Francois Gronet* took it a little while after this. When we had taken a full view of the Town, we rowed over the River, where we went ashore to a Beef Estantion or Farm, and kill'd a Cow, which we drest and eat. We staid there till the Evening Tide of Ebb, and then rowed down the River, and the 9th Day in the Morning arrived at *Puna.* In our way thither we went aboard the three Barks laden with Negroes, that lay at their Anchor in the River, and carried the Barks away with us. There were 1000 Negroes in the three Barks, all lusty young Men and Women. When we came to *Puna*, we sent a Canoa to Point *Arena*, to see if the Ships were come thither. The 12th Day she returned again, with Tidings that they were both there at Anchor. Therefore in the Afternoon we all went aboard of our Ships, and carried the Cloth-bark with us, and about forty of the stoutest Negro-Men, leaving their three Barks with the rest; and out of these also Capt. *Davis* and Capt. *Swan* chose about 14 or 15 a-piece, and turn'd the rest ashore.

¶ There was never a greater Opportunity put into the Hands of Men to enrich themselves than we had, to have gone with these Negroes, and settled our selves at *Santa Maria*, on the Isthmus of *Darien*, and employed them in getting Gold out of the Mines there. Which might have been done with ease: For about six Months before this, Capt. *Harris* (who was now with us) coming over Land from the *North-Seas*, with his Body of Privateers, had routed the *Spaniards* away from the Town and Gold-Mines of *Santa Maria*, so that they had never attempted to settle there again since: Add to this, that the *Indian* Neighbourhood, who were mortal Enemies to the *Spaniards*, and had been flush'd by their Successes against them, through the Assistance of the Privateers, for several Years, were our fast Friends, and ready to receive and assist us. We had, as I have said 1000 Negroes to work for us, we had 200 Tun of Flour that lay at the *Gallapagos*, there was the River of *Santa Maria*, where we could careen and fit our Ships; and might fortifie the Mouth so, that if all the strength the *Spaniards* have in *Peru* had come against us, we could have kept them out. If they lay with Guard-ships of Strength to keep us in, yet we had a great Country to live in, and a great Nation of *Indians* that were our Friends: Besides, which was the principal Thing, we had the *North-Seas* to befriend us; from whence we could export ourselves, or Effects, or import Goods or Men to our Assistance; for in a short time we should have had Assistance from all Parts of the *West-Indies*; many Thousands of Privateers from *Jamaica* and the *French* Islands especially would have flockt over to us; and long before this time we might have been Masters not only of those Mines, (the richest Gold-Mines ever yet found in *America*) but of all the Coast as high as *Quito*: And much more than I say might then probably have been done.

¶ But these may seem to the Reader but Golden Dreams: To leave them therefore; The 13th Day we sailed from Point *Arena* towards *Plata*, to seek our Bark that was sent to the Island *Lobos*, in search of Capt. *Eaton*. We were two Ships in Company, and two Barks; and the 16th Day we arrived at *Plata*, but found no Bark there, nor any Letter. The next Day we went over to the Main to fill Water, and in our Passage met our Bark: She had been a second time at the Island *Lobos*, and not finding us, was coming to *Plata* again. They had been in some want of Provision since they left us, and therefore they had been at *Santa Hellena*, and taken it; where they got as much Maize as served them three or four Days; and that with some Fish and Turtle which they struck, lasted them till they came to the Island *Lobos de Terra*. They got Boobies and Penguins Eggs, of which they laid in a store; and went from thence. to *Lobos de la Mar*, where they replenished their stock of Eggs, and salted up a few young Seal, for fear they should want: And being thus victualled, they returned again towards *Plata*. When our Water was fill'd we went over again to the Island *Plata*. There we parted the Cloths that were taken in the Cloth-Bark into two Lots or Shares; Capt. *Davis* and his Men had one part, and Capt. *Swan* and his Men had the other part. The Bark which the Cloth was in Capt. *Swan* kept for a Tender. At this time here were at *Plata* a great many large Turtles, which I judge came from the *Gallapago*'s, for I had never seen any here before, tho' I had been here several times. This was their Coupling-time, which is much sooner in the Year here than in the *West-Indies*, properly so called. Our Strikers brought aboard every Day more than we could eat. Captain *Swan* had no Striker, and therefore had no Turtle but what was sent him from Capt. *Davis*; and all his Flour too he had from Capt. *Davis*: but since our disappointment at *Guiaquil*, Capt. *Davis*'s Men murmured against Capt. *Swan*, and did not willingly give him any Provision, because he was not so forward to go thither as Captain *Davis*. However, at last, these Differences were made up, and we concluded to go into the Bay of *Panama*, to a Town called *La Velia*; but because we had not Canoas enough to land our Men, we were resolved to search some Rivers where the *Spaniards* have no Commerce, there to get *Indian* Canoas.

CHAPTER VII

They leave the Isle of Plata. *Cape* Passao. *The Coast between that and Cape St.* Francisco; *and from thence on to* Panama. *The River of* St. Jago. *The Red and the White* Cotton-tree. *The* Cabbage-tree. *The* Indians *of St.* Jago *River, and its Neighbourhood. The Isle of* Gallo. *The River and Village of* Tomaca. *Isle of* Gorgonia, *The* Pearl-Oysters *there and in other parts. The Land on the Main. Cape* Corientes. Point Garachina. Island Gallera. *The* Kings, *or* Pearl Islands, Pacheque St. Paul's Island. Lavelia. Nata. *The* Calm-fish. Oysters. *The pleasant Prospects in the Bay of* Panama. Old Panama. *The New City. The great Concourse there from* Lima *and* Portabel, &c. *upon the Arrival of the* Spanish Armada *in the* West-Indies. *The Course the* Armada *takes; with an incidental Account of the first inducements that made the* Privateers *undertake the passage over the Isthmus of* Darien *into the* South-Seas, *and of the particular beginning of their Correspondence with the* Indians *that inhabit that Isthmus. Of the Air and Weather at* Panama. *The Isles of* Perico. Tabago, *a pleasant Island. The* Mammee-tree. *The Village* Tabago. *A Spanish Stratagem or two of Capt.* Bond *their Engineer. The Ignorance of the* Spaniards *of these parts in Sea-Affairs. A Party of French Privateers arrive from over Land. Of the Commissions that are given out by the* French Governour *of* Petit Guavres. *Of the Gulph of St.* Michael, *and the Rivers of* Congos, Sambo, *and* Sta. Maria: *and an Error of the common Maps, in the placing Point* Garachina *and Cape St.* Lorenzo, *corrected. Of the Town and Gold Mines of* Sta. Maria; *and the Town of* Scuchadero, *Capt.* Townley's *Arrival with some more* English *Privateers over Land. Jars of* Pisco-Wine. *A Bark of Capt.* Knight's *joins them. Point* Garachina *again. Porto de Pinas. Isle of* Otoque. *The Pacquet from* Lima *taken. Other* English *and* French *Privateers arrive.* Chepelio, *one of the sweetest Islands in the World. The* Sapadillo Avogato Pear, Mammee Sappota. *Wild* Mammee *and* Star-Apple. Cheapo *River and Town. Some Traversings in the Bay of* Panama; *and an account of the Strength of the* Spanish Fleet, *and of the* Privateers, *and the* Engagement *between them.*

THE 23d Day of *Decemb.* 1684, we sailed from the Island *Plata*, towards the Bay of *Panama*: The Wind at S.S.E. a fine brisk Gale, and fine Weather. The next Morning we past by Cape *Passao*. This Cape is in lat. oo d. o8 m. South of the Equator. It runs out into the Sea with a high round Point, which seems to be divided in the midst. It is bald against the Sea, but within Land, and on both sides, it is full of short Trees. The Land in the Country is very high and mountainous, and it appears to be very woody. Between Cape *Passao* and Cape St. *Francisco*, the Land by the Sea is full of small Points, making as many little sandy Bays between them; and is of an indifferent heighth covered with Trees of divers sorts; so that sailing by this Coast you see nothing but a vast

Grove or Wood; which is so much the more pleasant, because the Trees are of several Forms, both in respect to their Growth and Colour.

¶ Our design was, as I said in my first Chapter, to search for Canoas in some River where the *Spaniards* have neither Settlement or Trade with the native *Indians*. We had *Spanish* Pilots, and *Indians* bred under the *Spaniards*, who were able to carry us into any Harbour or River belonging to the *Spaniards*, but were wholly unacquainted with those Rivers which were not frequented by the *Spaniards*. There are many such unfrequented Rivers between *Plata* and *Panama*: Indeed all the way from the Line to the Gulph of St. *Michaels*, or even to *Panama* it self, the Coast is not inhabited by any *Spaniards*, nor are the *Indians* that inhabit there any way under their Subjection: except only near the Isle *Gallo*, where on the Banks of a Gold River or two, there are some *Spaniards* who work there to find Gold.

¶ Now our Pilots being at a loss on these less frequented Coasts, we supplied that defect out of the *Spanish* Pilot-books, which we took in their Ships; These we found by Experience to be very good Guides. Yet nevertheless the Country in many Places by the Sea being low, and full of Openings, Creeks and Rivers, it is somewhat difficult to find any particular River that a Man designs to go to, where he is not well acquainted.

¶ This however could be no discouragement to us; for one River might probably be as well furnished with *Indian* Canoas as another; and if we found them, it was to us indifferent where, yet we pitch'd on the River St. *Jago*, not because there were not other Rivers as large, and as likely to be inhabited with *Indians* as it; but because that River was not far from *Gallo*, an Island where our Ships could anchor safely and ride securely. We past by Cape St. *Francisco*, meeting with great and continued Rains. The Land by the Sea to the North of the Cape, is low and extraordinary woody; the Trees are very thick, and seem to be of a prodigious heighth and bigness. From Cape St. *Francisco* the Land runs more Easterly into the Bay of *Panama*. I take this Cape to be its Bounds on the South-side, and the Isles of *Cobaya* or *Quibo* to bound it on the North-side. Between this Cape and the Isle *Gallo* there are many large and navigable Rivers. We past by them all till we came to the River St. *Jago*.

¶ This River is near 2 d. North of the Equator. It is large and navigable some Leagues up, and seven Leagues from the Sea it divides itself into two parts, making an Island that is four Leagues wide against the Sea. The widest Branch is that on the S.W. side of the Island. Both Branches are very deep, but the Mouth of the narrower is so choakt with sholes that at low Water even Canoas can't enter. Above the Island it is a League

wide, and the Stream runs pretty straight, and very swift. The Tide
flows about three Leagues up the River, but to what height I know not.
Probably the River hath its original from some of the rich Mountains near
the City *Quibo*, and it runs through a Country as rich in Soil, as perhaps
any in the World, especially when it draws within 10 or 12 Leagues of
the Sea. The Land there both on the Island, and on both sides of the
River, is of a black deep Mold, producing extraordinary great tall Trees
of many sorts, such as usually grow in these hot Climates. I shall only give
an account of the *Cotton* and *Cabbage-trees*, whereof there is great Plenty;
and they are as large of their kinds as ever I saw.

¶ There are two sorts of *Cotton-trees*, one is called the Red, the other the
White *Cotton-tree*. The White *Cotton-tree* grows like an Oak, but generally
much bigger and taller than our Oaks: The Body is straight and clear
from knots or boughs to the very head: there it spreads forth many great
Limbs just like an Oak. The Bark is smooth and of a grey colour: the
Leaves are as big as a large Plumb-Leaf, jagged at the edge; they are
oval, smooth, and of a dark green Colour. Some of these Trees have their
Bodies much bigger, 18 or 20 foot high, than nearer the Ground, being
big-bellied like Nine-pins. They bear a very fine sort of Cotton, called
Silk-Cotton. When this Cotton is ripe, the Trees appear like our Apple-
trees in *England*, when full of Blossoms. If I do not mistake, the Cotton
falls down in *November*, or *December*: then the Ground is covered white
with it. This is not substantial and continuous, like that which grows
upon the Cotton-shrubs in Plantations, but like the Down of Thistles; so
that I did never know any use made of it in the *West-Indies*, because it is
not worth the Labour of gathering it: but in the *East-Indies* the Natives
gather and use it for Pillows. It hath a small black Seed among it. The
Leaves of this Tree fall off the beginning of *April*; while the old Leaves
are falling off, the young ones spring out, and in a Week's Time the Tree
casts off her old Robes, and is cloathed in a new pleasant Garb. The red
Cotton-tree is like the other, but hardly so big: It bears no Cotton, but
its Wood is somewhat harder of the two, yet both sorts are soft spungy
Wood, fit for no use that I know, but only for Canoas, which being strait
and tall they are very good for; but they will not last long, especially if
not drawn ashore often and tarred; otherwise the Worm and the Water
soon rot them. They are the biggest Trees, or perhaps Weeds rather, in
the *West-Indies*. They are common in the *East* and *West-Indies* in good fat
Land.

¶ As the Cotton is the biggest Tree in the Woods, so the Cabbage-tree
is the tallest: The Body is not very big, but very high and strait. I have

measured one in the Bay of *Campeachy* 120 feet long as it lay on the Ground, and there are some much higher. It has no Limbs nor Boughs, but at the Head there are many Branches bigger than a Man's Arm. These Branches are not covered, but flat, with sharp edges; they are 12 or 14 Foot long. About two Foot from the Trunk, the Branches shoot forth small long Leaves, about an Inch broad, which grow so regularly on both sides of the Branch, that the whole Branch seems to be but one Leaf, made up of many small ones. The Cabbage-Fruit shoots out in the midst of these Branches, from the top of the Tree; it is invested with many young Leaves or Branches which are ready to spread abroad, as the old Branches drop and fall down. The Cabbage it self, when it is taken out of the Leaves which it seems to be folded in, is as big as the small of a Man's Leg, and a foot long; it is as white as Milk, and as sweet as a Nut, if eaten raw, and it is very sweet and wholsome if boiled. Besides, the Cabbage it self, there grow out between the Cabbage and the large Branches, small Twigs, as of a Shrub, about two Foot long from their Stump. At the end of those Twigs (which grow very thick together) there hang Berries hard and round, and as big as a Cherry. These the Trees shed every Year, and they are very good for Hogs: For this reason the *Spaniards* fine any who shall cut down any of these in their Woods. The Body of the Tree is full of rings round it, half a foot asunder from the bottom to the top. The Bark is thin and brittle; the Wood is black and very hard, the Heart or Middle of the Tree is white Pith. They do not climb to get the Cabbage, but cut them down; for should they gather it off the Tree as it stands, yet its Head being gone, it soon dies. These Trees are much used by Planters in *Jamaica*, to board the sides of the Houses, for it is but splitting the Trunk into four parts with an Axe, and there are so many Planks. Those Trees appear very pleasant, and they beautifie the whole Wood, spreading their green Branches above all other Trees.

¶ All this Country is subject to very great Rains, so that this part of *Peru* pays for the dry Weather which they have about *Lima* and all that Coast. I believe that is one reason why the *Spaniards* have made such small Discoveries, in this and other Rivers on this Coast. Another reason may be, because it lies not so directly in their way; for they do not coast it along in going from *Panama* to *Lima*, but first go Westward as far as to the Keys or Isles of *Cobaya*, for a westerly Wind, and from thence stand over towards Cape St. *Francisco*, not touching any where usually, till they come to *Manta* near Cape St. *Lorenzo*. In their return indeed from *Lima* to *Panama*, they may keep along the Coast hereabouts; but then their Ships are always laden; whereas the light Ships that go from *Panama*, are most at leisure to make Discoveries. A third Reason may be, the wildness and enmity of all the Natives on this Coast, who are naturally fortified by their Rivers and vast Woods, from whence with their Arrows they can easily annoy any that shall land there to assault them. At this River particularly there are no *Indians* live within 6 Leagues of the Sea, and all the Country so far is full of impassable Woods; so that to get at the *Indians*, or the Mines and Mountains, there is no way but by rowing up the River; and if any who are Enemies to the Natives attempt this, (as the *Spaniards* are always hated by them) they must all the way be exposed to the Arrows of those who would lie purposely in Ambush in the Woods for them. These wild *Indians* have small Plantations of Maiz, and good Plantain-Gardens; for Plantains are their chiefest Food. They have also a few Fowls and Hogs.

¶ It was to this River that we were bound, to seek for Canoas, therefore the 26th supposing our selves to be abrest of it, we went from our Ships with 4 Canoas. The 27th Day in the Morning we entered at half Flood into the smaller Branch of that River, and rowed up six Leagues before we met any Inhabitants. There we found two small Huts thatched with *Palmeto*-Leaves. The *Indians* seeing us rowing towards their Houses, got their Wives and little ones, with their Houshold-stuff, into their Canoas, and padled away faster than we could row; for we were forced to keep in the middle of the River because of our Oars, but they with their Paddles kept close under the Banks, and so had not the strength of the Stream against them, as we had. These Huts were close by the River on the East-side of it, just against the end of the Island. We saw a great many other Houses a League from us on the other side of the River; but the main Stream into which we were now come, seemed to be so swift, that we were afraid to put over, for fear we should not be able to get back again. We found only a Hog, some Fowls and Plantains in the Huts: We killed the Hog and the Fowls, which were drest presently. Their Hogs they got (as I suppose) from the *Spaniards* by some Accident, or from some Neighbouring *Indians* who converse with the *Spaniards*; for this that we took was of their *European* kind, which the *Spaniards* have introduced into *America* very plentifully, especially into the Islands *Jamaica*, *Hispaniola*, and *Cuba* above all, being very largely stored with them; where they feed in the Woods in the Day-time, and at Night come in at the sounding of a *Conch-shell*, and are put up in their Crauls or Pens, and yet some turn wild, which nevertheless are often decoyed in by the other, which being all marked, whenever they see an unmarked Hog in the Pen, they know it is a wild one, and shoot him presently. These *Crauls* I have not seen on the

Continent; where the *Spaniards* keep them tame at home. Among the *Wild Indians*, or in their Woods, are no Hogs, but Pecary and Warree, a sort I have mentioned before.

¶ After we had refreshed our selves, we returned toward the Mouth of the River. It was the Evening when we came from thence, and we got to the River's Mouth the next Morning before Day: Our Ships when we left them were ordered to go to *Gallo*, where they were to stay for us. *Gallo* is a small uninhabited Island lying in between two and three Degrees North Lat. It lieth in a wide Bay about three Leagues from the Mouth of the River *Tomaco*; and four Leagues and half from a small *Indian* Village called *Tomaco*: The Island *Gallo* is of an indifferent heighth; it is cloathed with very good Timber Trees, and is therefore often visited with Barks from *Guiaquil* and other Places: for most of the Timber carried from *Guiaquil* to *Lima*, is first fetcht from *Gallo*. There is a Spring of good Water at the N.E. end: at that Place there is a fine small sandy Bay, where there is good landing. The Road for Ships is against this Bay, where there is good secure riding in six or seven Fathom Water; and here Ships may careen. It is but shoal Water all about this Island; yet there is a Channel to come in at, where there is no less than four Fathom Water: You must go in with the Tide of Flood, and come out with Ebb, sounding all the way.

¶ *Tomaco* is a large River that takes its Name from an *Indian* Village so called: It is reported to spring from the rich Mountains about *Quito*. It is thick inhabited with *Indians*; and there are some *Spaniards* that live there, who Traffick with the *Indians* for Gold. It is shoal at the Mouth of the River, yet Barks may enter.

¶ This Village *Tomaco* is but small, and is seated not far from the Mouth of the River. It is a Place to entertain the *Spanish* Merchants that come to *Gallo* to load Timber, or to traffick with the *Indians* for Gold. At this place one *Doleman*, with seven or eight Men more, once of Capt. *Sharp's* Crew, were kill'd in the Year 1680. From the Branch of the River St. *Jago*, where we now lay, to *Tomaco*, is about five Leagues; the Land low, and full of Creeks, so that Canoas may pass within Land through those Creeks, and from thence into *Tomaco* River.

¶ The 28th Day we left the River of St. *Jago*, crossing some Creeks in our way with our Canoas; and came to an *Indian* House, where we took the Man and all his Family. We staid here till the Afternoon, and then rowed towards *Tomaco*, with the Man of this House for our Guide. We arrived at *Tomaco* about 12 a Clock at Night. Here we took all the Inhabitants of the Village, and a *Spanish* Knight, call'd Don *Diego de Pinas*. This Knight came in a Ship from *Lima* to lade Timber. The Ship was riding in a Creek about a Mile off, and there were only one *Spaniard* and 8 *Indians* aboard. We went in a Canoa with 7 Men, and took her; she had no Goods, but 12 or 13 Jars of good Wine, which we took out, and the next Day let the Ship go. Here an *Indian* Canoa came aboard with three Men in her. These Men could not speak *Spanish*, neither could they distinguish us from *Spaniards*; the wild *Indians* usually thinking all white Men to be *Spaniards*. We gave them 3 or 4 Callabashes of Wine, which they freely drank. They were streight-bodied, and well-limb'd Men, of a mean heighth; their Hair black, long-visag'd, small Noses and Eyes; and were thin-fac'd, ill-look'd Men, of a very dark Copper-colour. A little before Night Captain *Swan* and all of us returned to *Tomaco*, and left the Vessel to the Seamen. The 31st Day two of our Canoas, who had been up the River of *Tomaco*, returned back again to the Village. They had rowed seven or eight Leagues up, and found but one *Spanish* House, which they were told did belong to a Lady who lived at *Lima*; she had Servants here that traded with the *Indians* for Gold; but they seeing our Men coming, ran away: Yet our Men found there several Ounces of Gold in Callabashes.

¶ The first Day of *January* 1685, we went from *Tomaco* towards *Gallo*. We carried the Knight with us and two small Canoas which we took there, and while we were rowing over, one of our Canoas took a Pacquet-Boat that was sent from *Panama* to *Lima*. The *Spaniards* threw the Pacquet of Letters overboard with a Line and a Buoy to it, but our Men seeing it took it up, and brought the Letters, and all the Prisoners aboard our Ships, that were then at an Anchor at *Gallo*. Here we staid till the 6th Day, reading the Letters, by which we understood that the *Armada* from *Old Spain* was come to *Portabel*: And that the President of *Panama* had sent this Pacquet on purpose to hasten the Plate-Fleet thither from *Lima*.

¶ We were very joyful of this News, and therefore sent away the Pacquet-Boat with all her Letters; and we altered our former Resolutions of going to *Lavelia*. We now concluded to career our Ships as speedily as we could, that we might be ready to intercept this Fleet. The properest Place that we could think on for doing it was among the *King's-Islands* or *Pearl-Keys*, because they are near *Panama*, and all Ships bound to *Panama* from the Coast of *Lima* pass by them; so that being there we could not possibly miss the Fleet. According to these Resolutions we sailed the next Morning, in order to execute what we designed. We were two Ships and three Barks in Company, *viz.* Captain *Davis*, Captain *Swan*, a Fire-ship, and two small Barks, as Tenders; one on Capt. *Davis* his Ship, the other on Capt. *Swan*'s. We weigh'd before Day, and got out all but Capt. *Swan*'s

Tender, which never budged; for the Men were all asleep when we went out, and the Tide of Flood coming on before they waked, we were forced to stay for them till the next Day.

¶ The 8th Day in the Morning we descried a Sail to the West of us; the Wind was at South, and we chased her, and before Noon took her. She was a Ship of about 90 Tun laden with Flour; she came from *Truxillo*, and was bound to *Panama*. This Ship came very opportunely to us, for Flour began to grow scarce, and Captain *Davis* his Men grudg'd at what was given to Capt. *Swan*; who, as I said before, had none but what he had from Capt. *Davis*.

¶ We jogged on after this with a gentle Gale towards *Gorgonia*, an Island lying about 25 Leagues from the Island *Gallo*. The 9th Day we anchored at *Gorgonia*, on the West-side of the Island, in 38 Fathom clean Ground, not two Cables length from the shoar. *Gorgonia* is an uninhabited Island, in lat. about three degrees North: It is a pretty high Island, and very remarkable, by reason of two Saddles, or risings and fallings on the top. It is about 2 Leagues long, and a League broad; and it is four Leagues from the Main: At the West-end is another small Island. The Land against the Anchoring-place is low; there is a small sandy Bay and good landing. The Soil or Mould of it is black and deep, in the low Ground, but on the side of the high Land it is a kind of a red Clay. This Island is very well cloathed with large Trees of several sorts, that are flourishing and green all the Year. It's very well watered with small Brooks that issue from the high Land. Here are a great many little black Monkeys, some *Indian* Conies, and a few Snakes, which are all the Land Animals that I know there. It is reported of this Island that it Rains on every Day in the Year more or less; but that I can disprove: However, it is a very wet Coast, and it rains abundantly here all the Year long. There are but few fair Days; for there is little difference in the Seasons of the Year between the wet and dry; only in that Season which should be the dry time, the Rains are less frequent and more moderate than in the wet Season, for then it pours as out of a Sieve. It is deep Water and no anchoring any where about this Island, only at the West-side: The Tide riseth and falleth seven or eight foot up and down. Here are a great many Perewincles and Muscles to be had at low Water. Then the Monkeys come down by the Sea-side and catch them; digging them out of their Shells with their Claws.

¶ Here are Pearl-Oysters in great Plenty: They grow to the loose Rocks, in 4, 5 or 6 Fathom Water by Beards, or little small Roots, as a Muscle: These Oysters are commonly flatter and thinner than other Oysters;

otherwise much alike in shape. The Fish is not sweet nor very wholsome; it is as slimy as a Shell-Snail; they taste very copperish, if eaten raw, and are best boiled. The *Indians* who gather them for the *Spaniards*, hang the Meat of them on strings like Jews-ears, and dry them before they eat them. The Pearl is found at the Head of the Oyster, lying between the Meat and the Shell. Some will have 20 or 30 small Seed-Pearl, some none at all, and some will have one or two pretty large ones. The inside of the Shell is more glorious than the Pearl it self. I did never see any in the *South-Seas* but here. It is reported there are some at the South-end of *Callifornia*. In the *West-Indies*, the *Rancho Reys*, or *Rancheria*, spoken of in Chap. 3, is the Place where they are found most plentifully. 'Tis said there are some at the Island *Margarita*, near St. *Augustin*, a Town in the Gulph of *Florida*, &c. In the *East-Indies*, the Island *Ainam*, near the South-end of *China*, is said to have plenty of these Oysters, more productive of large round Pearl than those in other Places. They are found also in other parts of the *East-Indies*, and on the *Persian* Coast.

¶ At this Island *Gorgona* we rummaged our Prize, and found a few Boxes of Marmalade, and three or four Jars of Brandy, which were equally shared between Capt. *Davis* and Capt. *Swan*, and their Men. Here we fill'd all our Water, and Capt. *Swan* furnished himself with Flour: Afterward we turned ashore a great many Prisoners but kept the chiefest to put them ashore in a better Place.

¶ The 13th Day we sailed from hence towards the *King's-Islands*. We were now six Sail, two Men of War, two Tenders, a Fire-ship and the Prize. We had but little Wind, but what we had was the common Trade at South. The Land we sailed by on the Main, is very low towards the Sea-side, but in the Country there are very high Mountains.

¶ The 16th Day we passed by Cape *Corientes*. This Cape is in lat. 5 d. 10 m. it is high bluff Land, with three or four small Hillocks on the top. It appears at a distance like an Island. Here we found a strong Current running to the North, but whether it be always so, I know not. The Day after we passed by the Cape, we saw a small white Island, which we chaced, supposing it had been a Sail, till coming near we found our Error.

¶ The 21st Day we saw Point *Garachina*. This Point is in lat. 7 d. 20 m. North; it is pretty high Land, rocky, and destitute of Trees; yet within Land it is woody. It is fenced with Rocks against the Sea. Within the Point, by the Sea, at low Water, you may find store of Oysters and Muscles.

¶ The *King's-Islands*, or *Pearl-Keys*, are about twelve Leagues distant from this Point. Between Point *Garachina* and them, there is a small low flat barren Island called *Gallera*, at which Capt. *Harris* was sharing with his Men the Gold he took in his pillaging *Sancta Maria*, which I spoke of a little before, when on a sudden five *Spanish* Barks fitted out on purpose at *Panama*, came upon him; but he fought them so stoutly with one small Bark he had, and some few Canoas, boarding their Admiral particularly, that they were all glad to leave him. By this Island we anchored, and sent our Boats to the *King's-Islands* for a good careening Place.

¶ The *King's-Islands* are a great many low Woody Islands, lying N.W. by N. and S.E. by S. They are about 7 Leagues from the Main, and 14 Leagues in length, and from *Panama* about 12 Leagues. Why they are called the *King's-Islands*, I know not; they are sometimes, and mostly in Maps, called the *Pearl-Islands*. I cannot imagine wherefore they are called so, for I did never see one Pearl Oyster about them, nor any Pearl Oyster-shells; but on the other Oysters I have made many a Meal there: The northermost Island of all this range is called *Pachea*, or *Pacheque*. This is but a small Island distant from *Panama* 11 or 12 Leagues. The Southermost of them is called St. *Pauls*. Besides these two I know no more that are called by any particular Name, tho' there are many that far exceed either of the two in bigness. Some of these Islands are planted with Plantains and Bonano's; and there are Fields of Rice on others of them. The Gentlemen of *Panama*, to whom they belong, keep Negroes there to plant, weed, and husband the Plantations. Many of them, especially the largest, are wholly untill'd, yet very good fat Land, full of large Trees. These unplanted Islands shelter many Runaway-Negroes, who abscond in the Woods all Day, and in the Night boldly pillage the Plantain-Walks. Betwixt these Islands and the Main is a Channel of 7 or 8 Leagues wide; there is good depth of Water, and good anchoring all the way. The Islands border thick on each other; yet they make many small narrow deep Channels, fit only for Boats to pass between most of them. At the S.E. end, about a League from St. *Paul's* [sic] Island, there is a good Place for Ships to careen, or hale ashore. It is surrounded with the Land, and hath a good deep Channel on the North-side to go in at. The Tide riseth here about ten Foot perpendicular.

¶ We brought our Ships into this Place the 25th Day, but were forced to tarry for a Spring-Tide before we could have Water enough to clean them; therefore we first clean'd our Barks, that they might cruise before *Panama*, while we lay here. The 27th Day our Barks being clean we sent them out with 20 Men in each. The 4th Day after they returned with a Prize laden with Maiz, or *Indian* Corn, Salt-Beef and Fowls. She came

from *Lavelia*, and was bound to *Panama*. *Lavelia* is a Town we once designed to attempt. It is pretty large, and stands on the Bank of a River
on the North-side of the Bay of *Panama*, six or seven Leagues from the Sea.
¶ *Nata* is another such Town, standing in a Plain near another Branch
of the same River. In these Towns, and some others on the same Coast,
they breed Hogs, Fowls, Bulls and Cows, and plant Maiz purposely for
the support of *Panama*, which is supplied with Provision mostly from other
Towns and the neighbouring Islands.

¶ The Beef and Fowl our Men took, came to us in a good time, for we
had eaten but little Flesh since we left the Island *Plata*. The Harbour
where we careen'd was incompassed with three Islands, and our Ships
rode in the middle. That on which we haled our Ships ashore, was a
little Island on the North-side of the Harbour. There was a fine small
sandy Bay, but all the rest of the Island was invironed with Rocks, on
which at low Water we did use to gather Oysters, Clams, Muscles and
Limpits. The Clam is a sort of Oyster which grows so fast to the Rock,
that there is no separating it from thence, therefore we did open it where
it grows, and take out the Meat, which is very large, fat and sweet. Here
are a few common Oysters, such as we have in *England*, of which sort
I have met with none in these Seas but here, at Point *Garachina*, at *Puna*,
and on the *Mexican* Coast, in the lat. of 23 d. North. I have a Manuscript
of Mr. *Teat*, Capt. *Swan*'s chief Mate, which gives an account of Oysters
plentifully found in Port St. *Julian*, on the East-side and somewhat to the
North of the Streights of *Magellan*; but there is no mention made of what
Oysters they are. Here are some Guanoes, but we found no other sort
of Land-Animal. Here are also some Pigeons and Turtle-Doves. The rest
of the Islands that incompass this Harbour had of all these sorts of
Creatures. Our Men therefore did every Day go over in Canoas to them
to fish, fowl or hunt for Guanoes; but having one Man surprized once by
some *Spaniards* lying there in Ambush, and carried off by them to *Panama*,
we were after that more cautious of straggling.

¶ The 14th Day of *February* 1685, we made an end of cleaning our Ship,
fill'd all our Water, and stock'd our selves with Fire-wood. The 15th Day
we went out from among the Islands, and anchored in the Channel
between them and the Main, in 25 Fathom Water, soft oazy Ground. The
Plate-Fleet was not yet arrived; therefore we intended to cruise before
the City of *Panama*, which is from this Place about 25 Leagues. The next
day we sailed towards *Panama*, passing in the Channel between the *King's-
Islands* and the Main. It is very pleasant sailing here, having the Main on
one side, which appears in divers forms. It is beautified with many small

Hills, cloathed with Woods of divers sort of Trees, which are always green and flourishing. There are some few small high Islands within a League of the Main, scattering here and there one: These are partly woody, partly bare; and they as well as the Main, appear very pleasant. The *King's-Islands* are on the other side of this Channel, and make also a lovely Prospect as you sail by them. These, as I have already noted, are low and flat, appearing in several Shapes, according as they are naturally formed by many small Creeks and Branches of the Sea. The 16th day we anchored at *Pacheque*, in 17 Fathom Water, about a League from the Island, and sailed from thence the next Day, with the Wind at N.N.E. directing our course towards *Panama*.

¶ When we came abrest of *Old Panama* we anchored and sent our Canoa ashore with our Prisoner Don *Diego de Pinas*, with a Letter to the Governour, to treat about an Exchange for our Man they had spirited away, as I said; and another Captain *Harris* left in the River of St. *Maria* the Year before, coming over Land. Don *Diego* was desirous to go on this Errand in the Name, and with the Consent of the rest of our *Spanish* Prisoners; but by some accident he was killed before he got ashore, as we heard afterwards.

¶ *Old Panama* was formerly a famous Place, but it was taken by Sir *Henry Morgan* about the Year 1673, and at that time great part of it was burned to Ashes, and it was never re-edified since.

¶ *New Panama* is a very fair City, standing close by the Sea, about four Miles from the Ruines of the Old Town. It gives Name to a large Bay which is famous for a great many navigable Rivers, some whereof are very rich in Gold; it is also very pleasantly sprinkled with Islands, that are not only profitable to their Owners, but very delightful to the Passengers and Seamen that sail by them; some of which I have already described. It is incompassed on the backside with a pleasant Country, which is full of small Hills and Valleys, beautified with many Groves and Spots of Trees, that appear in the Savannahs like so many little Islands. This City is all compassed with a high Stone Wall; the Houses are said to be of Brick. Their Roofs appear higher than the top of the City Wall. It is beautified with a great many fair Churches and Religious Houses, besides the President's House, and other eminent Buildings; which altogether make one of the finest Objects that I did ever see, in *America* especially. There are a great many Guns on her Walls, most of which look toward the Land. They had none at all against the Sea, when I first entered those Seas with Capt. *Sawkins*, Capt. *Coxon*, Capt. *Sharp*, and others; for till then they did not fear any Enemy by Sea: But since that they have planted Guns clear round. This is a flourishing City by reason

it is a thoroughfair for all imported or exported Goods and Treasure, to
and from all Parts of *Peru* and *Chili*; whereof their Store-Houses are never
empty. The Road also is seldom or never without Ships. Besides, once
in three Years, when the *Spanish* Armada comes to *Portobel*, then the Plate-
Fleet also from *Lima* comes hither with the King's Treasure, and abundance of Merchant-Ships full of Goods and Plate; at that time the City is
full of Merchants and Gentlemen; the Seamen are busie in landing the
Treasure and Goods, and the Carriers, or Caravan Masters, imployed in
carrying it over Land on Mules (in vast droves every Day) to *Portobel*,
and bringing back *European* Goods from thence: Tho' the City be then
so full, yet during this heat of Business there is no hiring of an ordinary
Slave under a Piece of Eight a Day; Houses, also Chambers, Beds and
Victuals, are then extraordinary dear.

¶ Now I am on this Subject, I think it will not be amiss to give the
Reader an account of the Progress of the Armada from *Old-Spain*, which
comes thus every three Years into the *Indies*. Its first arrival is at *Carthagena*,
from whence, as I have been told, an Express is immediately sent over
Land to *Lima*, thro' the Southern Continent, and another by Sea to
Portobel, with two Pacquets of Letters, one for the Viceroy of *Lima*, the
other for the Viceroy of *Mexico*. I know not which way that of *Mexico*
goes after its arrival at *Portobel*, whether by Land or Sea: But I believe by
Sea to *La Vera Cruz*. That for *Lima* is sent by Land to *Panama*, and from
thence by Sea to *Lima*.

¶ Upon mention of these Pacquets I shall digress yet a little further, and
acquaint my Reader, that before my first going over into the *South-Seas*
with Captain *Sharp* (and indeed before any Privateers, (at least since
Drake and *Oxengham*) had gone that way which we afterwards went, except
La Sound, a *French* Captain, who by Capt. *Wright*'s Instructions had
ventured as far as *Cheapo* Town with a Body of Men, but was driven back
again,) I being then on Board Capt. *Coxon*, in Company with three or
four more Privateers, about four Leagues to the East of *Portobel*, we took
the Pacquets bound thither from *Carthagena*. We opened a great quantity
of the Merchants Letters, and found the Contents of many of them to be
very surprizing, the Merchants of several Parts of *Old-Spain* thereby
informing their Correspondents of *Panama*, and elsewhere, of a certain
Prophecy that went about *Spain* that Year, the Tenour of which was,
That there would be English *Privateers that Year in the* West-Indies, *who would
make such great Discoveries, as to open a Door into the* South-Seas; which
they supposed was fastest shut: And the Letters were accordingly full of
Cautions to their Friends to be very watchful and careful of their Coasts.

¶ This Door they spake of we all concluded must be the Passage over Land through the Country of the *Indians* of *Darien*, who were a little before this become our Friends, and had lately fallen out with the *Spaniards*, breaking off the Intercourse which for some time they had with them: And upon calling also to Mind the frequent Invitations we had from those *Indians* a little before this time, to pass through their Country, and fall upon the *Spaniards* in the *South-Seas*, we from henceforward began to entertain such Thoughts in earnest, and soon came to a Resolution to make those Attempts which we afterwards did with Capt. *Sharp, Coxon*, &c. So that the taking these Letters gave the first Life to those bold Undertakings: And we took the Advantage of the Fears the *Spaniards* were in from that Prophecy, or probable Conjecture, or whatever it were; for we sealed up most of the Letters again, and sent them ashore to *Portobel*.

¶ The occasion of this our late Friendship with those *Indians* was thus. About 15 Years before this time, Capt. *Wright* being cruising near that Coast, and going in among the *Samballoes* Isles to strike Fish and Turtle, took there a young *Indian* Lad as he was paddling about in a Canoa. He brought him aboard his Ship, and gave him the Name of *John Gret*, cloathing him, and intending to breed him among the *English*. But his *Moskito* Strikers, taking a fancy to the Boy, begg'd him of Capt. *Wright*, and took him with them at their return into their own Country, where they taught him their Art, and he married a Wife among them, and learnt their Language, as he had done some broken *English* while he was with Capt. *Wright*, which he improved among the *Moskitoes*, who corresponding so much with us, do all of them smatter *English* after a sort; but his own Language he had almost forgot. Thus he lived among them for many Years; till about six or eight Months before our taking these Letters, Capt. *Wright* being again among the *Samballoes*, took thence another *Indian* Boy about 10 or 12 Years old, the Son of a Man of some account among those *Indians*; and wanting a Striker, he went away to the *Moskito*'s Country, where he took *John Gret*, who was now very expert at it. *John Gret* was much pleased to see a Lad there of his own Country, and it came into his Mind to persuade Capt. *Wright*, upon this occasion, to endeavour a Friendship with those *Indians*; a thing our Privateers had long coveted, but never durst attempt, having such dreadful Apprehensions of their Numbers and Fierceness: But *John Gret* offered the Captain that he would go ashore and negotiate the Matter; who accordingly sent him in his Canoa till he was near the shoar, which of a sudden was covered with *Indians*, standing ready with their Bows and Arrows. *John Gret*, who had only a Clout about his middle, as the Fashion of the

Indians is, leapt then out of the Boat and swam, the Boat retiring a little way back; and the *Indians* ashore seeing him in that Habit, and hearing him call to them in their own Tongue, (which he had recovered by conversing with the Boy lately taken) suffered him quietly to land, and gathered all about to hear how it was with him. He told them particularly, that he was one of their Countrymen, and how he had been taken many Years ago by the *English*, who had used him very kindly; that they were mistaken in being so much afraid of that Nation, who were not Enemies to them, but to the *Spaniards*: To confirm this, he told them how well the *English* treated another young Lad of theirs, they had lately taken, such a one's Son; for this he had learnt of the Youth, and his Father was one of the Company that was got together on the shoar. He persuaded them therefore to make a League with these friendly People, by whose help they might be able to quell the *Spaniards*; assuring also the Father of the Boy, that if he would but go with him to the Ship, which they saw at anchor at an Island there (it was *Golden-Island*, the Eastermost of the *Samballoes*, a Place where there is good striking for Turtle) he should have his Son restored to him, and they might all expect a very kind Reception. Upon these Assurances 20 or 30 of them went off presently, in two or three Canoas laden with Plantains, Bonanoes, Fowls, &c. And Capt. *Wright* having treated them on board, went ashore with them, and was entertained by them, and Presents were made on each side. Capt. *Wright* gave the Boy to his Father in a very handsome *English* Dress, which he had caused to be made purposely for him; and an Agreement was immediately struck up between the *English* and these *Indians*, who invited the *English* through their Country into the *South-Seas*.

¶ Pursuant to this Agreement, the *English*, when they came upon any such Design, or for Traffick with them, were to give a certain Signal which they pitch't upon, whereby they might be known. But it happened that Mr. *La Sound*, the *French* Captain spoken of a little before, being then one of Capt. *Wright*'s Men, learnt this Signal, and staying ashore at *Petit-Guavres*, upon Capt. *Wright*'s going thither soon after, who had his Commission from thence, he gave the other *French* there such an account of the Agreement before-mentioned, and the easiness of entering the *South-Seas* thereupon, that he got at the Head of about 120 of them, who made that unsuccessful attempt upon *Cheapo*, as I said; making use of the Signal they had learnt for passing the *Indians* Country, who at that time could not distinguish so well between the several Nations of the *Europeans*, as they can since.

¶ From such small Beginnings arose those great stirs that have been since made over the *South-Seas, viz.* from the Letters we took, and from the Friendship contracted with these *Indians* by means of *John Gret.* Yet this Friendship had like to have been stifled in its Infancy; for within a few Months after an *English* trading Sloop came on this Coast from *Jamaica*, and *John Gret*, who by this time had advanced himself as a Grandee among these *Indians*, together with five or six more of that quality, went off to the Sloop in their long Gowns, as the Custom is for such to wear among them. Being received aboard, they expected to find every thing friendly, and *John Gret* talkt to them in *English*; but these *English* Men, having no Knowledge at all of what had happened, endeavoured to make them Slaves (as is commonly done) for upon carrying them to *Jamaica*, they could have sold them for 10 or 12 Pound a piece. But *John Gret*, and the rest, perceiving this, leapt all over board, and were by the others killed every one of them in the Water. The *Indians* on shoar never came to the knowledge of it; if they had, it would have endangered our Correspondence. Several times after, upon our conversing with 'em, they enquired of us what was become of their Country-men: But we told them we knew not, as indeed it was a great while after that we heard this Story; so they concluded the *Spaniards* had met with them, and killed, or taken them.

¶ But to return to the account of the Progress of the Armada which we left at *Carthagena*. After an appointed stay there of about 60 Days, as I take it, it goes thence to *Portobel*, where it lies 30 Days, and no longer. Therefore the Viceroy of *Lima*, on notice of the Armada's arrival at *Carthagena*, immediately sends away the King's Treasure to *Panama*, where it is landed, and lies ready to be sent to *Portobel* upon the first News of the Armada's arrival there. This is the reason partly of their sending Expresses so early to *Lima*, that upon the Armada's first coming to *Portobel*, the Treasure and Goods may lie ready at *Panama*, to be sent away upon the Mules, and it requires some time for the *Lima* Fleet to unlade, because the Ships ride not at *Panama*, but at *Perica*, which are three small Islands 2 Leagues from thence. The King's Treasure is said to amount commonly to about 24000000 of Pieces of Eight: Besides abundance of Merchants Money. All this Treasure is carried on Mules, and there are large Stables at both places to lodge them. Sometimes the Merchants to steal the Custom pack up Money among Goods, and send it to *Venta de Cruzes* on the River *Chagre*; from thence down the River, and afterwards by Sea to *Portobel*; in which Passage I have known a whole Fleet of Periago's and Canoas taken. The Merchants who are not ready to sail by the thirteenth Day after the Armada's arrival, are in danger to be left behind, for the

Ships all weigh the 30th Day precisely, and go to the Harbor's Mouth: Yet sometimes, on great importunity, the Admiral may stay a Week longer; for it is impossible that all the Merchants should get ready, for want of Men. When the Armada departs from *Portobel*, it returns again to *Carthagena*, by which time all the King's Revenue which comes out of the Country is got ready there. Here also meets them again a great Ship called the *Pattache*, one of the *Spanish* Galeons, which before their first arrival at *Carthagena* goes from the rest of the Armada on purpose to gather the Tribute of the Coast, touching at the *Margarita's* and other places in her way thence to *Carthagena*, as *Punta de Guaira Moracaybo*, *Dio de la Hacha*, and *Sancta Martha*; and at all these places takes in Treasure for the King. After the set stay at *Carthagena*, the Armada goes away to the *Havana* in the Isle of *Cuba*, to meet there the Flota, which is a small number of Ships that go to *La Vera Cruz*, and there takes in the Effects of the City and Country of *Mexico*, and what is brought thither in the Ship which comes thither every Year from the *Philippine* Islands; and having joined the rest at the *Havana*, the whole Armada sets sail for *Spain* through the Gulf of *Florida*. The Ships in the *South-Seas* lie a great deal longer at *Panama* before they return to *Lima*. The Merchants and Gentlemen which come from *Lima*, stay as little time as they can at *Portobel*, which is at the best but a sickly Place, and at this time is very full of Men from all parts. But *Panama*, as it is not over-charg'd with Men so unreasonably as the other, tho' very full, so it enjoys a good Air, lying open to the Sea-wind; which riseth commonly about 10 or 11 a Clock in the Morning, and continues till 8 or 9 a Clock at Night: then the Land-wind comes, and blows till 8 or 9 in the Morning.

¶ There are no Woods nor Marshes near *Panama*, but a brave dry Champion Land, not subject to Fogs nor Mists. The wet Season begins in the latter-end of *May*, and continues till *November*. At that time the Sea-breezes are at S.S.W. and the Land-winds at N. At the dry Season the Winds are most betwixt the E.N.E. and the N. Yet off in the Bay they are commonly at South; but of this I shall be more particular in my Chapter of Winds in the *Appendix*. The Rains are not so excessive about *Panama* it self, as on either side of the Bay; yet in the Months of *June*, *July* and *August*, they are severe enough. Gentlemen that come from *Peru* to *Panama*, especially in these Months, cut their Hair close, to preserve them from Fevers; for the place is sickly to them, because they come out of a Country which never hath any Rains or Fogs, but enjoys a constant serenity; but I am apt to believe this City is healthy enough to any other People. Thus much for *Panama*.

¶ The 20th Day we went and anchored within a League of the Islands *Perico* (which are only 3 little barren rocky Islands) in expectation of the President of *Panama*'s Answer to the Letter, I said, we sent him by Don *Diego*, treating about exchange of Prisoners; this being the Day on which he had given us his Parole to return with an Answer. The 21st day we took another Bark laden with Hogs, Fowls, Salt-Beef and Molossoes; she came from *Lavelia*, and was going to *Panama*. In the Afternoon we sent another Letter ashoar by a young *Mastiso* (a mixt brood of *Indians* and *Europeans*) directed to the President, and 3 or 4 Copies of it to be dispersed abroad among the common People. This Letter, which was full of Threats, together with the young Man's managing the Business, wrought so powerfully among the common People, that the City was in an uproar. The President immediately sent a Gentleman aboard, who demanded the Flour-Prize that we took off of *Gallo*, and all the Prisoners, for the Ransom of our two Men: but our Captains told him they would exchange Man for Man. The Gentleman said he had not Orders for that, but if we would stay till the next Day he would bring the Governour's Answer. The next Day he brought aboard our two Men, and had about 40 Prisoners in exchange.

¶ The 24th Day we ran over to the Island *Tabago*. *Tabago* is in the Bay, and about six Leagues South of *Panama*. It is about 3 Mile long, and 2 broad, a high mountainous Island. On the North-side it declines with a gentle descent to the Sea. The Land by the Sea is of a black Mold and deep; but towards the top of the Mountain it is strong and dry. The North-side of this Island makes a very pleasant shew, it seems to be a Garden of Fruit inclosed with many high Trees; the chiefest Fruits are Plantains and Bonano's. They thrive very well from the foot to the middle of it; but those near the top are but small, as wanting Moisture. Close by the Sea there are many Coco-Nut Trees, which make a very pleasant sight. Within the Coco-Nut-Trees there grow many *Mammet*-Trees. The *Mammet* is a large, tall, and straight-bodied Tree, clean, without knots or limbs, for 60 or 70 Foot, or more. The Head spreads abroad into many small Limbs, which grow pretty thick, and close together. The Bark is of a dark grey colour, thick and rough, full of large chops. The Fruit is bigger than a Quince; it is round, and covered with a thick Rind, of a grey colour: When the Fruit is ripe the Rind is yellow and tough; and it will then peel off like Leather; but before it is ripe it is brittle: the juice is then white and clammy; but when ripe not so. The ripe Fruit under the Rind is yellow as a Carrot, and in the middle are two large rough Stones, flat, and each of them much bigger than an

Almond. The Fruit smells very well, and the taste is answerable to the smell. The S.W. end of the Island hath never been cleared, but is full of Fire-wood, and Trees of divers sorts. There is a very fine small Brook of fresh Water, that springs out of the side of the Mountain, and gliding through the Grove of Fruit-trees, falls into the Sea on the North-side. There was a small Town standing by the Sea, with a Church at one end, but now the biggest part of it is destroyed by the Privateers. There is good anchoring right against the Town, about a Mile from the shoar, where you may have 16 or 18 Fathom Water, soft oazy Ground. There is a small Island close by the N.W. end of this called *Tabogilla*, with a small Channel to pass between. There is another woody Island about a Mile on the N.E. side of *Tabago*, and a good Channel between them: This Island hath no Name that ever I heard.

¶ While we lay at *Tabago*, we had like to have had a scurvy trick plaid us by a pretended Merchant from *Panama*, who came, as by stealth, to traffick with us privately; a thing common enough with the *Spanish* Merchants, both in the *North* and *South-Seas*, notwithstanding the severe Prohibition of the Governours; who yet sometimes connive at it, and will even trade with the Privateers themselves. Our Merchant was by agreement to bring out his Bark laden with Goods in the Night, and we to go and anchor at the South of *Perico*. Out he came, with a Fireship instead of a Bark, and approached very near, haling us with the Watch-word we had agreed upon. We suspecting the worst, call'd to them to come to an anchor, and upon their not doing so fired at them; when immediately their Men going out into the Canoas, set fire to their Ship, which blew up, and burnt close by us; so that we were forc'd to cut our Cables in all haste, and scamper away as well as we could.

¶ The *Spaniard* was not altogether so politick in appointing to meet us at *Perico*, for there we had Sea-room; whereas had he come thus upon us at *Tabago*, the Land-wind bearing hard upon us as it did, we must either have been burnt by the Fireship, or upon loosing our Cables have been driven ashore: But I suppose they chose *Perico*, rather for the Scene of their Enterprize, partly because they might there best sculk among the Islands, and partly because, if their Exploit fail'd, they could thence escape best from our Canoas to *Panama*, but two Leagues off.

¶ During this Exploit, Capt. *Swan* (whose Ship was less than ours, and so not so much aim'd at by the *Spaniards*) lay about a Mile off, with a Canoa at the Buoy of his Anchor, as fearing some Treachery from our pretended Merchant; and a little before the Bark blew up, he saw a small Float on the Water, and as it appeared, a Man on it, making towards his Ship; but the Man dived, and disappeared of a sudden, as thinking probably that he was discovered.

¶ This was supposed to be one coming with some combustible Matter to have stuck about the Rudder. For such a trick Capt. *Sharp* was served at *Coquimbo*, and his Ship had like to have been burnt by it, if, by meer Accident, it had not been discovered: I was then aboard Capt. *Sharp*'s Ship. Capt. *Swan* seeing the Blaze by us, cut his Cables as we did, his Bark did the like; so we kept under Sail all the Night, being more scared than hurt. The Bark that was on fire drove burning towards *Tabago*; but after the first blast she did not burn clear, only made a smother, for she was not well made, though Capt. *Bond* had the framing and management of it.

¶ This Capt. *Bond* was he of whom I made mention in my 4th Chapter. He, after his being at the Isles of Cape *Verd*, stood away for the *South-Seas*, at the Instigation of one *Richard Morton*, who had been with Capt. *Sharp* in the *South-Seas*. In his way he met with Capt. *Eaton*, and they two consorted a Day or two: At last *Morton* went aboard Capt. *Eaton*, and persuaded him to lose Capt. *Bond* in the Night, which Capt. *Eaton* did, *Morton* continuing aboard of Capt. *Eaton*, as finding his better Ship. Capt. *Bond* thus losing both his Consort *Eaton*, and *Morton* his Pilot, and his Ship being but an ordinary Sailer, he despaired of getting into the *South-Seas*; and had plaid such Tricks among the *Caribbee Isles*, as I have been told, that he did not dare to appear at any of the *English* Islands. Therefore he persuaded his Men to go to the *Spaniards*, and they consented to any thing that he should propose: So he presently steered away into the *West-Indies*, and the first Place where we came to an Anchor was at *Portobel*. He presently declared to the Governour, that there were *English* Ships coming into the *South-Seas*, and that if they questioned it, he offered to be kept a Prisoner, till time should discover the Truth of what he said; but they believed him, and sent him away to *Panama*, where he was in great Esteem. This several Prisoners told us.

¶ The *Spaniards* of *Panama* could not have fitted out their Fire-ship without this Capt. *Bond*'s Assistance; for it is strange to say how grosly ignorant the *Spaniards* in the *West-Indies*, but especially in the *South-Seas*, are of Sea-Affairs. They build indeed good Ships, but this is a small Matter: For any Ship of a good bottom will serve for these Seas on the South Coast. They rig their Ships but untowardly, have no Guns, but in 3 or 4 of the King's Ships, and are meanly furnished with Warlike Provisions, and much at a loss for the making any Fireships or other less useful Machines. Nay, they have not the sense to have their Guns run within the sides upon their discharge, but have Platforms without for the Men to stand on to charge them; so that when we come near we can fetch them down with small shot out of our Boats. A main reason of this is, that the Native *Spaniards* are too proud to be Seamen, but use the *Indians* for all those Offices: One *Spaniard*, it may be, going in the Ship to command it, and himself of little more knowledge than those poor ignorant Creatures: nor can they gain much Experience, seldom going far off to Sea, but coasting along the shores.

¶ But to proceed: In the Morning when it was light we came again to anchor close by our Buoys, and strove to get our Anchors again; but our Buoy-Ropes, being rotten, broke. While we were puzzling about our Anchors, we saw a great many Canoas full of Men pass between *Tabago*, and the other Island. This put us into a new Consternation: We lay still some time, till we saw that they came directly towards us, then we weighed and stood towards them: And when we came within hale, we found that they were *English* and *French* Privateers come out of the *North-Seas* through the Isthmus of *Darien*. They were 280 Men, in 28 Canoas; 200 of them *French*, the rest *English*. They were commanded by Captain *Gronet*, and Capt. *Lequie*. We presently came to an Anchor again, and all the Canoas came aboard. These Men told us, that there were 180 *English* Men more, under the command of Capt. *Townley*, in the Country of *Darien*, making Canoas (as these Men had been) to bring them into these Seas. All the *English* Men that came over in this Party were immediately entertained by Captain *Davis* and Captain *Swan* in their own Ships, and the *French* Men were ordered to have our Flour-Prize to carry them, and Captain *Gronet* being the eldest Commander was to command them there; and thus they were all disposed of to their Hearts content. Capt. *Gronet*, to retaliate this kindness, offered Capt. *Davis* and Capt. *Swan*, each of them a new Commission from the Governour of *Petit Guavres*. It hath been usual for many Years past, for the Governour of *P. Guavres* to send blank Commissions to Sea by many of his Captains, with Orders to dispose of them to whom they saw convenient. Those of *Petit Guavres* by this means making themselves the Sanctuary and Asylum of all People of desperate Fortunes; and increasing their own Wealth, and the Strength and Reputation of their Party thereby. Captain *Davis* accepted of one, having before only an old Commission, which fell to him by Inheritance at the decease of Capt. *Cook*; who took it from Captain *Tristian*, together with his Bark, as is before mentioned. But Captain *Swan* refused it, saying, He had an Order from the Duke of *York*, neither to give Offence to the *Spaniards*, nor to receive any affront from them;

and that he had been injur'd by them at *Baldivia*, where they had killed some of his Men, and wounded several more; so that he thought he had a lawful Commission of his own to right himself. I never read any of these *French* Commissions while I was in these Seas, nor did I then know the import of them; but I have learnt since, that the Tenor of them is, to give a Liberty to Fish, Fowl, and Hunt. The occasion of this is, that the Island *Hispaniola*, where the Garrison of *Petit-Guavres* is, belongs partly to the *French*, and partly to the *Spaniards*; and in time of Peace these Commissions are given as a Warrant to those of each side to protect them from the adverse Party: But in effect the *French* do not restrain them to *Hispaniola*, but make them a pretense for a general ravage in any part of *America*, by Sea or Land.

¶ Having thus disposed of our Associates, we intended to sail toward the Gulf of St. *Michael*, to seek Captain *Townley*; who by this time we thought might be entering into these Seas. Accordingly the second Day of *March* 1685, we sailed from hence towards the Gulf of St. *Michael*. This Gulf lies near 30 Leagues from *Panama*, towards the S.E. The way thither from *Panama* is, to pass between the *King's-Islands* and the Main. It is a place where many great Rivers having finished their Courses are swallowed up in the Sea. It is bounded on the S. with Point *Garachina*, which lieth in North lat. 6 d. 40 m. and on the North-side with Cape St. *Lorenzo*. Where by the way, I must correct a gross Error in our common Maps; which giving no Name at all to the South-Cape, which yet is the most considerable, and is the true Point *Garachina*, do give that name to the North-Cape, which is of small remark, only for those whose Business is into the Gulf; and the Name St. *Lorenzo*, which is the true Name of this Northern Point, is by them wholly omitted; the Name of the other Point being substituted into its place. The chief Rivers which run into this Gulf of St. *Michael*, are *Santa Maria*, *Sambo*, and *Congos*. The River *Congos* (which is the River I would have persuaded our Men to have gone up, as their nearest way in our Journey over Land, mentioned Chap 1.) comes directly out of the Country, and swallows up many small Streams that fall into it from both sides; and at last loseth itself on the North-side of the Gulf, a League within Cape St. *Lorenzo*. It is not very wide, but deep, and navigable some Leagues within Land. There are Sands without it; but a Channel for Ships. 'Tis not made use of by the *Spaniards*, because of the neighbourhood of *Santa Maria* River; where they have most Business on account of the Mines.

¶ The River of *Sambo* seems to be a great River, for there is a great Tide at its Mouth; but I can say nothing more of it, having never been in it.

This River falls into the Sea on the South-side of the Gulf, near Point *Garachina*. Between the Mouths of these two Rivers on either side, the Gulf runs in towards the Land somewhat narrower; and makes five or six small Islands, which are cloathed with great Trees, green and flourishing all the Year, and good Channels between the Islands. Beyond which, further in still, the shoar on each side closes so near, with two Points of low Mangrove Land, as to make a narrow or streight, scarce half a Mile wide. This serves as a Mouth or Entrance to the inner-part of the Gulf, which is a deep Bay two or three Leagues over every way, and about the East-end thereof are the Mouths of several Rivers, the chief of which is that of *Santa Maria*. There are many Outlets or Creeks besides this narrow Place I have described, but none navigable besides that. For this reason, the *Spanish* Guard-Ship, mentioned in Chap. 1. chose to lie between these two Points, as the only Passage they could imagine we should attempt; since this is the way that the Privateers have generally taken, as the nearest, between the *North* and *South-Seas*. The River of *Santa Maria* is the largest of all the Rivers of this Gulf: It is navigable eight or nine Leagues up; for so high the Tide flows. Beyond that Place the River is divided into many Branches, which are only fit for Canoas. The Tide rises and falls in this River about 18 foot.

¶ About six Leagues from the River's Mouth, on the South-side of it, the *Spaniards* about 20 Years ago, upon their first Discovery of the Gold Mines here, built the Town *Santa Maria*, of the same Name with the River. This Town was taken by Capt. *Coxon*, Capt. *Harris* and Capt. *Sharp*, at their entrance into these Seas; it being then but newly built. Since that time it is grown considerable; for when Captain *Harris*, the Nephew of the former, took it (as is said in Chap. 6.) he found in it all sorts of Tradesmen, with a great deal of Flour, and Wine, and abundance of Iron Crows and Pickaxes. These were Instruments for the Slaves to work in the Gold Mines; for besides what Gold and Sand they take up together, they often find great Lumps, wedg'd between the Rocks, as if it naturally grew there. I have seen a Lump as big as a Hen's Egg, brought by Captain *Harris* from thence, (who took 120 pound there) and he told me that there were Lumps a great deal bigger: But these they were forc'd to beat in pieces that they might divide them. These Lumps are not so solid, but that they have Crevises and Pores full of Earth and Dust. This Town is not far from the Mines, where the *Spaniards* keep a great many Slaves to work in the dry time of the Year: But in the rainy Season, when the Rivers do overflow, they cannot work so well. Yet the Mines are so nigh the Mountains, that as the Rivers soon rise, so they are soon down again; and presently after the Rain is the best searching for Gold in the Sands; for the violent Rains do wash down the Gold into the Rivers, where much of it settles to the bottom and remains. Then the Native *Indians* who live hereabouts get most; and of them the *Spaniards* buy more Gold than their Slaves get by working. I have been told that they get the value of five Shillings a Day, one with another. The *Spaniards* withdraw most of them with their Slaves, during the wet Season, to *Panama*. At this Town of *St. Maria*, Capt. *Townley* was lying with his Party, making Canoas, when Capt. *Gronet* came into these Seas; for it was then abandoned by the *Spaniards*.

¶ There is another small new Town at the Mouth of the River called the *Scuchaderoes*: It stands on the North-side of the open Place, at the Mouth of the River of St. *Maria*, where there is more Air than at the Mines, or at *Santa Maria* Town, where they are in a manner stifled with heat for want of Air.

¶ All about these Rivers, especially near the Sea, the Land is low, it is deep black Earth, and the Trees it produceth are extraordinary large and high. Thus much concerning the Gulf of St. *Michael*, whither we were bound.

¶ The second Day of *March*, as is said before, we weighed from *Perico*, and the same Night we anchor'd again at *Pacheque*. The third Day we sailed from thence steering towards the Gulf. Capt. *Swan* undertook to fetch off Capt. *Townley* and his Men: therefore he kept near the Main; but the rest of the Ships stood nearer the *Kings-Islands*. Captain *Swan* desired this Office, because he intended to send Letters over-land by the *Indians* to *Jamaica*, which he did; ordering the *Indians* to deliver his Letters to any *English* Vessel in the other Seas. At two a Clock we were again near the Place where we cleaned our Ships. There we saw two Ships coming out, who proved to be Captain *Townley* and his Men. They were coming out of the River in the Night, and took 2 Barks bound for *Panama*: the one was laden with Flour, the other with Wine, Brandy, Sugar, and Oil. The Prisoners that he took declared that the *Lima* Fleet was ready to sail. We went and anchored among the *Kings-Islands*, and the next Day Captain *Swan* returned out of the River of *Santa Maria*, being informed by the *Indians*, that Captain *Townley* was come over to the *Kings-Islands*. At this place Captain *Townley* put out a great deal of his Goods to make room for his Men. He distributed his Wine and Brandy some to every Ship, that it might be drank out, because he wanted the Jars to carry Water in. The *Spaniards* in these Seas carry all their Wine, Brandy and Oyl, in Jars that hold 7 or 8 Gallons. When they lade at *Pisco* (a Place about 40 Leagues to the Southward of *Lima*, and famous for

Wine) they bring nothing else but Jars of Wine, and they stow one Tier at the top of another so artificially, that we could hardly do the like without breaking them: Yet they often carry in this manner 1500 or 2000, or more in a Ship, and seldom break one. The 10th Day we took a small Bark that came from *Guiaquil*: She had nothing in her but Ballast. The 12th Day there came an *Indian* Canoa out of the River of *Santa Maria*, and told us, that there were 300 *English* and *French* Men more coming over Land from the *North-Seas*. The 15th Day we met a Bark, with five or six *English* Men in her, that belonged to Capt. *Knight*, who had been in the *South-Seas* five or six Months, and was now on the *Mexican* Coast. There he had espied this Bark; but not being able to come up with her in his Ship, he detach'd these five or six Men in a Canoa, who took her, but when they had done, could not recover their own Ship again, losing Company with her in the Night, therefore they came into the Bay of *Panama*, intending to go over-land back into the *North-Seas*, but that they luckily met with us: for the Isthmus of *Darien* was now become a common Road for Privateers to pass between the *North* and *South-Seas* at their Pleasure. This Bark of Captain *Knight*'s had in her 40 or 50 Jars of Brandy: she was now commanded by Mr. *Henry More*; but Captain *Swan* intending to promote Captain *Harris*, caused Mr. *More* to be turned out, alledging that it was very likely these Men were run away from their Commander. Mr. *More* willingly resigned her, and went aboard of Captain *Swan*, and became one of his Men.

¶ It was now the latter-end of the dry Season here; and the Water at the *Kings*, or *Pearl-Islands*, of which there was plenty when we first came hither, was now dried away. Therefore we were forced to go to Point *Garachina*, thinking to water our Ships there. Captain *Harris* being now Commander of the new Bark, was sent into the River of *Santa Maria*, to see for those Men that the *Indians* told us of, whilst the rest of the Ships sailed towards Point *Garachina*; where we arrived the 21st Day, and anchored two Mile from the Point, and found a strong Tide running out of the River *Sambo*. The next Day we ran within the Point, and anchored in four Fathom at low Water. The Tide riseth here eight or nine Foot: The Flood sets N.N.E. the Ebb S.S.W. The *Indians* that inhabit in the River *Sambo* came to us in Canoas, and brought Plantains and Bonanoes. They could not speak nor understand *Spanish*; therefore I believe they have no Commerce with the *Spaniards*. We found no fresh Water here neither; so we went from hence to *Port-Pinas*, which is seven Leagues S. by W. from hence.

¶ *Porto-Pinas* lieth in lat. 7 d. North. It is so called, because there are many Pine-trees growing there. The Land is pretty high, rising gently as it runs into the Country. This Country near the Sea is all covered with pretty high Woods: The Land that bounds the Harbour is low in the middle, but high and rocky on both sides. At the Mouth of the Harbour there are two small high Islands, or rather barren Rocks. The *Spaniards* in their Pilot-Books commend this for a good Harbour; but it lieth all open to the S.W. Winds, which frequently blow here in the wet Season: Beside, the Harbour within the Islands is a Place of but small extent, and hath a very narrow going in; what depth of Water there is in the Harbour I know not.

¶ The 25th Day we arrived at this Harbour of Pines, but did not go in with our Ship, finding it but an ordinary Place to lie at. We sent in our Boats to search it, and they found a Stream of good Water running into the Sea; but there were such great swelling Surges came into the Harbour, that we could not conveniently fill our Water there. The 26th Day we returned to Point *Garachina* again. In our way we took a small Vessel laden with Cacao: She came from *Guiaquil*. The 29th Day we arrived at Point *Garachina*: There we found Captain *Harris*, who had been in the River of *Santa Maria*; but he did not meet the Men that he went for: Yet he was informed again by the *Indians*, that they were making Canoas in one of the Branches of the River of *Santa Maria*. Here we shared our Cacao lately taken.

¶ Because we could not fill our Water here, we designed to go to *Tabago* again, where we were sure to be supplied. Accordingly on the 30th Day we set sail, being now nine Ships in Company; and had a small Wind at S.S.E. The first Day of *April*, being in the Channel between the *King's-Islands* and the Main, we had much Thunder, Lightning, and some Rain: This Evening we anchored at the Island *Pacheque*, and immediately sent four Canoas before us to the Island *Tabago*, to take some Prisoners for Information, and we followed the next Day. The 3d Day in the Evening we anchored by *Perica*, and the next Morning went to *Tabago*: where we found our four Canoas. They arrived there in the Night, and took a Canoa that came (as is usual) from *Panama* for Plantains. There were in the Canoa four *Indians* and a *Mulatta*. The *Mulatta*, because he said he was in the Fire-ship that came to burn us in the Night, was immediately hanged. These Prisoners confirmed, that one Capt. *Bond* an *English* Man, did command her.

¶ Here we filled our Water, and cut Firewood; and from hence we sent four Canoas over to the Main, with one of the *Indians* lately taken to guide them to a Sugar-work: For now we had Cacao, we wanted Sugar to make Chocolate. But the chiefest of their Business was to get Coppers, for each Ship having now so many Men, our Pots would not boil Victuals fast enough though we kept them boiling all the Day. About two or three Days after they returned aboard with three Coppers.

¶ While we lay here Capt. *Davis* his Bark went to the Island *Otoque*. This is another inhabited Island in the Bay of *Panama*; not so big as *Tabago*, yet there are good Plantain-walks on it, and some Negroes to look after them. These Negroes rear Fowls and Hogs for their Masters, who live at *Panama*; as at the *Kings-Islands*. It was for some Fowls or Hogs that our Men went thither; but by accident they met also with an Express that was sent to *Panama* with an account, that the *Lima* Fleet was at Sea. Most of the Letters were thrown overboard and lost; yet we found some that said positively, that the Fleet was coming with all the strength that they could make in the Kingdom of *Peru*; yet were ordered not to fight us, except they were forced to it: (though afterwards they chose to fight us, having first landed their Treasure at *Lavelia*) and that the Pilots of *Lima* had been in Consultation what course to steer to miss us.

¶ For the Satisfaction of those who may be curious to know, I have here inserted the Resolutions taken by the Committee of Pilots, as one of our Company translated them out of the *Spanish* of two of the Letters we took. The first Letter as follows.

Sir,

 Having been with his Excellency, and heard the Letter of Captain *Michael Sanches de Tena* read; wherein he says, there should be a meeting of the Pilots of *Panama* in the said City, they say 'tis not time, putting for objection the *Gallapagoes*: To which I answered, That it was fear of the Enemy, and that they might well go that way, I told this to his Excellency, who was pleased to command me to write this Course, which is as follows.

 The day for sailing being come, go forth to the West South West; from that to the West till you are forty Leagues off at Sea; then keep at the same distance to the N.W. till you come under the Line: from whence the Pilot must shape his Course for *Moro de Porco*, and for the Coast of *Lavelia* and *Natta*: where you may speak with the People, and according to the Information they give, you may keep the same Course for *Otoque*, from thence to *Tabago*, and so to *Panama*: This is what offers as to the Course.

¶ The Letter is obscure: But the Reader must make what he can of it. The Directions in the other Letter were to this Effect.

 The surest Course to be observed going forth from *Malabrigo*, is thus: You must sail W. by S. that you may avoid the sight of the Islands of *Lobos*; and if you should chance to see them, by reason of the Breezes, and should fall to Leward of the Lat. of *Malabrigo*, keep on a Wind as near as you can, and if necessary, go about, and stand in for the shoar; then tack and stand off, and be sure keep your Latitude; and when you are 40 Leagues to the Westward of the Island *Lobos*, keep that distance, till you come under the Line; and then, if the general Wind follow you farther, you must sail N.N.E. till you come into 3 degrees North. And if in this Lat. you should find the Breezes, make it your Business to keep the Coast, and so sail for *Panama*. If in your course you should come in sight of the Land before you are a-brest of Cape St. *Francisco*, be sure to stretch off again out of sight of Land, that you may not be discovered by the Enemy.

¶ The last Letter supposes the Fleet's setting out from *Malabrigo*, in about 8 deg. South Lat. (as the other doth its going immediately from *Lima*, 4 deg. further South) and from hence is that Caution given of avoiding *Lobos*, as near *Malabrigo*, in their usual way to *Panama*, and hardly to be kept out of sight, as the Winds are thereabouts; yet to be avoided by the *Spanish* Fleet at this time, because as they had twice before heard of the Privateers lying at *Lobos de la Mar*, they knew not but at that time we might be there in Expectation of them.

¶ The 10th Day we sailed from *Tabago* towards the *King's Islands* again, because our Pilots told us, that the King's Ships did always come this way. The 11th Day we anchored at the Place where we careen'd. Here we found Capt. *Harris*, who had gone a second time into the River of *Santa Maria*, and fetched the Body of Men that last came over Land, as the *Indians* had informed us: but they fell short of the Number they told us of. The 29th Day we sent 250 Men in 15 Canoas to the River *Cheapo*, to take the Town of *Cheapo*. The 21st Day all our Ships, but Captain *Harris*, who staid to clean his Ships, followed after. The 22d Day we arrived at the Island *Chepelio*.

¶ *Chepelio* is the pleasantest Island in the Bay of *Panama*: It is but seven Leagues from the City of *Panama*, and a League from the Main. This Island is about a Mile long, and almost so broad; it is low on the North-side, and riseth by a small ascent towards the South-side. The Soil is yellow, a kind of Clay. The high side is stony; the low Land is planted with all sorts of delicate Fruits, *viz.* Sapadilloes, Avogato-pears, Mammees, Mammee-Sappota's, Star-apples, &c. The midst of the Island is planted with Plantain-Trees, which are not very large, but the Fruit extraordinary sweet.

¶ The Sapadillo-Tree is as big as a large Pear-tree, the Fruit much like a Bergamot-pear, both in colour, shape and size; but on some Trees the Fruit is a little longer. When it is green or first gathered, the Juice is white and clammy, and it will stick like glew; then the Fruit is hard, but after it hath been gathered two or three Days, it grows soft and juicy, and then the juice is clear as Spring-Water, and very sweet; in the midst of the Fruit are two or three black Stones or Seeds, about the bigness of a Pumpkin-seed: This is an excellent Fruit.

¶ The *Avogato* Pear-tree is as big as most Pear-trees, and is commonly pretty high; the skin or bark black, and pretty smooth; the leaves large, of an oval shape, and the Fruit as big as a large Lemon. It is of a green colour, till it is ripe, and then it is a little yellowish. They are seldom fit to eat till they have been gathered two or three Days; then they become soft, and the Skin or Rind will peel off. The Substance in the inside is green, or a little yellowish, and as soft as Butter. Within the Substance there is a Stone as big as a Horse-Plumb. This Fruit hath no taste of it self, and therefore 'tis usually mixt with Sugar and Lime-juice, and beaten together in a Plate; and this is an excellent Dish. The ordinary way is to eat it with a little Salt and a roasted Plantain; and thus a Man that's Hungry, may make a good Meal of it. It is very wholsome eaten any way. It is reported that this Fruit provokes to Lust, and therefore is said to be much esteemed by the *Spaniards*: And I do believe they are much esteemed by them, for I have met with plenty of them in many Places in the *North-Seas*, where the *Spaniards* are settled, as in the Bay of *Campeachy*, on the Coast of *Cartagena*, and the Coast of *Caraccos*; and there are some in *Jamaica*, which were planted by the *Spaniards* when they possessed that Island.

¶ The *Mammee-Sappota* Tree is different from the *Mammee* described at the Island *Tabago* in this Chapter. It is not so big or so tall, neither is the Fruit so big or so round. The Rind of the Fruit is thin and brittle; the inside is a deep red, and it has a rough flat long Stone. This is accounted the principal Fruit of the *West-Indies*. It is very pleasant and wholsome. I have not seen any of these on *Jamaica*; but in many Places in the *West-Indies* among the *Spaniards*. There is another sort of Mammee-tree, which is called the wild Mammee: This bears a Fruit which is of no value, but the Tree is straight, tall, and very tough, and therefore principally used for making Masts.

¶ The Star Apple-tree grows much like the Quince Tree, but much bigger. It is full of leaves, and the leaf is broad of an oval shape, and of a very dark green colour. The Fruit is as big as a large Apple, which is commonly so covered with leaves, that a Man can hardly see it. They say this is a good Fruit; I did never taste any, but have seen both of the Trees and Fruit in many Places on the Main, on the North-side of the Continent, and in *Jamaica*. When the *Spaniards* possess'd that Island, they planted this and other sorts of Fruit, as the Sapadillo, Avogato-Pear, and the like; and of these Fruits there are still in *Jamaica* in those Plantations that were first settled by the *Spaniards*, as at the *Angles*, at 7 *Mile-Walk*, and 16 *Mile-Walk*. There I have seen these Trees which were planted by the *Spaniards*, but I did never see any Improvement made by the *English*, who seem in that little curious. The Road for Ships is on the North-side, where there is good anchoring half a Mile from the shoar. There is a Well close by the Sea on the North-side, and formerly there were three or four Houses close by it, but now they are destroyed. This Island stands right against the Mouth of the River *Cheapo*.

¶ The River *Cheapo* springs out of the Mountains near the North-side of the Country, and it being penn'd up on the South-side by other Mountains, bends its course to the Westward between both, till finding a Passage on the S.W. it makes a kind of a half Circle; and being swell'd to a considerable bigness, it runs with a slow Motion into the Sea, seven Leagues from *Panama*. This River is very deep, and about a Quarter of a Mile broad: but the Mouth of it is choaked up with Sands, so that no Ships can enter, but Barks may. There is a small *Spanish* Town of the same Name, within six Leagues of the Sea: it stands on the left Hand going from the Sea. This is it which I said Capt. *La Sound* attempted. The Land about it is Champion, with many small Hills cloathed with Woods; but the biggest Part of the Country is Savannah. On the South-side of the River it is all Wood-land for many Leagues together. It was to this Town that our 250 Men were sent. The 24th Day they returned out of the River, having taken the Town without any Opposition: but they found nothing in it. By the way going thither they took a Canoa, but most of the Men escaped ashoar upon one of the *King's Islands*: She was sent out well appointed with armed Men to watch our Motion. The 25th Day Capt. *Harris* came to us, having cleaned his Ship. The 26th Day we went again toward *Tabago*; our Fleet now, upon Capt. *Harris* joining us again, consisted of ten Sail. We arrived at *Tabago* the 28th Day: there our Prisoners were examined concerning the Strength of *Panama*; for now we thought our selves strong enough for such an Enterprize, being near 1000 Men. Out of these, on occasion, we could have landed 900: but our Prisoners gave us small Encouragement to it, for they assured us, that all the Strength of the Country was there, and that many Men were come from *Portobel*, besides its own Inhabitants, who of themselves were more in Number than we. These Reasons, together with the Strength of the Place (which hath a high Wall) deterred us from attempting it. While we lay there at *Tabago*, some of our Men burnt the Town on the Island.

¶ The 4th of *May* we sailed hence again bound for the *King's Islands*; and there we continued cruising from one end of these Islands to the other: till on the 22d Day, Capt. *Davis* and Capt. *Gronet* went to *Pacheque*, leaving the rest of the Fleet at Anchor at St *Paul's Island*. From *Pacheque* we sent two Canoas to the Island *Chepelio*, in hopes to get a Prisoner there. The 25th Day our Canoas returned from *Chepelio*, with three Prisoners which they took there: They were Seamen belonging to *Panama*, who said that Provision was so scarce and dear there, that the Poor were almost starved; being hindered by us from those common and daily Supplies of Plantains, which they did formerly enjoy from the Islands; especially from those two of *Chepelio* and *Tabago*: That the President of *Panama* had strictly ordered, that none should adventure to any of the Islands for Plantains: but Necessity had obliged them to trespass against the President's Order. They farther reported, that the Fleet from *Lima* was expected every Day; for it was generally talked that they were come from *Lima*: and that the Report at *Panama* was, that King *Charles* II of *England* was dead, and that the Duke of *York* was crowned King. The 27th Day Captain *Swan* and Captain *Townley* also came to *Pacheque*, where we lay, but Captain *Swan's* Bark was gone in among the *King's Islands* for Plantains. The Island *Pacheque*, as I have before related, is the Northermost of the *King's Islands*. It is a small low Island about a League round. On the South-side of it there are two or three small Islands, neither of them half a Mile round. Between *Pacheque* and these Islands is a small Channel not above six or seven Paces wide, and about a Mile long. Thro' this Capt. *Townley* made a bold Run, being prest hard by the *Spaniards* in the Fight I am going to speak of, though he was ignorant whether there was a sufficient Depth of Water or not. On the East-side of this Channel all our Fleet lay waiting for the *Lima* Fleet, which we were in hopes would come this way.

¶ The 28th Day we had a very wet Morning, for the Rains were come in, as they do usually in *May*, or *June*, sooner or later; so that *May* is here a very uncertain Month. Hitherto, till within a few Days, we had good fair Weather, and the Wind at N.N.E. but now the Weather was altered, and the Wind at S.S.W.

¶ However about eleven a Clock it cleared up, and we saw the *Spanish* Fleet about three Leagues W.N.W. from the Island *Pacheque*, standing close on a Wind to the Eastward; but they could not fetch the Island by a League. We were riding a League S.E. from the Island between it and the Main; only Capt. *Gronet* was about a Mile to the Northward of us near the Island: he weighed so soon as they came in sight, and stood over for the Main; and we lay still, expecting when he would tack and come to us: but he took care to keep himself out of Harm's way.

¶ Captain *Swan* and *Townley* came aboard of Capt. *Davis* to order how to engage the Enemy, who we saw came purposely to fight us, they being in all 14 Sail, besides Periagoes, rowing with 12 and 14 Oars apiece. Six Sail of them were Ships of good force: first the Admiral 48 Guns, 450 Men; the Vice-Admiral 40 Guns, 400 Men; the Rear-Admiral 36 Guns, 360 Men; a Ship of 24 Guns, 300 Men; one of 18 Guns, 250 Men; and one of eight Guns, 200 Men; two great Fireships, six Ships only with small Arms, having 800 Men on board them all; besides 2 or 3 hundred Men in Periagoes. This account of their Strength we had afterwards from Captain *Knight*, who being to the Windward on the Coast of *Peru*, took Prisoners, of whom he had this Information, being what they brought from *Lima*. Besides these Men, they had also some hundreds of *Old Spain* Men that came from *Portobel*, and met them at *Lavelia*, from whence they now came: and their strength of Men from *Lima* was 3000 Men, being all the strength they could make in that Kingdom; and for greater Security, they had first landed their Treasure at *Lavelia*.

¶ Our Fleet consisted of ten Sail: first Captain *Davis* 36 Guns, 156 Men, most *English*; Captain *Swan* 16 Guns, 140 Men, all *English*: These were the only Ships of force that we had; the rest having none but small Arms. Captain *Townley* had 110 Men, all *English*. Captain *Gronet* 308 Men, all *French*. Captain *Harris* 100 Men, most *English*. Captain *Branly* 36 Men, some *English*, some *French*; *Davis* his Tender eight Men; *Swan*'s Tender eight Men; *Townley*'s Bark 80 Men; and a small Bark of 30 Tuns made a Fireship, with a Canoas Crew in her. We had in all 960 Men. But Capt. *Gronet* came not to us till all was over, yet we were not discouraged at it, but resolved to fight them, for being to Windward of the Enemy, we had it at our Choice, whether we would fight or not. It was three a Clock in the Afternoon when we weighed, and being all under sail, we bore down right afore the Wind on our Enemies, who kept close on a Wind to come to us; but Night came on without any thing, beside the exchanging of a few Shot on each side. When it grew dark, the *Spanish* Admiral put out a Light, as a Signal for his Fleet to come to an Anchor. We saw the Light in the Admiral's Top, which continued about half an Hour, and then it was taken down. In a short time after we saw the Light again, and being to Windward we kept under sail, supposing the Light had been in the Admiral's Top; but as it proved this was only a Stratagem of theirs; for this Light was put out the second time at one of their Barks Topmast-head, and then she was sent to Leeward; which deceived us: for we thought still the Light was in the Admiral's Top, and by that means thought our selves to windward of them.

¶ In the Morning therefore, contrary to our expectation, we found they had got the Weather-gage of us, and were coming upon us with full Sail; so we ran for it, and after a running Fight all day, and having taken a turn almost round the Bay of *Panama*, we came to an Anchor again at the Isle of *Pacheque*, in the very same place from whence we set out in the Morning.

¶ Thus ended this day's Work, and with it all that we had been projecting for five or six Months; when instead of making our selves Masters of the *Spanish* Fleet and Treasure, we were glad to escape them; and owed that too, in a great measure, to their want of Courage to pursue their Advantage.

¶ The 30th day in the Morning when we looked out we saw the *Spanish* Fleet all together three Leagues to Leeward of us at an Anchor. It was but little Wind till 10 a Clock, and then sprung up a small Breeze at South, and the *Spanish* Fleet went away to *Panama*. What loss they had, I know not; we lost but one Man: And having held a Consult, we resolved to go to the Keys of *Quibo* or *Cobaya*, to seek Capt. *Harris*, who was forced away from us in the Fight; that being the place appointed for our Rendezvous upon any such accident. As for *Gronet*, he said his Men would not suffer him to joyn us in the Fight: But we were not satisfied with that excuse; so we suffered him to go with us to the Isles of *Quiboa*, and there cashiered our cowardly Companion. Some were for taking from him the Ship which we had given him: But at length he was suffered to keep it with his Men, and we sent them away in it to some other place.

CHAPTER VIII

They set out from Tabago. *Isle of* Chuche. *The Mountain called* Moro de Porcos. *The Coast to the Westward of the Bay of* Panama. *Isles of* Quibo, Quicaro, Rancheria. *The* Palma-Maria-tree. *The Isles* Canales *and* Cantarras. *They build Canoas for a new Expedition; and take* Puebla Nova. *Captain* Knight *joyns them. Canoas how made. The Coast and Winds between* Quibo *and* Nicoya. Volcan Vejo *again. Tornadoes, and the Sea rough.* Ria Lexa *Harbour. The City of* Leon *taken and burnt.* Ria Lexa *Creek; the Town and Commodities; the* Guava-Fruit, *and* Prickle-Pear: *A Ransom paid honourably upon Parole: The Town burnt. Captain* Davis *and others go off for the South Coast. A contagious Sickness at* Ria Lexa. *Terrible Tornadoes. The* Volcan of Guatimala; *the rich Commodities of that Country,* Indico, Otta *or* Anatta, Cochineel, Silvester. *Drift Wood, and Pumice-Stones. The Coast further on the*

ACCORDING to the Resolutions we had taken, we set out *June* the 1st, 1685, passing between Point *Garachina* and the *Kings Islands.* The Wind was at S.S.W. rainy Weather, with Tornadoes of Thunder and Lightning. The 3d day we passed by the Island *Chuche*, the last remainder of the Isles in the Bay of *Panama.* This is a small, low, round, woody Island, uninhabited; lying four Leagues S.S.W. from *Pacheca.*

¶ In our passage to *Quibo*, Captain *Branly* lost his Main-Mast; therefore he and all his Men left his Bark, and came aboard Captain *Davis* his Ship. Captain *Swan* also sprung his Main-top-Mast, and got up another; but while he was doing it, and we were making the best of our way, we lost sight of him, and were now on the North-side of the Bay; for this way all Ships must pass from *Panama*, whether bound towards the Coast of *Mexico* or *Peru.* The 10th day we passed by *Moro de Porcos*, or the *Mountain of Hogs.* Why so called, I know not: it is a high round Hill on the Coast of *Lavelia.*

¶ This side of the Bay of *Panama* runs out Westerly to the Islands of *Quibo*: There are on this Coast many Rivers and Creeks, but none so large as those on the South side of the Bay. It is a Coast that is partly mountainous, partly low Land, and very thick of Woods bordering on the Sea; but a few leagues within Land it consists mostly of Savannahs, which are stock'd with Bulls and Cows. The Rivers on this side are not wholly destitute of Gold, though not so rich as the Rivers on the other side of the Bay. The Coast is but thinly inhabited, for except the Rivers that lead up to the Towns of *Nata* and *Lavelia*, I know of no other Settlement between *Panama* and *Puebla Nova.* The *Spaniards* may travel by Land from *Panama* through all the Kingdom of *Mexico*, as being full of Savannahs; but towards the Coast of *Peru* they cannot pass further than the River *Cheapo*; the Land there being so full of thick Woods, and watered with so many great Rivers, besides less Rivers and Creeks, that the *Indians* themselves, who inhabit there, cannot travel far without much trouble.

¶ We met with very wet weather in our Voyage to *Quibo*; and with S.S.W. and sometimes S.W. Winds, which retarded our course. It was the 15th day of *June* when we arrived at *Quibo*, and found there Captain *Harris*, whom we sought. The Island *Quibo* or *Cabaya*, is in lat. 7. d. 14. m

North of the Equator. It is about six or seven Leagues long, and three or four broad. The Land is low, except only near the N.E. end. It is all over plentifully stored with great tall flourishing Trees of many sorts; and there is good Water on the East and North-East sides of the Island. Here are some Deer, and plenty of pretty large black Monkies, whose Flesh is sweet and wholsome: besides a few Guanoes, and some Snakes. I know no other sort of Land-Animal on the Island. There is a shole runs out from the S.E. point of the Island, half a Mile into the Sea; and a League to the North of this shole point, on the East-side, there is a Rock about a Mile from the shoar, which at the last quarter ebb appears above Water. Besides these two places, there is no danger on this side, but Ships may run within a quarter of a Mile of the shoar, and Anchor in 6, 8, 10, or 12 fathom, good clean Sand and Oaze.

¶ There are many other Islands, lying some on the S.W. side, others on the N. and N.E. sides of this Island; as the Island *Quicaro*, which is a pretty large Island S.W. of *Quibo*, and on the North of it is a small Island called the *Rancheria*; on which Island are plenty of *Palma-Maria* Trees. The *Palma-Maria* is a tall straight-bodied Tree, with a small Head, but very unlike the Palm-tree, notwithstanding the Name. It is greatly esteemed for making Masts, being very tough, as well as of a good length; for the grain of the Wood runs not straight along it, but twisting gradually about it. These Trees grow in many places of the *West-Indies*, and are frequently used both by the *English* and *Spaniards* there for that use. The Islands *Canales* and *Cantarras*, are small Islands lying on the N.E. of *Rancheria*. These have all Channels to pass between, and good Anchoring about them; and they are as well stored with Trees and Water as *Quibo*. Sailing without them all, they appear to be part of the Main. The Island *Quibo* is the largest and most noted; for although the rest have Names, yet they are seldom used only for distinction sake: these, and the rest of this knot, passing all under the common name of the *Keys* of *Quibo*. Captain *Swan* gave to several of these Islands, the Names of those *English* Merchants and Gentlemen who were Owners of his Ship.

¶ *June* 16th Captain *Swan* came to an Anchor by us: and then our Captains consulted about new methods to advance their Fortunes: and because they were now out of hopes to get any thing at Sea, they resolved to try what the Land would afford. They demanded of our Pilots, what Towns on the Coast of *Mexico* they could carry us to. The City of *Leon* being the chiefest in the Country (any thing near us) though a pretty way within Land, was pitch'd on. But now we wanted Canoas to Land our Men, and we had no other way but to cut down Trees, and make as many as we had occasion for, these Islands affording plenty of large Trees fit for our purpose. While this was doing, we sent 150 Men to take *Puebla Nova* (a Town upon the Main near the innermost of these Islands) to get Provision: It was in going to take this Town that Captain *Sawkins* was killed in the Year 1680, who was succeeded by *Sharp*. Our Men took the Town with much ease, although there was more strength of Men han when Captain *Sawkins* was kill'd. They returned again the 24th day, but got no Provision there. They took an empty Bark in their way, and brought her to us.

¶ The 5th day of *July* Captain *Knight*, mentioned in my last Chapter, came to us. He had been cruising a great way to the Westward, but got nothing beside a good Ship. At last, he went to the Southward, as high as the Bay of *Guiaquil*, where he took a Bark-log, or pair of Bark-logs as we call it, laden chiefly with Flour. She had other Goods, as Wine, Oyl, Brandy, Sugar, Soap, and Leather of Goats-skins: and he took out as much of each as he had occasion for, and then turned her away again. The Master of the Float told him, that the King's Ships were gone from *Lima* towards *Panama*: that they carried but half the King's Treasure with them, for fear of us, although they had all the strength that the Kingdom could afford: that all the Merchant-Ships which should have gone with them were laden and lying at *Payta*, where they were to wait for further Orders. Captain *Knight* having but few Men, did not dare to go to *Payta*, where, if he had been better provided, he might have taken them all; but he made the best of his way into the Bay of *Panama*, in hopes to find us there inriched with the Spoils of the *Lima* Fleet; but coming to the *Kings Islands*, he had advice by a Prisoner, that we had engaged with their Fleet, but were worsted, and since that made our way to the Westward; and therefore he came hither to seek us. He presently consorted with us, and set his Men to work to make Canoas. Every Ships company made for themselves, but we all helped each other to launch them, for some were made a Mile from the Sea.

¶ The manner of making a Canoa is, after cutting down a large long Tree, and squaring the uppermost side, and then turning it upon the flat side, to shape the opposite side for the bottom. Then again they turn her, and dig the inside; boring also three holes in the bottom, one before, one in the middle, and one abaft, thereby to gage the thickness of the bottom; for otherwise we might cut the bottom thinner than is convenient. We left the bottoms commonly about three Inches thick, and the sides two Inches thick below, and one and an half at the top. One or both of the ends we sharpen to a point.

¶ Capt. *Davis* made two very large Canoas; one was 36 Foot long, and five or six Feet wide; the other 32 Foot long, and near as wide as the other. In a Months time we finished our Business and were ready to sail. Here Capt. *Harris* went to lay his Ship a-ground to clean her, but she being old and rotten fell in pieces: And therefore he and all his Men went aboard of Capt. *Davis* and Capt. *Swan*. While we lay here we struck Turtle every day, for they were now very plentiful: But from *August* to *March* here are not many. The 18th day of *July John Rose*, a *Frenchman*, and 14 Men more, belonging to Capt. *Gronet*, having made a new Canoa, came in her to Capt. *Davis*, and desired to serve under him; and Capt. *Davis* accepted of them, because they had a Canoa of their own.

¶ The 20th day of *July* we sailed from *Quibo*, bending our course for *Ria Lexa*, which is the Port for *Leon*, the City that we now designed to attempt. We were now 640 Men in eight Sail of Ships, commanded by Capt. *Davis*, Capt. *Swan*, Capt. *Townley* and Capt. *Knight*, with a Fireship and three Tenders, which last had not a constant Crew. We past out between the River *Quibo* and the *Rancheria*, leaving *Quibo* and *Quicaro* on our Larboard side, and the *Rancheria*, with the rest of the Islands, and the Main, on our Starboard side. The Wind at first was at South South West: We coasted along shore, passing by the Gulf of *Nicoya*, the Gulf of *Dulce*, and by the Island *Caneo*. All this Coast is low Land overgrown with thick Woods, and there are but few Inhabitants near the shore. As we sailed to the Westward we had variable Winds, sometimes S.W. and at W.S.W. and sometimes at E.N.E. but we had them most commonly at S.W. we had a Tornado or two every Day, and in the Evening or in the Night, we had Land-winds at N.N.E.

¶ The 8th Day of *August*, being in the lat. of 11 d. 20 m. by observation, we saw a high Hill in the Country, towring up like a Sugar-loaf, which bore N.E. by N. We supposed it to be *Volcan Vejo*, by the smoak which ascended from its top; therefore we steered in North, and made it plainer, and then knew it to be that *Volcan*, which is the Sea-mark for the Harbour for *Ria Lexa*; for, as I said before in Chapter the 5th, it is a very remarkable Mountain. When we had brought this Mountain to bear N.E. we got out all our Canoas, and provided to embark into them the next Day.

¶ The 9th Day in the Morning, being about eight Leagues from the shore, we left our Ships under the charge of a few Men, and 520 of us went away in 31 Canoas, rowing towards the Harbour of *Ria Lexa*. We had fair Weather and little Wind till two a Clock in the Afternoon, then we had a Tornado from the shore, with much Thunder, Lightning and Rain, and such a gust of Wind, that we were all like to be foundred. In this extremity we put right afore the Wind, every Canoas Crew making what shift they could to avoid the Threatning Danger. The small Canoas being most light and buoyant, mounted nimbly over the Surges, but the great heavy Canoas lay like Logs in the Sea, ready to be swallowed by every foaming Billow. Some of our Canoas were half full of Water, yet kept two Men constantly heaving it out. The fierceness of the Wind continued about half an hour, and abated by degrees; and as the Wind died away, so the fury of the Sea abated: For in all hot Countries, as I have observed, the Sea is soon raised by the Wind, and as soon down again when the Wind is gone, and therefore it is a Proverb among the Seamen, *Up Wind, up Sea, Down Wind, down Sea*. At seven a Clock in the Evening it was quite calm, and the Sea as smooth as a Mill-pond. Then we tugg'd to get into the shore, but finding we could not do it before Day, we rowed off again to keep our selves out of sight. By that time it was Day, we were five Leagues from the Land, which we thought was far enough off shore. Here we intended to lye till the Evening, but at three a Clock in the Afternoon we had another Tornado, more fierce than that which we had the Day before. This put us in greater peril of our Lives, but did not last so long. As soon as the violence of the Tornado was over, we rowed in for the shore, and entred the Harbour in the Night: The Creek which leads towards *Leon* lieth on the S.E. side of the Harbour. Our Pilot being very well acquainted here, carried us into the Mouth of it, but could carry us no farther till Day, because it is but a small Creek, and there are other Creeks like it. The next Morning as soon as it was light, we rowed into the Creek, which is very narrow; the Land on both sides lying so low, that every Tide it is overflown with the Sea. This sort of Land produceth red Mangrove-Trees, which are here so plentiful and thick, that there is no passing thro' them. Beyond these Mangroves, on the firm Land, close by the side of the River, the *Spaniards* have built a Breast-work, purposely to hinder an Enemy from the Landing. When we came in sight of the Breast-work, we rowed as fast as we could to get ashore: The noise of our Oars alarmed the *Indians* who were set to watch, and presently they ran away towards the City of *Leon*, to give notice of our approach. We landed as soon as we could, and marched after them: 470 Men were drawn out to march to the Town, and I was left with 59 Men more to stay and guard the Canoas till their return.

¶ The City of *Leon* is 20 Mile up in the Country: The way to it plain and even, thro' a Champion Country, of long grassy Savannahs, and spots of high Woods. About five Mile from the Landing-place there is a Sugar-work, three Mile farther there is another, and two Mile beyond that, there is a fine River to ford, which is not very deep, besides which, there is no Water in all the way, till you come to an *Indian* Town, which is two Miles before you come to the City, and from thence it is a pleasant straight sandy way to *Leon*. This City stands in a Plain not far from a high pecked Mountain, which oftentimes casts forth fire and smoak from its top. It may be seen at Sea, and it is called the *Volcan* of *Leon*. The Houses of *Leon* are not high built, but strong and large, with Gardens about them. The Walls are Stone, and the Covering of Pan-tile: There are three Churches and a Cathedral, which is the head Church in these parts. Our Countryman Mr. *Gage*, who travelled in these parts, recommends it to the World as the pleasantest place in all *America*, and calls it the Paradice of the *Indies*. Indeed if we consider the Advantage of its Situation, we may find it surpassing most Places for Health and Pleasure in *America*, for the Country about it is of a sandy Soil, which soon drinks up all the Rain that falls, to which these parts are much subject. It is incompassed with Savannahs; so that they have the benefit of the Breezes coming from any quarter; all which makes it a very healthy Place. It is a place of no great Trade, and therefore not rich in Money. Their Wealth lies in their Pastures, and Cattle, and Plantations of Sugar. It is said that they make Cordage here of Hemp, but if they have any such Manufactory, it is at some distance from the Town, for here is no sign of any such thing.

¶ Thither our Men were now marching; they went from the Canoas about eight a Clock. Captain *Townley*, with 80 of the briskest Men, marched before, Captain *Swan* with 100 Men marched next, and Captain *Davis* with 170 Men marched next, and Captain *Knight* brought up the Rear. Captain *Townley*, who was near two Mile a-head of the rest, met about 70 Horsemen four Miles before he came to the City, but they never stood him. About three a Clock Captain *Townley*, only with his 80 Men, entered the Town, and was briskly charg'd in a broad Street, with 170 or 200 *Spanish* Horsemen, but two or three of their Leaders being knock'd down, the rest fled. Their Foot consisted of about 500 Men, which were drawn up in the Parade; for the *Spaniards* in these parts make a large square in every Town, tho' the Town it self be small. The Square is called the Parade: commonly the Church makes one side of it, and the Gentlemens Houses, with their Galleries about them, the other. But the Foot also seeing their Horse retire left an empty City to Captain *Townley*; beginning to save themselves by flight. Captain *Swan* came in about four a Clock, Captain *Davis* with his Men about five, and Captain *Knight* with as many Men as he could incourage to march, came in about six, but he

A PAGE OF DAMPIER'S JOURNAL (SLOANE MSS. 3236)

[*Note.* A comparison of this page with page 155 of the present edition shows that the text and marginal notes were subjected to considerable revision before publication of the book.]

left many Men tired on the Road; these, as is usual, came dropping in one or two at a time, as they were able. The next Morning the *Spaniards* kill'd one of our tired Men; he was a stout old Grey-headed Man, aged about 84, who had served under *Oliver* in the time of the *Irish* Rebellion; after which he was at *Jamaica*, and had followed Privateering ever since. He would not accept of the offer our Men made him to tarry ashoar, but said he would venture as far as the best of them: and when surrounded by the *Spaniards*, he refused to take Quarter, but discharged his Gun amongst them, keeping a Pistol still charged, so they shot him dead at a distance. His name was *Swan*; he was a very merry hearty old Man, and always used to declare he would never take Quarter: But they took Mr. *Smith* who was tired also; he was a Merchant belonging to Captain *Swan*, and being carried before the Governour of *Leon*, was known by a *Mulatta* Woman that waited on him. Mr. *Smith* had lived many years in the *Canaries*, and could speak and write very good *Spanish*, and it was there this *Mulatta* Woman remembred him. He being examined how many Men we were, said 1000 at the City, and 500 at the Canoas, which made well for us at the Canoas, who straggling about every day, might easily have been destroyed. But this so daunted the Governour, that he did never offer to molest our Men, although he had with him above 1000 Men, as Mr. *Smith* guessed. He sent in a Flag of Truce about Noon, pretending to Ransom the Town, rather than let it be burnt, but our Captains demanded 300000 Pieces of Eight for its Ransom, and as much Provision as would victual 1000 Men four Months, and Mr. *Smith* to be Ransomed for some of their Prisoners; but the *Spaniards* did not intend to Ransom the Town, but only capitulated day after day to prolong time, till they had got more Men. Our Captains therefore, considering the distance that they were from the Canoas, resolved to be marching down. The 14th day in the Morning, they ordered the City to be set on fire, which was presently done, and then they came away: but they took more time in coming down than in going up. The 15th day in the Morning, the *Spaniards* sent in Mr. *Smith*, and had a Gentlewoman in exchange. Then our Captains sent a Letter to the Governour, to acquaint him, that they intended next to visit *Ria Lexa*, and desired to meet him there: they also released a Gentleman, on his promise of paying 150 Beefs for his Ransom, and to deliver them to us at *Ria Lexa*; and the same day our Men came to their Canoas: where having staid all Night, the next Morning we all entred our Canoas, and came to the Harbour of *Ria Lexa*, and in the Afternoon our Ships came thither to an Anchor.

¶ The Creek that leads to *Ria Lexa*, lyeth from the N.W. part of the

Harbour, and it runs in Northerly. It is about two Leagues from the Island in the Harbours mouth to the Town; two thirds of the way it is broad, then you enter a narrow deep Creek, bordered on both sides with Red Mangrove Trees, whose limbs reach almost from one side to the other. A mile from the mouth of the Creek it turns away West. There the *Spaniards* have made a very strong Breast-work, fronting towards the mouth of the Creek, in which were placed 100 Soldiers to hinder us from landing: and 20 Yards below that Breast-work there was a Chain of great Trees placed cross the Creek, so that 10 Men could have kept off 500 or 1000.

¶ When we came in sight of the Breast-work we fired but two Guns, and they all ran away: and we were afterwards near half an hour cutting the Boom or Chain. Here we landed, and marched to the Town of *Ria Lexa*, or *Rea Lejo*, which is about a Mile from hence. This Town stands on a Plain by a small River. It is a pretty large Town with three Churches, and an Hospital that hath a fine Garden belonging to it: besides many large fair Houses, they all stand at a good distance one from another, with Yards about them. This is a very sickly place, and I believe hath need enough of an Hospital; for it is seated so nigh the Creeks and Swamps, that it is never free from a noisom smell. The Land about it is a strong yellow Clay: yet where the Town stands it seems to be Sand. Here are several sorts of Fruits, as Guavo's, Pine-apples, Melons, and Prickle-Pears. The Pine-apple and Melon are well known.

¶ The Guava Fruit grows on a hard scrubbed Shrub, whose Bark is smooth and whitish, the branches pretty long and small, the leaf somewhat like the leaf of a Hazel, the Fruit much like a Pear, with a thin rind; it is full of small hard Seeds, and it may be eaten while it is green, which is a thing very rare in the *Indies*: for most Fruit, both in the *East* or *West-Indies*, is full of clammy, white, unsavory juice, before it is ripe, though pleasant enough afterwards. When this Fruit is ripe it is yellow, soft, and very pleasant. It bakes as well as a Pear, and it may be codled, and it makes good Pies. There are of divers sorts, different in shape, taste, and colour. The inside of some is yellow, of others red. When this Fruit is eaten green, it is binding, when ripe, it is loosening.

¶ The Prickle-Pear, Bush, or Shrub, of about four or five Foot high, grows in many places of the *West-Indies*, as at *Jamaica*, and most other Islands there; and on the Main in several places. This prickly Shrub delights most in barren sandy grounds; and they thrive best in places that are near the Sea: especially where the Sand is saltish. The Tree, or Shrub, is three or four Foot high, spreading forth several branches; and on each branch two or three leaves. These leaves (if I may call them so) are round, as broad every way as the palm of a Man's hand, and as thick; their substance like Houseleek: these leaves are fenced round with strong prickles above an Inch long. The Fruit grows at the farther edge of the Leaf: it is as big as a large Plumb, growing small near the Leaf, and big towards the top, where it opens like a Medlar. This Fruit at first is green like the Leaf, from whence it springs with small Prickles about it; but when ripe it is of a deep red colour. The inside is full of small black Seeds, mixt with a certain red Pulp, like thick Syrup. It is very pleasant in taste, cooling, and refreshing; but if a Man eats 15 or 20 of them they will colour his Water, making it look like Blood. This I have often experienced, yet found no harm by it.

¶ There are many Sugar-works in the Country, and Estantions or Beef Farms: There is also a great deal of Pitch, Tar and Cordage, made in the Country, which is the chief of their Trade. This Town we approached without any opposition, and found nothing but empty Houses; besides such things as they could not, or would not carry away, which were chiefly about 500 Packs of Flour, brought hither in the great Ship that we left at *Amapalla*, and some Pitch, Tar and Cordage. These things we wanted, and therefore we sent them all aboard. Here we received 150 Beefs, promised by the Gentleman that was released coming from *Leon*; besides, we visited the Beef-Farms every Day, and the Sugar-Works, going in small Companies of 20 or 30 Men, and brought away every Man his Load; for we found no Horses, which if we had, yet the ways were so wet and dirty, that they would not have been serviceable to us. We stayed here from the 17th till the 24th day, and then some of our destructive Crew set fire to the Houses: I know not by whose order, but we marched away and left them burning; at the Breast-work we imbarked into our Canoas and returned aboard our Ships.

¶ The 25th day Capt. *Davis* and Capt. *Swan* broke off Consortship; for Capt. *Davis* was minded to return again on the Coast of *Peru*, but Capt. *Swan* desired to go farther to the Westward. I had till this time been with Capt. *Davis*, but now left him, and went aboard of Captain *Swan*. It was not from any dislike to my old Captain, but to get some knowledge of the Northern Parts of this Continent of *Mexico*: And I knew that Capt. *Swan* determined to coast it as far North, as he thought convenient, and then pass over for the *East-Indies*; which was a way very agreeable to my Inclination. Capt. *Townley*, with his two Barks, was resolved to keep us Company; but Capt. *Knight* and Capt. *Harris* followed Captain *Davis*.

The 27th day in the Morning Capt. *Davis* with his Ships went out of the Harbour, having a fresh Land Wind. They were in Company, Capt. *Davis*'s Ship with Capt. *Harris* in her; Capt. *Davis*'s Bark and Fireship, and Capt. *Knight* in his own Ship, in all four Sail. Capt. *Swan* took his last farewel of him by firing fifteen Guns, and he fired eleven in return of the Civility.

¶ We stayed here some time afterwards to fill our Water and cut Firewood; but our Men, who had been very healthy till now, began to fall down apace in Fevers. Whether it was the badness of the Water, or the unhealthiness of the Town was the cause of it we did not know; but of the two, I rather believe it was a Distemper we got at *Ria Lexa*; for it was reported that they had been visited with a Malignant Fever in that Town, which had occasioned many People to abandon it; and although this Visitation was over with them, yet their Houses and Goods might still retain somewhat of the Infection, and communicate the same to us.

¶ I the rather believe this, because it afterwards raged very much, not only among us, but also among Capt. *Davis* and his Men, as he told me himself since, when I met him in *England*: Himself had like to have died, as did several of his and our Men. The 3d day of *September* we turned ashore all our Prisoners and Pilots, they being unacquainted further to the West, which was the Coast that we designed to visit: for the *Spaniards* have a very little Trade by Sea beyond the River *Lempa*, a little to the North West of this place.

¶ About 10 a clock in the morning, the same day, we went from hence, steering Westward, being in company four Sail, as well as they who left us, *viz.* Captain *Swan* and his Bark, and Captain *Townley* and his Bark, and about 340 Men.

¶ We met with very bad weather as we sailed along this Coast: seldom a day past but we had one or two violent Tornadoes, and with them very frightful Flashes of Lightning and Claps of Thunder; I did never meet with the like before nor since. These Tornadoes commonly came out of the N.E. the Wind did not last long, but blew very fierce for the time. When the Tornadoes were over we had the Wind at W. sometimes at W.S.W. and S.W. and sometimes to the North of the West, as far as the N.W.

¶ We kept at a good distance off shoar, and saw no Land till the 14th day; but then, being in lat. 12 d. 50 m. the Volcan of *Guatimala* appeared in sight. This is a very high Mountain with two peeks or heads appearing like two Sugar-loaves. It often belches forth Flames of Fire and Smoak from between the two heads; and this, as the *Spaniards* do report, happens chiefly in tempestuous weather. It is called so from the City *Guatamala*, which stands near the foot of it, about eight Leagues from the *South-Sea*, and by report, 40 or 50 Leagues from the Gulf of *Matique* in the Bay of *Honduras*, in the North-Seas. This City is famous for many rich Commodities that are produced thereabouts (some almost peculiar to this Country) and yearly sent into *Europe*, especially four rich Dyes, Indico, Otta or Anatta, Silvester, and Cochineel.

¶ Indico is made of an Herb which grows a Foot and half or two Foot high, full of small branches; and the Branches full of Leaves, resembling the Leaves which grow on Flax, but more thick and substantial. They cut this Herb or Shrub and cast it into a large Cistern made in the ground for that purpose, which is half full of Water. The Indico Stalk or Herb remains in the Water till all the Leaves, and I think, the Skin, Rind, or Bark rot off, and in a manner dissolve: but if any of the Leaves should stick fast, they force them off by much labour, tossing and tumbling the Mass in the Water till all the pulpy substance is dissolved. Then the Shrub, or woody part, is taken out, and the Water, which is like Ink, being disturbed no more, settles, and the Indico falls to the bottom of the Cistern like Mud. When it is thus settled, they draw off the Water, and take the Mud and lay it in the Sun to dry: which there becomes hard, as you see it brought home.

¶ Otta, or Anatta, is a red sort of Dye. It is made of a red Flower that grows on Shrubs 7 or 8 Foot high. It is thrown into a Cistern of Water as the Indico is, but with this difference, that there is no stalk, nor so much as the head of the Flower, but only the Flower it self pull'd off from the head, as you peel Rose-leaves from the bud. This remains in the Water till it rots, and by much jumbling it dissolves to a liquid substance, like the Indico; and being settled, and the Water drawn off, the red Mud is made up into Rolls or Cakes, and laid in the Sun to dry. I did never see any made but at a place called the *Angels* in *Jamaica*, at Sir *Thomas Muddiford*'s Plantations, about 20 Years since; but was grubb'd up while I was there, and the Ground otherwise employed. I do believe there is none any where else on *Jamaica*: and even this probably was owing to the *Spaniards*, when they had that Island. Indico is common enough in *Jamaica*. I observed they planted it most in sandy Ground: they sow great Fields of it, and I think they sow it every Year; but I did never see the Seeds it bears. Indico is produced all over the *West-Indies*, on most of the *Caribbee Islands*, as well as the Main; yet no part of the Main yields such great quantities both of Indico and Otta as this Country about *Guatimala*. I believe that Otta is made now only by the *Spaniards*; for since the

destroying that at the *Angels* Plantation in *Jamaica*, I have not heard of
any Improvement made of this Commodity by our Country-men any
where; and as to *Jamaica*, I have since been informed, that 'tis wholly
left off there. I know not what quantities either of Indico or Otta are
made at *Cuba* or *Hispaniola*: but the place most used by our *Jamaica* Sloops
for these things is the Island *Porto Rico*, where our *Jamaica* Traders did
use to buy Indico for three Rials, and Otta for four Rials the Pound,
which is but 2*s*. 3*d*. of our Money: and yet at the same time Otta was
worth in *Jamaica* 5*s*. the Pound, and Indico 3*s*. 6*d*. the Pound; and even
this also paid in Goods; by which means alone they got 50 or 60 *per Cent*.
Our Traders had not then found the way of trading with the *Spaniards*
in the Bay of *Honduras*; but Captain *Coxon* went thither (as I take it) at
the beginning of the Year 1679, under pretence to cut Logwood, and
went into the Gulph of *Matique*, which is in the bottom of that Bay.
There he landed with his Canoas and took a whole Store-house full of
Indico and Otta in Chests, piled up in several parcels, and marked with
different marks ready to be shipt aboard two Ships that then lay in the
road purposely to take it in; but these Ships could not come at him, it
being shole-water. He opened some of the Chests of Indico, and supposing the other Chests to be all of the same Species, ordered his Men to
carry them away. They immediately set to work, and took the nearest at
hand; and having carried out one Heap of Chests, they seized on another
great Pile of a different Mark from the rest, intending to carry them away
next. But a *Spanish* Gentleman, their Prisoner, knowing that there was
a great deal more than they could carry away, desired them to take only
such as belonged to the Merchants, (whose Marks he undertook to shew
them) and to spare such as had the same Mark with those in that great
Pile they were then entring upon; because, he said, those Chests belonged
to the Ship-Captains, who following the Seas, as themselves did, he
hoped they would, for that reason, rather spare their Goods than the
Merchants. They consented to his Request; but upon their opening their
Chests (which was not before they came to *Jamaica*, where by connivance
they were permitted to sell them) they found that the *Don* had been too sharp
for them; the few Chests which they had taken of the same Mark with the
great Pile proving to be Otta, of greater value by far than the other; whereas
they might as well have loaded the whole Ship with Otta, as with Indico.
¶ The *Chochineel* is an Insect, bred in a sort of Fruit much like the
Prickle-Pear. The Tree or Shrub that bears it is like the Prickle-Pear-
Tree, about five Foot high, and so prickly; only the Leaves are not quite
so big, but the Fruit is bigger. On the top of the Fruit there grows a red

Flower: This Flower, when the Fruit is ripe, falls down on the top of the Fruit, which then begins to open, and covers it so, that no Rain nor Dew can wet the inside. The next day, or two days after its falling down, the Flower being then scorched away by the heat of the Sun, the Fruit opens as broad as the mouth of a Pint-Pot, and the inside of the Fruit is by this time full of small red Insects, with curious thin Wings. As they were bred here, so here they would die for want of food, and rot in their husks, (having by this time eaten up their Mother-Fruit) did not the *Indians*, who plant large Fields of these Trees, when once they perceive the Fruit open, take care to drive them out: for they spread under the branches of the Tree a large Linnen Cloth, and then with sticks they shake the branches, and so disturb the poor Insects, that they take wing to be gone, yet hovering still over the head of their native Tree, but the heat of the Sun so disorders them, that they presently fall down dead on the Cloth spread for that purpose, where the *Indians* let them remain two or three days longer, till they are thoroughly dry. When they fly up they are red, when they fall down they are black; and when first they are quite dry they are white as the sheet wherein they lie, though the Colour change a little after. These yield the much esteemed Scarlet. The Cochineel-trees are called by the *Spaniard* Toona's: They are planted in the Country about *Guatimala*, and about *Cheape* and *Guaxaca*, all three in the Kingdom of *Mexico*. The Silvester is a red Grain growing in a Fruit much resembling the Cochineel-fruit; as doth also the Tree that bears it. There first shoots forth a yellow Flower, then comes the Fruit, which is longer than the Cochineel-fruit. The Fruit being ripe opens also very wide. The inside being full of these small Seeds or Grains, they fall out with the least touch or shake. The *Indians* that gather them hold a Dish under to receive the Seed, and then shake it down. These Trees grow wild; and eight or ten of these Fruits will yield an Ounce of Seed: but of the Cochineel-fruits, three or four will yield an Ounce of Insects. The Silvester gives a colour almost as fair as the Cochineel; and so like it as to be often mistaken for it, but it is not near so valuable. I often made enquiry how the Silvester grows, and of the Cochineel; but was never fully satisfied, till I met a *Spanish* Gentleman that had lived 30 Years in the *West-Indies*, and some Years where these grow; and from him I had these relations. He was a very intelligent Person, and pretended to be well acquainted in the Bay of *Campeachy*; therefore I examined him in many particulars concerning that Bay, where I was well acquainted my self, living there three Years. He gave very true and pertinent answers to all my demands, so that I could have no distrust of what he related.

❡ When we first saw the Mountain of *Guatimala*, we were by judgment 25 Leagues distance from it. As we came nearer the Land it appeared higher and plainer, yet we saw no Fire, but a little Smoak proceeding from it. The Land by the Sea was of a good height, yet but low in comparison with that in the Country. The Sea for about eight or ten Leagues from the shoar was full of floating Trees, or Drift-Wood, as it is called, (of which I have seen a great deal, but no where so much as here,) and Pumice-stones floating, which probably are thrown out of the burning Mountains, and washed down to the shoar by the Rains, which are very violent and frequent in this Country; and on the side of *Honduras* it is excessively wet.

❡ The 24th Day we were in lat. 14 d. 30 m. North, and the Weather more settled. Then Captain *Townley* took with him 106 Men in nine Canoas, and went away to the Westward, where he intended to land, and romage in the Country for some refreshment for our sick Men, we having at this time near half our Men sick, and many were dead since we left *Ria Lexa*. We in the Ships lay still with our Topsails furled, and our Corses or lower Sails hal'd up this Day and the next, that Captain *Townley* might get the start of us.

❡ The 26th Day we made sail again, coasting to the Westward, having the Wind at North and fair weather. We ran along by a tract of very high Land, which came from the Eastward, more within Land than we could see; after we fell in with it, it bare us company for about 10 Leagues, and ended with a pretty gentle descent towards the West.

❡ There we had a perfect view of a pleasant low Country, which seemed to be rich in Pasturage for Cattle. It was plentifully furnished with Groves of green Trees, mixt among the grassy Savannahs: Here the Land was fenced from the Sea with high sandy Hills, for the Waves all along this Coast run high, and beat against the shoar very boisterously, making the Land wholly unapproachable in Boats or Canoas: So we coasted still along by this low Land, eight or nine Leagues farther, keeping close to the shoar for fear of missing Capt. *Townley*. We lay by in the Night, and in the Day made an easie sail.

❡ The 2d Day of *October* Captain *Townley* came aboard; he had coasted along shoar in his Canoas, seeking for an entrance, but found none. At last, being out of hopes to find any Bay, Creek, or River, into which he might safely enter; he put ashoar on a sandy Bay, but overset all his Canoas: He had one Man drowned, and several lost their Arms, and some of them that had not waxt up their Cartage or Catouche Boxes, wet all their Powder. Captain *Townley* with much ado got ashoar, and dragged the Canoas up dry on the Bay; then every Man searched his Catouche-box, and drew the wet Powder out of his Gun, and provided to march into the Country, but finding it full of great Creeks which they could not ford, they were forced to return again to their Canoas. In the night they made good Fires to keep themselves warm; the next morning 200 *Spaniards* and *Indians* fell on them, but were immediately repulsed, and made greater speed back than they had done forward. Captain *Townley* followed them, but not far for fear of his Canoas. These Men came from *Teguantapeque*, a Town that Captain *Townley* went chiefly to seek, because the *Spanish* Books make mention of a large River there; but whether it was run away at this time, or rather Captain *Townley* and his Men were short-sighted, I know not; but they could not find it.

❡ Upon his return we presently made sail, coasting still Westward, having the Wind at E.N.E. fair weather and a fresh gale. We kept within two Mile of the shoar, sounding all the way; and found at six Miles distance from Land 19 Fathom; at eight Miles distance 21 Fathom, gross Sand. We saw no opening, nor sign of any place to land at, so we sailed about 20 Leagues farther, and came to a small high Island called *Tangola*, where there is good anchoring. The Island is indifferently well furnished with Wood and Water, and lieth about a League from the shoar. The Main against the Island is pretty high champion Savannah Land by the Sea; but two or three Leagues within Land it is higher, and very woody.

❡ We coasted a League farther and came to *Guatulco*. This Port is in lat. 15 d. 30 m. it is one of the best in all this Kingdom of *Mexico*. Near a Mile from the mouth of the Harbour, on the East-side, there is a little Island close by the shoar; and on the West-side of the mouth of the Harbour there is a great hollow Rock, which by the continual working of the Sea in and out makes a great noise, which may be heard a great way. Every Surge that comes in forceth the Water out of a little hole on its top, as out of a Pipe, from whence it flies out just like the blowing of a Whale; to which the *Spaniards* also liken it. They call this Rock and Spout the *Buffadore*: upon what account I know not. Even in the calmest Seasons the Sea beats in there, making the Water spout at the hole: so that this is always a good Mark to find the Harbour by. The Harbour is about three Mile deep, and one Mile broad; it runs in N.W. But the West-side of the Harbour is best to ride in for small Ships; for there you may ride land-locked: whereas any where else you are open to the S.W. Winds, which often blow here. There is good clean ground any where, and good gradual soundings from 16 to 6 Fathom; it is bounded with a smooth sandy shoar, very good to land at; and at the bottom of the

Harbour there is a fine Brook of fresh Water running into the Sea. Here formerly stood a small *Spanish* Town, or Village, which was taken by Sir *Francis Drake*: but now there is nothing remaining of it, beside a little Chapel standing among the Trees, about 200 paces from the Sea. The Land appears in small short ridges parallel to the shoar, and to each other; the innermost still gradually higher than that nearer the shoar; and they are all cloathed with very high flourishing Trees, that it is extraordinary pleasant and delightful to behold at a distance: I have no where seen any thing like it.

¶ At this place Captain *Swan*, who had been very sick, came ashoar, and all the sick Men with him, and the Surgeon to tend them. Captain *Townley* again took a company of Men with him, and went into the Country to seek for Houses or Inhabitants. He marched away to the Eastward, and came to the River *Capalita*: which is a swift River, yet deep near the mouth, and is about a League from *Guatulco*. There two of his Men swam over the River, and took three *Indians* that were placed there, as Centinels, to watch for our coming. These could none of them speak *Spanish*; yet our Men by Signs made them understand, that they desired to know if there was any Town or Village near; who by the Signs which they made gave our Men to understand, that they could guide them to a Settlement: but there was no understanding by them, whether it was a *Spanish* or *Indian* Settlement, nor how far it was thither. They brought these *Indians* aboard with them, and the next Day, which was the 6th Day of *October*, Captain *Townley* with 140 Men (of whom I was one) went ashoar again, taking one of these *Indians* with us for a Guide to conduct us to this Settlement. Our Men that stay'd aboard fill'd our Water, and cut Wood, and mended our Sails: and our *Moskito* Men struck three or four Turtle every Day. They were a small sort of Turtle, and not very sweet, yet very well esteemed by us all, because we had eaten no Flesh a great while. The 8th Day we returned out of the Country, having been about 14 Miles directly within Land before we came to any Settlement. There we found a small *Indian* Village, and in it a great quantity of Vinello's drying in the Sun.

¶ The Vinello is a little Cod full of small black Seeds; it is four or five Inches long, about the bigness of the stem of a Tobacco Leaf, and when dried much resembling it: so that our Privateers at first have often thrown them away when they took any, wondering why the *Spaniards* should lay up Tobacco stems. This Cod grows on a small Vine, which climbs about and supports it self by the neighbouring Trees: it first bears a yellow Flower, from whence the Cod afterwards proceeds. It is first green, but when ripe it turns yellow; then the *Indians* (whose Manufacture it is, and who sell it cheap to the *Spaniards*) gather it, and lay it in the Sun, which makes it soft; then it changes to a Chestnut-colour. Then they frequently press it between their fingers, which makes it flat. If the *Indians* do any thing to them beside, I know not; but I have seen the *Spaniards* sleek them with Oil.

¶ These Vines grow plentifully at *Bocca-toro*, where I have gathered and tried to cure them, but could not: which makes me think that the *Indians* have some Secret that I know not of to cure them. I have often askt the *Spaniards* how they were cured, but I never could meet with any could tell me. One Mr. *Cree* also, a very curious Person, who spoke *Spanish* well, and had been a Privateer all his Life, and seven Years a Prisoner among the *Spàniards* at *Portobel* and *Cartagena*, yet upon all his enquiry could not find any of them that understood it. Could we have learnt the Art of it, several of us would have gone to *Bocca-toro* Yearly, at the dry season and cured them, and freighted our Vessel. We there might have had Turtle enough for food, and store of Vinello's. Mr. *Cree* first shewed me those at *Bocca-toro*. At, or near a Town also, called *Caihooca*, in the Bay of *Campeachy*, these Cods are found. They are commonly sold for Three pence a Cod among the *Spaniards* in the *West-Indies*, and are sold by the Druggist, for they are much used among Chocolate to perfume it. Some will use them among Tobacco, for it gives a delicate scent. I never heard of any Vinello's but here in this Country, about *Caihooca*, and at *Bocca-toro*.

¶ The *Indians* of this Village could speak but little *Spanish*. They seemed to be a poor innocent People: and by them we understood, that there are very few *Spaniards* in these parts; yet all the *Indians* hereabout are under them. The Land from the Sea to their Houses is black Earth, mixt with some Stones and Rocks; all the way full of very high Trees.

¶ The 10th Day we sent four Canoas to the Westward, who were ordered to lie for us at Port *Angels*; where we were in hopes that by some means or other they might get Prisoners, that might give us a better account of the Country than at present we could have; and we followed them with our Ships, all our Men being now pretty well recovered of the Fever, which had raged amongst us ever since we departed from *Ria Lexa*.

CHAPTER IX

*They set out from Guatulco. The Isle Sacrificio. Port Angels. Jaccals. A narrow Escape.
The Rock Algatross, and the neighbouring Coast. Snooks, a sort of Fish. The Town of Acapulco.
Of the Trade it drives with the Philippine Islands. The Haven of Acapulco. A Tornado.
Port Marquis. Capt. Townley makes a fruitless Attempt. A long sandy Bay, but very rough
Seas. The Palm-tree, great and small. The Hill of Petaplan. A poor Indian Village. Jew-fish.
Chequetan, a good Harbour. Estapa; Muscles there. A Caravan of Mules taken. A Hill near
Thelupan. The Coast hereabouts. The Volcan, Town, Valley, and Bay of Colima. Sallagua
Port. Orrha. Ragged Hills. Coronada, or the Crown-Land. Cape Corrientes. Isles of
Chametly. The City Purification. Valderas; or the Valley of Flags. They miss their design
on this Coast. Captain Townley leaves them with the Darien Indians. The Point and Isles of
Pontique. Other Isles of Chametley. The Penguin-fruit, the yellow and the red. Seals here.
Of the River of Cullacan, and the Trade of a Town there with California. Massaclau. River
and Town of Rosario. Caput Cavalli, and another Hill. The difficulty of Intelligence on this
Coast. The River of Oletta. River of St. Jago. Maxentelba Rock, and Zelisco Hill. Sancta
Pechaque Town in the River of St. Jago. Of Compostella. Many of them cut off at Sancta
Pechaque. Of California; whether an Island or not: and of the North-West and North-East
Passage. A Method proposed for Discovery of the North-West and North-East Passages. Isle
of Santa Maria. A prickly Plant. Capt. Swan proposes a Voyage to the East-Indies. Valley of
Balderas again, and Cape Corrientes. The reason of their ill Success on the Mexican Coast, and
Departure thence for the East-Indies.*

IT was the 12th of *October*, 1685, when we set out of the Harbour of
Guatulco with our Ships. The Land here lies along West, and a little
Southerly for about 20 or 30 Leagues, and the Sea-winds are commonly at W.S.W. sometimes at S.W. the Land-winds at N. We had now
fair weather, and but little wind. We coasted along to the Westward,
keeping as near the shore as we could for the benefit of the Land-winds,
for the Sea-winds were right against us; and we found a Current setting
to the Eastward which kept us back, and obliged us to anchor at the
Island *Sacrificio*, which is a small green Island about half a Mile long. It
lieth about a League to the West of *Guatulco*, and about half a Mile from
the Main. There seems to be a fine Bay to the West of the Island; but
it is full of Rocks. The best riding is between the Island and the Main:
there you will have five or six Fathom Water. Here runs a pretty strong
Tide; the Sea riseth and falleth five or six Foot up and down.

¶ The 18th Day we sailed from hence, coasting to the Westward after our Canoas. We kept near the shoar, which was all sandy Bays; the Country pretty high and woody, and a great Sea tumbling in upon the shoar. The 22d Day two of our Canoas came aboard, and told us they had been a great way to the Westward, but could not find Port *Angels*. They had attempted to land the Day before, at a place where they saw a great many Bulls and Cows feeding, in hopes to get some of them; but the Sea ran so high, that they over-set both Canoas, and wet all their Arms, and lost four Guns, and had one Man drown'd, and with much ado got off again. They could give no account of the other two Canoas, for they lost company the first Night that they went from *Guatulco*, and had not seen them since.

¶ We were now abrest of *Port Angels*, though our Men in the Canoas did not know it; therefore we went in and anchored there. This is a broad open Bay, with two or three Rocks at the West-side. Here is good anchoring all over the Bay, in 30 or 20 or 12 fathom Water; but you must ride open to all Winds, except the Land-Winds, till you come into 12 or 13 fathom Water; then you are sheltered from the W.S.W. which are the common Trade Winds. The Tide riseth here about five Foot; the Flood sets to the N.E. and the Ebb to the S.W. The landing in this Bay is bad; the place of landing is close by the West-side, behind a few Rocks; here always goes a great Swell. The *Spaniards* compare this Harbour for goodness to *Guatulco*, but there is a great difference between them. For *Guatulco* is almost Landlocked, and this an open road, and no one would easily know it by their Character of it, but by its Marks and its Latitude, which is 15 d. North. For this reason our Canoas, which were sent from *Guatulco* and ordered to tarry here for us, did not know it, (not thinking this to be that fine Harbour) and therefore went farther; two of them, as I said before, returned again, but the other two were not yet come to us. The Land that bounds this Harbour is pretty high, the Earth sandy and yellow, in some places red; it is partly Woodland, partly Savannahs. The Trees in the Woods are large and tall, and the Savannahs are plentifully stored with very kindly Grass. Two Leagues to the East of this place is a Beef Farm, belonging to *Don Diego de la Rosa*.

¶ The 23d Day we landed about 100 Men and marched thither, where we found plenty of fat Bulls and Cows, feeding in the Savannahs, and in the House good store of Salt and Maiz; and some Hogs, and Cocks and Hens: but the Owners or Overseers were gone. We lay here two or three Days feasting on fresh Provision, but could not contrive to carry any quantity aboard, because the Way was so long, and our Men but weak, and a great wide River to ford. Therefore we return'd again from thence the 26th Day, and brought every one a little Beef or Pork for the Men that stay'd aboard. The two Nights that we stay'd ashoar at this place we heard great droves of Jaccals, as we suppos'd them to be, barking all Night long, not far from us. None of us saw these; but I do verily believe they were Jaccals; tho' I did never see those Creatures in *America*, nor hear any but at this time. We could not think that there were less than 30 or 40 in a company. We got aboard in the Evening; but did not yet hear any news of our two Canoas.

¶ The 27th Day in the Morning we sailed from hence, with the Land-Wind at N. by W. The Sea-Wind came about Noon at W.S.W. and in the Evening we anchored in 16 Fathom Water, by a small rocky Island, which lieth about half a Mile from the Main, and six Leagues Westward from Port *Angels*. The *Spaniards* give no account of this Island in their Pilot-book. The 28th Day we sailed again with the Land Wind: in the Afternoon the Sea-breeze blew hard, and we sprung our Main Top-mast. This Coast is full of small Hills and Valleys, and a great Sea falls in upon the Shore. In the Night we met with the other two of our Canoas that went from us at *Guatulco*. They had been as far as *Acapulco* to seek *Port Angels*. Coming back from thence they went into a River to get Water, and were encountered by 150 *Spaniards*, yet they filled their Water in spight of them, but had one Man shot through the Thigh. Afterward they went into a Lagune, or Lake of Salt-water, where they found much dried Fish, and brought some aboard. We being now abreast of that place, sent in a Canoa mann'd with twelve Men for more Fish. The Mouth of this Lagune is not Pistol-shot wide, and on both sides are pretty high Rocks, so conveniently placed by Nature, that many Men may abscond behind; and within the Rocks and Lagune opens wide on both sides. The *Spaniards* being alarmed by our two Canoas that had been there two or three Days before, came armed to this Place to secure their Fish; and seeing our Canoa coming, they lay snug behind the Rocks, and suffered the Canoa to pass in, then they fired their Volley, and wounded five of our Men. Our People were a little surprized at this sudden Adventure, yet fired their Guns, and rowed farther into the Lagune, for they durst not adventure to come out again thro' the narrow Entrance, which was near a Quarter of a Mile in length. Therefore they rowed into the Middle of the Lagune, where they lay out of Gun-shot, and looked about to see if there was not another Passage to get out at, broader than that by which they entred, but could see none. So they lay still two Days and three Nights, in hopes that we should come to seek them; but we lay off at Sea, about three Leagues distant, waiting for their return, supposing by their long absence, that they had made some greater Discovery, and were gone farther than the Fish-Range; because it is usual with Privateers when they enter upon such Designs, to search farther than they proposed, if they meet any Encouragement. But Captain *Townley* and his Bark being nearer the Shore, heard some Guns fired in the Lagune. So he mann'd his Canoa, and went towards the Shore, and beating the *Spaniards* away from the Rocks, made a free Passage for our Men to come out of their Pound, where else they must have been starved or knocked on the Head by the *Spaniards*. They came aboard their Ships again the 31st of *October*. This Lagune is about the Lat. of 16 d. 40 m. North.

¶ From hence we made sail again, coasting to the Westward, having fair Weather and a Current setting to the West. The second Day of *November* we past by a Rock, called by the *Spaniards* the *Algatross*. The Land hereabout is of an indifferent height, and woody, and more within the Country mountainous. Here are seven or eight white Cliffs by the Sea, which are very remarkable, because there are none so white and so thick together on all the Coast. They are five or six Mile to the West of the *Algatross* Rock. There is a dangerous Shoal lieth S. by W. from these Cliffs, four or five Mile off at Sea. Two Leagues to the West of these Cliffs there is a pretty large River, which forms a small Island at its Mouth. The Channel on the East-side is but shoal and sandy, but the West Channel is deep enough for Canoas to enter. On the Banks of this Channel the *Spaniards* have made a Breast-work, to hinder an Enemy from landing or filling Water.

¶ The 3d Day we anchored abrest of this River, in 14 Fathom Water, about a Mile and half off Shore. The next Morning we mann'd our Canoas, and went ashore to the Breast-work with little Resistance, altho' there were about 200 Men to keep us off. They fired about twenty or thirty Guns at us, but seeing we were resolved to land, they quitted the Place; one chief Reason why the *Spaniards* are so frequently routed by us, although many times much our Superiors in Numbers, and in many places fortified with Breast-works, is, their want of small Fire-arms, for they have but few on all the Sea Coasts, unless near their larger Garrisons. Here we found a great deal of Salt, brought hither, as I judge, for to salt Fish, which they take in the Lagunes. The Fish I observed here mostly, were what we call Snooks, neither a Sea-fish nor fresh Water-fish, but very numerous in these salt Lakes. This Fish is about a Foot long, and round, and as thick as the small of a Man's Leg, with a pretty long Head: It hath Scales of a whitish Colour, and is good Meat. How the *Spaniards* take them I know not, for we never found any Nets, Hooks or Lines; neither yet any Bark, Boat, or Canoa among them, on all this Coast, except the Ship I shall mention at *Acapulco*.

¶ We marched two or three Leagues into the Country, and met with but one House, where we took a *Mulatto* Prisoner, who informed us of a Ship that was lately arrived at *Acapulco*; she came from *Lima*. Capt. *Townely* wanting a good Ship, thought now he had an opportunity of getting one, if he could persuade his Men to venture with him into the Harbour of *Acapulco*, and fetch this *Lima* Ship out. Therefore he immediately proposed it, and found not only all his own Men willing to assist him, but many of Captain *Swan*'s Men also. Captain *Swan* opposed it, because Provision being scarce with us, he thought our time might be much better employed in first providing our selves with Food, and here was plenty of Maiz in the River, where we now were, as we were informed by the same Prisoner, who offered to conduct us to the Place where it was. But neither the present Necessity, nor Captain *Swan*'s Persuasion availed any thing, no nor yet their own Interest; for the great Design we had then in Hand, was to lie and wait for a rich Ship which comes to *Acapulco* every Year richly laden from the *Philippine* Islands. But it was necessary we should be well stored with Provisions, to enable us to cruise about, and wait the Time of her coming. However, *Townley*'s Party prevailing, we only filled our Water here, and made ready to be gone. So the 5th Day in the Afternoon we sailed again, coasting to the Westward, towards *Acapulco*. The 7th Day in the Afternoon, being about twelve Leagues from the Shoar, we saw the high Land of *Acapulco*, which is very remarkable: for there is a round Hill standing between two other Hills; the Westermost of which is the biggest and highest, and hath two Hillocks like two Paps on its Top: the Eastermost Hill is higher and sharper than the Middlemost. From the middle Hill the Land declines toward the Sea, ending in a high round Point. There is no Land shaped like this on all the Coast. In the Evening Captain *Townley* went away from the Ships with 140 Men in twelve Canoes, to try to get the *Lima* Ship out of *Acapulco* Harbour.

¶ *Acapulco* is a pretty large Town, 17 deg. North of the Equator. It is the Sea-Port for the City of *Mexico*, on the West-side of the Continent; as *La Vera Cruz*, or St. *John d'Ulloa* in the Bay of *Nova Hispania*, is on the North-side. This Town is the only place of Trade on all this Coast; for there is little or no Traffick by Sea on all the N.W. Part of this vast Kingdom, here being, as I have said, neither Boats, Barks nor Ships, (that I could ever see) unless only what come hither from other Parts, and some Boats near the S.E. End of *California*; as I guess, by the Intercourse between that and the Main, for Pearl-fishing.

¶ The Ships that Trade hither are only three, two that constantly go once a Year between this and *Manila* in *Luconia*, one of the *Philippine* Islands, and one Ship more every Year to and from *Lima*. This from *Lima* commonly arrives a little before *Christmas*; she brings them Quick-silver, Cacoa, and Pieces of Eight. Here she stays till the *Manila* Ships arrive, and then takes in a Cargo of Spices, Silks, Callicoes, and Muslins, and other *East-India* Commodities, for the Use of *Peru*, and then returns to *Lima*. This is but a small Vessel of twenty Guns, but the two *Manila* Ships are each said to be above 1000 Tun. These make their Voyages alternately, so that one or other of them is always at the *Manila*'s. When either of them sets out from *Acapulco*, it is at the latter End of *March*, or the Beginning of *April*; she always touches to refresh at *Guam*, one of the *Ladrone* Islands, in about sixty Days space after she sets out. There she stays but two or three Days, and then prosecutes her Voyage to *Manila*, where she commonly arrives some time in *June*. By that time the other is ready to sail from thence, laden with *East-India* Commodities. She stretcheth away to the North as far as 36, or sometimes into 40 d. of North Lat. before she gets a Wind to stand over to the *American* Shoar. She falls in first with the Coast of *California*, and then coasts along the Shoar to the South again, and never misses a Wind to bring her away from thence quite to *Acapulco*. When she gets the length of Cape St. *Lucas*, which is the Southermost Point of *California*, she stretches over to Cape *Corrientes*, which is in about the 20th Degree of North Lat. from thence she coasts along till she comes to *Sallagua*, and there she sets ashoar Passengers that are bound to the City of *Mexico*: From thence she makes her best way, coasting still along Shoar, till she arrives at *Acapulco*, which is commonly about *Christmas*, never more than eight or ten Days before or after. Upon the Return of this Ship to the *Manila*, the other which stayeth there till her Arrival, takes her turn back to *Acapulco*. Sir *John Narborough* therefore was imposed on by the *Spaniards*, who told him that there were eight Sail, or more, that used this Trade.

¶ The Port of *Acapulco* is very commodious for the Reception of Ships, and so large, that some Hundreds may safely ride there without damnifying each other. There is a small low Island crossing the Mouth of the Harbour; it is about a Mile and a half long, and half a Mile broad, stretching East and West. It leaves a good wide deep Channel at each End, where Ships may safely go in or come out, taking the Advantage of the Winds; they must enter with the Sea-wind, and go out with the Land-wind, for these

Winds seldom or never fail to succeed each other alternately in their proper Season of the Day or Night. The Westermost Channel is the narrowest, but so deep, there is no anchoring, and the *Manila* Ships pass in that way, but the Ships from *Lima* enter on the S.W. Channel. This Harbour runs in North about three Miles, then growing very narrow, it turns short about to the West, and runs about a Mile farther, where it ends. The Town stands on the N.W. side; at the Mouth of this narrow Passage, close by the Sea, and at the End of the Town there is a Platform with a great many Guns. Opposite to the Town, on the East-side, stands a high strong Castle, said to have forty Guns of a very great Bore. Ships commonly ride near the Bottom of the Harbour, under the Command both of the Castle and the Platform.

¶ Capt. *Townley*, who, as I said before, with 140 Men, left our Ships on a design to fetch the *Lima* Ship out of the Harbour, had not rowed above three or four Leagues before the Voyage was like to end with all their Lives; for on a sudden they were encountred with a violent Tornado from the Shore, which had like to have foundered all the Canoas: but they escaped that Danger, and the second Night got safe into *Port Marquis*. *Port Marquis* is a very good Harbour, a League to the East of *Acapulco* Harbour. Here they staid all the next Day to dry themselves, their Cloaths, their Arms and Ammunition, and the next Night they rowed softly into *Acapulco* Harbour; and because they would not be heard, they hal'd in their Oars, and paddled as softly as if they had been seeking Manatee. They paddled close to the Castle; then struck over to the Town, and found the Ship riding between the Breast-work and the Fort, within about a hundred Yards of each. When they had well viewed her, and considered the Danger of the Design, they thought it not possible to accomplish it; therefore they paddled softly back again, till they were out of command of the Forts, and then they went to Land, and fell in among a Company of *Spanish* Soldiers (for the *Spaniards* having seen them the Day before, had set Guards along the Coast) who immediately fired at them, but did them no damage, only made them retire farther from the Shore. They lay afterwards at the Mouth of the Harbour till it was Day, to take a view of the Town and Castle, and then returned aboard again, being tired, hungry and sorry for their Disappointment.

¶ The 11th Day we made sail again further on to the Westward, with the Land-wind, which is commonly at N.E. but the Sea-winds are at S.W. We passed by a long sandy Bay of above twenty Leagues. All the way along it the Sea falls with such Force on the Shore, that it is impossible to come near it with Boat or Canoa; yet it is good clean Ground, and good anchoring a Mile or two from the Shore. The Land by the Sea is low and indifferent fertile, producing many sorts of Trees, especially the spreading Palm, which grows in spots from one End of the Bay to the other.

¶ The Palm-Tree is as big as an ordinary Ash, growing about twenty or thirty Foot high. The Body is clear from Boughs or Branches, till just at the Head; there it spreads forth many large green Branches, not much unlike the Cabbage-Tree before described. These Branches also grow in many places, (as in *Jamaica*, *Darien*, the Bay of *Campeachy*, &c.) from a Stump not above a Foot or two high; which is not the Remains of a Tree cut down; for none of these sort of Trees will ever grow again when they have once lost their Head; but these are a sort of Dwarf-palm, and the Branches which grow from the Stump, are not so large as those that grow on the great Tree. These smaller Branches are used both in the *East* and *West-Indies* for thatching Houses: They are very lasting and serviceable, much surpassing the Palmeto. For this Thatch, if well laid on, will endure five or six Years; and this is called by the *Spaniards* the *Palmeto-Royal*. The *English* at *Jamaica* give it the same Name. Whether this be the same which they in *Guinea* get the Palm-wine from, I know not; but I know that it is like this.

¶ The Land in the Country is full of small peeked barren Hills, making as many little Valleys, which appear flourishing and green. At the West-end of this Bay is the Hill of *Petaplan*, in lat, 17 d. 30 m. N. This is a round Point stretching out into the Sea: At a Distance it seems to be an Island. A little to the West of this Hill are several round Rocks, which we left without us, steering in between them and the round Point, where we had eleven Fathom Water. We came to an Anchor on the N.W. side of the Hill, and went ashore, about 170 Men of us, and marched into the Country twelve or fourteen Miles. There we came to a poor *Indian* Village that did not afford us a Meal of Victuals. The People all fled, only a *Mulatta* Woman, and three or four small Children, who were taken and brought aboard. She told us that a Carrier (one who drives a Caravan of Mules) was going to *Acapulco*, laden with Flour and other Goods, but stopt in the Road for fear of us, a little to the West of this Village, (for he had heard of our being on this Coast) and she thought he still remained there: And therefore it was we kept the Woman to be our Guide to carry us to that Place. At this Place where we now lay, our *Moskito*-men struck some small Turtle, and many small *Jew-fish*.

¶ The *Jew-fish* is a very good Fish, and I judge so called by the *English*, because it hath Scales and Fins, therefore a clean Fish, according to the

Levitical Law, and the *Jews* at *Jamaica* buy them, and eat them very freely. It is a very large Fish, shaped much like a Cod, but a great deal bigger; one will weigh three, or four, or five Hundred Weight. It hath a large Head, with great Fins and Scales, as big as an Half-Crown, answerable to the bigness of his Body. It is very sweet Meat, and commonly fat. This Fish lives among the Rocks; there are plenty of them in the *West-Indies*, about *Jamaica*, and the Coast of *Caraccos*; but chiefly in these Seas, especially more Westward.

¶ We went from hence with our Ships the 18th [sic] day, and steered West about two Leagues farther, to a Place called *Chequetan*. A Mile and half from the shore there is a small Key, and within it is a very good Harbour where Ships may careen; there is also a small River of fresh Water, and Wood enough.

¶ The 14th Day in the Morning we went with 95 Men in six Canoas to seek for the Carrier, taking the *Mulatto*-Woman for our Guide; but Captain *Townley* would not go with us. Before Day we landed at a Place called *Estapa*, a League to the West of *Chequetan*. The Woman was well acquainted here, having been often at this Place for Muscles, as she told us; for here are great Plenty of them. They seem in all respects like our *English* Muscles. She carried us through the pathless Wood by the side of a River, for about a League: Then we came into a Savannah full of Bulls and Cows; and here the Carrier before-mentioned was lying at the Estantion-House with his Mules, not having dared to advance all this while, as not knowing where we lay; so his own fear made him, his Mules, and all his Goods, become a Prey to us. He had 40 Packs of Flour, some Chocolate, a great many small Cheeses, and abundance of Earthern Ware. The Eatables we brought away, but the Earthen Vessels we had no occasion for, and therefore left them. The Mules were about 60: We brought our Prize with them to the Shore, and so turned them away. Here we also kill'd some Cows, and brought with us to our Canoas. In the Afternoon our Ships came to an Anchor half a Mile from the Place where we landed; and then we went aboard. Captain *Townley* seeing our good Success, went ashore with his Men to kill some Cows; for here were no Inhabitants near to oppose us. The Land is very woody, of a good fertile Soil, watered with many small Rivers; yet it hath but few Inhabitants near the Sea. Captain *Townley* killed 18 Beefs, and after he came aboard, our Men, contrary to Captain *Swan*'s Inclination, gave Captain *Townley* part of the Flour which we took ashore. Afterwards we gave the Woman some Cloaths for her, and her Children, and put her and two of them ashore; but one of them, a very pretty Boy, about seven or eight

Years old Captain *Swan* kept. The Woman cried, and begg'd hard to have him; but Captain *Swan* would not, but promised to make much of him, and was as good as his Word. He proved afterwards a very fine Boy for Wit, Courage, and Dexterity; I have often wondered at his Expressions and Actions.

¶ The 21st Day in the Evening, we sailed hence with the Land-Wind. The Land-Winds on this part of the Coast are at N. and the Sea-Winds at W.S.W. We had fair Weather, and coasted along to the Westward. The Land is high, and full of ragged Hills; and West from these ragged Hills the Land makes many pleasant and fruitful Valleys among the Mountains. The 25th Day we were abreast of a very remarkable Hill, which towring above the rest of his Fellows, is divided in the top, and makes two small Parts. It is in lat. 18 d. 8 m. North. The *Spaniards* make mention of a Town called *Thelupan* near this Hill, which we would have visited if we could have found the way to it. The 26th Day Captain *Swan* and Captain *Townley*, with 200 Men, of whom I was one, went in our Canoas to seek for the City of *Colima*, a rich Place by report, but how far within Land I could never learn: For as I said before, here is no Trade by Sea, and therefore we could never get Guides to inform us, or conduct us to any Town, but one or two, on this Coast: and there is never a Town that lieth open to the Sea but *Acapulco*; and therefore our search was commonly fruitless, as now; for we rowed above 20 Leagues along shoar, and found it a very bad Coast to Land. We saw no House, nor sign of Inhabitants, although we past by a fine Valley, called the Valley of *Maguella*; only at two Places, the one at our first setting out on this Expedition, and the other at the end of it, we saw a Horseman set, as we supposed, as a Centinel, to watch us. At both Places we landed with difficulty, and at each Place we followed the track of the Horse on the Sandy Bay; but where they entered the Woods we lost the track, and although we diligently searcht for it, yet we could find it no more; so we were perfectly at a loss to find out the Houses or Town they came from. The 28th Day, being tired and hopeless to find any Town, we went aboard our Ships, that were now come abrest of the Place where we were; for always when we leave our Ships, we either order a certain Place of Meeting, or else leave them a Sign to know where we are, by making one or more great Smoaks; yet we had all like to have been ruined by such a signal as this, in a former Voyage under Captain *Sharp*, when we made that unfortunate Attempt upon *Arica*, which is mentioned in the *History of the Buccaneers*. For upon the routing our Men, and taking several of them, some of those so taken told the *Spaniards*, that it was agreed between them and their Companions on board, to make two great Smoaks at a distance from each other, as soon as the Town should be taken, as a signal to the Ship, that it might safely enter the Harbour. The *Spaniards* made these Smoaks presently: I was then among those who staid on board; and whether the signal was not so exactly made, or some other Discouragement happened, I remember not, but we forbore going in, till we saw our scattered Crew coming off in their Canoas. Had we entered the Port upon the false Signal, we must have been taken or sunk; for we must have past close by the Fort, and could have had no Wind to bring us out, till the Land-Wind should rise in the Night.

¶ But to our present Voyage: After we came aboard we saw the Volcan of *Colima*. This is a very high Mountain, in about 18 d. 36 m. North, standing five or six Leagues from the Sea, in the midst of a pleasant Valley. It appears with two sharp Peeks, from each of which there do always issue Flames of Fire or Smoak. The Valley in which this Volcan stands, is called the Valley of *Colima*, from the Town it self which stands there not far from the Volcan. The Town is said to be great and rich, the chief of all its Neighbourhood: And the Valley in which it is seated, by the relation which the *Spaniards* give of it, is the most pleasant and fruitful Valley in all the Kingdom of *Mexico*. This Valley is about ten or twelve Leagues wide by the Sea, where it makes a small Bay: but how far the Vale runs into the Country I know not. It is said to be full of Cacoa-Gardens, Fields of Corn, Wheat, and Plantain-Walks. The neighbouring Sea is bounded with a sandy shoar; but there is no going ashoar for the violence of the Waves. The Land within it is low all along, and woody for about two Leagues from the East-side; at the end of the Woods there is a deep River runs out into the Sea, but it hath such a great Bar, or sandy Shoal, that when we were here, no Boat or Canoa could possibly enter, the Sea running so high upon the Bar: otherwise, I judge, we should have made some farther Discovery into this pleasant Valley. On the West-side of the River the Savannah-land begins, and runs to the other side of the Valley. We had but little Wind when we came aboard, therefore we lay off this Bay that Afternoon and the Night ensuing.

¶ The 29th Day our Captains went away from our Ships with 200 Men, intending at the first convenient Place to land and search about for a Path: For the *Spanish* Books make mention of two or three other Towns hereabouts, especially one called *Sallagua*, to the West of this Bay. Our Canoas rowed along as near the shoar as they could, but the Sea went so high that they could not land. About 10 or 11 a Clock, two Horsemen came near the shoar, and one of them took a Bottle out of his Pocket, and drank to our Men. While he was drinking, one of our Men snatch'd up his Gun, and let drive at him, and kill'd his Horse: So his Consort immediately set Spurs to his Horse and rode away, leaving the other to come after a Foot. But he being booted, made but slow haste; therefore two of our Men stript themselves, and swam ashoar to take him. But he had a Macheat, or long Knife, wherewith he kept them both from seizing him, they having nothing in their Hands wherewith to defend themselves, or offend him. The 30th Day our Men came all aboard again, for they could not find any Place to land in.

¶ The first Day of *December* we passed by the Port of *Sallagua*. This Port is in lat. 18 d. 52 m. It is only a pretty deep Bay, divided in the middle with a rocky Point, which makes, as it were, two Harbours. Ships may ride securely in either, but the West Harbour is the best: there is good Anchoring any where in 10 or 12 Fathom, and a Brook of fresh Water runs into the Sea. Here we saw a great new thatched House, and a great many *Spaniards* both Horse and Foot, with Drums beating, and Colours flying in defiance of us, as we thought. We took no notice of them till the next Morning, and then we landed about 200 Men to try their Courage; but they presently withdrew. The Foot never stay'd to exchange one shot, but the Horsemen stay'd till two or three were knock'd down, and then they drew off, our Men pursuing them. At last two of our Men took two Horses that had lost their Riders, and mounting them, rode after the *Spaniards* full drive till they came among them, thinking to have taken a Prisoner for Intelligence, but had like to have been taken themselves: for four *Spaniards* surrounded them, after they had discharged their Pistols, and unhorsed them; and if some of our best Footmen had not come to their rescue, they must have yielded, or have been killed. They were both cut in two or three Places, but their Wounds were not mortal. The four *Spaniards* got away before our Men could hurt them, and mounting their Horses, speeded after their Consorts, who were marched away into the Country. Our Men finding a broad Road leading into the Country, followed it about four Leagues in a dry stony Country, full of short Wood; but finding no sign of Inhabitants, they returned again. In their way back they took two *Mulatto*'s, who were not able to march as fast as their Consorts; therefore they had skulked in the Woods, and by that means thought to have escaped our Men. These Prisoners informed us, that this great Road did lead to a great City called *Oarrha*, from whence many of those Horsemen before spoken of came: That this city was distant from hence, as far as a Horse will go in four Days; and that there is no place of Consequence nearer: That the Country is very poor, and thinly inhabited.

They said also, that these Men came to assist the *Phillipine* Ship, that was every Day expected here, to put ashore Passengers for *Mexico*. The *Spanish* Pilot-Books mention a Town also called *Sallagua* hereabouts; but we could not find it, nor hear any thing of it by our Prisoners.

¶ We now intended to cruise off Cape *Corrientes*, to wait for the *Phillipine* Ship. So the 6th Day of *December* we set sail, coasting to the Westward, towards Cape *Corrientes*. We had fair Weather, and but little Wind; the Sea-Breezes at N.W. and the Land-wind at N. The Land is of an indifferent Heighth, full of ragged Points, which at a Distance appear like Islands: The Country is very woody, but the Trees are not high, nor very big.

¶ Here I was taken sick of a Fever and Ague that afterwards turned to a Dropsy, which I laboured under a long time after; and many of our Men died of this Distemper, though our Surgeons used their greatest Skill to preserve their Lives. The Dropsy is a general Distemper on this Coast, and the Natives say, that the best Remedy they can find for it, is the Stone or Cod of an Allegator (of which they have four, one near each Leg, within the Flesh) pulverized and drunk in Water: This Receipt we also found mentioned in an Almanack made at *Mexico*: I would have tried it, but we found no Allegators here, though there are several.

¶ There are many good Harbours between *Sallagua* and Cape *Corrientes*; but we passed by them all. As we drew near the Cape, the Land by the Sea appeared of an indifferent heighth, full of white Cliffs; but in the Country the Land is high and barren, and full of sharp peeked Hills, unpleasant to the sight. To the West of this ragged Land is a Chain of Mountains running parallel with the Shore; they end on the West with a gentle Descent; but on the East-side they keep their heighth, ending with a high steep Mountain, which hath three small sharp peeked Tops, somewhat resembling a Crown; and therefore called by the *Spaniards*, *Coronada*, the *Crown Land*.

¶ The 11th Day we were fair in sight of Cape *Corrientes*, it bore N. by W. and the *Crown Land* bore North. The Cape is of an indifferent heighth, with steep Rocks to the Sea. It is flat and even on the Top, cloathed with Woods: The Land in the Country is high and doubled. This Cape lieth in 20 d. 8 m. North. I find its Longitude from *Tenariff* to be 230 d. 56 m. but I keep my Longitude Westward, according to our Course; and according to this reckoning, I find it is from the *Lizard* in *England* 121 d. 41 m. so that the Difference of time is eight Hours, and almost six Minutes.

¶ Here we had resolved to cruize for the *Philipine* Ship, because she always makes this Cape in her Voyage homeward. We were, (as I have said) four Ships in Company; Captain *Swan*, and his Tender; Captain *Townley*, and his Tender. It was so ordered, that Captain *Swan* should lye eight or ten Leagues off shore, and the rest about a League distant each from other, between him and the Cape, that so we might not miss the *Philippine* Ship; but we wanted Provision, and therefore we sent Capt. *Townley*'s Bark, with 50 or 60 Men to the West of the Cape, to search about for some Town or Plantations, where we might get Provision of any sort. The rest of us in the mean time cruising in our Stations. The 17th Day the Bark came to us again, but had got nothing, for they could not get about the Cape, because the Wind on this Coast is commonly between the N.W. and the S.W. which makes it very difficult getting to the Westward; but they left four Canoas with 46 Men at the Cape, who resolved to row to the Westward. The 18th Day we sailed to the Keys of *Chametly* to fill our Water. The Keys or Islands of *Chametly* are about 16 or 18 Leagues to the Eastward of Cape *Corrientes*. They are small, low, and woody, invironed with Rocks, there are five of them lying in the form of an half Moon, not a Mile from the shore, and between them and the Main is very good Riding, secure from any wind. The *Spaniards* do report, that here live Fishermen, to fish for the Inhabitants of the City of *Purification*. This is said to be a large Town, the best hereabouts; but is 14 Leagues up in the Country.

❡ The 20th instant we entred within these Islands, passing in on the S.E. side, and anchored between the Islands and the Main, in five Fathom clean Sand. Here we found good fresh Water and Wood, and caught plenty of Rock-fish with Hook and Line, a sort of Fish I described at the Isle of *John Fernando*, but we saw no sign of Inhabitants, besides three or four old Hutts; therefore I do believe that the *Spanish* or *Indian* Fishermen come hither only at *Lent*, or some other such Season, but that they do not live here constantly. The 21st Day Captain *Townley* went away, with about 60 Men, to take an *Indian* Village, seven or eight Leagues from hence to the Westward more towards the Cape, and the next Day we went to cruise off the Cape, where Capt. *Townley* was to meet us. The 24th Day, as we were cruising off the Cape, the four Canoas before-mentioned, which Captain *Townley*'s Bark left at the Cape, came off to us. They, after the Bark left them, past to the West of the Cape, and rowed into the Valley *Valderas*, or perhaps *Val d'Iris*; for it signifies the *Valley of Flags*.

❡ This Valley lies in the bottom of a pretty deep Bay, that runs in between Cape *Corrientes* on the S.E. and the point of *Pontique* on the N.W. which two places are about 10 Leagues asunder. The Valley is about three Leagues wide; there is a level sandy Bay against the Sea, and good smooth landing. In the midst of the Bay is a fine River, whereinto Boats may enter; but it is brackish at the latter-end of the dry Season, which is in *February*, *March*, and part of *April*. I shall speak more of the Seasons in my Chapter of Winds, in the Appendix. This Valley is bounded within Land, with a small green Hill, that makes a very gentle descent into the Valley, and affords a very pleasant prospect to Sea-ward. It is inriched with fruitful Savannahs, mixt with Groves of Trees fit for any uses, beside Fruit-Trees in abundance, as Guava's, Oranges and Limes, which here grow wild in such plenty, as if Nature had designed it only for a Garden. The Savannahs are full of fat Bulls and Cows, and some Horses, but no House in sight.

¶ When our Canoas came to this pleasant Valley, they landed 37 Men, and marched into the Country seeking for some Houses. They had not gone past three Mile before they were attackt by 150 *Spaniards*, Horse and Foot: There was a small thin Wood close by them, into which our Men retreated, to secure themselves from the fury of the Horse: Yet the *Spaniards* rode in among them, and attackt them very furiously, till the *Spanish* Captain, and 17 more, tumbled dead off their Horses: then the rest retreated, being many of them wounded. We lost four Men, and had two desperately wounded. In this action, the Foot, who were armed with Lances and Swords, and were the greatest number, never made any attack; the Horsemen had each a brace of Pistols, and some short Guns. If the Foot had come in, they had certainly destroy'd all our Men. When the Skirmish was over, our Men placed the two wounded Men on Horses, and came to their Canoas. There they kill'd one of the Horses, and dress'd it, being afraid to venture into the Savannah to kill a Bullock, of which there was store. When they had eaten, and satisfied themselves, they returned aboard. The 25th Day, being *Christmas*, we cruised in pretty near the Cape, and sent in three Canoas with the Strikers to get Fish, being desirous to have a *Christmas* Dinner. In the Afternoon they returned aboard with three great *Jew-fish*, which feasted us all; and the next Day we sent ashoar our Canoas again, and got three or four more.

¶ Captain *Townley*, who went from us at *Chametly*, came aboard the 28th Day, and brought about 40 Bushels of Maiz. He had landed to the Eastward of Cape *Corrientes*, and march'd to an *Indian* Village that is four or five Leagues in the Country. The *Indians* seeing him coming, set two Houses on fire that were full of Maiz, and run away; yet he and his Men got in other Houses as much as they could bring down on their Backs, which he brought aboard.

¶ We cruised off the Cape till the first Day of *January* 1686 and then made towards the Valley *Valderas*, to hunt for Beef, and before Night we Anchored in the bottom of the Bay, in 60 Fathom Water a Mile from the shoar. Here we stay'd hunting till the 7th Day, and Captain *Swan* and Captain *Townley* went ashoar every Morning with about 240 Men, and marched to a small Hill; where they remained with 50 or 60 Men to watch the *Spaniards*, who appeared in great Companies on other Hills not far distant, but did never attempt any thing against our Men. Here we kill'd and salted above two months Meat, besides what we spent fresh; and might have kill'd as much more, if we had been better stor'd with Salt. Our hopes of meeting the *Philippine* Ship were now over; for we did all conclude, that while we were necessitated to hunt here for Provisions, she was past by to the Eastward, as indeed she was, as we did understand afterwards by Prisoners. So this design fail'd, through Captain *Townley*'s eagerness after the *Lima* Ship, which he attempted in *Acapulco* Harbour, as I have related. For though we took a little Flour hard by, yet the same Guide which told us of that Ship, would have conducted us where we might have had store of Beef and Maiz: but instead thereof, we lost both our time, and the opportunity of providing our selves; and so we were forced to be victualling when we should have been cruising off Cape *Corrientes*, in expectation of the *Manila* Ship.

¶ Hitherto we had coasted along here with two different designs; the one was to get the *Manila* Ship, which would have inriched us beyond measure; and this Captain *Townley* was most for. Sir *Thomas Cavendish* formerly took the *Manila* Ship off Cape *St. Lucas* in *California*, (where we also would have waited for her, had we been early enough stored with Provisions, to have met her there) and threw much rich Goods overboard. The other design, which Captain *Swan* and our Crew were most for, was to search along the Coast for rich Towns, and Mines chiefly of Gold and Silver, which we were assured were in this Country, and we hoped near the shoar: not knowing (as we afterwards found) that it was in effect an Inland Country, its Wealth remote from the *South-Sea* Coast, and having little or no Commerce with it, its Trade being driven Eastward with *Europe* by *La Vera Cruz*. Yet we had still some expectation of Mines, and so resolved to steer on farther Northward; but Captain *Townley*, who had no other design in coming on this Coast, but to meet this Ship, resolved to return again towards the Coast of *Peru*.

¶ In all this Voyage on the *Mexican* Coast, we had with us a Captain, and two or three of his Men of our friendly *Indians* of the Isthmus of *Darien*; who having conducted over some Parties of our Privateers, and

expressing a desire to go along with us, were received, and kindly entertained aboard our Ships; and we were pleas'd in having, by this means,
Guides ready provided, should we be for returning over Land, as several
of us thought to do, rather than sail round about. But at this time, we
of Captain *Swan*'s Ship designing farther to the North-West, and Captain
Townley going back, we committed these our *Indian* Friends to his care, to
carry them home. So here we parted; he to the Eastward, and we to the
Westward, intending to search as far to the Westward as the *Spaniards*
were settled.

¶ It was the 7th Day of *January* in the Morning when we sailed from this
pleasant Valley. The Wind was at N.E. and the weather fair. At eleven
a Clock the Sea-wind came at N.W. Before Night we passed by Point
Pontique; this is the West-point of the Bay of the Valley of *Valderas*, and is
distant from Cape *Corrientes* 10 Leagues. This Point is in lat. 20 d. 50 m.
North; it is high, round, rocky and barren. At a distance it appears like
an Island. A League to the West of this Point are two small barren Islands,
called the Islands of *Pontique*. There are several high, sharp, white
Rocks, that lie scattering about them: We pass'd between these rocky
Islands on the left, and the Main on the right, for there is no danger. The
Sea-coast beyond this Point runs Northward for about 18 Leagues, making
many ragged Points, with small sandy Bays between them. The Land by
the Sea-side is low and pretty woody; but in the Country, full of high,
sharp, barren, rugged, unpleasant Hills.

¶ The 14th Day we had sight of a small white Rock, which appears
very much like a Ship under sail. This Rock is in lat. 21 d. 15 m. it is
three Leagues from the Main. There is a good Channel between it and
the Main, where you will have 12 or 14 Fathom Water near the Island;
but running nearer the Main, you will have gradual Soundings, till you
come in with the shoar. At Night we anchored in six Fathom Water, near
a League from the Main, in good oazy Ground. We caught a great many
Cat-fish here, and at several places on this Coast, both before and after this.

¶ From this Island the Land runs more northerly, making a fair sandy
Bay; but the Sea falls in with such violence on the shoar, that there is no
landing, but very good Anchoring on all the Coast, and gradual Soundings.
About a League off shoar you will have six Fathom, and four Mile off
shoar you will have seven Fathom Water. We came to an Anchor every
Evening; and in the Mornings we sailed off with the Land-wind, which
we found at N.E. and the Sea-breezes at N.W.

¶ The 20th Day we anchored about three Miles on the East-side of the
Islands *Chametly*, different from those of that name before-mentioned; for

these are six small Islands, in lat. 23 d. 11 m. a little to the South of the Tropick of *Cancer*, and about 3 Leagues from the Main, where a Salt Lake hath its out-let into the Sea. These Isles are of an indifferent heighth: Some of them have a few shrubby Bushes; the rest are bare of any sort of Wood. They are rocky round by the Sea, only one or two of them have sandy Bays on the North-side. There is a sort of Fruit growing on these Islands called Penguins; and 'tis all the Fruit they have.

❡ The Penguin-Fruit is of two sorts, the yellow and the red. The yellow Penguin grows on a green stem, as big as a Man's Arm, above a Foot high from the Ground: The Leaves of this Stalk are half a Foot long, and an Inch broad; the Edges full of sharp Prickles. The Fruit grows at the head of the Stalk, in two or three great clusters, 16 or 20 in a cluster. The Fruit is as big as a Pullet's Egg, of a round form, and in colour yellow. It has a thick Skin or rind, and the inside is full of small black seeds, mixt among the Fruit. It is sharp pleasant Fruit. The red Penguin is of the bigness and colour of a small dry Onion, and is in shape much like a Nine-pin; for it grows not on a Stalk, or Stem, as the other, but one End on the ground, the other standing upright. Sixty or seventy grow thus together as close as they can stand one by another, and all from the same Root, or cluster of Roots. These Penguins are encompass'd or fenced with long Leaves, about a Foot and an half, or two Foot long, and prickly like the former; and the Fruit too is much alike. They are both wholsome, and never offend the Stomach; but those that eat many, will find a heat or tickling in their Fundament. They grow so plentifully in the Bay of *Campeachy*, that there is no passing for their high prickly Leaves.

❡ There are some Guanoes on these Islands, but no other sort of Land-Animal. The Bays about the Islands are sometimes visited with Seal; and this was the first place where I had seen any of these Animals, on the North-side of the Equator, in these Seas. For the Fish on this sandy Coast lye most in the Lagunes or Salt-lakes, and Mouths of Rivers; but the Seals come not so much there, as I judge: For this being no rocky Coast, where Fish resort most, there seems to be but little Food for the Seals, unless they will venture upon Cat-fish.

❡ Capt. *Swan* went away from hence with 100 Men in our Canoas, to the Northward, to seek for the River *Coolecan*, possibly the same with the River of *Pastla*, which some Maps lay down in the Province or Region of *Cullacan*. This River lieth in about 24 d. N. lat. We were informed, that there is a fair rich *Spanish* Town seated on the East-side of it, with Savannahs about it, full of Bulls and Cows; and that the Inhabitants of this Town pass over in Boats to the Island *California*, where they fish for Pearl.

I have been told since by a *Spaniard* that said he had been at the Island *California*, that there are great plenty of Pearl Oysters there, and that the Native *Indians* of *California*, near the Pearl-fishery, are mortal Enemies to the *Spaniards*. Our Canoas were absent three or four Days, and said they had been above 30 Leagues but found no River; that the Land by the Sea was low, and all sandy Bay; but such a great Sea, that there was no landing. They met us in their return in the lat. 23 d. 30 m. coasting along shore after them towards *Cullacan*; so we returned again to the Eastward. This was the farthest that I was to the N. on this Coast.

¶ Six or seven Leagues N.N.W. from the Isles of *Chametly*, there is a small narrow entrance into a Lake, which runs about 12 Leagues easterly, parallel with the shore, making many small low Mangrove Islands. The Mouth of this Lake is in lat. about 23 d. 30 m. It is called by the *Spaniards Rio de Sall*: for it is a salt Lake. There is Water enough for Boats and Canoas to enter, and smooth landing after you are in. On the West-side of it, there is an House, and an Estantion, or Farm of large Cattle. Our Men went into the Lake and landed, and coming to the House, found seven or eight Bushels of Maiz: but the Cattle were driven away by the *Spaniards*, yet there our Men took the Owner of the Estantion, and brought him aboard. He said, that the Beefs were driven a great way in the Country, for fear we should kill them. While we lay here, Capt. *Swan* went into this Lake again, and landed 150 Men on the N.E. side, and marched into the Country: About a Mile from the Landing-place, as they were entring a dry *Salina*, or Salt-pond, they fired at two *Indians* that cross'd the way before them; one of them being wounded in the Thigh, fell down, and being examined, he told our Men, that there was an *Indian* Town four or five Leagues off, and that the way which they were going would bring them thither. While they were in Discourse with the *Indian* they were attack'd by 100 *Spanish* Horsemen, who came with a design to scare them back, but wanted both Arms and Hearts to do it.

¶ Our Men past on from hence, and in their way marched through a Savannah of long dry Grass. This the *Spaniards* set on fire, thinking to burn them, but that did not hinder our Men from marching forward, though it did trouble them a little. They rambled for want of Guides all this Day, and part of the next, before they came to the Town the *Indian* spoke of. There they found a company of *Spaniards* and *Indians*, who made head against them, but were driven out of the Town after a short Dispute. Here our Surgeon and one Man more were wounded with Arrows, but none of the rest were hurt. When they came into the Town they found two or three *Indians* wounded, who told them that the Name of the Town was *Massaclan*; that there were a few *Spaniards* living in it, and the rest were *Indians*; that five Leagues from this Town there were two rich Gold Mines, where the *Spaniards* of *Compostalla*, which is the chiefest Town in these Parts, kept many Slaves and *Indians* at work for Gold. Here our Men lay that Night, and the next Morning packt up all the Maiz that they could find, and brought it on their Backs to the Canoas, and came aboard.

¶ We lay here till the 2d of *February*, and then Captain *Swan* went away with about 80 Men to the River *Rosario*; where they landed, and marched to an *Indian* Town of the same Name. They found it about nine Mile from the Sea; the way to it fair and even. This was a fine little Town, of about 60 or 70 Houses, with a fair Church; and it was chiefly inhabited with *Indians*, they took Prisoners there, which told them, That the River *Rosario* is rich in Gold, and that the Mines are not above two Leagues from the Town. Captain *Swan* did not think it convenient to go to the Mines, but made haste aboard with the Maiz which he took there, to the quantity of about 80 or 90 Bushels; and which to us, in the scarcity we were in of Provisions, was at that time more valuable than all the Gold in the World; and had he gone to the Mines, the *Spaniards* would probably have destroyed the Corn before his return. The 3d of *February*, we went with our Ships also towards the River *Rosario*, and anchored the next Day against the River's Mouth, seven Fathom, good oazy ground, a League from the shoar. This River is in lat. 22 d. 51 m. N. When you are at an Anchor against this River, you will see a round Hill, like a Sugar-loaf, a little way within Land, right over the River, and bearing N.E. by N. To the Westward of that Hill there is another pretty long Hill, called by the *Spaniards Caput Cavalli*, or the Horse's head.

¶ The 7th Day Captain *Swan* came aboard with the Maiz which he got. This was but a small quantity for so many Men as we were, especially considering the place we were in, being strangers, and having no Pilots to direct or guide us into any River; and we being without all sort of Provision, but what we were forced to get in this manner from the shoar. And though our Pilot-Book directed us well enough to find the Rivers, yet for want of Guides to carry us to the Settlements, we were forced to search two or three Days before we could find a place to land: for, as I have said before, besides the Seas being too rough for landing in many places, they have neither Boat, Bark, nor Canoa, that we could ever see or hear of: and therefore as there are no such Landing-places in these Rivers, as there are in the *North-Seas*; so when we were landed, we did not know which way to go to any Town, except we accidentally met with a path. Indeed, the *Spaniards* and *Indians*, whom we had aboard, knew the Names of several Rivers and Towns near them, and knew the Towns when they saw them; but they knew not the way to go to them from the Sea.

¶ The 8th Day, Captain *Swan* sent about 40 Men to seek for the River *Oleta*, which is to the Eastward of the River *Rosario*. The next Day we followed after with the Ships, having the Wind at W.N.W. and fair weather. In the Afternoon our Canoas came again to us, for they could not find the River *Oleta*; therefore we designed next for the River St. *Jago*, to the Eastward still. The 11th Day in the Evening, we anchored against the mouth of the River, in seven Fathom Water, good soft oazy ground, and about two Mile from the shoar. There was a high white Rock without us, called *Maxentelbo*. This Rock at a distance appears like a Ship under sail; it bore from us W.N.W. distant about three Leagues. The Hill *Zelisco* bore S.E. which is a very high Hill in the Country, with a Saddle or Bending on the top. The River St. *Jago* is in lat. 22 d. 15 m. It is one of the principal Rivers on this Coast; there is 10 Foot Water on the Bar at low Water, but how much it flows here I know not. The mouth of this River is near half a Mile broad, and very smooth entring. Within the mouth it is broader, for there are three or four Rivers more meet there, and issue all out together, it is brackish a great way up; yet there is fresh Water to be had, by digging or making Wells in the sandy Bay, two or three Foot deep, just at the mouth of the River.

¶ The 11th Day Captain *Swan* sent 70 Men in four Canoas into this River, to seek a Town; for although we had no intelligence of any, yet the Country appearing very promising, we did not question but they would find Inhabitants before they returned. They spent two Days in rowing up and down the Creeks and Rivers; at last they came to a large Field of Maiz, which was almost ripe: they immediately fell to gathering as fast as they could, and intended to lade the Canoas; but seeing an *Indian* that was set to watch the Corn, they quitted that troublesome and tedious work, and seiz'd him, and brought him aboard, in hopes by his information, to have some more easie and expedite way of a Supply, by finding Corn ready cut and dried. He being examined, said, that there was a Town called *Santa Pecaque*, four Leagues from the place where he was taken; and that if we designed to go thither, he would undertake to be our Guide. Captain *Swan* immediately ordered his Men to make ready, and the same Evening went away with eight Canoas and 140 Men, taking the *Indian* for their Guide.

¶ He rowed about five Leagues up the River, and landed the next

Morning. The River at this place was not above Pistol-shot wide, and the Banks pretty high on each side, and the Land plain and even. He left 23 Men to guard the Canoas, and marcht with the rest to the Town. He set out from the Canoas at six a Clock in the Morning, and reach'd the Town by 10. The way through which he passed was very plain, part of it Wood-land, part Savannahs. The Savannahs were full of Horses, Bulls and Cows. The *Spaniards* seeing him coming run all away; so he entred the Town without the least opposition.

¶ This Town of *Santa Pecaque* stands on a Plain, in a Savannah, by the side of a Wood, with many Fruit-Trees about it. It is but a small Town, but very regular, after the *Spanish* mode, with a Parade in the midst. The Houses fronting the Parade had all Balconies: there were two Churches; one against the Parade, the other at the end of the Town. It is inhabited most with *Spaniards*. Their chiefest Occupation is Husbandry. There are also some Carriers, who are imployed by the Merchants of *Compostella*, to trade for them to and from the Mines.

¶ *Compostella* is a rich Town, about 21 Leagues from hence. It is the chiefest in all this part of the Kingdom, and is reported to have 70 white Families; which is a great matter in these parts; for it may be, that such a Town hath not less than 500 Families of copper-coloured People, besides the white. The Silver Mines are about five or six Leagues from *Santa Pecaque*; where, as we were told, the Inhabitants of *Compostella* had some hundreds of Slaves at work. The Silver here, and all over the Kingdom of *Mexico*, is said to be finer and richer in proportion than that of *Potosi* or *Peru*, tho' the Oar be not so abundant; and the Carriers of this Town of *Santa Pecaque*, carry the Oar to *Compostella*, where it is refined. These Carriers, or Sutlers, also furnish the Slaves at the Mines with Maiz, whereof here was great plenty now in the Town designed for that use: Here was also Sugar, Salt, and Salt-fish.

¶ Captain *Swan's* only business at *Santa Pecaque* was to get Provision; therefore he ordered his Men to divide themselves into two parts, and by turns carry down the Provision to the Canoas; one half remaining in the Town to secure what they had taken, while the other half were going and coming. In the Afternoon they caught some Horses, and the next Morning, being the 17th Day, 57 Men, and some Horses, went laden with Maiz to the Canoas. They found them, and the Men left to guard them, in good order; though the *Spaniards* had given them a small diversion, and wounded one Man: but our Men of the Canoas landed, and drove them away. These that came loaded to the Canoas left seven Men more there, so that now they were 30 Men to guard the Canoas.

At Night the other returned; and the 18th Day in the Morning, the half which staid the Day before at the Town, took their turn of going with every Man his burthen, and 24 Horses laden. Before they returned, Captain *Swan*, and his other Men at the Town, caught a Prisoner, who said, that there were near a thousand Men of all colours, *Spaniards* and *Indians*, *Negroes* and *Mulatto's*, in Arms, at a place called St. *Jago*, but three Leagues off, the chief Town on this River; that the *Spaniards* were armed with Guns and Pistols, and the copper-coloured with Swords and Lances. Captain *Swan*, fearing the ill consequence of separating his small Company, was resolved the next Day to march away with the whole Party; and therefore he ordered his Men to catch as many Horses as they could, that they might carry the more Provision with them. Accordingly, the next Day, being the 19th Day of *February* 1686, Captain *Swan* called out his Men betimes to be gone; but they refused to go, and said, that they would not leave the Town till all the Provision was in the Canoas: Therefore he was forced to yield to them, and suffered half the Company to go as before: They had now 54 Horses laden, which Captain *Swan* ordered to be tied one to another, and the Men to go in two bodies, 25 before, and as many behind; but the Men would go at their own rate, every Man leading his Horse. The *Spaniards* observing their manner of marching, had laid an Ambush about a Mile from the Town, which they managed with such success, that falling on our body of Men, who were guarding the Corn to the Canoas, they killed them every one. Capt. *Swan* hearing the report of their Guns, ordered his Men, who were then in the Town with him, to march out to their assistance; but some opposed him, despising their Enemies, till two of the *Spaniards* Horses that had lost their Riders, came galloping into the Town in a great fright, both bridled and saddled, with each a pair of Holsters by their sides, and one had a Carabine newly discharged; which was an apparent token that our Men had been engaged, and that by Men better armed than they imagined they should meet with. Therefore Captain *Swan* immediately march'd out of the Town, and his Men all followed him; and when he came to the place where the Engagement had been, he saw all his Men that went out in the Morning lying dead. They were stript, and so cut and mangled, that he scarce knew one Man. Captain *Swan* had not more Men then with him, than those were who lay dead before him, yet the *Spaniards* never came to oppose him, but kept at a great distance; for 'tis probable, the *Spaniards* had not cut off so many men of ours, but with the loss of a great many of their own. So he marched down to the Canoas, and came aboard the Ship with the Maiz that was already in the Canoas. We had about 50 Men killed, and among the rest, my ingenious Friend Mr. *Ringrose* was one, who wrote that Part of the *History of the Buccaneers*, which relates to Capt. *Sharp*. He was at this time Cape-Merchant, or Super-Cargo of Capt. *Swan*'s Ship. He had no mind to this Voyage; but was necessitated to engage in it or starve.

¶ This loss discouraged us from attempting any thing more hereabouts. Therefore Capt. *Swan* proposed to go to Cape St. *Lucas* on *California* to careen. He had two reasons for this: First, that he thought he could lye there secure from the *Spaniards*, and next, that if he could get a Commerce with the *Indians* there, he might make a discovery in the Lake of *California*, and by their Assistance try for some of the Plate of *New Mexico*.

¶ This Lake of *California* (for so the Sea, Channel or Streight, between that and the Continent, is called) is but little known to the *Spaniards*, by what I could ever learn; for their Drafts do not agree about it. Some of them do make *California* an Island, but give no manner of account of the Tides flowing in the Lake, or what depth of Water there is, or of the Harbours, Rivers, or Creeks, that border on it: Whereas on the West-side of the Island towards the *Asiatick* Coast, their Pilot-Book gives an account of the Coast from Cape St. *Lucas* to 40 d. North. Some of their Drafts newly made do make *California* to join to the Main. I do believe that the *Spaniards* do not care to have this Lake discovered, for fear lest other *European* Nations should get knowledge of it, and by that means visit the Mines of *New Mexico*. We heard that not long before our arrival here, the *Indians* in the Province of *New Mexico* made an Insurrection, and destroyed most of the *Spaniards* there, but that some of them flying towards the Gulph or Lake of *California*, made Canoas in that Lake, and got safe away; though the *Indians* of the Lake of *California*, seem to be at perfect Enmity with the *Spaniards*. We had an old intelligent *Spaniard* now aboard, who said that he spoke with a Friar that made his Escape among them.

¶ *New Mexico*, by report of several *English* Prisoners there and *Spaniards* I have met with, lieth N.W. from *Old Mexico* between 4 and 500 Leagues, and the biggest Part of the Treasure which is found in this Kingdom, is in that Province; but without doubt there are plenty of Mines in other Parts, as well in this Part of the Kingdom where we now were, as in other Places; and probably, on the Main, bordering on the Lake of *California*; although not yet discovered by the *Spaniards*, who have Mines enough, and therefore, as yet, have no reason to discover more.

¶ In my Opinion here might be very advantageous Discoveries made by any that would attempt it: for the *Spaniards* have more than they can well manage. I know yet, they would lie like the *Dog in the Manger*; although not able to eat themselves, yet they would endeavour to hinder others. But the Voyage thither being so far, I take that to be one reason that hath hindred the Discoveries of these Parts: yet it is possible, that a Man may find a nearer way hither than we came; I mean by the North-West.

¶ I know there have been divers Attempts made about a North-West Passage, and all unsuccessful: yet I am of Opinion, that such a Passage may be found. All our Countrymen that have gone to discover the N.W. Passage, have endeavoured to pass to the Westward, beginning their search along *Davis's* or *Hudson's Bay*. But if I was to go on this Discovery, I would go first into the *South-Seas*, bend my course from thence along by *California*, and that way seek a Passage back into the *West-Seas*. For as others have spent the Summer, in first searching on this more known side nearer home, and so before they got through, the time of the Year obliged them to give over their Search, and provide for a long Course back again, for fear of being left in the Winter; on the contrary, I would search first on the less known Coast of the South-Sea-side, and then as the Year past away, I should need no retreat, for I should come farther into my Knowledge, if I succeeded in my Attempt, and should be without that Dread and Fear which the others must have in passing from the known to the unknown: who, for ought I know, gave over their Search just as they were on the Point of accomplishing their Desires.

¶ I would take the same Method if I was to go to discover the North-East Passage. I would winter about *Japan*, *Corea*, or the North-East Part of *China*; and taking the Spring and Summer before me, I would make my first Trial on the Coast of *Tartary*, wherein, if I succeeded, I should come into some known Parts, and have a great deal of time before me to reach *Archangel* or some other Port. Captain *Wood*, indeed, says, this N. East Passage is not to be found for Ice: but how often do we see that sometimes Designs have been given over as impossible, and at another time, and by other ways, those very things have been accomplished; but enough of this.

¶ The next Day after that fatal Skirmish near *Santa Pecaque*, Captain *Swan* ordered all our Water to be filled, and to get ready to sail. The 21st Day we sailed from hence, directing our Course towards *California*: we had the Wind at N.W. and W.N.W. a small Gale, with a great Sea out of the West. We past by three Islands called the *Maria's*. After we past these Islands we had much Wind at N.N.W. and N.W. and at N. with thick rainy Weather. We beat till the 6th Day of *February*, but it was against a brisk Wind, and proved labour in vain. For we were now within reach of the Land Trade-wind, which was opposite to us: but would we go to *California* upon the Discovery or otherwise, we should bear sixty or seventy Leagues off from the Shoar; where we should avoid the Land-winds, and have the Benefit of the true easterly Trade-wind.

¶ Finding therefore that we got nothing, but rather lost ground, being then 21 d. 5 m. N. we steered away more to the eastward again for the Islands *Maria*'s, and the 7th Day we came to an anchor at the East-end of the middle Island, in eight Fathom Water, good clean Sand.

¶ The *Maria*'s are three uninhabited Islands in Lat. 21 d. 40 m. they are distant from Cape St. *Lucas* on *California*, forty Leagues, bearing East-South-East, and they are distant from Cape *Corientes* twenty Leagues, bearing upon the same Points of the Compass with Cape St. *Lucas*. They stretch N.W. and S.E. about fourteen Leagues. There are two or three small high Rocks near them: The westermost of them is the biggest Island of the three; and they are all three of an indifferent heighth. The Soil is stony and dry; the Land in most places is covered with a shrubby sort of Wood, very thick and troublesome to pass through. In some places there is plenty of strait large Cedars, though speaking of the Places where I have found Cedars, *Chap*. 3. I forgot to mention this place. The *Spaniards* make mention of them in other places: but I speak of those which I have seen. All round by the Sea-side it is sandy; and there is produced a green prickly Plant, whose Leaves are much like the Penguin-leaf, and the Root like the Root of a *Sempervive*, but much larger. This Root being bak'd in an Oven is good to eat: and the *Indians* on *California*, as I have been informed, have great part of their Subsistence from these Roots. We made an Oven in a sandy Bank, and baked of these Roots, and I eat of them: but none of us greatly cared for them. They taste exactly like the Roots of our *English* Burdock boil'd, of which I have eaten. Here are plenty of Guanoes and Raccoons (a large sort of Rat) and *Indian* Conies, and abundance of large Pigeons and Turtle-Doves. The Sea is also pretty well stored with Fish, and Turtle or Tortoise, and Seal. This is the second Place on this Coast where I did see any Seal: and this place helps to confirm what I have observed, that they are seldom seen but where there is plenty of Fish. Capt. *Swan* gave the middle Island the Name of *Prince George's Island*.

¶ The 8th Day we run near the Island, and anchored in five Fathom, and moored Head and Stern, and unrigg'd both Ship and Bark, in order to careen. Here Capt. *Swan* proposed to go into the *East-Indies*. Many were well pleased with the Voyage; but some thought, such was their

Ignorance, that he would carry them out of the World; for about two thirds of our Men did not think there was any such way to be found; but at last he gained their Consents.

¶ At our first coming hither we did eat nothing but Seal; but after the first two or three Days our Strikers brought aboard Turtle every Day; on which we fed all the time that we lay here, and saved our Maiz, for our Voyage. Here also we measured all our Maiz, and found we had about eighty Bushels. This we divided into three parts; one for the Bark, and two for the Ship; our Men were divided also, a hundred Men aboard the Ship, and fifty aboard the Bark, besides three or four Slaves in each.

¶ I had been a long time sick of a Dropsy, a Distemper, whereof, as I said before, many of our Men died; so here I was laid and covered all but my Head in the hot Sand: I endured it near half an Hour, and then was taken out and laid to sweat in a Tent. I did sweat exceedingly while I was in the Sand, and I do believe it did me much good, for I grew well soon after.

¶ We staid here till the 26th Day, and then both Vessels being clean, we sailed to the Valley of *Balderas* to water, for we could not do it here now. In the wet Season indeed here is Water enough, for the Brooks then run down plentifully; but now, though there was Water, yet it was bad filling, it being a great way to fetch it from the Holes where it lodged. The 28th Day we anchored in the Bottom of the Bay in the Valley of *Balderas*, right against the River, where we watered before; but this River was brackish now in the dry Season; and therefore we went two or three Leagues nearer Cape *Corrientes*, and anchored by a small round Island, not half a Mile from the Shoar. The Island is about four Leagues to the northward of the Cape; and the Brook where we filled our Water is just within the Island, upon the Main. Here our Strikers struck nine or ten *Jew-fish*; some we did eat, and the rest we salted; and the 29th Day we fill'd thirty-two Tuns of very good Water.

¶ Having thus provided our selves, we had nothing more to do, but to put in Execution our intended Expedition to the *East-Indies*, in hopes of some better success there, than we had met with on this little frequented Coast. We came on it full of Expectations; for besides the Richness of the Country, and the Probability of finding some Sea-Ports worth visiting, we persuaded our selves that there must needs be Shipping and Trade here, and that *Acapulco* and *La Vera Cruz* were to the Kingdom of *Mexico*, what *Panama* and *Portobel* are to that of *Peru*, *viz*. Marts for carrying on a constant Commerce between the South and North-Seas, as indeed they are. But whereas we expected that this Commerce should be managed by Sea, we found our selves mistaken: that of *Mexico* being almost wholly a Land trade, and managed more by Mules than by Ships: So that instead of profit we met with little on this Coast, besides Fatigues, Hardships and Losses, and so were the more easily induced to try what better Fortune we might have in the *East-Indies*. But to do right to Capt. *Swan*, he had no Intention to be as a Privateer in the *East-Indies*; but, as he hath often assured me with his own Mouth, he resolved to take the first Opportunity of returning to *England*: So that he feigned a Compliance with some of his Men, who were bent upon going to cruize at *Manila*, that he might have leisure to take some favourable Opportunity of quitting the Privateer Trade.

CHAPTER X

Their Departure from Cape Corientes *for the* Ladrone *Islands, and the* East-Indies. *Their Course thither, and Accidents by the way: with a Table of each Day's Run, &c. Of the different Accounts of the Breadth of these Seas.* Guam, *one of the* Ladrone *Islands. The Coco-Nut Tree, Fruit, &c. The* Toddi, *or Arack that distils from it; with other Uses that are made of it.* Coire-Cables. *The Lime, or Crab-Limon. The Bread-fruit. The Native Indians of* Guam. *Their Proes, a remarkable sort of Boats: and of those used in the* East-Indies. *The State of* Guam: *and the Provisions with which they were furnished there.*

I HAVE given an Account in the last Chapter of the Resolutions we took of going over to the *East-Indies*. But having more calmly considered on the Length of our Voyage, from hence to *Guam*, one of the *Ladrone* Islands, which is the first place that we could touch at, and there also being not certain to find Provisions, most of our Men were almost daunted at the Thoughts of it; for we had not sixty Day's Provision, at a little more than half a Pint of Maiz a Day for each Man, and no other Provision, except three Meals of salted *Jew-fish*; and we had a great many Rats aboard, which we could not hinder from eating part of our Maiz. Beside, the great Distance between Cape *Corientes* and *Guam*: which is variously set down. The *Spaniards*, who have the greatest Reason to know best, make it to be between 2300 and 2400 Leagues; our Books also reckon it differently, between 90 and 100 Degrees, which all comes short indeed of 2000 Leagues; but even that was a Voyage enough to frighten us, considering our scanty Provisions. Capt. *Swan*, to encourage his Men to go with him, persuaded them that the *English* Books did give the best Account of the Distance; his Reasons were many, although but weak. He urged among the rest, that Sir *Thomas Candish* and Sir *Francis Drake* did run it in less than fifty Days, and that he did not question but that our Ships were better Sailers, than those which were built in that Age, and that he did not doubt to get there in little more than forty Days: This being the best time in the Year for Breezes, which undoubtedly is the Reason that the *Spaniards* set out from *Acapulco* about this time; and that although they are sixty Days in their Voyage; it is because, they are great Ships deep laden, and very heavy Sailers; besides, they wanting nothing, are in no great haste in their way, but sail with a great deal of their usual Caution. And when they come near the Island *Guam*, they lie by in the Night for a Week, before they make Land. In prudence we also should have contriv'd to lie by in the Night when we came near Land, for otherwise we might have run ashoar, or have out-sailed the Islands, and lost sight of them before Morning. But our bold Adventurers seldom proceed with such wariness when in any straights.

¶ But of all Capt. *Swan*'s Arguments, that which prevailed most with them was, his promising them, as I have said, to cruize off the *Manila*'s. So he and his Men being now agreed, and they encouraged with the Hope of Gain, which works its way thro' all Difficulties, we set out from Cape *Corrientes*, *March* the 31st, 1686. We were two Ships in Company, Capt. *Swan*'s Ship and a Bark commanded under Capt. *Swan*, by Capt. *Teat*, and we were 150 Men, 100 aboard of the Ship, and 50 aboard the Bark, besides Slaves, as I said.

¶ We had a small Land-wind at E.N.E. which carried us three or four Leagues, then the Sea-wind came at W.N.W. a fresh Gale, so we steered away S.W. By six a Clock in the Evening we were about nine Leagues S.W. from the Cape, then we met a Land-wind which blew fresh all Night; and the next Morning about 10 a-Clock we had the Sea-breeze at N.N.E. so that at Noon we were thirty Leagues from the Cape. It blew a fresh Gale of Wind which carried us off into the true Trade-wind, (of the Difference of which Trade-winds I shall speak in the Chapter of Winds in the Appendix) for although the constant Sea-breeze near the Shoar is at W.N.W. yet the true Trade off at Sea, when you are clear of the Land-winds, is at E.N.E. At first we had it at N.N.E. so it came about northerly, and then to the East as we run off. At 250 Leagues distance from the Shoar we had it at E.N.E. and there it stood till we came within forty Leagues of *Guam*. When we had eaten up our three Meals of salted *Jew-fish*, in so many Days time we had nothing but our small Allowance of Maiz.

¶ After the 31st Day of *March* we made great Runs every Day, having very fair clear Weather, and a fresh Trade-wind, which we made use of

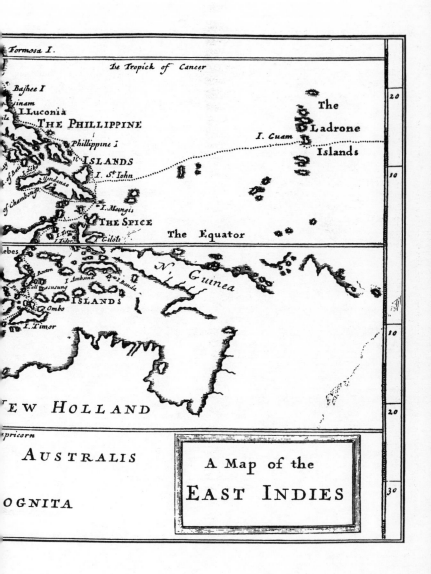

A Map of the
EAST INDIES

with all our Sails, and we made many good *Observations* of the Sun. At our first setting out, we steer'd into the Lat. of 13 Degrees, which is near the Lat. of *Guam*; then we steered West, keeping in that Lat. By that time we had sailed twenty Days, our Men seeing we had made such great Runs, and the Wind like to continue, repined because they were kept at such short Allowance. Captain *Swan* endeavoured to persuade them to have a little Patience; yet nothing but an Augmentation of their daily Allowance would appease them. Captain *Swan*, though with much Reluctance, gave way to a small Enlargement of our Commons, for now we had about ten Spoonfuls of boil'd *Maiz* a Man, once a Day, whereas before we had but eight: I do believe that this short Allowance did me a great deal of good, though others were weakened by it; for I found that my Strength increased, and my Dropsy wore off. Yet I drank three times every Twenty-four Hours; but many of our Men did not drink in nine or ten Days time, and some not in twelve Days; one of our Men did not drink in seventeen Days time, and said he was not adry when he did drink; yet he made water every Day more or less. One of our Men in the midst of these Hardships was found guilty of Theft, and condemned for the same to have three Blows from each Man in the Ship, with a Two-Inch and a half Rope on his bare Back. Captain *Swan* began first, and struck with a good Will; whose Example was followed by all of us.

¶ It was very strange, that in all this Voyage we did not see one Fish, not so much as a Flying-fish, nor any sort of Fowl, but at one time, when we were by my account 4975 Miles West from Cape *Corientes*, then we saw a great Number of Boobies, which we supposed came from some Rocks not far from us, which were mentioned in some of our Sea-Charts, but we did not see them.

¶ After we had run the 1900 Leagues by our reckoning, which made the *English* account to *Guam*, the Men began to murmur against Captain *Swan*, for persuading them to come this Voyage; but he gave them fair words, and told them that the *Spanish* Account might probably be the truest, and seeing the Gale was likely to continue, a short time longer would end our troubles.

¶ As we drew nigh the Island, we met with some small Rain, and the Clouds settling in the West, were an apparent token that we were not far from Land; for in these Climates, between or near the Tropicks, where the Trade-wind blows constantly, the Clouds which fly swift over Head, yet seem near the Limb of the Horizon to hang without much motion or alteration, where the Land is near. I have often taken notice of it,

especially if it is high Land, for you shall then have the Clouds hang about
it without any visible Motion.

¶ The 20th Day of *May*, our Bark being about three Leagues a-head of
our Ship, sailed over a rocky shole, on which there was but four Fathom
Water, and abundance of Fish swimming about the Rocks. They imagined
by this that the Land was not far off; so they clapt on a Wind with the
Bark's Head to the North, and being past the Shole, lay by for us. When
we came up with them, Captain *Teat* came aboard us, and related what
he had seen. We were then in lat. 12 d. 55 m. steering West. The Island
Guam is laid down in Lat. 13 d. N. by the *Spaniards*, who are Masters of it,
keeping it as a baiting-Place as they go to the *Philippine* Islands. Therefore
we clapt on a Wind and stood to northward, being somewhat troubled
and doubtful whether we were right, because there is no Shole laid down
in the *Spanish* Drafts about the Island *Guam*. At four a-Clock, to our great
Joy, we saw the Island *Guam*, at about eight Leagues distance.

¶ It was well for Captain *Swan* that we got sight of it before our Provision
was spent, of which we had but enough for three Days more; for, as I was
afterwards informed, the Men had contrived, first to kill Captain *Swan*
and eat him when the Victuals was gone, and after him all of us who were
accessary in promoting the undertaking this Voyage. This made Capt.
Swan say to me after our arrival at *Guam*. *Ah!* Dampier, *you would have
made them but a poor Meal*; for I was as lean as the Captain was lusty and
fleshy. The Wind was at E.N.E. and the Land bore at N.N.E. therefore
we stood to the Northward, till we brought the Island to bear East, and
then we turned to get in to an anchor.

¶ The account I have given hitherto of our Course from Cape *Corrientes*
in the Kingdom of *Mexico*, (for I have mentioned another Cape of that
Name in *Peru*, South of the Bay of *Panama*) to *Guam*, one of the *Ladrone*
Islands, hath been in the gross. But for the Satisfaction of those who may
think it serviceable to the fixing the Longitudes of these Parts, or to any
other Use in Geography or Navigation, I have here subjoyned a particular
Table of every Days Run, which was as follows.

	Day	Course.	Dist	S.	W.	Lat.	Winds.
March	31	S W 5 d W	27	17	20	20 : 11	W N W
April	1	S W 5 W	106	68	81	R. 19 : 2	N W : N N W
	2	S W 1 W	142	98	101	R. 17 : 25	N b W
	3	W by S	102	19	100	Ob. 17 : 6	N
	4	W 12 S	140	29	136	Ob. 16 : 37	N : N N E
	5	W 20 S	160	54	150	Ob. 15 : 43	N
	6	W 10 S	108	18	106	Ob. 15 : 25	N E
	7	W 15 S	89	23	86	Ob. 15 : 2	N E : E N E
	8	W 2 S	64	5	63	R. 14 : 57	E N E
	9	W 4 S	94	6	93	Ob. 14 : 51	E N E
	10	W 5 S	138	12	137	Ob. 14 : 39	E N E
	11	W 5 S	124	10	123	Ob. 14 : 29	E N E
	12	W 5 S	170	14	169	R. 14 : 15	E N E ·
	13	W 5 S	170	14	169	R. 14 : 1	E N E
	14	W 5 S	180	15	177	R. 13 : 46	E N E
	15	W 6 S	174	18	172	R. 13 : 28	E N E cloudy
	16	W 6 S	182	19	180	R. 13 : 9	E N E misty
	17	W 6 S	216	22	214	R. 12 : 47	E N E rain

The Sum of the Westings hitherto is —— 2283 which make Deg. of Longitude —— 39 d. 5 m.

From hence my Course is most West, sometimes Southerly, sometimes Northerly.

	Day	Course.	Dist	N or S.	W.	Lat.	Winds.
April	18	W	192	0	192	R. 12 : 47	E by N
	19	W	180	0	180	R. 12 : 47	E cloudy
	20	W	177	0	170	R. 12 : 47	E N E
	21	W	171	0	171	R. 12 : 47	E N E
	22	W	180	0	180	R. 12 : 47	E by N
	23	R. W. Ob. W 4 N	170	11 N	168	R. 12 : 47 Ob. 12 : 58	E by N
	24	R. W.	146	0	146	R. 12 : 58	E by N

	Day	Course.	Dist	N or S.	W.	Lat.	Winds.
April	25	W	146	0	146	R. 12 : 58	E by N
	26	W 3 N	185	9 N	184	Ob. 13 : 7	E by N
	27	W	140	0	140	Ob. 13 : 7	E by N
	28	W	167	0	167	R. 13 : 7	E by N
	29	W. 2 N.	172	5	171	Ob. 13 : 12	E
	30	W	172	0	173	Ob. 13 : 12	E N E
May	1	W	196	0	196	R. 13 : 12	E by N
	2	W	100	0	160	Ob. 13 : 12	E by N
	3	W	154	0	154	R. 13 : 12	E N E
	4	R. W. Ob. W. 2 S	153	5 S	152	R. 13 : 12 Ob. 13 : 7	E N E
	5	W 2 N	180	7 N	179	Ob. 13 : 14	E N E
	6	W 2 N	172	9 N	171	Ob. 13 : 22	E N E
	7	W	160	0	160	Ob. 13 : 22	E N E
	8	W 3 S	149	7 S	148	Ob. 13 : 15	E by N
	9	W 4 S	134	9 S	133	Ob. 13 : 6	E N E
	10	W	128	0	128	R. 13 : 6	E N E
	11	W 5 S	112	9	111	Ob. 12 : 57	E N E
	12	W	128	0	128	R. 12 : 57	E N E
	13	W	129	0	129	R. 12 : 57	E N E
	14	W	128	0	128	R. 12 : 57	E N E
	15	W 4 N	188	8 N	117	Ob. 13 : 5	E N E
	16	W 6 S	114	11 S	113	Ob. 12 : 54	E N E
	17	W 3 S	109	5 S	108	Ob. 12 : 49	E N E
	18	W	120	0	120	R. 12 : 49	E N E
	19	W	127	0	137	R. 12 : 49	E N E
	20	W	134	0	130	R. 12 : 50	E
	21	NW 7 W	13	8 N	10	R. 12 : 59	E N E

Summ of all the Westings —— 7323.
Making Deg. of Longitude in all —— 125 d. 11 m.

¶ Now the Island *Guam* bore N.N.E. eight Leagues dist. this gives 22 m. to my lat. and takes 9 from my Meridian dist. so that the Island is in Lat. 13 : 21; and the Merid. dist. from *Corientes* 7302 Miles; which, reduced into degrees, makes 125 d. 11 m.

¶ The Table consists of seven Columns. The first is of the Days of the Month. The 2d Column contains each Day's course, or the Point of the Compass we ran upon. The 3d gives the distance or length of such course in *Italian* or Geometrical Miles, (at the rate of 60 to a degree) or the Progress the Ship makes every Day; and is reckoned always from noon to noon. But because the course is not always made upon the same Rumb in a direct Line, therefore the 4th and 5th Columns shew how many Miles we ran to the South every Day, and how many to the West; which last was our main Run in this Voyage. By the 17th of *April* we were got pretty near into the Latitude *Guam*, and our Course then lying along that parallel, our northing and southing consequently were but little, according as the Ship deviated from its direct course; and such deviation is thenceforward exprest by N. or S. in the 5th Column, and the Ship's keeping straight on the West-Rumb, by 0, that is to say, no northing or southing. The 6th Column shews the Latitude we were in every Day, where R. signifies the *dead Reckoning*, by the running of the Logs, and Ob. shews the Lat. by Observation. The 7th Column shews the Wind and Weather.

¶ To these I would have added an 8th Column, to shew the Variation of the Needle; but as it was very small in this course, so neither did we make any observation of it, above once, after we were set out from the *Mexican* Coast. At our departure from Cape *Corientes*, we found it to be 4 d. 28 m. easterly: and the Observation we made of it afterwards, when we had gone about a third of the Voyage, shewed it to be so near the same, to be decreasing: Neither did we observe it at *Guam*, for Capt. *Swan* who had the instruments in his Cabbin, did not seem much to regard it: Yet I am inclined to think that at *Guam*, the Variation might be either none at all, or even increasing to the westward.

¶ To conclude, *May* 20th at noon (when we begin to call it 21st) we were in lat. 12 d. 50 m. N. by R. having run since the noon before 134 Miles directly West. We continued the same Course till two that Afternoon, for which I allow 10 Miles more West still, and then, finding the parallel we ran upon to be too much southerly, we clapt on a Wind and sailed directly North, till five in the Afternoon, having at that time run eight Mile, and increased our Latitude so many Minutes, making it 12 d. 58 m. We then saw the Island *Guam* bearing N.N.E. distant from us about eight

Leagues, which gives the Latitude of the Island 13 d. 20 m. And according to the account foregoing, its Longitude is 125 d. 11 m. West from the Cape *Corrientes* on the Coast of *Mexico*, allowing 58 or 59 *Italian* miles to a degree in these Latitudes, at the common rate of 60 Miles to a degree of the Equator, as before computed.

¶ As a Corollary from hence it will follow, that upon a supposal of the Truth of the general allowance, Seamen make of 60 *Italian* Miles to an Equinoctial Degree, that the *South-Sea* must be of a greater breadth by 25 degrees than it's commonly reckoned by Hydrographers, who make it only about 100, more or less. For since we found (as I shall have occasion to say) the distance from *Guam* to the eastern Parts of *Asia*, to be much the same with the common reckoning; it follows by way of necessary Consequence from hence, that the 25 degrees of Longitude, or thereabouts, which are under-reckoned in the distance between *America* and the *East-Indies* westward, are over-reckoned in the breadth of *Asia* and *Africk*, the *Atlantick* Sea, or the *American* Continent, or all together; and so that Tract of the Terraqueous Globe, must be so much shortned. And for a further confirmation of the fact, I shall add, that as to the *Æthiopick* or *Indian* Sea, its breadth must be considerably less than 'tis generally calculated to be; if it be true what I have heard over and over, from several able Seamen, whom I have conversed with in these parts, that Ships sailing from the *Cape of Good Hope* to *New Holland*, (as many Ships bound to *Java*, or thereabouts, keep that Latitude) find themselves there, (and sometimes to their cost) running aground when they have thought themselves to be a great way off; and 'tis from hence possibly, that the *Dutch* call that part of this Coast the Land of *Indraught*, (as if it magnetically drew Ships too fast to it) and give cautions to avoid it: But I rather think, 'tis the nearness of the Land, than any Whirlpool, or the like, that surprizes them. As to the breadth of the *Atlantick* Sea, I am from good hands assured, that it is over-reckoned by six, seven, eight, or ten degrees; for besides the con-current Accounts of several experienced Men, who have confirmed the same to me: Mr. *Canby* particularly, who hath sailed as a Mate in a great many Voyages, from Cape *Lopez*, on the Coast of *Guinea*, to *Barbadoes*, and is much esteem'd as a very sensible Man, hath often told me, that he constantly found the distance to be between 60 and 62 degrees; whereas 'tis laid down in 68, 69, 70, and 72 degrees, in the common Draughts.

¶ As to the supposition it self, which our Seamen make, in the allowing but 60 Miles to a degree, I am not ignorant how much this hath been canvased of late years especially, and that the prevailing Opinion hath been that about 70, or upwards, should be allowed. But till I can see some better grounds for the exactness of those trials, that have been made on Land by Mr. *Norwood* and others, considering the inequality of the Earth's Surface, as well as the obliquity of the way; in their allowing for which I am somewhat doubtful of their measures. Upon the whole matter, I cannot but adhere to the general Sea-calculation, confirmed as to the main by daily experience, till some more certain Estimate shall be made, than those hitherto attempted. For we find our selves, when we sail North or South, to be brought to our intended place, in a time agreeable enough with what we expect upon the usual supposition, making all reasonable allowance, for the little unavoidable deviations East or West: and there seems no reason why the same Estimate should not serve us in crossing the Meridians, which we find so true in Sailing under them. As to this Course of ours to *Guam* particularly, we should rather increase than shorten our Estimate of the length of it, considering that the easterly Wind and Current being so strong, and bearing therefore our Log after us, as is usual in such cases; should we therefore, in casting up the run of the Log, make allowance for so much space as the Log it self drove after us (which is commonly three or four Miles in 100, in so brisk a gale as this was) we must have reckoned more than 125 degrees; but in this Voyage we made no such allowance: (though it be usual to do it) so that how much soever this Computation of mine exceeds the common Draughts, yet it is of the shortest, according to our Experiment and Calculation.

¶ But to proceed with our Voyage: The Island *Guam* or *Guabon*, (as the Native *Indians* pronounce it) is one of the *Ladrone* Islands, belongs to the *Spaniards*, who have a small Fort with six Guns in it, with a Governour, and 20 or 30 Soldiers. They keep it for the relief and refreshment of their *Philippine* Ships, that touch here in their way from *Acapulco* to *Manila*, but the Winds will not so easily let them take this way back again. The *Spaniards* of late have named *Guam*, the Island *Maria*; it is about 12 Leagues long, and four broad, lying N. and S. It is pretty high Champion Land.

¶ The 21st Day of *May*, 1686, at 11 a Clock in the Evening, we anchored near the middle of the Island *Guam*, on the West-side, a Mile from the shore. At a distance it appears flat and even, but coming near it you will find it stands shelving, and the East-side, which is much the highest, is fenced with steep Rocks, that oppose the Violence of the Sea, which continually rages against it, being driven with the constant Trade-wind, and on that side there is no Anchoring. The West-side is pretty low, and full of small sandy Bays, divided with as many rocky Points. The Soil of the Island is reddish, dry and indifferent fruitful. The Fruits are chiefly

Rice, Pine-Apples, Water-melons, Musk-melons, Oranges and Limes, Coco-nuts, and a sort of Fruit called by us Bread-fruit.

¶ The Coco-nut Trees grow by the Sea, on the Western-side in great Groves, three or four Miles in length, and a Mile or two broad. This Tree is in shape like the Cabbage-tree, and at a distance they are not to be known each from other, only the Coco-nut Tree is fuller of Branches; but the Cabbage-tree generally is much higher, tho' the Coco-nut Trees in some places are very high.

¶ The Nut or Fruit grows at the head of the Tree, among the Branches and in Clusters, 10 or 12 in a Cluster. The Branch to which they grow is about the bigness of a Man's Arm, and as long, running small towards the end. It is of a yellow Colour, full of Knots, and very tough. The Nut is generally bigger than a Man's Head. The outer Rind is near two Inches thick, before you come to the Shell; the Shell it self is black, thick, and very hard. The Kernel in some Nuts is near an Inch thick, sticking to the inside of the Shell clear round, leaving a hollow in the middle of it, which contains about a Pint, more or less, according to the bigness of the Nut, for some are much bigger than others.

¶ This Cavity is full of sweet, delicate, wholsom and refreshing Water. While the Nut is growing, all the inside is full of this Water, without any Kernel at all; but as the Nut grows towards its Maturity, the Kernel begins to gather and settle round on the inside of the Shell, and is soft like Cream; and as the Nut ripens, it increaseth in substance and becomes hard. The ripe Kernel is sweet enough, but very hard to digest, therefore seldom eaten, unless by Strangers, who know not the effects of it; but while it is young and soft like Pap, some Men will eat it, scraping it out with a Spoon, after they have drunk the Water that was within it. I like the Water best when the Nut is almost ripe, for it is then sweetest and briskest.

¶ When these Nuts are ripe and gathered, the outside Rind becomes of a brown rusty colour; so that one would think that they were dead and dry; yet they will sprout out like Onions, after they have been hanging in the Sun three or four Months, or thrown about in a House or Ship, and if planted afterward in the Earth, they will grow up to a Tree. Before they thus sprout out, there is a small spungy round knob grows in the inside, which we call an Apple. This at first is no bigger than the top of one's Finger, but increaseth daily, sucking up the Water till it is grown so big as to fill up the Cavity of the Coco-nut, and then it begins to sprout forth. By this time the Nut that was hard, begins to grow oily and soft, thereby giving passage to the Sprout that springs from the Apple, which

Nature hath so contrived, that it points to the hole in the Shell, (of which there are three, till it grows ripe, just where it's fastned by its stalk to the Tree; but one of these holes remain open, even when it is ripe) through which it creeps and spreads forth its Branches. You may let these teeming Nuts sprout out a Foot and half, or two Foot high before you plant them, for they will grow a great while like an Onion out of their own Substance.

¶ Beside the Liquor or Water in the Fruit, there is also a sort of Wine drawn from the Tree called Toddy, which looks like Whey. It is sweet and very pleasant, but it is to be drunk within 24 Hours after it is drawn, for afterwards it grows sowre. Those that have a great many Trees, draw a Spirit from the sowre Wine, called Arack. Arack is distill'd also from Rice, and other things in the *East-Indies*; but none is so much esteemed for making Punch as this sort, made of Toddy, or the Sap of the Coco-nut Tree, for it makes most delicate Punch; but it must have a dash of Brandy to hearten it, because this Arack is not strong enough to make good Punch of it self. This sort of Liquor is chiefly used about *Goa*; and therefore it has the Name of *Goa* Arack. The way of drawing the Toddy from the Tree, is by cutting the top of a Branch that would bear Nuts; but before it has any Fruit; and from thence the Liquor which was to feed its Fruit, distils into the hole of a Callabash that is hung upon it.

¶ This Branch continues running almost as long as the Fruit would have been growing, and then it dries away. The Tree hath usually three fruitful Branches, which if they be all tapp'd thus, then the Tree bears no Fruit that Year; but if one or two only be tapped, the other will bear Fruit all the while. The Liquor which is thus drawn is emptied out of the Callabash duly Morning and Evening, so long as it continues running, and is sold every Morning and Evening in most Towns in the *East-Indies*, and great Gain is produced from it even this way; but those that distil it and make Arrack, reap the greatest profit. There is also great profit made of the Fruit, both of the Nut and the Shell.

¶ The Kernel is much used in making Broath. When the Nut is dry, they take off the Husk, and giving two good Blows on the middle of the Nut, it breaks in two equal parts, letting the Water fall on the Ground; then with a small Iron Rasp made for the purpose, the Kernel or Nut is rasped out clean, which being put into a little fresh Water, makes it become white as Milk. In this milky Water, they boil a Fowl, or any other sort of Flesh, and it makes very savory Broath. *English* Seamen put this Water into boiled Rice, which they eat instead of Rice-milk, carrying Nuts purposely to Sea with them. This they learnt from the Natives.

¶ But the greatest use of the Kernel is to make Oyl, both for burning and for frying. The way to make the Oyl is to grate or rasp the Kernel, and steep it in fresh Water; then boil it, and scum off the Oyl at top as it rises: But the Nuts that make the Oyl ought to be a long time gathered, so as that the Kernel may be turning soft and oily.

¶ The Shell of this Nut is used in the *East-Indies* for Cups, Dishes, Ladles, Spoons, and in a manner for all eating and drinking Vessels. Well-shaped Nuts are often brought home to *Europe*, and much esteemed. The Husk of the Shell is of great use to make Cables; for the dry Husk is full of small Strings and Threads, which being beaten, become soft, and the other Substance which was mixt among it falls away like Saw-dust, leaving only the Strings. These are afterwards spun into long Yarns, and twisted up into Balls for Convenience: and many of these Rope-Yarns joined together make good Cables. This Manufactory is chiefly used at the *Maldive-Islands*, and the Threads sent in Balls into all places that trade thither, purposely for to make Cables. I made a Cable at *Achin* with some of it. These are called *Coire* Cables; they will last very well. But there is another sort of *Coire* Cables (as they are called) that are black, and more strong and lasting; and are made of strings that grow like Horse-hair, at the heads of certain Trees, almost like the Coco-nut Tree. This sort comes most from the Island *Timor*. In the *South-Seas* the *Spaniards* do make Oakam to caulk their Ships, with the Husk of the Coco-nut, which is more serviceable than that made of Hemp, and they say it will never rot. I have been told by Captain *Knox*, who wrote the Relation of *Ceylon*, that in some places of *India* they make a sort of coarse Cloth of the husk of the Coco-nut, which is used for Sails. I my self have seen a sort of coarse Sail-cloth made of such a kind of substance; but whether the same or no I know not.

¶ I have been the longer on this subject, to give the Reader a particular Account of the use and profit of a Vegetable, which is possibly of all others the most generally serviceable to the Conveniences, as well as the Necessities of humane Life. Yet this Tree, that is of such great use, and esteemed so much in the *East-Indies*, is scarce regarded in the *West-Indies*, for want of the knowledge of the benefit which it may produce. And 'tis partly for the sake of my Country-men, in our *American* Plantations, that I have spoken so largely of it. For the hot Climates there are a very proper Soil for it: and indeed it is so hardy, both in the raising it, and when grown, that it will thrive as well in dry sandy ground as in rich Land. I have found them growing very well in low sandy Islands (on the West of *Sumatra*) that are over-flowed with the Sea every Spring-tide; and though the Nuts there are not very big, yet this is no loss, for the Kernel

is thick and sweet; and the Milk, or Water in the inside, is more pleasant
and sweet than of the Nuts that grow in rich ground, which are commonly
large indeed, but not very sweet. These at *Guam* grow in dry ground, are
of a middle size, and I think the sweetest that I did ever taste. Thus much
for the Coco-nut.

¶ The Lime is a sort of bastard or Crab-limon. The Tree, or Bush that
bears it, is prickly, like a Thorn, growing full of small Boughs. In *Jamaica*,
and other places, they make of the Lime-Bush Fences about Gardens, or
any other Inclosure, by planting the Seeds close together, which growing
up thick, spread abroad, and make a very good Hedge. The Fruit is like
a Lemon, but smaller; the Rind thin, and the inclosed Substance full of
Juice. The Juice is very tart, yet of a pleasant taste if sweetned with
Sugar. It is chiefly used for making Punch, both in the *East* and *West-
Indies*, as well ashoar as at Sea, and much of it is for that purpose yearly
brought home to *England*, from our *West-India* Plantations. It is also used
for a particular kind of Sauce, which is called Pepper-Sauce, and is made
of Cod-Pepper, commonly call'd *Guinea*-Pepper, boiled in Water, and then
pickled with Salt, and mixed with Lime-juice to preserve it. Limes grow
plentiful in the *East* and *West-Indies*, within the Tropicks.

¶ The Bread-fruit (as we call it) grows on a large Tree, as big and high
as our largest Apple-Trees. It hath a spreading Head full of Branches,
and dark Leaves. The Fruit grows on the Boughs like Apples: it is as
big as a Penny-loaf, when Wheat is at five Shillings the Bushel. It is of
a round shape, and hath a thick tough Rind. When the Fruit is ripe, it
is yellow and soft; and the taste is sweet and pleasant. The Natives of
this Island use it for Bread: they gather it when full grown, while it is
green and hard; then they bake it in an Oven, which scorcheth the rind
and makes it black: but they scrape off the outside black Crust, and there
remains a tender thin Crust, and the inside is soft, tender and white, like
the Crumb of a Penny Loaf. There is neither Seed nor Stone in the inside,
but all is of a pure substance like Bread: it must be eaten new, for if it is
kept above 24 Hours, it becomes dry, and eats harsh and choaky; but 'tis
very pleasant before it is too stale. This Fruit lasts in season eight
Months in the Year; during which time the Natives eat no other sort
of Food of Bread-kind. I did never see of this Fruit any where but
here. The Natives told us, that there is plenty of this Fruit growing on
the rest of the *Ladrone* Islands; and I did never hear of any of it any where
else.

¶ They have here some Rice also: but the Island being of a dry Soil,
and therefore not very proper for it, they do not sow very much. Fish

is scarce about this Island; yet on the shole that our Bark came over there was great plenty, and the Natives commonly go thither to fish.

¶ The Natives of this Island are strong-bodied, large-limb'd, and well-shap'd. They are Copper-coloured, like other *Indians*: their Hair is black and long, their Eyes meanly proportioned; they have pretty high Noses; their Lips are pretty full, and their Teeth indifferent white. They are long-visaged, and stern of countenance; yet we found them to be affable and courteous. They are many of them troubled with a kind of Leprosie. This Distemper is very common at *Mindanao*: therefore I shall speak more of it in my next Chapter. They of *Guam* are otherwise very healthy, especially in the dry season: but in the wet season, which comes in in *June*, and holds till *October*, the Air is more thick and unwholsome; which occasions Fevers: but the Rains are not violent nor lasting. For the Island lies so far westerly from the *Philippine* Islands, or any other Land, that the westerly Winds do seldom blow so far; and when they do, they do not last long: but the easterly Winds do constantly blow here, which are dry and healthy; and this Island is found to be very healthful, as we were informed while we lay by it. The Natives are very ingenious beyond any People, in making Boats, or Proes, as they are called in the *East-Indies*, and therein they take great delight. These are built sharp at both ends; the bottom is of one piece, made like the bottom of a little Canoa, very neatly dug, and left of a good substance. This bottom-part is instead of a Keel. It is about 26 or 28 Foot long; the under-part of this Keel is made round, but inclining to a wedge, and smooth; and the upper-part is almost flat, having a very gentle hollow, and is about a Foot broad: From hence both sides of the Boat are carried up to about five Foot high with narrow Plank, not above four or five Inches broad, and each end of the Boat turns up round, very prettily. But what is very singular, one side of the Boat is made perpendicular, like a Wall, while the other side is rounding, made as other Vessels are, with a pretty full belly. Just in the middle it is about four or five Foot broad aloft, or more, according to the length of the Boat. The Mast stands exactly in the middle, with a long Yard that peeps up and down like a Mizen-yard. One end of it reacheth down to the end or head of the Boat, where it is placed in a notch, that is made there purposely to receive it, and keep it fast. The other end hangs over the Stern: To this Yard the Sail is fastened. At the Foot of the Sail there is another small Yard, to keep the Sail out square, and to roll up the Sail on when it blows hard; for it serves instead of a Reef to take up the Sail to what degree they please, according to the strength of the Wind. Along the Belly-side of the Boat, parallel with it, at about six or seven Foot distance, lies another small Boat, or Canoa, being a Log of very light Wood, almost as long as the great Boat, but not so wide, being not above a Foot and an half wide at the upper part, and very sharp like a Wedge at each end. And there are two Bamboes of about eight or 10 Foot long, and as big as one's Leg, placed over the great Boat's side, one near each end of it, and reaching about six or seven Foot from the side of the Boat: By the help of which, the little Boat is made firm and contiguous to the other. These are generally called by the *Dutch*, and by the *English* from them, *Out-layers*. The use of them is to keep the great Boat upright from over-setting; because the Wind here being in a manner constantly East, (or if it were at West it would be the same thing) and the Range of these Islands, where their business lies too and fro, being mostly North and South, they turn the flat side of the Boat against the Wind, upon which they sail, and the Belly-side, consequently with its little Boat, is upon the Lee: And the Vessel having a Head at each end, so as to sail with either of them foremost (indifferently) they need not tack, or go about, as all our Vessels do, but each end of the Boat serves either for Head or Stern as they please. When they ply to Windward, and are minded to go about, he that steers bears away a little from the Wind, by which means the Stern comes to the Wind; which is now become the Head, only by shifting the end of the Yard. This Boat is steered with a broad Paddle, instead of a Rudder. I have been the more particular in describing these Boats, because I do believe, they sail the best of any Boats in the World. I did here for my own satisfaction, try the swiftness of one of them; sailing by our Log, we had 12 Knots on our Reel, and she run it all out before the half Minute-Glass was half out; which, if it had been no more, is after the rate of 12 Mile an Hour; but I do believe she would have run 24 Mile an Hour. It was very pleasant to see the little Boat running along so swift by the others side.

¶ The Native *Indians* are no less dextrous in managing than in building these Boats. By report they will go from hence to another of the *Ladrone* Islands about 30 Leagues off, and there do their Business, and return again in less than 12 Hours. I was told that one of these Boats was sent Express to *Manila*, which is above 400 Leagues, and performed the Voyage in four Days time. There are of these Proes or Boats used in many places of the *East-Indies*, but with a Belly and a little Boat on each side. Only at *Mindanao* I saw one like these, with the Belly and a little Boat only on one side, and the other flat, but not so neatly built.

¶ The *Indians* of *Guam* have neat little Houses, very handsomly thatch'd with Palmeto-thatch. They inhabit together in Villages built by the Sea, on the West-side, and have *Spanish* Priests to instruct them in the Christian Religion.

¶ The *Spaniards* have a small Fort on the West-side, near the South-end, with six Guns in it. There is a Governour, and 20 or 30 *Spanish* Soldiers. There are no more *Spaniards* on this Island, beside two or three Priests. Not long before we arrived here, the Natives rose on the *Spaniards* to destroy them, and did kill many: But the Governour with his Soldiers at length prevailed, and drove them out of the Fort: So when they found themselves disappointed of their intent, they destroyed the Plantations and Stock, and then went away to other Islands: There were then three or 400 *Indians* on this Island; but now there are not above 100; for all that were in this Conspiracy went away. As for these who yet remain, if they were not actually concerned in that broil, yet their Hearts also are bent against the *Spaniards*: for they offered to carry us to the Fort, and assist us in the Conquest of the Island; but Capt. *Swan* was not for molesting the *Spaniards* here.

¶ Before we came to an anchor here, one of the Priests came aboard in the Night with three *Indians*. They first haled us to know from whence we came, and what we were: to whom answer was made in *Spanish*, that we were *Spaniards*, and that we came from *Acapulco*. It being dark they could not see the make of our Ship, nor very well discern what we were: Therefore we came aboard; but perceiving the mistake they were in, in taking us for a *Spanish* Ship, they endeavoured to get from us again, but we held their Boat fast, and made them come in. Capt. *Swan* received the Priest with much Civility, and conducting him into the great Cabbin, declared, That the reason of our coming to this Island was want of Provision, and that he came not in any hostile manner, but as a Friend to purchase with his Money what he wanted: And therefore desired the Priest to write a Letter to the Governour, to inform him what we were, and on what account we came. For having him now aboard, the Captain was willing to detain him as an Hostage, till we had Provision. The *Padre* told Captain *Swan*, that Provision was now scarce on the Island; but he would engage, that the Governour would do his utmost to furnish us.

¶ In the Morning the *Indians*, in whose Boat or Proe the Friar came aboard, were sent to the Governour with two Letters; one from the Friar, and another very obliging one from Capt. *Swan*, and a Present of four yards of Scarlet-cloath, and a piece of broad Silver and Gold-Lace. The Governour lives near the South-end of the Island on the West-side; which was about five Leagues from the place where we were; therefore we did not expect an Answer till the Evening, not knowing then how nimble they were. Therefore when the *Indian* Canoa was dispatched away to the Governour, we hoised out two of our Canoas, and sent one a fishing, and the other ashore for Coco-nuts. Our fishing Canoa got nothing; but the Men that went ashore for Coco-nuts came off laden.

¶ About 11 a Clock, that same Morning, the Governour of the Island sent a Letter to Capt. *Swan*, complimenting him for his Present, and promising to support us with as much Provision as he could possibly spare; and as a Token of his Gratitude, he sent a Present of six Hogs, of a small sort, most excellent Meat, the best I think, that ever I eat: They are fed with Coco-nuts, and their Flesh is as hard as Brisket-Beef. They were doubtless of that breed in *America* which came originally from *Spain*. He sent also 12 Musk-melons, larger than ours in *England*, and as many Water-melons, both sorts here being a very excellent Fruit; and sent an order to the *Indians* that lived in a Village not far from our Ship, to bake every Day as much of the Bread-fruit as we did desire, and to assist us in getting as many dry Coco-nuts as we would have; which they accordingly did, and brought off the Bread-Fruit every Day hot, as much as we could eat. After this the Governour sent every Day a Canoa or two with Hogs and Fruit, and desired for the same Powder, Shot and Arms; which were sent according to his Request. We had a delicate large *English* Dog, which the Governour did desire, and had it given him very freely by the Captain, though much against the grain of many of his Men, who had a great value for that Dog. Captain *Swan* endeavoured to get this Governour's Letter of Recommendation to some Merchants at *Manila*, for he had then a design to go to Fort St. *George*, and from thence intended to trade to *Manila*: but this his design was concealed from the Company. While we lay here, the *Acapulco* Ship arrived in sight of the Island, but did not come in the sight of us; for the Governour sent an *Indian* Proe, with advice of our being here. Therefore she stood off to the Southward of the Island, and coming foul of the same shole that our Bark had run over before, was in great danger of being lost there, for she struck off her Rudder, and with much ado got clear; but not till after three Days labour. For tho' the shole be so near the Island, and the *Indians* go off and fish there every Day, yet the Master of the *Acapulco* Ship, who should (one would think) know these Parts, was utterly ignorant of it. This their striking on the shole we heard afterward, when we were on the Coast of *Manila*; but these *Indians* of *Guam* did speak of her being in sight of the Island while we lay there, which put our Men in a great heat to go out after her, but Captain *Swan* persuaded them out of that humour, for he was now wholly averse to any Hostile action.

¶ The 30th Day of *May*, the Governour sent his last Present, which was some Hogs, a Jar of pickled Mangoes, a Jar of excellent pickled Fish, and a Jar of fine Rusk, or Bread of fine Wheat-Flower, baked like Bisket, but not so hard. He sent besides, six or seven Packs of Rice, desiring to be excused from sending any more Provision to us, saying he had no more on the Island that he could spare. He sent word also, that the West Monsoon was at hand, that therefore it behoved us to be jogging from hence, unless we were resolved to return back to *America* again. Captain *Swan* returned him thanks for his kindness and advice, and took his leave; and the same Day sent the Friar ashoar, that was seized on at our first arrival, and gave him a large Brass Clock, an Astrolable, and a large Telescope; for which Present the Friar sent us aboard six Hogs, and a roasting Pig, three or four Bushels of Potatoes, and 50 Pound of *Manila* Tobacco. Then we prepared to be gone, being pretty well furnished with Provision to carry us to *Mindano*, where we designed next to touch. We took aboard us as many Coco-nuts as we could well stow, and we had a good stock of Rice, and about 50 Hogs in salt.

CHAPTER XI

They resolve to go to Mindanao. *Their departure from* Guam. *Of the* Philippine *Islands. The Isle* Luconia, *and its chief Town and Port,* Manilo, Manila, *or* Manilbo. *Of the rich Trade we might establish with these Islands. St. John's Island. They arrive at* Mindanao. *The Island described. Its Fertility. The* Libby *Trees, and the* Sago *made of them. The Plantain Tree, Fruit, Liquor, and Cloath. A smaller Plantain at* Mindanao. *The* Bonano. *Of the Clove-bark, Cloves and Nutmegs, and the Methods taken by the* Dutch *to monopolize the Spices. The Betel-Nut, and* Arek-Tree. *The* Durien, *and the* Jaca-Tree *and Fruit. The Beasts of* Mindanao. *Centepees or* Forty Legs, *a venomous Insect, and others. Their Fowls, Fish, &c. The Temperature of the Climate, with the Course of the Winds, Tornadoes, Rain, and Temper of the Air throughout the Year.*

WHILE we lay at *Guam*, we took up a Resolution of going to *Mindanao*, one of the *Philippine* Islands, being told by the Friar and others, that it was exceedingly well stored with Provisions; that the Natives were *Mahometans*, and that they had formerly a Commerce with the *Spaniards*, but that now they were at Wars with them. This Island was therefore thought to be a convenient place for us to go; for besides that it was in our way to the *East-Indies*, which we had resolved to visit; and that the Westerly *Monsoon* was at hand, which would oblige us to shelter somewhere in a short time, and that we could not expect good Harbours in a better place than in so large an Island as *Mindanao*: besides all this, I say, the Inhabitants of *Mindanao* being then, as we were told, (tho' falsly) at Wars with the *Spaniards*, our Men, who it should seem were very squeamish of plundering without Licence, derived hopes from thence of getting a Commission there from the Prince of the Island, to plunder the *Spanish* Ships about *Manila*, and so to make *Mindanao* their common Rendezvous. And if Captain *Swan* was minded to go to an *English* Port, yet his Men, who thought he intended to leave them, hoped to get Vessels and Pilots at *Mindanao* fit for their turn, to cruize on the Coast of *Manila*. As for Captain *Swan*, he was willing enough to go thither, as best suiting his own design; and therefore this Voyage was concluded on by general consent.

¶ Accordingly *June* 2d, 1686, we left *Guam*, bound for *Mindanao*. We had fair Weather, and a pretty smart gale of Wind at East, for 3 or 4 Days, and then it shifted to the S.W. being rainy, but it soon came about again to the East, and blew a gentle gale; yet it often shuffled about to the S.E. For though in the *East-Indies* the Winds shift in *April*, yet we found this to be the shifting Season for the Winds here; the other shifting Season being in *October*, sooner or later, all over *India*. As to our Course from *Guam* to the *Philippine* Islands, we found it (as I intimated before) agreeable enough with the account of our common Draughts.

¶ The 21st Day of *June* we arrived at the Island *St. John*, which is one of the *Philippine* Islands. The *Philippines* are a great company of large Islands, taking up about 13 deg. of Lat. in length, reaching near upon, from 3 d. of North Lat. to the 19th degree, and in breadth about 6 deg. of Longitude. They derive this Name from *Phillip* II. King of *Spain*; and even now do they most of them belong to that Crown.

¶ The chiefest Island in this Range is *Luconia*, which lies on the North of them all. At this Island *Magellan* died on the Voyage that he was making round the World. For after he had past those Streights between the South-end of *America* and *Terra del Fuego*, which now bear his Name, and had ranged down in the *South-Seas* on the back of *America*; from thence stretching over to the *East-Indies*, he fell in with the *Ladrone* Islands, and from thence steering East still, he fell in with these *Philippine* Islands, and anchored at *Luconia*; where he warr'd with the native *Indians*, to bring them in Obedience to his Master the King of *Spain*, and was by them kill'd with a poysoned Arrow. It is now wholly under the *Spaniards*, who have several Towns there. The chief is *Manilo*, which is a large Sea-port Town near the S.E. end, opposite to the Island *Mindora*. It is a place of great Strength and Trade: The two great *Acapulco* Ships before mentioned fetching from hence all sorts of *East-India* Commodities; which are brought hither by Foreigners, especially by the *Chinese*, and the *Portugese*. Sometimes the *English* Merchants of Fort *St. George* send their Ships hither as it were by stealth, under the charge of *Portuguese* Pilots and Mariners: For as yet we cannot get the *Spaniards* there to a Commerce with us or the *Dutch*, although they have but few Ships of their own. This seems to arise from a Jealousie or Fear of discovering the Riches of these Islands, for most, if not all the *Philippine* Islands, are rich in Gold: And the *Spaniards* have no place of much strength in all these Islands that I could ever hear of, besides *Manilo* it self. Yet they have Villages and Towns on several of the Islands, and Padres or Priests to instruct the native *Indians*, from whom they get their Gold.

¶ The *Spanish* Inhabitants of the smaller Islands especially, would willingly trade with us if the Government was not so severe against it: for they have no Goods but what are brought from *Manilo* at an extraordinary dear rate. I am of the Opinion, that if any of our Nations will seek a Trade with them, they would not lose their labour; for the *Spaniards* can and will smuggle (as our Seamen call trading by stealth) as well as any Nation that I know; and our *Jamaicans* are to their profit sensible enough of it. And I have been informed that Captain *Goodlud of London*, in a Voyage which he made from *Mindanao* to *China*, touch'd at some of these Islands, and was civilly treated by the *Spaniards*, who bought some of his Commodities, giving him a very good Price for the same.

¶ There are about 12 or 14 more large Islands lying to the Southward of *Luconia*; most of which, as I said before, are inhabited by the *Spaniards*. Besides these there are an infinite number of small Islands of no account, and even the great Islands, many of them, are without Names; or at least so variously set down, that I find the same Islands named by divers Names.

¶ The Island St. *John* and *Mindanao* are the southermost of all these Islands, and are the only Islands in all this Range that are not subject to the *Spaniards*.

¶ St. *John*'s Island is on the East-side of the *Mindanao*, and distant from it 3 or 4 Leagues. It is in lat. about 7 or 8 North. This Island is in length about 38 Leagues, stretching N.N.W. and S.S.E. and it is in breadth about 24 Leagues, in the middle of the Island. The northermost end is broader, and the southermost is narrower: This Island is of a good heighth, and is full of many small Hills. The Land at the South-East-end (where I was ashoar) is of a black fat Mould; and the whole Island seems to partake of the same fatness, by the vast number of large Trees that it produceth; for it looks all over like one great Grove.

¶ As we were passing by the S.E. end we saw a Canoa of the Natives under the shoar; therefore one of our Canoas went after to have spoken with her; but she run away from us, seeing themselves chaced, put their Canoa ashoar, leaving her, fled into the Woods; nor would be allured to come to us, altho' we did what we could to entice them; besides these Men, we saw no more here, nor sign of any Inhabitants at this end.

¶ When we came aboard our Ship again, we steered away for the Island *Mindanao*, which was now fair in sight of us: it being about 10 leagues distant from this part of St. *John*'s. The 22d day we came within a league of the East-side of the Island *Mindanao*, and having the Wind at S.E. we steered toward the North-end, keeping on the East-side, till we came into the lat. of 7 d. 40 m. and there we anchored in a small Bay, about a Mile from the Shoar, in 10 Fathom Water, rocky foul Ground.

¶ Some of our Books gave us an account, that *Mindanao* City and Isle lies in 7 d. 40 m. We guest that the middle of the Island might lie in this lat. but we were at a great loss where to find the City, whether on the East or West-side. Indeed, had it been a small Island, lying open in the Eastern Wind, we might probably have searched first on the West-side; for commonly the Islands within the Tropicks, or within the bounds of the Trade-Winds, have their Harbours on the West-side, as best sheltered; but the Island *Mindanao* being guarded on the East-side by St. *John*'s Island, we might as reasonably expect to find the Harbour and City on this side, as any where else: but coming into the Lat. in which we judg'd the City might be, found no Canoas, or People, that might give us any umbrage of a City, or place of Trade near at hand, tho' we coasted within a League of the Shoar.

¶ The Island *Mindanao* is the biggest of all the *Philippine* Islands except *Luconia*. It is about 60 Leagues long, and 40 or 50 broad. The South-end is in about 5 d. N. and the N.W. end reacheth almost to 8 d. N. It is a very mountainous Island, full of Hills and Valleys. The Mould in general is deep and black and extraordinary fat and fruitful. The sides of the Hills are stony, yet productive enough of very large tall Trees. In the heart of the Country there are some Mountains that yield good Gold. The Valleys are well moistned with pleasant Brooks, and small Rivers of delicate Water; and have Trees of divers sorts flourishing and green all the Year. The Trees in general are very large, and most of them are of kinds unknown to us.

¶ There is one sort which deserves particular notice; called by the Natives *Libby*-Trees. These grow wild in great Groves of 5 or 6 Miles long, by the sides of the Rivers. Of these Trees Sago is made, which the poor

Country People eat instead of Bread 3 or 4 Months in the Year. This Tree for its body and shape is much like the Palmeto-Tree, or the Cabbage-Tree, but not so tall as the latter. The Bark and Wood is hard and thin like a Shell, and full of white Pith, like the Pith of an Elder. This Tree they cut down, and split it in the middle and scrape out all the Pith; which they beat lustily with a Wooden Pestle in a great Mortar or Trough, and then put it into a Cloth or Strainer held over a Trough; and pouring Water in among the Pith, they stir it about in the Cloth: So the Water carries all the Substance of the Pith through the Cloth down into the Trough, leaving nothing in the Cloth but a light sort of Husk, which they throw away; but that which falls into the Trough settles in a short time to the bottom like Mud; and then they draw off the Water, and take up the muddy Substance, wherewith they make Cakes; which being bak'd proves very good Bread.

¶ The *Mindanao* People live 3 or 4 Months of the Year on this Food for their Bread-kind. The Native *Indians* of *Teranate*, and *Tidore*, and all the *Spice-Islands*, have plenty of these Trees, and use them for Food in the same manner; as I have been inform'd by Mr. *Caril Rofy*, who is now Commander of one of the King's Ships. He was one of our Company at this time; and being left with Captain *Swan* at *Mindanao*, went afterwards to *Teranate*, and lived there among the *Dutch* a Year or two. The Sago which is transported into other parts of the *East-Indies*, is dried in small pieces like little Seeds or Comfits, and commonly eaten with Milk of Almonds, by those that are troubled with the Flux; for it is a great binder, and very good in that Distemper.

¶ In some places of *Mindanao* there is plenty of Rice; but in the hilly Land they plant Yams, Potatoes, and Pumpkins; all which thrive very well. The other Fruits of this Island are Water-Melons, Musk-Melons, Plantains, Bonanoes, Guavas, Nutmegs, Cloves, Betel-Nuts, Durians, Jacks, or Jacas, Coco-Nuts, Oranges, &c.

¶ The Plantain I take to be the King of all Fruit, not except the Coco it self. The Tree that bears this Fruit is about 3 Foot, or 3 Foot and an half round, and about 10 or 12 Foot high. These Trees are not raised from Seed, (for they seem not to have any) but from the Roots of other old Trees. If these young Suckers are taken out of the Ground, and planted in another place, it will be 15 Months before they bear, but if let stand in their own native Soil they will bear in 12 Months. As soon as the Fruit is ripe the Tree decays, but then there are many young ones growing up to supply its place. When this Tree first springs out of the Ground, it comes up with two Leaves; and by that time it is a Foot high, two more spring up in the inside of them; and in a short time after two more within them; and so on. By that time the Tree is a Month old, you may perceive a small body almost as big as one's Arm, and then there are eight or ten Leaves, some of them four or five Foot high. The first Leaves that it shoots forth are not above a Foot long, and half a Foot broad; and the Stem that bears them no bigger than one's Finger; but as the Tree grows higher the Leaves are larger. As the young Leaves spring up in the inside, so the old Leaves spread off, and their tops droop downward, being of a greater length and breadth, by how much they are nearer the Root, and at last decay and rot off: but still there are young Leaves spring up out of the top, which makes the Tree look always green and flourishing. When the Tree is full grown, the leaves are 7 or 8 Foot long, and a Foot and half broad; towards the end they are smaller, and end with a round point. The Stem of the Leaf is as big as a Man's Arm, almost round, and about a Foot in length, between the Leaf and the Body of the Tree. That part of the Stem which comes from the Tree, if it be the outside Leaf, seems to inclose half the Body as it were with a thick Hide; and right against it, on the other side of the Tree, is another such answering to it. The next two Leaves, in the inside of these, grow opposite to each other in the same manner, but so that if the two outward grow North and South, these grow East and West, and those still within them keep the same order. Thus the Body of this Tree seems to be made up of many thick Skins, growing one over another, and when it is full grown, there springs out of the top a strong Stem, harder in substance than any other part of the Body. This Stem shoots forth at the Heart of the Tree, is as big as a Man's Arm, and as long; and the Fruit grows in clusters round it, first blossoming and then shooting forth the Fruit. It is so excellent, that the *Spaniards* give it the preheminence of all other Fruit, as most conducing to Life. It grows in a Cod about 6 or 7 Inches long, and as big as a Man's Arm. The Shell, Rind or Cod, is soft, and of a yellow colour when ripe. It resembles in shape a Hogs-gut Pudding. The inclosed Fruit is no harder than Butter in Winter, and is much of the colour of the purest yellow Butter. It is of a delicate taste, and melts in one's Mouth like Marmalet. It is all pure Pulp, without any Seed, Kernel or Stone. This Fruit is so much esteemed by all *Europeans* that settle in *America*, that when they make a new Plantation, they commonly begin with a good Plantain-walk, as they call it, or a Field of Plantains; and as their Family increaseth, so they augment the Plantain-walk, keeping one Man purposely to prune the Trees, and gather the Fruit as he sees convenient. For the Trees continue bearing, some or other, most part of the Year; and this is many times the whole Food on which a whole Family subsists. They thrive only in rich fat ground, for poor sandy will not bear them. The *Spaniards* in their Towns in *America*, as at *Havana, Cartagena, Portobel*, &c. have their Markets full of Plantains, it being the common Food for poor People: Their common price is half a Riol, or 3*d.* a Dozen. When this Fruit is only used for Bread, it is roasted or boil'd when it's just full grown, but not yet ripe, or turn'd yellow. Poor People, or Negroes, that have neither Fish nor Flesh to eat with it, make Sauce with Cod-pepper, Salt and Lime-juice, which makes it eat very savory; much better than a crust of Bread alone. Sometimes for a change they eat a roasted Plantain, and a ripe raw Plaintain together, which is instead of Bread and Butter. They eat very pleasant so, and I have made many a good Meal in this Manner. Sometimes our *English* take 5 or 7 ripe Plantains, and mashing them together, make them into a lump, and boil them instead of a Bag-pudding; which they call a Buff-Jacket: and this is a very good way for a change. This Fruit makes also very good Tarts; and the green Plantains slic'd thin, and dried in the Sun, and grated, will make a sort of Flour which is very good to make Puddings. A ripe Plantain slic'd and dried in the Sun may be preserved a great while; and then eat like Figs, very sweet and pleasant. The *Darien Indians* preserve them a long time, by drying them gently over the Fire; mashing them first, and moulding them into lumps. The *Moskito Indians* will take a ripe Plantain and roast it; then take a pint and half of Water in a Calabash, and squeeze the Plantain in pieces with their Hands, mixing it with the Water; then they drink it all off together: This they call *Mishlaw*, and it's pleasant and sweet, and nourishing: somewhat like Lambs-wool (as 'tis call'd) made with Apples and Ale: and of this Fruit alone many thousand of *Indian* Families in the *West-Indies* have their whole subsistence. When they make Drink with them, they take 10 or 12 ripe Plantains and mash them well in a Trough: then they put 2 Gallons of Water among them; and this in 2 Hours time will ferment and froth like Wort. In 4 Hours it is fit to drink, and then they bottle it, and drink it as they have occasion: but this will not keep above 24 or 30 Hours. Those therefore that use this Drink, brew it in this manner every Morning. When I went first to *Jamaica* I could relish no other drink they had there. It drinks brisk and cool, and is very pleasant. This Drink is windy, and so is the Fruit eaten raw; but boil'd or roasted it is not so. If this Drink is kept above 30 Hours it grows sharp: but if then it be put out in the Sun, it will become very good Vinegar. This Fruit grows all over the *West-Indies* (in the proper Climates) at *Guniea*, and in the *East-Indies*.

¶ As the Fruit of this Tree is of great use for Food, so is the Body no less serviceable to make Cloaths; but this I never knew till I came to this Island. The ordinary People of *Mindanao* do wear no other Cloth. The Tree never bearing but once, and so being fell'd when the Fruit is ripe, they cut it down close by the Ground if they intend to make Cloth with it. One blow with a Hatchet, or long Knife, will strike it asunder; then they cut off the top, leaving the trunk 8 or 10 foot long, stripping off the outer Rind, which is thickest towards the lower end, having stript 2 or 3 of these Rinds, the Trunk becomes in a manner all of one bigness, and of a whitish colour: Then they split the Trunk in the middle; which being done, they split the two halves again, as near the middle as they can. This they leave in the Sun 2 or 3 Days, in which time part of the juicy substance of the Tree dries away, and then the ends will appear full of small Threads. The Women, whose employment it is to make the Cloth, take hold of those Threads one by one, which rend away easily from one end of the Trunk to the other, in bigness like whited-brown Thread; for the Threads are naturally of a determinate bigness, as I observed their Cloth to be all of one substance and equal fineness; but 'tis stubborn when new, wears out soon, and when wet, feels a little slimy. They make their pieces 7 or 8 Yards long, their Warp and Woof all one thickness and substance.

¶ There is another sort of Plantains in that Island, which are shorter and less than the others, which I never saw any where but here. These are full of black Seeds mixt quite through the Fruit. They are binding, and are much eaten by those that have Fluxes. The Country People gave them us for that use, and with good success.

¶ The *Bonano* Tree is exactly like the Plantain for shape and bigness, not easily distinguishable from it but by its Fruit, which is a great deal smaller, and not above half so long as a Plantain, being also more mellow and soft, less luscious, yet of a more delicate taste. They use this for the making Drink oftner than Plantains, and it is best when used for Drink, or eaten as Fruit; but it is not so good for Bread, nor doth it eat well at all when roasted or boil'd; so 'tis only necessity that makes any use it this way. They grow generally where Plantains do, being set intermixt with them purposely in their Plantain-walks. They have plenty of Clove-bark, of which I saw a Ship-load; and as for Cloves, *Raja Laut*, whom I shall have occasion to mention, told me, that if the *English* would settle there, they could order Matters so in a little time, as to send a Ship-load of Cloves from thence every Year. I have been informed that they grow on the Boughs of a Tree about as big as a Plumb-tree, but I never happened to see any of them.

¶ I have not seen the Nutmeg-trees any where; but the Nutmegs this Island produceth are fair and large, yet they have no great store of them, being unwilling to propagate them or the Cloves, for fear that should invite the *Dutch* to visit them, and bring them into subjection, as they have done the rest of the neighbouring Islands where they grow. For the *Dutch* being seated among the Spice-Islands, have monoplized all the Trade into their own Hands, and will not suffer any of the Natives to dispose of it, but to themselves alone. Nay, they are so careful to preserve it in their own Hands, that they will not suffer the Spice to grow in the uninhabited Islands, but send Soldiers to cut the Trees down. Captain *Rofy* told me, that while he lived with the *Dutch*, he was sent with other Men to cut down the Spice-Trees; and that he himself did at several times cut down 7 or 800 Trees. Yet altho' the *Dutch* take such care to destroy them, there are many uninhabited Islands that have great plenty of Spice-Trees, as I have been informed by *Dutch* Men that have been there, particularly by a Captain of a *Dutch* Ship that I met with at *Achin*, who told me, that near the Island *Banda* there is an Island where the Cloves falling from the Trees do lie and rot on the ground, and they are at the time when the Fruit falls, 3 or 4 Inches thick under the Trees. He and some others told me, that it would not be a hard matter for an *English* Vessel to purchase a Ship's Cargo of Spice, of the Natives of some of these Spice-Islands.

¶ He was a free Merchant that told me this. For by that name the *Dutch* and *English* in the *East-Indies*, distinguish those Merchants who are not Servants to the Company. The free Merchants are not suffered to trade to the Spice-Islands, nor to many other places where the *Dutch* have Factories; but on the other Hand, they are suffered to trade to some places where the *Dutch* Company themselves may not trade, as to *Achin* particularly, for there are some Princes in the *Indies*, who will not trade with the Company for fear of them. The Seamen that go to the Spice Islands are obliged to bring no Spice from thence for themselves, except a small matter for their own use, about a pound or two. Yet the Masters of those Ships do commonly so order their business, that they often secure a good quantity, and send it ashoar to some place near *Batavia*, before they come into that Harbour, (for it is always brought thither first before it's sent to *Europe*,) and if they meet any Vessel at Sea that will buy their Cloves, they will sell 10 or 15 Tuns out of 100, and yet seemingly carry their Complement to *Batavia*; for they will pour Water among the remaining part of their Cargo, which will swell them to that degree, that the Ships Hold will be as full again, as it was before any were sold. This

Trick they use when ever they dispose of any clandestinely; for the Cloves when they first take them in are extraordinary dry, and so will imbibe a great deal of Moisture. This is but one Instance, of many hundreds, of little deceitful Arts the *Dutch* Sea-men have in these Parts among them, of which I have both seen and heard several. I believe there are no where greater Thieves; and nothing will persuade them to discover one another; for should any do it, the rest would certainly knock him on the Head. But to return to the Products of *Mindanao*.

¶ The Betel-nut is much esteemed here, as it is in most places of the *East-Indies*. The Betel-Tree grows like the Cabbage-Tree, but it is not so big, nor so high. The Body grows strait, about 12 or 14 foot high without Leaf or Branch, except at the Head. There it spreads forth long Branches, like other Trees of the like nature, as the Cabbage-Tree, the Coco-Nut Tree, and the Palm. These Branches are about 10 or 12 foot long, and their stems near the head of the Tree, as big as a Man's Arm. On the top of the Tree among the Branches the Betel-Nut grows on a tough stem as big as a Man's Finger, in clusters much as the Coco-Nuts do, and they grow 40 or 50 in a cluster. This Fruit is bigger than a Nutmeg, and is much like it, but rounder. It is much used all over the *East-Indies*. Their way is to cut it in four pieces, and wrap one of them up in an Arek-leaf, which they spread with a soft Paste made of Lime or Plaster, and then chew it altogether. Every Man in these parts carries his Lime-box by his side, and dipping his Finger into it, spreads his Betel and Arek-leaf with it. The Arek is a small Tree or Shrub, of a green Bark, and the Leaf is long and broader than a Willow. They are packt up to sell into Parts that have them not, to chew with the Betel. The Betel-Nut is most esteem'd when it is young, and before it grows hard, and then they cut it only in two pieces with the green Husk or Shell on it. It is then exceeding juicy, and therefore makes them spit much. It tastes rough in the Mouth, and dies the Lips red, and makes the Teeth black, but it preserves them, and cleanseth the Gums. It is also accounted very wholsom for the Stomach; but sometimes it will cause great Giddiness in the Head of those that are not us'd to chew it. But this is the Effect only of the old Nut, for the young Nuts will not do it. I speak of my own experience.

¶ This Island produceth also Durians and Jacks. The Trees that bear the Durians, are as big as Apple-Trees, full of Boughs. The Rind is thick and rough; the Fruit is so large that they grow only about the Bodies, or on the Limbs near the Body, like the Cacao. The Fruit is about the Bigness of a large Pumpkin, covered with a thick green rough Rind. When it is ripe, the Rind begins to turn yellow, but it is not fit to eat till it opens at the top. Then the Fruit in the inside is ripe, and sends forth an excellent Scent. When the Rind is opened, the Fruit may be split into four quarters; each quarter hath several small Cells, that inclose a certain quantity of the Fruit, according to the bigness of the Cell, for some are larger than others. The largest of the Fruit may be as big as a Pullet's Egg. 'Tis as white as Milk, and as soft as Cream, and the Taste very delicious as those that are accustomed to them; but those who have not been used to eat them, will dislike them at first, because they smell like roasted Onions. This Fruit must be eaten in its prime, (for there is no eating of it before it is ripe) and even then 'twill not keep above a day or two before it putrifies, and turns black, or of a dark colour, and then it is not good. Within the Fruit there is a Stone as big as a small Bean, which hath a thin Shell over it. Those that are minded to eat the Stones or Nuts, roast them, and then a thin Shell comes off, which incloses the Nut; and it eats like a Chesnut.

¶ The Jack or Jaca is much like the Durian, both in bigness and shape. The Trees that bear them also are much alike, and so is their manner of the Fruits growing. But the inside is different; for the Fruit of the Durian is white, that of the Jack is yellow, and fuller of Stones. The Durian is most esteemed; yet the Jack is a very pleasant Fruit, and the Stones or Kernels are good roasted.

¶ There are many other sorts of Grain, Roots and Fruits in this Island, which to give a particular description of would fill up a large Volume.

¶ In this Island are also many sorts of Beasts, both wild and tame; as Horses, Bulls, and Cows, Buffaloes, Goats, Wild Hogs, Deer, Monkies, Guano's, Lizards, Snakes, &c. I never saw or heard of any Beasts of Prey here, as in many other places. The Hogs are ugly Creatures; they have all great Knobs growing over their Eyes, and there are multitudes of them in the Woods. They are commonly very poor, yet sweet. Deer are here very plentiful in some places, where they are not disturbed.

¶ Of the venomous kind of Creatures here are Scorpions, whose sting is in their Tail; and Centapes, call'd by the *English* 40 Legs, both which are also common in the *West-Indies*, in *Jamaica*, and elsewhere. These Centapees are 4 or 5 Inches long, as big as a Goose-Quill, but flattish; of a Dun or reddish colour on the Back, but Belly whitish, and full of Legs on each side the Belly. Their Sting or Bite is more raging than the Scorpion. They lie in old Houses, and dry Timber. There are several sorts of Snakes, some very poisonous. There is another sort of Creature like a Guano both in colour and shape, but four times as big, whose Tongue is like a small Harpoon, having two beards like the beards of a Fish-hook.

They are said to be very venomous, but I know not their Names. I have seen them in other places also, as at *Pulo Condore*, or the Island *Condore*, and at *Achin*, and have been told that they are in the Bay of *Bengal*.

¶ The Fowls of this Country are Ducks and Hens: Other tame Fowl I have not seen nor heard of any. The wild Fowl, are Pidgeons, Parrots, Parakits, Turtle-Doves, and abundance of small Fowls. There are Bats as big as a Kite.

¶ There are a great many Harbours, Creeks, and good Bays for Ships to ride in; and Rivers navigable for Canoas, Proes or Barks, which are all plentifully stored with Fish of divers sorts, so is also the adjacent Sea. The chiefest Fish are Boneta's, Snooks, Cavally's, Bremes, Mullets, 10 Pounders, &c. Here are also plenty of Sea Turtle, and small Manatee, which are not near so big as those in the *West-Indies*. The biggest that I saw would not weigh above 600 Pound; but the flesh both of the Turtle and Manatee are very sweet.

¶ The Weather at *Mindanao* is temperate enough as to heat, for all it lies so near the Equator; and especially on the borders near the Sea. There they commonly enjoy the Breezes by Day, and cooling Land-Winds at Night. The Winds are easterly one part of the Year, and westerly the other. The easterly Winds begin to blow in *October*, and it is the middle of *November* before they are settled. These Winds bring fair Weather. The westerly Winds begin to blow in *May*, but are not settled till a Month afterwards. The West-Winds always bring Rain, Tornadoes, and very tempestuous Weather. At the first coming in of these Winds they blow but faintly; but then the Tornadoes rise one in a Day, sometimes two. These are Thunder-showers which commonly come against the Wind, bringing with them a contrary Wind to what did blow before. After the Tornadoes are over, the Wind shifts about again, and the Sky becomes clear, yet then in the Valleys and the sides of the Mountains, there riseth a thick Fog, which covers the Land. The Tornadoes continue thus for a Week or more; then they come thicker, two or three in a Day, bringing violent gusts of Wind, and terrible claps of Thunder. At last they come so fast, that the Wind remains in the Quarter from whence these Tornadoes do rise, which is out of the West, and there it settles till *October* or *November*. When these westward Winds are thus settled, the Sky is all in mourning, being covered with black Clouds, pouring down excessive Rains sometimes mixt with Thunder and Lightning, that nothing can be more dismal. The Winds raging to that degree, that the biggest Trees are torn up by the Roots, and the Rivers swell and overflow their Banks, and drown the low Land, carrying great Trees into the Sea. Thus it continues sometimes a Week together, before the Sun or Stars appear. The fiercest of this Weather is in the latter end of *July* and in *August*, for then the Towns seem to stand in a great Pond, and they go from one House to another in Canoas. At this time the Water carries away all the filth and nastiness from under their Houses. Whilst this tempestuous Season lasts, the Weather is cold and chilly. In *September* the Weather is more moderate, and the Winds are not so fierce, nor the Rain so violent. The Air thenceforward begins to be more clear and delightsome; but then in the Morning there are thick Fogs, continuing till 10 or 11 a Clock before the Sun shines out, especially when it has rained in the Night. In *October* the easterly-Winds begin to blow again, and bring fair Weather till *April*. Thus much concerning the natural state of *Mindanao*.

CHAPTER XII

Of the Inhabitants, and Civil State of the Isle of Mindanao. *The* Mindanayans, Hillanoones, Sologues, *and* Alfoores. *Of the* Mindanayans, *properly so called; Their Manners and Habits. The Habits and Manners of their Women. A Comical Custom at* Mindanao. *Their Houses, their Diet, and Washings. The Languages spoken there, and Transactions with the* Spaniards. *Their fear of the* Dutch, *and seeming desire of the* English. *Their Handy-crafts, and peculiar sort of Smiths Bellows. Their Shipping, Commodities, and Trade. The* Mindanao *and* Manila Tobacco. *A sort of Leprosie there, and other Distempers. Their Marriages. The* Sultan *of* Mindanao, *his Poverty, Power, Family,* &c. *The Proes or Boats here.* Raja Laut *the General, Brother to the* Sultan, *and his Family. Their way of Fighting. Their Religion.* Raja Laut*'s Devotion. A Clock or Drum in their Mosques. Of their* Circumcision, *and the Solemnity then used. Of other their Religious Observations and Superstitions. Their abhorrence of Swines-Flesh,* &c.

THIS Island is not subject to one Prince, neither is the Language one and the same; but the People are much alike, in colour, strength, and stature. They are all or most of them of one Religion, which is Mahometanism, and their customs and manner of living are alike. The *Mindanao* People, more particularly so called, are the greatest Nation in the Island, and trading by Sea with other Nations, they are therefore the more civil. I shall say but little of the rest, being less known to me, but so much as hath come to my knowledge, take as follows. There are besides the *Mindanayans*, the *Hilanoones*, (as they call them) or the *Mountaneers*, the *Sologues* and *Alfoores*.

¶ The *Hilanoones* live in the heart of the Country: They have little or no commerce by Sea, yet they have Proe's that row with 12 or 14 Oars apiece. They enjoy the benefit of the Gold Mines; and with their Gold buy foreign Commodities of the *Mindanao* People. They have also plenty of Bees-Wax, which they exchange for other Commodities.

¶ The *Sologues* inhabit the N.W. end of the Island. They are the least Nation of all; they Trade to *Manila* in Proes, and to some of the Neighbouring Islands, but have no Commerce with the *Mindanao* People.

¶ The *Alfoores* are the same with the *Mindanayans*, and were formerly under the subjection of the Sultan of *Mindanao*, but were divided between the Sultan's Children, and have of late had a Sultan of their own; but having by Marriage contracted an alliance with the Sultan of *Mindanao*, this has occasioned that Prince to claim them again as his Subjects; and he made War with them a little after we went away, as I afterwards understood.

¶ The *Mindanayans* properly so called, are Men of mean statures; small Limbs, straight Bodies, and little Heads. Their Faces are oval, their Foreheads flat, with black small Eyes, short low Noses, pretty large Mouths; their Lips thin and red, their Teeth black, yet very sound, their Hair black and straight, the colour of their Skin tawney, but inclining to a brighter yellow than some other *Indians*, especially the Women. They have a Custom to wear their Thumb-nails very long, especially that on their left Thumb, for they do never cut it but scrape it often. They are indued with good natural Wits, are ingenious, nimble, and active, when they are minded; but generally very lazy and thievish, and will not work except forced by Hunger. This laziness is natural to most *Indians*; but these People's laziness seems rather to proceed not so much from their natural Inclinations, as from the severity of their Prince, of whom they stand in awe: For he dealing with them very arbitrarily, and taking from them what they get, this damps their Industry, so they never strive to have any thing but from Hand to Mouth. They are generally proud, and walk very stately. They are civil enough to Strangers, and will easily be acquainted with them, and entertain them with great freedom; but they are implacable to their Enemies, and very revengeful if they are injured, frequently poisoning secretly those that have affronted them.

¶ They wear but few Cloaths; their Heads are circled with a short Turbat, fringed or laced at both ends; it goes once about the Head, and is tied in a knot, the laced ends hanging down. They wear Frocks and Breeches, but no Stockings nor Shooes.

¶ The Women are fairer than the Men; and their Hair is black and long; which they tie in a knot, that hangs back in their Poles. They are more round visaged than the Men, and generally well featured; only their

Noses are very small, and so low between their Eyes, that in some of the Female Children the rising that should be between the Eyes is scarce discernable; neither is there any sensible rising in their Foreheads. At a distance they appear very well; but being nigh, these Impediments are very obvious. They have very small Limbs. They wear but two Garments; a Frock, and a sort of Petticoat; the Petticoat is only a piece of Cloth, sowed both ends together: but it is made two Foot too big for their Wastes, so that they may wear either end uppermost: that part that comes up to their Waste, because it is so much too big, they gather it in their Hands, and twist it till it fits close to their Wastes, tucking in the twisted part between their Waste and the edge of the Petticoat, which keeps it close. The Frock fits loose about them, and reaches down a little below the Waste. The Sleeves are a great deal longer than their Arms, and so small at the end, that their Hands will scarce go through. Being on, the Sleeve fits in folds about the Wrist, wherein they take great Pride.

¶ The better sort of People have their Garments made of long Cloth; but the ordinary sort wear Cloth made of Plantain-tree, which they call *Saggen*, by which Name they call the Plantain. They have neither Stocking or Shooe, and the Women have very small Feet.

¶ The Women are very desirous of the Company of Strangers, especially of White Men; and doubtless would be very familiar, if the Custom of the Country did not debar them from that freedom, which seems coveted by them. Yet from the highest to the lowest they are allowed liberty to converse with, or treat Strangers in the sight of their Husbands.

¶ There is a kind of begging Custom at *Mindanao*, that I have not met elsewhere with in all my Travels; and which I believe is owing to the little Trade they have; which is thus: When Strangers arrive here, the *Mindanao* Men will come aboard, and invite them to their Houses, and inquire who has a *Comrade*, (which word I believe they have from the *Spaniards*) or a *Pagally*, and who has not. A *Comrade* is a familiar Male-friend; a *Pagally* is an innocent Platonick Friend of the other Sex. All Strangers are in a manner oblig'd to accept of this Acquaintance and Familiarity, which must be first purchased with a small Present, and afterwards confirmed with some Gift or other to continue the Acquaintance: and as often as the Stranger goes ashore, he is welcome to his *Comrade* or *Pagally*'s House, where he may be entertained for his Money, to Eat, Drink, or Sleep; and complimented, as often as he comes ashore, with Tobacco and Betel-Nut, which is all the Entertainment he must expect *gratis*. The richest Mens Wives, are allowed the freedom to converse with her *Pagally* in publick, and may give or receive Presents from him. Even the Sultans and the Generals Wives, who are always coopt up, will yet look out of their Cages when a Stranger passeth by, and demand of him if he wants a *Pagally*: and to invite him to their Friendship, will send a Present of Tobacco and Betel-nut to him by their Servants.

¶ The chiefest City on this Island is called by the same name of *Mindanao*. It is seated on the South-side of the Island, in lat. 7 d. 20 m. N. on the Banks of a small River, about two Mile from the Sea. The manner of building is somewhat strange: yet generally used in this part of the *East-Indies*. Their Houses are all built on Posts, about 14, 16, 18, or 20 Foot high. These Posts are bigger or less, according to the intended magnificence of the Superstructure. They have but one Floor, but many Partitions or Rooms, and a Ladder or Stairs to go up out of the Streets. The Roof is large, and covered with Palmeto or Palm-leaves. So there is a clear passage like a Piazza (but a filthy one) under the House. Some of the poorer People that keep Ducks or Hens, have a fence made round the Posts of their Houses, with a Door to go in and out; and this Under-room serves for no other use. Some use this place for the common draught of their Houses, but building mostly close by the River in all parts of the *Indies*, they make the River receive all the filth of their House; and at the time of the Land-floods, all is washed very clean.

¶ The Sultan's House is much bigger than any of the rest. It stands on about 180 great Posts or Trees, a great deal higher than the common Building, with great broad Stairs made to go up. In the first Room he hath about 20 Iron Guns, all Saker and Minion, placed on Field-Carriages. The General, and other great Men have some Guns also in their Houses. About 20 paces from the Sultan's House there is a small low House, built purposely for the Reception of Ambassadors or Merchant Strangers. This also stands on Posts, but the Floor is not raised above three or four Foot above the Ground, and is neatly matted purposely for the Sultan and his Council to sit on; for they use no Chairs, but sit cross-legg'd like Taylors on the Floor.

¶ The common Food at *Mindanao* is Rice, or Sago, and a small Fish or two. The better sort eat Buffalo, or Fowls ill drest, and abundance of Rice with it. They use no Spoons to eat their Rice, but every Man takes a handful out of the Platter, and by wetting his Hand in Water, that it may not stick to his Hand, squeezes it into a lump, as hard as possibly he can make it, and then crams it into his Mouth. They all strive to make these lumps as big as their Mouth can receive them; and seem to vie with each other, and glory in taking in the biggest lump; so that sometimes they almost choak themselves. They always wash after Meals, or if they touch any thing that is unclean; for which reason they spend abundance of Water in their Houses. This Water, with the washing of their Dishes, and what other filth they make, they pour down near their Fire-place: for their Chambers are not boarded, but floored with split Bamboes, like Lathe, so that the Water presently falls underneath their dwelling Rooms, where it breeds Maggots, and makes a prodigious stink. Besides this filthiness, the sick People ease themselves, and make Water in their Chambers; there being a small hole made purposely in the Floor, to let it drop through. But healthy sound People commonly ease themselves, and make Water in the River. For that reason you shall always see abundance of People, of both Sexes in the River, from Morning till Night; some easing themselves, others washing their Bodies or Cloaths. If they come into the River purposely to wash their Cloaths, they strip and stand naked till they have done; then put them on, and march out again: both Men and Women take great delight in swimming, and washing themselves, being bred to it from their Infancy. I do believe it is very wholsom to wash Mornings and Evenings in these hot Countries, at least three or four Days in the Week: For I did use my self to it when I lived afterwards at *Ben-cooly*, and found it very refreshing and comfortable. It is very good for those that have Fluxes to wash and stand in the River Mornings and Evenings. I speak it experimentally; for I was brought very low with that distemper at *Achin*; but by washing constantly Mornings and Evenings I found great benefit, and was quickly cured by it.

¶ In the City of *Mindanao* they speak two Languages indifferently; their own *Mindanao* Language, and the *Malaya*: but in other parts of the Island they speak only their proper Language, having little Commerce abroad. They have Schools, and instruct their Children to read and write, and bring them up in the *Mahometan* Religion. Therefore many of the Words, especially their Prayers, are in *Arabick*; and many of the words of civilty the same as in *Turkey*; and especially when they meet in the Morning, or take leave of each other, they express themselves in that Language.

¶ Many of the old People, both Men and Women, can speak *Spanish*, for the *Spaniards* were formerly settled among them, and had several Forts on this Island; and then they sent two Friars to the City, to convert the Sultan of *Mindanao* and his People. At that time these People began to learn *Spanish*, and the *Spaniards* incroached on them, and endeavoured to bring them into subjection; and probably before this time had brought them all under their Yoak, if they themselves had not been drawn off from this Island to *Manila*, to resist the *Chinese*, who threatned to invade them there. When the *Spaniards* were gone, the old Sultan of *Mindanao*, Father to the present, in whose time it was, razed and demolished their Forts, brought away their Guns, and sent away the Friars; and since that time will not suffer the *Spaniards* to settle on the Islands.

¶ They are now most afraid of the *Dutch*, being sensible how they have inslaved many of the Neighbouring Islands. For that Reason they have a long time desired the *English* to settle among them, and have offered them any convenient Place to build a Fort in, as the General himself told us; giving this Reason, that they do not find the *English* so incroaching as the *Dutch* or *Spanish*. The *Dutch* are no less jealous of their admitting the *English*, for they are sensible what detriment it would be to them if the *English* should settle here.

¶ There are but few Tradesmen at the City of *Mindanao*. The chiefest Trades are Goldsmiths, Blacksmiths, and Carpenters. There are but two or three Goldsmiths; these will work in Gold or Silver, and make any thing that you desire: but they have no Shop furnished with Ware ready-made for Sale. Here are several Blacksmiths who work very well, considering the Tools that they work with. Their Bellows are much different from ours. They are made of a wooden Cylinder, the trunk of a Tree, about three Foot long, bored hollow like a Pump, and set upright on the ground, on which the Fire it self is made. Near the lower end there is a small hole, in the side of the Trunk next the Fire, made to receive a Pipe, through which the wind is driven to the Fire by a great bunch of fine Feathers fastned to one end of the Stick, which closing up the inside of the Cylinder, drives the Air out of the Cylinder through the Pipe: Two of these Trunks or Cylinders are placed so nigh together, that a Man standing between them may work them both at once alternately, one with each Hand. They have neither Vice nor Anvil, but a great hard Stone or a piece of an old Gun, to hammer upon: yet they will perform their work, making both common Utensils and Iron-works about Ships to admiration. They work altogether with Charcoal. Every Man almost is a Carpenter, for they can work with the Ax and Adds. Their Ax is but small, and so made that they can take it out of the Helve, and by turning it make an Adds of it. They have no Saws; but when they make Plank, they split the Tree in two, and make a Plank of each part, plaining it with the Ax and Adds. This requires much pains, and takes up a great deal of time; but they work cheap, and the goodness of the Plank thus hewed, which hath its Grain preserv'd entire, makes amends for their cost and pains.

¶ They build good and serviceable Ships or Barks for the Sea, some for

Trade, others for Pleasure; and some Ships of War. Their trading Vessels they send chiefly to *Manila*. Thither they transport Bees-wax, which, I think, is the only Commodity, besides Gold that they vend there. The Inhabitants of the City of *Mindanao* get a great deal of Bees-wax themselves: but the greatest quantity they purchase is of the Mountaneers, from whom they also get the Gold which they send to *Manila*; and with these they buy their Callicoes, Muslins, and *China* Silk. They send sometimes their Barks to *Borneo* and other Islands; but what they transport thither, or import from thence, I know not. The *Dutch* come hither in Sloops from *Ternate* and *Tidore*, and buy Rice, Bees-wax, and Tobacco: for here is a great deal of Tobacco grows on this Island, more than in any Island or Country in the *East-Indies*, that I know of, *Manila* only excepted. It is an excellent sort of Tobacco; but these People have not the Art of managing this Trade to their best advantage, as the *Spaniards* have at *Manila*. I do believe the Seeds were first brought hither from *Manila* by the *Spaniards*, and even thither, in all probability, from *America*: the difference between the *Mindanao* and *Manila* Tobacco is, that the *Mindanao* Tobacco is of a darker colour; and the Leaf larger and grosser than the *Manila* Tobacco, being propagated or planted in a fatter Soil. The *Manila* Tobacco is of a bright yellow colour, of an indifferent size, not strong, but pleasant to Smoak. The *Spaniards* at *Manila* are very curious about this Tobacco, having a peculiar way of making it up neatly in the Leaf. For they take two little Sticks, each about a Foot long, and flat, and placing the Stalks of the Tobacco Leaves in a row, 40 or 50 of them between the two Sticks, they bind them hard together, so that the Leaves hang dangling down. One of these bundles is sold for a Rial at Fort St. *George*: but you may have 10 or 12 Pound of Tobacco at *Mindanao* for a Rial; and the Tobacco is as good, or rather better than the *Manila* Tobacco, but they have not that vent for it as the *Spaniards* have.

¶ The *Mindanao* People are much troubled with a sort of Leprosie, the same as we observed at *Guam*. This Distemper runs with a dry Scurf all over their Bodies, and causeth great itching in those that have it, making them frequently scratch and scrub themselves, which raiseth the outer Skin in small whitish flakes, like the Scales of little Fish, when they are raised on end with a Knife. This makes their Skin extraordinary rough, and in some you shall see broad white Spots in several parts of their Body. I judge such have had it, but were cured; for their Skins were smooth, and I did not perceive them to scrub themselves: yet I have learnt from their own Mouths that these Spots were from this Distemper. Whether they use any means to cure themselves, or whether it goes away of it self,

I know not: but I did not perceive that they made any great matter of it, for they did never refrain any Company for it; none of our People caught it of them, for we were afraid of it, and kept off. They are sometimes troubled with the Small-Pox, but their ordinary Distempers are Fevers, Agues, Fluxes, with great pains, and gripings in their Guts. The Country affords a great many Drugs and Medicinal Herbs, whose Virtues are not unknown to some of them that pretend to cure the Sick.

¶ The *Mindanao* Men have many Wives: but what Ceremonies are used when they marry I know not. There is commonly a great Feast made by the Bridegroom to entertain his Friends, and the most part of the Night is spent in Mirth.

¶ The Sultan is absolute in his Power over all his Subjects. He is but a poor Prince; for as I mentioned before, they have but little Trade, and therefore cannot be rich. If the Sultan understands that any Man has Money, if it be but 20 Dollars, which is a great matter among them, he will send to borrow so much Money, pretending urgent occasions for it; and they dare not deny him. Sometimes he will send to sell one thing or another that he hath to dispose of, to such whom he knows to have Money, and they must buy it, and give him his price; and if afterwards he hath occasion for the same thing, he must have it if he sends for it. He is but a little Man, between 50 or 60 Years old, and by relation very good-natured, but over-ruled by those about him. He has a Queen, and keeps about 29 Women, or Wives more, in whose company he spends most of his time. He has one Daughter by his Sultaness or Queen, and a great many Sons and Daughters by the rest. These walk about the Streets, and would be always begging things of us; but it is reported, that the young Princess is kept in a Room, and never stirs out, and that she did never see any Man but her Father and *Raja Laut* her Uncle, being then about Fourteen Years old.

¶ When the Sultan visits his Friends he is carried in a small Couch on four Mens shoulders, with eight or ten armed Men to guard him; but he never goes far this way; for the Country is very woody, and they have but little Paths, which renders it the less commodious. When he takes his pleasure by Water, he carries some of his Wives along with him. The Proes that are built for this purpose, are large enough to entertain 50 or 60 Persons or more. The Hull is neatly built, with a round Head and Stern, and over the Hull there is a small slight House built with Bamboes; the sides are made up with split Bamboes, about four Foot high, with little Windows in them of the same, to open and shut at their pleasure. The Roof is almost flat, neatly thatched with Palmeto Leaves. This

House is divided into two or three small Partitions or Chambers, one
particularly for himself. This is neatly Matted underneath and round the
sides; and there is a Carpet and Pillows for him to sleep on. The second
Room is for his Women, much like the former. The third is for the
Servants, who tend them with Tobacco and Betel-Nut; for they are
always chewing or smoaking. The fore and after-parts of the Vessel are
for the Marriners to sit and row. Besides this, they have Outlayers, such
as those I described at *Guam*; only the Boats and Outlayers here are
larger. These Boats are more round, like a Half-Moon almost; and the
Bamboes or Outlayers that reach from the Boat are also crooked. Besides,
the Boat is not flat on one side here, as at *Guam*; but hath a Belly and
Outlayers on each side: and whereas at *Guam* there is a little Boat fasten'd
to the Outlayers, that lies in the Water; the Beams or Bamboes here are
fastened traverse-wise to the Outlayers on each side, and touch not the
Water like Boats, but 1, 3 or 4 Foot above the Water, and serve for the
Barge-Men to sit and row and paddle on; the inside of the Vessel, except
only just afore and abaft, being taken up with the Apartments for the
Passengers. There run a-cross the Outlayers two tire of Beams for the
Padlers to sit on, on each side the Vessel. The lower tire of these Beams
is not above a Foot from the Water: so that upon any the least reeling
of the Vessel, the Beams are dipt in the Water, and the Men that sit are
wet up to their Waste: their Feet seldom escaping the Water. And thus
as all our Vessels are rowed from within, these are paddled from without.
¶ The Sultan hath a Brother called *Raja Laut*, a brave Man. He is the
second Man in the Kingdom. All Strangers that come hither to trade
must make their Address to him, for all Sea-Affairs belong to him. He
licenseth Strangers to import or export any Commodity, and 'tis by his
Permission that the Natives themselves are suffered to trade: Nay, the
very Fishermen must take a Permit from him: So that there is no Man
can come into the River or go out but by his leave. He is two or three
Years younger than the Sultan, and a little Man like him. He has eight
Women, by some of whom he hath Issue. He hath only one Son, about
twelve or fourteen Years old, who was circumcised while we were there.
His eldest Son died a little before we came hither, for whom he was still
in great Heaviness. If he had lived a little longer he should have married
the young Princess; but whether this second Son must have her I know
not, for I did never hear any Discourse about it. *Raja Laut* is a very sharp
Man; he speaks and writes *Spanish*, which he learned in his Youth. He
has by often conversing with Strangers, got a great sight into the Customs
of other Nations, and by *Spanish* Books has some Knowledge of *Europe*.

He is General of the *Mindanayans*, and is accounted an expert Soldier, and a very stout Man; and the Women in their Dances, sing many Songs in his Praise.

¶ The Sultan of *Mindanao* sometimes makes War with his Neighbours the *Mountaneers* or *Alfoores*. Their Weapons are Swords, Lances, and some Hand-Cressets. The Cresset is a small thing like a Baggonet, which they always wear in War or Peace, at work or play, from the greatest of them to the poorest, or the meanest Persons. They do never meet each other so as to have a pitcht Battle, but they build small Works or Forts of Timber, wherein they plant little Guns, and lie in sight of each other two or three Months, skirmishing every Day in small Parties, and sometimes surprizing a Breast-work; and whatever side is like to be worsted, if they have no probability to escape by flight, they sell their Lives as dear as they can; for there is seldom any quarter given, but the Conquerour cuts and hacks his Enemies to pieces.

¶ The Religion of these People is Mahometanism; *Friday* is their Sabbath; but I did never see any difference that they make between this Day and any other Day; only the Sultan himself goes then to the Mosque twice. *Raja Laut* never goes to the Mosque, but prays at certain Hours, Eight or Ten times in a Day; where-ever he is, he is very punctual to his Canonical Hours, and if he be aboard will go ashore, on purpose to pray. For no Business nor Company hinders him from this Duty. Whether he is at home or abroad, in a House or in the Field, he leaves all his Company, and goes about 100 Yards off, and there kneels down to his Devotion. He first kisses the Ground, then prays aloud, and divers time in his Prayers he kisses the Ground, and does the same when he leaves off. His Servants, and his Wives and Children talk and sing, or play how they please all the time, but himself is very serious. The meaner sort of People have little Devotion: I did never see any of them at their Prayers, or go into a Mosque.

¶ In the Sultan's Mosque there is a great Drum with but one Head called a *Gong*; which is instead of a Clock. This *Gong* is beaten at 12 a Clock, at 3, 6, and 9; a Man being appointed for that Service. He has a Stick as big as a Man's Arm, with a great Knob at the end, bigger than a Man's Fist, made with Cotton, bound fast with small Cords: with this he strikes the *Gong* as hard as he can, about twenty strokes; beginning to strike leisurely the first five or six strokes; then he strikes faster, and at last strikes as fast as he can; and then he strikes again slower and slower so many more strokes: Thus he rises and falls three times, and then leaves off till three Hours after. This is done Night and Day.

¶ They circumcise the Males at 11 or 12 Years of Age, or older; and many are circumcised at once. This Ceremony is performed with a great deal of Solemnity. There had been no Circumcision for some Years before our being here; and then there was one for *Raja Laut*'s Son. They choose to have a general Circumcision when the Sultan, or General, or some other great Person hath a Son fit to be circumcised; for with him a great many more are circumcised. There is notice given about eight or ten Days before for all Men to appear in Arms. And great Preparation is made against the solemn Day. In the Morning before the Boys are circumcised, Presents are sent to the Father of the Child, that keeps the Feast; which, as I said before, is either the Sultan, or some great Person: and about 10 or 11 a Clock the *Mahometan* Priest does his Office. He takes hold of the Fore-skin with two Sticks, and with a pair of Scissars snips it off. After this most of the Men, both in City and Country being in Arms before the House, begin to act as if they were ingaged with an Enemy, having such Arms as I described. Only one acts at a time, the rest make a great Ring of 2 or 300 Yards round about him. He that is to exercise comes into the Ring with a great Shriek or two, and a horrid Look; then he fetches two or three large stately strides, and falls to work. He holds his broad Sword in one Hand, and his Lance in the other, and traverses his Ground, leaping from one side of the Ring to the other; and in a menacing Posture and Look, bids Defiance to the Enemy, whom his Fancy frames to him; for there is nothing but Air to oppose him. Then he stamps and shakes his Head, and grinning with his Teeth makes many ruful Faces. Then he throws his Lance, and nimbly snatches out his Cresset, with which he hacks and hews the Air like a Mad-man, often shrieking. At last, being almost tired with motion, he flies to the middle of the Ring, where he seems to have his Enemy at his Mercy, and with two or three Blows cuts on the Ground as if he was cutting off his Enemy's Head. By this time he is all of a Sweat, and withdraws triumphantly out of the Ring, and presently another enters with the like Shrieks and Gestures. Thus they continue combating their imaginary Enemy all the rest of the Day; towards the conclusion of which the richest Men act, and at last the General, and then the Sultan concludes this Ceremony: He and the General, with some other great Men, are in Armour, but the rest have none. After this the Sultan returns home, accompanied with abundance of People, who wait on him there till they are dismist. But at the time when we were there, there was an after-game to be played; for the General's Son being then circumcised, the Sultan intended to give him a second Visit in the Night, so they all waited to attend him thither. The

General also provided to meet him in the best manner, and therefore desired Capt. *Swan* with his Men to attend him. Accordingly Capt. *Swan* ordered us to get our Guns, and wait at the General's House till further Orders. So about 40 of us waited till Eight a Clock in the Evening: When the General with Capt. *Swan*, and about 1000 Men, went to meet the Sultan, with abundance of Torches that made it as light as Day. The manner of the March was thus: First of all there was a Pageant, and upon it two dancing Women gorgeously apparalled, with Coronets on their Heads, full of glittering Spangles, and Pendants of the same, hanging down over their Breast and Shoulders. These are Women bred up purposely for dancing: Their Feet and Legs are but little employed, except sometimes to turn round very gently; but their Hands, Arms, Head and Body, are in continual Motion, especially their Arms, which they turn and twist so strangely, that you would think them to be made without Bones. Besides the two dancing Women, there were two old Women in the Pageant holding each a lighted Torch in their Hands, close by the two dancing Women, by which Light the glittering Spangles appeared very gloriously. This Pageant was carried by six lusty Men: Then came six or seven Torches, lighting the General and Captain *Swan*, who marched side by side next, and we that attended Captain *Swan* followed close after, marching in order six and six abreast, with each Man his Gun on his Shoulder, and Torches on each side. After us came twelve of the General's Men with old *Spanish* Match-locks, marching four in a row. After them about forty Lances, and behind them as many with great Swords, marching all in Order. After them came abundance only with Cressets by their sides, who marched up close without any order. When we came near the Sultan's House, the Sultan and his Men met us, and we wheel'd off to let them pass. The Sultan had three Pageants went before him: In the first Pageant were four of his Sons, who were about ten or eleven Years old. They had gotten abundance of small Stones, which they roguishly threw about on the People's Heads. In the next were four young Maidens, Nieces to the Sultan, being his Sister's Daughters; and in the third, there was three of the Sultan's Children, not above six Years old. The Sultan himself followed next, being carried in his Couch, which was not like your *Indians Palankins*, but open, and very little and ordinary. A multitude of People came after, without any order: But as soon as he was past by, the General, and Capt. *Swan*, and all our Men, closed in just behind the Sultan, and so all marched together to the General's House. We came thither between 10 and 11 a Clock, where the biggest part of the Company were immediately dismist; but the Sultan and his Children, and his

Nieces, and some other Persons of Quality, entered the General's House. They were met at the Head of the Stairs by the General's Women, who with a great deal of Respect conducted them into the House. Captain *Swan*, and we that were with him, followed after. It was not long before the General caused his dancing Women to enter the Room and divert the Company with that Pastime. I had forgot to tell you that they have none but vocal Musick here, by what I could learn, except only a row of a kind of Bells without Clappers, 16 in Number, and their weight increasing gradually from about three to ten pound weight. These are set in a row on a Table in the General's House, where for seven or eight Days together before the Circumcision Day, they were struck each with a little Stick, for the biggest part of the Day making a great noise, and they ceased that Morning. So these dancing Women sung themselves, and danced to their own Musick. After this the General's Women, and the Sultan's Sons, and his Nieces danced. Two of the Sultan's Nieces were about 18 or 19 Years old, the other two were three or four Years younger. These young Ladies were very richly drest, with loose Garments of Silk, and small Coronets on their Heads. They were much fairer than any Women I did ever see there, and very well featured; and their Noses, tho' but small, yet higher than the other Womens, and very well proportioned. When the Ladies had very well diverted themselves and the Company with dancing, the General caused us to fire some Sky-rockets, that were made by his and Capt. *Swan*'s Order, purposely for this Night's Solemnity; and after that the Sultan and his Retinue went away with a few Attendants, and we all broke up, and thus ended this Day's Solemnity: but the Boys being sore with their Amputation, went straddling for a Fortnight after.

¶ They are not, as I said before, very curious, or strict in observing any Days, or Times of particular Devotions, except it be *Ramdam* time, as we call it. The *Ramdam* time was then in *August*, as I take it, for it was shortly after our Arrival here. In this time they fast all Day, and about seven a Clock in the Evening they spend near an Hour in Prayer. Towards the latter End of their Prayer they loudly invoke their Prophet for about a quarter of an Hour, both old and young bawling out very strangely, as if they intended to fright him out of his Sleepiness or neglect of them. After their Prayer is ended, they spend some time in Feasting before they take their Repose. Thus they do every Day for a whole Month at least; for sometimes 'tis two or three Days longer before the *Ramdam* ends: For it begins at the New-Moon, and lasts till they see the next New-Moon, which sometimes in thick hazy Weather is not till three or four Days after the Change, as it happen'd while I was at *Achin*, where they continued the *Ramdam* till the New-Moon's Appearance. The next Day after they have seen the New-Moon, the Guns are all discharged about Noon, and then the time ends.

¶ A main part of their Religion consists in washing often, to keep themselves from being defiled; or after they are defiled to cleanse themselves again. They also take great care to keep themselves from being polluted, by tasting or touching any thing that is accounted unclean; therefore Swines Flesh is very abominable to them; nay, any one that hath either tasted of Swines Flesh, or touched those Creatures, is not permitted to come into their Houses in many Days after, and there is nothing will scare them more than a Swine. Yet there are wild Hogs in the Islands, and those so plentiful, that they will come in Troops out of the Woods in the Night into the very City, and come under their Houses, to romage up and down the Filth that they find there. The Natives therefore would even desire us to lie in wait for the Hogs to destroy them, which we did frequently, by shooting them and carrying them presently on board, but were prohibited their Houses afterwards.

¶ And now I am on this Subject, I cannot omit a Story concerning the General. He once desired to have a Pair of Shoes made after the *English* Fashion, though he did very seldom wear any: So one of our Men made him a Pair, which the General liked very well. Afterwards some body told him, that the Thread wherewith the Shoes were sowed, were pointed with Hogs-bristles. This put him into a great Passion; so he sent the Shoes to the Man that made them, and sent him withal more Leather to make another Pair, with Threads pointed with some other Hair, which was immediately done, and then he was well pleased.

CHAPTER XIII

Their coasting along the Isle of Mindanao, *from a Bay on the East-side to another at the S.E. end. Tornadoes and boisterous Weather. The S.E. Coast, and its Savannah and plenty of Deer. They coast along the South-side to the River of* Mindanao *City, and anchor there. The Sultan's Brother and Son come aboard them, and invite them to settle there. Of the Feasibleness and probable Advantage of such a Settlement from the neighbouring Gold and Spice-Islands. Of the best way to* Mindanao *by the South-Sea and* Terra Australis; *and of an accidental Discovery there by Captain* Davis, *and a Probability of a greater. The Capacity they were in to settle here. The* Mindanayans *measure their Ship. Captain* Swan's *Present to the Sultan: his Reception of it, and Audience given to Capt.* Swan, *with Raja Laut, the Sultan's Brother's Entertainment of him. The Contents of two* English *Letters shewn them by the Sultan of* Mindanao. *Of the Commodities and the Punishments there. The General's Caution how to demean themselves; at his Persuasion*

HAVING in the two last Chapters given some account of the Natural, Civil, and Religious State of *Mindanao*, I shall now go on with the Prosecution of our Affairs during our stay here.

¶ 'Twas in a Bay on the N. East-side of the Island that we came to an Anchor, as hath been said. We lay in this Bay but one Night, and part of the next Day. Yet there we got Speech with some of the Natives, who by signs made us to understand, that the City *Mindanao* was on the West-side of the Island. We endeavoured to persuade one of them to go with us to be our Pilot, but he would not: Therefore in the Afternoon we loosed from hence, steering again to the South-east, having the Wind at S.W. When we came to the S.E. end of the Island *Mindanao*, we saw two small Islands about three Leagues distant from it. We might have passed between them and the main Island, as we learnt since; but not knowing them, nor what dangers we might encounter there, we chose rather to sail to the Eastward of them. But meeting very strong westerly Winds, we got nothing forward in many Days. In this time we first saw the Islands *Meangis*, which are about sixteen Leagues distant from the *Mindanao*, bearing S.E. I shall have occasion to speak more of them hereafter.

¶ The 4th Day of *July* we got into a deep Bay, four Leagues N.W. from the two small Islands before-mentioned. But the Night before, in a violent Tornado, our Bark being unable to bear any longer, bore away, which put us in some Pain for fear she was overset, as we had like to have been our selves. We anchored on the South-West-side of the Bay, in fifteen Fathom Water, about a Cables length from the Shore. Here we were forced to shelter our selves from the Violence of the Weather, which was so boisterous with Rains and Tornadoes, and a strong westerly Wind, that we were very glad to find this Place to anchor in, being the only Shelter on this Side from the West-Winds.

¶ This Bay is not above two Miles wide at the Mouth, but farther in it is three Leagues wide, and seven Fathom deep; running in N.N.W. There is a good Depth of Water about four or five Leagues in, but rocky foul Ground for about two Leagues in, from the Mouth on both sides of the Bay, except only in that place where we lay. About three Leagues in from the Mouth, on the Eastern-side, there are fair sandy Bays, and very good anchoring in four, five, and six Fathom. The Land on the East-side is high, mountainous and woody, yet very well watered with small Brooks, and there is one River large enough for Canoas to enter. On the West-side of the Bay, the Land is of a mean heighth with a large Savannah, bordering on the Sea, and stretching from the Mouth of the Bay, a great way to the Westward.

¶ This Savannah abounds with long Grass, and it is plentifully stock'd with Deer. The adjacent Woods are a Covert for them in the Heat of the Day; but Mornings and Evenings they feed in the open Plains, as thick as in our Parks in *England*. I never saw any where such Plenty of wild Deer, tho' I have met with them in several parts of *America*, both in the North and South-Seas.

¶ The Deer live here pretty peaceably and unmolested; for there are no Inhabitants on that side of the Bay. We visited this Savannah every Morning, and killed as many Deer as we pleased, sometimes 16 or 18 in a Day; and we did eat nothing but Venison all the time we stayed here.

¶ We saw a great many Plantations by the sides of the Mountains, on the East-side of the Bay, and we went to one of them, in hopes to learn of the Inhabitants whereabouts the City was, that we might not over-sail it in the Night, but they fled from us.

¶ We lay here till the 12th Day before the Winds abated of their fury, and then we sailed from hence, directing our Course to the Westward. In the Morning we had a Land-Wind at North. At a 11 a Clock the Sea-breeze came at West, just in our Teeth, but it being fair Weather, we kept on our way, turning and taking the advantage of the Land-breezes by Night, and the Sea-breezes by Day.

¶ Being now past the S.E. part of the Island, we coasted down on the South-side, and we saw abundance of Canoas a fishing, and now and then a small Village. Neither were these Inhabitants afraid of us (as the former) but came aboard; yet we could not understand them, nor they us, but by signs: And when we mentioned the Word *Mindanao*, they would point towards it.

¶ The 18th Day of *July* we arrived before the River of *Mindanao*, the Mouth of which lies in lat 6 d. 22 m. N. and is laid in 231 d. 12 m. Longitude West, from the *Lizard* in *England*. We anchored right against the River in 15 Fathom Water, clear hard Sand; about two Miles from the shore, and three or four Miles from a small Island, that lay without us to the Southward. We fired seven or nine Guns, I remember not well which, and were answered again with three from the shore; for which we gave one again. Immediately after our coming to an Anchor, *Raja Laut* and one of the Sultan's Sons came off in a Canoa, being rowed with ten Oars, and demanded in *Spanish* what we were? and from whence we came? Mr. *Smith* (he who was taken Prisoner at *Leon* in *Mexico*) answered in the same Language, that we were *English*, and that we had been a great while out of *England*. They told us that we were welcome, and asked us a great many Questions about *England*; especially concerning our *East-India* Merchants; and whether we were sent by them to settle a Factory here? Mr. *Smith* told them that we came hither only to buy Provision. They seemed a little discontented when they understood that we were not come to settle among them: For they had heard of our Arrival on the East-side of the Island a great while before, and entertained hopes that we were sent purposely out of *England* hither to settle a Trade with them; which it should seem they are very desirous of. For Capt. *Goodlud* had been here not long before to treat with them about it; and when he went away told them (as they said) that in a short time they might expect an Ambassador from *England* to make a full Bargain with them.

¶ Indeed upon mature Thoughts, I should think we could not have done better, than to have complied with the desire they seemed to have of our settling here; and to have taken up our Quarters among them. For as thereby we might better have consulted our own Profit and Satisfaction, than by the other loose roving way of Life; so it might probably have proved of Publick Benefit to our Nation, and been a means of introducing an *English* Settlement and Trade, not only here, but through several of the Spice-Islands, which lie in its Neighbourhood.

¶ For the Islands *Meangis*, which I mentioned in the beginning of this Chapter, lye within twenty Leagues of *Mindanao*. These are three small Islands that abound with Gold and Cloves, if I may credit my Author Prince *Jeoly*, who was born on one of them, and was at that time a Slave in the City of *Mindanao*. He might have been purchased by us of his Master for a small matter, as he was afterwards by Mr. *Moody*, (who came hither to trade, and laded a Ship with Clove-Bark) and by transporting him home to his own Country, we might have gotten a Trade there. But of Prince *Jeoly* I shall speak more hereafter. These Islands are as yet probably unknown to the *Dutch*, who as I said before, indeavour to ingross all the Spice into their own Hands.

¶ There was another Opportunity offered us here of settling on another Spice-Island that was very well inhabited: For the Inhabitants fearing the *Dutch*, and understanding that the *English* were settling at *Mindanao*, their Sultan sent his Nephew to *Mindanao* while we were there to invite us thither: Capt. *Swan* conferr'd with him about it divers times, and I do believe he had some Inclination to accept the Offer; and I am sure most of the Men were for it: But this never came to a Head, for want of a true understanding between Capt. *Swan* and his Men, as may be declared hereafter.

¶ Beside the Benefit which might accrue from this Trade with *Meangis*, and other the Spice-Islands, the *Philippine* Islands themselves, by a little Care and Industry, might have afforded us a very beneficial Trade, and all these Trades might have been managed from *Mindanao*, by settling there first. For that Island lyeth very convenient for Trading either to the Spice-Islands, or to the rest of the *Philippine* Islands: since as its Soil is much of the same Nature with either of them, so it lies as it were in the Center of the Gold and Spice-Trade in these Parts; the Islands North of *Mindanao* abounding most in Gold, and those South of *Meangis* in Spice.

¶ As the Island *Mindanao* lies very convenient for Trade, so considering its Distance, the way thither may not be over-long and tiresome. The Course that I would choose should be to set out of *England* about the latter-end of *August*, and to pass round *Terra del Fuego*, and so stretching over towards *New Holland*, coast it along that shoar till I came near to *Mindanao*; or first I would coast down near the *American* Shore, as far as I found convenient, and then direct my Course accordingly for the Island. By this I should avoid coming near any of the *Dutch* Settlements, and be sure to meet always with a constant brisk easterly Trade-Wind, after I was once past *Terra del Fuego*. Whereas in passing about the Cape of *Good Hope*, after you are shot over the *East-Indian* Ocean, and are come to the Islands, you must pass through the Streights of *Malacca* or *Sandy*, or else some other Streights East from *Java*, where you will be sure to meet with Country-winds, go on which side of the Equator you please; and this would require ordinarily seven or eight Months for the Voyage, but the other I should hope to perform in six or seven at most. In your return from thence also you must observe the same Rule as the *Spaniards* do in going from *Manila* to *Acapulco*; only as they run towards the North-Pole for variable Winds, so you must run to the Southward, till you meet with a Wind that will carry you over to *Terra del Fuego*. There are Places enough to touch at for Refreshment, either going or coming. You may touch going thither on either side of *Terra Patagonia*, or, if you please, at the *Gallapagoes Islands*,

where there is Refreshment enough; and returning you may probably
touch somewhere on *New-Holland*, and so make some profitable Discovery
in these Places without going out of your way. And to speak my Thoughts
freely, I believe 'tis owing to the neglect of this easie way that all that vast
Tract of *Terra Australis* which bounds the *South-Sea* is yet undiscovered:
Those that cross that Sea seeming to design some Business on the *Peruvian*
or *Mexican* Coast, and so leaving that at a distance. To confirm which,
I shall add what Captain *Davis* told me lately, That after his Departure
from us at the Haven of *Ria Lexa* (as is mentioned in the 8th Chap.) he
went, after several Traverses, to the *Gallapagoes*, and that standing thence
Southward for Wind, to bring him about *Terra del Fuego*, in the Lat. of
27 South, about 500 Leagues from *Copayapo*, on the Coast of *Chili*, he saw
a small sandy Island just by him; and that they saw to the Westward of
it a long Tract of pretty high Land, tending away toward the North West
out of sight. This might probably be the Coast of *Terra Australis Incognita*.
¶ But to return to *Mindanao*; as to the Capacity we were then in, of
settling our selves at *Mindanao*, although we were not sent out of any such
design of settling, yet we were as well provided, or better, considering all
Circumstances, than if we had. For there was scarce any useful Trade,
but some or other of us understood it. We had Sawyers, Carpenters,
Joyners, Brickmakers, Bricklayers, Shoemakers, Taylors, &c. we only
wanted a good Smith for great Work; which we might have had at
Mindanao. We were very well provided with Iron, Lead, and all sorts of
Tools, as Saws, Axes, Hammers, &c. We had Powder and Shot enough,
and very good small Arms. If we had designed to build a Fort, we could
have spared 8 or 10 Guns out of our Ship, and Men enough to have
managed it, and any Affair of Trade beside. We had also a great Advantage above raw Men that are sent out of *England* into these places,
who proceed usually too cautiously, coldly and formally, to compass any
considerable Design, which Experience better teaches than any Rules
whatsoever; besides the danger of their Lives in so great and sudden a
change of Air: whereas we were all inured to hot Climates, hardened by
many Fatigues, and in general, daring Men, and such as would not be
easily baffled. To add one thing more, our Men were almost tired, and
began to desire a *quietus est*; and therefore they would gladly have seated
themselves any where. We had a good Ship too, and enough of us (beside
what might have been spared to manage our new Settlement) to bring
the News with the Effects to the Owners in *England*: for Captain *Swan*
had already five Thousand Pound in Gold, which he and his Merchants
received for Goods sold mostly to Captain *Harris* and his Men: which if

he had laid but part of it out in Spice, as probably he might have done, would have satisfy'd the Merchants to their Hearts content. So much by way of digression.

¶ To proceed therefore with our first Reception at *Mindanao*, *Raja Laut* and his Nephew sat still in their Canoa, and would not come aboard us; because, as they said, they had no Orders for it from the Sultan. After about half an Hour's Discourse, they took their leaves; first inviting Captain *Swan* ashore, and promising to assist him in getting Provision; which they said at present was scarce, but in three or four Month's time the Rice would be gathered in, and then he might have as much as he pleased: and that in the mean time he might secure his Ship in some convenient place, for fear of the westerly Winds, which they said would be very violent at the latter-end of this Month, and all the next, as we found them.

¶ We did not know the Quality of these two Persons till after they were gone; else we should have fir'd some Guns at their departure: When they were gone, a certain Officer under the Sultan came aboard, and measured our Ship. A Custom derived from the *Chinese*, who always measure the length and breadth, and the depth of the Hold of all Ships that come to load there: by which means they know how much each Ship will carry. But what reason this Custom is used either by the *Chinese*, or *Mindanao* Men, I could never learn: unless the *Mindanayans* design by this means to improve their Skill in Shipping, against they have a Trade.

¶ Captain *Swan*, considering that the Season of the Year would oblige us to spend some time at this Island, thought it convenient to make what Interest he could with the Sultan; who might afterwards either obstruct, or advance his Designs. He therefore immediately provided a Present to send ashore to the Sultan, *viz.* Three Yards of Scarlet-Cloath, Three Yards of broad Gold Lace, a Turkish Scimiter and a Pair of Pistols: And to *Raja Laut* he sent Three Yards of Scarlet-Cloth, and Three Yards of Silver Lace. This Present was carried by Mr. *Henry More* in the Evening. He was first conducted to *Raja Laut*'s House; where he remained till report thereof was made to the Sultan, who immediately gave order for all things to be made ready to receive him.

¶ About nine a Clock at Night, a Messenger came from the Sultan to bring the Present away. Then Mr. *More* was conducted all the way with Torches and armed Men, till he came to the House where the Sultan was. The Sultan with eight or ten Men of his Council were seated on Carpets, waiting his coming. The Present that Mr. *More* brought was laid down before them, and was very kindly accepted by the Sultan, who caused Mr. *More* to sit down by them, and asked a great many Questions of him. The discourse was in *Spanish* by an Interpreter. This Conference lasted about an hour, and then he was dismist, and returned again to *Raja Laut*'s House. There was a Supper provided for him, and the Boat's Crew; after which he returned aboard.

¶ The next day the Sultan sent for Capt. *Swan*: He immediately went ashore with a Flag flying in the Boat's-head, and two Trumpets sounding all the way. When he came ashore, he was met at his Landing by two principal Officers, guarded along with Soldiers and abundance of People gazing to see him. The Sultan waited for him in his Chamber of Audience, where Captain *Swan* was treated with Tobacco and Betel, which was all his Entertainment.

¶ The Sultan sent for two *English* Letters for Captain *Swan* to read, purposely to let him know, that our *East-India* Merchants did design to settle here, and that they had already sent a Ship hither. One of these Letters was sent to the Sultan from *England*, by the *East-India* Merchants. The chiefest things contained in it, as I remember, for I saw it afterwards in the Secretarys hand, who was very proud to shew it to us, was to desire some Priviledges, in order to the building of a Fort there. This Letter was written in a very fair Hand; and between each Line, there was a Gold Line drawn. The other Letter was left by Captain *Goodlud*, directed to any *English*-men who should happen to come thither. This related wholly to Trade, giving an account, at what rate he had agreed with them for Goods of the Island, and how *European* Goods should be sold to them with an account of their Weights and Measures, and their difference from ours.

¶ The Rate agreed on for *Mindanao* Gold, was 14 *Spanish* Dollars, (which is a current Coin all over *India*) the *English* Ounce, and 18 Dollars the *Mindanao* Ounce. But for Bees-wax and Clove-bark, I do not remember the Rates, neither do I well remember the Rates of *Europe* Commodities; but I think the Rate of Iron was not above 4 Dollars a Hundred. Captain *Goodlud*'s Letter concludes thus. *Trust none of them, for they are all Thieves, but* Tace *is Latin for a Candle.* We understood afterwards that Captain *Goodlud* was robb'd of some Goods by one of the General's Men, and that he that robb'd him was fled into the Mountains, and could not be found while Captain *Goodlud* was here. But the Fellow returning back to the City some time after our arrival here, *Raja Laut* brought him bound to Captain *Swan*, and told him what he had done, desiring him to punish him for it as he pleased; but Captain *Swan* excused himself, and said it did not belong to him, therefore he would have nothing to do with it.

However, the General *Raja Laut*, would not pardon him, but punished him according to their own Custom, which I did never see but at this time.
¶ He was stript stark naked in the Morning at Sun-rising, and bound to a Post, so that he could not stir Hand nor Foot, but as he was mov'd; and was placed with his Face Eastward against the Sun. In the Afternoon they turn'd his Face towards the West, that the Sun might still be in his Face; and thus he stood all Day, parcht in the Sun (which shines here excessively hot) and tormented with the Moskito's or Gnats: After this the General would have killed him, if Captain *Swan* had consented to it. I did never see any put to Death; but I believe they are barbarous enough in it. The General told us himself that he put two Men to Death in a Town where some of us were with him; but I heard not the manner of it. Their common way of punishing is to strip them in this manner, and place them in the Sun; but sometimes they lay them flat on their Backs on the Sand, which is very hot; where they remain a whole Day in the scorching Sun, with the Moskito's biting them all the time.
¶ This Action of the General in offering Captain *Swan* the Punishment of the Thief, caus'd Captain *Swan* afterwards to make him the same offer of his Men, when any had offended the *Mindanao* Men: but the General left such Offenders to be punished by Captain *Swan*, as he thought convenient. So that for the least Offence Captain *Swan* punished his Men, and that in the sight of the *Mindanaians*; and I think sometimes only for revenge; as he did once punish his chief Mate Mr. *Teat*, he that came Captain of the Bark to *Mindanao*. Indeed at that time Captain *Swan* had his Men as much under command as if he had been in a King's Ship: and had he known how to use his Authority, he might have led them to any Settlement, and have brought them to assist him in any design he had pleased.
¶ Captain *Swan* being dismiss'd from the Sultan, with abundance of Civility, after about two Hours Discourse with him, went thence to *Raja Laut*'s House. *Raja Laut* had then some Difference with the Sultan, and therefore he was not present at the Sultan's Reception of our Captain; but waited his return, and treated him and all his Men with boyled Rice and Fowls. He then told Captain *Swan* again, and urged it to him, that it would be best to get his Ship into the River as soon as he could, because of the usual tempestuous Weather at this time of the Year; and that he should want no assistance to further him in any thing. He told him also, that as we must of necessity stay here some time, so our Men would often come ashore; and he therefore desired him to warn his Men to be careful to give no affront to the Natives; who, he said, were very revengful. That

their Customs being different from ours, he feared that Captain *Swan*'s Men might some time or other offend them, though ignorantly; that therefore he gave him this friendly warning, to prevent it: That his House should always be open to receive him or any of his Men, and that he knowing our Customs, would never be offended at any thing. After a great deal of such Discourse he dismist the Captain and his Company, who took their leave and came aboard.

¶ Captain *Swan* having seen the two Letters, did not doubt but that the *English* did design to settle a Factory here: therefore he did not much scruple the Honesty of these People, but immediately ordered us to get the Ship into the River. The River upon which the City of *Mindanao* stands is but small, and hath not above 10 or 11 foot Water on the Bar at a Spring-tide: Therefore we lightned our Ship, and the Spring coming on, we with much ado got her into the River, being assisted by 50 or 60 *Mindanaian* Fishermen, who liv'd at the Mouth of the River; *Raja Laut* himself being aboard our Ship to direct them. We carried her about a quarter of a Mile up, within the Mouth of the River, and there moored her, head and stern in a hole, where we always rode afloat. After this the Citizens of *Mindanao* came frequently aboard, to invite our Men to their Houses, and to offer us Pagallies. 'Twas a long time since any of us had received such Friendship, and therefore we were the more easily drawn to accept of their kindnesses; and in a very short time most of our Men got a Comrade or two, and as many Pagallies; especially such of us as had good Clothes, and store of Gold, as many had, who were of the number of those that accompanied Captain *Harris* over the Isthmus of *Darien*, the rest of us being poor enough. Nay, the very poorest and meanest of us could hardly pass the Streets, but we were even hal'd by Force into their Houses, to be treated by them: altho' their Treats were but mean, *viz*. Tobacco, or Betel-nut, or a little sweet spiced Water; yet their seeming Sincerity, Simplicity, and the manner of bestowing these Gifts, made them very acceptable. When we came to their Houses, they would always be praising the *English*, as declaring that the *English* and *Mindanaians* were all one. This they exprest by putting their two fore-fingers close together, and saying, that the *English* and *Mindanaians* were *samo, samo*, that is, *all one*. Then they would draw their fore-fingers half a foot asunder, and say the *Dutch* and they were *Bugeto*, which signifies so, that they were at such distance in point of Friendship: And for the *Spaniards*, they would make a greater Representation of distance than for the *Dutch*: Fearing these, but having felt, and smarted from the *Spaniards*, who had once almost brought them under.

¶ Captain *Swan* did seldom go into any House at first, but into *Raja Laut*'s. There he dined commonly every day; and as many of his Men as were ashore, and had no Money to entertain themselves, resorted thither about 12 a Clock, where they had Rice enough boiled and well drest, and some scraps of Fowls, or bits of Buffaloe, drest very nastily. Captain *Swan* was served a little better, and his two Trumpeters sounded all the time that he was at dinner. After dinner *Raja Laut* would sit and discourse with him most part of the Afternoon. It was now the *Ramdam* time, therefore the General excused himself, that he could not entertain our Captain with Dances, and other Pastimes, as he intended to do when this solemn Time was past; besides, it was the very heighth of the wet Season, and therefore not so proper for Pastimes.

¶ We had now very tempestuous Weather, and excessive Rains, which so swell'd the River, that it overflowed its Banks; so that we had much ado to keep our Ship safe: For every now and then we should have a great Tree come floating down the River and sometimes lodge against our Bows, to the endangering the breaking our Cables, and either the driving us in, over the Banks, or carrying us out to Sea; both which would have been very dangerous to us, especially being without Ballast.

¶ The City is about a Mile long (of no great breadth) winding with the Banks of the River on the right Hand going up, tho' it hath many Houses on the other Side too. But at this time it seemed to stand as in a Pond, and there was no passing from one House to another but in Canoas. This tempestuous rainy Weather happened the latter-end of *July*, and lasted most part of *August*.

¶ When the bad Weather was a little asswaged, Captain *Swan* hired a House to put our Sails and Goods in, while we careen'd our Ship. We had a great deal of Iron and Lead, which was brought ashore into this House. Of these Commodities Captain *Swan* sold to the Sultan or General, 8 or 10 Tuns, at the Rates agreed on by Captain *Goodlud*, to be paid in Rice. The *Mindanaians* are no good Accomptants; therefore the *Chinese* that live here, do cast up their Accompts for them. After this, Captain *Swan* bought Timber-trees of the General, and set some of our Men to saw them into Planks, to sheath the Ship's bottom. He had two Whip-Saws on Board, which he brought out of *England*, and four or five Men that knew the use of them, for they had been Sawyers in *Jamaica*.

¶ When the *Ramdam* time was over, and the dry time set in a little, the General, to oblige Captain *Swan*, entertained him every Night with Dances. The dancing Women that are purposely bred up to it, and make it their Trade, I have already described. But beside them all the Women in general are much addicted to Dancing. They dance 40 or 50 at once; and that standing all round in a Ring, joined Hand in Hand, and singing and keeping time. But they never budge out of their places, nor make any motion till the Chorus is sung; then all at once they throw out one Leg, and bawl out aloud; and sometimes they only clap their Hands when the Chorus is sung. Captain *Swan*, to retaliate the General's Favours, sent for his Violins, and some that could dance English Dances; wherewith the General was very well pleased. They commonly spent the biggest part of the Night in these sort of Pastimes.

¶ Among the rest of our Men that did use to dance thus before the General, there was one *John Thacker*, who was a Seaman bred, and could neither write nor read; but had formerly learnt to dance in the Musick-houses about *Wapping*: This Man came into the *South-Seas* with Captain *Harris*, and getting with him a good Quantity of Gold, and being a pretty good Husband of his Share, had still some left, besides what he laid out in a very good Suit of Cloaths. The General supposed by his Garb and his dancing, that he had been of noble Extraction; and to be satisfy'd of his Quality, asked of one of our Men, if he did not guess aright of him? The Man of whom the General asked this Question told him, he was much in the right; and that most of our Ship's Company were of the like Extraction; especially all those that had fine Cloaths; and that they came aboard only to see the World, having Money enough to bear their Ex-pences where-ever they came; but that for the rest, those that had but mean Clothes, they were only common Seamen. After this, the General shew'd a great deal of Respect to all that had good Clothes, but especially to *John Thacker*, till Captain *Swan* came to know the Business, and marr'd all; undeceiving the General, and drubbing the Nobleman: For he was so much incensed against *John Thacker*, that he could never endure him afterwards; tho' the poor Fellow knew nothing of the Matter.

¶ About the middle of *November* we began to work on our Ship's Bottom, which we found very much eaten with the Worm: For this is a horrid place for Worms. We did not know this till after we had been in the River a Month; and then we found our Canoas Bottoms eaten like Honey-combs; our Bark, which was a single Bottom, was eaten thro'; so that she could not swim. But our Ship was sheathed, and the Worm came no further than the Hair between the sheathing Plank, and the main Plank. We did not mistrust the General's Knavery 'till now: for when he came down to our Ship, and found us ripping off the sheathing Plank, and saw the firm Bottom underneath, he shook his Head, and seemed to be dis-contented; saying, he did never see a Ship with two Bottoms before. We were told that in this place, where we now lay, a *Dutch* Ship was eaten up in 2 Months time, and the General had all her Guns; and it is probable he did expect to have had ours: Which I do believe was the main Reason that made him so forward in assisting us to get our Ship into the River, for when we came out again we had no Assistance from him. We had no Worms till we came to this place: For when we careen'd at the *Marias*, the Worm had not touch'd us; nor at *Guam*, for there we scrubb'd; nor after we came to the Island *Mindanao*; for at the S.E. end of the Island we heel'd and scrubb'd also. The *Mindanaians* are so sensible of these destructive Insects, that whenever they come from Sea, they immediately hale their Ship into a dry Dock, and burn her bottom, and there let her lye dry till they are ready to go to Sea again. The Canoas or Proes they hale up dry, and never suffer them to be long in the Water. It is reported that those Worms which get into a Ship's bottom in the salt Water, will dye in the fresh Water; and that the fresh Water Worms will dye in salt Water; but in the brackish Water both sorts will increase prodigiously. Now this place where we lay was sometimes brackish Water, yet commonly fresh; but what sort of Worm this was I know not. Some Men are of Opinion, that these Worms breed in the Plank; but I am perswaded they breed in the Sea: For I have seen Millions of them swimming in the Water, particularly in the Bay of *Panama*; for there Captain *Davis*, Captain *Swan* and my self, and most of our Men, did take notice of them divers times, which was the reason of our Cleaning so often while we were there: and these were the largest Worms that I did ever see. I have also seen them in *Virginia*, and in the Bay of *Campeachy*; in the latter of which places the Worms eat prodigiously. They are always in Bays, Creeks, Mouths of Rivers, and such places as are near the shore; being never found far out at Sea, that I could ever learn: yet a Ship will bring them lodg'd in its Plank for a great way.

¶ Having thus ript off all our Worm-eaten Plank, and clapt on new, by the beginning of *December* 1686, our Ship's-bottom was sheathed and tallowed, and the 10th day we went over the Bar and took aboard the Iron and Lead that we could not sell, and began to fill our Water, and fetch aboard Rice for our Voyage: but C. *Swan* remain'd ashore still, and was not yet determin'd when to sail, or whither. But I am well assured that he did never intend to cruize about *Manila*, as his Crew designed; for I did once ask him, and he told me, That what he had already done of that kind he was forc'd to; but now being at Liberty, he would never more engage in any such Design: For, said he, there is no Prince on Earth is able to wipe off the Stain of such Actions. What other Designs he had I know not, for he was commonly very cross; yet he did never propose doing any thing else, but only ordered the Provision to be got aboard in order to sail; and I am confident if he had made a motion to go to any *English* Factory, most of his Men would have consented to it, tho' probably some would have still opposed it. However, his Authority might soon have over-swayed those that were refractory; for it was very strange to see the Awe that these Men were in of him, for he punish'd the most stubborn and daring of his Men. Yet when we had brought the Ship out into the Road, they were not altogether so submissive as while it lay in the River, tho' even then it was that he punished Captain *Teat*.

¶ I was at that time a hunting with the General for Beef, which he had a long time promised us. But now I saw that there was no Credit to be given to his Word; for I was a Week out with him and saw but four Cows, which were so wild, that we did not get one. There were five or six more of our Company with me; these who were young Men, and had *Dalilah*'s there, which made them fond of the Place, all agreed with the General to tell Captain *Swan* that there were Beeves enough, only they were wild. But I told him the Truth, and advised him not to be too credulous of the General's Promises. He seemed to be very angry, and stormed behind the General's Back, but in his Presence was very mute, being a Man of small Courage.

¶ It was about the 20th Day of *December* when we returned from hunting, and the General designed to go again to another place to hunt for Beef; but he stayed till after *Christmas-day*, because some of us designed to go with him; and Captain *Swan* had desired all his Men to be aboard that Day, that we might keep it solemnly together: And accordingly he sent aboard a Buffaloe the Day before, that we might have a good Dinner. So the 25th Day about 10 a Clock, Captain *Swan* came aboard, and all his Men who were ashore: For you must understand that near a third of our Men lived constantly ashore, with their Comrades and Pagallies, and some with Women-Servants, whom they hired of their Masters for Concubines. Some of our Men also had Houses, which they hired or bought, for Houses are very cheap, for 5 or 6 Dollars. For many of them having more Money than they knew what to do with, eased themselves here of the trouble of telling it, spending it very lavishly, their Prodigality making the People impose upon them, to the making the rest of us pay the dearer for what we bought, and to endangering the like Impositions upon such *Englishmen* as may come here hereafter. For the *Mindanayans* knew how to get our Squires Gold from them (for we had no Silver,) and when our Men wanted Silver, they would change now and then an Ounce of

Gold, and could get for it no more than ten or eleven Dollars for a *Mindanao* Ounce, which they would not part with again under eighteen Dollars. Yet this, and the great Prices the *Mindanayans* set on their Goods, were not the only way to lessen their Stocks; for their Pagallies and Comrades would often be begging somewhat of them, and our Men were generous enough, and would bestow half an Ounce of Gold at a time, in a Ring for their Pagallies, or in a Silver Wrist-band, or Hoop to come about their Arms, in hopes to get a Night's Lodging with them.

¶ When we are all aboard on *Christmas-Day*, Captain *Swan* and his two Merchants; I did expect that Captain *Swan* would have made some Proposals, or have told us his Designs; but he only dined and went ashore again, without speaking any thing of his mind. Yet even then I do think that he was driving on a design, of going to one of the Spice-Islands, to load with Spice; for the young Man before mentioned, who I said was sent by his Unkle, the Sultan of a Spice-Island near *Ternate*, to invite the *English* to their Island, came aboard at this time, and after some private discourse with Captain *Swan*, they both went ashore together. This young Man did not care that the *Mindanaians* should be privy to what he said. I have heard Captain *Swan* say that he offered to load his Ship with Spice, provided he would build a small Fort, and leave some Men to secure the Island from the *Dutch*; but I am since informed, that the *Dutch* have now got possession of the Island.

¶ The next day after *Christmas*, the General went away again, and 5 or 6 *Englishmen* with him, of whom I was one, under pretence of going a hunting; and we all went together by Water in his Proe, together with his Women and Servants, to the hunting-place. The General always carried his Wives and Children, his Servants, his Money and Goods with him: so we all imbarked in the Morning, and arrived there before Night. I have already described the Fashion of their Proes, and the Rooms made in them. We were entertained in the General's Room or Cabbin. Our Voyage was no so far, but that we reached our Fort before Night.

¶ At this time one of the General's Servants had offended, and was punished in this manner: He was bound fast flat on his Belly, on a Bambou belonging to the Prow, which was so near the Water, that by the Vessels motion, it frequently delved under Water, and the Man along with it; and sometimes when hoisted up, he had scarce time to blow before he would be carried under Water again.

¶ When we had rowed about two Leagues, we entred a pretty large deep River, and rowed up a League further, the Water salt all the way. There was a pretty large Village, the Houses built after the Country fashion.

We landed at this Place, where there was a House made ready immediately for us. The General and his Women lay at one end of the House, and we at the other end, and in the Evening all the Women in the Village danced before the General.

¶ While we staid here, the General with his Men went out every Morning betimes, and did not return till four or five a Clock in the Afternoon, and he would often complement us, by telling us what good Trust and Confidence he had in us, saying that he left his Women and Goods under our Protection, and that he thought them as secure with us six, (for we had all our Arms with us) as if he had left 109 of his own Men to guard them. Yet for all this great Confidence, he always left one of his principal Men, for fear some of us should be too familiar with his Women.

¶ They did never stir out of their own Room when the General was at Home, but as soon as he was gone out, they would presently come into our Room, and sit with us all Day, and ask a Thousand Questions of us concerning our *English* Women, and our Customs. You may imagine that before this time, some of us had attained so much of their Language as to understand them, and give them Answers to their Demands. I remember that one day they asked how many Wives the King of *England* had? We told them but one, and that our *English* Laws did not allow of any more. They said it was a strange Custom, that a Man should be confined to one Woman; some of them said it was a very bad Law, but others again said it was a good Law; so there was a great Dispute among them about it. But one of the General's Women said positively, That our Law was better than theirs, and made them all silent by the Reason which she gave for it. This was the *War Queen*, as we called her, for she did always accompany the General when ever he was called out to engage his Enemies, but the rest did not.

¶ By this Familiarity among the Women, and by often discoursing them, we came to be acquainted with their Customs and Priviledges. The General lies with his Wives by turns; but she by whom he had the first Son, has a double Portion of his Company: For when it comes to her turn, she has him two Nights, whereas the rest have him but one. She with whom he is to lye at Night, seems to have a particular Respect shewn her by the rest all the precedent day; and for a Mark of distinction, wears a striped silk Handkerchief about her Neck, by which we knew who was Queen that day.

¶ We lay here about 5 or 6 Days, but did never in all that time see the least sign of any Beef, which was the Business we came about, neither were we suffered to go out with the General to see the wild Kine, but we wanted for nothing else: However, this did not please us, and we often importuned him to let us go out among the Cattle. At last he told us, That he had provided a Jar of Rice-drink to be merry with us, and after that we should go with him.

¶ This Rice-drink is made of Rice boiled and put into a Jar, where it remains a long time steeping in Water. I know not the manner of making it, but it is very strong pleasant Drink. The Evening when the General designed to be merry, he caused a Jar of this Drink to be brought into our Room, and he began to drink first himself, then afterwards his Men; so they took turns till they were all as drunk as Swine, before they suffered us to drink. After they had enough, then we drank, and they drank no more, for they will not drink after us. The General leapt about our Room a little while; but having his Load, soon went to sleep.

¶ The next Day we went out with the General into the Savannah, where he had near 100 Men making of a large Pen to drive the Cattle into. For that is the manner of their Hunting, having no Dogs. But I saw not above eight or ten Cows; and those as wild as Deer, so that we got none this Day: yet the next Day some of his Men brought in three Heifers, which they kill'd in the Savannah. With these we returned aboard, they being all that we got there.

¶ Captain *Swan* was much vexed at the General's Actions; for he promised to supply us with as much Beef as we should want, but now either could not, or would not make good his Promise. Besides, he failed to perform his Promise in a Bargain of Rice, that we were to have for the Iron which we sold him, but he put us off still from time to time, and would not come to any Account. Neither were these all his Tricks; for a little before his Son was circumcised, (of which I spake in the foregoing Chapter) he pretended a great streight for Money, to defray the Charges of that Day; and therefore desired Captain *Swan* to lend him about twenty Ounces of Gold; for he knew that Captain *Swan* had a considerable quantity of Gold in his possession, which the General thought was his own, but indeed he had none but what belonged to the Merchants. However he lent it the General; but when he came to an account with Captain *Swan*, he told him, that it was usual at such solemn times to make Presents, and that he received it as a Gift. He also demanded Payment for the Victuals that our Captain and his Men did eat at his House. These things startled Captain *Swan*, yet how to help himself he knew not. But all this, with other inward Troubles, lay hard on our Captain's Spirits, and put him very much out of Humour; for his own Company were pressing him every Day to be gone, because now was the heighth of the easterly Monsoon, the only Wind to carry us farther into the *Indies*.

¶ About this time some of our Men, who were weary and tired with wandring, ran away into the Country and absconded, they being assisted, as was generally believed by *Raja Laut*. There were others also, who fearing we should not go to an *English* Port, bought a Canoa, and designed to go in her to *Borneo*: For not long before the *Mindanao* Vessel came from thence, and brought a Letter directed to the chief of the *English* Factory at *Mindanao*. This Letter the General would have Captain *Swan* have opened, but he thought it might come from some of the *East-India* Merchants whose Affairs he would not intermeddle with, and therefore did not open it. I since met with Captain *Bowry* at *Achin*, and telling him this Story, he said that he sent that Letter, supposing that the *English* were settled there at *Mindanao*; and by this Letter we also thought that there was an *English* Factory at *Borneo*: So here was a mistake on both sides. But this Canoa, wherewith some of them thought to go to *Borneo*, Captain *Swan* took from them, and threatned the Undertakers very hardly. However, this did not so far discourage them, for they secretly bought another; but their Designs taking Air, they were again frustrated by Captain *Swan*.

¶ The whole Crew were at this time under a general Disaffection, and full of very different Projects; and all for want of Action. The main Division was between those that had Money and those that had none. There was a great difference in the Humours of these; for they that had Money lived ashore, and did not care for leaving *Mindanao*; whilst those that were poor lived aboard, and urged Capt. *Swan* to go to Sea. These began to be unruly as well as dissatisfy'd, and sent ashore the Merchants Iron to sell for Rack and Honey, to make Punch, wherewith they grew drunk and quarrelsome: Which disorderly Actions deterred me from going aboard; for I did ever abhor Drunkenness, which now our Men that were aboard abandon'd themselves wholly to.

¶ Yet these Disorders might have been crush'd, if Capt. *Swan* had used his Authority to suppress them: But he with his Merchants living always ashore, there was no Command; and therefore every Man did what he pleased, and encouraged each other in his Villanies. Now Mr. *Harthop*, who was one of Captain *Swan*'s Merchants, did very much importune him to settle his Resolutions, and declare his Mind to his Men; which at last he consented to do. Therefore he gave warning to all his Men to come aboard the 13th Day of *January*, 1687.

¶ We did all earnestly expect to hear what Captain *Swan* would propose, and therefore were very willing to go aboard. But unluckily for him, two Days before this Meeting was to be, Captain *Swan* sent aboard his Gunner, to fetch something ashore out of his Cabbin. The Gunner rummaging to find what he was sent for, among other things took out the Captain's Journal from *America* to the Island *Guam*, and laid down by him. This Journal was taken up by one *John Read*, a *Bristol* Man, whom I have mentioned in my 4th Chapter. He was a pretty Ingenious young Man, and of a very civil carriage and behaviour. He was also accounted a good Artist, and kept a Journal, and was now prompted by his Curiosity, to peep into Captain *Swan*'s Journal, to see how it agreed with his own; a thing very usual among the Seamen that keep Journals, when they have an opportunity, and especially young Men, who have no great experience. At the first opening of the Book he light on a place in which Captain *Swan* had inveighed bitterly against most of his Men, especially against another *John Reed* a *Jamaica* Man. This was such stuff as he did not seek after: But hitting so pat on this Subject, his curiosity led him to pry further; and therefore while the Gunner was busie, he convey'd the Book away, to look over it at his leisure. The Gunner having dispatch'd his business, lock'd up the Cabbin-door, not missing the Book, and went ashore. Then *John Reed* shewed it to his Namesake, and to the rest that were aboard, who were by this time the biggest part of them ripe for mischief; only wanting some fair pretence to set themselves to work about it. Therefore looking on what was written in this Journal to be matter sufficient for them to accomplish their Ends, Captain *Teat*, who as I said before, had been abused by Captain *Swan*, laid hold on this opportunity to be revenged for his Injuries, and aggravated the matter to the heighth; perswading the Men to turn out Captain *Swan* from being Commander, in hopes to have commanded the Ship himself. As for the Sea-men they were easily perswaded to any thing; for they were quite tired with this long and tedious Voyage, and most of them despaired of ever getting home, and therefore did not care what they did, or whither they went. It was only want of being busied in some Action that made them so uneasie; therefore they consented to what *Teat* proposed, and immediately all that were aboard bound themselves by Oath to turn Captain *Swan* out, and to conceal this Design from those that were ashore, until the Ship was under Sail; which would have been presently, if the Surgeon or his Mate had been aboard; but they were both ashore, and they thought it no Prudence to go to Sea without a Surgeon: Therefore the next Morning they sent ashore one *John Cookworthy*, to hasten off either the Surgeon or his Mate, by pretending that one of the Men in the Night broke his Leg by falling into the Hold. The Surgeon told him that he intended to come aboard the next Day with the Captain, and would not come before; but sent his Mate, *Herman Coppinger*.

¶ This Man sometime before this, was sleeping at his Pagallies, and a Snake twisted himself about his Neck; but afterwards went away without hurting him. In this Country it is usual to have the Snakes come into the Houses and into the Ships too; for we had several came aboard our Ship when we lay in the River. But to proceed, *Herman Coppinger* provided to go aboard; and the next Day, being the time appointed for Captain *Swan* and all his Men to meet aboard, I went aboard with him, neither of us distrusted what was designing by those aboard, till we came thither. Then we found it was only a Trick to get the Surgeon off; for now, having obtained their Desires, the Canoa was sent ashore again immediately, to desire as many as they could meet to come aboard; but not to tell the Reason, lest Captain *Swan* should come to hear of it.

¶ The 13th Day in the Morning they weighed, and fired a Gun: Capt. *Swan* immediately sent aboard Mr. *Nelly*, who was now his chief Mate, to see what the matter was: To him they told all their Grievances, and shewed him the Journal. He perswaded them to stay till the next Day, for an Answer from Captain *Swan* and the Merchants. So they came to an Anchor again, and the next Morning Mr. *Harthop* came aboard: He perswaded them to be reconciled again, or at least to stay and get more Rice: But they were deaf to it, and weighed again while he was aboard. Yet at Mr. *Harthop*'s Perswasion they promised to stay till two a Clock in the Afternoon for Captain *Swan*, and the rest of the Men, if they would come aboard; but they suffered no Man to go ashore, except one *William Williams* that had a wooden Leg, and another that was a Sawyer.

¶ If Capt. *Swan* had yet come aboard, he might have dash'd all their Designs; but he neither came himself, as a Captain of any Prudence and Courage would have done, nor sent till the time was expired. So we left Captain *Swan* and about 36 Men ashore in the City, and six or eight that run away; and about 16 we had buried there, the most of which died by Poison. The Natives are very expert at Poisoning, and do it upon small occasions: Nor did our Men want for giving Offence, through their general Rogueries, and sometimes by dallying too familiarly with their Women, even before their Faces. Some of their Poisons are slow and lingering; for we had some now aboard who were poison'd there; but died not till some Months after.

CHAPTER XIV

They depart from the River of Mindanao. *Of the time lost or gain'd in sailing round the World: With a Caution to Seamen, about the Allowance they are to take for the difference of the Sun's declination. The South-Coast of* Mindanao. Chambongo *Town and Harbour, with its neighbouring Keys. Green Turtle. Ruins of a* Spanish *Fort. The Westermost-point of* Mindanao. *Two Proes of the* Sologues *laden from* Manila. *An Isle to the West of* Sebo. *Walking-Canes. Isle of* Batts, *very large; and numerous Turtle and Manatee. A dangerous Shoal. They sail by* Panay *belonging to the* Spaniards, *and others of the* Philippine *Islands. Isle of* Mindora. *Two Barks taken. A further Account of the Isle* Luconia, *and the City and Harbour of* Manila. *They go off* Pulo Condore *to lie there. The Sholes of* Pracel, &c. Pulo Condore. *The Tar-tree. The Mango. Grape-tree. The Wild or Bastard-Nutmeg. Their Animals. Of the Migration of the Turtle from place to place. Of the commodious Situation of* Pulo Condore; *its Water, and its* Cochinchinese *Inhabitants. Of the* Malayan *Tongue. The Custom of prostituting their Women in these Countries, and in* Guinea. *The Idolatry here, at* Tunquin, *and among the* Chinese *Seamen, and of a Procession at* Fort St. George. *They refit their Ship. Two of them dye of Poyson they took at* Mindanao. *They take in Water, and a Pilot for the Bay of* Siam. Pulo Uby; *and Point of* Cambodia. *Two* Cambodian *Vessels. Isles in the Bay of* Siam. *The tight Vessels and Seamen of the Kingdom of* Champa. *Storms. A* Chinese Jonk *from* Palimbam *in* Sumatra. *They come again to* Pulo Condore. *A bloody Fray with a* Malayan *Vessel. The Surgeon's and the Author's desires of leaving their Crew.*

THE 14th Day of *January* 1687, at three of the Clock in the Afternoon, we sailed from the River of *Mindanao*, designing to cruise before *Manila*.

¶ It was during our stay at *Mindanao*, that we were first made sensible of the change of time, in the course of our Voyage. For having travell'd so far Westward, keeping the same Course with the Sun, we must consequently have gain'd something insensibly in the length of the particular Days, but have lost in the tale, the bulk, or number of the Days or Hours. According to the different Longitudes of *England* and *Mindanao*, this Isle being West from the *Lizzard*, by common Computation, about 210 Degrees, the difference of time at our Arrival at *Mindanao* ought to be about 14 Hours: And so much we should have anticipated our reckoning, having gained it by bearing the Sun company. Now the natural Day in every particular place must be consonant to itself: But this going about with, or against the Sun's course, will of necessity make a difference in the Calculation of the civil Day between any two places. Accordingly, at *Mindanao*, and all other places in the *East-Indies*, we found them reckoning a Day before us, both Natives and *Europeans*; for the *Europeans* coming eastward by the Cape of *Good Hope*, in a Course contrary to the Sun and us, where-ever we met they were a full Day before us in their Accounts. So among the *Indian Mahometans* here, their *Friday*, the Day of their Sultan's going to their Mosques, was *Thursday* with us; though it were *Friday* also with those who came eastward from *Europe*. Yet at the *Ladrone* Islands, we found the *Spaniards* of *Guam* keeping the same Computation with our selves; the reason of which I take to be, that they settled that Colony by a Course westward from *Spain*; the *Spaniards* going first to *America*, and thence to the *Ladrones* and *Philippines*. But how the reckoning was at *Manila*, and the rest of the *Spanish* Colonies in the *Philippine* Islands, I know not; whether they keep it as they brought it, or corrected it by the Accounts of the Natives, and of the *Portugueze*, *Dutch* and *English*, coming the contrary way from *Europe*.

¶ One great Reason why Seamen ought to keep the difference of time as exact as they can, is, that they may be the more exact in their Latitudes. For our Tables of the Sun's declination, being calculated for the Meridians of the places in which they were made, differ about 12 Minutes from those parts of the World that lie on their opposite Meridians, in the Months of *March* and *September*; and in proportion to the Sun's declination, at other times of the Year also. And should they run farther as we did, the difference would still increase upon them, and be an occasion of great Errours. Yet even able Seamen in these Voyages are hardly made sensible of this, tho' so necessary to be observed, for want of duly attending to the reason of it, as it happened among those of our Crew; who after we had past 180 Degrees, began to decrease the difference of declination, whereas they ought still to have increased it, for it all the way increased upon us.

¶ We had the Wind at N.N.E. fair clear Weather, and a brisk Gale. We coasted to the westward, on the South-side of the Island of *Mindanao*, keeping within four or five Leagues of the Shore. The Land from hence trends away W. by S. It is of a good heighth by the Sea, and very woody, and in the Country we saw high Hills.

¶ The next Day we were abrest of *Chambongo*; a Town in this Island, and 30 Leagues from the River of *Mindanao*. Here is said to be a good Harbour, and a great Settlement, with plenty of Beef and Buffaloe. It is reported that the *Spaniards* were formerly fortified here also: There are two Shoals lie off this place, two or three Leagues from the Shoar. From hence the Land is more low and even; yet there are some Hills in the Country.

¶ About six Leagues before we came to the West-end of the Island

Mindanao, we fell in with a great many small low Islands or Keys, and about two or three Leagues to the Southward of these Keys, there is a long Island stretching N.E. and S.W. about 12 Leagues. This Island is low by the Sea on the North-side, and has a Ridge of Hills in the middle, running from one end to the other. Between this Isle and the small Keys, there is a good large Channel: Among the Keys also there is a good depth of Water, and a violent Tide; but on what point of the Compass it flows, I know not, nor how much it riseth and falls.

¶ The 17th Day we anchored on the East-side of all these Keys, in eight fathom Water, clean Sand. Here are plenty of green Turtle, whose Flesh is as sweet as any in the *West-Indies*: But they are very shy. A little to the westward of these Keys, on the Island *Mindanao*, we saw abundance of Coco-nut-Trees: Therefore we sent our Canoa ashore, thinking to find Inhabitants, but found none, nor sign of any; but great Tracts of Hogs, and great Cattle; and close by the Sea there were Ruins of an old Fort; the Walls thereof were of a good heighth, built with Stone and Lime, and by the Workmanship seem'd to be *Spanish*. From this place the Land trends W.N.W. and it is of an indifferent heighth by the Sea. It run on this point of the Compass four or five Leagues, and then the Land trends away N.N.W. five or six Leagues farther, making with many bluff Points.

¶ We weigh'd again the 14th Day, and went thro' between the Keys; but met such uncertain Tides, that we were forced to anchor again. The 22d Day we got about the westermost Point of all *Mindanao*, and stood to the northward, plying under the Shore, and having the Wind at N.N.E. a fresh Gale. As we sailed along further, we found the Land to trend N.N.E. On this part of the Island the Land is high by the Sea, with full bluff Points, and very woody. There are some small sandy Bays, which afford Streams of fresh Water.

¶ Here we met with two Prows belonging to the *Sologues*, one of the *Mindanaian* Nations before-mentioned. They came from *Manila* laden with Silks and Callicoes. We kept on this western part of the Island steering northerly, till we came abrest of some other of the *Philippine* Islands, that lay to the northward of us, then steered away towards them; but still keeping on the West-side of them, and we had the Winds at N.N.E.

¶ The 3d of *February* we anchored in a good Bay on the West-side of the Island, in Lat. 9 d. 55 min. where we had 13 Fathom-water, good soft Ooze. This Island hath no Name that we could find in any Book, but lieth on the West-side of the Island *Sebo*. It is about eight or ten Leagues long, mountainous and woody. At this place Captain *Read*, who was the same Captain *Swan* had so much railed against in his Journal, and was now made Captain in his room (as Captain *Teat* was made Master, and Mr. *Henry More* Quarter-Master) ordered the Carpenters to cut down our Quarter-Deck to make the Ship snug, and the fitter for sailing. When that was done we heeled her, scrubbed her Bottom, and tallowed it. Then we fill'd all our Water, for here is a delicate small run of Water.

¶ The Land was pretty low in this Bay, the Mould black and fat, and the Trees of several Kinds, very thick and tall. In some places we found plenty of Canes, such as we use in *England* for Walking-Canes. These were short-jointed, not above two Foot and a half, or two Foot 10 Inches the longest, and most of them not above two Foot. They run along on the Ground like a Vine; or taking hold of their Trees, they climb up to their very tops. They are 15 or 20 Fathom long, and much of a bigness from the Root, till within five or six Fathom of the end. They are of a pale green Colour, cloathed over with a Coat of short thick hairy Substance, of a dun Colour; but it comes off by only drawing the Cane through your Hand. We did cut many of them, and they proved very tough heavy Canes.

¶ We saw no Houses, nor sign of Inhabitants; but while we lay here, there was a Canoa with six Men came into this Bay; but whither they were bound, or from whence they came, I know not. They were *Indians*, and we could not understand them.

¶ In the middle of this Bay, about a Mile from the Shore, there is a small low woody Island, not above a Mile in Circumference; our Ship rode about a Mile from it. This Island was the Habitation of an incredible number of great Batts, with Bodies as big as Ducks, or large Fowl, and with vast Wings: For I saw at *Mindanao* one of this sort, and I judge that the Wings stretch'd out in length, could not be less assunder than 7 or 8 Foot from tip to tip; for it was much more than any of us could fathom with our Arms extended to the utmost. The Wings are for Substance like those of other Batts, of a Dun or Mouse colour. The Skin or Leather of them hath Ribs running along it, and draws up in 3 or 4 Folds; and at the joints of those Ribs and the extremities of the Wings, there are sharp and crooked Claws, by which they may hang on any thing. In the Evening as soon as the Sun was set, these Creatures would begin to take their flight from this Island, in swarms like Bees, directing their flight over to the Main Island; and whither afterwards I know not. Thus we should see them rising up from the Island till Night hindred our sight; and in the Morning as soon as it was light, we should see them returning again like a Cloud, to the small Island, till Sun rising. This Course they kept constantly while we lay here, affording us every Morning and Evening an

Hour's Diversion in gazing at them, and talking about them; but our Curiosity did not prevail with us to go ashore to them, our selves and Canoas being all the day-time taken up in business about our Ship. At this Isle also we found plenty of Turtle and Manatee, but no Fish.

¶ We stay'd here till the 10th of *February*, 1687, and then having compleated our Business, we sailed hence with the Wind at North. But going out we struck on a Rock, where we lay two Hours: It was very smooth Water, and the Tide of Flood, or else we should there have lost our Ship. We struck off a great piece of our Rudder, which was all the damage that we received, but we more narrowly mist losing our Ships this time, than in any other in the whole Voyage. This is a very dangerous Shoal, because it does not break, unless probably it may appear in foul Weather. It lies about two Miles to the westward, without the small Batt-Island. Here we found the Tide of Flood setting to the southward, and the Ebb to the northward.

¶ After we were past this Shoal, we coasted along by the rest of the *Philippine* Islands, keeping on the West-side of them. Some of them appeared to be very mountainous dry Land. We saw many Fires in the Night as we passed by *Panay*, a great Island settled by *Spaniards*, and by the Fires up and down it seems to be well settled by them; for this is a *Spanish* Custom, whereby they give Notice of any Danger or the like from Sea; and 'tis probable they had seen our Ship the Day before. This is an unfrequented Coast, and 'tis rare to have any Ship seen there. We touched not at *Panay*, nor any where else; tho' we saw a great many small Islands to the westward of us, and some Shoals, but none of them laid down in our Draughts.

¶ The 18th Day of *Feb.* we anchored at the N.W. end of the Island *Mindora*, in 10 Fathom-water, about three quarters of a Mile from the Shore. *Mindora*, is a large Island; the middle of it lying in Lat. 13. about 40 Leagues long, stretching N.W. and S.E. It is high and mountainous, and not very woody. At this Place where we anchored the Land was neither very high nor low. There was a small Brook of Water, and the Land by the Sea was very woody, and the Trees high and tall, but a League or two farther in, the Woods are very thin and small. Here we saw great Tracks of Hog and Beef, and we saw some of each, and hunted them; but they were wild, and we could kill none.

¶ While we were here, there was a Canoa with four *Indians* came from *Manila*. They were very shy of us a while: But at last, hearing us speak *Spanish*, they came to us, and told us, that they were going to a Fryar, that liv'd at an *Indian* Village towards the S.E. end of the Island. They told us also, that the Harbour of *Manila* is seldom or never without 20 or 30 Sail of Vessels, most *Chinese*, some *Portugueze*, and some few the *Spaniards* have of their own. They said, that when they had done their business with the Fryar they would return to *Manila*, and hope to be back again at this place in four Days time. We told them that we came for a Trade with the *Spaniards* at *Manila*, and should be glad if they would carry a Letter to some Merchant there, which they promised to do. But this was only a pretence of ours, to get out of them what intelligence we could as to their Shipping, Strength, and the like, under Colour of seeking a Trade; for our business was to pillage. Now if we had really designed to have traded there, this was as fair an opportunity as Men could have desired: For these Men could have brought us to the Fryar that they were going to, and a small Present to him would have engaged him to do any kindness for us in the way of Trade: For the *Spanish* Governours do not allow of it, and we must trade by stealth.

¶ The 21st Day we went from hence with the wind at E.N.E. a small gale. The 23d Day in the Morning we were fair by the S.E. end of the Island *Luconia*, the place that had been so long desired by us. We presently saw a Sail coming from the northward, and making after her we took her in two Hours time. She was a *Spanish* Bark, that came from a place called *Pangasanam*, a small Town on the N. end of *Luconia*, as they told us; probably the same with *Pongassiny*, which lies on a Bay at the N.W. side of the Island. She was bound to *Manila*, but had no Goods aboard; and therefore we turned her away.

¶ The 23d we took another *Spanish* Vessel that came from the same place as the other. She was laden with Rice and Cotton-Cloth, and bound for *Manila* also. These Goods were purposely for the *Acapulco* Ship: The Rice was for the Men to live on while they lay there, and in their return: and the Cotton-cloth was to make Sail. The Master of this Prize was Boat-swain of the *Acapulco* Ship which escaped us at *Guam*, and was now at *Manila*. It was this Man that gave us the Relation of what Strength it had, how they were afraid of us there, and of the accident that happen'd to them, as is before mentioned in the 10th Chapter. We took these two Vessels within seven or eight Leagues of *Manila*.

¶ *Luconia* I have spoken of already: but I shall now add this further account of it. It is a great Island, taking up between 6 and 7 degrees of Lat. in length, and its breadth near the middle is about 60 Leagues, but the ends are narrow. The North-end lies in about 19 d. North Lat. and the S. end is about 12 d. 30 m. This great Island hath abundance of small Keys or Islands lying about it; especially at the North-end. The South-

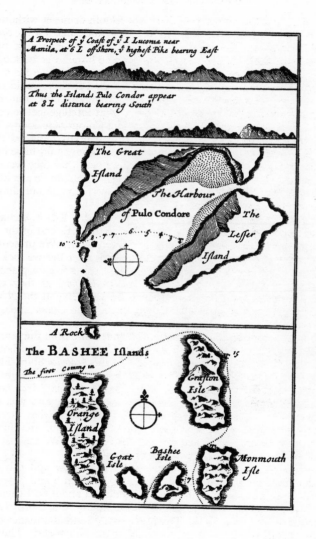

A Prospect of ye Coast of ye I Lucenia near
Manila, at 6 L off Shore, ye highest Pike bearing East

Thus the Islands Pulo Condor appear
at 8 L distance bearing South

The Great
Island
The Harbour
of Pulo Condore
The
Lesser
Island
10   9   8   7   6   5   4   3   2

A Rock
The BASHEE Islands
The first coming in
15
Grafton
Isle
Orange
Island
Goat
Isle
Bashee
Isle
Monmouth
Isle

side fronts towards the rest of the *Philippine* Islands: Of these that are its nearest Neighbours, *Mindora* lately mention'd, is the chief, and gives Name to the Sea or Streight that parts it and the other Islands from *Luconia*: being called the Streights of *Mindora*.

¶ The Body of the Island *Luconia* is composed of many spacious plain Savannahs, and large Mountains. The North-end seems to be more plain and even, I mean freer from Hills, than the South-end: but the Land is all along of a good heighth. It does not appear so flourishing and green as some of the other Islands in this Range; especially that of St. *John*, *Mindanao*, *Batt*-Island, &c. yet in some places it is very woody. Some of the Mountains of this Island afford Gold, and the Savannahs are well stockt with Herds of Cattle, especially Buffaloes. These Cattle are in great plenty all over the *East-Indies*; and therefore 'tis very probable that there were many of these here even before the *Spaniards* came hither. But now there are also plenty of other Cattle, as I have been told, as Bullocks, Horses, Sheep, Goats, Hogs, &c. brought hither by the *Spaniards*.

¶ It is pretty well inhabited with *Indians*, most of them, if not all, under the *Spaniards*, who now are Masters of it. The Native *Indians* do live together in Towns; and they have Priests among them to instruct them in the *Spanish* Religion.

¶ *Manila* the Chief, or perhaps the only City, lies at the Foot of a Ridge of high Hills, facing upon a spacious Harbour near the S.W. Point of the Island, in about the Lat. of 14 d. North. It is environ'd with a high strong Wall, and very well fortify'd with Forts and Breast-works. The Houses are large, strongly built, and covered with Pan-tile. The Streets are large and pretty regular; with a Parade in the midst, after the *Spanish* Fashion. There are a great many fair Buildings, besides Churches and other Religious Houses; of which there are not a few.

¶ The Harbour is so large, that some Hundreds of Ships may ride here; and is never without many, both of their own and Strangers. I have already given you an account of the two Ships going and coming between this Place and *Acapulco*. Besides them, they have some small Vessels of their own; and they do allow the *Portuguese* to trade here, but the *Chinese* are the chiefest Merchants, and they drive the greatest Trade; for they have commonly twenty, thirty or forty Jonks in the Harbour at a time, and a great many Merchants constantly residing in the City, besides Shop-keepers, and Handy-crafts-men in abundance. Small Vessels run up near the Town, but the *Acapulco* Ships and others of greater Burthen, lie a League short of it, where there is a strong Fort also, and Store-houses to put Goods in.

¶ I had the major Part of this Relation two or three Years after this time, from Mr. *Coppinger* our Surgeon; for he made a Voyage hither from *Porto-Nova*, a Town on the Coast of *Coromandel*; in a *Portuguese* Ship, as I think. Here he found ten or twelve of Captain *Swan*'s Men; some of those that we left at *Mindanao*. For after we came from thence, they bought a Proe there, by the Instigation of an *Irishman*, who went by the Name of *John Fitz-Gerald*, a Person that spoke *Spanish* very well; and so in this their Proe they came hither. They had been here but eighteen Months when Mr. *Coppinger* arrived here, and Mr. *Fitz-Gerald* had in this time gotten a *Spanish* Mustesa Woman to Wife, and a good Dowry with her. He then professed Physick and Surgery, and was highly esteemed among the *Spaniards* for his supposed Knowledge in those Arts; for being always troubled with sore Shins while he was with us, he kept some Plaisters and Salves by him; and with these he set up upon his bare natural Stock of Knowledge, and his Experience in Kibes. But then he had a very great Stock of Confidence withal to help out the other, and being an *Irish Roman* Catholick, and having the *Spanish* Language, he had a great Advantage of all his Consorts; and he alone lived well there of them all. We were not within sight of this Town, but I was shewn the Hills that overlooked it, and drew a Draft of them as we lay off at Sea; which I have caused to be engraven among a few others that I took my self. *See the Table* (p. 261).

¶ The time of the Year being now too far spent to do any thing here, it was concluded to sail from hence to *Pulo Condore*, a little Parcel of Islands, on the Coast of *Cambodia*, and carry this Prize with us, and there careen if we could find any convenient Place for it, designing to return hither again by the latter End of *May*, and wait for the *Acapulco* Ship that comes about that time. By our Drafts (which we were guided by, being Strangers to these Parts) this seemed to us then to be a Place out of the way, where we might lie snug for a while, and wait the time of returning for our Prey. For we avoided as much as we could the going to lie by at any great Place of Commerce, lest we should become too much exposed, and perhaps be assaulted by a Force greater than our own.

¶ So having set our Prisoners ashore, we sailed from *Luconia* the 26th Day of *February*, with the Wind E.N.E. and fair Weather, and a brisk Gale. We were in Lat. 14 d. N. when we began to steer away for *Pulo Condore*, and we steer'd S. by W. In our way thither we went pretty near the Shoals of *Pracel*, and other Shoals which are very dangerous. We were very much afraid of them, but escaped them without so much as seeing them, only at the very South-end of the *Pracel* Shoals we saw three little sandy Islands or Spots of Sand standing just above Water within a Mile of us.

¶ It was the 13th Day of *March* before we came in sight of *Pulo Condore*, or the Island *Condore*, as *Pulo* signifies. The 14th Day about Noon we anchored on the North-side of the Island, against a sandy Bay two Mile from the Shore, in ten Fathom clean hard Sand, with both Ship and Prize. *Pulo Condore* is the Principal of a Heap of Islands, and the only inhabited one of them. They lie in Lat. 8 d. 40 m. North, and about twenty Leagues South and by East from the Mouth of the River of *Cambodia*. These Islands lie so near together, that at a distance they appear to be but one Island.

¶ Two of these Islands are pretty large, and of a good heighth, they may be seen fourteen or fifteen Leagues at Sea; the rest are but little Spots. The biggest of the two (which is the inhabited one) is about four or five Leagues long, and lies East and West. It is not above three Mile broad at the broadest Place, in most places not above a Mile wide. The other large Island is about three Mile long, and half a Mile wide. This Island stretcheth N. and S. It is so conveniently placed at the West-end of the biggest Island, that between both there is formed a very commodious Harbour. The Entrance of this Harbour is on the North-side, where the two Islands are near a Mile asunder. There are three or four small Keys, and a good deep Channel between them and the biggest Island. Towards the South-end of the Harbour the two Islands do in a manner close up, leaving only a small Passage for Boats and Canoas. There are no more Islands on the North-side, but five or six on the South-side of the great Island. *See the Table* (p. 261).

¶ The Mold of these Islands for the biggest Part is blackish, and pretty deep, only the Hills are somewhat stony. The Eastern Part of the biggest Island is sandy, yet all cloathed with Trees of divers sorts. The Trees do not grow so thick as I have seen them in some Places, but they are generally large and tall, and fit for any use.

¶ There is one sort of Tree much larger than any other on this Island, and which I have not seen any where else. It is about three or four Foot Diameter in the Body, from whence is drawn a sort of clammy Juice, which being boiled a little becomes perfect Tar; and if you boil it much it will become hard as Pitch. It may be put to either use; we used it both ways, and found it to be very serviceable. The way that they get this Juice, is by cutting a great Gap horizontally in the Body of the Tree half through, and about a Foot from the Ground; and then cutting the Upper-part of the Body aslope inwardly downward, till in the middle of the Tree it meets with the Traverse cutting or plain. In this plain horizontal semi-circular Stump, they make a hollow like a Bason, that may contain a

Quart or two. Into this Hole the Juice which drains from the wounded Upper-part of the Tree falls; from whence you must empty it every Day. It will run thus for some Months, and then dry away, and the Tree will recover again.

¶ The Fruit-trees that Nature hath bestowed on these Isles are Mangoes; and Trees bearing a sort of Grape, and other Trees bearing a kind of wild or bastard Nutmegs. These all grow wild in the Woods, and in very great plenty.

¶ The Mangoes here grow on Trees as big as Apple-trees: Those at *Fort St. George* are not so large. The Fruit of these is as big as a small Peach; but long and smaller towards the Top: It is of a yellowish Colour when ripe; it is very juicy, and of a pleasant Smell, and delicate Taste. When the Mango is young they cut them in two pieces, and pickle them with Salt and Vinegar, in which they put some Cloves of Garlick. This is an excellent Sauce, and much esteemed; it is called Mango-*Achar*. *Achar* I presume signifies Sauce. They make in the *East-Indies*, especially at *Siam* and *Pegu*, several sorts of *Achar*, as of the young Tops of Bamboes, &c. Bambo-*Achar* and Mango-*Achar* are most used. The Mangoes were ripe when we were there, (as were also the rest of these Fruits) and they have then so delicate a Fragrancy, that we could smell them out in the thick Woods if we had but the Wind of them, while we were a good way from them, and could not see them; and we generally found them out this way. Mangoes are common in many Places of the *East-Indies*; but I did never know any grow wild only at this Place. These, though not so big as those I have seen at *Achin* and at *Maderas* or *Fort St. George*, are yet every whit as pleasant as the best sort of their Garden Mangoes.

¶ The Grape-tree grows with a strait Body, of a Diameter about a Foot or more, and hath but few Limbs or Boughs. The Fruit grows in Clusters, all about the Body of the Tree, like the Jack, Durian, and Cacao Fruits. There are of them both red and white. They are much like such Grapes as grow on our Vines, both in shape and colour; and they are of a very pleasant winy taste. I never saw these but on the two biggest of these Islands; the rest had no Tar-trees, Mangoes, Grape-trees, nor wild Nutmegs.

¶ The wild Nutmeg-tree is as big as a Walnut-tree; but it does not spread so much. The Boughs are gross, and the Fruit grows among the Boughs as the Walnut, and other Fruits. This Nutmeg is much smaller than the true Nutmeg, and longer also. It is inclosed with a thin Shell, and a sort of Mace, encircling the Nut within the Shell. This bastard Nutmeg is so much like the true Nutmeg in shape, that at our first Arrival here we thought it to be the true one; but it hath no manner of smell nor taste.

¶ The Animals of these Islands are some Hogs, Lizards and Guanoes; and some of those Creatures mentioned in *Chap.* XI, which are like, but much bigger than the Guanoes.

¶ Here are many sorts of Birds, as Parrots, Parakites, Doves and Pigeons. Here are also a sort of wild Cocks and Hens: They are much like our tame Fowl of that kind; but a great deal less, for they are about the bigness of a Crow. The Cocks do crow like ours, but much more small and shrill; and by their crowing we do first find them out in the Woods where we shoot them. Their flesh is very white and sweet.

¶ There are a great many Limpits and Muscles, and plenty of green Turtle.

¶ And upon this mention of Turtle again, I think it not amiss to add some Reasons to strengthen the Opinion that I have given concerning these Creatures removing from Place to Place. I have said in *Chap.* V, that they leave their common feeding-places, and go to places a great way from thence to lay, as particularly to the Island *Ascension*. Now I have discoursed with some since that Subject was printed, who are of Opinion, that when the laying-time is over, they never go from thence, but lie somewhere in the Sea about the Island, which I think is very improbable: for there can be no Food for them there, as I could soon make appear; as particularly from hence, that the Sea about the Isle of *Ascension* is so deep as to admit of no anchoring but at one place, where there is no sign of Grass: and we never bring up with our sounding Lead any Grass or Weeds out of very deep Seas, but Sand, or the like, only. But if this be granted, that there is Food for them, yet I have a great deal of reason to believe that the Turtle go from hence; for after the laying-time you shall never see them, and where-ever Turtle are, you will see them rise, and hold their Head above Water to breath, once in seven or eight Minutes, or at longest in ten or twelve. And if any Man does but consider how Fish take their certain Seasons of the Year to go from one Sea to another, this would not seem strange; even Fowls also having their Seasons to remove from one place to another.

¶ These Islands are pretty well watered with small Brooks of fresh Water, that run flush into the Sea for ten Months in the Year. The latter-end of *March* they begin to dry away, and in *April* you shall have none in the Brooks, but what is lodged in deep Holes; but you may dig Wells in some places. In *May*, when the Rain comes, the Land is again replenished with Water, and the Brooks run out into the Sea.

¶ These Islands lie very commodiously in the way to and from *Japan*,

China, *Manila*, *Tunquin*, *Cochinchina*, and in general all this most easterly Coast of the *Indian* Continent; whether you go through the Streights of *Malacca*, or the Streights of *Sunda*, between *Sumatra* and *Java*: and one of them you must pass in the common way from *Europe*, or other parts of the *East-Indies*; unless you mean to fetch a great Compass round most of the *East-India* Islands, as we did. Any Ship in distress may be refreshed and recruited here very conveniently; and besides ordinary Accommodations, be furnished with Masts, Yards, Pitch and Tar. It might also be a convenient Place to usher in a Commerce with the neighbouring Country of *Cochinchina*, and Forts might be built to secure a Factory; particularly at the Harbour, which is capable of being well fortified. This Place therefore being upon all these Accounts so valuable, and withal so little known, I have here inserted a Draft of it, which I took during our stay there.

¶ The Inhabitants of this Island are by Nation *Cochinchinese*, as they told us, for one of them spoke good *Malayan*: which Language we learnt a smattering of, and some of us so as to speak it pretty well, while we lay at *Mindanao*; and this is the common Tongue of Trade and Commerce (though it be not in several of them the Native Language) in most of the *East-India* Islands, being the *Lingua Franca*, as it were, of these Parts. I believe it is the vulgar Tongue at *Malacca*, *Sumatra*, *Java*, and *Borneo*; but at *Celebes*, the *Philippine*-Islands, and the Spice-Islands, it seems borrowed for the carrying on of Trade.

¶ The Inhabitants of *Pulo Condore* are but a small People in Stature, well enough shaped, and of a darker Colour than the *Mindanayans*. They are pretty long Visaged; their Hair is black and streight, their Eyes are but small and black, their Noses of a mean bigness, and pretty high, their Lips thin, their Teeth white, and little Mouths. They are very civil People, but extraordinary poor. Their chiefest Employment is to draw the Juice of those Trees that I have described to make Tar. They preserve it in wooden Troughs; and when they have their Cargo, they transport it to *Cochinchina*, their Mother-Country. Some others of them employ themselves to catch Turtle, and boil up their Fat to Oil, which they also transport home. These People have great large Nets, with wide Mashes to catch the Turtle. The *Jamaica* Turtlers have such; and I did never see the like Nets but at *Jamaica* and here.

¶ They are so free of their Women, that they would bring them aboard and offer them to us; and many of our Men hired them for a small Matter. This is a Custom used by several Nations in the *East-Indies*, as at *Pegu*, *Siam*, *Cochinchina*, and *Cambodia*, as I have been told. It is used at *Tunquin* also to my Knowledge; for I did afterwards make a Voyage thither, and most of our Men had Women aboard all the time of our abode there. In *Africa* also, on the Coast of *Guinea*, our Merchants, Factors, and Seamen that reside there, have their black Misses. It is accounted a piece of Policy to do it; for the chief Factors and Captains of Ships have the great Men's Daughters offered them, the *Mandarins* or Noblemens at *Tunquin*, and even the King's Wives in *Guinea*; and by this sort of Alliance the Country People are engaged to a greater Friendship: And if there should arise any difference about Trade, or any thing else, which might provoke the Natives to seek some treacherous Revenge, (to which all these Heathen Nations are very prone) then these *Dalilahs* would certainly declare it to their white Friends, and so hinder their Country-men's Design.

❡ These People are Idolaters: But their manner of Worship I know not. There are a few scattering Houses and Plantations on the great Island, and a small Village on the South-side of it; where there is a little Idol Temple, and an Image of an Elephant about five Foot high, and in bigness proportionable, placed on one side of the Temple; and a Horse not so big, placed on the other side of it; both standing with their Heads towards the South. The Temple it self was low and ordinary, built of Wood, and thatched like one of their Houses; which are but very meanly.

❡ The Images of the Horse and the Elephant were the most general Idols that I observed in the Temples of *Tunquin*, when I travelled there. There were other Images also, of Beasts, Birds and Fish. I do not remember I saw any Humane Shape there; nor any such monstrous Representations as I have seen among the *Chinese*. Where-ever the *Chinese* Seamen or Merchants come (and they are very numerous all over these Seas) they have always hideous Idols on board their Jonks or Ships, with Altars, and Lamps burning before them. These Idols they bring ashore with them: And beside those they have in common, every Man hath one in his own House. Upon some particular solemn Days I have seen their *Bonzies*, or Priests, bring whole Armfuls of painted Papers, and burn them with a great deal of Ceremony, being very careful to let no Piece escape them. The same Day they killed a Goat which had been purposely fatting a Month before; this they offer or present before their Idol, and then dress it and feast themselves with it. I have seen them do this in *Tunquin*, where I have at the same time been invited to their Feasts; and at *Bancouli*, in the Isle of *Sumatra*, they sent a Shoulder of the sacrificed Goat to the *English*, who eat of it, and asked me to do so too; but I refused.

❡ When I was at *Maderas*, or *Fort St. George*, I took notice of a great Ceremony used for several Nights successively by the Idolaters inhabiting the Suburbs: Both Men and Women (these very well clad) in a great Multitude went in solemn Procession with lighted Torches, carrying their Idols about with them. I knew not the meaning of it. I observed some went purposely carrying Oil to sprinkle into the Lamps, to make them burn the brighter. They began their Round about 11 a Clock at Night, and having paced it gravely about the Streets till two or three a Clock in the Morning, their Idols were carried with much Ceremony into the Temple by the Chief of the Procession, and some of the Women I saw enter the Temple, particularly. Their Idols were different from those of *Tunquin, Cambodia,* &c. being in Humane Shape.

¶ I have said already that we arrived at these Islands the 14th Day of *March,* 1687. The next Day we searched about for a Place to careen in; and the 16th Day we entered the Harbour, and immediately provided to careen. Some Men were set to fell great Trees to saw into Planks; others went to unrigging the Ship; some made a House to put our Goods in, and for the Sail-maker to work in. The Country People resorted to us, and brought us of the Fruits of the Island, with Hogs, and sometimes Turtle; for which they received Rice in exchange, which we had a Ship-load of, taken at *Manila.* We bought of them also a good Quantity of their pitchy Liquor, which we boiled, and used about our Ship's Bottom. We mixed it first with Lime, which we made here, and it made an excellent Coat, and stuck on very well.

¶ We staid in this Harbour from the 16th Day of *March*, till the 16th of *April*; in which time we made a new Suit of Sails of the Cloth that was taken in the Prize. We cut a spare Main-top-mast, and sawed Plank to sheath the Ship's Bottom; for she was not sheathed all over at *Mindanao*, and that old Plank that was left on then we now ript off, and clapt on new.

¶ While we lay here two of our Men died, who were poisoned at *Mindanao*, they told us of it when they found themselves poisoned, and had lingered ever since. They were open'd by our Doctor, according to their own Request before they died, and their Livers were black, light and dry, like Pieces of Cork.

¶ Our Business being finished, here, we left the *Spanish* Prize taken at *Manila*, and most of the Rice, taking out enough for ourselves; and on the 17th Day we went from hence to the Place where we first anchored, on the North-side of the great Island, purposely to water; for there was a great Stream when we first came to the Island, and we thought it was so now. But we found it dried up, only it stood in Holes, two or three Hogsheads or a Tun in a Hole: Therefore we did immediately cut Bamboes, and made Spouts, through which we conveyed the Water down to the Sea-side; by taking it up in Bowls, and pouring it into these Spouts or Troughs. We conveyed some of it thus near half a Mile. While we were filling our Water, Capt. *Read* engaged an old Man, one of the Inhabitants of this Island, the same who I said could speak the *Malayan* Language, to be his Pilot to the Bay of *Siam*; for he had often been telling us, that he was well acquainted there, and that he knew some Islands there, where there were Fishermen lived, who he thought could supply us with Salt-fish to eat at Sea; for we had nothing but Rice to eat. The easterly Monsoon was not yet done; therefore it was concluded to spend some time there, and then take the advantage of the beginning of the western Monsoon, to return to *Manila* again.

¶ The 21st Day of *April* 1687, we sailed from *Pulo Condore*, directing our Course W. by S. for the Bay of *Siam*. We had fair Weather, and a fine moderate Gale of Wind at E.N.E.

¶ The 23d Day we arrived at *Pulo Ubi*, or the Island *Ubi*. This Island is about 40 Leagues to the westward of *Pulo Condore*; it lies just at the entrance of the Bay of *Siam*, at the S.W. point of Land, that makes the Bay; namely, the Point of *Cambodia*. This Island is about seven or eight Leagues round, and it is higher Land than any of *Pulo Condore* Isles. Against the South-East-part of it there is a small Key, about a Cables length from the main Island. This *Pulo Ubi* is very woody, and it has good Water on the North-side, where you may anchor; but the best anchoring is on the East-side against a small Bay; then you will have the little Island to the southward of you.

¶ At *Pulo Ubi* we found two small Barks laden with Rice. They belonged to *Cambodia*, from whence they came not above two or three Days before, and they touched here to fill Water. Rice is the general Food of all these Countries, therefore it is transported by Sea from one Country to another, as Corn in these parts of the World. For in some Countries they produce more than enough for themselves, and send what they can spare to those Places where there is but little.

¶ The 24th Day we went into the Bay of *Siam*: This is a large deep Bay, of which and of this Kingdom I shall at present speak but little, because I design a more particular account of all this Coast, to wit, of *Tunquin*, *Cochinchina*, *Siam*, *Champa*, *Cambodia*, and *Malacca*, making all the most easterly part of the Continent of *Asia*, lying *South* of *China*: But to do it in the Course of this Voyage, would too much swell this Volume; and I shall chuse therefore to give a separate Relation of what I know or have learnt of them, together with the neighbouring Parts of *Sumatra*, *Java*, &c. where I have spent some time.

¶ We ran down into the Bay of *Siam*, till we came to the Islands that our *Pulo Condore* Pilot told us of, which lie about the middle of the Bay: But as good a Pilot as he was, he run us a-ground; yet we had no damage. Capt. *Read* went ashore at these Islands, where he found a small Town of Fishermen; but they had no Fish to sell, and so we returned empty.

¶ We had yet fair Weather, and very little Wind; so that being often becalmed, we were till the 13th Day of *May* before we got to *Pulo Ubi* again. There we found two small Vessels at an Anchor on the East-side: They were laden with Rice and Laquer, which is used in Japanning of Cabinets. One of these came from *Champa*, bound to the Town of *Malacca*, which belongs to the *Dutch*, who took it from the *Portugueze*; and this shews that they have a Trade with *Champa*. This was a very pretty neat Vessel, her bottom very clean and curiously coated, she had about forty Men all armed with Cortans, or broad Swords, Lances, and some Guns, that went with a Swivel upon their Gunnal. They were of the Idolaters, Natives of *Champa*, and some of the briskest, most sociable, without Fearfulness or Shyness, and the most neat and dextrous about their Shipping, of any such I have met with in all my Travels. The other Vessel came from the River of *Cambodia*, and was bound towards the Streights of *Malacca*. Both of them stopt here, for the westerly-winds now began to blow, which were against them, being somewhat bleated.

¶ We anchored also on the East-side, intending to fill Water. While we lay here we had very violent Wind at S.W. and a strong Current setting right to windward. The fiercer the Wind blew, the more strong the Current set against it. This Storm lasted till the 20th Day, and then it began to abate.

¶ The 21st Day of *May* we went back from hence towards *Pulo Condore*. In our way we overtook a great Jonk that came from *Palimbam*, a Town on the Island *Sumatra*: She was full laden with Pepper which they bought there, and was bound to *Siam*: But it blowing so hard, she was afraid to venture into that Bay, and therefore came to *Pulo Condore* with us, where we both anchored *May* the 24th. This Vessel was of the *Chinese* make, full of little Rooms or Partitions, like our Well-boats. I shall describe them in the next Chapter. The Men of this Jonk told us, that the *English* were settled on the Island *Sumatra*, at a Place called *Sillabar*; and the first Knowledge we had that the *English* had any Settlement on *Sumatra* was from these.

¶ When we came to an Anchor, we saw a small Bark at an Anchor near the Shore; therefore Capt. *Read* sent a Canoa aboard her, to know from whence they came; and supposing that it was a *Malayan* Vessel, he ordered the Men not to go aboard, for they are accounted desperate Fellows, and their Vessels are commonly full of Men, who all wear Cressets, or little Daggers by their sides. The Canoas Crew not minding the Captain's Orders went aboard, all but one Man that stayed in the Canoa. The *Malayans*, who were about 20 of them, seeing our Men all armed, thought that they came to take their Vessel; therefore at once, on a Signal given, they drew out their Cressets, and stabbed five or six of our Men before they knew what the matter was. The rest of our Men leapt over-board, some into the Canao, and some into the Sea, and so got away. Among the rest, one *Daniel Wallis* leapt into the Sea, who could never swim before nor since; yet now he swam very well a good while before he was taken up. When the Canoas came aboard, Capt. *Read* mann'd two Canoas, and went to be revenged on the *Malayans*; but they seeing him coming, did cut a Hole in the Vessel's bottom, and went ashore in their Boat. Capt. *Read* followed them, but they ran into the Woods and hid themselves. Here we staid ten or eleven Days, for it blew very hard all the time. While we staid here *Herman Coppinger* our Surgeon went ashore, intending to live here; but Capt. *Read* sent some Men to fetch him again. I had the same Thoughts, and would have gone ashore too, but waited for a more convenient Place. For neither he nor I, when we were last on board at *Mindanao*, had any Knowledge of the Plot that was laid to leave Capt. *Swan*, and run away with the Ship; and being sufficiently weary of this mad Crew, we were willing to give them the slip at any Place from whence we might hope to get a Passage to an *English* Factory. There was nothing else of Moment happened while we staid here.

CHAPTER XV

The Habits of a Tartarian *Officer and his Retinue. Their Presents, excellent Beef.* Samciu, *a sort
of* Chinese Arack, *and* Hocciu *a kind of* Chinese Mum, *and the Jars it is bottled in. Of the
Isle of* Formosa, *and the five Islands; to which they gave the Names of* Orange, Monmouth,
Grafton, Bashee, *and* Goat-Islands, *in general, the* Bashee-Islands. *A Digression concerning the
different depths of the Sea near high or low Lands, Soil,* &c. *as before. The Soil, Fruits and Animals
of these Islands. The Inhabitants and their Cloathing. Rings of a yellow Metal like Gold. Their
Houses built on remarkable Precipices. Their Boats and Employments. Their Food, of Goats-Skins,
Entrails,* &c. *Parcht Locusts.* Bashee, *or Sugar-cane Drink. Of their Language and Original,
Launces and* Buffaloe *Coats. No Idols, nor civil Form of Government. A young Man buried alive
by them; supposed to be for Theft. Their Wives and Children, and Husbandry. Their Manners,
Entertainments, and Traffick. Of the Ships first Entercourse with these People, and Bartering with
them. Their Course among the Islands; their stay there, and provision to depart. They are driven
off by a violent Storm, and return. The Natives Kindness to six of them left behind. The Crew
discouraged by those Storms, quit their design of Crusing off* Manila *for the* Acapulco *Ship; and
'tis resolved to fetch a Compass to Cape* Comorin, *and so for the* Red-Sea.

HAVING filled our Water, cut our Wood, and got our Ship in a
sailing Posture, while the blustering hard Winds lasted, we took
the first Opportunity of a settled Gale to sail towards *Manila*.
Accordingly *June* the 4th, 1687, we loosed from *Pulo Condore*, with the
Wind at S.W. fair Weather at a brisk Gale. The *Pepper*-Jonk bound to
Siam remained there, waiting for an easterly Wind; but one of his Men,
a kind of a bastard *Portuguese*, came aboard our Ship, and was entertained
for the sake of his Knowledge in the several Languages of these Countries.
The Wind continued in the S.W. but 24 Hours, or a little more, and then
came about to the North, and then to the N.E.; and the Sky became
exceeding clear. Then the Wind came at East, and lasted betwixt E. and
S.E. for eight or ten Days. Yet we continued plying to Windward,
expecting every Day a shift of Wind, because these Winds were not
according to the Season of the Year.

¶ We were now afraid lest the Currents might deceive us, and carry us
on the Shoals of *Pracel*, which were near us, a little to the N.W. but we
passed on to the eastward, without seeing any sign of them; yet we were
kept much to the northward of our intended Course. And the easterly
Winds still continuing, we despaired of getting to *Manila*; and therefore
began to project some new Design; and the result was, to visit the Island
Plata, about the Lat. of 20 Deg. 40 Min. North; and not far from us at
this time.

¶ It is a small low Island, environ'd with Rocks clear round it, by report.
It lyeth so in the way between *Manila* and *Canton*, the Head of a Province,
and a Town of great Trade in *China*, that the *Chinese* do dread the Rocks

about it, more than the *Spaniards* did formerly dread *Bermudas*; for many of their Jonks coming from *Manila* have been lost there, and with abundance of Treasure in them; as we were informed by all the *Spaniards* that ever we convers'd with in these Parts. They told us also, that in these Wrecks most of the Men were drowned, and that the *Chinese* did never go thither to take up any of the Treasure that was lost there, for fear of being lost themselves. But the danger of the Place did not daunt us; for we were resolved to try our Fortunes there, if the Winds would permit; and we did beat for it five or six Days; but at last were forced to leave that Design also for want of Winds; for the S.E. Winds continuing, forced us on the Coast of *China*.

❡ It was the 25th Day of *June* when we made the Land; and running in towards the Shore we came to an Anchor the same Day, on the N.E. end of St. *John*'s Island.

❡ This Island is in Lat. about 22 d. 30 min. North, lying on the S. Coast of the Province of *Quantung* or *Canton* in *China*. It is of an indifferent heighth, and pretty plain, and the Soil fertile enough. It is partly woody, partly Savannahs or Pasturage for Cattle; and there is some moist arable Land for Rice. The Skirts or outer-part of the Island, especially that part of it which borders on the main Sea, is woody: The middle-part of it is good thick grassy Pasture, with some Groves of Trees; and that which is cultivated Land is low wet Land, yielding plentiful Crops of Rice; the only Grain that I did see here. The tame Cattle which this Island affords, are *China*-Hogs, Goats, Buffaloes, and some Bullocks. The Hogs of this Island are all black; they have but small Heads, very short thick Necks, great Bellies, commonly touching the Ground, and short Legs. They eat but little Food, yet they are most of them very fat; probably because they Sleep much. The tame Fowls are Ducks, and Cocks and Hens. I saw no wild Fowl but a few small Birds.

❡ The Natives of this Island are *Chinese*. They are subject to the Crown of *China*, and consequently at this time to the *Tartars*. The *Chinese* in general are tall, strait-bodied, raw-boned Men. They are long Visaged, and their Foreheads are high; but they have little Eyes. Their Noses are pretty large, with a rising in the middle. Their Mouths are of a mean size, pretty thin Lips. They are of an ashy Complexion; their Hair is black, and their Beards thin and long, for they pluck the Hair out by the Roots, suffering only some few very long straggling Hairs to grow about their Chin, in which they take great Pride, often combing them, and sometimes tying them up in a knot, and they have such Hairs too growing down from each side of their upper-Lip like Whiskers. The ancient

Chinese were very proud of the Hair of their Heads, letting it grow very long, and stroking it back with their Hands curiously, and then winding the Plats all together round a Bodkin, thrust through it at the hinder-part of the Head; and both Men and Women did thus. But when the *Tartars* conquered them, they broke them of this Custom they were so fond of by main Force; insomuch that they resented this Imposition worse than their Subjection, and rebelled upon it; but being still worsted, were forced to acquiesce; and to this Day they follow the Fashion of their Masters the *Tartars*, and shave all their Heads, only reserving one Lock, which some tye up, others let it hang down to a great or small length as they please. The *Chinese* in other Countries still keep their old Custom, but if any of the *Chinese* is found wearing long Hair in *China*, he forfeits his Head; and many of them have abandoned their Country to preserve their Liberty of wearing their Hair, as I have been told by themselves.

¶ The *Chinese* have no Hats, Caps, or Turbans; but when they walk abroad, they carry a small Umbrello in their Hands, wherewith they fence their Head from the Sun or the Rain, by holding it over their Heads. If they walk but a little way, they carry only a large Fan made of Paper, or Silk, of the same Fashion as those our Ladies have, and many of them are brought over hither; one of these every Man carried in his Hand if he do but cross the Street, skreening his Head with it, if he hath not an Umbrello with him.

¶ The common Apparel of the Men, is a loose Frock and Breeches. They seldom wear Stockings, but they have Shoes, or a sort of Slippers rather. The Men's Shoes are made diversly. The Women have very small Feet, and consequently but little Shoes; for from their Infancy their Feet are kept swathed up with Bands, as hard as they can possibly endure them; and from the time they can go till they have done growing they bind them up every Night. This they do purposely to hinder them from growing, esteeming little Feet to be a great Beauty. But by this unreasonable Custom they do in a manner lose the use of their Feet, and instead of going they only stumble about their Houses, and presently squat down on their Breeches again, being as it were confined to sitting all Days of their Lives. They seldom stir abroad, and one would be apt to think, that as some have conjectured, their keeping up their fondness for this Fashion were a Stratagem of the Mens, to keep them from gadding and gossipping about, and confine them at home. They are kept constantly to their Work, being fine Needle Women, and making many curious Embroideries, and they make their own Shoes; but if any Stranger be desirous to bring away any for Novelty's sake, he must be a great Favourite to get a pair of

Shoes of them, though he give twice their Value. The poorer sort of Women trudge about Streets, and to the Market, without Shoes or Stockings; and these cannot afford to have little Feet, being to get their living with them.

¶ The *Chinese*, both Men and Women, are very ingenious; as may appear by the many curious things that are brought from thence, especially the *Porcelaine*, or *China* earthen-Ware. The *Spaniards* of *Manila*, that we took on the Coast of *Luconia*, told me, that this Commodity is made of Conch-shells; the inside of which looks like Mother of Pearl. But the *Portuguese* lately mentioned, who had lived in *China*, and spoke that and the neigh-bouring Languages very well, said, That it was made of a fine sort of Clay that was dug in the Province of *Canton*. I have often made enquiry about it, but could never be well satisfied in it: But while I was on the Coast of *Canton* I forgot to enquire about it. They make very fine Lacquer-ware also, and good Silks; and they are curious at Painting and Carving.

¶ *China* affords Drugs in great abundance, especially *China*-Root; but this is not peculiar to that Country alone; for there is much of this Root growing at *Jamaica*, particularly at 16 *Mile-walk*, and in the Bay of *Honduras* it is very plentiful. There is a great store of Sugar made in this Country; and Tea in abundance is brought from thence; being much used there, and in *Tunquin* and *Cochinchina* as common drinking; Women sitting in the Streets, and selling Dishes of Tea hot and ready made; they call it *Chau*, and even the poorest People sip it. But the Tea at *Tonqueen* of *Cochinchina* seems not so good, or of so pleasant a bitter, or of so fine a Colour, or such virtue as this in *China*; for I have drank of it in these Countries; unless the fault be in the way of making it, for I made none there my self; and by the high red Colour it looks as if they made a Decoction of it, or kept it stale. Yet at *Japan* I was told there is a great deal of pure Tea, very good.

¶ The *Chinese* are very great Gamesters, and they will never be tired with it, playing Night and Day, till they have lost all their Estates; then it is usual with them to hang themselves. This was frequently done by the *Chinese* Factors at *Manila*, as I was told by *Spaniards* that lived there. The *Spaniards* themselves are much addicted to Gaming, and are very expert at it; but the *Chinese* are too subtle for them, being in general a very cunning People.

¶ But a particular Account of them and their Country would fill a Volume; nor doth my short Experience of them qualifie me to say much of them. Wherefore I confine my self chiefly to what I observed at St. *John*'s Island, where we lay some time, and visited the Shore every Day to buy Provision, as Hogs, Fowls, and Buffaloe. Here was a small Town standing in a wet swampy Ground, with many filthy Ponds amongst the Houses, which were built on the Ground as ours are, not on Posts as at *Mindanao*. In these Ponds were plenty of Ducks; the Houses were small and low, and covered with Thatch, and the insides were but ill furnished, and kept nastily: And I have been told by one who was there, that most of the Houses in the City of *Canton* it self are but poor and irregular.

¶ The Inhabitants of this Village seem to be most Husbandmen: They were at this time very busy in sowing their Rice, which is their chiefest Commodity. The Land in which they choose to sow the Rice is low and wet, and when plowed the Earth was like a mass of Mud. They plow their Land with a small Plow, drawn by one Buffaloe, and one Man both holds the Plow and drives the Beast. When the Rice is ripe and gathered in, they tread it out of the Ear with Buffaloes, in a large round Place made with a hard Floor fit for that purpose, where they chain three or four of these Beasts, one at the Tail of the other, and driving them round in a Ring, as in a Horse-mill, they so order it that the Buffaloes may tread upon it all.

¶ I was once ashore at this Island, with seven or eight *Englishmen* more, and having occasion to stay some time, we killed a Shote, or young Porker, and roasted it for our Dinners. While we were busy dressing of our Pork, one of the Natives came and sat down by us; and when the Dinner was ready, we cut a good Piece and gave it him, which he willingly received. But by Signs he begged more, and withal pointed into the Woods; yet we did not understand his meaning, nor much mind him, till our Hunger was pretty well asswaged; although he did still make signs, and walking a little way from us, he beckoned to us to come to him; which at last I did, and two or three more. He going before, led the way in a small blind Path, through a Thicket, into a small Grove of Trees, in which there was an old Idol Temple about ten Foot square: The Walls of it were about six Foot high, and two Foot thick, made of Bricks. The Floor was paved with broad Bricks, and in the middle of the Floor stood an old rusty Iron Bell on its Brims. This Bell was about two Foot high, standing flat on the Ground; the Brims on which it stood were about sixteen Inches Diameter. From the Brims it did taper away a little towards the Head, much like our Bells; but that the Brims did not turn out so much as ours do. On the Head of the Bell there were three Iron Bars as big as a Man's Arm, and about ten Inches long from the Top of the Bell, where the Ends joined as in a Center, and seemed of one Mass with the Bell, as if cast together. These Bars stood all parallel to the

Ground, and their farther Ends, which stood triangularly and opening from each other at equal Distances, like the Fliers of our Kitchen-Jacks, were made exactly in the Shape of the Paw of some monstrous Beast, having sharp Claws on it. This it seems was their God; for as soon as our zealous Guide came before the Bell, he fell flat on his Face and beckoned to us, seeming very desirous to have us do the like. At the Inner-side of the Temple, against the Walls, there was an Altar of white hewn Stone. The Table of the Altar was about three Foot long, sixteen Inches broad, and three Inches thick. It was raised about two Foot from the Ground, and supported by three small Pillars of the same white Stone. On this Altar there were several small earthen Vessels; one of them was full of small Sticks that had been burned at one end. Our Guide made a great many signs for us to fetch and to leave some of our Meat there, and seemed very importunate, but we refused. We left him there, and went aboard; I did see no other Temple nor Idol here.

❡ While we lay at this Place, we saw several small *China* Jonks sailing in the *Lagune* between the Islands and the Main, one came and anchored by us. I and some more of our Men went aboard to view her: She was built with a square flat Head as well as Stern, only the Head or Fore-part was not so broad as the Stern. On her Deck she had little thatcht Houses like Hovels, covered with Palmeto Leaves, and raised about three Foot high, for the Seamen to creep into. She had a pretty large Cabbin, wherein there was an Altar and a Lamp burning. I did but just look in, and saw not the Idol. The Hold was divided into many small Partitions, all of them made so tight, that if a Leak should spring up in any one of them, it could go no farther, and so could do but little damage, but only to the Goods in the Bottom of that Room where the Leak springs up. Each of these Rooms belong to one or two Merchants, or more; and every Man freights his Goods in his own Room; and probably lodges there, if he be on Board himself. These Jonks have only two Masts, a Main-mast and a Fore-mast. The Fore-mast has a square Yard and a square Sail, but the Main-mast has a Sail narrow aloft, like a Sloops-sail, and in fair Weather they use a Top-sail, which is to hale down on the Deck in foul Weather, Yard and all; for they do not go up to furl it. The Main-mast in their biggest Jonks seem to me as big as any Third-Rate Man of Wars Mast in *England*, and yet not pieced as ours, but made of one grown Tree; and in all my Travels I never saw any single Tree-masts so big in the Body, and so long, and yet so well tapered, as I have seen in the *Chinese* Jonks.

❡ Some of our Men went over to a pretty large Town on the Continent of *China*, where we might have furnished our selves with Provision, which was a thing we were always in want of, and was our chief Business here; but we were afraid to lie in this Place any longer, for we had some signs of an approaching Storm; this being the time of the Year in which Storms are expected on this Coast; and here was no safe Riding. It was now the time of the Year for the S.W. Monsoon, but the Wind had been whiffling about from one part of the Compass to another for two or three Days, and sometimes it would be quite calm. This caused us to put to Sea, that we might have Sea-room at least; for such flattering Weather is commonly the fore-runner of a Tempest.

¶ Accordingly we weighed Anchor, and set out; yet we had very little Wind all the next Night. But the Day ensuing, which was the 4th Day of *July*, about Four a-Clock in the Afternoon, the Wind came to the N.E. and freshned upon us, and the Sky looked very black in that quarter, and the black Clouds began to rise apace and moved towards us; having hung all the Morning in the Horizon. This made us take in our Top-sails, and the Wind still increasing, about Nine a-Clock we rift our Main-sail and Fore-sail; at Ten we furl'd our Fore-sail, keeping under a Main-sail and Mizen. At Eleven a-Clock we furl'd our Main-sail, and ballasted our Mizen; at which time it began to rain, and by Twelve a-Clock at Night it blew exceeding hard, and the Rain poured down as through a Sieve. It thundered and lightned prodigiously, and the Sea seemed all of a Fire about us; for every Sea that broke sparkled like Lightning. The violent Wind raised the Sea presently to a great heighth, and it ran very short, and began to break in on our Deck. One Sea struck away the Rails of our Head, and our Sheet-Anchor, which was stowed with one Flook or bending of the Iron over the Ships Gunnal, and lasht very well down to the Side, was violently washt off, and had like to have struck a Hole in our Bow, as it lay beating against it. Then we were forced to put right before the Wind to stow our Anchor again; which we did with much ado; but afterwards we durst not adventure to bring our Ship to the Wind again, for fear of foundring, for the turning the Ship either to or fro from the Wind is dangerous in such violent Storms. The Fierceness of the Weather continued till Four a-Clock that Morning; in which time we did cut away two Canoas that were towing astern.

¶ After Four a-Clock the Thunder and the Rain abated, and then we saw a *Corpus Sant* at our Main-top-mast Head, on the very Top of the Truck of the Spindle. This sight rejoiced our Men exceedingly; for the height of the Storm is commonly over when the *Corpus Sant* is seen aloft; but when they are seen lying on the Deck, it is generally accounted a bad Sign.

¶ A *Corpus Sant* is a certain small glittering Light; when it appears as this did, on the very Top of the Main-mast or at a Yard-arm, it is like a Star; but when it appears on the Deck, it resembles a great Glow-worm. The *Spaniards* have another Name for it (though I take even this to be a *Spanish* or *Portuguese* Name, and a Corruption only of *Corpus Sanctum*) and I have been told that when they see them, they presently go to Prayers, and bless themselves for the happy Sight. I have heard some ignorant Seamen discoursing how they have seen them creep, or, as they say, travel about in the Scuppers, telling many dismal Stories that hapned at such times: but I did never see any one stir out of the place where it was first fixt, except upon Deck, where every Sea washeth it about: Neither did I ever see any but when we have had hard Rain as well as Wind; and therefore do believe it is some Jelly: but enough of this.

¶ We continued scudding right before Wind and Sea from Two till Seven a-Clock in the Morning, and then the Wind being much abated, we set our Mizen again, and brought our Ship to the Wind, and lay under a Mizen till Eleven. Then it fell flat calm, and it continued so for about two Hours: but the Sky looked very black and rueful, especially in the S.W. and the Sea tossed us about like an Egg-shell, for want of Wind. About One a-Clock in the Afternoon the Wind sprung up at S.W. out of the Quarter from whence we did expect it: therefore we presently brailed up our Mizen; and wore our Ship: But we had no sooner put our Ship before the Wind, but it blew a Storm again, and rain'd very hard, though not so violently as the Night before: but the Wind was altogether as boisterous, and so continued till Ten or Eleven a-Clock at Night. All which time we scudded and run before the Wind very swift, though only with our bare Poles, that is, without any Sail abroad. Afterwards the Wind died away by degrees, and before Day we had but little Wind, and fine clear Weather.

¶ I was never in such a violent Storm in all my Life; so said all the Company. This was near the Change of the Moon: it was two or three Days before the Change. The 6th Day in the Morning, having fine handsome Weather, we got up our Yards again, and began to dry our selves and our Cloaths, for we were all well sopt. This Storm had deadned the Hearts of our Men so much, that instead of going to buy more Provision at the same place from whence we came before the Storm, or of seeking any more for the Island *Prata*, they thought of going somewhere to shelter before the Full Moon, for fear of another such Storm at that time: For commonly, if there is any very bad Weather in the Month, it is about two or three Days before or after the Full or Change of the Moon.

¶ These Thoughts, I say, put our Men on thinking where to go, and the Drafts or Sea-plats being first consulted, it was concluded to go to certain Islands lying in Lat. 23 d. N. called *Piscadores*. For there was not a Man aboard that was any thing acquainted on these Coasts; and therefore all our Dependance was on the Drafts, which only pointed out to us where such and such Places or Islands were, without giving us any account what Harbour, Roads or Bays there were, or the Produce, Strength or Trade of them; these we were forced to seek after our selves.

¶ The *Piscadores* are a great many inhabited Islands, lying near the Island *Formosa*, between it and *China*, in or near the Lat. of 23 d. N. Lat. almost as high as the Tropick of *Cancer*. These *Piscadore* Islands are moderately high, and appear much like our *Dorsetshire* and *Wiltshire-Downs* in *England*. They produce thick short Grass, and a few Trees. They are pretty well watered, and they feed abundance of Goats, and some great Cattle. There are abundance of Mounts and old Fortifications on them: but of no use now, whatever they have been.

¶ Between the two eastermost Islands there is a very good Harbour, which is never without Jonks riding in it: and on the West-side of the eastermost Island there is a large Town and Fort commanding the Harbour. The Houses are but low, yet well built, and the Town makes a fine Prospect. This is a Garrison of the *Tartars*, wherein are also three or four Hundred Soldiers; who live here three Years, and then they are mov'd to some other Place.

¶ On the Island, on the West-side of the Harbour, close by the Sea, there is a small Town of *Chinese*; and most of the other Islands have some *Chinese* living on them more or less.

¶ Having, as I said before, concluded to go to these Islands, we steered away for them, having the Wind at W.S.W. a small Gale. The 20th Day of *July* we had first sight of them, and steered in among them; finding no place to anchor in till we came into the Harbour before-mentioned. We blundering in, knowing little of our way, and we admired to see so many Jonks going and coming, and some at an Anchor, and so great a Town as the neighbouring Eastermost Town, the *Tartarian* Garrison; for we did not expect, nor desire to have seen any People, being in Care to lie conceal'd in these Seas; however seeing we were here, we boldly run into the Harbour, and presently sent ashore our Canoa to the Town.

¶ Our People were met by an Officer at their Landing; and our Quartermaster, who was the chiefest Man in the Boat, was conducted before the Governour, and examined of what Nation we were, and what was our Business here. He answer'd, That we were *English*, and were bound to

Amoy or *Anhay*, which is a City standing on a navigable River in the Province of *Fokein* in *China*, and is a place of vast Trade, there being a huge Multitude of Ships there, and in general on all these Coasts, as I have heard of several that have been there. He said also, that having received some Damage by a Storm, we therefore put in here to refit, before we could adventure to go farther; and that we did intend to lie here till after the Full-Moon, for fear of another Storm. The Governour told him, that we might better refit our Ship at *Amoy* than here, and that he heard that two *English* Vessels were arrived there already; and that he should be very ready to assist us in any thing; but we must not expect to trade there, but must go to the Places allowed to entertain Merchant-Strangers, which were *Amoy* and *Macao*. *Macao* is a Town of great Trade also, lying in an Island at the very Mouth of the River of *Canton*. It is fortified and garrisoned by a large *Portuguese* Colony, but yet under the *Chinese* Government, whose People inhabit one Moiety of the Town, and lay on the *Portuguese* what Tax they please; for they dare not disoblige the *Chinese*, for fear of losing their Trade. However, the Governour very kindly told our Quarter-master, that whatsoever we wanted, if that Place could furnish us, we should have it. Yet that we must not come ashore on that Island, but he would send aboard some of his Men, to know what we wanted, and they should also bring it off to us. That nevertheless we might go on shore on other Islands to buy Refreshments of the *Chinese*. After the Discourse was ended, the Governour dismist him, with a small Jar of Flour, and three or four large Cakes of very fine Bread, and about a Dozen Pine-Apples and Water-Melons (all very good in their kind) as a Present to the Captain.

¶ The next Day an eminent Officer came aboard, with a great many Attendants. He wore a black Silk Cap of a particular make, with a Plume of black and white Feathers, standing up almost round his Head behind, and all his outside Cloaths were black Silk: He had a loose black Coat, which reached to his Knees, and his Breeches were of the same; and underneath his Coat he had two Garments more, of other coloured Silk. His Legs were covered with small black limber Boots. All his Attendants were in a very handsome Garb of black Silk, all wearing those small black Boots and Caps. These Caps were like the Crown of a Hat made of Palmeto-leaves, like our Straw-hats; but without Brims, and coming down but to their Ears. These had no Feathers, but had an oblong Button on the top, and from between the Button and the Cap, there fell down all round their Head as low as the Cap reached, a sort of coarse Hair like Horse-hair, dyed (as I suppose) of a light red colour.

¶ The Officer brought aboard, as a Present from the Governour, a young Heifer, the fattest and kindliest Beef, that I did ever taste in any foreign Country; 'twas small, yet full grown; two large Hogs, four Goats, two Baskets of fine Flour, 20 great flat Cakes of fine well-tasted Bread, two great Jars of Arack, (made of Rice as I judged) called by the *Chinese*, *Sam Shu*; and 55 Jars of *Hoc Shu*, as they call it, and our *Europeans* from them. This is a strong Liquor, made of Wheat, as I have been told. It looks like Mum, and tastes much like it, and is very pleasant and hearty. Our Seamen love it mightily, and will lick their Lips with it: for scarce a Ship goes to *China*, but the Men come home fat with soaking this Liquor, and bring store of Jars of it home with them. It is put into small white thick Jars, that hold near a Quart: The double Jars hold about two Quarts. These Jars are small below, and thence rise up with a pretty full belly, closing in pretty short at top, with a small thick mouth. Over the mouth of the Jar they put a thin Chip cut round, just so as to cover the mouth, over that a piece of Paper, and over that they put a great lump of Clay, almost as big as the Bottle or Jar it self, with a hollow in it, to admit the neck of the Bottle, made round, and about four Inches long; this is to preserve the Liquor. If the Liquor take any vent it will be sowre presently, so that when we buy any of it of the Ships from *China* returning to *Maderas*, or Fort St. *George*, where it is then sold, or of the *Chinese* themselves, of whom I have bought it at *Achin*, and *Bencouli* in *Sumatra*, if the Clay be crackt, or the Liquor motherly, we make them take it again. A Quart Jar there is worth Six-pence. Besides this Present from the Governour, there was a Captain of a Jonk sent two Jars of *Arack*, and abundance of Pine-apples and Water-melons.

¶ Captain *Read* sent ashore, as a present to the Governour a curious *Spanish* Silver-hilted Rapier, an *English* Carbine, and a Gold Chain, and when the Officer went ashore, three Guns were fired. In the Afternoon the Governour sent off the same Officer again, to compliment the Captain for his Civility, and promised to retaliate his kindness before we departed; but we had such blustring Weather afterward, that no Boat could come aboard.

¶ We stayed here till the 29th Day, and then sailed from hence with the Wind at S.W. and pretty fair Weather. We now directed our Course for some Islands we had chosen to go to, that lye between *Formosa* and *Luconia*. They are laid down in our Plots without any name, only with a figure of 5, denoting the number of them. It was supposed by us, that these Islands had no Inhabitants, because they had not any name by our Hydrographers. Therefore we thought to lye there secure, and be pretty near the Island *Luconia*, which we did still intend to visit.

¶ In going to them we sailed by the South West-end of *Formosa*, leaving it on our Larboard-side. This is a large Island; the South-end is in Lat. 21. d. 20 m. and the North-end in the 25 d. 10 m. North Lat. the Longitude of this Isle is laid down from 142 d. 5 m. to 143 d. 16 m. reckoning East from the Pike of *Tenariffe*, so that 'tis but narrow; and the Tropick of *Cancer* crosses it. It is a high and woody Island, and was formerly well inhabited by the *Chinese*, and was then frequently visited by English Merchants, there being a very good Harbour to secure their Ships. But since the *Tartars* have conquered *China*, they have spoiled the Harbour, (as I have been informed) to hinder the *Chinese* that were then in Rebellion, from fortifying themselves there; and ordered the Foreign Merchants to come and trade on the Main.

¶ The sixth Day of *August* we arrived at the five Islands that we were bound to, and anchored on the East-side of the northermost Island, in 15 Fathom, a Cable's length from the Shore. Here, contrary to our Expectation, we found abundance of Inhabitants in sight; for there were three large Towns all within a League of the Sea; and another larger Town than any of the three, on the backside of a small Hill close by also, as we found afterwards. These Islands lie in Lat. 20 d. 20 m. North Lat. by my Observation, for I took it there, and I find their Longitude according to our Drafts, to be 141 d. 50 m. These Islands having no particular Names in the Drafts, some or other of us made use of the Seamens priviledge, to give them what Names we please. Three of the Islands were pretty large; the westermost is the biggest. This the Dutchmen who were among us called the Prince of *Orange*'s Island, in honour of his present Majesty. It is about seven or eight Leagues long, and about two Leagues wide; and it lies almost N. and S. The other two great Islands are about 4 or 5 Leagues to the eastward of this. The northermost of them, where we first anchored, I called the Duke of *Grafton*'s Isle, as soon as we landed on it; having married my Wife out of his Dutchess's Family, and leaving her at *Arlington*-house, at my going Abroad. This Isle is about 4 Leagues long, and one League and an half wide, stretching North and South. The other great Island our Seamen called the Duke of *Monmouth*'s Island. This is about a League to the southward of *Grafton*-Isle. It is about three Leagues long, and a League wide, lying as the other. Between *Monmouth* and the South-end of *Orange*-Island, there are two small Islands of a roundish Form, lying East and West. The eastermost Island of the two, our Men unanimously called *Bashee* Island, from a Liquor which we drank there plentifully every Day, after we came to an Anchor at it. The other, which is the smallest of all, we called *Goat* Island, from the great number of Goats there; and to the northward of them all, are two high Rocks.

¶ *Orange*-Island, which is the biggest of them all, is not inhabited. It is high Land, flat and even on the top, with steep Cliffs against the Sea; for which Reason we could not go ashore there, as we did on all the rest.

¶ I have made it my general Observation, that where the Land is fenced with steep Rocks and Cliffs against the Sea, there the Sea is very deep, and seldom affords Anchor-ground; and on the other side where the Land falls away with a declivity into the Sea, (altho' the Land be extraordinary high within,) yet there are commonly good Soundings, and consequently Anchoring; and as the visible declivity of the Land appears near, or at the edge of the Water, whether pretty steep, or more sloping, so we commonly find our Anchor-ground to be, more or less deep or steep; therefore we come nearer the Shore, or anchor farther off, as we see convenient; for there is no Coast in the World, that I know, or have heard of, where the Land is of a continual heighth, without some small Valleys or Declivities, which lie intermixt with the high Land. They are the subsidings of Valleys or low Lands, that make Dents in the Shore and Creeks, small Bays, and Harbours, or little Coves, &c. which afford good anchoring, the surface of the Earth being there lodged deep under Water. Thus we find many good Harbours on such Coasts, where the Land bounds the Sea with steep Cliffs, by reason of the Declivities, or subsiding of the Land between these Cliffs: But where the Declension from the Hills or Cliffs is not within Land, between Hill and Hill, but, as on the Coast of *Chili* and *Peru*, the Declivity is toward the Main Sea, or into it, the Coast being perpendicular, or very steep from the neighbouring Hills, as in those Countries from the *Andes*, that run along the Shore, *there* is a deep Sea, and few or no Harbours or Creeks. All that Coast is too steep for anchoring, and hath the fewest Roads fit for Ships of any Coast I know. The Coasts of *Gallicia*, *Portugal*, *Norway* and *Newfoundland*, &c. are Coasts like the *Peruvian*, and the high Islands of the *Archipelago*; but yet not so scanty of good Harbours; for where there are short Ridges of Land, there are good Bays at the extremities of those Ridges, where they plunge into the Sea; as on the Coast of *Caraccos*, &c. The Island of *John Fernando*, and the Island St. *Hellena*, &c. are such high Land with deep Shore: and in general, the plunging of any Land under Water, seems to be in proportion to the rising of its continuous part above Water, more or less steep; and it must be a Bottom almost level, or very gently declining, that affords good anchoring, Ships being soon driven from their Moorings on a steep Bank: Therefore we never strive to anchor where we see the Land high, and bounding the Sea with steep Cliffs; and for this reason, when we came in sight of *States*-Island near *Terra del Fuego*, before we entered into the South-Seas, we did not so much as think of anchoring after we saw what Land it was, because of the steep Cliffs which appeared against the Sea: yet there might be little Harbours or Coves for Shallops, or the like, to anchor in, which we did not see or search after.

¶ As high steep Cliffs bounding on the Sea have this ill consequence, that they seldom afford anchoring; so they have this benefit, that we can see them far off, and sail close to them, without danger: for which reason we call them bold Shores; whereas low Land on the contrary, is seen but a little way, and in many places we dare not come near it, for fear of running a-ground before we see it. Besides there are in many places Shoals thrown out by the course of great Rivers, that from the low Land fall into the Sea.

¶ This which I have said, that there is usually good anchoring near low Lands, may be illustrated by several Instances. Thus on the South-side of the Bay of *Campeachy*, there is mostly low Land, and there also is good anchoring all along Shore; and in some places to the eastward of the Town of *Campeachy*, we shall have so many fathom as we are Leagues off from Land; that is, from 9 or 10 Leagues distance till you come within 4 Leagues: and from thence to Land it grows but shallower. The Bay of *Honduras* also is low Land, and continues mostly so, as we past along from thence to the Coasts of *Portobel*, and *Cartagena*, till we came as high as *Santa Martha*; afterwards the Land is low again, till you come towards the Coast of *Caraccos*, which is a high Coast and bold Shore. The Land about *Surinam* on the same Coast is low and good anchoring, and that over on the Coast of *Guinea* is such also. And such too is the Bay of *Panama*, where the Pilot-Book orders the Pilot always to sound, and not to come within such a depth, be it by Night or Day. In the same Seas, from the high Land of *Guatimala* in *Mexico*, to *California*, there is mostly low Land and good anchoring. In the Main of *Asia*, the Coast of *China*, the Bay of *Siam* and *Bengal*, and all the Coast of *Coromandel*, and the Coast about *Malacca*, and against it the Island *Sumatra*, on that side, are mostly low anchoring Shores. But on the West-side of *Sumatra*, the Shore is high and bold; so most of the Islands lying to the eastward of *Sumatra*; as the Islands *Borneo*, *Celebes*, *Gilolo*, and abundance of Islands of less note, lying scattering up and down those Seas, are low Land, and have good anchoring about them, with many Shoals scattered to and fro among them; but the Islands lying against the *East-Indian* Ocean, especially the West-sides of them, are high Land and steep, particularly the West-parts, not only of

Sumatra, but also of *Java*, *Timor*, &c. Particulars are endless; but in general, 'tis seldom but high Shores and deep Waters; and on the other side, low Land and shallow Seas are found together.

¶ But to return from this Digression, to speak of the rest of these Islands. *Monmouth* and *Grafton* Isles are very hilly, with many of those steep inhabited Precipices on them, that I shall describe particularly. The two small Islands are flat and even; only the *Bashee* Island hath one steep scraggy Hill, but *Goat*-Island is all flat and very even.

¶ The Mold of these Islands in the Valley, is blackish in some places, but in most red. The Hills are very rocky: The Valleys are well watered with Brooks of fresh Water, which run into the Sea in many different places. The Soil is indifferent fruitful, especially in the Valleys; producing pretty great plenty of Trees (tho' not very big) and thick Grass. The sides of the Mountains have also short Grass, and some of the Mountains have Mines within them; for the Natives told us, that the yellow Metal they shewed us, (as I shall speak more particularly) came from these Mountains; for when they held it up, they would point towards them.

¶ The Fruit of the Islands are a few Plantains, Bonanoes, Pine-apples, Pumkins, Sugar-canes, &c. and there might be more if the Natives would, for the Ground seems fertile enough. Here are great plenty of Potatoes, and Yams, which is the common Food for the Natives, for Bread-kind: For those few Plantains they have, are only used as Fruit. They have some Cotton growing here of the small Plants.

¶ Here are plenty of Goats, and abundance of Hogs; but few Fowls, either wild or tame. For this I have always observed in my Travels, both in the *East* and *West-Indies*, that in those Places where there is plenty of Grain, that is, of Rice in one, and Maiz in the other, there are also found great abundance of Fowls; but on the contrary, few Fowls in those Countries where the Inhabitants feed on Fruits and Roots only. The few wild Fowls that are here, are Parakites, and some other small Birds. Their tame Fowl are only a few Cocks and Hens.

¶ *Monmouth* and *Grafton* Islands are very thick inhabited; and *Bashee* Island hath one Town on it. The Natives of these Islands are short squat People; they are generally round-visaged, with low Fore-heads, and thick Eye-brows; their Eyes of a hazel colour, and small, yet bigger than the *Chinese*; short low Noses, and their Lips and Mouths middle proportioned; Their Teeth are white; their Hair is black, and thick, and lank, which they wear but short; it will just cover their Ears, and so it is cut round very even. Their Skins are of a very dark Copper-colour.

¶ They wear no Hat, Cap, nor Turbat, nor any thing to keep off the

Sun. The Men for the biggest part have only a small Clout to cover their Nakedness; some of them have Jackets made of Plantain-leaves, which were as rough as any Bear's-skin: I never saw such rugged Things. The Women have a short Petticoat made of Cotton, which comes a little below their Knees. It is a thick sort of stubborn Cloth, which they make themselves of their Cotton. Both Men and Women do wear large Ear-rings, made of that yellow Metal before mentioned. Whether it were Gold or no I cannot positively say; I took it to be so, it was heavy and of the colour of our paler Gold. I would fain have brought away some to have satisfied my Curiosity; but I had nothing wherewith to buy any. Captain *Read* bought two of these Rings with some Iron, of which the People are very greedy; and he would have bought more, thinking he was come to a very fair Market, but that the paleness of the Metal made him and his Crew distrust its being right Gold. For my part, I should have ventured on the purchase of some, but having no property in the Iron, of which we had great store on board, sent from *England* by the Merchants along with Captain *Swan*, I durst not barter it away.

¶ These Rings when first polished look very gloriously, but time makes them fade, and turn to a pale yellow. Then they make a soft Paste of red Earth, and smearing it over their Rings, they cast them into a quick Fire, where they remain till they be red hot; then they take them out and cool them in Water, and rub off the Paste; and they look again of a glorious Colour and Lustre.

¶ These People make but small low Houses. The Sides which are made of small Posts, watled with Boughs, are not above 4 Foot and a half high: the Ridge-pole is about 7 or 8 Foot high. They have a Fire-place at one end of their Houses, and Boards placed on the Ground to lye on. They inhabit together in small Villages built on the sides and tops of rocky Hills, 3 or 4 rows of Houses one above another, and on such steep Pre-cipices, that they go up to the first Row with a wooden Ladder, and so with a Ladder still from every Story up to that above it, there being no way to ascend. The Plain on the first Precipice may be so wide, as to have room both for a Row of Houses that stand all along on the Edge or Brink of it, and a very narrow Street running along before their Doors, between the Row of Houses and the Foot of the next Precipice; the Plain of which is in a manner level to the tops of the Houses below, and so for the rest. The common Ladder to each Row or Street comes up at a narrow Passage left purposely about the middle of it; and the Street being bounded with a Precipice also at each end, 'tis but drawing up the Ladder, if they be assaulted, and then there is no coming at them from below, but by climbing up as against a perpendicular Wall: And that they may not be assaulted from above, they take care to build on the side of such a Hill, whose back-side hangs over the Sea, or is some high, steep, perpendicular Precipice, altogether inaccessible. These Precipices are natural; for the Rocks seem too hard to work on; nor is there any sign that Art hath been employed about them. On *Bashee* Island there is one such, and built upon, with its back next the Sea. *Grafton* and *Monmouth* Isles are very thick set with these Hills and Towns; and the Natives, whether for fear of Pirates, or Foreign Enemies, or Factions among their own Clans, care not for Building but in these Fastnesses; which I take to be the Reason that *Orange* Isle, though the largest, and as fertile as any, yet being level, and exposed, hath no Inhabitants. I never saw the like Precipices and Towns.

¶ These People are pretty ingenious also in building Boats. Their small Boats are much like our *Deal* Yalls, but not so big; and they are built with very narrow Plank, pinn'd with wooden Pins, and some Nails. They have also some pretty large Boats, which will carry 40 or 50 Men. These they Row with 12 or 14 Oars of a side. They are built much like the small ones, and they row doubled banked; that is, two Men setting on one Bench, but one Rowing on one side, the other on the other side of the Boat. They understand the use of Iron, and work it themselves. Their Bellows are like those at *Mindanao*.

¶ The common Imployment for the Men is Fishing; but I did never see them catch much: Whether it is more plenty at other times of the Year I know not. The Women do manage their Plantations.

¶ I did never see them kill any of their Goats or Hogs for themselves, yet they would beg the Paunches of the Goats that they themselves did sell to us: And if any of our surly Seamen did heave them into the Sea, they would take them up again and the Skins of the Goats also. They would not meddle with Hogs-guts, if our Men threw away any besides what they made Chitterlings and Sausages of. The Goat-skins these People would carry ashore, and making a Fire they would singe off all the Hair, and afterwards let the Skin lie and parch on the Coals, till they thought it eatable; and then they would knaw it, and tear it in pieces with their Teeth, and at last swallow it. The Paunches of the Goats would make them an excellent Dish; they drest it in this manner. They would turn out all the chopt Grass and Crudities found in the Maw into their Pots, and set it over the Fire, and stir it about often: This would smoak and puff, and heave up as it was boiling; Wind breaking out of the Ferment, and making a very savoury Stink. While this was doing, if they had any

Fish, as commonly they had two or three small Fish, these they would make very clean (as hating Nastiness belike) and cut the Flesh from the Bone, and then mince the Flesh as small as possibly they could, and when that in the Pot was well boiled, they would take it up, and strewing a little Salt into it, they would eat it, mixt with their raw minced Flesh. The Dung in the Maw would look like so much boil'd Herbs minc'd very small; and they took up their Mess with their Fingers, as the *Moors* do their Pillaw, using no Spoons.

¶ They had another Dish made of a sort of Locusts, whose Bodies were about an Inch and an half long, and as thick as the top of one's little Finger; with large thin Wings, and long and small Legs. At this time of the Year these Creatures came in great Swarms to devour their Potato-leaves, and other Herbs; and the Natives would go out with small Nets, and take a Quart at one sweep. When they had enough, they would carry them home, and parch them over the Fire in an earthen Pan; and then their Wings and Legs would fall off, and their Heads and Backs would turn red like boil'd Shrimps, being before brownish. Their Bodies being full, would eat very moist, their Heads would crackle in one's Teeth. I did once eat of this Dish, and liked it well enough; but their other Dish my Stomach would not take.

¶ Their common Drink is Water; as it is of all other *Indians*: Besides which they make a sort of Drink with the Juice of the Sugar-cane, which they boil, and put some small black sort of Berries among it. When it is well boiled, they put it into great Jars, and let it stand three or four Days and work. Then it settles, and becomes clear, and is presently fit to drink. This is an excellent Liquor, and very much like *English* Beer, both in Colour and Taste. It is very strong, and I do believe very wholesome: For our Men, who drank briskly of it all day for several Weeks, were frequently drunk with it, and never sick after it. The Natives brought a vast deal of it every Day to those aboard and ashore: For some of our Men were ashore at work on *Bashee*-Island; which Island they gave that Name to from their drinking this Liquor there; that being the Name which the Natives call'd this Liquor by: and as they sold it to our Men very cheap, so they did not spare to drink it as freely. And indeed from the plenty of this Liquor, and their plentiful use of it, our Men call'd all these Islands, the *Bashee* Islands.

¶ What Language these People do speak I know not: for it had no affinity in sound to the *Chinese*, which is spoke much through the Teeth; nor yet to the *Malayan* Language. They called the Metal that their Ear-rings were made of *Bullawan*, which is the *Mindanao* word for Gold;

therefore probably they may be related to the *Philippine Indians*; for that is the general Name for Gold among all those *Indians*. I could not learn from whence they have their Iron; but it is most likely they go in their great Boats to the North-end of *Luconia*, and trade with the *Indians* of that Island for it. Neither did I see any thing beside Iron, and pieces of Buffaloes Hides, which I could judge that they bought of Strangers: Their Cloaths were of their own Growth and Manufacture.

¶ These Men had Wooden Lances, and a few Lances headed with Iron; which are all the Weapons that they have. Their Armour is a piece of Buffaloe-hide, shaped like our Carters Frocks, being without Sleeves, and sewed both sides together, with holes for the Head and the Arms to come forth. This Buff-Coat reaches down to their Knees: It is close about their Shoulders, but below it is three Foot wide, and as thick as a Board.

¶ I could never perceive them to worship any thing, neither had they any Idols; neither did they seem to observe any one Day more than other. I could never perceive that one Man was of greater Power than another; but they seemed to be all equal; only every Man ruling in his own House, and the Children respecting and honouring their Parents.

¶ Yet 'tis probable that they have some Law, or Custom, by which they are govern'd; for while we lay here we saw a young Man buried alive in the Earth; and 'twas for Theft, as far as we could understand from them. There was a great deep hole dug, and abundance of People came to the Place to take their last Farewell of him: Among the rest, there was one Woman who made great Lamentation, and took off the condemn'd Person's Ear-rings. We supposed her to be his Mother. After he had taken his leave of her and some others, he was put into the Pit, and covered over with Earth. He did not struggle, but yielded very quietly to his Punishment; and they ramm'd the Earth close upon him, and stifled him.

¶ They have but one Wife, with whom they live and agree very well; and their Children live very obediently under them. The Boys go out a fishing with their Fathers; and the Girles live at home with their Mothers: And when the Girles are grown pretty strong, they send them to their Plantations, to dig Hames and Potatoes, of which they bring home on their Heads every Day enough to serve the whole Family; for they have no Rice nor Maize.

¶ Their Plantations are in the Valleys, at a good distance from their Houses; where every Man has a certain spot of Land, which is properly his own. This he manageth himself for his own use; and provides enough, that he may not be beholding to his Neighbour.

¶ Notwithstanding the seeming nastiness of their Dish of Goats-Maw, they are in their Persons a very neat cleanly People, both Men and Women: And they are withal the quietest and civilest People that I did ever meet with. I could never perceive them to be angry with one another. I have admired to see 20 or 30 Boats aboard our Ship at a time, and yet no difference among them; but all civil and quiet, endeavouring to help each other on occasion: No noise, nor appearance of distaste: and although sometimes cross Accidents would happen, which might have set other Men together by the Ears, yet they were not moved by them. Sometimes they will also drink freely, and warm themselves with their Drink; yet neither then could I ever perceive them out of Humour. They are not only thus civil among themselves, but very obliging and kind to Strangers; nor were their Children rude to us, as is usual. Indeed the Women, when we came to their Houses, would modestly beg any Rags or small pieces of Cloth, to swaddle their young ones in, holding their Children out to us; and begging is usual among all these wild Nations. Yet neither did they beg so importunately as in other Places; nor did the Men ever beg any thing at all. Neither, except once at the first time that we came to an Anchor (as I shall relate) did they steal any thing; but dealt justly, and with great sincerity with us; and make us very welcome to their Houses with *Bashee* drink. If they had none of this Liquor themselves, they would buy a Jar of Drink of their Neighbours, and sit down with us: for we could see them go and give a piece or two of their Gold for some Jars of *Bashee*. And indeed among wild *Indians*, as these seem to be, I wonder'd to see buying and selling, which is not so usual; nor to converse so freely, as to go aboard Strangers Ships with so little caution: Yet their own small Trading may have brought them to this. At these Entertainments, they and their Family, Wife and Children, drank out of small Calabashes: and when by themselves, they drink about from one to another; but when any of us came among them, then they would always drink to one of us.

¶ They have no sort of Coin; but they have small Crumbs of the Metal before described, which they bind up very safe in Plantain-Leaves, or the like. This Metal they exchange for what they want, giving a small quantity of it, about two or three Grains, for a Jar of Drink that would hold five or six Gallons. They have no Scales, but give it by guess. Thus much in general.

¶ To proceed therefore with our Affairs: I have said before, that we anchored here the 6th Day of *August*. While we were furling our Sails, there came near 100 Boats of the Natives aboard, with three or four Men

in each; so that our Deck was full of Men. We were at first afraid of
them, and therefore got up 20 or 30 small Arms on our Poop, and kept
three or four Men as Centinels, with Guns in their Hands, ready to fire
on them if they had offered to molest us. But they were pretty quiet, only
they pickt up such old Iron that they found on our Deck, and they also
took out our Pump-Bolts, and Linch-Pins out of the Carriages of our
Guns, before we perceived them. At last, one of our Men perceived one
of them very busy getting out one of our Linch-Pins; and took hold of
the Fellow, who immediately bawl'd out, and all the rest presently leaped
over-board, some into their Boats, others into the Sea; and they all made
away for the Shoar. But when we perceived their Fright, we made much
of him that was in hold, who stood trembling all the while; and at last
we gave him a small Piece of Iron, with which he immediately leapt over-
board and swam to his Consorts; who hovered about our Ship to see the
Issue. Then we beckned to them to come aboard again, being very loth
to lose a Commerce with them. Some of the Boats came aboard again,
and they were always very honest and civil afterward.

¶ We presently after this sent a Canoa ashore, to see their manner of
living, and what Provision they had: The Canoa's Crew were made very
welcome with *Bashee* drink, and saw abundance of Hogs, some of which
they bought, and returned aboard. After this the Natives brought aboard
both Hogs and Goats to us in their own Boats; and every Day we should
have fifteen or twenty Hogs and Goats in Boats aboard by our side. These
we bought for a small matter; we could buy a good fat Goat for an old
Iron Hoop, and a Hog of seventy or eighty Pound weight for two or
three Pound of Iron. Their drink also they brought off in Jars, which we
bought for old Nails, Spikes and Leaden Bullets. Beside the fore-mentioned Commodities, they brought aboard great quantities of Yams and
Potatoes; which we purchased for Nails, Spikes or Bullets. It was one
Man's Work to be all Day cutting out Bars of Iron into small Pieces with
a cold Chisel: And these were for the great Purchases of Hogs and Goats,
which they would not sell for Nails, as their Drink and Roots. We never
let them know what Store we have, that they may value it the more.
Every Morning, as soon as it was light, they would thus come aboard with
their Commodities; which we bought as we had occasion. We did commonly furnish our selves with as many Goats and Roots as served us all
the Day; and their Hogs we bought in large quantities, as we thought
convenient; for we salted them. Their Hogs were very sweet; but I never
saw so many meazled ones.

¶ We filled all our Water at a curious Brook close by us, in *Grafton*'s Isle, where we first anchored. We stayed there about three or four Days, before we went to other Islands. We sailed to the southward, passing on the East-side of *Grafton* Island, and then passed through between that and *Monmouth* Island; but we found no anchoring till we came to the North-end of *Monmouth* Island, and there we stopt during one Tide. The Tide runs very strong here, and sometimes makes a short chopping Sea. Its course among these Islands is S. by E. and N. by W. The Flood sets to the North, and Ebb to the South, and it riseth and falleth eight Foot.

¶ When we went from hence, we coasted about two Leagues to the southward, on the West-side of *Monmouth* Island; and finding no Anchor-ground, we stood over to the *Bashee* Island, and came to an Anchor on the North-east part of it, against a small sandy Bay, in seven Fathom clean hard Sand, and about a quarter of a Mile from the Shore. Here is a pretty wide Channel between these two Islands, and Anchoring all over it. The Depth of Water is twelve, fourteen and sixteen Fathom.

¶ We presently built a Tent ashore, to mend our Sails in, and stay'd all the rest of our time here, *viz.* from the 13th Day of *August* till the 26th Day of *September*. In which time we mended our Sails, and scrubb'd our Ship's Bottom very well; and every Day some of us went to their Towns, and were kindly entertained by them. Their Boats also came aboard with their Merchandize to sell, and lay aboard all Day; and if we did not take it off their Hands one Day, they would bring the same again the next.

¶ We had yet the Winds at S.W. and S.S.W. mostly fair Weather. In *October* we did expect the Winds to shift to the N.E. and therefore we provided to sail (as soon as the eastern Monsoon was settled) to cruize off of *Manila*. Accordingly we provided a Stock of Provision. We salted seventy or eighty good fat Hogs, and bought Yams and Potatoes good store to eat at Sea.

¶ About the 24th Day of *September* the Winds shifted about to the East, and from thence to the N.E. fine fair Weather. The 25th it came at N. and began to grow fresh, and the Sky began to be clouded, and the Wind freshned on us.

¶ At Twelve a-Clock at Night it blew a very fierce Storm. We were then riding with our best Bower a Head; and though our Yards and Top-mast were down, yet we drove. This obliged us to let go our Sheet-anchor, veering out a good Scope of Cable, which stopt us till Ten or Eleven a-Clock the next Day. Then the Wind came on so fierce, that she drove again, with both Anchors a-head. The Wind was now at N. by W. and we kept driving till Three or Four a-Clock in the Afternoon: And it was well for us that there were no Islands, Rocks or Sands in our way, for if there had, we must have been driven upon them. We used our utmost Endeavours to stop here, being loth to go to Sea, because we had six of our Men ashore, who could not get off now. At last we were driven out into deep Water, and then it was in vain to wait any longer: Therefore we hove in our Sheet-Cable, and got up our Sheet-Anchor, and cut away our best Bower, (for to have heav'd her up then would have gone near to have foundred us) and so put to Sea. We had very violent Weather the Night ensuing, with very hard Rain, and we were forced to scud with our bare Poles till Three a-Clock in the Morning. Then the Wind slacken'd, and we brought our Ship to under a Mizen, and lay with our Head to the Westward. The 27th Day the Wind abated much, but it rained very hard all Day, and the Night ensuing. The 28th Day the Wind came about to the N.E. and it cleared up, and blew a hard Gale, but it stood not there, for it shifted about to the eastward, thence to the S.E. then to the South, and at last settled at S.W. and then we had a moderate Gale and fair Weather.

¶ It was the 29th Day when the Wind came to the S.W. Then we made all the Sail we could for the Island again. The 30th Day we had the Wind at West, and saw the Islands; but could not get in before Night. Therefore we stood off to the southward till two a-Clock in the Morning; then we tackt and stood in all the Morning, and about Twelve a-Clock, the 1st Day of *October*, we anchored again at the Place from whence we were driven.

¶ Then our six Men were brought aboard by the Natives, to whom we gave three whole Bars of Iron for their Kindness and Civility, which was an extraordinary Present to them. Mr. *Robert Hall* was one of the Men that was left ashore. I shall speak more of him hereafter. He and the rest of them told me, that after the Ship was out of sight, the Natives began to be more kind to them than they had been before, and persuaded them to cut their Hair short, as theirs was, offering to each of them if they would do it, a young Woman to Wife, and a small Hatchet and other Iron Utensils fit for a Planter, in Dowry; and withal shewed them a Piece of Land for them to manage. They were courted thus by several of the Town where they then were: but they took up their head Quarters at the House of him with whom they first went ashoar. When the Ship appeared in sight again, then they importuned them for some Iron, which is the chief thing that they covet, even above their Ear-rings. We might have bought all their Ear-rings, or other Gold they had, with our Iron-bars, had we been assured of its Goodness; and yet when it was touched and compared with other Gold, we could not discern any Difference, though it looked so pale in the Lump; but the seeing them polish it so often, was a new Discouragement.

¶ This last Storm put our Men quite out of heart: for although it was not altogether so fierce as that which we were in on the Coast of *China*, which was still fresh in Memory, yet it wrought more powerfully, and frighted them from their Design of cruising before *Manila*, fearing another Storm there. Now every Man wisht himself at home, as they had done a hundred times before: But Captain *Read*, and Captain *Teat* the Master, persuaded them to go towards Cape *Comorin*, and then they would tell them more of their Minds, intending doubtless to cruize in the *Red-Sea*; and they easily prevailed with the Crew.

¶ The eastern Monsoon was now at hand, and the best way had been to go through the Streights of *Malacca*: But Captain *Teat* said it was dangerous, by reason of many Islands and Shoals there, with which none of us were acquainted. Therefore he thought it best to go round on the East-side of all the *Philippine* Islands, and so keeping South toward the *Spice-Islands*, to pass out into the *East-Indian* Ocean about the Island *Timor*.

¶ This seemed to be a very tedious way about, and as dangerous altogether for Shoals; but not for meeting with *English* or *Dutch* Ships, which was their greatest Fear. I was well enough satisfied, knowing that the farther we went, the more Knowledge and Experience I should get, which was the main Thing that I regarded; and should also have the more variety of Places to attempt an Escape from them, being fully resolved to take the first Opportunity of giving them the slip.

CHAPTER XVI

They depart from the Bashee-*Islands, and passing by some others, and the N.-End of* Luconia. *St.* John's *Isle, and other of the* Philippines. *They stop at the two Isles near* Mindanao; *where they re-fit their Ship, and make a Pump after the Spanish Fashion. By the young Prince of the Spice-Island they have News of Capt.* Swan, *and his Men, left at* Mindanao. *The Author proposes to the Crew to return to him; but in vain. The Story of his Murder at* Mindanao. *The Clove-Islands.* Ternate. Tidore, *&c. The Island* Celebes, *and Dutch Town of* Macasser. *They coast along the East-side of* Celebes, *and between it and other Islands and Shoals, with great difficulty. Shy Turtle. Vast Cockles. A wild Vine of great Virtue for Sores. Great Trees; one excessively big. Beacons instead of Buoys on the Sholes. A Spout: a Description of them, with a Story of one. Uncertain Tornadoes. Turtle. The Island* Bouton, *and its chief Town and Harbour* Callasusung. *The Inhabitants. Visits given and received by the Sultan. His Device in the Flag*

THE 3d Day of *October* 1687, we sailed from these Islands, standing to the southward, intending to sail through among the Spice-Islands. We had fair Weather, and the Wind at West. We first steer'd S.S.W. and passed close by certain small Islands that lie just by the North-end of the Island *Luconia*. We left them all on the West of us, and past on the East-side of it, and the rest of the *Philippine* Islands, coasting to the southward.

¶ The N. East-end of the Island *Luconia* appears to be good Champion Land, of an indifferent heighth, plain and even for many Leagues; only it has some pretty high Hills standing upright by themselves in these Plains; but no Ridges of Hills, or Chains of Mountains joining one to another. The Land on this side seems to be most Savannah, or Pasture: The S. East-part is more mountainous and woody.

¶ Leaving the Island *Luconia*, and with it our Golden Projects, we sailed on to the Southward, passing on the East-side of the rest of the *Philippine* Islands. These appear to be more mountainous, and less woody, till we came in sight of the Island St. *John*; the first of that Name I mentioned: the other I spake of on the Coast of *China*. This I have already described to be a very woody Island. Here the Wind coming southerly, forced us to keep farther from the Islands.

¶ The 14th Day of *October* we came close by a small low woody Island, that lieth East from the S.E. end of *Mindanao*, distant from it about 20 Leagues. I do not find it set down in any Sea-Chart.

¶ The 15th Day we had the Wind at N.E. and we steered West for the Island *Mindanao*, and arrived at the S.E. end again on the 16th Day. There we went in and anchored between two small Islands, which lie in about 5 d. 10 m. North Lat. I mentioned them when we first came on this Coast. Here we found a fine small Cove, on the N.W. end of the eastermost Island, fit to careen in, or hale ashore; so we went in there, and presently unrigged our Ship, and provided to hale our Ship ashore, to clean her Bottom. These Islands are about three or four Leagues from the Island *Mindanao*; they are about four or five Leagues in Circumference, and of a pretty good heighth. The Mold is black and deep; and there are two small Brooks of fresh Water.

¶ They are both plentifully stored with great high Trees; therefore our Carpenters were sent ashore to cut down some of them for our use; for here they made a new Boltsprit, which we did set here also, our old one being very faulty. They made a new Fore-yard too, and a Fore-top-mast: And our Pumps being faulty, and not serviceable, they did cut a Tree to make a Pump. They first squared it, then sawed it in the middle, and then hollowed each side exactly. The two hollow sides were made big enough to contain a Pump-box in the midst of them both, when they were joined together; and it required their utmost Skill to close them exactly to the making a tight Cylinder for the Pump-box; being unaccustomed to such Work. We learnt this way of Pump-making from the *Spaniards*; who make their Pumps that they use in their Ships in the *South-Seas* after this manner; and I am confident that there are no better Hand-pumps in the World than they have.

¶ While we lay here, the young Prince that I mentioned in the 13th Chapter came aboard He understanding that we were bound farther to the southward, desired us to transport him and his Men to his own Island. He shewed it to us in our Draft, and told us the Name of it; which we put down in our Draft, for it was not named there; but I quite forgot to put it into my Journal.

¶ This Man told us, that not above six Days before this, he saw Captain *Swan*, and several of his Men that we left there, and named the Names of some of them, who he said were all well, and that now they were at the City of *Mindanao*; but that they had all of them been out with *Raja Laut*, fighting under him in his Wars against his Enemies the *Alfoores*; and that most of them fought with undaunted Courage; for which they were highly honoured and esteemed, as well by the Sultan, as by the General *Raja Laut*; that now Capt. *Swan* intended to go with his Men to Fort St. *George*, and that in order thereto, he had proffered forty Ounces of Gold for a Ship; but the Owner and he were not yet agreed; and that he feared that the Sultan would not let him go away till the Wars were ended.

¶ All this the Prince told us in the *Malayan* Tongue, which many of us had learnt; and when he went away he promised to return to us again in three Days time, and so long Capt. *Read* promised to stay for him (for we had now almost finished our Business) and he seemed very glad of the Opportunity of going with us.

¶ After this I endeavoured to perswade our Men to return with the Ship to the River of *Mindanao*, and offer their Service again to Captain *Swan*. I took an Opportunity when they were filling of Water, there being then half the Ship's Company ashore; and I found all these very willing to do it. I desired them to say nothing, till I had tried the Minds of the other half, which I intended to do the next Day, it being their turn to fill Water then; But one of these Men, who seemed most forward to invite back Captain *Swan*, told Captain *Read* and Captain *Teat* of the Project, and they presently disswaded the Men from any such Designs. Yet fearing the worst, they made all possible haste to be gone.

¶ I have since been informed, that Captain *Swan* and his Men staied there a great while afterward; and that many of the Men got Passages from thence in *Dutch* Sloops to *Ternate*, particularly Mr. *Rofy*, and Mr. *Nelly*. There they remained a great while, and at last got to *Batavia* (where the *Dutch* took their Journals from them) and so to *Europe*; and that some of Capt. *Swan*'s Men died at *Mindanao*; of which Number Mr. *Harthrope*, and Mr. *Smith*, Captain *Swan*'s Merchants were two. At last Captain *Swan* and his Surgeon going in a small Canoa aboard of a *Dutch* Ship then in the Road, in order to get Passage to *Europe*, were overset by the Natives at the Mouth of the River; who waited their coming purposely to do it, but unsuspected by them; where they both were killed in the Water. This was done by the General's Order, as some think, to get his Gold, which he did immediately seize on. Others say, it was because the General's House was burnt a little before, and Captain *Swan* was suspected to be the Author of it; and others say, That it was Captain *Swan*'s Threats occasioned his own Ruin; for he would often say passionately, that he had been abused by the General, and that he would have Satisfaction for it; Saying also, that now he was well acquainted with their Rivers, and knew how to come in at any time; that he also knew their manner of Fighting, and the Weakness of their Country; and therefore he would go away, and get a Band of Men to assist him, and returning thither again, he would spoil and take all that they had, and their Country too. When the General had been informed of these Discourses, he would say, What, is Captain *Swan* made of Iron, and able to resist a whole Kingdom? Or does he think that we are afraid of him, that he speaks thus? Yet did he never touch him, till now the *Mindanayans* killed him. It is very probable there might be somewhat of Truth in all this; for the Captain was passionate; and the General greedy of Gold. But whatever was the Occasion, so he was killed, as several have assured me, and his Gold seized on, and all his Things; and his Journal also from *England*, as far as Cape *Corrientes* on the Coast of *Mexico*. This Journal was afterwards sent away from thence by Mr. *Moody* (who was there both a little before and a little after the Murder) and he sent it to *England* by Mr. *Goddard*, Chief-Mate of the *Defence*.

¶ But to our purpose: Seeing I could not perswade them to go to Captain *Swan* again, I had a great desire to have had the Prince's Company: But Captain *Read* was afraid to let his fickle Crew lie long. That very Day that the Prince had promised to return to us, which was *November* 2. 1687. we sailed hence, directing our Course South-West, and having the Wind at N.W.

¶ This Wind continued till we came in sight of the Island *Celebes*; then it veered about to the West, and to the southward of the West. We came up with the N.E. end of the Island *Celebes* the 9th Day, and there we found the Current setting to the westward so strongly that we could hardly get on the East-side of that Island.

¶ The Island *Celebes* is a very large Island, extended in length from North to South, about 7 degrees of Lat. and in breadth it is about 3 degrees. It lies under the Equator, the North-end being in Lat. 1 d. 30 m. North, and the South-end in Lat. 5 d. 30 m. South, and by common account the North-point in the Bulk of this Island, lies nearest North and South, but at the North-East-end there runs out a long narrow Point, stretching N.E. about thirty Leagues; and about thirty Leagues to the eastward of this long Slip, is the Island *Gilolo*, on the West-side of which are four small Islands, close by it, which are very well stored with Cloves. The two chiefest are *Ternate* and *Tidore*; and as the Isle of *Ceylon* is reckoned the only Place for Cinnamon, and that of *Banda* for Nutmegs, so these are thought by some to be the only Clove-Islands in the World; but this is a great Error, as I have already shewn.

¶ At the South-end of the Island *Celebes* there is a Sea or Gulph, of about seven or eight Leagues wide, and forty or fifty long, which runs up the Country almost directly to the North; and this Gulph hath several small Islands along the middle of it. On the West-side of the Island, almost at the South-end of it, the Town of *Macasser* is seated. A Town of great Strength and Trade, belonging to the *Dutch*.

¶ There are great Inlets and Lakes on the East-side of the Island; as also abundance of small Islands, and Sholes lying scattered about it. We saw a high peeked Hill at the N. end: But the Land on the East-side is low all along; for we cruized almost the length of it. The Mold on this side is black and deep, and extraordinary fat and rich, and full of Trees: And there are many Brooks of Water run out into the Sea. Indeed all this

East-side of the Island seems to be but one large Grove of extraordinary great high Trees.

¶ Having with much ado got on this East-side, coasting along to the Southward, and yet having but little Wind, and even that little against us, at S.S.W. and sometimes Calm, we were a long time going about the Island.

¶ The 22d Day we were in Lat. 1 d. 20 m. South, and being about three Leagues from the Island standing to the Southward, with a very gentle Land-Wind, about 2 or 3 a Clock in the Morning, we heard a clashing in the Water, like Boats rowing: And fearing some sudden Attack, we got up all our Arms, and stood ready to defend our selves. As soon as it was Day we saw a great Proe, built like the *Mindanayan* Proes, with about 60 Men in her; and six smaller Proes. They lay still about a Mile to windward of us, to view us; and probably designed to make a Prey of us when they first came out; but they were now afraid to venture on us.

¶ At last we shewed them *Dutch* Colours, thinking thereby to allure them to come to us: For we could not go to them; but they presently rowed in toward the Island, and went into a large Opening; and we saw them no more; nor did we ever see any other Boats or Men, but only one fishing Canoa, while we were about this Island; neither did we see any House on all the Coast.

¶ About five or six Leagues to the South of this Place, there is a great Range of both large and small Islands; and many Shoals also that are not laid down in our Drafts; which made it extremely troublesome for us to get through. But we past between them all and the Island *Celebes*, and anchored against a sandy Bay in eight Fathom sandy Ground, about half a Mile from the main Island; being then in Lat. 1 d. 50 m. South.

¶ Here we staied several Days, and sent out our Canoas a striking of Turtle every Day; for here is great plenty of them; but they were very shy, as they were generally where-ever we found them in the *East-India* Seas. I know not the reason of it, unless the Natives go very much a striking here: For even in the *West-Indies* they are shy in Places that are much disturbed: And yet on *New-Holland* we found them shy, as I shall relate; though the Natives there do not molest them.

¶ On the Shole without us we went and gathered Shell-fish at low Water. There were a monstrous sort of Cockles; the Meat of one of them would suffice seven or eight Men. It was very good wholsome Meat. We did also beat about in the Woods on the Island, but found no Game. One of our Men, who was always troubled with sore Legs, found a certain Vine that supported it self by clinging about other Trees. The Leaves reach six or seven Foot high, but the Strings or Branches 11 or 12. It had a very green Leaf, pretty broad and roundish, and of a thick Substance. These Leaves pounded small and boiled with Hog's Lard, make an excellent Salve. Our Men knowing the Virtues of it, stockt themselves here: There were scarce a Man in the Ship but got a Pound or two of it; especially such as were troubled with old Ulcers, who found great Benefit by it. This Man that discovered these Leaves here, had his first Knowledge of them in the Isthmus of *Darien*, he having had his Receipt from one of the *Indians* there: And he had been ashore in divers Places since, purposely to seek these Leaves, but did never find any but here. Among the many vast Trees hereabouts, there was one exceeded all the rest. This Capt. *Read* caused to be cut down, in order to make a Canoa, having lost our Boats, all but one small one, in the late Storms; so six lusty Men, who had been Logwood cutters in the Bays of *Campeachy* and *Honduras* (as Captain *Read* himself, and many more of us had) and so were very expert at this work, undertook to fell it, taking their turn, three always cutting together; and they were one whole Day, and half the next before they got it down. This Tree, though it grew in a Wood, was yet 18 Foot in Circumference, and 44 Foot of clean Body, without Knot or Branch: And even there it had no more than one or two Branches, and then ran clear again 10 Foot higher; there it spread it self into many great Limbs and Branches, like an Oak, very green and flourishing: Yet it was perisht at the Heart, which marr'd it for the Service intended.

¶ So leaving it, and having no more Business here, we weighed, and went from hence the next Day, it being the 29th Day of *November*. While we lay here we had some Tornadoes, one or two every Day, and pretty fresh Land-winds which were at West. The Sea-breezes are small and uncertain, sometimes out of the N.E. and so veering about to the East and South-East. We had the Wind at North-East when we weighed, and we steered off S.S.W. In the Afternoon we saw a Shole a-head of us, and altered our Course to the S.S.E. In the Evening at 4 a Clock, we were close by another great Shole; therefore we tackt, and stood in for the Island *Celebes* again, for fear of running on some of the Sholes in the Night. By Day a Man might avoid them well enough, for they had all Beacons on them, like Huts built on tall Posts, above High-water Mark, probably set up by the Natives of the Island *Celebes*, or those of some other neighbouring Islands; and I never saw any such elsewhere. In the Night we had a violent Tornado out of the S.W. which lasted about an Hour.

¶ The 30th Day we had a fresh Land-Wind, and steered away South, passing between the two Shoals, which we saw the Day before. These

Shoals lye in Lat. 3 d. South, and about ten Leagues from the Island *Celebes*. Being past them, the Wind died away, and we lay becalmed till the Afternoon: Then we had a hard Tornado out of the South-West, and towards the Evening we saw two or three Spouts, the first I had seen since I came into the *East-Indies*; in the *West-Indies* I had often met with them. A Spout is a small ragged piece or part of a Cloud hanging down about a Yard, seemingly from the blackest part thereof. Commonly it hangs down sloping from thence, or sometimes appearing with a small bending, or elbow in the middle. I never saw any hang perpendicularly down. It is small at the lower-end, seeming no bigger than one's Arm, but still fuller towards the Cloud, from whence it proceeds.

¶ When the Surface of the Sea begins to work, you shall see the Water, for about 100 Paces in Circumference, foam and move gently round till the whirling Motion increases: And then it flies upward in a Pillar, about 100 Paces in Compass at the bottom, but lessening gradually upwards to the smallness of the Spout it self, there where it reacheth the lower-end of the Spout, through which the rising Sea-water seems to be conveyed into the Clouds. This visibly appears by the Clouds increasing in bulk and blackness. Then you shall presently see the Cloud drive along, although before it seemed to be without any Motion: The Spout also keeping the same Course with the Cloud, and still sucking up the Water as it goes along, and they make a Wind as they go. Thus it continues for the space of half an Hour, more or less, until the sucking is spent, and then breaking off, all the Water which was below the Spout, or pendulous piece of Cloud, falls down again into the Sea, making a great Noise with its fall and clashing Motion in the Sea.

¶ It is very dangerous for a Ship to be under a Spout when it breaks, therefore we always endeavour to shun it, by keeping at a distance, if possibly we can. But for want of Wind to carry us away, we are often in great fear and danger, for it is usually calm when Spouts are at work; except only just where they are. Therefore Men at Sea, when they see a Spout coming, and know not how to avoid it, do sometimes fire Shot out of their great Guns into it, to give it air or vent, that so it may break; but I did never hear that it proved to be of any Benefit.

¶ And now being on this Subject, I think it not amiss to give you an account of an Accident that happened to a Ship once on the Coast of *Guinea*, sometime in or about the Year 1674. One Captain *Records* of *London*, bound for the Coast of *Guinea*, in a Ship of 300 Tuns, and 16 Guns, called the *Blessing*; when he came into the Lat. 7 or 8 degrees North, he saw several Spouts, one of which came directly towards the Ship, and he having no Wind to get out of the way of the Spout, made ready to receive it by furling his Sails. It came on very swift and broke a little before it reached the Ship; making a great Noise, and raising the Sea round it, as if a great House or some such Thing, had been cast into the Sea. The Fury of the Wind still lasted, and took the Ship on the Starboard-bow with such Violence, that it snapt off the Boltsprit and Fore-mast both at once, and blew the Ship all along, ready to over-set it, but the Ship did presently right again, and the Wind whirling round, took the Ship a second time with the like Fury as before, but on the contrary side, and was again like to over-set her the other way. The Mizen-mast felt the Fury of this second Blast, and was snapt short off, as the Fore-mast and Boltsprit had been before. The Main-mast, and Main-top-mast, received no Damage, for the Fury of the Wind (which was presently over) did not reach them. Three Men were in the Fore-top when the Fore-mast broke, and one on the Boltsprit, and fell with them into the Sea, but all of them were saved. I had this Relation from M. *John Canby*, who was then Quarter-master, and Steward of her; one *Abraham Wise* was Chief Mate, and *Leonard Jefferies* second Mate.

¶ We are usually very much afraid of them: Yet this was the only Damage that ever I heard done by them. They seem terrible enough, the rather because they come upon you while you lie becalmed, like a Log in the Sea, and cannot get out of their way: But though I have seen, and been beset by them often, yet the Fright was always the greatest of the Harm.

¶ *December* the 1st, we had a gentle Gale at E.S.E. we steered South; and at Noon I was by Observation in Lat. 3 d. 34 m. South. Then we saw the Island *Bouton*, bearing South-West, and about ten Leagues distant. We had very uncertain and unconstant Winds: The Tornadoes came out of the S.W. which was against us; and what other Winds we had were so faint, that they did us little Kindness; but we took the Advantage of the smallest Gale, and got a little way every Day. The 4th Day at Noon I was by Observation in Lat. 4 d. 30 m. South.

¶ The 5th Day we got close by the N.W. end of the Island *Bouton*, and in the Evening, it being fair Weather, we hoised out our Canoa, and sent the *Moskito* Men, of whom we had two or three, to strike Turtle, for here are plenty of them; but they being shy, we chose to strike them in the Night (which is customary in the *West-Indies* also) for every time they come up to breath, which is once in 8 or 10 Minuts, they blow so hard, that one may hear them at 30 or 40 Yards distance; by which means the Striker knows where they are, and may more easily approach them then in the Day; for the Turtle sees better than he hears; but on the contrary, the Manatee's hearing is quickest.

¶ In the Morning they returned with a very large Turtle, which they took near the Shore; and withal an *Indian* of the Island came aboard with them. He spake the *Malayan* Language; by which we did understand him. He told us, that two Leagues farther to the Southward of us, there was a good Harbour, in which we might anchor: So having a fair Wind, we got thither by Noon.

¶ This Harbour is in Lat. 4 d. 54 m. South; lying on the East-side of the Island *Bouton*. Which Island lies near the S.E. end of the Island *Celebes*, distant from it about three or four Leagues. It is of a long form, stretching S.W. and N.E. above 25 Leagues long, and 10 broad. It is pretty high Land, and appears pretty even, and flat and very woody.

¶ There is a large Town within a League of the anchoring-Place, called *Callasusung*, being the chief, if there were more; which we knew not. It is about a Mile from the Sea, on the top of a small Hill, in a very fair Plain, incompassed with Coco-nut Trees. Without the Trees there is a strong Stone-Wall clear round the Town. The Houses are built like the Houses at *Mindanao*; but more neat: And the whole Town was very clean and delightsome.

¶ The Inhabitants are small, and well shaped. They are much like the *Mindanaians* in shape, colour, and habit; but more neat and tight. They speak the *Malayan* Language, and are all *Mahometans*. They are very obedient to the Sultan, who is a little Man, about forty or fifty Years old, and hath a great many Wives and Children.

¶ About an Hour after we came to an Anchor, the Sultan sent a Messenger aboard, to know what we were, and what our Business. We gave him an account; and he returned ashore, and in a short time after he came aboard again, and told us, that the Sultan was very well pleased when he heard that we were *English*; and said, that we should have any thing that the Island afforded; and that he himself would come aboard in the Morning. Therefore the Ship was made clean, and every thing put in the best order to receive him.

¶ The 6th Day in the Morning betimes a great many Boats and Canoas came aboard, with Fowls, Eggs, Plantains, Potatoes, &c. but they would dispose of none till they had Orders for it from the Sultan, at his coming. About 10 a-Clock the Sultan came aboard in a very neat Proe, built after the *Mindanao* Fashion. There was a large white Silk Flag at the Head of the Mast, edged round with a deep red for about two or three Inches broad, and in the middle there was neatly drawn a Green Griffon, trampling on a winged Serpent, that seemed to struggle to get up, and threatened his Adversary with open Mouth, and with a long Sting that was ready to be darted into his Legs. Other *East-Indian* Princes have their Devices also.

¶ The Sultan with three or four of his Nobles, and three of his Sons, sat in the House of the Proe. His Guards were ten Musqueteers, five standing on one side of the Proe, and five on the other side; and before the Door of the Proe-house stood one with a great broad Sword and a Target, and two more such at the after-part of the House; and in the Head and Stern of the Proe stood four Musqueteers more, two at each end.

¶ The Sultan had a Silk Turbat, laced with narrow Gold Lace by the sides, and broad Lace at the end: which hung down on one side the Head, after the *Mindanayan* Fashion. He had a Sky-coloured Silk pair of Breeches, and a piece of red Silk thrown cross his Shoulders, and hanging loose about him; the greatest part of his Back and Waste appearing naked. He had neither Stocking nor Shoe. One of his Sons were about 15 or 16 Year old, the other two were young things; and they were always in the Arms of one or other of his Attendants.

¶ Captain *Read* met him at the side, and led him into his small Cabin, and fired five Guns for his welcome. As soon as he came aboard he gave leave to his Subjects to Traffick with us; and then our People bought what they had a Mind to. The Sultan seem'd very well pleased to be visited by the *English*; and said he had coveted to have a sight of *English-men*, having heard extraordinary Characters of their just and honourable Dealing: But he exclaimed against the *Dutch*, (as all the *Mindanayans*, and all the *Indians* we met with do) and wished them at a greater distance.

¶ For *Macasser* is not very far from hence, one of the chiefest Towns that the *Dutch* have in those parts. From thence the *Dutch* come sometimes hither to purchase Slaves. The Slaves that these People get here and sell to the *Dutch*, are some of the idolatrous Natives of the Island, who not being under the Sultan, and having no Head, live straggling in the Country, flying from one Place to another to preserve themselves from the Prince and his Subjects, who hunt after them to make them Slaves. For the civilized *Indians* of the Maritime Places, who trade with Foreigners, if they cannot reduce the inland People to the Obedience of their Prince, they catch all they can of them and sell them for Slaves; accounting them to be but as Savages, just as the *Spaniards* do the poor *Americans*.

¶ After two or three Hours Discourse, the Sultan went ashore again, and five Guns were fired at his Departure also. The next Day he sent for Captain *Read* to come ashore, and he with seven or eight Men went to wait on the Sultan. I could not slip an Opportunity of seeing the Place; and so accompanied them. We were met at the Landing-place by two of the chief Men, and guided to a pretty neat House, where the Sultan waited our coming. The House stood at the further-end of all the Town before-mentioned, which we past through; and abundance of People were gazing on us as we past by. When we came near the House, there were forty poor naked Soldiers with Musquets made a Lane for us to pass through. This House was not built on Posts, as the rest were, after the *Mindanayan* way; but the Room in which we were entertained was on the Ground, covered with Mats to sit on. Our Entertainment was Tobacco and Betel-nut, and young Coco-nuts; and the House was beset with Men, and Women and Children, who thronged to get near the Windows to look on us.

¶ We did not tarry above an Hour before we took our leaves and departed. This Town stands in a sandy Soil; but what the rest of the Island is I know not, for none of us were ashore but at this Place.

¶ The next Day the Sultan came aboard again, and presented Captain *Read* with a little Boy, but he was too small to be serviceable on board; and so Captain *Read* returned Thanks, and told him he was too little for him. Then the Sultan sent for a bigger Boy, which the Captain accepted. This Boy was a very pretty tractable Boy; but what was wonderful in him, he had two Rows of Teeth, one within another on each Jaw. None of the other People were so, nor did I ever see the like. The Captain was presented also with two He-goats, and was promised some Buffaloe, but I do believe that they have but few of either on the Island. We did not see any Buffaloe, nor many Goats, neither have they much Rice, but their chiefest Food is Roots. We bought here about a Thousand Pound Weight of Potatoes. Here our Men bought also abundance of Crockadores, and fine large Parakites, curiously coloured, and some of them the finest I ever saw.

¶ The Crockadore is as big as a Parrot, and shaped much like it, with such a Bill; but it is as white as Milk, and hath a Bunch of Feathers on his Head like a Crown. At this Place we bought a Proe also of the *Mindanayan* make, for our own use, which our Carpenters afterwards altered, and made a delicate Boat fit for any Service. She was sharp at both ends, but we saw'd off one, and made that end flat, fastening a Rudder to it, and she rowed and sailed incomparably.

¶ We staied here but till the 12th Day, because it was a bad Harbour and foul Ground, and a bad time of the Year too, for the Tornadoes began to come in thick and strong. When we went to weigh our Anchor, it was hooked in a Rock, and we broke our Cable, and could not get our Anchor, though we strove hard for it; so we went away and left it there. We had the Wind at N.N.E. and we steered towards the S.E. and fell in with four or five small Islands, that lie in 5 d. 40 m. South Lat. and about five or six Leagues from *Callasusung* Harbour. These Islands appeared very Green with Coco-nut Trees, and we saw two or three Towns on them, and heard a Drum all Night, for we were got in among Shoals, and could not get out again till the next Day. We knew not whether the Drum were for fear of us, or that they were making merry, as 'tis usual in these Parts to do all the Night, singing and dancing till Morning.

¶ We found a pretty strong Tide here, the Flood setting to the southward, and the Ebb to the northward. These Shoals, and many other that are not laid down in our Drafts, lie on the South-West-side of the Islands where we heard the Drum, about a League from them. At last we past between the Islands, and tried for a Passage on the East-side. We met with divers Sholes on this side also, but found Channels to pass through; so we steer'd away for the Island *Timor*, intending to pass out by it. We had the Winds commonly at W.S.W. and S.W. hard Gales and rainy Weather.

¶ The 16th Day we got clear of the Shoals, and steered S. by E. with the Wind at W.S.W. but veering every half Hour, sometimes at S.W. and then again at W. and sometimes at N.N.W. bringing much Rain, with Thunder and Lightning.

¶ The 20th Day we passed by the Island *Omba*, which is a pretty high Island, lying in Lat. 8 d. 20 m. and not above five or six Leagues from the N.E. part of the Island *Timor*. It is about 13 or 14 Leagues long, and five or six Leagues wide.

¶ About seven or eight Leagues to the West of *Omba*, is another pretty large Island, but it had no Name in our Plats; yet by the Situation it should be that which in some Maps is called *Pentare*. We saw on it abundance of Smoaks by Day, and Fires by Night, and a large Town on the North-side of it, not far from the Sea; but it was such bad Weather that we did not go ashore. Between *Omba* and *Pentare*, and in the mid Channel, there is a small low sandy Island, with great Sholes on either side; but there is a very good Channel close by *Pentare*, between that and the Sholes about the small Isle. We were three Days beating off and on, not having a Wind, for it was at South South West.

¶ The 23d Day in the Evening, having a small Gale at North, we got through, keeping close by *Pentare*. The Tide of Ebb here set out to the Southward, by which we were helped through, for we had but little Wind.

But this Tide, which did us a kindness in setting us through, had like to have ruined us afterwards; for there are two small Islands lying at the South-end of the Channel we came through, and towards these Islands the Tide hurried us so swiftly, that we very narrowly escaped being driven ashore; for the little Wind we had before at North dying away, we had not one breath of Wind when we came there, neither was there any Anchor-Ground. But we got out our Oars and rowed, yet all in vain; for the Tide set wholly on one of these small Islands, that we were forced with might and main Strength to bear off the Ship, by thrusting with our Oars against the Shore, which was a steep Bank, and by this means we presently drove away clear of Danger; and having a little Wind in the Night at North, we steered away S.S.W. In the Morning again we had the Wind at W.S.W. and steered S. and the Wind coming to the W.N.W. we steered S.W. to get clear of the S.W. end of the Island *Timor*. The 29th Day we saw the N.W. point of *Timor* S.E. by E. distant about eight Leagues.

¶ *Timor* is a long high mountainous Island stretching N.E. and S.W. It is about 70 Leagues long, and 15 or 16 wide, the middle of the Island is in Lat. about 9 d. South I have been informed that the *Portuguese* do trade to this Island; but I know nothing of its produce besides Coire for making Cables, of which there is mention Chap. X.

¶ The 27th Day we saw two small Islands which lie near the S.W. end of *Timor*. They bear from us S.E. We had very hard Gales of Wind, and still with a great deal of Rain; the Wind at W. and W.S.W.

¶ Being now clear of all the Islands, we stood off South, intending to touch at *New-Holland*, a part of *Terra Australis Incognita*, to see what that Country would afford us. Indeed as the Winds were, we could not now keep our intended Course (which was first westerly, and then northerly) without going to *New-Holland*, unless we had gone back again among the Islands: But this was not a good time of the Year to be among any Islands to the South of the Equator, unless in a good Harbour.

¶ The 31st Day we were in Lat. 13 d. 20 m. still standing to the southward, the Wind bearing commonly very hard at W. we keeping upon it under two Courses, and our Mizen, and sometimes a Main-top-sail Rift. About 10 a Clock at Night we tackt and stood to the Northward, for fear of running on a Shoal which is laid down in our Drafts in Lat. 13 d. 50 m. or thereabouts: It bearing S. by W. from the East-end of *Timor*; and so the Island bore from us by our Judgments and Reckoning. At 3 a Clock we tackt again, and stood S. by W. and S.S.W.

¶ In the Morning as soon as it was Day, we saw the Shoal right a-head:

It lies in 13 d. 50 m. by all our Reckonings. It is a small spit of Sand, just appearing above the Water's edge, with several Rocks about it, eight or ten Foot high above Water. It lies in a triangular Form; each side being about a League and half. We stemm'd right with the middle of it, and stood within half a Mile of the Rocks, and sounded; but found no Ground. Then we went about and stood to the North two Hours; and then tackt and stood to the southward again, thinking to weather it, but could not. So we bore away on the North-side, till we came to the East-point, giving the Rocks a small Birth: Then we trimm'd sharp, and stood to the Southward, passing close by it, and sounded again but found no Ground.

¶ This Shoal is laid down in our Drafts not above 16 or 20 Leagues from *New-Holland*; but we did run afterwards 60 Leagues due South before we fell in with it; and I am very confident, that no part of *New-Holland* hereabouts lies so far northerly by 40 Leagues, as 'tis laid down in our Drafts. For if *New-Holland* were laid down true, we must of necessity have been driven near 40 Leagues to the westward of our Course; but this is very improbable, that the Current should set so strong to the westward, seeing we had such a constant westerly Wind. I grant, that when the Monsoon shifts first, the Current does not presently shift, but runs afterwards near a Month; but the Monsoon had been shifted at least two Months now. But of the Monsoons and other Winds, and of the Currents elsewhere, in their proper Place. As to these here, I do rather believe that the Land is not laid down true, than that the Current deceived us; for it was more probable we should have been deceived before we met with a Shole, than afterwards; for on the Coast of *New-Holland* we found the Tides keeping their constant Course; the Flood running N. by E. and the Ebb S. by E.

¶ The 4th Day of *January*, 1688, we fell in with the Land of *New-Holland* in the Lat. of 16 d. 50 m. having, as I said before, made our Course due South from the Shoal that we past by the 31st Day of *December*. We ran in close by it, and finding no convenient anchoring, because it lies open to the N.W. we ran along shore to the Eastward, steering N.E. by E. for so the Land lies. We steered thus about 12 Leagues; and then came to a Point of Land, from whence the Land trends East and southerly, for 10 or 12 Leagues; but how afterwards I know not. About 3 Leagues to the eastward of this Point, there is a pretty deep Bay, with abundance of Islands in it, and a very good place to anchor in, or to hale ashoar. About a League to the eastward of that Point we anchored *January* the 5th, 1688, two Mile from the Shore, in 29 Fathom, good hard Sand, and clean Ground.

¶ *New-Holland* is a very large Tract of Land. It is not yet determined whether it is an Island or a main Continent; but I am certain that it joins neither to *Asia*, *Africa*, nor *America*. This part of it that we saw is all low even Land, with sandy Banks against the Sea, only the Points are rocky, and so are some of the Islands in this Bay.

¶ The Land is of a dry sandy Soil, destitute of Water, except you make Wells; yet producing divers sorts of Trees; but the Woods are not thick, nor the Trees very big. Most of the Trees that we saw are Dragon-Trees as we supposed; and these too are the largest Trees of any there. They are about the bigness of our large Apple-trees, and about the same heighth; and the Rind is blackish, and somewhat rough. The Leaves are of a dark Colour; the Gum distils out of the Knots or Cracks that are in the Bodies of the Trees. We compared it with some Gum-Dragon or Dragon's Blood that was aboard, and it was of the same colour and taste. The other sort of Trees were not known by any of us. There was pretty long Grass growing under the Trees; but it was very thin. We saw no Trees that bore Fruit or Berries.

¶ We saw no sort of Animal, nor any Track of Beast, but once; and that seemed to be the Tread of a Beast as big as a great Mastiff-Dog. Here are a few small Land-birds, but none bigger than a Black-bird; and but few Sea-fowls. Neither is the Sea very plentifully stored with Fish, unless you reckon the Manatee and Turtle as such. Of these Creatures there is plenty; but they are extraordinary shy; though the Inhabitants cannot trouble them much having neither Boats nor Iron.

¶ The Inhabitants of this Country are the miserablest People in the World. The *Hodmadods* of *Monomatapa*, though a nasty People, yet for Wealth are Gentlemen to these; who have no Houses, and skin Garments, Sheep, Poultry, and Fruits of the Earth, Ostrich Eggs, &c. as the *Hodmadods* have: And setting aside their Humane Shape, they differ but little from Brutes. They are tall, strait-bodied, and thin, with small long Limbs. They have great Heads, round Foreheads, and great Brows. Their Eyelids are always half closed, to keep the Flies out of their Eyes; they being so troublesome here, that no fanning will keep them from coming to one's Face; and without the Assistance of both Hands to keep them off, they will creep into ones Nostrils, and Mouth too, if the Lips are not shut very close; so that from their Infancy being thus annoyed with these Insects, they do never open their Eyes as other People: And therefore they cannot see far, unless they hold up their Heads, as if they were looking at somewhat over them.

¶ They have great Bottle-Noses, pretty full Lips, and wide Mouths. The two Fore-teeth of their Upper-jaw are wanting in all of them, Men and Women, old and young; whether they draw them out, I know not: Neither have they any Beards. They are long-visaged, and of a very unpleasing Aspect, having no one graceful Feature in their Faces. Their Hair is black, short and curl'd, like that of the Negroes; and not long and lank like the common *Indians*. The Colour of their Skins, both of their Faces and the rest of their Body, is Coal-black, like that of the Negroes of *Guinea*.

¶ They have no sort of Cloaths, but a piece of the Rind of a Tree tied like a Girdle about their Waists, and a handful of long Grass, or three or four small green Boughs full of Leaves, thrust under their Girdle, to cover their Nakedness.

¶ They have no Houses, but lie in the open Air without any covering; the Earth being their Bed, and the Heaven their Canopy. Whether they cohabit one Man to one Woman, or promiscuously, I know not; but they do live in Companies, 20 or 30 Men, Women, and Children together. Their only Food is a small sort of Fish, which they get by making Wares of Stone across little Coves or Branches of the Sea; every Tide bringing in the small Fish, and there leaving them for a Prey to these People, who constantly attend there to search for them at Low-water. This small Fry I take to be the top of their Fishery: They have no Instruments to catch great Fish, should they come; and such seldom stay to be left behind at Low-water: Nor could we catch any Fish with our Hooks and Lines all the while we lay there. In other Places at Low-water they seek for Cockles, Muscles, and Periwincles: Of these Shell-fish there are fewer still; so that their chiefest dependance is upon what the Sea leaves in their Wares; which, be it much or little they gather up, and march to the Places of their Abode. There the old People that are not able to stir abroad by reason of their Age, and the tender Infants, wait their return; and what Providence has bestowed on them, they presently broil on the Coals, and eat it in common. Sometimes they get as many Fish as makes them a plentiful Banquet; and at other times they scarce get every one a taste: But be it little or much that they get, every one has his part, as well the young and tender, the old and feeble, who are not able to go abroad, as the strong and lusty. When they have eaten they lie down till the next Low-water, and then all that are able march out, be it Night or Day, rain or shine, 'tis all one; they must attend the Wares, or else they must fast: For the Earth affords them no Food at all. There is neither Herb, Root, Pulse nor any sort of Grain for them to eat, that we saw; nor any sort of Bird or Beast that they can catch, having no Instruments wherewithal to do so.

¶ I did not perceive that they did worship any thing. These poor Creatures have a sort of Weapon to defend their Ware, or fight with their Enemies, if they have any that will interfere with their poor Fishery. They did at first endeavour with their Weapons to frighten us, who lying ashore deterr'd them from one of their Fishing-places. Some of them had wooden Swords, others had a sort of Lances. The Sword is a piece of Wood shaped somewhat like a Cutlass. The Lance is a long strait Pole sharp at one end, and hardened afterwards by heat. I saw no Iron, nor any other sort of Metal; therefore it is probable they use Stone-Hatchets, as some *Indians* in *America* do, described in Chap. IV.

¶ How they get their Fire I know not; but probably as *Indians* do, out of Wood. I have seen the *Indians* of *Bon-Airy* do it, and have my self tried the Experiment: They take a flat piece of Wood that is pretty soft, and make a small dent in one side of it, then they take another hard round Stick, about the bigness of one's little Finger, and sharpening it at one end like a Pencil, they put that sharp end in the hole or dent of the flat soft piece, and then rubbing or twirling the hard piece between the Palms of their Hands, they drill the soft piece till it smoaks, and at last takes Fire.

¶ These People speak somewhat thro' the Throat; but we could not understand one word that they said. We anchored, as I said before, *January* the 5th, and seeing Men walking on the Shore, we presently sent a Canoa to get some Acquaintance with them: for we were in hopes to get some Provision among them. But the Inhabitants, seeing our Boat coming, run away and hid themselves. We searched afterwards three Days in hopes to find their Houses; but found none: yet we saw many places where they had made Fires. At last, being out of hopes to find their Habitations, we searched no farther; but left a great many Toys ashore, in such places where we thought that they would come. In all our search we found no Water, but old Wells on the sandy Bays.

¶ At last we went over to the Islands, and there we found a great many of the Natives: I do believe there were 40 on one Island, Men, Women and Children. The Men at our first coming ashore, threatned us with their Lances and Swords; but they were frighted by firing one Gun, which we fired purposely to scare them. The Island was so small that they could not hide themselves: but they were much disordered at our Landing, especially the Women and Children: for we went directly to their Camp. The lustiest of the Women snatching up their Infants ran away howling, and the little Children run after squeaking and bawling; but the Men stood still. Some of the Women, and such People as could not go from us, lay still by a Fire, making a doleful noise, as if we had been coming to devour them: but when they saw we did not intend to harm them, they were pretty quiet, and the rest that fled from us at our first coming, returned again. This their place of Dwelling was only a Fire, with a few Boughs before it, set up on that side the Winds was of.

¶ After we had been here a little while, the Men began to be familiar, and we cloathed some of them, designing to have had some service of them for it: for we found some Wells of Water here, and intended to carry 2 or 3 Barrels of it aboard. But it being somewhat troublesome to carry to the Canoas, we thought to have made these Men to have carry'd it for us, and therefore we gave them some old Cloaths; to one an old pair of Breeches, to another a ragged Shirt, to the third a Jacket that was scarce worth owning; which yet would have been very acceptable at some places where we had been, and so we thought they might have been with these People. We put them on them, thinking that this finery would have brought them to work heartily for us; and our Water being filled in small long Barrels, about six Gallons in each, which were made purposely to carry Water in, we brought these our new Servants to the Wells, and put a Barrel on each of their Shoulders for them to carry to the Canoa. But all the signs we could make were to no purpose, for they stood like Statues, without motion, but grinn'd like so many Monkeys, staring one upon another: For these poor Creatures seem not accustomed to carry Burthens; and I believe that one of our Ship-boys of 10 Years old, would carry as much as one of them. So we were forced to carry our Water our selves, and they very fairly put the Cloaths off again, and laid them down, as if Cloaths were only to work in. I did not perceive that they had any great liking to them at first, neither did they seem to admire any thing that we had.

¶ At another time our Canoa being among these Islands seeking for Game, espy'd a drove of these Men swimming from one Island to another; for they have no Boats, Canoas, or Bark-logs. They took up Four of them, and brought them aboard; two of them were middle-aged, the other two were young Men about 18 or 20 Years old. To these we gave boiled Rice, and with it Turtle and Manatee boiled. They did greedily devour what we gave them, but took no notice of the Ship, or any thing in it, and when they were set on Land again, they ran away as fast as they could. At our first coming, before we were acquainted with them, or they with us, a Company of them who liv'd on the Main, came just against our Ship, and standing on a pretty high Bank, threatned us with their Swords and Lances, by shaking them at us: At last the Captain ordered the Drum to be beaten, which was done of a sudden with much vigour, purposely to scare the poor Creatures. They hearing the noise, ran away as fast as they could drive; and when they ran away in haste, they would cry *Gurry*, *Gurry*, speaking deep in the Throat. Those Inhabitants also that live on the Main, would always run away from us; yet we took several of them. For, as I have already observed, they had such bad Eyes, that they could not see us till we came close to them. We did always give them Victuals, and let them go again, but the Islanders, after our first time of being among them, did not stir for us.

¶ When we had been here about a Week, we hal'd our Ship into a small sandy Cove, at a Spring-tide, as far as she would float; and at low Water she was left dry, and the Sand dry without us near half a Mile; for the Sea riseth and falleth here about five fathom. The Flood runs North by East, and the Ebb South by West. All the Neep-tides we lay wholly a-ground, for the Sea did not come near us by about a hundred Yards. We had therefore time enough to clean our Ships bottom, which we did very well. Most of our Men lay ashore in a Tent, where our Sails were mending; and our Strikers brought home Turtle and Manatee every Day, which was our constant Food.

¶ While we lay here, I did endeavour to persuade our Men to go to some *English* Factory; but was threatned to be turned ashore, and left here for it. This made me desist, and patiently wait for some more convenient place and opportunity to leave them, than here: Which I did hope I should accomplish in a short time; because they did intend, when they went from hence, to bear down towards Cape *Comorin*. In their way thither they designed also to visit the Island *Cocos*, which lieth in Lat. 12 d. 12 m. North, by our Drafts; hoping there to find of that Fruit; the Island having its Name from thence.

CHAPTER XVII

Leaving New-Holland *they pass by the Island* Cocos, *and touch at another woody Island near it. A Land Animal like large Craw-fish. Coco-Nuts, floating in the Sea. The Island* Triste *bearing* Coco's, *yet over-flown every Spring-tide. They anchor at a small Island near that of* Nassaw. Hog-Island, *and others. A Proe taken belonging to* Achin. Nicobar-Island, *and the rest called by that Name. Ambergreece, good and bad. The Manners of the Inhabitants of these Islands. They anchor at* Nicobar-Isle. *Its Situation, Soil, and pleasant mixture of its Bays, Trees, &c. The* Melory-Tree *and Fruit, used for Bread. The Natives of* Nicobar-Island, *their Form, Habit, Language, Habitations; no form of Religion or Government: Their Food and Canoas. They clean the Ship. The Author projects and gets leave to stay ashore here, and with him two* English-men*

MARCH the 12th, 1688, we sailed from *New-Holland*, with the Wind
at N.N.W. and fair weather. We directed our course to the
northward, intending, as I said, to touch at the Island *Cocos*: But
we met with the Winds at N.W., W.N.W. and N.N.W. for several Days;
which obliged us to keep a more easterly course than was convenient to
find that Island. We had soon after our setting out very bad weather,
with much Thunder and Lightning, Rain and high blustring Winds.

¶ It was the 26th Day of *March* before we were in the Lat. of the Island
Cocos, which is in 12 d. 12 m. and then, by Judgment, we were 40 or 50
Leagues to the East of it; and the Wind was now at S.W. Therefore we
did rather chuse to bear away towards some Islands on the West-side of
Sumatra, than to beat against the Wind for the Island *Cocos*. I was very
glad of this; being in hopes to make my escape from them to *Sumatra*, or
to some other Place.

¶ We met nothing of remark in this Voyage, beside the catching two
great Sharks, till the 28th Day. Then we fell in with a small woody
Island, in Lat. 10 d. 20 m. Its Longitude from *New-Holland*, from whence
we came, was, by my account, 12 d. 6 m. West. It was deep Water about
the Island, and therefore no Anchoring; but we sent two Canoas ashore;
one of them with the Carpenters, to cut a Tree to make another Pump;
the other Canoa went to search for fresh Water, and found a fine small
Brook near the S.W. point of the Island; but there the Sea fell in on the
Shore so high, that they could not get it off. At Noon both our Canoas
returned aboard; and the Carpenters brought aboard a good Tree, which
they afterwards made a Pump with, such a one as they made at *Mindanao*.
The other Canoa brought aboard as many Boobies, and Men of War
Birds, as sufficed all the Ships Company when they were boiled. They
got also a sort of Land-Animal, somewhat resembling a large Craw-fish
without its great Claws. These Creatures lived in Holes in the dry sandy
Ground, like Rabbits. Sir *Francis Drake* in his Voyage round the World
makes mention of such that he found at *Ternate*, or some other of the
Spice-Islands, or near them. They were very good sweet Meat, and so
large that two of them were more than a Man could eat; being almost as

thick as one's Leg. Their Shells were of a dark brown; but red when boiled.

¶ This Island is of a good heighth, with steep Cliffs against the S. and S.W. and a sandy Bay on the North-side; but very deep Water steep to the Shore. The Mould is blackish, the Soil fat, producing large Trees of divers sorts.

¶ About one a-Clock in the Afternoon we made sail from this Island, with the Wind at S.W. and we steered N.W. Afterwards the Winds came about at N.W. and continued between the W.N.W. and the N.N.W. several Days. I observed, that the Winds blew for the most part out of the West, or N.W. and then we had always rainy Weather with Tornadoes, and much Thunder and Lightning; but when the Wind came any way to the southward, it blew but faint, and brought fair weather.

¶ We met nothing of remark till the 7th Day of *April*, and then, being in Lat. 7 d. S. we saw the Land of *Sumatra* at a great distance, bearing North. The 8th Day we saw the East-end of the Island *Sumatra* very plainly; we being then in Lat. 6 d. S. The 10th Day, being in Lat. 5 d. 11 m. and about seven or eight Leagues from the Island *Sumatra*, on the West side of it, we saw abundance of Coco-Nuts swimming in the Sea; and we hoysed out our Boat, and took up some of them; as also a small Hatch, or Scuttle rather, belonging to some Bark. The Nuts were very sound, and the Kernel sweet, and in some the Milk or Water in them, and was yet sweet and good.

¶ The 12th Day we came to a small Island called *Triste*, in Lat. (by Observation) 4 d. South; it is about 14 or 15 Leagues to the West of the Island *Sumatra*. From hence to the northward there are a great many small uninhabited Islands, lying much at the same distance from *Sumatra*. This Island *Triste* is not a Mile round, and so low, that the Tide flows clear over it. It is of a sandy Soil, and full of Coco-nut Trees. The Nuts are but small; yet sweet enough, full, and more ponderous than I ever felt any of that bigness; notwithstanding that every Spring-tide the Salt-water goes clear over the Island.

¶ We sent ashore our Canoas for Coco-nuts, and they returned aboard laden with them three times. Our Strikers also went out and struck some Fish, which was boiled for Supper. They also killed two young Alligators, which we salted for the next Day.

¶ I had no Opportunity at this place to make any Escape as I would have done, and gone over hence to *Sumatra*, could I have kept a Boat to me. But there was no compassing this; and so the 15th Day we went from hence, steering to the Northward on the West-side of *Sumatra*. Our

Food now was Rice, and the Meat of the Coco-nuts rasped, and steep'd in Water; which made a sort of Milk, into which we did put our Rice, making a pleasant Mess enough. After we parted from *Triste* we saw other small Islands, that were also full of Coco-nut Trees.

¶ The 19th Day, being in Lat. 3 d. 25 m. S. the S.W. point of the Island *Nassaw* bore N. about five Mile dist. This is a pretty large uninhabited Island; in Lat. 3 d. 20 m. S. and is full of high Trees. About a Mile from the Island *Nassaw* there is a small Island full of Coco-nut Trees. There we anchored the 29th Day to replenish our stock of Coco-nuts. A Riff of Rocks lies almost round this Island, so that our Boats could not go ashore, nor come aboard at low Water; yet we got aboard four Boat-load of Nuts. This Island is low like *Triste*, and the anchoring is on the North-side; where you have 14 Fathom, a Mile from shore, clean Sand.

¶ The 21st Day we went from hence, and kept to the northward, coasting still on the West-side of the Island *Sumatra*; and having the Winds between the W. and S.S.W. with unsettled Weather; sometimes Rains and Tornadoes, and sometimes fair Weather.

¶ The 25th Day we crost the Equator, still coasting to the northward, between the Island *Sumatra*, and a Range of small Islands, lying 14 or 15 Leagues off it. Amongst all these Islands, *Hog*-Island is the most considerable. It lies in Lat. 3 d. 40 m. North. It is pretty high even Land, cloathed with tall flourishing Trees; we past it by the 28th Day.

¶ The 29th we saw a Sail to the North of us, which we chased: but it being little Wind, we did not come up with her till the 30th Day. Then, being within a League of her, Captain *Read* went into a Canoa and took her, and brought her aboard. She was a Proe with four Men in her, belonging to *Achin*, whither she was bound. She came from one of these Coco-nut Islands that we past by, and was laden with Coco-nuts, and Coco-nut Oil. Captain *Read* ordered his Men to take aboard all the Nuts, and as much of the Oil as he thought convenient, and then cut a hole in the bottom of the Proe, and turned her loose, keeping the Men Prisoners.

¶ It was not for the Lucre of the Cargo, that Captain *Read* took this Boat, but to hinder me and some others from going ashore; for he knew that we were ready to make our escapes, if an opportunity presented it self; and he thought, that by his abusing and robbing the Natives, we should be afraid to trust our selves among them. But yet this proceeding of his turned to our great advantage, as shall be declared hereafter.

¶ *May* the 1st, we ran down by the North-West-end of the Island *Sumatra*, within seven or eight Leagues of the shore. All this West-side of *Sumatra* which we thus coasted along, our *Englishmen* at *Fort St. George*, call the *West-Coast* simply, without adding the name of *Sumatra*. The Prisoners who were taken the Day before shewed us the Islands that lie off of *Achin* Harbour, and the Channels through which Ships go in; and told us also that there was an *English* Factory at *Achin*. I wish'd my self there, but was forced to wait with patience till my time was come.

¶ We were now directing our course towards the *Nicobar* Islands, intending there to clean the Ship's Bottom, in order to make her sail well.

¶ The 4th Day in the evening, we had sight of one of the *Nicobar* Islands. The southermost of them lies about 40 Leagues N.N.W. from the N.W. end of the Island *Sumatra*. This most southerly of them is *Nicobar* it self, but all the Cluster of Islands lying South of the *Andeman* Islands are called by our Seamen the *Nicobar* Islands.

¶ The Inhabitants of these Islands have no certain Converse with any Nation; but as Ships pass by them, they will come aboard in their Proes, and offer their Commodities to Sale, never inquiring of what Nation they are; for all white People are alike to them. Their chiefest Commodities are Ambergreece and Fruits.

¶ Ambergreece is often found by the Native *Indians* of these Islands, who know it very well; as also know how to cheat ignorant Strangers with a certain Mixture like it. Several of our Men bought such of them for a small Purchase. Captain *Weldon* also about this time touched at some of these Islands, to the North of the Island where we lay; and I saw a great deal of such Ambergreece, that one of his Men bought there; but it was not good, having no smell at all. Yet I saw some there very good and fragrant.

¶ At that Island where Captain *Weldon* was, there were two Fryars sent thither to convert the *Indians*. One of them came away with Captain *Weldon*; the other remained there still. He that came away with Captain *Weldon* gave a very good Character of the Inhabitants of that Island, *viz.* that they were very honest, civil, harmless People; That they were not addicted to Quarrelling, Theft, or Murder; That they did marry, or at least live as Man and Wife, one Man with one Woman, never changing till Death made the Separation; That they were punctual and honest in performing their Bargains; And that they were inclined to receive the Christian Religion. This Relation I had afterwards from the Mouth of a Priest at *Tonqueen*, who told me that he received this Information by a Letter from the Fryar that Capt. *Weldon* brought away from thence. But to proceed.

¶ The 5th Day of *May* we ran down on the West-side of the Island *Nicobar*, properly so called, and anchored at the N.W. end of it, in a small

Bay, in eight Fathom Water, not half a Mile from the Shore. The Body of this Island is in 7 d. 30 m. North Lat. It is about 12 Leagues long, and 3 or 4 broad. The South-end of it is pretty high, with steep Cliffs against the Sea; the rest of the Island is low, flat, and even. The Mold of it is black, and deep; and it is very well watered with small running Streams. It produceth abundance of tall Trees, fit for any uses; for the whole bulk of it seems to be but one entire Grove. But that which adds most to its Beauty off at Sea, are the many Spots of Coco-nut Trees which grow round it in every small Bay. The Bays are half a Mile, or a Mile long, more or less; and these Bays are intercepted, or divided from each other, with as many little rocky Points of Wood-land.

¶ As the Coco-nut Trees do thus grow in Groves, fronting to the Sea, in the Bays, so there is another sort of Fruit-Trees in the Bays, bordering on the back-side of the Coco-Trees, farther from the Sea. It is called by the Natives, a Melory-Tree. This Tree is as big as our large Apple-Trees, and as high. It hath a blackish Rind, and a pretty broad Leaf. The Fruit is as big as the Bread-fruit at *Guam*, described in Chapter X. or a large Penny-Loaf. It is shaped like a Pear, and hath a pretty tough smooth Rind, of a light green Colour. The inside of the Fruit is in Substance much like an Apple; but full of small Strings, as big as a brown Thread. I did never see of these Trees any where but here.

¶ The Natives of this Island are tall well-limb'd Men; pretty long visaged, with black Eyes; their Noses middle proportioned, and the whole Symmetry of their Faces agreeing very well. Their Hair is black and lank, and their Skins of a dark Copper-colour. The Women have no Hair on their Eye-brows. I do believe it is pluck'd up by the Roots; for the Men had Hair growing on their Eye-brows, as other People.

¶ The Men go all naked, save only a long narrow piece of Cloath, or Sash, which going round their Wastes, and thence down between their Thighs, is brought up behind, and tuck'd in at that part which goes about the Waste. The Women have a kind of a short Petticoat reaching from their Waste to their Knees.

¶ Their Language was different from any that I had ever heard before; yet they had some few *Malayan* words, and some of them had a word or two of *Portuguese*; which probably they might learn aboard of their Ships, passing by this place: for when these Men see a Sail, they do presently go aboard of them in their Canoas. I did not perceive any Form of Religion that they had; they had neither Temple, nor Idol, nor any manner of outward veneration to any Deity, that I did see.

¶ They inhabit all round the Island by the Sea-side, in the Bays; there being four or five Houses, more or less, in each Bay. Their Houses are built on Posts, as the *Mindanayans* are. They are small, low, and of a square form. There is but one Room in each House, and this Room is about eight Foot from the Ground; and from thence the Roof is raised about eight Foot higher. But instead of a sharp ridge, the top is exceeding neatly arched with small Rafters about the bigness of a Man's Arm, bent round like a Half-Moon, and very curiously thatch'd with Palmeto-leaves.

¶ They live under no Government that I could perceive; for they seem to be equal, without any distinction; every Man ruling in his own House. Their Plantations are only those Coco-nut Trees which grow by the Sea-side; there being no cleared Land farther in on the Island: for I observ'd that when past the Fruit-Trees, there were no Paths to be seen going into the Woods. The greatest use which they make of their Coco-Trees is to draw *Toddy* from them, of which they are very fond.

¶ The Melory Trees seem to grow wild; they have great earthen Pots to boil the Melory Fruit in, which will hold 12 or 14 Gallons. These Pots they fill with the Fruit; and putting in a little Water, they cover the Mouth of the Pot with Leaves, to keep the steem while it boils. When the Fruit is soft they peel off the Rind, and scrape the Pulp from the strings with a flat stick made like a Knife; and then make it up in great lumps, as big as a *Holland* Cheese; and then it will keep six or seven Days. It looks yellow, and tastes well, and is their chiefest Food: For they have no Yams, Potatoes, Rice, nor Plantains (except a very few;) yet they have a few small Hogs, and a very few Cocks and Hens like ours. The Men imploy themselves in Fishing; but I did not see much Fish that they got: Every House hath at least two or three Canoas belonging to it, which they draw up ashore.

¶ The Canoas that they go a fishing in are sharp at both ends; and both the sides and the bottom are very thin and smooth. They are shaped somewhat like the Proes at *Guam*, with one side flattish, and the other with a pretty big belly; and they have small slight Outlagers on one side. Being thus thin and light they are better managed with Oars than with Sails: Yet they sail well enough, and are steered with a Paddle. There commonly go 20 or 30 Men in one of these Canoas; and seldom fewer than 9 or 10. Their Oars are short, and they do not paddle but row with them as we do. The Benches they sit on when they row are made of split Bamboes, laid a-cross, and so neat together, that they look like a Deck. The Bamboes lie moveable; so that when any go in to row they take up a Bambo in the place where they would sit; and lay it by to make room for their Legs. The Canoas of those of the rest of these Islands were like those of *Nicobar*: and probably they were alike in other things; for we saw no difference at all in the Natives of them, who came hither while we were here.

¶ But to proceed with our Affairs: It was, as I said before, the 5th Day of *May*, about 10 in the Morning, when we anchored at this Island: Captain *Read* immediately ordered his Men to heel the Ship in order to clean her: which was done this Day and the next. All the Water-Vessels were fill'd they intended to go to Sea at Night: for the Winds being yet at N.N.E. the Captain was in hopes to get over to Cape *Comorin* before the Wind shifted. Otherwise it would have been somewhat difficult for him to get thither, because the westerly Monsoon was not at hand.

¶ I thought now was my time to make my Escape, by getting leave, if possible, to stay here: for it seémed not very feazable to do it by stealth; and I had no reason to despair of getting leave: this being a place where my stay could, probably, do our Crew no harm, should I design it. Indeed one reason that put me on the thoughts of staying at this particular place, besides the present opportunity of leaving Captain *Read*, which I did always intend to do as soon as I could, was that I had here also a prospect of advancing a profitable Trade for Ambergreece with these People, and of gaining a considerable Fortune to my self: For in a short time I might have learned their Language, and by accustoming my self to row with them in the Proes or Canoas, especially by conforming my self to their Customs and Manners of Living, I should have seen how they got their Ambergreece, and have known what quantities they get, and the time of the Year when most is found. And then afterwards I thought it would be easie for me to have transported my self from thence, either in some Ship that past this way, whether *English*, *Dutch*, or *Portuguese*; or else to have gotten one of the Young Men of the Island, to have gone with me in one of their Canoas to *Achin*; and there to have furnished my self with such Commodities, as I found most coveted by them; and therewith, at my return, to have bought their Ambergreece.

¶ I had, till this time, made no open show of going ashore here: but now, the Water being fill'd, and the Ship in a readiness to sail, I desired Captain *Read* to set me ashore on this Island. He, supposing that I could not go ashore in a place less frequented by Ships than this, gave me leave: which probably he would have refused to have done, if he thought I should have gotten from hence in any short time; for fear of my giving an account of him to the *English* or *Dutch*. I soon got up my Chest and Bedding, and immediately got some to row me ashore; for fear lest his mind should change again.

¶ The Canoa that brought me ashore, landed me on a small sandy Bay, where there were two Houses, but no Person in them. For the Inhabitants were removed to some other House, probably, for fear of us; because the Ship was close by: and yet both Men and Women came aboard the Ship without any sign of fear. When our Ship's Canoa was going aboard again, they met the Owner of the Houses coming ashore in his Boat. He made a great many signs to them to fetch me off again: but they would not understand him. Then he came to me, and offered his Boat to carry me off; but I refused it. Then he made signs for me to go up into the House, and, according as I did understand him by his signs, and a few *Malayan* words that he used, he intimated that somewhat would come out of the Woods in the Night, when I was asleep, and kill me, meaning probably some wild Beast. Then I carried my Chest and Cloaths up into the House.

¶ I had not been ashore an Hour before Captain *Teat* and one *John Damarel*, with three or four armed Men more, came to fetch me aboard again. They need not have sent an armed *Posse* for me; for had they but sent the Cabbin-boy ashore for me, I would not have denied going aboard. For tho' I could have hid my self in the Woods, yet then they would have abused, or have killed some of the Natives, purposely to incense them against me. I told them therefore that I was ready to go with them, and went aboard with all my Things.

¶ When I came aboard I found the Ship in an uproar; for there were three Men more, who taking Courage by my Example, desired leave also to accompany me. One of them was the Surgeon Mr. *Coppinger*, the other was Mr. *Robert Hall*, and one named *Ambrose*; I have forgot his Sirname. These Men had always harboured the same Designs as I had. The two last were not much opposed; but Captain *Read* and his Crew would not part with the Surgeon. At last the Surgeon leapt into the Canoa, and taking up my Gun, swore he would go ashore, and that if any Man did oppose it, he would shoot him: But *John Oliver*, who was then Quartermaster, leapt into the Canoa, taking hold of him, took away the Gun, and with the Help of two or three more, they dragged him again into the Ship.

¶ Then Mr. *Hall* and *Ambrose* and I were again sent ashore; and one of the Men that rowed us ashore stole an Ax, and gave it to us, knowing it was a good Commodity with the *Indians*. It was now dark, therefore we lighted a Candle, and I being the oldest Stander in our new Country, conducted them into one of the Houses, where we did presently hang up our Hammocks. We had scarce done this before the Canoa came ashore again, and brought the four *Malayan* Men belonging to *Achin*, (which we took in the Proe we took off of *Sumatra*) and the *Portuguese* that came to our Ship out of the *Siam* Jonk at *Pulo Condore*: The Crew having no occasion for these, being leaving the *Malayan* Parts, where the *Portuguese* Spark served as an Interpreter; and not fearing now that the *Achinese* could be serviceable to us in bringing us over to their Country, forty Leagues off; nor imagining that we durst make such an Attempt, as indeed it was a bold one. Now we were Men enough to defend our selves against the Natives of this Island, if they should prove our Enemies: though if none of these Men had come ashore to me, I should not have feared any Danger: Nay, perhaps less, because I should have been cautious of giving any Offence to the Natives. And I am of the Opinion, that there are no People in the World so barbarous as to kill a single Person that falls accidentally into their Hands, or comes to live among them; except they have before been injured, by some Outrage or Violence committed against them. Yet even then, or afterwards, if a Man could but preserve his Life from their first Rage, and come to treat with them, (which is the hardest thing, because their way is usually to abscond, and rushing suddenly upon their Enemy to kill him at unawares) one might, by some slight, insinuate one's self into their Favours again; especially by shewing some Toy or Knack that they did never see before: which any *European*, that has seen the World, might soon contrive to amuse them withal: as might be done, generally even with a lit-Fire struck with a Flint and Steel.

¶ As for the common Opinion of *Authropophagi*, or Man-eaters, I did never meet with any such People: All Nations or Families in the World, that I have seen or heard of, having some sort of Food to live on, either Fruit, Grain, Pulse or Roots, which grow naturally, or else planted by them; if not Fish and Land-Animals besides; (yea, even the People of *New-Holland* had Fish amidst all their Penury) and would scarce kill a Man purposely to eat him. I know not what barbarous Customs may formerly have been in the World; and to sacrifice their Enemies to their Gods, is a thing hath been much talked of, with Relation to the Savages of *America*. I am a Stranger to that also, if it be, or have been customary in any Nation there; and yet, if they sacrifice their Enemies, it is not necessary they should eat them too. After all, I will not be peremptory in the Negative, but I speak as to the Compass of my own Knowledge, and know some of these Cannibal Stories to be false, and many of them have been disproved since I first went to the *West-Indies*. At that time how barbarous were the poor *Florida Indians* accounted, which now we find to be civil enough? What strange Stories have we heard of the *Indians*, whose Islands were called the Isles of *Cannibals*? Yet we find that they do trade very civilly with the *French* and *Spaniards*; and have done so with us. I do own that they have formerly endeavoured to destroy our Plantations at *Barbadoes*, and have since hindred us from settling in the Island *Santa Loca* by destroying two or three Colonies successively of those that were settled there; and even the Island *Tabago* has been often annoyed and ravaged by them, when settled by the *Dutch*, and still lies waste (though a delicate fruitful Island) as being too near the *Caribbees* on the Continent, who visit it every Year. But this was to preserve their own right, by endeavouring to keep out any that would settle themselves on those Islands, where they had planted themselves; yet even these People would not hurt a single Person, as I have been told by some that have been Prisoners among them. I could instance also in the *Indians* of *Bocca Toro*, and *Bocca Drago*, and many other Places where they do live, as the *Spaniards* call it, wild and savage: yet there they have been familiar with Privateers, but by Abuses have withdrawn their Friendship again. As for these *Nicobar* People, I found them affable enough, and therefore I did not fear them; but I did not much care whether I had gotten any more Company or no.

⁋ But however I was very well satisfied, and the rather, because we were now Men enough to row our selves over to the Island *Sumatra*; and accordingly we presently consulted how to purchase a Canoa of the Natives.

⁋ It was a fine clear Moon-light Night, in which we were left ashore. Therefore we walked on the sandy Bay to watch when the Ship would weigh and be gone, not thinking our selves secure in our new-gotten Liberty till then. About Eleven or Twelve a-Clock we saw her under Sail, and then we returned to our Chamber, and so to sleep. This was the 6th of *May*.

⁋ The next Morning betimes, our Landlord, with four or five of his Friends, came to see his new Guests, and was somewhat surprized to see so many of us, for he knew of no more but my self. Yet he seemed to be very well pleased, and entertain'd us with a large Calabash of Toddy, which he brought with him. Before he went away again, (for wheresoever we came they left their Houses to us, but whether out of Fear or Superstition I know not) we bought a Canoa of him for an Ax, and we did presently put our Chests and Cloaths in it, designing to go to the South-end of the Island, and lye there till the Monsoon shifted, which we expected every Day.

⁋ When our Things were stowed away, we with the *Achinese* entered with

Joy into our new Frigot, and launched off from the Shore. We were no sooner off, but our Canoa overset, bottom upwards. We preserved our Lives well enough by swimming, and dragg'd also our Chests and Cloaths ashore; but all our things were wet. I had nothing of value but my Journal and some Drafts of Land of my own taking, which I much prized, and which I had hitherto carefully preserved. Mr. *Hall* had also such another Cargo of Books and Drafts, which were now like to perish. But we presently opened our Chests and took out our Books, which, with much ado, we did afterwards dry; but some of our Drafts that lay loose in our Chests were spoiled.

¶ We lay here afterwards three Days, making great Fires to dry our Books. The *Achinese* in the mean time fixt our Canoa, with Outlagers on each side; and they also cut a good Mast for her, and made a substantial Sail with Mats.

¶ The Canoa being now very well fixt, and our Books and Cloaths dry, we launched out a second time, and rowed towards the East-side of the Island, leaving many Islands to the North of us. The *Indians* of the Island accompanied us with eight or ten Canoas against our desire; for we thought that these Men would make Provision dearer at that side of the Island we were going to, by giving an account what rates we gave for it at the Place from whence we came, which was owing to the Ship's being there; for the Ship's Crew were not so thrifty in bargaining (as they seldom are) as single Persons, or a few Men might be apt to be, who would keep to one bargain. Therefore to hinder them from going with us, Mr. *Hall* scared one Canoa's Crew by firing a shot over them. They all leapt over-board, and cried out, but seeing us row away, they got into their Canoa again and came after us.

¶ The firing of that Gun made all the Inhabitants of the Island to be our Enemies. For presently after this we put ashore at a Bay where were four Houses, and a great many Canoas: But they all went away, and came near us no more for several Days. We had then a great Loaf of Melory which was our constant Food; and if we had a mind to Coco-Nuts, or Toddy, our *Malayans* of *Achin* would climb the Trees, and fetch as many Nuts as we would have, and a good Pot of Toddy every Morning. Thus we lived till our Melory was almost spent; being still in hopes that the Natives would come to us, and sell it as they had formerly done. But they came not to us; nay, they opposed us where-ever we came, and often shaking their Lances at us, made all the shew of Hatred that they could invent.

¶ At last, when we saw that they stood in Opposition to us, we resolved to use Force to get some of their Food, if we could not get it other ways. With this Resolution we went into our Canoa to a small Bay on the North-part of the Island; because it was smooth Water there and good landing; but on the other side, the Wind being yet on that Quarter, we could not land without Jeopardy of oversetting our Canoa, and wetting our Arms, and then we must have lain at the Mercy of our Enemies, who stood 2 or 300 Men in every Bay, where they saw us coming, to keep us off.

¶ When we set out, we rowed directly to the North-end, and presently were followed by seven or eight of their Canoas. They keeping at a distance, rowed away faster than we did, and got to the Bay before us; and there, with about 20 more Canoas full of Men, they all landed, and stood to hinder us from landing. But we rowed in, within a hundred Yards of them. Then we lay still, and I took my Gun, and presented at them; at which they all fell down flat on the Ground. But I turn'd my self about, and to shew that we did not intend to harm them, I fired my Gun off towards the Sea; so that they might see the Shot graze on the Water. As soon as my Gun was loaded again, we rowed gently in; at which some of them withdrew. The rest standing up, did still cut and hew the Air, making Signs of their Hatred; till I once more frighted them with my Gun, and discharged it as before. Then more of them sneak'd away, leaving only five or six Men on the Bay. Then we rowed in again, and Mr. *Hall* taking his Sword in his Hand, leapt ashore; and I stood ready with my Gun to fire at the *Indians*, if they had injur'd him: But they did not stir, till he came to them and saluted them.

¶ He shook them by the Hand, and by such Signs of Friendship as he made, the Peace was concluded, ratified and confirmed by all that were present: And others that were gone, were again call'd back, and they all very joyfully accepted of a Peace. This became universal over all the Island, to the great joy of the Inhabitants. There was no ringing of Bells nor Bonfires made, for that is not the Custom here; but Gladness appeared in their Countenances, for now they could go out and fish again, without fear of being taken. This Peace was not more welcome to them than to us; for now the Inhabitants brought their Melory again to us; which we bought for old Rags, and small stripes of Cloath, about as broad as the Palm of one's Hand. I did not see above five or six Hens, for they have but few on the Island. At some places we saw some small Hogs, which we could have bought of them reasonably; but we would not offend our *Achinese* Friends, who were Mahometans.

¶ We stayed here two or three Days and then rowed toward the South-end of the Island, keeping on the East-side, and we were kindly received by the Natives where-ever we came. When we arrived at the South-end of the Island, we fitted our selves with Melory and Water. We bought three or four Loaves of Melory, and about twelve large Coco-nut-shells, that had all the Kernel taken out, yet were preserved whole, except only a small hole at one end; and all these held for us about three Gallons and a half of Water. We bought also two or three Bamboes, that held about four or five Gallons more: This was our Sea-store.

¶ We now designed to go for *Achin*, a Town on the N.W. end of the Island *Sumatra*, distant from hence about 40 Leagues, bearing South-South-East. We only waited for the western Monsoon, which we had expected a great while, and now it seemed to be at Hand; for the Clouds began to hang their Heads to the eastward, and at last moved gently that way; and though the Wind was still at East, yet this was an infallible Sign that the western Monsoon was nigh.

CHAPTER XVIII

The Author, with some others put to Sea in an open Boat, designing for Achin. *Their Accommodations for their Voyage. Change of Weather; a Halo about the Sun, and a violent Storm. Their great Danger and Distress.* Cudda, *a Town and Harbour on the Coast of* Malacca. Pulo Way. *Golden Mountain on the Isle of* Sumatra: *River and Town of* Passange-Jonca *on* Sumatra, *near* Diamond-point; *where they go ashore very sick, and are kindly entertained by the* Oromkay, *and Inhabitants. They go thence to* Achin. *The Author is examined before the* Shabander; *and takes Physick of a* Malayan *Doctor. His long Illness. He sets out towards* Nicobar *again, but returns suddenly to* Achin *Road. He makes several Voyages thence, to* Tonqueen, *to* Malacca, *to* Fort St. George, *and to* Bencouli, *an English Factory on* Sumatra. *An Account of the Ship's Crew who set the Author ashore at* Nicobar. *Some go to* Trangambar, *a Danish Fort on* Coromandel; *others to* Fort St. George; *many to the* Mogul's Camp. *Of the* Peuns; *and how* John Oliver *made himself a Captain.* Capt. Read, *with the rest, having plundered a rich* Portuguese *Ship near* Ceylon, *goes to* Madagascar, *and ships himself off thence in a* New-York *Ship. The Traverses of the rest to* Johanna, &c. *Their Ship, the* Cygnet *of* London, *now lies sunk in* Augustin Bay *at* Madagascar. *Of Prince* Jeoly *the painted Man, whom the Author brought with him to* England, *and who died at* Oxford. *Of his Country the Isle of* Meangis; *the Cloves there,* &c. *The Author is made Gunner of* Bencouli, *but is forced to slip away from thence to come for* England.

I T was the 15th Day of *May* 1688, about four a Clock in the Afternoon, when we left *Nicobar* Island, directing our Course towards *Achin*, being eight Men of us in Company, *viz.* three *English*, four *Malayans*, who were born at *Achin*, and the mungrel *Portuguese*.

¶ Our Vessel, the *Nicobar* Canoa, was not one of the biggest, nor of the least size: She was much about the Burden of one of our *London* Wherries below Bridge, and built sharp at both ends, like the fore-part of a Wherry. She was deeper than a Wherry, but not so broad, and was so thin and light, that when empty, four Men could launch her, or hale her ashore on a sandy Bay. We had a good substantial Mast, and a Mat Sail, and good Outlagers lash'd very fast and firm on each side the Vessel, being made of strong Poles. So that while these continued firm the Vessel could not overset, which she would easily have done without them, and with them too had they not been made very strong; and we were therefore much beholding to our *Achinese* Companions for this Contrivance.

¶ These Men were none of them so sensible of the Danger as Mr. *Hall* and my self, for they all confided so much in us, that they did not so much as scruple any thing that we did approve of. Neither was Mr. *Hall* so well provided as I was, for before we left the Ship, I had purposely consulted our Draft of the *East-Indies*, (for we had but one in the Ship) and out of that I had written in my Pocket-book an account of the bearing and distance of all the *Malacca* Coast, and that of *Sumatra*, *Pegu*, and *Siam*, and also brought away with me a Pocket-Compass for my Direction in any Enterprize that I should undertake.

¶ The Weather at our setting out was very fair, clear and hot. The Wind was still at S.E. a very small Breeze, just fanning the Air, and the Clouds were moving gently from West to East, which gave us hopes that the Winds were either at West already abroad at Sea, or would be so in a very short time. We took this Opportunity of fair Weather, being in hopes to accomplish our Voyage to *Achin*, before the western Monsoon was set in strong, knowing that we should have very blustering Weather after this fair Weather, especially at the first coming of the western Monsoon.

¶ We rowed therefore away to the Southward, supposing that when we were clear from the Island we should have a true Wind, as we call it; for the Land hales the Wind; and we often find the Wind at Sea different from what it is near the Shore. We rowed with four Oars, taking our turns: Mr. *Hall* and I steered also by turns, for none of the rest were capable of it. We rowed the first Afternoon, and the Night ensuing, about twelve Leagues by my Judgment. Our Course was South-South-East; but the 16th Day in the Morning, when the Sun was an Hour high, we saw the Island from whence we came, bearing N.W. by N. Therefore I found we had gone a point more to the East than I intended, for which reason we steered S. by E.

¶ In the Afternoon at 4 a Clock, we had a gentle Breeze at W.S.W. which continued so till nine, all which time we laid down our Oars, and steered away S.S.E. I was then at the Helm, and I found by the ripling of the Sea, that there was a strong Current against us. It made a great noise that might be heard near half a Mile. At 9 a Clock it fell calm, and so continued till ten. Then the Wind sprung up again, and blew a fresh Breeze all Night.

¶ The 17th Day in the Morning we lookt out for the Island *Sumatra*, supposing that we were now within 20 Leagues of it; for we had rowed and sailed, by our reckoning, 24 Leagues from *Nicobar* Island; and the distance from *Nicobar* to *Achin* is about 40 Leagues. But we lookt in vain for the Island *Sumatra*; for turning our selves about, we saw, to our Grief, *Nicobar* Island lying W.N.W. and not above eight Leagues distant. By this it was visible, that we had met a very strong Current against us in the Night. But the Wind freshned on us, and we made the best use of it while the Weather continued fair. At Noon we had an Observation of the Sun, my lat. was 6 d. 55 m. and Mr. *Hall*'s was 7 d. N.

¶ The 18th Day the Wind freshned on us again, and the Sky began to be clouded. It was indifferent clear till Noon, and we thought to have had an Observation; but we were hindered by the Clouds that covered the Face of the Sun, when it came on the Meridian. This often happens that we are disappointed of making Observations, by the Sun's being clouded at Noon, though it shines clear both before and after, especially in Places near the Sun; and this obscuring of the Sun at Noon, is commonly sudden and unexpected, and for about half an Hour or more.

¶ We had then also a very ill Presage, by a great Circle about the Sun (five or six times the Diameter of it) which seldom appears, but storms of Wind, or much Rain ensue. Such Circles about the Moon are more frequent, but of less import. We do commonly take great notice of these that are about the Sun, observing if there be any Breach in the Circle, and in what Quarter the Breach is; for from thence we commonly find the greatest Stress of the Wind will come. I must confess that I was a little anxious at the sight of this Circle, and wish'd heartily that we were near some Land. Yet I shewed no sign of it to discourage any Consorts, but made a Virtue of Necessity, and put a good Countenance on the Matter.

¶ I told Mr. *Hall*, that if the Wind became too strong and violent, as I feared it would, it being even then very strong, we must of necessity steer away before the Wind and Sea, till better Weather presented; and that as the Winds were now, we should, instead of about twenty Leagues to

Achin, be driven sixty or seventy Leagues to the Coast of *Cudda* or *Queda*, a Kingdom, and Town, and Harbour of Trade on the Coast of *Malacca*.

¶ The Winds therefore bearing very hard, we rolled up the Foot of our Sail on a Pole fastned to it, and settled our Yard within three Foot of the Canoa sides, so that we had now but a small Sail; yet it was still too big, considering the Wind; for the Wind being on our Broad-side, prest her down very much, though supported by her Outlagers; insomuch that the Poles of the Outlagers going from the Sides of their Vessel, bent as if they would break; and should they have broken, our overturning and perishing had been inevitable. Besides, the Sea encreasing, would soon have filled the Vessel this way. Yet thus we made a shift to bear up with the side of the Vessel against the Wind for a while: But the Wind still increasing, about One a-Clock in the Afternoon we put away right before Wind and Sea, continuing to run thus all the Afternoon, and part of the Night ensuing. The Wind continued increasing all the Afternoon, and the Sea still swelled higher, and often broke, but did us no damage; for the Ends of the Vessel being very narrow, he that steered received and broke the Sea on his Back, and so kept it from coming in so much as to endanger the Vessel: Though much Water would come in, which we were forced to keep heaving out continually. And by this time we saw it was well that we had altered our Course, every Wave would else have filled and sunk us, taking the side of the Vessel: And though our Outlagers were well lash'd down to the Canoas Bottom with Rattans, yet they must probably have yielded to such a Sea as this; when even before they were plunged under Water, and bent like Twigs.

¶ The Evening of this 18th Day was very dismal. The Sky look'd very black, being covered with dark Clouds, the Wind blew hard, and the Seas ran high. The Sea was already roaring in a white Foam about us; a dark Night coming on, and no Land in sight to shelter us, and our little Ark in danger to be swallowed by every Wave; and, what was worst of all, none of us thought our selves prepared for another World. The Reader may better guess than I can express, the Confusion that we were all in. I had been in many imminent Dangers before now, some of which I have already related, but the worst of them all was but a Play-game in comparison with this. I must confess that I was in great Conflicts of Mind at this time. Other Dangers came not upon me with such a leisurely and dreadful Solemnity. A sudden Skirmish or Engagement, or so, was nothing when one's Blood was up, and pushed forwards with eager Expectations. But here I had a lingring View of approaching Death, and little or no hopes of escaping it; and I must confess that my Courage, which I had hitherto kept up, failed me here; and I made very sad Reflections on my former Life, and looked back with Horrour and Detestation on Actions which before I disliked, but now I trembled at the remembrance of. I had long before this repented me of that roving Course of Life, but never with such Concern as now. I did also call to mind the many miraculous Acts of God's Providence towards me in the whole Course of my Life, of which kind I believe few Men have met with the like. For all these I returned Thanks in a peculiar Manner, and this once more desired God's Assistance, and composed my Mind as well as I could in the Hopes of it, and as the Event shew'd, I was not disappointed of my Hopes.

¶ Submitting our selves therefore to God's good Providence, and taking all the Care we could to preserve our Lives, Mr. *Hall* and I took turns to steer, and the rest took turns to heave out the Water, and thus we provided to spend the most doleful Night I ever was in. About Ten a-Clock it began to thunder, lighten and rain; but the Rain was very welcome to us, having drank up all the Water we brought from the Island.

¶ The Wind at first blew harder than before, but within half an Hour it abated, and became more moderate; and the Sea also assuaged of its Fury; and then by a lighted Match, of which we kept a Piece burning on purpose, we looked on our Compass, to see how we steered, and found our Course to be still East. We had no occasion to look on the Compass before, for we steered right before the Wind, which if it shifted we had been obliged to have altered our Course accordingly. But now it being abated, we found our Vessel lively enough with that small Sail which was then aboard, to hale to our former Course S.S.E. which accordingly we did, being now in hopes again to get to the Island *Sumatra*.

¶ But about Two a-Clock in the Morning of the 19th Day, we had another Gust of Wind, with much Thunder, Lightning and Rain, which lasted till Day, and obliged us to put before the Wind again, steering thus for several Hours. It was very dark, and the hard Rain soaked us so thoroughly, that we had not one dry Thread about us. The Rain chill'd us extreamly; for any fresh Water is much colder than that of the Sea. For even in the coldest Climates the Sea is warm, and in the hottest Climates the Rain is cold and unwholsome for Man's Body. In this wet starveling Plight we spent the tedious Night. Never did poor Mariners on a Lee-shore more earnestly long for the dawning Light than we did now. At length the Day appeared; but with such dark black Clouds near the Horizon, that the first Glimpse of the Dawn appeared 30 or 40 Degrees high; which was dreadful enough; for it is a common Saying among

Seamen, and true, as I have experienc'd, that a *high Dawn* will have *high Winds*, and a *low Dawn small Winds*.

¶ We continued our Course still East, before Wind and Sea, till about Eight a-Clock in the Morning of this 19th Day; and then one of our *Malayan* Friends cried out, *Pulo Way*. Mr. *Hall*, and *Ambrose* and I, thought the Fellow had said *Pull away*, an Expression usual among *English* Seamen when they are rowing. And we wondered what he meant by it, till we saw him point to his Consorts; and then we looking that way, saw Land appearing, like an Island, and all our *Maylayans* said it was an Island at the N.W. end of *Sumatra*, called *Way*; for *Pulo Way* is the Island *Way*. We, who were dropping with wet, cold and hungry, were all over-joyed at the Sight of the Land, and presently marked its bearing. It bore South, and the Wind was still at West, a strong Gale; but the Sea did not run so high as in the Night. Therefore we trimmed our small Sail no bigger than an Apron, and steered with it. Now our Outlagers did us a great Kindness again, for although we had but a small Sail, yet the Wind was strong, and prest down our Vessel's Side very much: But being supported by the Outlagers, we could brook it well enough, which otherwise we could not have done.

¶ About Noon we saw more Land beneath the supposed *Pulo Way*; and steering towards it, before Night we saw all the Coast of *Sumatra*, and found the Errors of our *Achinese*; for the high Land that we first saw, which then appear'd like an Island, was not *Pulo Way*, but a great high Mountain on the Island *Sumatra*, called by the *English*, the *Golden Mountain*. Our Wind continued till about Seven a-Clock at Night; then it abated, and at Ten a-Clock it died away: And then we stuck to our Oars again, though all of us quite tired with our former Fatigues and Hardships.

¶ The next Morning, being the 20th Day, we saw all the low Land plain, and judged ourselves not above eight Leagues off. About Eight a-Clock in the Morning we had the Wind again at West, a fresh Gale, and steering in still for the Shore, at Five a-Clock in the Afternoon we run to the Mouth of a River on the Island *Sumatra*, called *Passange Jonca*. It is 34 Leagues to the Eastward of *Achin*, and six Leagues to the West of *Diamond Point*, which makes with three Angles of a Rhombus, and is low Land.

¶ Our *Malayans* were very well acquainted here, and carried us to a small Fishing Village, within a Mile of the River's Mouth, called also by the Name of the River *Passange Jonca*. The Hardships of this Voyage, with the scorching Heat of the Sun at our first setting out, and the cold Rain, and our continuing wet for the last two Days, cast us all into Fevers, so that now we were not able to help each other, nor so much as to get our Canoa up to the Village; but our *Malayans* got some of the Townsmen to bring her up.

¶ The News of our Arrival being noised abroad, one of the *Oramki*'s, or Noblemen of the Island, came in the Night to see us. We were then lying in a small Hut at the end of the Town, and it being late, this Lord only viewed us, and having spoken with our *Malayans*, went away again; but he returned to us again the next Day, and provided a large House for us to live in, till we should be recovered of our Sickness, ordering the Towns-People to let us want for nothing. The *Achinese Malayans* that came with us, told them all the Circumstances of our Voyage; how they were taken by our Ship, and where, and how we that came with them were Prisoners aboard the Ship, and had been set ashore together at *Nicobar*, as they were. It was for this reason probably, that the Gentlemen of *Sumatra* were thus extraordinary kind to us, to provide every thing that we had need of; nay, they would force us to accept of Presents from them, that we knew not what to do with; as young Buffaloes, Goats, &c. for these we would turn loose at Night, after the Gentlemen that gave them to us were gone, for we were prompted by our *Achinese* Consorts to accept of them, for fear of disobliging by our Refusal. But the Coco-Nuts, Plantains, Fowls, Eggs, Fish, and Rice, we kept for our use. The *Malayans* that accompanied us from *Nicobar*, separated themselves from us now, living at one end of the House by themselves, for they were *Mahometans*, as all those of the Kingdom of *Achin* are; and though during our Passage by Sea together, we made them be contented to drink their Water out of the same Coco-shell with us; yet being now no longer under that Necessity, they again took up their accustomed Nicety and Reservedness. They all lay sick, and as their Sickness increased, one of them threatned us, that if any of them died, the rest would kill us, for having brought them this Voyage; yet I question whether they would have attempted, or the Country People have suffered it. We made a shift to dress our own Food, for none of these People, though they were very kind in giving us any thing that we wanted, would yet come near us, to assist us in dressing our Victuals: Nay, they would not touch any thing that we used. We had all Fevers, and therefore took turns to dress Victuals, according as we had Strength to do it, or Stomachs to eat it. I found my Fever to increase, and my Head so distempered, that I could scarce stand, therefore I whetted and sharpned my Penknife, in order to let my self Blood; but I could not, for my Knife was too blunt.

¶ We stayed here ten or twelve Days, in hopes to recover our Health, but finding no Amendment, we desired to go to *Achin*. But we were delayed by the Natives, who had a desire to have kept Mr. *Hall* and my self to sail in their Vessels to *Malacca, Cudda,* or to other Places whither they Trade. But finding us more desirous to be with our Countrymen in our Factory at *Achin*, they provided a large Proe to carry us thither, we not being able to manage our own Canoa. Besides, before this, three of our *Malayan* Comrades were gone very sick into the Country, and only one of them and the *Portuguese* remained with us, accompanying us to *Achin*, and they both as sick as we.

¶ It was the Beginning of *June*, 1686, [*sic*] when we left *Passange Jonca*. We had four Men to row, one to steer, and a Gentleman of the Country, that went purposely to give an Information to the Government of our Arrival. We were but three Days and Nights in our Passage, having Sea-breezes by Day, and Land-winds by Night, and very fair Weather.

¶ When we arrived at *Achin*, I was carried before the *Shebander*, the chief Magistrate in the City. One Mr. *Dennis Driscal*, an *Irishman*, and a Resident there, in the Factory which our *East-India* Company had there then, was Interpreter. I being weak, was suffered to stand in the *Shebander*'s Presence: For it is their custom to make Men sit on the Floor, as they do, cross-legg'd like Taylors: But I had not strength then to pluck up my Heels in that manner. The *Shebander* asked of me several Questions, especially how we durst adventure to come in a Canoa from the *Nicobar* Islands to *Sumatra*. I told him, that I had been accustomed to Hardships and Hazards, therefore I did with much Freedom undertake it. He enquired also concerning our Ship, whence she came, &c. I told him, from the *South-Seas*; that she had ranged about the *Philippine* Islands, &c. and was now gone towards *Arabia*, and the *Red-Sea*. The *Malayans* also and *Portuguese* were afterwards examined, and confirmed what I declared, and in less than half an Hour I was dismist with Mr. *Driscal*, who then lived in the *English East-India* Company's Factory. He provided a Room for us to lie in, and some Victuals.

¶ Three Days after our Arrival here, our *Portuguese* died of a Fever. What became of our *Malayans* I know not: *Ambrose* lived not long after, Mr. *Hall* also was so weak, that I did not think he would recover. I was the best; but still very sick of a Fever, and little likely to live. Therefore Mr. *Driscal*, and some other *Englishmen*, persuaded me to take some purging Physick of a *Malayan* Doctor. I took their Advice, being willing to get Ease: But after three Doses, each a large Calabash of nasty stuff, finding no Amendment, I thought to desist from more Physick; but was persuaded to take one Dose more; which I did, and it wrought so violently, that I thought it would have ended my Days. I struggled till I had been about twenty or thirty times at Stool: But it working so quick with me, with little Intermission, and my Strength being almost spent, I even threw my self down once for all, and had above sixty Stools in all before it left off working. I thought my *Malayan* Doctor, whom they so much commended, would have killed me out-right. I continued extraordinary weak for some Days after his drenching me thus: But my Fever left me for above a Week: After which, it returned upon me again for a Twelve Month, and a Flux with it.

¶ However, when I was a little recovered from the Effects of my Drench, I made a shift to go abroad: And having been kindly invited to Capt. *Bowrey*'s House there, my first Visit was to him; who had a Ship in the Road, but lived ashore. This Gentleman was extraordinary kind to us all, particularly to me, and importuned me to go his Boatswain to *Persia*; whither he was bound, with a Design to sell his Ship there, as I was told, though not by himself. From thence he intended to pass with the Caravan to *Aleppo*, and so home for *England*. His Business required him to stay some time longer at *Achin*; I judge, to sell some Commodities that he had not yet disposed of. Yet he chose rather to leave the Disposal of them to some Merchant there, and make a short Trip to the *Nicobar* Islands in the mean time, and on his return to take in his Effects, and so proceed towards *Persia*. This was a sudden Resolution of Capt. *Bowry*'s, presently after the Arrival of a small Frigot from *Siam*, with an Ambassador from the King of *Siam* to the Queen of *Achin*. The Ambassador was a *Frenchman* by Nation. The Vessel that he came in was but small, yet very well mann'd, and fitted for a Fight. Therefore it was generally supposed here, that Captain *Bowry* was afraid to lie in *Achin* Road, because the *Siamers* were now at Wars with the *English*, and he was not able to defend his Ship if he should be attack'd by them.

¶ But whatever made him think of going to the *Nicobar* Islands, he provided to sail; and took me, Mr. *Hall*, and *Ambrose* with him, though all of us so sick and weak, that we could do him no service. It was some time about the Beginning of *June* when we sailed out of *Achin* Road: But we met with the Winds at N.W. with turbulent Weather, which forced us back again in two Days time. Yet he gave us each 12 *Mess* apiece, a Gold Coin, each of which is about the Value of 15*d*. *English*. So he gave over that Design: And some *English* Ships coming into *Achin* Road, he was not afraid of the *Siamers*, who lay there.

¶ After this, he again invited me to his House at *Achin*, and treated me always with Wine and good Cheer, and still importuned me to go with him to *Persia*: But I being very weak, and fearing the westerly Winds would create a great deal of trouble, did not give him a positive Answer; especially because I thought I might get a better Voyage in the *English* Ships newly arrived, or some others now expected here. It was this Captain *Bowry* who sent the Letter from *Borneo*, directed to the Chief of the *English* Factory at *Mindanao*, of which mention is made in Chapter XIII.

¶ A short time after this, Captain *Welden* arrived here from *Fort St. George*, in a Ship called the *Curtana*, bound to *Tonqueen*. This being a more agreeable Voyage than to *Persia*, at this time of the Year; besides, that the Ship was better accommodated, especially with a Surgeon, and I being still sick; I therefore chose rather to serve Captain *Welden* than Captain *Bowry*. But to go on with a particular Account of that Expedition, were to carry my Reader back again: Whom having brought thus far towards *England* in my Circum-Navigation of the Globe, I shall not weary him with new Rambles, nor so much swell this Volume, as I must to describe the Tour I made in those remote Parts of the *East-Indies*, from and to *Sumatra*. So that my Voyage to *Tonqueen* at this time, as also another to *Malacca* afterwards, with my Observations in them, and the Descriptions of those and the neighbouring Countries; as well as the Description of the Island *Sumatra* itself, and therein the Kingdom and City of *Achin*, *Bencouli*, &c. I shall refer to another place, where I may give a particular Relation of them. In short, it may suffice, that I set out to *Tonqueen* with Captain *Welden* about *July* 1688, and returned to *Achin* in the *April* following. I staid here till the latter-end of *September* 1689, and making a short Voyage to *Malacca*, came thither again about *Christmas*. Soon after that, I went to *Fort St. George*, and staying there about five Months, I returned once more to *Sumatra*; not to *Achin*, but *Bencouli*, an *English* Factory on the West Coast; of which I was Gunner about five Months more.

¶ So that having brought my Reader to *Sumatra*, without carrying him back, I shall bring him on next way from thence to *England*: And of all that occurr'd between my first setting out from this Island in 1688, and my final Departure from it at the Beginning of the Year 1691, I shall only take notice at present of two Passages; which I think I ought not to omit.

¶ The first is, that at my return from *Malacca*, a little before *Christmas*, 1689, I found at *Achin* one Mr. *Morgan*, who was one of our Ship's Crew that left me ashoar at *Nicobar*, now Mate of a *Danish* Ship of *Trangambar*; which is a Town on the Coast of *Coromandel*, near Cape *Comarin*, belonging to the *Danes*: And receiving an account of our Crew from him and others, I thought it might not be amiss to gratify the Reader's Curiosity there-with; who would probably be desirous to know the Success of those

Ramblers, in their new-intended Expedition towards the *Red-Seas*. And withal I thought it might not be unlikely that these Papers might fall into the Hands of some of our *London* Merchants, who were concerned in fitting out that Ship; which I said formerly was called the *Cygnet of London*, sent on a Trading Voyage into the *South-Seas*, under the Command of Captain *Swan*: And that they might be willing to have a particular Information of the Fate of their Ship. And by the way, even before this meeting with Mr. *Morgan*, while I was at *Tonqueen*, *Jan.* 1689, I met with an *English* Ship in the River of *Tonqueen*, called the *Rainbow of London*, Captain *Poole* Commander; by whose Mate, Mr. *Barlow*, who was returning in that Ship to *England*, I sent a Pacquet, which he undertook to deliver to the Merchants, Owners of the *Cygnet*, some of which he said he knew: Wherein I gave a particular Account of all the Course and Transactions of their Ship, from the time of my first meeting it in the *South-Seas*, and going aboard it there, to its leaving me ashoar at *Nicobar*. But I never could hear that either that, or other Letters which I sent at the same time, were received.

¶ To proceed therefore with Mr. *Morgan*'s Relation: He told me, That when they in the *Cygnet* went away from *Nicobar*, in pursuit of their intended Voyage to *Persia*, they directed their Course towards *Ceylon*. But not being able to weather it, the westerly Monsoon being hard against them, they were obliged to seek Refreshment on the Coast of *Coromandel*. Here this mad fickle Crew were upon new Projects again. Their Designs meeting with such Delays and Obstructions, that many of them grew weary of it, and about half of them went ashoar. Of this Number, Mr. *Morgan*, who told me this, and Mr. *Herman Coppinger* the Surgeon, went to the *Danes* at *Trangambar*, who kindly received them. There they lived very well; and Mr. *Morgan* was employed as a Mate in a Ship of theirs at this time to *Achin*: and Captain *Knox* tells me, that he since commanded the *Curtana*, the Ship that I went in to *Tonqueen*, which Captain *Welden* having sold to the Mogul's Subjects, they employed Mr. *Morgan* as Captain to trade in her for them; and it is an usual thing for the trading *Indians* to hire *Europeans* to go Officers on board their Ships; especially Captains and Gunners.

¶ About two or three more of these that were set ashore, went to *Fort St. George*; but the main Body of them were for going into the Mogul's Service. Our Seamen are apt to have great Notions of I know not what Profit and Advantages to be had in serving the Mogul; nor do they want for fine Stories to encourage one another to it. It was what these Men had long been thinking and talking of as a fine thing; but now they went upon it in good earnest. The place where they went ashore was at a Town of the *Moors*: Which Name our Seamen give to all the Subjects of the great Mogul, but especially his *Mahometan* Subjects; calling the Idolaters, *Gentous* or *Rashbouts*. At this *Moors* Town they got a Peun to be their Guide to the Mogul's nearest Camp; for he hath always several Armies in his vast Empire.

¶ These Peuns are some of the *Gentous* or *Rashbouts*, who in all places along the Coast, especially in Sea-port Towns, make it their Business to hire themselves to wait upon Strangers, be they Merchants, Seamen, or what they will. To qualify them for such Attendance, they learn the *European* Languages, *English*, *Dutch*, *French*, *Portuguese*, &c. according as they have any of the Factories of these Nations in their Neighbourhood, or are visited by their Ships. No sooner doth any such Ship come to an Anchor, and the Men come ashore, but a great many of these Peuns are ready to proffer their Service. 'Tis usual for the Strangers to hire their Attendance during their Stay there, giving them about a Crown a Month of our Money, more or less. The richest sort of Men will ordinarily hire two or three Peuns to wait upon them; and even the common Seamen, if able, will hire one apiece to attend them, either for Conveniency or Ostentation; or sometimes one Peun between two of them. These Peuns serve them in many Capacities, as Interpreters, Brokers, Servants to attend at Meals, and go to Market and on Errands, &c. Nor do they give any trouble, eating at their own Homes and lodging there; when they have done their Masters Business for them, expecting nothing but their Wages, except that they have a certain Allowance of about a Fanam, or 3*d.* in a Dollar, which is an 18th Part profit, by way of Brokerage for every Bargain they drive; they being generally employed in buying and selling. When the Strangers go away, their Peuns desire them to give them their Names in Writing, with a Certificate of their honest and diligent serving them: And these they shew to the next Comers, to get into Business; some being able to produce a large Scrowl of such Certificates.

¶ But to proceed; the *Moors* Town, where these Men landed, was not far from *Cunnimere*, a small *English* Factory on the *Coromandel* Coast. The Governour whereof having Intelligence by the *Moors* of the landing of these Men, and their intended March to the Mogul's Camp, sent out a Captain with his Company to oppose it. He came up with them, and gave them hard Words: But they being thirty or forty resolute Fellows, not easily daunted, he durst not attack them, but returned to the Governour, and the News of it was soon carried to *Fort St. George*. During their

March, *John Oliver*, who was one of them, privately told the Peun who guided them, that himself was their Captain. So when they came to the Camp, the Peun told this to the General: And when their Stations and Pay were assigned them, *John Oliver* had a greater Respect paid him than the rest; and whereas their Pay was ten Pagodas a Month each Man, (a Pagoda is two Dollars, or 9*s*. *English*) his Pay was twenty Pagodas: Which Stratagem and Usurpation of his, occasioned him no small Envy and Indignation from his Comrades.

¶ Soon after this, two or three of them went to *Agra*, to be of the Mogul's Guard. A while after the Governour of *Fort St. George* sent a Message to the main Body of them, and a Pardon, to withdraw them from thence; which most of them accepted, and came away. *John Oliver*, and the small Remainder, continued in the Country; but leaving the Camp, went up and down plundering the Villages, and fleeing when they were pursued; and this was the last News I heard of them. This Account I had partly by Mr. *Morgan*, from some of those Deserters he met with at *Trangambar*; partly from others of them, whom I met with my self afterwards at *Fort St. George*. And these were the Adventures of those who went up into the Country.

¶ Captain *Read* having thus lost the best half of his Men, sailed away with the rest of them, after having filled his Water, and got Rice, still intending for the *Red-Sea*. When they were near *Ceylon*, they met with a *Portuguese* Ship richly laden, out of which they took what they pleas'd, and then turn'd her away again. From thence they pursu'd their Voyage: but the westerly Winds bearing hard against them, and making it hardly feizable for them to reach the *Red-Sea*, they stood away for *Madagascar*. There they entered into the Service of one of the petty Princes of that Island, to assist him against his Neighbours with whom he was at Wars. During this Interval, a small Vessel from *New-York* came hither to purchase Slaves: Which Trade is driven here, as it is upon the Coast of *Guinea*; one Nation or Clan selling others that are their Enemies. Captain *Read*, with about five or six more, stole away from their Crew, and went aboard this *New-York* Ship; and Captain *Teat* was made Commander of the Residue. Soon after which, a Brigantine from the *West-Indies*, Captain *Knight* Commander, coming thither with a design to go to the *Red-Sea* also, these of the *Cygnet* consorted with them, and they went together to the Island *Johanna*. Thence going together towards the *Red-Sea*, the *Cygnet* proving leaky, and sailing heavily, as being much out of Repair, Captain *Knight* grew weary of her Company, and giving her the slip in the Night, went away for *Achin*: for having heard that there was plenty of Gold there, he went thither with a Design to cruize: And it was from one Mr. *Humes*, belonging to the *Ann* of *London*, Capt. *Freke* Commander, who had gone aboard Captain *Knight*, and whom I saw afterwards at *Achin*, that I had this Relation. Some of Captain *Freke*'s Men, their own Ship being lost, had gone aboard the *Cygnet* at *Johanna*: And after Capt. *Knight* had left her, she still pursued her Voyage towards the *Red-Sea*: But the Winds being against them, and the Ship in so ill a Condition, they were forced to bear away for *Coromandel*, where Captain *Teat* and his own Men went ashore to serve the Mogul. But the Strangers of Captain *Freke*'s Ship, who kept still aboard the *Cygnet*, undertook to carry her for *England*: and the last News I heard of the *Cygnet* was from Captain *Knox*, who tells me, that she now lies sunk in St. *Augustin*'s Bay in *Madagascar*. This Digression I have made, to give an account of our Ship.

¶ The other Passage I shall speak of, that occurred during this Interval of the Tour I made from *Achin*, is with Relation to the painted Prince, whom I brought with me into *England*, and who died at *Oxford*. For while I was at *Fort St. George*, about *April* 1690, there arrived a Ship called the *Mindanao*-Merchant, laden with Clove-bark from *Mindanao*. Three of Captain *Swan*'s Men that remain'd there when we went from thence, came in her: From whence I had the Account of Captain *Swan*'s Death, as is before related. There was also one Mr. *Moody*, who was Supercargo of the Ship. This Gentleman bought at *Mindanao* the painted Prince *Jeoly* (mentioned in *Chap.* XIII.) and his Mother; and brought them to *Fort St. George*, where they were much admired by all that saw them. Some time after this, Mr. *Moody*, who spoke the *Malayan* Language very well, and was a Person very capable to manage the Company's Affairs, was ordered by the Governour of *Fort St. George* to prepare to go to *Indrapore*, an *English* Factory on the West Coast of *Sumatra*, in order to succeed Mr. *Gibbons*, who was the chief of that Place.

¶ By this time I was very intimately acquainted with Mr. *Moody*, and was importun'd by him to go with him, and to be Gunner of the Fort there. I always told him I had a great desire to go to the Bay of *Bengal*, and that I had now an offer to go thither with Captain *Metcalf*, who wanted a Mate, and had already spoke to me. Mr. *Moody*, to encourage me to go with him, told me, that if I would go with him to *Indrapore*, he would buy a small Vessel there, and send me to the Island *Meangis*, Commander of her; and that I should carry Prince *Jeoly* and his Mother with me, (that being their Country) by which means I might gain a Commerce with his People for Cloves.

¶ This was a design that I liked very well, and therefore I consented to go thither. It was some time in *July* 1690, when we went from *Fort St. George* in a small Ship, called the *Diamond*, Capt. *Howel* Commander. We were about fifty or sixty Passangers in all; some ordered to be left at *Indrapore*, and some at *Bencouli*: Five or six of us were Officers, the rest Soldiers to the Company. We met nothing in our Voyage that deserves notice, till we came abrest of *Indrapore*. And then the Wind came at N.W. and blew so hard that we could not get in, but were forced to bear away to *Bencouli*, another *English* Factory on the same Coast, lying fifty or sixty Leagues to the southward of *Indrapore*.

¶ Upon our arrival at *Bencouli* we saluted the Fort, and were welcomed by them. The same Day we came to an Anchor, and Captain *Howel*, and Mr. *Moody* with the other Merchants went ashoar, and were all kindly received by the Governour of the Fort. It was two Days before I went ashoar, and then I was importuned by the Governour to stay there, to be Gunner of this Fort; because the Gunner was lately dead: And this being a place of greater Import than *Indrapore*, I should do the Company more Service here than there. I told the Governour, if he would augment my Sallary, which by Agreement with the Governour of *Fort St. George* I was to have had at *Indrapore*, I was willing to serve him, provided Mr. *Moody* would consent to it. As to my Sallary, he told me, I should have 24 Dollars *per* Month, which was as much as he gave to the old Gunner.

¶ Mr. *Moody* gave no Answer till a Week after, and then, being ready to be gone to *Indrapore*, he told me I might use my own Liberty, either to stay here, or go with him to *Indrapore*. He added, that if I went with him, he was not certain as yet to perform his Promise, in getting a Vessel for me to go to *Meangis*, with *Jeoly* and his Mother: But he would be so fair to me, that because I left *Maderas* on his Account, he would give me the half share of the two painted People, and leave them in my Possession, and at my Disposal. I accepted of the Offer, and Writings were immediately drawn between us.

¶ Thus it was that I came to have this painted Prince, whose Name was *Jeoly*, and his Mother. They were born on a small Island called *Meangis*, which is once or twice mentioned in *Chap.* XIII. I saw the Island twice, and two more close by it: Each of the three seemed to be about four or five Leagues round, and of a good heighth. *Jeoly* himself told me, that they all three abounded with Gold, Cloves and Nutmegs: For I shewed him some of each sort several times, and he told me in the *Malayan* Language, which he spake indifferent well, *Meangis Hadda Madochala se Bullawan*: That is, there is abundance of Gold at *Meangis*. *Bullawan*, I have observed to be the common Word for Gold at *Mindanao*; but

whether the proper *Malayan* Word I know not, for I found much difference
between the *Malayan* Language as it was spoken at *Mindanao*, and the
Language on the Coast of *Malacca* and *Achin*. When I shewed him Spice,
he would not only tell me that there was *Madochala*, that is, abundance;
but to make it appear more plain, he would also show me the Hair of his
Head, a thing frequent among all the *Indians* that I have met with, to
show their Hair, when they would express more than they can number.
He told me also, that his Father was *Raja* of the Island where they lived:
That there were not above Thirty Men on the Island, and about one
Hundred Women: That he himself had five Wives and eight Children,
and that one of his Wives painted him.

¶ He was painted all down the Breast, between his Shoulders behind;
on his Thighs (mostly) before; and in the Form of several broad Rings,
or Bracelets round his Arms and Legs. I cannot liken the Drawings to
any Figure of Animals, or the like; but they were very curious, full of
great variety of Lines, Flourishes, Chequered-Work, &c. keeping a very
graceful Proportion, and appearing very artificial, even to Wonder,
especially that upon and between his Shoulder-blades. By the Account
he gave me of the manner of doing it, I understood that the Painting was
done in the same manner, as the *Jerusalem* Cross is made in Mens Arms,
by pricking the Skin, and rubbing in a Pigment. But whereas Powder is
used in making the *Jerusalem* Cross, they at *Meangis* use the Gum of a
Tree beaten to Powder, called by the *English*, Dammer, which is used
instead of Pitch in many parts of *India*. He told me, that most of the
Men and Women on the Island were thus painted: And also that they
had all Ear-rings made of Gold, and Gold Shackles about their Legs
and Arms: That their common Food, of the Produce of the Land, was
Potatoes and Yams: That they had plenty of Cocks and Hens; but no
other tame Fowl. He said, that Fish (of which he was a great Lover, as
wild *Indians* generally are) was very plentiful about the Island; and that
they had Canoas, and went a fishing frequently in them; and that they
often visited the other two small Islands, whose Inhabitants spake the
same Language as they did; which was so unlike the *Malayan*, which he
had learnt while he was a Slave at *Mindanao*, that when his Mother and
he were talking together in their *Meangian* Tongue, I could not understand
one Word they said. And indeed all the *Indians* who spake *Malayan*, who
are the trading and politer sort, lookt on these *Meangians* as a kind of
Barbarians; and upon any occasion of dislike, would call them *Bobby*, that
is, Hogs; the greatest Expression of Contempt that can be, especially
from the Mouth of *Malayans*, who are generally *Mahometans*; and yet the

Malayans every where call a Woman *Babby*, by a Name not much different, and *Mamma* signifies a Man; tho' these two last Words properly denote Male and Female: And as *Ejam* signifies a Fowl, so *Ejam Mamma* is a Cock, and *Ejam Babbi* is a Hen. But this by the way.

¶ He said also that the Customs of those other Isles, and their manner of living, was like theirs, and that they were the only People with whom they had any Converse: And that one time as he, with his Father, Mother and Brother, with two or three Men more were going to one of these other Islands, they were driven by a strong Wind on the Coast of *Mindanao*, where they were taken by the Fishermen of that Island, and carried ashore, and sold as Slaves; they being first stript of their Gold Ornaments. I did not see any of the Gold that they wore, but there were great Holes in their Ears, by which it was manifest that they had worn some Ornaments in them. *Jeoly* was sold to one *Michael* a *Mindanayan*, that spoke good *Spanish*, and commonly waited on *Raja Laut*, serving him as our Interpreter, where the *Raja* was at a loss in any word, for *Michael* understood it better. He did often beat and abuse his painted Servant, to make him work, but all in vain; for neither fair means, threats nor blows, would make him work as he would have him. Yet he was very timerous, and could not endure to see any sort of Weapons; and he often told me that they had no Arms at *Meangis*, they having no Enemies to fight with.

¶ I knew this *Michael* very well while we were at *Mindanao*: I suppose that Name was given him by the *Spaniards*, who baptized many of them at the time when they had footing at that Island: But at the departure of the *Spaniards*, they were *Mahometans* again as before. Some of our People lay at this *Michael*'s House, whose Wife and Daughter were *Pagallies* to some of them. I often saw *Jeoly* at his Master *Michael*'s House, and when I came to have him so long after, he remembered me again. I did never see his Father nor Brother, nor any of the others that were taken with them; but *Jeoly* came several times aboard our Ship when we lay at *Mindanao*, and gladly accepted of such Victuals as we gave him; for his Master kept him at very short Commons.

¶ Prince *Jeoly* lived thus a Slave at *Mindanao* four or five Years, till at last Mr. *Moody* bought him and his Mother for 60 Dollars, and as is before related, carried him to *Fort St. George*, and from thence along with me to *Bencouli*. Mr. *Moody* stayed at *Bencouli* about three Weeks, and then went back with Captain *Howel*, to *Indrapore*, leaving *Jeoly* and his Mother with me. They lived in a House by themselves without the Fort. I had no Employment for them; but they both employed themselves. She used to make and mend their own Cloaths, at which she was not very expert, for they wear no Cloaths at *Meangis*, but only a Cloath about their Wastes: And he busied himself in making a Chest with four Boards, and a few Nails that he begged of me. It was but an ill-shaped odd Thing, yet he was as proud of it as if it had been the rarest Piece in the World. After some time they were both taken sick, and though I took as much care of them as if they had been my Brother and Sister, yet she died. I did what I could to comfort *Jeoly*; but he took on extremely, insomuch that I feared him also. Therefore I caused a Grave to be made presently, to hide her out of his sight. I had her shrouded decently in a piece of new Callico; but *Jeoly* was not so satisfied, for he wrapt all her Cloaths about her, and two new pieces of Chints that Mr. *Moody* gave her, saying that they were his Mother's, and she must have 'em. I would not disoblige him for fear of endangering his Life; and I used all possible means to recover his Health; but I found little Amendment while we stay'd here.

¶ In the little printed Relation that was made of him when he was shown for a Sight in *England*, there was a romantick Story of a beautiful Sister of his a Slave with them at *Mindanao*; and of the Sultan's falling in Love with her; but these were Stories indeed. They reported also that this Paint was of such Virtue, that Serpents, and venomous Creatures would flee from him, for which reason, I suppose, they represented so many Serpents scampering about in the printed Picture that was made of him. But I never knew any Paint of such Virtue: and as for *Jeoly*, I have seen him as much afraid of Snakes, Scorpions, or Centapees, as my self.

¶ Having given this account of the Ship that left me at *Nicobar*, and of my painted Prince whom I brought with me to *Bencouli*, I shall now proceed on with the Relation of my Voyage thence to *England*, after I have given this short Account of the occasion of it, and the manner of my getting away.

¶ To say nothing therefore now of that Place, and my Employment there as Gunner of the Fort, the Year 1690 drew towards an end, and not finding the Governour keep to his Agreement with me, nor seeing by his Carriage towards others any great Reason I had to expect he would, I began to wish my self away again. I saw so much Ignorance in him, with respect to his charge, being much fitter to be a Book-keeper than Governour of a Fort; and yet so much Insolence and Cruelty with respect to those under him, and Rashness in his Management of the *Malayan* Neighbourhood, that I soon grew weary of him, not thinking my self very safe, indeed, under a Man whose Humours were so brutish and barbarous. I forbear to mention his Name after such a Character; nor do I care to fill these Papers with particular Stories of him: But therefore give this intimation, because as it is the interest of the Nation in general, so is it especially of the Honourable *East-India* Company, to be informed of abuses in their Factories. And I think the Company might receive great Advantage by strictly enquiring into the Behaviour of those whom they entrust with any Command. For beside the Odium, which reflects back upon the Superiours from the mis-doings of their Servants, how undeservedly so ever, there are great and lasting Mischiefs proceed from the Tyranny or ignorant rashness of some petty Governours. Those under them are discouraged from their Service by it, and often go away to the *Dutch*, the Mogul, or the *Malayan* Princes, to the great detriment of our Trade; and even the Trade and the Forts themselves are many times in danger by indiscreet Provocations given to the neighbouring Nations, who are best managed, as all Mankind are, by Justice, and fair dealings; nor any more implacably revengeful than those *Malayans*, who live in the neighbourhood of *Bencouli*, which Fort hath been more than once in danger of being surprized by them. I speak not this out of disgust to this particular Governour; much less would I seem to reflect on any others, of whom I know nothing amiss: But as it is not to be wondered at, if some should not know how to demean themselves in places of Power, for which neither their Education nor their Business possibly have sufficiently qualified them, so it will be the more necessary for the Honourable Company to have the closer Eye over them, and as much as may be, to prevent or reform any Abuses they may be guilty of; and 'tis purely out of my Zeal for theirs and the Nation's Interest, that I have given this Caution, having seen too much occasion for it.

❡ I had other Motives also for my going away. I began to long after my native Country, after so tedious a Ramble from it: and I proposed no small Advantage to my self from my painted Prince, whom Mr. *Moody* had left entirely to my disposal, only reserving to himself his right to one half share in him. For beside what might be gained by shewing him in *England*, I was in hopes that when I had got some Money, I might there obtain what I had in vain sought for in the *Indies*, *viz.* A Ship from the Merchants, wherewith to carry him back to *Meangis*, and re-instate him there in his own Country, and by his Favour and Negotiation to establish a Traffick for the Spices and other products of those Islands.

❡ Upon these Projects, I went to the Governour and Council, and desired that I might have my discharge to go for *England* with the next Ship that came. The Council thought it reasonable, and they consented to it; he also gave me his word that I should go. Upon the 2d of *January* 1691, there came to anchor in *Bencouli* Road, the *Defence*, Capt. *Heath* Commander, bound for *England*, in the Service of the Company. They had been at *Indrapore*, where Mr. *Moody* then was, and he had made over his share in Prince *Jeoly* to Mr. *Goddard* chief Mate of the Ship. Upon his coming on shore, he shewed me Mr. *Moody*'s Writings, and lookt upon *Jeoly*, who had been sick for three Months: In all which time I tended him as carefully as if he had been my Brother. I agreed Matters with Mr. *Goddard*, and sent *Jeoly* on board, intending to follow him as I could, and desiring Mr. *Goddard*'s Assistance to fetch me off, and conceal me aboard the Ship, if there should be occasion; which he promised to do, and the Captain promised to entertain me. For it proved, as I had foreseen, that upon Captain *Heath*'s Arrival, the Governour repented him of his Promise, and would not suffer me to depart. I importuned him all I could; but in vain: so did Capt. *Heath* also, but to no purpose. In short, after several Essays, I slipt away, at Midnight (understanding the Ship was to sail away the next Morning, and that they had taken leave of the Fort) and creeping through one of the Port-holes of the Fort, I got to the shore, where the Ship's Boat waited for me, and carried me on board. I brought with me my Journal, and most of my written Papers; but some Papers and Books of value I left in haste, and all my Furniture; being glad I was my self at Liberty, and had hopes of seeing *England* again.

CHAPTER XIX

The Author's departure from Bencouli, *on board the* Defence, *under Captain* Heath, *Of a Fight between some* French Men of War *from* Ponticheri, *and some* Dutch Ships *from* Pallacat, *joined with some* English, *in sight of* Fort St. George. *Of the bad Water taken in at* Bencouli; *and the strange sickness and death of the Seamen, supposed to be occasioned thereby. A Spring at* Bencouli *recommended. The great Exigencies on board: A Consult held and a Proposal made to go to* Johanna. *A Resolution taken to prosecute their Voyage to the Cape of* Good Hope. *The Wind favours them. The Captain's Conduct. They arrive at the Cape, and are helped into Harbour by the* Dutch. *A Description of the Cape, its Prospect, Soundings, Table-Mount, Harbour, Soil, &c. large Pomgranates, and good Wines. The Land-Animals. A very beautiful kind of* Onager, *or wild Ass striped regularly black and white. Ostrages. Fish. Scales. The* Dutch Fort *and Factory. Their fine Garden. The Traffick here.*

BEING thus got on board the *Defence*, I was concealed there, till a Boat which came from the Fort laden with Pepper was gone off again. And then we set sail for the Cape of *Good-Hope*, *Jan.* 25, 1691, and made the best of our way, as Wind and Weather would permit;

expecting there to meet three *English* Ships more bound home from the *Indies*: For the War with the *French* having been proclaimed at *Fort St. George*, a little before Capt. *Heath* came from thence, he was willing to have Company home, if he could.

¶ A little before this War was proclaimed, there was an Engagement in the Road of *Fort St. George* between some *French* Men of War and some *Dutch* and *English* Ships at anchor in the Road: which because there is such a plausible Story made of it in Monsieur *Duquesne's* late Voyage to the *East-Indies*, I shall give a short account of, as I had it particularly related to me by the Gunner's Mate of Capt. *Heath's* Ship, a very sensible Man, and several others of his Men, who were in the Action. The *Dutch* have a Fort on the Coast of *Coromandel*, called *Pallacat*, about 20 Leagues to the northward of *Fort St. George*. Upon some occasion or other the *Dutch* sent some Ships thither to fetch away their Effects, and transport them to *Batavia*. Acts of Hostility were already begun between the *French* and *Dutch*; and the *French* had at this time a Squadron newly arrived in *India*, and lying at *Ponticheri*, a *French* Fort on the same Coast Southward of *Fort St. George*. The *Dutch* in returning to *Batavia*, were obliged to coast it along by *Fort St. George* and *Ponticheri*, for the sake of the Wind; but when they came near this last, they saw the *French* Men of War lying at anchor there; and should they have proceeded along the Shore, or stood out to Sea, expected to be pursued by them. They therefore turned back again; for though their Ships were of a pretty good Force, yet were they unfit for Fight, as having great Loads of Goods, and many Passengers, Women and Children, on board; so they put in at *Fort St. George*, and desiring the Governour's Protection, had leave to anchor in the Road, and to send their Goods and useless People ashore. There were then in the Road a few small *English* Ships; and Captain *Heath*, whose Ship was a very stout Merchant-man, and which the *French* Relater calls the *English* Admiral, was just come from *China*; but very deep laden with Goods, and the Deck full of Canisters of Sugar, which he was preparing to send ashore. But before he could do it, the *French* appeared; coming into the Road with their Lower-Sails and Top-Sails, and had with them a Fireship. With this they thought to have burnt the *Dutch* Commodore, and might probably enough have done it as she lay at anchor, if they had had the Courage to have come boldly on; but they fired their Ship at a distance, and the *Dutch* sent and towed her away, where she spent her self without any Execution. Had the *French* Men of War also come boldly up, and grappled with their Enemies, they might have done something considerable, for the Fort could not have played on them, without damaging our Ships as well as theirs. But instead of this, the *French* dropt anchor out of reach of the shot of the Fort, and there lay exchanging shot with their Enemies Ships, with so little Advantage to themselves, that after about four Hours fighting, they cut their Cables, and went away in haste and disorder, with all their Sails loose, even their Top-gallant Sails, which is not usual, but when Ships are just next to running away.

¶ Captain *Heath*, notwithstanding his Ship was so heavy and incumbred, behaved himself very bravely in the Fight; and upon the going off of the *French*, went aboard the *Dutch* Commodore and told him, that if he would pursue them, he would stand out with them to Sea, though he had very little Water aboard; but the *Dutch* Commander excused himself, saying he had Orders to defend himself from the *French*, but none to chase them, or go out of his way to seek them. And this was the Exploit which the *French* have thought fit to brag of. I hear that the *Dutch* have taken from them since their Fort of *Ponticheri*.

¶ But to proceed with our Voyage: We had not been at Sea long before our Men began to droop, in a sort of Distemper that stole insensibly on them, and proved fatal to above thirty, who died before we arrived at the Cape. We had sometimes two, and once three Men thrown over-board in a Morning. This Distemper might probably arise from the badness of the Water which we took in at *Bencouli*: For I did observe while I was there that the River-water, wherewith our Ships were watered, was very unwholsome, it being mixt with the Water of many small Creeks, that proceeded from low Land, and whose Streams were always very black, they being nourished by the Water that drained out of the low swampy unwholsome Ground.

¶ I have observed not only there, but in other hot Countries also both in the *East* and *West-Indies*, that the Land-floods which pour into the Channels of the Rivers, about the Season of the Rains, are very un-wholsome. For when I lived in the Bay of *Campeachy*, the Fish were found dead in heaps on the shores of the Rivers and Creeks, at such a Season; and many we took up half dead; of which sudden Mortality there appeared no cause, but only the malignity of the Waters draining off the Land. This happens chiefly, as I take it, where the Water drains through thick Woods and Savannahs of long Grass, and swampy Grounds, with which some hot Countries abound: And I believe it receives a strong Tincture from the Roots of several kind of Trees, Herbs, &c. And especially where there is any stagnancy of the Water, it soon corrupts; and possibly the Serpents and other poisonous Vermin and Insects may not a little con-tribute to its bad Qualities: At such times it will look very deep-coloured, yellow, red, or black, &c. The Season of the Rains was over, and the Land-floods were abating upon the taking up this Water in the River of *Bencouli*: But would the Seamen have given themselves the trouble they might have fill'd their Vessels with excellent good Water at a Spring on the backside of the Fort, not above 2 or 300 paces from the Landing-Place; and with which the Fort is served. And I mention this as a caution to any Ships that shall go to *Bencouli* for the future; and withal I think it worth the care of the Owners or Governours of the Factory, and that it would tend much to the Preservation of their Seamen's Lives, to lay Pipes to convey the Fountain Water to the Shore, which might easily be done with a small charge: And had I staid longer there I would have undertaken it   I had a design also of bringing it into the Fort, tho' much higher: for it would be a great Convenience and Security to it, in case of a Siege.

¶ Besides the badness of our Water, it was stowed among the Pepper in the Hold, which made it very hot. Every Morning when we came to take our Allowance, it was so hot that a Man could hardly suffer his Hands in it, or hold a Bottle full of it in his Hands. I never any where felt the like, nor could have thought it possible that Water should heat to that degree in a Ship's Hold. It was exceeding black too, and looked more like Ink than Water. Whether it grew so black with standing, or was tinged with the Pepper, I know not, for this Water was not so black when it was first taken up. Our Food also was very bad; for the Ship had been out of *England* upon this Voyage above three Years; and the salt Provision brought from thence, and which we fed on, having been so long in Salt, was but ordinary Food for sickly Men to feed on.

¶ Captain *Heath*, when he saw the Misery of his Company, ordered his own Tamarinds, of which he had some Jars aboard, to be given some to each Mess, to eat with their Rice. This was a great refreshment to the Men, and I do believe it contributed much to keep us on our Legs.

¶ This Distemper was so universal, that I do believe there was scarce a Man in the Ship, but languished under it; yet it stole so insensibly on us, that we could not say we were sick, feeling little or no Pain, only a Weakness, and but little Stomach. Nay, most of those that died in this Voyage, would hardly be perswaded to keep their Cabbins, or Hammocks, till they could not stir about; and when they were forced to lye down, they made their Wills, and piked off in two or three Days.

¶ The loss of these Men, and the weak languishing Condition that the rest of us were in, rendered us uncapable to govern our Ship, when the Wind blew more than ordinary. This often happened when we drew near the Cape, and as oft put us to our trumps to manage the Ship. Captain *Heath*, to encourage his Men to their Labour, kept his Watch as constantly as any Man, though sickly himself, and lent an helping Hand on all occasions. But at last, almost despairing of gaining his Passage to the Cape by reason of the Winds coming southerly, and we having now been sailing eight or nine weeks, he called all our Men to consult about our Safety, and desired every Man, from the highest to the lowest, freely to give his real Opinion and Advice, what to do in this dangerous Juncture; for we were not in a Condition to keep out long; and could we not get to Land quickly, must have perished at Sea. He consulted therefore whether it were best to beat for the Cape, or bear away for *Johanna*, where we might expect relief, that being a Place where our outward bound *East-India* Ships usually touch, and whose Natives are very familiar: But other Places, especially St. *Laurence*, or *Madagascar*, which was nearer, was unknown to us. We were now so nigh the Cape, that with a fair Wind we might expect to be there in four or five Days; but as the Wind was now, we could not hope to get thither. On the other side this Wind was fair to carry us to *Johanna*; but then *Johanna* was a great way off, and if the Wind should continue as it was, to bring us into a true Trade-Wind, yet we could not get thither under a Fortnight; and if we should meet Calms, as we might probably expect, it might be much longer. Besides, we should lose our Passage about the Cape till *October* or *November*, this being about the latter-end of *March*, for after the 10th of *May* 'tis not usual to beat about the Cape to come home. All Circumstances therefore being weighed and considered, we at last unanimously agreed to prosecute our Voyage towards the Cape, and with Patience wait for a shift of Wind.

¶ But Captain *Heath*, having thus far sounded the Inclination of his weak Men, told them, that it was not enough that they all consented to beat for the Cape, for our desires were not sufficient to bring us thither; but that there would need a more than ordinary labour and management from those that were able. And withal, for their Encouragement he promised a Month's Pay *Gratis*, to every Man that would engage to assist on all Occasions, and be ready upon call, whether it were his turn to watch or not; and this Money he promised to pay at the Cape. This Offer was first embraced by some of the Officers, and then as many of the Men as found themselves in a Capacity, listed themselves in a Roll to serve their Commander.

¶ This was wisely contrived of the Captain, for he could not have compelled them in their weak Condition, neither would fair Words alone, without some hopes of a Reward, have engaged them to so much extra-ordinary Work; for the Ship, Sail and Rigging were much out of repair. For my part, I was too weak to enter my self into that List, for else our common Safety, which I plainly saw lay at stake, would have prompted me to do more than any such reward would do. In a short time after this it pleased God to favour us with a fine Wind, which being improved to the best Advantage by the incessant labour of these new-listed Men, brought us in a short time to the Cape.

¶ The Night before we entered the Harbour, which was about the beginning of *April*, being near the Land, we fired a Gun every Hour, to give notice that we were in distress. The next Day a *Dutch* Captain came aboard in his Boat, who seeing us so weak as not to be able to trim our Sails to turn into the Harbour; though we did tolerably well at Sea before the Wind, and being requested by our Captain to assist him, sent ashore for a hundred lusty Men, who immediately came aboard, and brought our Ship in to an Anchor. They also unbent our Sails, and did every thing for us that they were required to do, for which Capt. *Heath* gratified them to the full.

¶ These Men had better Stomachs than we, and eat freely of such Food as the Ship afforded; and they having the freedom of our Ship, to go too and fro between Decks, made prize of what they could lay their Hands on, especially Salt-Beef, which our Men, for want of Stomachs in the Voyage, had hung up 6, 8, or 10 pieces in a Place. This was conveyed away before we knew it, or thought of it: Besides, in the Night there was a Bale of Muzlins broke open, and a great deal conveyed away: but whether the Muzlins were stolen by our own Men or the *Dutch*, I cannot say; for we had some very dexterous Thieves in our Ship.

¶ Being thus got safe to an Anchor, the Sick were presently sent ashore to Quarters provided for them, and those that were able remained aboard, and had good fat Mutton, or fresh Beef, sent aboard every Day. I went ashore also with my painted Prince, where I remained with him till the time of sailing again, which was about six Weeks. In which time I took the Opportunity to inform my self what I could concerning this Country, which I shall in the next Place give you a brief Account of, and so make what haste I can home.

¶ The Cape of *Good-Hope* is the utmost Bounds of the Continent of *Africa* towards the South, lying in 34 d. 30 m. S. lat. in a very temperate Climate. I look upon this Latitude to be one of the mildest and sweetest for its temperature of any whatsoever; and I cannot here but take notice of a common prejudice our *European* Seamen have as to this Country, that they look upon it as much colder than Places in the same Latitude to the North of the Line. I am not of their Opinion as to that: And their thinking so, I believe, may easily be accounted for from hence, that whatever way they come to the Cape, whether going to the *East-Indies* or returning back, they pass through a hot Climate; and coming to it thus out of an extremity of Heat, 'tis no wonder if it appear the colder to them. Some impute the coldness of the South-wind here to its blowing off from Sea. On the contrary, I have always observed the Sea-winds to be warmer than Land-winds, unless it be when a bloom, as we call it, or hot blast blow from thence. Such an one we felt in this very Voyage, as we went from Cape *Verd* Islands, towards the *South-Seas*; which I forgot to mention in its proper Place, Chap. 4th. For one Afternoon about the 19th of *January* 1683, in the lat. of 37 South we felt a brisk Gale coming from off the Coast of *America*, but so violent hot, that we thought it came from some burning Mountain on the Shore, and was like the heat from the Mouth of an Oven. Just such another Gleam I felt one Afternoon also, as I lay at Anchor at the *Groin* in *July* 1694, it came with a Southerly-wind, both these were followed by a Thunder-shower. These were the only great Blooms I ever met with in my Travels. But setting these aside, which are Exceptions, I have made it my general Observation, that the Sea-winds are a great deal warmer than those which blow from Land; unless where the Wind blows from the Poles, which I take to be the true cause of the coldness of the South-wind at the Cape, for it is cold at Sea also. And as for the coldness of Land-winds, as the South-West parts of *Europe* are very sensible of it from the northern and eastern Winds; so on the opposite Coast of *Virginia*, they are as much pinched with the North-West Winds, blowing excessively cold from over the Continent; though its Lat. be not much greater than this of the Cape.

¶ But to proceed: This large Promontory consists of high and very remarkable Land; and off at Sea it affords a very pleasant and agreeable Prospect. And without doubt the Prospect of it was very agreeable to those *Portuguese* who first found out this way by Sea to the *East-Indies*; when after coasting along the vast Continent of *Africk*, towards the *South-Pole*, they had the comfort of seeing the Land and their Course end in this Promontory: Which therefore they called the Cape *de Bon Esperance*, or of *Good Hope*, finding that they might now proceed easterly.

¶ There is good sounding off this Cape 50 or 60 Leagues at Sea to the Southward, and therefore our *English* Seamen standing over as they usually do, from the Coast of *Brazil*, content themselves with their Soundings, concluding thereby that they are abrest of the Cape, they often pass by without seeing it, and begin to shape their Course north-ward. They have several other Signs whereby to know when they are near it, as by the Sea-fowl they meet at Sea, especially the Algatrosses, a very large long winged Bird, and the Mangovolucres, a smaller Fowl. But the greatest Dependance of our *English* Seamen now is upon their observing the Variation of the Compass, which is very carefully minded when they come near the Cape, by taking the Sun's Amplitude Mornings and Evenings. This they are so exact in, that by the Help of the Azimuth Compass, an Instrument more peculiar to the Seamen of our Nation, they know when they are abrest of the Cape, or are either to the East or the West of it: And for that reason, though they should be to south-ward of all the Soundings, or fathomable Ground, they can shape their Course right, without being obliged to make the Land. But the *Dutch* on the contrary, having settled themselves on this Promontory, do always touch here in their *East-India* Voyages, both going and coming.

¶ The most remarkable Land at Sea is a high Mountain, steep to the Sea, with a flat even Top, which is called the Table Land. On the West-side of the Cape, a little to the northward of it, there is a spacious Harbour, with a low flat Island lying off it, which you may leave on either Hand, and pass in or out securely at either end. Ships that anchor here ride near the main Land, leaving the Island at a farther Distance without them. The Land by the Sea against the Harbour is low; but back with high Mountains a little way in, to the southward of it.

¶ The Soil of this Country is of a brown Colour; not deep, yet indifferently productive of Grass, Herbs and Trees. The Grass is short, like that which grows on our *Wiltshire* or *Dorsetshire* Downs. The Trees hereabouts are but small and few; the Country also farther from the Sea, does not much abound in Trees, as I have been inform'd. The Mould or Soil also is much like this near the Harbour, which though it cannot be said to be very fat or rich Land, yet it is very fit for Cultivation, and yields good Crops to the industrious Husbandman, and the Country is pretty well settled with *Farms*, *Dutch* Families, and *French* Refugees, for twenty or thirty Leagues up the Country; but there are but few Farms near the Harbour.

¶ Here grows plenty of Wheat, Barly, Pease, &c. Here are also Fruits of many kinds, as Apples, Pears, Quinces, and the largest Pomgranates that I did ever see.

¶ The chief Fruits are Grapes. These thrive very well, and the Country is of late Years so well stockt with Vineyards, that they make abundance of Wine, of which they have enough and to spare; and do sell great

Quantities to Ships that touch here. This Wine is like a *French* High-Country White-wine, but of a pale yellowish Colour; it is sweet, very pleasant and strong.

¶ The tame Animals of this Country are Sheep, Goats, Hogs, Cows, Horses, &c. The Sheep are very large and fat, for they thrive very well here: This being a dry Country, and the short Pasturage very agreeable to these Creatures, but it is not so proper for great Cattle; neither is the Beef in its kind so sweet as the Mutton. Of wild Beasts, it is said, here are several sorts, but I saw none. However, it is very likely there are some wild Beasts, that prey on the Sheep, because they are commonly brought into the Houses in the Night, and penn'd up.

¶ There is a very beautiful sort of wild Ass in this Country, whose Body is curiously striped with equal Lists of white and black; the Stripes coming from the Ridge of his Back, and ending under the Belly, which is white. These Stripes are two or three Fingers broad, running parallel with each other, and curiously intermixt, one white and one black, over from the Shoulder to the Rump. I saw two of the Skins of these Beasts, dried and preserved to be sent to *Holland* as a Rarity. They seemed big enough to inclose the Body of a Beast, as big as a large Colt of a Twelvemonth old.

¶ Here are a great many Ducks, Dunghil-Fowls, &c. and Ostriges are plentifully found in the dry Mountains and Plains. I eat of their Eggs here, and those of whom I bought them told me that these Creatures lay their Eggs in the Sand, or at least on dry Ground, and so leave them to be hatch'd by the Sun. The Meat of one of their Eggs will suffice two Men very well. The Inhabitants do preserve the Eggs that they find to sell to Strangers. They were pretty scarce when I was here, it being the Beginning of their Winter; whereas I was told they lay their Eggs about *Christmas*, which is their Summer.

¶ The Sea hereabouts affords plenty of Fish of divers sorts; especially a small sort of Fish, not so big as a Herring; whereof they have such great Plenty, that they pickle great Quantities yearly, and send them to *Europe*. Seals are also in great Numbers about the Cape; which, as I have still observed, is a good sign of the Plentifulness of Fish, which is their Food.

¶ The *Dutch* have a strong Fort by the Sea-side, against the Harbour, where the Governour lives. At about Two or Three Hundred Paces distance from thence, on the West-side of the Fort, there is a small *Dutch* Town, in which I told about fifty or sixty Houses; low, but well built, with Stone-walls; there being plenty of Stone drawn out of a Quarry close by.

¶ On the backside of the Town, as you go towards the Mountains, the

Dutch East-India Company have a large House, and a stately Garden walled in with a high Stone-wall.

¶ This Garden is full of divers sorts of Herbs, Flowers, Roots, and Fruits, with curious spacious Gravel-walks and Arbours; and is watered with a Brook that descends out of the Mountains: which being cut into many Channels, is conveyed into all parts of the Garden. The Hedges which make the Walks are very thick, and nine or ten Foot high: They are kept exceeding neat and even by continual pruning. There are lower Hedges within these again, which serve to separate the Fruit-Trees from each other, but without shading them: and they keep each sort of Fruit by themselves, as Apples, Pears, abundance of Quinces, Pomgranates, &c. These all prosper very well, and bear good Fruit, especially the Pom-granate. The Roots and Garden-Herbs have also their distinct places, hedged in apart by themselves; and all in such order, that it is exceeding pleasant and beautiful. There are a great Number of Negro-Slaves brought from other parts of the World; some of which are continually weeding, pruning, trimming and looking after it. All Strangers are allowed the Liberty to walk there; and by the Servants leave, you may be admitted to taste of the Fruit: but if you think to do it clandestinely, you may be mistaken, as I knew one was when I was in the Garden, who took five or six Pomgranates, and was espy'd by one of the Slaves, and threatned to be carried before the Governour: I believe it cost him some Money to make his peace, for I heard no more of it. Further up from the Sea, beyond the Garden, towards the Mountains, there are several other small Gardens and Vineyards belonging to private Men: but the Mountains are so nigh, that the Number of them are but small.

¶ The *Dutch* that live in the Town get considerably by the Ships that frequently touch here, chiefly by entertaining Strangers that come ashoar to refresh themselves; for you must give 3s. or a Dollar a Day for your Entertainment; the Bread and Flesh is as cheap here as in *England*; besides, they buy good Penny-worths of the Seamen, both outward and homeward bound, which the Farmers up the Country buy of them again at a dear Rate; for they have not an Opportunity of buying things at the best Hand, but must buy of those that live at the Harbour; the nearest Settlements, as I was informed, being twenty Miles of.

¶ Notwithstanding the great Plenty of Corn and Wine, yet the extra-ordinary high Taxes which the Company lays on Liquors, makes it very dear; and you can buy none but at the Tavern, except it be by stealth. There are but three Houses in the Town that sell strong Liquor, one of which is this Wine-House or Tavern; there they sell only Wine; another

sells Beer and Mum; and the Third sells Brandy and Tobacco, all extraordinary dear. A Flask of Wine, which holds three Quarts, will cost
eighteen Stivers, for so much I paid for it; yet I bought as much for eight
Stivers in another place, but it was privately at an unlicensed House, and
the Person that sold it would have been ruined had it been known. And
thus much for the Country and the *European* Inhabitants.

CHAPTER XX

*Of the natural Inhabitants of the Cape of Good Hope, the Hodmadods or Hottantots. Their
Personage, Garb, besmearing themselves; their Cloathing, Houses, Food, way of Living, and
Dancing at the Full of the Moon: Compared in those respects with other Negroes and Wild Indians.
Captain Heath refreshes his Men at the Cape, and getting some more Hands, departs in company
with the James and Mary, and the Josiah. A great swelling Sea from S.W. They arrive at
Santa Hellena, and there meet with the Princess Ann, homeward bound. The Air, Situation,
and Soil of that Island. Its first Discovery, and change of Masters since. How the English got it.
Its Strength, Town, Inhabitants, and the Product of their Plantations. The Santa Hellena
Manatee no other than the Sea-Lion. Of the English Women at this Isle. The English Ships
refresh their Men here; and depart all together. Of the different Courses from hence to England.
Their Course and Arrival in the English Channel and the Downs.*

THE natural Inhabitants of the Cape are the *Hodmadods*, as they are
commonly called, which is a Corruption of the Word *Hottantot*; for
this is the Name by which they call to one another, either in their
Dances, or on any occasion; as if every one of them had this for his Name.
The Word probably hath some Signification or other in their Language,
whatever it is.

¶ These *Hottantots* are People of a middle Stature, with small Limbs and
thin Bodies, full of Activity. Their Faces are of a flat oval Figure, of the
Negro make, with great Eye-brows, black Eyes, but neither are their Noses
so flat, nor their Lips so thick, as the *Negroes* of *Guinea*. Their Complexion
is darker than the common *Indians*; though not so black as the *Negroes* or
New Hollanders; neither is their Hair so much frizled.

¶ They besmear themselves all over with Grease, as well to keep their
Joints supple, as to fence their half-naked Bodies from the Air, by stopping
up their Pores. To do this the more effectually, they rub Soot over the
greased Parts, especially their Faces, which adds to their natural Beauty,
as Painting does in *Europe*; but withal sends from them a strong Smell,
which though sufficiently pleasing to themselves, is very unpleasant to

others. They are glad of the worst of Kitchen-stuff for this purpose, and use it as often as they can get it.

¶ This Custom of anointing the Body is very common in other Parts of *Africa*, especially on the Coast of *Guinea*, where they generally use Palm-Oil, anointing themselves from Head to Foot; but when they want Oil, they make use of Kitchen-stuff, which they buy of the *Europeans* that trade with them. In the *East-Indies* also, especially on the Coast of *Cudda* and *Malacca*, and in general, on almost all the easterly Islands, as well on *Sumatra*, *Java*, &c. as on the *Philipine* and Spice-Islands, the *Indian* Inhabitants anoint themselves with Coco-nut Oil two or three times a Day, especially Mornings and Evenings. They spend sometimes half an Hour in chafing the Oil, and rubbing it into their Hair and Skin, leaving no place unsmear'd with Oil, but their Face, which they daub not like these *Hottantots*. The *Americans* also in some places do use this Custom, but not so frequently, perhaps for want of Oil and Grease to do it. Yet some *American Indians* in the North-Seas frequently daub themselves with a Pigment made with Leaves, Roots, or Herbs, or with a sort of red Earth, giving their Skins a yellow, red, or green Colour, according as the Pigment is. And these smell unsavourly enough to People not accustomed to them; though not so rank as those who use Oil or Grease.

¶ The *Hottantots* do wear no covering on their Heads, but deck their Hair with small Shells. Their Garments are Sheep-skins wrapt about their Shoulders like a Mantle, with the woolly Sides next their Bodies. The Men have besides this Mantle a Piece of Skin like a small Apron, hanging before them. The Women have another Skin tucked about their Waists, which comes down to their Knees like a Petticoat; and their Legs are wrapt round with Sheeps-guts two or three Inches thick, some up as high as to their Calves, others even from their Feet to their Knees, which at a small Distance seems to be a sort of Boots. These are put on when they are green; and so they grow hard and stiff on their Legs, for they never pull them off again, till they have occasion to eat them; which is when they journey from home, and have no other Food; then these Guts which have been worn, it may be, six, eight, ten or twelve Months, make them a good Banquet: This I was informed of by the *Dutch*. They never pull off their Sheep-skin Garments, but to lowse themselves, for by continual wearing them they are full of Vermin, which obliges them often to strip and sit in the Sun two or three Hours together in the heat of the Day, to destroy them. Indeed most *Indians* that live remote from the Equator, are molested with Lice, though their Garments afford less shelter for Lice than these *Hottantots* Sheep-skins do. For all those *Indians* who live in cold Countries, as in the North and South-parts of *America*, have some sort of Skin or other to cover their Bodies, as Deer, Otter, Beaver or Seal-skins, all which they as constantly wear, without shifting themselves, as these *Hottantots* do their Sheep-skins. And hence they are lowsy too, and strong scented, though they do not daub themselves at all, or but very little; or even by reason of their Skins they smell strong.

¶ The *Hottantots* Houses are the meanest that I did ever see. They are about nine or ten Foot high, and ten or twelve from side to side. They are in a manner round, made with small Poles stuck into the Ground, and brought together at the top, where they are fastened. The sides and top of the House are filled up with Boughs coarsely watled between the Poles, and all is covered over with long Grass, Rushes, and pieces of Hides; and the House at a distance appears just like a Hay-cock. They leave only a small hole on one side about three or four Foot high, for a Door to creep in and out at; but when the Wind comes in at this Door, they stop it up, and make another hole in the opposite side. They make the Fire in the middle of the House, and the Smoak ascends out of the Crannies, from all parts of the House. They have no Beds to lie on, but tumble down at Night round the Fire.

¶ Their Houshold Furniture is commonly an earthen Pot or two to boil Victuals, and they live very miserably and hard; it is reported that they will fast two or three Days together when they travel about the Country.

¶ Their common Food is either Herbs, Flesh, or Shell-fish, which they get among the Rocks, or other places at low Water: For they have no Boats, Barklogs, nor Canoas to go a fishing in; so that their chief Sub-sistence is on Land-Animals, or on such Herbs as the Land naturally produceth. I was told by my *Dutch* Landlord, that they kept Sheep and Bullocks here before the *Dutch* settled among them; and that the Inland *Hottantots* have still great stocks of Cattle, and sell them to the *Dutch* for Rolls of Tobacco: And that the price for which they sell a Cow or Sheep, was as much twisted Tobacco, as would reach from the Horns or Head, to the Tail; for they are great lovers of Tobacco, and will do any thing for it. This their way of trucking was confirmed to me by many others, who yet said that they could not buy their Beef this cheap way, for they had not the Liberty to deal with the *Hottantots*, that being a Priviledge which the *Dutch East-India* Company reserved to themselves. My Landlord having a great many Lodgers, fed us most with Mutton, some of which he bought of the Butcher, and there is but one in the Town; but most of it he killed in the Night, the Sheep being brought privately by the *Hottantots*, who assisted in Skinning and Dressing, and had the Skin and

Guts for their Pains. I judge these Sheep were fetched out of the Country, a good way off, for he himself would be absent a Day or two to procure them, and two or three *Hottantots* with him. These of the *Hottantots* that live by the *Dutch* Town, have their greatest Subsistence from the *Dutch*, for there is one or more of them belonging to every House. These do all sorts of servile Work, and there take their Food and Grease. Three or Four more of the nearest Relations sit at the Doors or near the *Dutch* House, waiting for the scraps and fragments that come from the Table; and if between Meals the *Dutch* People have any occasion for them, to go on Errands, or the like, they are ready at Command; expecting little for their Pains; but for a Stranger they will not budge under a Stiver.

¶ Their Religion, if they have any, is wholly unknown to me; for they have no Temple nor Idol, nor any Place of Worship that I did see or hear of. Yet their mirth and nocturnal Pastimes at the new and full of the Moon, lookt as if they had some Superstition about it. For at the Full especially they sing and dance all Night, making a great Noise: I walked out to their Huts twice at these times, in the Evening, when the Moon arose above the Horizon, and viewed them for an Hour or more. They seem all very busie, both Men, Women and Children, dancing very odly on the green Grass by their Houses. They traced to and fro promiscuously, often clapping their Hands and singing aloud. Their Faces were sometimes to the East, sometimes to the West: Neither did I see any Motion or Gesture that they used when their Faces were towards the Moon, more than when their Backs were toward it. After I had thus observed them for a while, I returned to my Lodging, which was not above 2 or 300 Paces from their Huts; and I heard them singing in the same manner all Night. In the grey of the Morning I walked out again, and found many of the Men and Women still singing and dancing; who continued their Mirth till the Moon went down, and then they left off: Some of them going into their Huts to sleep, and others to their Attendance in their *Dutch* Houses. Other Negroes are less circumspect in their Night-Dances, as to the precise time of the Full-Moon, they being more general in these nocturnal Pastimes, and use them oftner; as do many People also in the *East* and *West-Indies*: Yet there is a difference between colder and warmer Countries as to their Divertisements. The warmer Climates being generally very productive of delicate Fruits, &c. and these uncivilized People caring for little else than what is barely necessary, they spend the greatest part of their time in diverting themselves, after their several Fashions; but the *Indians* of colder Climates are not so much at leisure, the Fruits of the Earth being scarce with them, and they necessitated to be continually Fishing, Hunting, or Fowling for their Subsistence; not as with us for Recreation.

¶ As for these *Hottantots*, they are a very lazy sort of People, and though they live in a delicate Country, very fit to be manured, and where there is Land enough for them, yet they choose rather to live as their Fore-fathers, poor and miserable, than be at Pains for Plenty. And so much for the *Hottantots*: I shall now return to our own Affairs.

¶ Upon our Arrival at the Cape, Captain *Heath* took an House to live in, in order to recover his Health. Such of his Men as were able did so too, for the rest he provided Lodgings and paid their Expences. Three or Four of our Men, who came ashore very sick, died, but the rest, by the Assistance of the Doctors of the Fort, a fine Air, and good Kitchen and Cellar Physick, soon recovered their Healths. Those that subscribed to be at all calls, and assisted to bring in the Ship, received Captain *Heath's* Bounty, by which they furnished themselves with Liquor for their home-ward Voyage. But we were now so few, that we could not sail the Ship; therefore Captain *Heath* desired the Governour to spare him some Men; and as I was informed, had a promise to be supplied out of the homeward bound *Dutch East-India* Ships, that were now expected every Day, and we waited for them. In the mean time in came the *James* and *Mary*, and the *Josiah* of *London*, bound home. Out of these we thought to have been furnished with Men; but they had only enough for themselves; therefore we waited yet longer for the *Dutch* Fleet, which at last arrived; but we could get no Men from them.

¶ Captain *Heath* was therefore forced to get Men by stealth, such as he could pick up, whether Soldiers or Seamen. The *Dutch* knew our want of Men, therefore near forty of them, those that had a design to return to *Europe*, came privately and offered themselves, and waited in the Night at Places appointed, where our Boats went and fetched three or four aboard at a time, and hid them, especially when any *Dutch* Boat came aboard our Ship. Here at the Cape I met my Friend *Daniel Wallis*, the same who leapt into the Sea and swam at *Pulo Condore*. After several Traverses to *Madagascar*, *Don Mascarin*, *Ponticherri*, *Pegu*, *Cunnimere*, *Maderas*, and the River of *Hugli*, he was now got hither in a homeward bound *Dutch* Ship. I soon perswaded him to come over to us, and found means to get him aboard our Ship.

¶ About the 23d of *May* we sailed from the Cape, in the Company of the *James and Mary*, and the *Josiah*, directing our Course towards the Island *Santa Hellena*. We met nothing of remark in this Voyage, except a great swelling Sea, out of the S.W. which taking us on the Broad-side, made us rowl sufficiently. Such of our Water-casks as were between Decks, running from side to side, were in a short time all staved, and the Deck well washed with the fresh Water. The Shot tumbled out the Lockers and Garlands; and rung a loud Peal, rumbling from side to side, every rowl that the Ship made; neither was it an easie matter to reduce them again within Bounds. The Guns, being carefully looked after and lashed fast, never budged, but the Tackles or Pulleys, and Lashings, made great Musick too. The sudden and violent Motion of the Ship, made us fearful lest some of the Guns should have broken loose, which must have been very detrimental to the Ship's sides. The Masts were also in great danger to be rowled by the board; but no harm happened to any of us, besides the loss of three or four Buts of Water, and a Barrel or two of good Cape Wine, which was staved in the great Cabbin.

¶ This great tumbling Sea, took us shortly after we came from the Cape. The violence of it lasted but one Night; yet we had a continual Swelling came out of the S.W. almost during all the Passage to *Santa Hellena*; which was an eminent Token that the S.W. Winds were now violent in the higher Latitudes towards the South Pole; for this was the time of the Year for those Winds. Notwithstanding this boisterous Sea coming thus obliquely upon us, we had fine clear Weather, and a moderate Gale at S.E. or between that and the East, till we came to the Island *Santa Hellena*, where we arrived the 20th Day of *June*. There we found the *Princess Ann* at an Anchor waiting for us.

¶ The Island *Santa Hellena* lies in about 16 Degrees South Lat. The Air is commonly serene and clear, except in the Months that yield Rain; yet we had one or two very rainy Days, even while we were here. Here are moist Seasons to plant and sow, and the Weather is temperate enough as to Heat, though so near the Equator, and very healthy.

¶ The Island is but small, not above nine or ten Leagues in length, and stands 3 or 400 Leagues from the main Land. It is bounded against the Sea with steep Rocks, so that there is no landing but at two or three Places. The Land is high and mountainous, and seems to be very dry and poor; yet they are fine Valleys, proper for Cultivation. The Mountains appear bare, only in some Places you may see a few low Shrubs, but the Valleys afford some Trees fit for Building, as I was informed.

¶ This Island is said to have been first discovered and settled by the *Portuguese*, who stockt it with Goats and Hogs. But it being afterwards deserted by them, it lay waste, till the *Dutch* finding it convenient to relieve their *East-India* Ships, settled it again; but they afterwards relinquished it for a more convenient Place; I mean the Cape of *Good Hope*.

Then the *English East-India* Company settled their Servants there, and began to fortify it, but they being yet weak, the *Dutch* about the Year 1672 came hither, and re-took it, and kept it in their Possession. This News being reported in *England*, Captain *Monday* was sent to re-take it, who by the advice and conduct of one that had formerly lived there, landed a Party of armed Men in the Night in a small Cove, unknown to the *Dutch* then in Garrison, and climbing the Rocks, got up into the Island, and so came in the Morning to the Hills hanging over the Fort, which stands by the Sea in a small Valley. From thence firing into the Fort, they soon made them surrender. There were at this time two or three *Dutch East-India* Ships, either at Anchor, or coming thither, when our Ships were there. These, when they saw that the *English* were Masters of the Island again, made sail to be gone; but being chaced by the *English* Frigots, two of them became rich Prizes to Capt. *Monday* and his Men.

¶ The Island hath continued ever since in the Hands of the *English East-India* Company, and hath been greatly strengthened both with Men and Guns; so that at this Day it is secure enough from the Invasion of any Enemy. For the common Landing-Place is a small Bay, like a Half Moon, scarce 500 Paces wide, between the two Points. Close by the Sea-side are good Guns planted at equal distances, lying along from one end of the Bay to the other; besides a small Fort, a little further in from the Sea, near the midst of the Bay. All which makes the Bay so strong, that it is impossible to force it. The small Cove where Captain *Monday* landed his Men when he took the Island from the *Dutch*, is scarce fit for a Boat to land at; and yet that is now also fortified.

¶ There is a small *English* Town within the great Bay, standing in a little Valley, between two high steep Mountains. There may be about twenty or thirty small Houses, whose Walls are built with rough Stones: The inside Furniture is very mean. The Governour hath a pretty tolerable handsome low House, by the Fort; where he commonly lives, having a few Soldiers to attend him, and to guard the Fort. But the Houses in the Town before-mentioned stand empty, save only when Ships arrive here; for their Owners have all Plantations farther in the Island, where they constantly employ themselves. But when Ships arrive, they all flock to the Town, where they live all the time that the Ships lie here; for then is their Fair or Market, to buy such Necessaries as they want, and to sell off the Product of their Plantations.

¶ Their Plantations afford Potatoes, Yames, and some Plantains and Bonanoes. Their Stock consists chiefly of Hogs, Bullocks, Cocks and Hens, Ducks, Geese, and Turkeys, of which they have great plenty, and sell them at a lower rate to the Sailors, taking in exchange, Shirts, Drawers, or any light Cloaths; pieces of Callico, Silks, or Muzlins: Arack, Sugar, and Lime-juice, is also much esteemed and coveted by them. But now they are in hopes to produce Wine and Brandy, in a short time; for they do already begin to plant Vines for that end, there being a few *French* Men there to manage that Affair. This I was told, but I saw nothing of it, for it rained so hard when I was ashore, that I had not the opportunity of seeing their Plantations. I was also informed, that they get Manatee or Sea-Cows here, which seemed very strange to me. Therefore enquiring more strictly into the matter, I found the *Santa Hellena* Manatee to be, by their shapes, and manner of lying ashore on the Rocks, those Creatures called Sea-lyons; for the Manatee never come ashore, neither are they found near any rocky Shores, as this Island is, there being no feeding for them in such places. Besides, in this Island there is no River for them to drink at, tho' there is a small Brook runs into the Sea, out of the Valley by the Fort.

¶ We stayed here five or six Days; all which time the Islanders lived at the Town, to entertain the Seamen; who constantly flock ashore, to enjoy themselves among their Country People. Our touching at the Cape had greatly drained the Seamen of their loose Coins, at which these Islanders as greatly repined; and some of the poorer sort openly complained against such doings, saying, it was fit that the *East-India* Company should be acquainted with it, that they might hinder their Ships from touching at the Cape. Yet they were extreamly kind, in hopes to get what was remaining. They are most of them very poor: but such as could get a little Liquor to sell to the Seamen at this time got what the Seamen could spare; for the Punch-houses were never empty. But had we all come directly hither, and not touched at the Cape, even the poorest People among them would have gotten something by entertaining sick Men. For commonly the Seamen coming home, are troubled, more or less with scorbutick Distempers: and their only hopes are to get refreshment and health at this Island; and these hopes seldom or never fail them, if once they get footing here. For the Islands afford abundance of delicate Herbs, wherewith the Sick are first bathed to supple their Joints, and then the Fruits and Herbs, and fresh food soon after cure them of their scorbutick Humours. So that in a Week's time Men that have been carried ashore in Hammocks, and they who were wholly unable to go, have soon been able to leap and dance. Doubtless the serenity and wholesomness of the Air contributes much to the carrying off of these Distempers; for here is constantly a fresh breeze. While we stayed here, many of the Seamen got Sweethearts. One young Man belonging to the *James* and *Mary*, was married, and brought his Wife to *England* with him. Another brought his Sweetheart to *England*, they being each engaged by Bonds to marry at their Arrival in *England*; and several other of our Men, were over Head and Ears in Love with the *Santa Hellena* Maids, who tho' they were born there, yet very earnestly desired to be released from that Prison, which they have no other way to compass, but by marrying Seamen, or Passengers that touch here. The young Women born here, are but one remove from *English*, being the Daughters of such. They are well shaped, proper and comely, were they in a Dress to set them off.

¶ My stay ashore here was but two Days, to get Refreshments for my self and *Jeoly*, whom I carried ashore with me: and he was very diligent to pick up such things as the Islands afforded, carrying ashore with him a Bag, which the People of the Isle filled with Roots for him. They flock'd about him, and seemed to admire him much. This was the last place where I had him at my own disposal, for the Mate of the Ship, who had Mr. *Moody*'s share in him, left him entirely to my management, I being to bring him to *England*. But I was no sooner arrived in the *Thames*, but he was sent ashore to be seen by some eminent Persons; and I being in want of Money, was prevailed upon to sell first, part of my share in him, and by degrees all of it. After this I heard he was carried about to be shown as a Sight, and that he died of the Small-pox at *Oxford*.

¶ But to proceed, our Water being filled, and the Ship all stock'd with fresh Provision, we sailed from hence in Company of the *Princess Ann*, the *James and Mary*, and the *Josiah*, *July* the 2d, 1691, directing our course towards *England*, and designing to touch no where by the way. We were now in the way of the Trade Winds, which we commonly find at E.S.E. or S.E. by E. or S.E. till we draw near the Line, and sometimes till we are eight or ten degrees to the North of the Line. For which reason Ships might shape their course so, as to keep on the *African* shore, and pass between Cape *Verd* and Cape *Verd* Islands; for that seems to be the directest course to *England*. But experience often shews us, that the farthest way about is the nearest way home, and so it is here. For by striving to keep near the *African* Shore, you meet with the Winds more uncertain, and subject to calms; whereas in keeping the mid-way between *Africa* and *America*, or rather nearer the *American* Continent, till you are North of the Line, you have a brisk constant gale.

¶ This was the way that we took, and in our passage before we got to the Line, we saw three Ships, and making towards them, we found two of them to be *Portuguese*, bound to *Brazil*. The third kept on a Wind, so that we could not speak with her; but we found by the *Portuguese* it was an *English* Ship, called the *Dorothy*, Capt. *Thwart* Commander, bound to the *East-Indies*. After this we kept Company still with our Three Consorts till we came near *England*, and then were separated by bad weather; but before we came within sight of Land we got together again, all but the *James and Mary*. She got into the Channel before us, and went to *Plymouth*, and there gave an account of the rest of us; whereupon our Men of War who lay there, came out to join us, and meeting us, brought us off of *Plymouth*. There our Consort the *James and Mary* came to us again, and from thence we all sailed in company of several Men of War towards *Portsmouth*. There our first Convoy left us, and went in thither. But we did not want Convoys, for our Fleets were then repairing to their Winter Harbours, to be laid up; so that we had the company of several *English* Ships to the *Downs*, and a Squadron also of *Dutch* sailed up the Channel, but kept off farther from our *English* Coast, they being bound home to *Holland*. When we came as high as the *South Foreland*, we left them standing on their Course, keeping on the Back of the *Goodwin-Sands*; and we lufft in for the *Downs*, where we anchored *September* the 16th, 1691.

INDEX OF PERSONS, PLACES AND SHIPS MENTIONED IN WILLIAM DAMPIER'S "NEW VOYAGE ROUND THE WORLD"

A CATALOG OF SELECTED DOVER

BOOKS IN ALL FIELDS OF INTEREST

CONCERNING THE SPIRITUAL IN ART, Wassily Kandinsky. Pioneering work by father of abstract art. Thoughts on color theory, nature of art. Analysis of earlier masters. 12 illustrations. 80pp. of text. 5⅜ x 8½.   0-486-23411-8

CELTIC ART: The Methods of Construction, George Bain. Simple geometric techniques for making Celtic interlacements, spirals, Kells-type initials, animals, humans, etc. Over 500 illustrations. 160pp. 9 x 12. (Available in U.S. only.)   0-486-22923-8

AN ATLAS OF ANATOMY FOR ARTISTS, Fritz Schider. Most thorough reference work on art anatomy in the world. Hundreds of illustrations, including selections from works by Vesalius, Leonardo, Goya, Ingres, Michelangelo, others. 593 illustrations. 192pp. 7⅛ x 10¼.   0-486-20241-0

CELTIC HAND STROKE-BY-STROKE (Irish Half-Uncial from "The Book of Kells"): An Arthur Baker Calligraphy Manual, Arthur Baker. Complete guide to creating each letter of the alphabet in distinctive Celtic manner. Covers hand position, strokes, pens, inks, paper, more. Illustrated. 48pp. 8¼ x 11.   0-486-24336-2

EASY ORIGAMI, John Montroll. Charming collection of 32 projects (hat, cup, pelican, piano, swan, many more) specially designed for the novice origami hobbyist. Clearly illustrated easy-to-follow instructions insure that even beginning papercrafters will achieve successful results. 48pp. 8¼ x 11.   0-486-27298-2

BLOOMINGDALE'S ILLUSTRATED 1886 CATALOG: Fashions, Dry Goods and Housewares, Bloomingdale Brothers. Famed merchants' extremely rare catalog depicting about 1,700 products: clothing, housewares, firearms, dry goods, jewelry, more. Invaluable for dating, identifying vintage items. Also, copyright-free graphics for artists, designers. Co-published with Henry Ford Museum & Greenfield Village. 160pp. 8¼ x 11.   0-486-25780-0

THE ART OF WORLDLY WISDOM, Baltasar Gracian. "Think with the few and speak with the many," "Friends are a second existence," and "Be able to forget" are among this 1637 volume's 300 pithy maxims. A perfect source of mental and spiritual refreshment, it can be opened at random and appreciated either in brief or at length. 128pp. 5⅜ x 8½.   0-486-44034-6

JOHNSON'S DICTIONARY: A Modern Selection, Samuel Johnson (E. L. McAdam and George Milne, eds.). This modern version reduces the original 1755 edition's 2,300 pages of definitions and literary examples to a more manageable length, retaining the verbal pleasure and historical curiosity of the original. 480pp. 5¾₆ x 8¼.   0-486-44089-3

ADVENTURES OF HUCKLEBERRY FINN, Mark Twain, Illustrated by E. W. Kemble. A work of eternal richness and complexity, a source of ongoing critical debate, and a literary landmark, Twain's 1885 masterpiece about a barefoot boy's journey of self-discovery has enthralled readers around the world. This handsome clothbound reproduction of the first edition features all 174 of the original black-and-white illustrations. 368pp. 5⅜ x 8½.   0-486-44322-1

STICKLEY CRAFTSMAN FURNITURE CATALOGS, Gustav Stickley and L. & J. G. Stickley. Beautiful, functional furniture in two authentic catalogs from 1910. 594 illustrations, including 277 photos, show settles, rockers, armchairs, reclining chairs, bookcases, desks, tables. 183pp. 6½ x 9¼. 0-486-23838-5

AMERICAN LOCOMOTIVES IN HISTORIC PHOTOGRAPHS: 1858 to 1949, Ron Ziel (ed.). A rare collection of 126 meticulously detailed official photographs, called "builder portraits," of American locomotives that majestically chronicle the rise of steam locomotive power in America. Introduction. Detailed captions. xi+ 129pp. 9 x 12. 0-486-27393-8

AMERICA'S LIGHTHOUSES: An Illustrated History, Francis Ross Holland, Jr. Delightfully written, profusely illustrated fact-filled survey of over 200 American light-houses since 1716. History, anecdotes, technological advances, more. 240pp. 8 x 10¾. 0-486-25576-X

TOWARDS A NEW ARCHITECTURE, Le Corbusier. Pioneering manifesto by founder of "International School." Technical and aesthetic theories, views of industry, economics, relation of form to function, "mass-production split" and much more. Profusely illustrated. 320pp. 6⅛ x 9¼. (Available in U.S. only.) 0-486-25023-7

HOW THE OTHER HALF LIVES, Jacob Riis. Famous journalistic record, exposing poverty and degradation of New York slums around 1900, by major social reformer. 100 striking and influential photographs. 233pp. 10 x 7⅞. 0-486-22012-5

FRUIT KEY AND TWIG KEY TO TREES AND SHRUBS, William M. Harlow. One of the handiest and most widely used identification aids. Fruit key covers 120 deciduous and evergreen species; twig key 160 deciduous species. Easily used. Over 300 photographs. 126pp. 5⅜ x 8½. 0-486-20511-8

COMMON BIRD SONGS, Dr. Donald J. Borror. Songs of 60 most common U.S. birds: robins, sparrows, cardinals, bluejays, finches, more—arranged in order of increasing complexity. Up to 9 variations of songs of each species.
Cassette and manual 0-486-99911-4

ORCHIDS AS HOUSE PLANTS, Rebecca Tyson Northen. Grow cattleyas and many other kinds of orchids—in a window, in a case, or under artificial light. 63 illus-trations. 148pp. 5⅜ x 8½. 0-486-23261-1

MONSTER MAZES, Dave Phillips. Masterful mazes at four levels of difficulty. Avoid deadly perils and evil creatures to find magical treasures. Solutions for all 32 exciting illustrated puzzles. 48pp. 8¼ x 11. 0-486-26005-4

MOZART'S DON GIOVANNI (DOVER OPERA LIBRETTO SERIES), Wolfgang Amadeus Mozart. Introduced and translated by Ellen H. Bleiler. Standard Italian libretto, with complete English translation. Convenient and thoroughly portable—an ideal companion for reading along with a recording or the performance itself. Introduction. List of characters. Plot summary. 121pp. 5¼ x 8½. 0-486-24944-1

FRANK LLOYD WRIGHT'S DANA HOUSE, Donald Hoffmann. Pictorial essay of residential masterpiece with over 160 interior and exterior photos, plans, eleva-tions, sketches and studies. 128pp. 9¼ x 10¾. 0-486-29120-0

THE CLARINET AND CLARINET PLAYING, David Pino. Lively, comprehensive work features suggestions about technique, musicianship, and musical interpretation, as well as guidelines for teaching, making your own reeds, and preparing for public performance. Includes an intriguing look at clarinet history. "A godsend," *The Clarinet,* Journal of the International Clarinet Society. Appendixes. 7 illus. 320pp. 5⅜ x 8½. 0-486-40270-3

HOLLYWOOD GLAMOR PORTRAITS, John Kobal (ed.). 145 photos from 1926-49. Harlow, Gable, Bogart, Bacall; 94 stars in all. Full background on photographers, technical aspects. 160pp. 8⅜ x 11¼. 0-486-23352-9

THE RAVEN AND OTHER FAVORITE POEMS, Edgar Allan Poe. Over 40 of the author's most memorable poems: "The Bells," "Ulalume," "Israfel," "To Helen," "The Conqueror Worm," "Eldorado," "Annabel Lee," many more. Alphabetic lists of titles and first lines. 64pp. 5$^{3}/_{16}$ x 8¼. 0-486-26685-0

PERSONAL MEMOIRS OF U. S. GRANT, Ulysses Simpson Grant. Intelligent, deeply moving firsthand account of Civil War campaigns, considered by many the finest military memoirs ever written. Includes letters, historic photographs, maps and more. 528pp. 6⅛ x 9¼. 0-486-28587-1

ANCIENT EGYPTIAN MATERIALS AND INDUSTRIES, A. Lucas and J. Harris. Fascinating, comprehensive, thoroughly documented text describes this ancient civilization's vast resources and the processes that incorporated them in daily life, including the use of animal products, building materials, cosmetics, perfumes and incense, fibers, glazed ware, glass and its manufacture, materials used in the mummification process, and much more. 544pp. 6⅛ x 9¼. (Available in U.S. only.) 0-486-40446-3

RUSSIAN STORIES/RUSSKIE RASSKAZY: A Dual-Language Book, edited by Gleb Struve. Twelve tales by such masters as Chekhov, Tolstoy, Dostoevsky, Pushkin, others. Excellent word-for-word English translations on facing pages, plus teaching and study aids, Russian/English vocabulary, biographical/critical introductions, more. 416pp. 5⅜ x 8½. 0-486-26244-8

PHILADELPHIA THEN AND NOW: 60 Sites Photographed in the Past and Present, Kenneth Finkel and Susan Oyama. Rare photographs of City Hall, Logan Square, Independence Hall, Betsy Ross House, other landmarks juxtaposed with contemporary views. Captures changing face of historic city. Introduction. Captions. 128pp. 8¼ x 11. 0-486-25790-8

NORTH AMERICAN INDIAN LIFE: Customs and Traditions of 23 Tribes, Elsie Clews Parsons (ed.). 27 fictionalized essays by noted anthropologists examine religion, customs, government, additional facets of life among the Winnebago, Crow, Zuni, Eskimo, other tribes. 480pp. 6⅛ x 9¼. 0-486-27377-6

TECHNICAL MANUAL AND DICTIONARY OF CLASSICAL BALLET, Gail Grant. Defines, explains, comments on steps, movements, poses and concepts. 15-page pictorial section. Basic book for student, viewer. 127pp. 5⅜ x 8½. 0-486-21843-0

THE MALE AND FEMALE FIGURE IN MOTION: 60 Classic Photographic Sequences, Eadweard Muybridge. 60 true-action photographs of men and women walking, running, climbing, bending, turning, etc., reproduced from rare 19th-century masterpiece. vi + 121pp. 9 x 12. 0-486-24745-7

ANIMALS: 1,419 Copyright-Free Illustrations of Mammals, Birds, Fish, Insects, etc., Jim Harter (ed.). Clear wood engravings present, in extremely lifelike poses, over 1,000 species of animals. One of the most extensive pictorial sourcebooks of its kind. Captions. Index. 284pp. 9 x 12.   0-486-23766-4

1001 QUESTIONS ANSWERED ABOUT THE SEASHORE, N. J. Berrill and Jacquelyn Berrill. Queries answered about dolphins, sea snails, sponges, starfish, fishes, shore birds, many others. Covers appearance, breeding, growth, feeding, much more. 305pp. 5¼ x 8¼.   0-486-23366-9

ATTRACTING BIRDS TO YOUR YARD, William J. Weber. Easy-to-follow guide offers advice on how to attract the greatest diversity of birds: birdhouses, feeders, water and waterers, much more. 96pp. 5³/₁₆ x 8¼.   0-486-28927-3

MEDICINAL AND OTHER USES OF NORTH AMERICAN PLANTS: A Historical Survey with Special Reference to the Eastern Indian Tribes, Charlotte Erichsen-Brown. Chronological historical citations document 500 years of usage of plants, trees, shrubs native to eastern Canada, northeastern U.S. Also complete identifying information. 343 illustrations. 544pp. 6½ x 9¼.   0-486-25951-X

STORYBOOK MAZES, Dave Phillips. 23 stories and mazes on two-page spreads: Wizard of Oz, Treasure Island, Robin Hood, etc. Solutions. 64pp. 8¼ x 11.
                                                          0-486-23628-5

AMERICAN NEGRO SONGS: 230 Folk Songs and Spirituals, Religious and Secular, John W. Work. This authoritative study traces the African influences of songs sung and played by black Americans at work, in church, and as entertainment. The author discusses the lyric significance of such songs as "Swing Low, Sweet Chariot," "John Henry," and others and offers the words and music for 230 songs. Bibliography. Index of Song Titles. 272pp. 6½ x 9¼.   0-486-40271-1

MOVIE-STAR PORTRAITS OF THE FORTIES, John Kobal (ed.). 163 glamor, studio photos of 106 stars of the 1940s: Rita Hayworth, Ava Gardner, Marlon Brando, Clark Gable, many more. 176pp. 8⅜ x 11¼.   0-486-23546-7

YEKL and THE IMPORTED BRIDEGROOM AND OTHER STORIES OF YIDDISH NEW YORK, Abraham Cahan. Film Hester Street based on *Yekl* (1896). Novel, other stories among first about Jewish immigrants on N.Y.'s East Side. 240pp. 5⅜ x 8½.   0-486-22427-9

SELECTED POEMS, Walt Whitman. Generous sampling from *Leaves of Grass.* Twenty-four poems include "I Hear America Singing," "Song of the Open Road," "I Sing the Body Electric," "When Lilacs Last in the Dooryard Bloom'd," "O Captain! My Captain!"–all reprinted from an authoritative edition. Lists of titles and first lines. 128pp. 5³/₁₆ x 8¼.   0-486-26878-0

SONGS OF EXPERIENCE: Facsimile Reproduction with 26 Plates in Full Color, William Blake. 26 full-color plates from a rare 1826 edition. Includes "The Tyger," "London," "Holy Thursday," and other poems. Printed text of poems. 48pp. 5¼ x 7.
                                                          0-486-24636-1

THE BEST TALES OF HOFFMANN, E. T. A. Hoffmann. 10 of Hoffmann's most important stories: "Nutcracker and the King of Mice," "The Golden Flowerpot," etc. 458pp. 5⅜ x 8½.   0-486-21793-0

THE BOOK OF TEA, Kakuzo Okakura. Minor classic of the Orient: entertaining, charming explanation, interpretation of traditional Japanese culture in terms of tea ceremony. 94pp. 5⅜ x 8½.   0-486-20070-1

FRENCH STORIES/CONTES FRANÇAIS: A Dual-Language Book, Wallace Fowlie. Ten stories by French masters, Voltaire to Camus: "Micromegas" by Voltaire; "The Atheist's Mass" by Balzac; "Minuet" by de Maupassant; "The Guest" by Camus, six more. Excellent English translations on facing pages. Also French-English vocabulary list, exercises, more. 352pp. 5⅜ x 8½. 0-486-26443-2

CHICAGO AT THE TURN OF THE CENTURY IN PHOTOGRAPHS: 122 Historic Views from the Collections of the Chicago Historical Society, Larry A. Viskochil. Rare large-format prints offer detailed views of City Hall, State Street, the Loop, Hull House, Union Station, many other landmarks, circa 1904-1913. Introduction. Captions. Maps. 144pp. 9⅜ x 12¼. 0-486-24656-6

OLD BROOKLYN IN EARLY PHOTOGRAPHS, 1865-1929, William Lee Younger. Luna Park, Gravesend race track, construction of Grand Army Plaza, moving of Hotel Brighton, etc. 157 previously unpublished photographs. 165pp. 8⅞ x 11¾. 0-486-23587-4

THE MYTHS OF THE NORTH AMERICAN INDIANS, Lewis Spence. Rich anthology of the myths and legends of the Algonquins, Iroquois, Pawnees and Sioux, prefaced by an extensive historical and ethnological commentary. 36 illustrations. 480pp. 5⅜ x 8½. 0-486-25967-6

AN ENCYCLOPEDIA OF BATTLES: Accounts of Over 1,560 Battles from 1479 B.C. to the Present, David Eggenberger. Essential details of every major battle in recorded history from the first battle of Megiddo in 1479 B.C. to Grenada in 1984. List of Battle Maps. New Appendix covering the years 1967-1984. Index. 99 illustrations. 544pp. 6½ x 9¼. 0-486-24913-1

SAILING ALONE AROUND THE WORLD, Captain Joshua Slocum. First man to sail around the world, alone, in small boat. One of great feats of seamanship told in delightful manner. 67 illustrations. 294pp. 5⅜ x 8½. 0-486-20326-3

ANARCHISM AND OTHER ESSAYS, Emma Goldman. Powerful, penetrating, prophetic essays on direct action, role of minorities, prison reform, puritan hypocrisy, violence, etc. 271pp. 5⅜ x 8½. 0-486-22484-8

MYTHS OF THE HINDUS AND BUDDHISTS, Ananda K. Coomaraswamy and Sister Nivedita. Great stories of the epics; deeds of Krishna, Shiva, taken from puranas, Vedas, folk tales; etc. 32 illustrations. 400pp. 5⅜ x 8½. 0-486-21759-0

MY BONDAGE AND MY FREEDOM, Frederick Douglass. Born a slave, Douglass became outspoken force in antislavery movement. The best of Douglass' autobiographies. Graphic description of slave life. 464pp. 5⅜ x 8½. 0-486-22457-0

FOLLOWING THE EQUATOR: A Journey Around the World, Mark Twain. Fascinating humorous account of 1897 voyage to Hawaii, Australia, India, New Zealand, etc. Ironic, bemused reports on peoples, customs, climate, flora and fauna, politics, much more. 197 illustrations. 720pp. 5⅜ x 8½. 0-486-26113-1

THE PEOPLE CALLED SHAKERS, Edward D. Andrews. Definitive study of Shakers: origins, beliefs, practices, dances, social organization, furniture and crafts, etc. 33 illustrations. 351pp. 5⅜ x 8½. 0-486-21081-2

THE MYTHS OF GREECE AND ROME, H. A. Guerber. A classic of mythology, generously illustrated, long prized for its simple, graphic, accurate retelling of the principal myths of Greece and Rome, and for its commentary on their origins and significance. With 64 illustrations by Michelangelo, Raphael, Titian, Rubens, Canova, Bernini and others. 480pp. 5⅜ x 8½. 0-486-27584-1

CATALOG OF DOVER BOOKS

LIGHT AND SHADE: A Classic Approach to Three-Dimensional Drawing, Mrs. Mary P. Merrifield. Handy reference clearly demonstrates principles of light and shade by revealing effects of common daylight, sunshine, and candle or artificial light on geometrical solids. 13 plates. 64pp. 5⅜ x 8½. 0-486-44143-1

ASTROLOGY AND ASTRONOMY: A Pictorial Archive of Signs and Symbols, Ernst and Johanna Lehner. Treasure trove of stories, lore, and myth, accompanied by more than 300 rare illustrations of planets, the Milky Way, signs of the zodiac, comets, meteors, and other astronomical phenomena. 192pp. 8⅜ x 11. 0-486-43981-X

JEWELRY MAKING: Techniques for Metal, Tim McCreight. Easy-to-follow instructions and carefully executed illustrations describe tools and techniques, use of gems and enamels, wire inlay, casting, and other topics. 72 line illustrations and diagrams. 176pp. 8¼ x 10⅞. 0-486-44043-5

MAKING BIRDHOUSES: Easy and Advanced Projects, Gladstone Califf. Easy-to-follow instructions include diagrams for everything from a one-room house for bluebirds to a forty-two-room structure for purple martins. 56 plates; 4 figures. 80pp. 8¾ x 6⅜. 0-486-44183-0

LITTLE BOOK OF LOG CABINS: How to Build and Furnish Them, William S. Wicks. Handy how-to manual, with instructions and illustrations for building cabins in the Adirondack style, fireplaces, stairways, furniture, beamed ceilings, and more. 102 line drawings. 96pp. 8¾ x 6⅜. 0-486-44259-4

THE SEASONS OF AMERICA PAST, Eric Sloane. From "sugaring time" and strawberry picking to Indian summer and fall harvest, a whole year's activities described in charming prose and enhanced with 79 of the author's own illustrations. 160pp. 8¼ x 11. 0-486-44220-9

THE METROPOLIS OF TOMORROW, Hugh Ferriss. Generous, prophetic vision of the metropolis of the future, as perceived in 1929. Powerful illustrations of towering structures, wide avenues, and rooftop parks–all features in many of today's modern cities. 59 illustrations. 144pp. 8¼ x 11. 0-486-43727-2

THE PATH TO ROME, Hilaire Belloc. This 1902 memoir abounds in lively vignettes from a vanished time, recounting a pilgrimage on foot across the Alps and Apennines in order to "see all Europe which the Christian Faith has saved." 77 of the author's original line drawings complement his sparkling prose. 272pp. 5⅜ x 8½. 0-486-44001-X

THE HISTORY OF RASSELAS: Prince of Abissinia, Samuel Johnson. Distinguished English writer attacks eighteenth-century optimism and man's unrealistic estimates of what life has to offer. 112pp. 5⅜ x 8½. 0-486-44094-X

A VOYAGE TO ARCTURUS, David Lindsay. A brilliant flight of pure fancy, where wild creatures crowd the fantastic landscape and demented torturers dominate victims with their bizarre mental powers. 272pp. 5⅜ x 8½. 0-486-44198-9

Paperbound unless otherwise indicated. Available at your book dealer, online at **www.doverpublications.com**, or by writing to Dept. GI, Dover Publications, Inc., 31 East 2nd Street, Mineola, NY 11501. For current price information or for free catalogs (please indicate field of interest), write to Dover Publications or log on to **www.doverpublications.com** and see every Dover book in print. Dover publishes more than 500 books each year on science, elementary and advanced mathematics, biology, music, art, literary history, social sciences, and other areas.